Homeland Security

Safeguarding the U.S. from Domestic Catastrophic Destruction

By CW Productions Ltd.

Edited by:

Richard White, Ph.D., Tina Bynum, DM, and Stan Supinski, Ph.D.

Cover art: *New York City Freedom Tower, Mandritoiu,* courtesy of Shutterstock.com

Previously published as The U.S. Department of Homeland Security: An Overview, by Richard White, Tina Markowski, and Kevin Collins © 2010

Printed in the United States of America.

10 9 8 7 6 5 4 3 2

ISBN 978-1-48357-456-1

2005420444

EH

Please visit our web site at *www.cwpnow.com*

CW Productions Ltd.
Colorado Springs, CO
A Homeland Security Education Company

Preface

Welcome to the third edition of our textbook. As indicated by the new title, this edition is significantly different than the previous two, and accordingly stocked with mostly new material. Whereas the first two editions described "what" was being done in the name of homeland security, this one explains "why". In keeping with our previous approach, we do not ascribe ourselves as "authors" but "editors" because the bulk of material is drawn directly from government documents, either primary sources or publicly available derivatives. Two of our foremost derivative sources were reports published by the Congressional Research Service (CRS) and Government Accountability Office (GAO). They have access to information, unclassified as it may be, well beyond the means of the general public. We would also like to acknowledge the many public websites that were also instrumental in completing this text. And while we were only "editors", we think this book offers its own unique contributions to the field of homeland security. First, it delivers both a comprehensive yet concise treatment of a very broad subject spanning numerous separate fields, from national security to military operations to law enforcement to emergency management, to name only a few. Second, and most importantly, it offers insight into the exact nature of homeland security. Because it was brought to the forefront of national attention by an act of terrorism, homeland security has become confused with terrorism. While terrorism certainly remains a concern to homeland security, it is not the root concern. As we try to make eminently clear in this textbook, the homeland security concern predates 9/11, stemming back to the 1995 Tokyo Subway Attacks which saw the first employment of a weapon of mass destruction by non-state actors. As our title suggests, the homeland security concern is domestic catastrophic destruction. 9/11 demonstrated how it could be achieved by subverting critical infrastructure. Hurricane Katrina demonstrated how it could be accomplished without malicious intent. While we give due attention to the terrorist motive, we don't give it the undue attention it has gained by becoming almost synonymous with homeland security. In this regard, we hope to set the record straight and make it clear what homeland security "is", and what it "is not". Homeland security is not terrorism, nor is it mass killings. While closely related, homeland security, terrorism, and mass killings are distinctly separate. We hope to demonstrate that in this book. More importantly, we hope to impart a clarity of understanding that will give you, the reader, a corresponding advantage in your academic and professional pursuits supported by this knowledge.

About the Authors

Richard White, Ph.D.

Rick White is an Assistant Research Professor at the University of Colorado at Colorado Springs. His Ph.D. is in Engineering Security. He has published works on critical infrastructure risk management. Rick's interest in homeland security stems back to 9/11 when he was teaching at the Air Force Academy and watched together with his cadets as the hijacked aircraft crashed into the Twin Towers. A retired Air Force officer, Rick has developed and taught homeland security courses for colleges, universities, and various government agencies over the years. Other textbooks include *Homeland Defense: An Overview* (Pearson 2007), *Introduction to Joint and Coalition Warfare* (FastPlanet 2005), and *United States Military Power* (FastPlanet 2004).

Tina Bynum , DM

Tina Bynum is the University Program Director for the College of Security Studies at Colorado Technical University where she develops and manages the curriculum for homeland security, criminal justice, and public administration programs at the undergraduate, graduate, and doctoral levels. She is an editorial review board member for the Journal for Homeland Security Education and is a member of the International Society for Preparedness, Resilience and Security (INSPRS). A retired firefighter and emergency medical technician, Dr. Bynum also plays key roles in local emergency planning and exercising under the Homeland Security Exercise and Evaluation Program (HSEEP) protocols and teaches courses in criminal justice, emergency and fire management services, public administration, and homeland security. While serving as the Associate Director for the University of Colorado's Trauma, Health and Hazards Center, she developed a peer support program to build resilience and assist recovery from high-risk occupational traumatic experiences that was implemented in local police and fire departments. This program has gone on to serve the needs of military personnel returning from combat. Dr. Bynum also co-authored The *United States Department of Homeland Security, An Overview* (2Ed, 2010).

Stan Supinski, Ph.D.

Stan Supinski is the Deputy Director of Partnership Programs and faculty member for the Naval Postgraduate School, Center for Homeland Defense and Security. He has taught and directed Homeland security courses for a variety of institutions, to include Long Island University, the University of Denver and the University of Massachusetts. He also founded and formerly directed the Homeland Security/Defense Education Consortium on behalf of NORAD/US Northern Command. Dr. Supinski is a retired US Air Force officer, having served as a professor of Russian at the US Air Force Academy and as an intelligence officer in various locations worldwide.

Contents

Contents

Part IV: Mission Components

Part V: Mission Partners

Appendices

Contents

List of Tables

Contents

List of Tables (continued)

Contents

List of Figures

Contents

List of Figures (continued)

Contents

List of Figures (continued)

Part I: Hard Lessons

This section explores the events that created and shaped U.S. homeland security policy. It begins shortly after the end of the Cold War in 1991. After a four-decade standoff between the United States and Soviet Union, there was a global sense of relief and great expectation that the world would become a much safer place after the threat of imminent nuclear war had subsided. Those illusions were shattered in March 1995 after a religious cult attempted to murder thousands of Japanese commuters aboard the Tokyo subway system using Sarin nerve gas. It was the first time a non-state actor employed a weapon of mass destruction, marking a watershed moment in history when small groups attained the destructive power of nations. The implication was not lost on Congress which, spurred by the Oklahoma City bombing a few months later, chartered a number of commissions to investigate the prospects of WMD attack on U.S. soil. Because the Tokyo subway attacks sought to topple the Japanese government, they were, by definition, acts of terrorism. The congressional committees subsequently blurred the distinction between act and motive, labeling a WMD attack by non-state actors as "terrorism". The committees also introduced the term "homeland security" to describe various organizational proposals to prevent and respond to WMD attack. In February 2001, the Hart-Rudman Commission recommended creation of a National Homeland Security Agency. These recommendations would've gone unheeded except for 9/11. On September 11th, 2001, nineteen hijackers inflicted as much damage as the Imperial Japanese Navy on December 7th, 1941; 3,000 dead and $40 billion in direct damages. The 9/11 Commission characterized the attack as one of "surpassing disproportion". However, instead of using WMD, the attackers achieved WMD effects by subverting the nation's transportation infrastructure, turning passenger jets into guided missiles. The enduring lesson from 9/11 is that the critical infrastructure essential to an industrial economy also contains the means for catastrophic destruction. What makes critical infrastructure particularly vulnerable, and therefore a tempting target, is that little of it was designed to withstand deliberate attack, and much of it, due to the Internet revolution, is susceptible to cyber attack. Moreover, the national security system built during the Cold War to counter threats from nation states, suffered a collective "failure of imagination" to counter threats from non-state actors. Accordingly, the U.S. Federal government underwent its largest reorganization since the end of World War II and created a new Department of Homeland Security. But in its rush to close the gap exposed by this new threat, the Federal government overlooked the consequences posed by an even older threat. In August 2005, Hurricane Katrina forced the evacuation of a major U.S. city and killed over 1,400 of its citizens. It was another hard lesson that catastrophic destruction comes in both natural and manmade forms.

Chapter 1

Turning Point

Learning Outcomes

Careful study of this chapter will help a student do the following:

- Explain the significance of the 1995 Tokyo subway attacks.
- Describe the legal definition of terrorism.
- Compare the different classes of weapons of mass destruction.
- Discuss how the 1995 Tokyo subway attacks precipitated U.S. homeland security policy.

"The 1995 Sarin nerve gas attack on the Tokyo subway marked a turning point in the history of terrorism."

- 1999 Gilmore Commission Report

Introduction

Providing for the common defense is a purpose of U.S. government enumerated in the Preamble to the Constitution. For over two hundred years the nation's military defended the country from other nations who sought to do us harm. But as weapons of war developed into weapons of mass destruction (WMD), a new threat began to emerge towards the end of the 20th century that the nation's military could not counter. That threat was nuclear terrorism, or more generally speaking, the employment of WMD by non-state actors. This chapter examines the turning point when the nation first realized its vulnerability, and events surrounding the evolution from national security to homeland security.

From the Frying Pan into the Fire

With the dissolution of the Soviet Union in August 1991, the United States emerged from the Cold War as the world's sole remaining superpower. After forty-four years of facing down the Soviet Union in global brinkmanship, it seemed the United States could finally step back from the nuclear abyss that threatened at a moment's notice to turn the Cold War into World War III. As events would turn out though, it seemed that the United States had jumped from the frying pan into the fire.

Loose Nukes

By 1991, the Soviet Union had amassed a stockpile of 35,000 nuclear warheads[1] [1] strategically located in the Soviet Republics of Russia, Ukraine, Belarus, and Kazakhstan. The failed coup in Moscow in August 1991 and subsequent disintegration of the Soviet Union raised concerns about the safety and security of nuclear weapons in the former Soviet Republics. [2, pp. 3-4] In 1968, the United States and Soviet Union signed the nuclear Nonproliferation Treaty (NPT) agreeing to keep nuclear weapons from countries that did not have them. [3] Fearing that those weapons and their secrets might now fall into the hands of rogue nations, in November 1991, senators Sam Nunn (D-GA), and Richard Lugar (R-IN) sponsored the Soviet Nuclear Threat Reduction Act authorizing $400 million to assist former members of the Soviet Union with 1) destroying nuclear, chemical, and other weapons of mass destruction, 2) providing secure transport for weapons on their way to destruction, and 3) establishing verifiable safeguards against proliferation of these weapons. [2, pp. 3-4]

[1] By 1991, the United States had amassed over 20,000 nuclear warheads. [1]

Initially, many in Congress saw U.S. assistance under Nunn-Lugar as an emergency response to impending chaos in the former Soviet Union. Even after the sense of immediate crisis passed in 1992 and 1993, many analysts and members of Congress remained concerned about the potential for diversion or a loss of control of nuclear and other weapons. Russia's economy was extremely weak and press accounts reported that nuclear materials from Russia were appearing on the black market in Western Europe. Consequently, many began to view the Cooperative Threat Reduction Program as part of a long-term threat reduction and nonproliferation effort in keeping with the 1968 Nonproliferation Treaty. This view changed, though, after 1995 Tokyo Subway Attack. [2, p. 5]

1995 Tokyo Subway Attack

Sarin is an odorless, colorless liquid that attacks the nervous system.

At 6:00 am on the morning of March 20, 1995, Ken'ichi Hirose was driven to the Yotsuya subway station in Tokyo. Upon arrival, Hirose boarded a westbound train to Shinjuku Station where he caught a northbound train to Ikebukuro Station. While waiting to board his next train, Hirose bought a sports tabloid then sought to isolate himself among the crowd. After surveying the other passengers to confirm nobody was looking, Hirose removed two plastic bags filled with clear liquid and wrapped them in the newspaper. The bags were filled with the deadly nerve agent Sarin. Ken'ichi Hirose was part of a five-man team dispatched by Shoko Asahara to attack the Japanese government. [4]

Shibuya Asahara proclaimed himself "Christ" and sought to take on the sins of the world in advance of a nuclear Armageddon from which he would emerge as "emperor" of Japan. On March 20, 1995, Asahara sought to hasten his prophesied apocalypse by murdering thousands of commuters transiting Tokyo's Kasumigaseki and Nagatacho districts, home to the Japanese government. Asahara also hoped it would put an end to a police investigation into murder charges against the cult. To attain his designs, Asahara would release the chemical agent Sarin within the crowded and confined Tokyo subway. [4]

Sarin is an odorless, colorless liquid that attacks the nervous system. Developed as a pesticide in 1938 Germany, it is outlawed by the 1993 Chemical Weapons Convention. Sarin quickly vaporizes when exposed to the atmosphere, posing a threat to victims either through inhalation or direct contact. Sarin is fatal even at very low concentrations; a single drop the size of a pinhead can kill an adult. Death follows quickly in one to ten minutes. [5]

On the morning of March 20, 1995, five members of Aum Shinrikyo, Ken'ichi Hirose, Ikuo Hayashi, Toru Toyoda, Masato Yokoyama, and Yasuo Hayashi, picked up their bags of Sarin and set out for the rush hour commute aboard the Tokyo subway. Hirose was a thirty-year-old doctor of Physics. Hayashi was a medical doctor held in esteem at the Ministry of Science and Technology before quitting his job and joining Aum. Toyoda was a Physics student who graduated with honors from the University of Tokyo and was about to begin doctoral studies when he joined Aum. Yokoyama was a thirty-one-year-old Applied Physics major who worked at an electronics firm before joining Aum. Thirty-seven year old Hayashi, the oldest member of the group, studied Artificial Intelligence at university and traveled to India to study yoga before joining Aum. Five men, all highly educated and psychologically sound, set out that Monday morning to launch a chemical attack on the world's busiest commuter transport system at the peak of morning rush hour. [4]

Each perpetrator carried two bags of Sarin, except Yasuo Hayashi who carried three. Carrying their bags of sarin and umbrellas with sharpened tips, the perpetrators boarded their appointed trains. At prearranged stations, the sarin bags wrapped in newspaper were dropped and punctured several times with the sharpened tip of an umbrella. Each perpetrator then got off the train and exited the station to rendezvous with pre-arranged getaway cars. They left behind them packets of Sarin leaking out onto train cars packed with passengers. [4]

Ken'ichi Hirose was aboard the second car of the A777 heading inward to the government district. As he was about to release the Sarin, Hirose caught the unwanted attention of a schoolgirl. He paused. To ward off her attention, Hirose decided to move up to the third car, taking his packet with him. As the train approached Ochanomizu Station, Hirose dropped the packet to the floor, whispered an Aum mantra, then punctured it with the tip of his umbrella. Hirose poked the packet with such force that he bent the tip of his sharpened umbrella. Still, both bags were successfully broken, and the Sarin began to leak across the train floor. Hirose immediately departed and fled for his waiting getaway car. [4]

Ikuo Hayashi arrived at Sendagi Station and purchased a copy of the Japan Communist Party newspaper to wrap his bags of Sarin. At 7:48 am he boarded the first car of the A725K inbound to Tokyo's central business district. Hayashi wore a surgical mask commonly worn by Japanese during cold and flu season. At Shin-Ochanomizu Station he dropped his packet to the floor and poked it with his umbrella. In his haste to flee, though, Hayashi succeeded in puncturing only one of the two bags. Sarin leaked out across the train as Hayashi moved quickly to join his getaway driver. [4]

Masato Yokoyama stopped on his way to Shinjuku Station to buy a paper to wrap his bags of Sarin. Yokoyama put on a wig and fake glasses before boarding the fifth car of the B801 inbound to the government district on the Marunouchi Line. As his train approached Yotsuya Station, Yokoyama dropped his packet to the floor and began poking it. He succeeded in making only a single puncture in one of the bags. As Yokoyama fled the scene, the single bag leaked Sarin slowly across the floor. [4]

Toru Toyoda picked up a newspaper and wrapped his Sarin bags on the way to Naka-Meguro Station. At 7:59 am he boarded the first car of the B711T inbound to Tokyo's central district. Sitting close to the door, Toyoda set the Sarin packet on the floor. When the train arrived at the next station, Ebisu, Toyoda punctured the bags as he disembarked. He was on the train a total of two minutes, the quickest drop of the day. [4]

In order to prove his loyalty, Yasuo Hayashi carried three bags of Sarin. These he wrapped in newspaper before boarding the train at 07:43. Hayashi took the third car of the A720S departing Ueno Station. Shortly after boarding, he dropped his packet to the floor. Two stops later, Hayashi punctured the bags as he departed the train at Akihabara Station. Hayashi made the most punctures of any of the perpetrators. [4]

As the Sarin started vaporizing, passengers within the packed cars began to fall sick. Victims would later report feeling nauseous and experiencing blurred vision. Neither knowing nor understanding what was happening, instinct took control and compelled them to flight. As the trains pulled into the next station, victims pushed their way out of the contaminated cars, unwittingly spreading the agent onto the crowded platforms. One passenger, noticing a liquid-soaked package on the floor, kicked it out the door onto the Kodenmacho Station platform. Soon, waiting commuters began feeling the effects and started pushing towards the exits. Some collapsed on the platform before they could make it. [4]

Unaware what was happening, the contaminated trains continued towards central Tokyo. Only after people started collapsing did agents realize something was seriously wrong and ordered all trains stopped. But not before thousands had been exposed. Hundreds collapsed outside the station entrances and lay on the ground waiting for assistance. Ambulances transported 688 to nearby hospitals. More than 4,000 made their own way, including the "worried well". Hospitals were overwhelmed. [4]

Of the 5,510 who sought treatment, 17 were deemed critical, 37 severe, and 984 moderate. By mid-afternoon, the mildly affected victims had recovered from vision problems and were released. Most of the remaining patients were well enough to go home the next day. Twelve people were not so fortunate and eventually died from their exposure. Most of them were station attendants who had sought to help stricken passengers. Experts suggest that if the attackers had been more successful in deploying the Sarin, thousands could have died. [4]

In 2008, victims were authorized payment of damages because the attack had been directed at the Japanese government. By 2009, 5,259 had applied for benefits under the law. Of those, 47 were certified disabled, and 1,077 certified having serious injuries or illnesses. Surveys of the victims showed that many still suffer from post-traumatic stress disorder. In one survey, 27% of 837 respondents complained they felt insecure whenever riding a train. [4]

The Tokyo subway attack was a seminal event; it was the first time a non-state group had used a weapon of mass destruction against civilians.

The Terrorism Threat

The Tokyo subway attack was a seminal event; it was the first time a non-state group had used a weapon of mass destruction against civilians. The incident appeared to underscore both the vulnerabilities and potentially catastrophic consequences of unprotected societies and ill-prepared governments in the face of indiscriminate attacks employing weapons of mass destruction. Two years earlier, the bombing of New York City's World Trade Center by Islamic fundamentalists had demonstrated that the United States itself was not immune to acts of terrorism intent on causing large numbers of casualties. Indeed, the six persons who perished in that attack and the approximately 1,000 others who were injured paled in comparison to the tens of thousands who might have been harmed had the terrorists' plans to topple one of the towers into the other actually had succeeded. If any further evidence were needed of this potential, it was provided less than a month after the Tokyo attack when Timothy McVeigh used a large truck bomb to demolish the Alfred P. Murrah Federal office building in Oklahoma City, killing 168 persons and injuring hundreds more. [6, p. 1]

Terrorism. "Acts dangerous to human life that are a violation of the criminal laws of the United States or of any State, that appear to be intended to intimidate or coerce a civilian population; influence the policy of a government by intimidation or coercion; or to affect the conduct of a government by mass destruction, assassination, or kidnapping."

- Title 18 United States Code, Section 2331

Until the 1993 attack on the World Trade Center, most Americans thought that terrorism was something that happened elsewhere. However frequently U.S. citizens and interests were the target of terrorists abroad, many nonetheless believed that the United States itself was somehow immune to such violence within its own borders. Terrorism, accordingly, was regarded as a sporadic—albeit attention-grabbing—problem that occasionally affected Americans traveling or living overseas and concerned only those U.S. government agencies with specific diplomatic and national security responsibilities. If the 1993 World Trade Center bombing shattered that complacency, then the explosion in Oklahoma City two years later dramatically underscored the breadth of grievances felt toward the U.S. government. The list of potential adversaries had seemed suddenly to grow from the foreign radicals and religious extremists located in other regions of the world about whom we had always worried, to include wholly domestic threats, such as those posed by the militantly antigovernment, white supremacist organizations that had come to light in the aftermath of the Oklahoma City tragedy. [6, p. 6]

In the wake of the New York and Oklahoma City bombings and Tokyo subway attacks, there was a dramatic shift in the perceived threat of WMD terrorism.

In the wake of the New York and Oklahoma City bombings and Tokyo subway attacks, there was a dramatic shift in the perceived threat of WMD terrorism. A number of developments account for this sudden shift in direction and appreciation for what had been previously dismissed as a far less realistic threat scenario. [6, p. 7]

First, terrorism had arguably shown a marked trend toward greater lethality. While some observers pointed optimistically to the decline in the number of international terrorist incidents during the 1990s as a noteworthy and salutary development in the struggle against terrorism, the percentage of terrorist incidents with fatalities had paradoxically increased. For example, at least one person was killed in 29% of terrorist incidents in 1995. That represented the highest ratio of fatalities to incidents recorded over the previous thirty years. [6, p. 7]

Second, the dangers posed specifically by chemical and biological weapons became increasingly apparent. In part, this was a function of the demise of the Cold War preoccupation with the nuclear dimension of international relations. Perhaps more significant, however, was the possibility that, given the ongoing travails of the Russian economy, poorly paid, disgruntled former Soviet scientists might attempt to sell their expertise in chemical, biological and nuclear weapons on the "open market" to terrorists or rogue states. [6, p. 8]

Finally, a precedent for mass destruction had been set in the guise of the 1995 Aum nerve gas attack. That incident represented the first widely known attempt by a non-state group to use WMD with the specific intent of causing mass civilian casualties. Moreover, Aum's use of such an exotic weapon as sarin may have raised the stakes for terrorists everywhere, who might feel driven to emulate or create their own version of the Tokyo attack to attract attention to themselves and their causes. [6, p. 9]

In the wake of these incidents, a new era of terrorism was perceived by experts and government officials alike who foresaw a potentially bloodier and more destructive age of violence emerging as we approached the twenty-first century. The changes in terrorism that they described raised concerns in the United States, especially within Congress and the Executive Branch, about the implications of evolving terrorist threats that were now seen to include use of WMD. [6, p. 1]

WMD is defined in 18USC S2332a. Current convention recognizes chemical, biological, radiological, and nuclear agents as general classes of WMD.

WMD Terrorism

According to 18USC S2332a, a weapon of mass destruction is "any weapon that is designed or intended to cause death or serious bodily injury through the release, dissemination, or impact of toxic or poisonous chemicals, or their precursors; any weapon involving a biological agent, toxin, or vector; or any weapon that is designed to release radiation or radioactivity at a level dangerous to human life." For simplicity, current convention recognizes chemical, biological, radiological, and nuclear (CBRN) agents as general classes of WMD. 18USC S2332a makes it illegal to employ WMD against U.S. citizens, anywhere in the world.

Chemical weapons are defined in 18USC S229F as "chemicals, precursors, munitions, or devices specifically designed to cause death or other harm through the toxic properties of the chemicals." Under 18USC S229F, it is illegal to develop, produce, acquire, or transfer chemical weapons. Chemical agents are generally classified by their effects. Thus nerve agents attack the body's nervous system, blood agents block oxygen transfer in the blood, blister agents cause blisters, and choking agents attack the respiratory system. Experts also recognize that a host of toxic industrial chemicals (TICs) essential to manufacturing processes may also be employed as weapons. [7, pp. II-10 - II-11] In 2005, the National Planning Scenarios were released, examining possible attack scenarios and their potential consequences. Of the fifteen listed scenarios, four related to chemical attacks. Two pertained to the release of chemical agents. The other two involved the release of toxic industrial chemicals. The deliberate destruction of a chlorine storage tank produced the most casualties, estimated at 17,500 according to the scenario. The nerve agent attack resulted in the second most casualties, estimated at 6,000 according to that scenario. In both scenarios, rescue operations were hampered by the difficulty of operating in a contaminated environment. [8]

Biological weapons are defined in 18USC S178 as "any microorganism or infectious substance, or any naturally occurring, bioengineered or synthesized component of any such microorganism or infectious substance, capable of causing death, disease, or other biological malfunction in a human, animal, plant, or other living organism; deterioration of food, water, equipment, supplies, or materials of any kind; or deleterious alteration of the environment." As with chemical weapons, it is illegal to develop, produce, stockpile, transfer, acquire, retain, or possess a biological agent or delivery system for use as a weapon. Biological agents include three basic categories: pathogens, toxins, and bioregulators. Pathogens are disease producing microorganisms such as bacteria, rickettsia, or viruses. Pathogens can occur naturally or can be altered with biotechnology. Toxins are poisons formed by a vegetable or animal, but can be produced synthetically also. Bioregulators affect cell processes in the body. Used as a bioweapon, they can cause severe adverse effects or death. [7, pp. II-18] The fifteen National Planning Scenarios describe five different types of biological incidents, four of them stemming from some form of attack. According to the Planning Scenarios, an anthrax attack could result in 13,000 casualties. Alternatively, the deliberate introduction of foot and mouth disease could kill an untold number of livestock. Either attack would be hugely disruptive to the national economy. [8]

18USC S2332a makes it illegal to employ WMD against U.S. citizens, anywhere in the world.

Radiological Dispersal Devices (RDDs), or "dirty bombs" are covered by the definition for WMD found in 18USC S2332a. Specifically, they include "any weapon that is designed or intended to release radiation or radioactivity at a level dangerous to human life; or any device or object that is capable of and designed or intended to endanger human life through the release of radiation or radioactivity." 18USC S2332h makes it illegal to knowingly produce, construct, acquire, transfer, receive, possess, import, export, possess, or threaten to use an RDD. The Planning Scenarios have only one RDD scenario. An RDD is not considered particularly destructive, but it is considered highly disruptive. According to the scenario, an RDD released in a major urban area could contaminate up to thirty-six city blocks. Essentially, the area of contamination would have to be evacuated until such time as it could be decontaminated. Decontamination could take years and cost billions of dollars. [8, pp. 11-1 - 11-4]

Nuclear weapons are also covered by the definition for WMD found in 18USC S232a. The Planning Scenarios postulate a situation in which a terrorist group assemble a gun-type nuclear device from highly enriched uranium (HEU) stolen from a former Soviet facility. The materials are smuggled into the United States and assembled near a major metropolitan center. The improvised nuclear device (IND) is transported by van to the central business district and detonated. The estimated 10-kiloton blast would incinerate most everything within half mile of the detonation. Blast damage would gradually taper off out to four miles from the epicenter. Electromagnetic pulse (EMP) would render any surviving electronics inoperative within three miles of the detonation. Those outside the blast radius but within twelve miles of detonation could be affected by radiation exposure. Winds could carry radioactive fallout as far as 150 miles and contaminate as much as 3,000 square miles. [8, pp. 1-1 - 1-5] Dissimilar circumstances make it difficult to draw comparisons with the August 6, 1945 bombing of Hiroshima with a similar type device, but casualties from the blast, radiation, and fallout might be expected to exceed 100,000. Of course, recovery would take decades and cost hundreds of billions of dollars.

As serious and potentially catastrophic a CBRN attack might prove, it is highly unlikely it could ever completely undermine national security. However, because of the extreme consequences that could result from a successful CBRN attack, event the remotest likelihood of one cannot be dismissed as insignificant.

Still, most experts agree that even if terrorists want to employ WMD, they don't necessarily have the requisite scientific knowledge or technical capabilities to implement their violent ambitions. Accordingly, as easy as some may argue it is for terrorists to culture anthrax spores or brew up a concoction of deadly nerve gas, the effective dissemination or dispersal of these viruses and poisons still presents serious technological hurdles that greatly inhibit their effective use. Indeed, the ultimate failure of the Tokyo subway attacks seems to affirm this position. [6, p. 38]

It should also be noted that, as serious and potentially catastrophic as a domestic terrorist CBRN attack might prove, it is highly unlikely that it could ever completely undermine the national security, much less threaten the survival, of the United States as a nation. Indeed, following the 1995 nerve gas attack, the Japanese government did not fall, widespread disorder did not ensue, nor did society collapse. There is no reason to assume that the outcome would be any different in the United States. [6, pp. 37-38]

However, because of the extreme consequences that could result from a successful CBRN attack, even the remotest likelihood of one cannot be dismissed as insignificant. The challenge in responding to the threat of potential terrorist use of CBRN weapons is to craft defense capabilities to respond to an incident if it occurs that are not only both cost-effective and appropriate, but dynamic enough to respond as effectively as possible in a wide a range of circumstances or scenarios. [6, pp. 34-35] The problem was, the Federal government was not ready.

U.S. Counterterrorism Posture

At the time of the Tokyo Subway Attacks, the U.S. response to a terrorist incident was seen as a highly coordinated interagency operation that included federal, state, and local participation. Primary federal agencies besides the Department of Justice (DoJ), Federal Bureau of Investigation (FBI), and Federal Emergency Management Agency (FEMA) included the Department of Defense (DoD), Department of Energy (DoE), the Environmental Protection Agency (EPA), and the Department of Health and Human Services (DHHS). [9, pp. CRS-6]

The National Security Council was the center of U.S. government efforts to coordinate the national response to threats or acts of domestic terrorism. The NSC Principals Committee, the Deputies Committee, and the Counterterrorism and National Preparedness Policy Coordination Committee (PCC) constituted the major policy and decision making bodies involved in the federal response to terrorism. [9, pp. CRS-7]

In the wake of the Tokyo subway attacks and Oklahoma City bombing, President Clinton in June 1995 signed PDD-39 updating U.S. policy on counterterrorism. PDD-39 designated the FBI as the Lead Federal Agency for responding to terrorist attacks on U.S. soil. FEMA was assigned responsibility for coordinating the Federal response to a WMD attack.

The PCC had four standing subordinate groups to coordinate policy in specific areas. The Counterterrorism and Security Group (CSG) coordinated policy for preventing and responding to foreign terrorism, either internationally or domestically. The Preparedness and Weapons of Mass Destruction Group provided policy coordination for preventing WMD attacks in the United States and developing response and consequence management capabilities to deal with domestic WMD incidents. The Information Infrastructure Protection and Assurance Group handled policy for preventing and responding to major threats to America's cyberspace, and the Continuity of Federal Operations Group was charged with policy coordination for assuring the continued operation of Constitutional offices and federal departments and agencies. [9, pp. CRS-7 - CRS-8]

When the NSC was advised of the threat of a terrorist incident or actual event, the appropriate subordinate group would convene to formulate recommendations for the Counterterrorism and Preparedness PCC who in turn would provide policy analysis for the Deputies Committee. The Deputies Committee would ensure that the issues being brought before the Principals Committee and NSC were properly analyzed and prepared for a decision by the President. [9, pp. CRS-8]

In the wake of the Tokyo subway attacks and Oklahoma City bombing, President Clinton in June 1995 signed Presidential Decision Directive #39 (PDD-39) updating U.S. policy on counterterrorism. Among its provisions, PDD-39 designated the FBI the Lead Federal Agency for responding to terrorist attacks on U.S. soil. PDD-39 also assigned FEMA primary responsibility for coordinating federal efforts in responding to the consequences of a WMD attack. [9, pp. CRS-5]

The FBI's first step when a terrorist threat was discovered was to initiate a threat credibility assessment. The FBI would take immediate steps to identify, acquire, and plan for the use of federal resources to augment the State and local authorities if the threat was deemed highly credible or an incident was verified. The FBI will designate a Federal On-Scene Commander (OSC) who would function as the incident manager for the U.S. Government. The FBI would operate from a Joint Operations Center (JOC) and report back to the Strategic Information Operations Center (SIOC) at FBI Headquarters in Washington DC. If necessary, the FBI could call upon a Domestic Emergency Support Team (DEST) comprised of representatives from other Federal agencies to help advise on the incident. In the event of a WMD incident, the FBI on-scene commander could request DoD support through the Attorney General. [9, pp. CRS-9 - CRS-13]

Concerned about the overall leadership and coordination of programs to combat terrorism, Congress established three separate commissions to investigate the prospects for WMD attack on U.S. soil.

Homeland Security

Concerned about the overall leadership and coordination of programs to combat terrorism, Congress established three separate commissions to include the Advisory Panel to Assess Domestic Response Capabilities for Terrorism Involving Weapons of Mass Destruction (also known as the Gilmore Panel because it was chaired by Governor James Gilmore III of Virginia); the United States Commission on National Security in the 21st Century (also known as the Hart-Rudman Commission because it was chaired by former Senators Gary Hart and Warren Rudman); and the National Commission on Terrorism (also known as the Bremer Commission because it Chairman was former Ambassador Paul Bremer). [10, p. 37]

The Bremer Commission raised the issue that the National Coordinator, the senior official responsible for coordinating all U.S. counterterrorism efforts, didn't have sufficient authority to ensure the President's priorities were reflected in agencies' budgets. The United States didn't have a single counterterrorism budget. Instead, counterterrorism programs existed in the individual budgets of 45 departments and agencies of the federal government. [11]

In December 2000, the second report of the Gilmore Commission issued a finding that the organization of the federal government's programs for combating terrorism was fragmented, uncoordinated, and politically unaccountable. It linked the lack of a national strategy to the fact that no entity had the authority to direct all of the agencies that may be engaged. At the federal level, no entity had the authority even to direct the coordination of relevant federal efforts. As a consequence, the Gilmore Commission recommended that the next President should establish a National Office for Combating Terrorism in the Executive Office of the President, and should seek a statutory basis for this office. [12]

The Gilmore Commission recommended that the National Office for Combating Terrorism should have a broad and comprehensive scope, with responsibility for the full range of deterring, preventing, preparing for, and responding to international as well as domestic terrorism. The director of the office should be the principal spokesman of the Executive Branch on all matters related to federal programs for combating terrorism and should be appointed by the President and confirmed by the Senate. The office should have a substantial and professional staff, drawn from existing National Security Council offices and other relevant agencies. The Gilmore Commission argued that the office should have at least five major sections, each headed by an Assistant Director:

1. Domestic Preparedness Programs
2. Intelligence
3. Health and Medical Programs
4. Research, Development, Test, and Evaluation (RDT&E), and National Standards
5. Management and Budget [12]

In February 2001, the Hart-Rudman Commission recommended the creation of a National Homeland Security Agency .

The Hart-Rudman Commission decried the fact that responsibility for homeland security resided at all levels of the U.S. government—local, state, and federal. That within the federal government, almost every agency and department was involved in some aspect of homeland security, but none was organized to focus on the scale of the contemporary threat to the homeland. The Hart-Rudman Commission recommended an organizational realignment that:

- Designated a single person, accountable to the President, to be responsible for coordinating and overseeing various U.S. government activities related to homeland security;
- Consolidated certain homeland security activities to improve their effectiveness and coherence;
- Established planning mechanisms to define clearly specific responses to specific types of threats; and
- Ensured that the appropriate resources and capabilities were available. [13]

In February 2001, the Hart-Rudman Commission recommended the creation of a National Homeland Security Agency (NHSA) with responsibility for planning, coordinating, and integrating various U.S. government activities involved in homeland security. [13] Sadly, the recommendation came too little too late. Less than seven months later the nation would suffer a terrorist attack of catastrophic proportions on its own soil. What few had foreseen was how it would be accomplished not by WMD, but by subverting the nation's infrastructure.

Conclusion

The United States stepped back from the brink of nuclear annihilation at the end of the Cold War only to face the threat of nuclear terrorism at the outset of the 21st century. The incident that brought this terrible prospect to the forefront of national security concern was the Tokyo subway bombing in 1995. It was the first employment of WMD by a non-state agent. Taken together with the increasing frequency and ferocity of terrorist attacks against the United States itself, the Tokyo subway bombing suddenly made the unthinkable not only thinkable, but credible. So as the United States prepared for a new century, it also started preparing for the prospect of a domestic terrorist attack employing a CBRN agent. As various advisory committees investigated the matter and advised Congress, they developed the concept of homeland security and the recommendation for a homeland security agency. What made it happen was what nobody expected would happen.

Challenge Your Understanding

The following questions are designed to challenge your understanding of the material presented in this chapter. Some questions may require additional research outside this book in order to provide a complete answer.

1. What was the historic significance of the Tokyo subway attacks?
2. Why are the Tokyo subway attacks considered an act of terrorism?
3. Do you have to be a terrorist to employ a WMD agent? Explain your answer.
4. What type of WMD agent do you think would be easiest to acquire? Explain your answer.
5. What type of WMD agent do you think would be most physically destructive? Explain your answer.
6. What type of WMD agent do you think could possibly cause the most deaths? Explain your answer.
7. Would you rather have one enemy with many WMD, or many enemies with one WMD? Explain.
8. Identify five differences between a soldier fighting for a country and a terrorist fighting for a cause.
9. Identify five differences between the 1995 Tokyo subway attacks and the 1995 Oklahoma City bombing.
10. Identify five differences between the 1995 Tokyo subway attacks and the 2007 Virginia Tech shooting.

Chapter 2

Lost Opportunities

Learning Outcomes

Careful study of this chapter will help a student do the following:

- Explain why Osama bin Laden declared war on the U.S.
- Describe the difficulties in arresting or killing Osama bin Laden.
- Compare the differences between an attack on U.S. soil and an attack against U.S. foreign interests.
- Discuss how 9/11 might have been prevented.

"A direct attack against American citizens on American Soil is likely over the next quarter century."

- Phase III Report of the U.S. Commission on National Security/21st Century

February 15, 2001

Introduction

On September 11th, 2001, the unthinkable happened, but not in the manner anybody imagined. This chapter examines the opportunities missed in the gathering storm that would become 9/11.

Al Qaeda was conceived in 1988 by Osama Bin Laden, the seventeenth child of a Saudi construction magnate.

New Priorities

After a bitterly contested election, George W. Bush was inaugurated the 46th President of the United States in January 2001. He campaigned on a platform that included bringing integrity and honor back to the White House, increasing the size of the military, cutting taxes, improving education, and aiding minorities. [1] Under the direction of his newly appointed National Security Advisor, Condoleezza Rice, the incoming national security team focused their priorities on China, missile defense, the Middle East peace process, and the Persian Gulf. In January 2001, Rice was briefed by the outgoing National Security Advisor, Sandy Berger, and told she would find herself spending more time on terrorism in general, and al Qaeda in particular. [2, p. 199]

Al Qaeda

Al Qaeda was conceived in 1988 by Osama Bin Laden, the seventeenth child of a Saudi construction magnate. [2, p. 55] In 1980, Bin Laden left university to help the mujahideen fight the Soviets in Afghanistan. [3] In December 1979, the Soviet Union sent the 40th Army into the Afghan capital of Kabul to prop up the pro-Soviet government of Nur Mohammad Taraki. [4] Arriving in Pakistan, bin Laden joined Abdullah Azzam and used money and machinery from his own construction company to help the mujahideen. By 1984, bin Laden and Azzam established Maktab al-Khidamat (MAK) to funnel money, arms, and fighters from around the Arab world into Afghanistan. [3] After nine years, the Soviets had killed 850,000-1.5 million Afghan civilians at a cost to their own forces of 14,453 killed and 11,654 wounded, but were still no nearer to suppressing the mujahideen insurgency. Unwilling or unable to sustain a counter-insurgency, Soviet forces withdrew from Afghanistan in April 1988. [4] As they departed, Bin Laden and Azzam agreed that the organization they created should not be allowed to dissolve. Accordingly, they established what they called a base or foundation, "al Qaeda" as a potential general headquarters for future jihad. Though Azzam had been considered number one in the MAK, by August 1988 bin Laden was clearly the leader of al Qaeda [2, pp. 55-56]

Bin Laden

In 1990, bin Laden returned home to Saudi Arabia. On August 2, 1990, Saddam Hussein launched the Iraqi invasion of Kuwait. With nothing to stop Iraqi forces from crossing into Saudi Arabia, the royal family felt at risk. Bin Laden, whose efforts in Afghanistan had earned him celebrity and respect, proposed to the Saudi monarchy that he summon mujahideen for a jihad to retake Kuwait. He was rebuffed, and the Saudis joined the U.S.-led coalition. [2, p. 57] On August 7, 1990, the U.S. 82nd Airborne landed in Dhahran Saudi Arabia, and took up positions barely 400 miles from Medina, the second holiest site in Islam. [3] Bin Laden and a number of Muslim clerics began to publicly denounce the arrangement. The Saudi government exiled the clerics and undertook to silence bin Laden by, among other things, confiscating his passport. With help from a dissident member of the royal family, bin Laden managed to get out of the country and make his way to Sudan. [2, p. 57]

In response to Saddam Hussein's invasion of Kuwait on August 2, 1990, the U.S. 82nd Airborne deployed to Dhahran Saudi Arabia, and took up positions barely 400 miles from Medina, the second holiest site in Islam. Bin Laden and a number of Muslim clerics began to publicly denounce the arrangement.

Exile in Sudan

Previously, In 1989, bin Laden had been invited by Hassan al Turabi, head of the National Islamic Front, to assist him in Sudan. After making his escape from Saudi Arabia in 1991, bin Laden moved to Khartoum and set about building a large set of complex and intertwined business and terrorist enterprises. In time, his business ventures would encompass numerous companies and a global network of bank accounts and nongovernmental institutions. Fulfilling his bargain with Turabi, bin Laden used his construction company to build a new highway from Khartoum to Port Sudan on the Red Sea coast. Meanwhile, al Qaeda finance officers and top operatives used their positions in bin Laden's companies to acquire weapons, explosives, and technical equipment for terrorist purposes. In early 1992, al Qaeda issued a fatwa, a religious edict calling for jihad against the Western "occupation" of Islamic lands, specifically singling out U.S. forces for attack. During bin Laden's time in Sudan, al Qaeda was suspected of supporting attacks against U.S. forces in Yemen, Somalia, and Saudi Arabia. [2, pp. 57-61] In 1995 al Qaeda was implicated in an assassination attempt against Egyptian President Hosni Mubarak. Subsequent pressure from Saudi Arabia, Egypt, and the United States forced the expulsion of bin Laden from Sudan. Because his citizenship had been revoked in 1994, bin Laden could not return to Saudi Arabia. Instead, he chose to return to Pakistan and eventually make his way back to Afghanistan. [3]

Return to Afghanistan

When bin Laden arrived in Pakistan in May 1996, the Taliban were still fighting to gain control of Afghanistan. After the Soviets departed in April 1988, Afghanistan erupted in civil war between competing militias. In 1994, the Taliban arose as a political-religious force, and with financial backing from Pakistan and Saudi Arabia, succeeded in rising to power in September 1996. [5] Under the protection of the Taliban leader, Mullah Muhammed Omar, bin Laden re-established al Qaeda operations in Kandahar, Afghanistan. Through his connections, bin Laden brought much needed financial support to the Taliban. In return, bin Laden and al Qaeda were given a sanctuary in which to train and indoctrinate fighters and terrorists, import weapons, and plot and staff terrorist schemes. The Taliban seemed to open the doors to all who wanted to come to Afghanistan to train in the camps. It is estimated some 10,000 to 20,000 fighters underwent instruction at bin Laden supported camps in Afghanistan from 1996 to 2001. [2, pp. 65-67]

Shortly after arriving in Afghanistan in 1996, bin Laden issued a fatwa declaring war against the United States.

War on the United States

Shortly after arriving in Afghanistan in 1996, bin Laden issued a fatwa declaring war against the United States. U.S. forces remained in Saudi Arabia to protect the kingdom from any further aggression by Saddam Hussein. [3] In his 1996 fatwa, bin Laden decried the "occupation of the land of the two Holy Places—the foundation of the house of Islam, the place of the revelation, the source of the message and the place of the noble Ka'ba, the Qiblah of all Muslims—by the armies of the American Crusaders and their allies." [6] Two years later, after al Qaeda had regathered its strength, bin Laden issued a second fatwa in February 1998. The second fatwa declared the killing of North Americans and their allies an "individual duty for every Muslim" to "liberate the al Aqsa Mosque (in Jerusalem) and the holy mosque (in Mecca) from their grip". At the public announcement of the fatwa, bin Laden called North Americans "very easy targets", and told journalists "You will see the results of this in a very short time." On August 7, 1998, two truck bombs were exploded outside U.S. embassies in Nairobi, Kenya, and Dar es Salaam, Tanzania. Together, the explosions killed 224 people including 12 Americans, and injured 4,500 more. The attacks were linked to al Qaeda, and bin Laden was placed on the FBI's list of Ten Most Wanted. [3]

Cat and Mouse

Al Qaeda and bin Laden had come to the attention of the U.S. before the African embassy bombings. The CIA had even conceived a kidnapping plan to deliver bin Laden to an Arab court to answer for his role in the failed assassination attempt on Egypt's president. Because CIA senior management didn't think the plan would work, it was never executed. Still, the CIA maintained surveillance of bin Laden and al Qaeda. It was because of this monitoring they were able to quickly trace the embassy bombings back to bin Laden. Debate about what to do settled very soon on one option: Tomahawk cruise missiles. [2, pp. 114-118] Two weeks later, on March 20, 1998, Navy vessels in the Arabian Sea fired about 75 cruise missiles at four training camps inside Afghanistan. One camp was where bin Laden met with other leaders. According to the CIA, bin Laden departed the camp just hours before the cruise missiles hit. [7] At the same time he authorized the cruise missile attacks, President Clinton issued a Memorandum of Notification authorizing the CIA to capture bin Laden. A second memorandum issued in December authorized the CIA to capture or kill bin Laden. As the agency examined alternative plans throughout 1999, all were discarded as either unlikely to succeed or likely to cause significant collateral damage. [2, pp. 126 -143] At the turn of the new century, al Qaeda was implicated in failed attacks against targets in Jordan, and the USS The Sullivans. Jordanian police foiled the first, and the boat filled with explosives sank before detonating. Together with a failed attack on Los Angeles International Airport they were collectively called the "Millennium Plot". [8] While reviewing these actions in January 2000, National Security Advisor Sandy Berger was advised that more al Qaeda attacks were not a question of "if" but rather of "when" and "where". The warning placed increased pressure on efforts to capture or kill bin Laden. The State Department was thwarted by the Taliban's refusal to give him over. CIA progress was slowed by attempts to recruit Taliban rivals in southern Afghanistan. Military options were stymied by absence of a friendly operating base in the area. President Clinton noted the lack of progress in March 2000 when he wrote in the margin of his daily briefing that "the United States could surely do better." [2, pp. 182-190] On October 12, 2000, a speed boat laden with explosives rammed the USS Cole in Yemen, killing 17 sailors and heavily damaging the destroyer. While al Qaeda was suspected in the attack, the absence of "smoking gun" evidence prevented the White House from delivering an ultimatum to the Taliban to give up bin Laden. Further action was subsequently deferred to the new Bush Administration after belatedly winning one of the closest presidential contests in U.S. history. [2, pp. 190-198]

On October 12, 2000, a speed boat laden with explosives rammed the USS Cole in Yemen, killing 17 sailors and heavily damaging the destroyer.

The Planes Operation

By early 1999, al Qaeda was already a potent adversary of the United States. Bin Laden and his chief of operations, Abu Hafs al Masri, also known as Mohammed Atef, occupied undisputed leadership positions atop al Qaeda's organizational structure. Within this structure, al Qaeda's worldwide terrorist operations relied heavily on the ideas and work of enterprising and strong willed field commanders who enjoyed considerable autonomy. Khalid Sheikh Mohammed (KSM) was one such commander. [2, p. 145] KSM was involved in the "Bojinka" plot, a 1995 plan to bomb 12 U.S. commercial jets in midair over the Pacific as they flew home from the Philippines. The plot was discovered, however, and KSM's accomplices arrested in Manila. KSM evaded capture and made his way to Afghanistan in 1996. Shortly after arriving, he managed a meeting with bin Laden and Mohammed Atef. KSM presented several ideas for attack against the United States. One proposal involved hijacking ten planes to attack targets on both the East and West coasts of the United States. In addition to the Twin Towers and Pentagon, the planes were to hit the White House, CIA and FBI headquarters, unidentified nuclear power plants, and the tallest buildings in California and Washington State. The tenth plane was to kill every adult male passenger before landing and denouncing U.S. Middle East policies in front of the media. Bin Laden listened, but did not commit. [9, pp. 1-2] He had just arrived in Afghanistan himself, and had yet to re-establish al Qaeda operations. It wasn't until after the African embassy bombings in 1998 that planning for the 9/11 operation began in earnest. In March/April 1999, bin Laden summoned KSM to Kandahar and told him al Qaeda would support his proposal, but he had to scale it back. KSM and bin Laden agreed to four targets: the Twin Towers, Pentagon, White House, and U.S. Capitol. The plot was now referred to within al Qaeda as the "Planes Operation". [2, pp. 148-154]

al Qaeda's worldwide terrorist operations relied heavily on the ideas and work of enterprising and strong willed field commanders who enjoyed considerable autonomy. Khalid Sheikh Mohammed (KSM) was one such commander. KSM presented several ideas for attack against the United States.

Recruitment

Bin Laden soon selected four individuals to serve as suicide operatives: Nawaf al Hazmi, Khalid al Mihdhar, Walid Muhammad Salih bin Attash, also known as Khallad, and Abu Bara Taizi. Hazmi and Mihdhar were Saudi nationals; Khallad and Abu Bara were from Yemen. KSM knew the Yemeni nationals would have trouble obtaining U.S. visas. Therefore, KSM decided to split the operation into two parts. Hazmi and Mihdhar would go to the United States, and Khallad and Abu Bara would go to Malaysia to carry out a smaller version of the Bojinka plot. The four spent most the rest of the year at the Mes Aynak training camp in Afghanistan before they flew to Kuala Lumpur where they were to study airport security and conduct surveillance of U.S. carriers. On January 15, 2000, Hazmi and Mihdhar took off for Los Angeles to complete plans for the U.S. portion of the attack. Khallad and Abu Bara remained behind, but they would never complete their portion of the Planes Operation; in the spring of 2000, bin Laden cancelled the Malaysia part of the operation because it was too difficult to coordinate with the U.S. part. Meanwhile, those plans continued. [9, pp. 2-3]

While KSM was deploying his initial operatives for the 9/11 attacks to Kuala Lumpur, a group of four Western-educated men who would prove ideal for the attacks were making their way from Hamburg Germany to al Qaeda camps in Afghanistan. The four were Mohamed Atta, Marwan al Shehhi, Ziad Jarrah, and Ramzi Binalshibh. Atta, Shehhi, and Jarrah would become pilots for the 9/11 attacks, while Binalshibh would act as a key coordinator for the plot. [9, p. 3]

Binalshibh, Atta, and Jarrah met with Bin Laden's deputy, Mohamed Atef, who directed them to return to Germany and enroll in flight training. Atta was chosen as the emir, or leader, of the mission. He met with Bin Laden to discuss the targets: the World Trade Center, which represented the U.S. economy; the Pentagon, a symbol of the U.S. military; and the U.S. Capitol, the perceived source of U.S. policy in support of Israel. The White House was also on the list, as Bin Laden considered it a political symbol and wanted to attack it as well. In early 2000, Shehhi, Atta, and Binalshibh met with KSM in Karachi for training that included learning about life in the United States and how to read airline schedules. [9, p. 4]

In March/April 1999, bin Laden summoned KSM to Kandahar and told him al Qaeda would support his proposal, but he had to scale it back. KSM and bin Laden agreed to four targets: the Twin Towers, Pentagon, White House, and U.S. Capitol. The plot was now referred to within al Qaeda as the "Planes Operation".

By early March 2000, all four new al Qaeda recruits were back in Hamburg. They began researching flight schools in Europe, but quickly found that training in the United States would be cheaper and faster. Atta, Shehhi, and Jarrah obtained U.S. visas, but Binalshibh—the sole Yemeni in the group—was rejected repeatedly. In the spring of 2000, Atta, Shehhi, and Jarrah prepared to travel to the United States to begin flight training. Binalshibh would remain behind and help coordinate the operation, serving as a link between KSM and Atta. [9, p. 4]

Training

While the Hamburg operatives were just joining the 9/11 plot, Nawaf al Hazmi and Khalid al Mihdhar were already living in the United States. Having arrived in Los Angeles in January, they moved to San Diego in February. KSM contends that he directed the two to settle in San Diego after learning from a phone book about language and flight schools there. Hazmi and Mihdhar were supposed to learn English and then enroll in flight schools, but they made only cursory attempts at both. Mihdhar paid for an English class that Hazmi took for about a month. The two al Qaeda operatives also took a few short flying lessons. According to their flight instructors, they were interested in learning to fly jets and did not realize that they had to start training on small planes. In June 2000, Mihdhar abruptly returned to his family in Yemen, apparently without permission. KSM was very displeased and wanted to remove him from the operation, but Bin Laden interceded, and Mihdhar remained part of the plot. [9, pp. 4-6]

On the East Coast, in May and June 2000, the three operatives from Hamburg who had succeeded in obtaining visas began arriving in the United States. Mohamed Atta and Marwan Shehhi flew into New Jersey; Ziad Jarrah flew into Florida. Atta and Shehi looked into flight schools in New Hampshire and New Jersey, and, after spending about a month in New York City, visited the Airman Flight School in Norman, Oklahoma. For some reason, Atta and Shehhi decided not to enroll there. Instead, they went to Venice, Florida, where Jarrah had already started his training at Florida Flight Training Center. Atta and Shehhi enrolled in a different flight school, Huffman Aviation, and began training almost daily. Jarrah obtained his single engine private pilot certificate in early August; Atta and Shehhi received their pilots' licenses a few weeks later. Their instructors described Atta and Shehhi as aggressive and rude, and in a hurry to complete their training. [9, p. 6]

The plot called for four pilots. By the fall of 2000, Atta, Shehhi, and Jarrah were progressing in their training.

The plot called for four pilots. By the fall of 2000, Atta, Shehhi, and Jarrah were progressing in their training. It was clear, though, that Hazmi and Mihdhar would not learn to fly aircraft. In their place was sent a young Saudi named Hani Hanjour. Hanjour had studied in the United States intermittently since 1991, and had undergone enough flight training in Arizona to obtain his commercial pilot certificate in April 1999. In 2000, he was training for al Qaeda at the al Faruq camp in Afghanistan. Recognizing his skills, Hanjour was sent to KSM for inclusion in the plot. On December 8, 2000, Hani Hanjour joined Nawaf al Hazmi in San Diego; Khalid al Mihdhar was still absent in Yemen. Together, Hanjour and Hazmi relocated to Mesa Arizona where Hanjour spent most of his previous time in the United States. By early 2001, Hanjour was training in a Boeing 737 simulator. Because his performance struck his flight instructors as sub-standard, they discouraged Hanjour from continuing, but he persisted. By the end of March, Hanjour finished training and drove east with Hazmi. On April 1 they were stopped and issued a speeding ticket in Oklahoma. A few days later they arrived in Northern Virginia and rented an apartment in Alexandria outside Washington DC. In May they moved to Paterson New Jersey to be closer to New York City. [9, pp. 7-8]

Back in Florida, the Hamburg pilots—Atta, Shehhi, and Jarrah—continued to train. By the end of 2000, they also were starting to train on jet aircraft simulators. Around the beginning of the New Year, all three of them left the United States on various foreign trips. Atta traveled to Germany for an early January 2001 meeting with Ramzi Binalshibh. Atta reported that the pilots had completed their training and were awaiting further instruction from al Qaeda. After the meeting, Atta returned to Florida and Binalshibh headed to Afghanistan to brief the al Qaeda leadership. [9, p. 7]

While the pilots trained in the United States, Bin Laden and al Qaeda leaders in Afghanistan started selecting the muscle hijackers—those operatives who would storm the cockpit and control the passengers on the four hijacked planes. (The term "muscle" hijacker appears in the interrogation reports of 9/11 conspirators KSM and Binalshibh, and has been widely used to refer to the non-pilot hijackers.) The so-called muscle hijackers actually were not physically imposing, as the majority of them were between 5'5" and 5'7" in height and slender in build. In addition to Hazmi and Mihdhar, the first pair to enter the United States, there were 13 other muscle hijackers, all but one from Saudi Arabia. They were Satam al Suqami, Wail and Waleed al Shehri (two brothers), Abdul Aziz al Omari, Fayez Banihammad (from the UAE), Ahmed al Ghamdi, Hamza al Ghamdi, Mohand al Shehri, Saeed al Ghamdi, Ahmad al Haznawi, Ahmed al Nami, Majed Moqed, and Salem al Hazmi (the brother of Nawaf al Hazmi). [9, p. 8]

While the pilots trained in the United States, Bin Laden and al Qaeda leaders in Afghanistan started selecting the muscle hijackers—those operatives who would storm the cockpit and control the passengers on the four hijacked planes.

The muscle hijackers received special training in Afghanistan on how to conduct hijackings, disarm air marshals, and handle explosives and knives. Next KSM sent them to the UAE, where his nephew, Ali Abdul Aziz Ali, and another al Qaeda member, Mustafa al Hawsawi, would help them buy plane tickets to the United States. In late April 2001, the muscle hijackers started arriving in the United States, specifically in Florida, Washington, DC, and New York. They traveled mostly in pairs and were assisted upon arrival by Atta and Shehhi in Florida or Hazmi and Hanjour in DC and New York. The final pair, Salem al Hazmi and Abdulaziz al Omari, arrived New York on June 29 and likely were picked up the following day by Salem's brother, Nawaf, as evidenced by Nawaf's minor traffic accident while heading east on the George Washington Bridge. Finally, on July 4, Khalid al Mihdhar, who had abandoned Nawaf al Hazmi back in San Diego 13 months earlier, re-entered the United States. Mihdhar promptly joined the group in Paterson, New Jersey. [9, pp. 8-9]

In addition to assisting the newly-arrived muscle hijackers, the pilots busied themselves during the summer of 2001 with cross-country surveillance flights and additional flight training. In addition to the test flights, some of the operatives obtained additional training. The 9/11 operatives were now split between two locations: southern Florida and Paterson, New Jersey. Atta had to coordinate the two groups, especially with Nawaf al Hazmi, who was considered Atta's second-in-command for the entire operation. Their first in-person meeting probably took place in June, when Hazmi flew round-trip between Newark and Miami. [9, p. 9]

The next step for Atta was a mid-July status meeting with Binalshibh at a small resort town in Spain. According to Binalshibh, the two discussed the progress of the plot, and Atta disclosed that he would still need about five or six weeks before he would be able to provide the date for the attacks. Atta also reported that he, Shehhi, and Jarrah had been able to carry box cutters onto their test flights; they had determined that the best time to storm the cockpit would be about 10-15 minutes after takeoff, when they noticed that cockpit doors were typically opened for the first time. Atta also said that the conspirators planned to crash their planes into the ground if they could not strike their targets. Atta himself planned to crash his aircraft into the streets of New York if he could not hit the World Trade Center. After the meeting, Binalshibh left to report the progress to the al Qaeda leadership in Afghanistan, and Atta returned to Florida on July 19. [9, pp. 9-10]

On August 15, 2001, a flight school reported to the FBI that one of its students, Zacarias Moussaoui only wanted to learn how to take off and land the airplane, that he had no background in aviation, and that he had paid in cash for the course.

In early August, Atta spent a day waiting at the Orlando airport for one additional muscle hijacker intended for the operation, Mohamed al Kahtani. Kahtani was turned away by U.S. immigration officials and failed to join the operation. On August 13, another in-person meeting of key players in the plot apparently took place, as Atta, Nawaf al Hazmi, and Hanjour gathered in Las Vegas. Two days later, the FBI learned about the strange behavior of Zacarias Moussaoui, who was now training on flight simulators in Minneapolis. [9, p. 10]

On August 15, 2001, the flight school reported its suspicions about Moussaoui to the FBI, including that he only wanted to learn how to take off and land the airplane, that he had no background in aviation, and that he had paid in cash for the course. The Minneapolis FBI opened an investigation on Moussaoui, believing that he was seeking flight training to commit a terrorist act. . [10, p. 101] On August 16, 2001, Moussaoui was arrested by FBI and INS agents in Minnesota and charged with an immigration violation. Materials itemized when he was arrested included a laptop computer, two knives, flight manuals pertaining to Boeing's 747 aircraft, a flight simulator computer program, fighting gloves and shin guards, and a computer disk with information about crop dusting. [11] Without any firm evidence of terrorist intentions, and unable to obtain a warrant to search Moussaoui's laptop, the FBI began plans to deport Moussaoui to France and ask French authorities to search his belongings. [10, p. 101]

Moussaoui's arrest occurred about a month after an FBI field agent in Phoenix sent an electronic communication to headquarters suggesting that bin Laden affiliated agents were attending flight schools with possible intent of targeting civil aviation. Later referred to as the "Phoenix Memo", the message was transmitted to the FBI Counterterrorism Division and New York Division on July 10, 2001. The message was sent after conducting surveillance on four students attending aviation colleges and universities in Arizona. While some of the subjects confessed to being al Qaeda members, none were associated with the Planes Operation. The Phoenix Memo did not raise any particular alarm at the FBI because it gave no specific evidence and was marked for "routine" action. [10, pp. 60-64]

On August 16, 2001, Moussaoui was arrested and charged with an immigration violation. Moussaoui's arrest occurred about a month after an FBI field agent sent what was later called the "Phoenix Memo" to headquarters suggesting that bin Laden affiliated agents were attending flight schools with possible intent of targeting civil aviation.

Just over two weeks before the attacks, the conspirators purchased their flight tickets. Between August 26 and September 5, they bought tickets on the Internet, by phone, and in person. Once the ticket purchases were made, the conspirators returned excess funds to al Qaeda. The last step was to travel to the departure points for the attacks. [9, p. 10]

The teams assembled according to their assigned targets. Operatives attacking the Pentagon gathered in Laurel Maryland near Dulles Airport where they were scheduled to take American Airlines Flight 77. On September 10th they stayed the night at a hotel in Herndon, Virginia. Operatives assigned to attack the White House gathered in Newark where they were scheduled to take United Airlines Flight 93. Just after midnight on September 9, Jarrah received a speeding ticket as he headed north through Maryland along Interstate 95, towards his team's staging point in New Jersey. The two teams targeting the Twin Towers both staged out of Boston. By September 9, Marwan al Shehhi and the team he would lead against United Airlines Flight 175 had arrived in Boston. The team that Mohammed Atta would lead against American Airlines Flight 11 was also assembled in Boston. Then, for reasons unknown, on September 10, Atta picked up Abdul Aziz al Omari, one of the Flight 11 muscle hijackers, from his Boston hotel and drove to Portland, Maine. They would take a commuter flight to Boston during the early hours of September 11 to connect to Flight 11. The Portland detour almost prevented Atta and Omari from making Flight 11 out of Boston. In fact, the luggage they checked in Portland failed to make it onto the plane.

On the morning of September 11, after years of planning and many months of intensive preparation, all four terrorist teams were in place to execute the attacks of that day. [9, pp. 10-11]

Conclusion

Though the 9/11 attacks were unforeseen, it is plausible they might still have been prevented. Before the attacks occurred, bin Laden was a known terrorist with an avowed mission to kill Americans, wanted by the U.S. government. Attempts to capture or kill him, though, were ultimately thwarted by a lack of will; while the CIA dallied in tribal negotiations, the administration was unwilling to risk the collateral damage attendant to overt military operations. Still, the Planes Operation might have been foiled during any number instances at home, particularly when 1) known al Qaeda operatives crossed U.S. borders, 2) the FBI received the Phoenix Memo warning of a potential strike against U.S. civil aviation, coupled with 3) the arrest of Zacarias Moussaoui while attending flight school, and 4) when plot members were ticketed for speeding. These lost opportunities, and more such on the day of the attacks, would figure prominently in shaping the nation's homeland security policy.

Challenge Your Understanding

The following questions are designed to challenge your understanding of the material presented in this chapter. Some questions may require additional research outside this book in order to provide a complete answer.

1. Why did Osama bin Laden declare war on the United States?
2. Describe the two different attacks Osama bin Laden successfully mounted against the U.S. before 9/11.
3. Identify five similarities between the 2000 attack on the USS Cole and the 1983 Beirut barracks bombing.
4. Identify five differences between the 2000 attack on the USS Cole and the 1993 World Trade Center attack.
5. Would you classify the following attacks as a criminal act or act of war? Explain your answers.
   a. 1983 Beirut barracks bombing
   b. 1993 attack on the World Trade Center
   c. 2000 attack on the USS Cole
6. Why didn't the U.S. simply arrest Osama bin Laden after the 2000 attack on the USS Cole?
7. Why didn't the U.S. simply kill Osama bin Laden after the 2000 attack on the USS Cole?
8. List three reasons why an attack on U.S. soil would be harder than an attack against U.S. foreign interests.
9. List three reasons why Osama bin Laden would want to mount an attack on U.S. soil.
10. Do you think 9/11 was preventable? Explain your answer.

Chapter 3

We Have Some Planes

Learning Outcomes

Careful study of this chapter will help a student do the following:

- Describe the 9/11 attacks.
- Explain the significance of the targets.
- Assess whether a similar attack would be successful today.
- Demonstrate the relationship between 9/11 and the 1995 Tokyo subway attacks.

"American 11: We have some planes. Just stay quiet, and you'll be okay. We are returning to the airport."

- 2004 9/11 Commissioner Report

Introduction

Tuesday, September 11, 2001, dawned temperate and nearly cloudless in the eastern United States. Millions of men and women readied themselves for work. Some made their way to the Twin Towers, the signature structures of the World Trade Center complex in New York City. Others went to Arlington, Virginia, to the Pentagon. Across the Potomac River, the United States Congress was back in session. At the other end of Pennsylvania Avenue, people began to line up for a White House tour. In Sarasota, Florida, President George W. Bush went for an early morning run.

For those heading to an airport, weather conditions could not have been better for a safe and pleasant journey. Among the travelers were Mohamed Atta and Abdul Aziz al Omari, who arrived at the airport in Portland Maine.

Table 3-1: 9/11 Hijackers & Flights

	AA Flt. 11, Boston Logan			AA Flt. 77, Dulles
1.	Mohammed Atta*		11.	Hani Hanjour*
2.	Abul Aziz al Omari		12.	Khalid al Midhhar
3.	Satam al Suqami		13.	Majed Moqed
4.	Wail al Shehri		14.	Nawaf al Hazmi
5.	Waleed al Shehri		15.	Salem al Hazmi
	UA Flt. 175, Boston Logan			UA Flt. 93, Newark
6.	Marwan al Shehhi*		16.	Ziad Jarrah*
7.	Fayez Banihammad		17.	Saeed al Ghamdi
8.	Mohand al Shehri		18.	Ahmed al Nami
9.	Ahmed al Ghamndi		19.	Ahad al Haznawi
10.	Hamza al Ghamdi			

*Designated Pilot

Boston: American 11 and United 175

On Tuesday, September 11, 2001, Mohammed Atta and Abul Aziz al Omari arrived at the airport in Portland Maine to catch a 6:00 a.m. flight to Boston's Logan International Airport. [1, p. 253]

When he checked in for his flight to Boston, Atta was selected by a computerized prescreening system known as CAPPS (Computer Assisted Passenger Prescreening System), created to identify passengers who should be subject to special security measures. Under security rules in place at the time, the only consequence of Atta's selection by CAPPS was that his checked bags were held off the plane until it was confirmed that he had boarded the aircraft. [1, p. 1]

At 6:45 a.m., Atta and Omari arrived in Boston. Between 6:45 and 7:40, Atta and Omari, along with Satam al Suqami, Wail al Shehri, and Waleed al Shehri, checked in and boarded American Airlines Flight 11, bound for Los Angeles. The flight was scheduled to depart at 7:45. [1, p. 2]

Elsewhere at Logan Airport, Marwan al Shehhi, Fayez Banihammad, Mohand al Shehri, Ahmed al Ghamdi, and Hamza al Ghamdi checked in for United Airlines Flight 175, also bound for Los Angeles. Their flight was scheduled to depart at 08:00. [1, p. 2]

As Atta's team passed through passenger screening, three members--Suqami, Wail al Shehri, and Waleed al Shehri--were selected by CAPPS. Their selection affected only the handling of their checked bags, not their screening at the checkpoint. All five men cleared the checkpoint and made their way to the gate for American 11. Atta, Omari, and Suqami took their seats in business class. The Shehri brothers had adjacent seats in row 2 in the first-class cabin. They boarded American 11 between 7:31 and 7:40. The aircraft pushed back from the gate at 7:40. [1, p. 2]

On the morning of September 11, 2001, eight of the nineteen hijackers were flagged by the Computer Assisted Passenger Prescreening System (CAPPS). Under security rules in place at the time, the only consequence was that their checked bags were held off the plane until it was confirmed that they had boarded

Shehhi and his team, none of whom had been selected by CAPPS, boarded United 175 between 7:23 and 7:28. Their aircraft pushed back from the gate just before 8:00. [1, p. 2]

Washington Dulles: American 77

At 7:15 a.m., Khalid al Mihdhar and Majed Moqed checked in with the American Airlines ticket counter at Dulles International Airport in Virginia. Both were ticketed for Flight 77 bound for Los Angeles. Within 20 minutes, three other members of the team checked in including Hani Hanjour, Nawaf al Hazmi, and Salem al Hazmi. Hani Hanjour, Khalid al Mihdhar, and Majed Moqed were flagged by CAPPS. The Hazmi brothers were also selected for extra security by the airline's customer service representative at the check-in counter. He did so because one of the brothers did not have photo identification nor could he understand English, and because the agent found both passengers to be suspicious. The only consequence of their selection was that their checked bags were held off the plane until it was confirmed that they had boarded the aircraft. [1, p. 3]

The five hijackers proceeded to the Main Terminal's west security screening point. The checkpoint featured closed-circuit television that recorded all passengers, including the hijackers as they were screened. Both Mihdhar and Moqed set off the metal detector and were directed to a second metal detector. Mihdhar did not trigger the alarm and was permitted through the checkpoint. Moqed set it off, a screener wanded him with a hand-held magnetic detector. He passed this inspection. About 20 minutes later, Hani Hanjour, Nawaf al Hazmi, and Salem al Hazmi entered the screening area. Nawaf al Hazmi set off both the first and second metal detectors and was then hand-wanded before being passed. In addition, his over-the-shoulder carry-on bag was swiped by an explosive trace detector and then passed. [1, p. 3]

At Washington Dulles, three of the hijackers set off metal detectors and were directed to secondary screening. All three passed inspection with a hand-held magnetic detector.

At 7:50 a.m., Majed Moqed and Khalid al Mihdhar boarded American 77 and were seated in 12A and 12B in coach. Hani Hanjour, assigned to seat 1B in first class, soon followed. The Hazmi brothers, sitting in 5E and 5F, joined Hanjour in the first-class cabin. [1, pp. 3-4]

Newark: United 93

At Newark Airport in New Jersey, another hijacking team assembled. Between 7:03 and 7:39, Saeed al Ghamdi, Ahmed al Nami, Ahad al Haznawi, and Ziad Jarrah checked in at the United Airlines Ticket counter for Flight 93, going to Los Angeles. Haznawi was selected by CAPPS. His checked bag was screened for explosives and then loaded on the plane. [1, p. 4]

The four men passed though the security checkpoint and boarded their plane between 7:39 and 7:48. All four had seats in the first-class cabin. Jarrah was in seat 1B, closest to the cockpit; Nami was in 3C, Ghamdi in 3D, and Haznawi in 6B. [1, p. 4]

The 19 men were aboard four transcontinental flights. They were planning to hijack these planes and turn them into large guided missiles, loaded with up to 11,400 gallons of jet fuel. By 8:00 a.m. on the morning of Tuesday, September 11, 2001, they had defeated all the security layers that America's civil aviation security system then had in place to prevent hijacking. [1, p. 4]

The Hijacking of American 11

American Airlines Flight 11 provided nonstop service from Boston to Los Angeles. On September 11, Captain John Ogonowski and First Officer Thomas McGuinness piloted the Boeing 767. It carried its full capacity of nine flight attendants. Eighty-one passengers boarded the flight with them, including the five terrorists. [1, p. 4]

American Flight 11 took off at 7:59. Just before 8:14, it had climbed to 26,000 feet, not quite its initial assigned cruising altitude of 29,000 feet. All communications and flight profile data were normal. About this time, the "Fasten Seatbelt" sign would usually have been turned off and the flight attendants would have begun preparing for cabin service. [1, p. 4]

At this time, American 11 had its last routine communication with the ground when it acknowledged navigational instructions from the FAA's air traffic control (ATC) center in Boston. Sixteen seconds after that transmission, ATC instructed the aircraft's pilots to climb to 35,000 feet. That message and all subsequent attempts to contact the flight were not acknowledged. From this and other evidence, it is believed the hijacking began at 8:14 or shortly thereafter. [1, p. 4]

By 8:00 a.m. on the morning of Tuesday, September 11, 2001, the nineteen hijackers had defeated all the security layers that America's civil aviation security system then had in place to prevent hijacking.

Reports from two flight attendants in the coach cabin, Betty Ong and Madeline "Amy" Sweeney, tell us most of what we know about how the hijacking happened. As it began, some of the hijackers--most likely Wail al Shehri and Waleed al Shehri, who were seated in row 2 in first class--stabbed the two unarmed flight attendants who would have been preparing for cabin service. [1, p. 5]

It's not known exactly how the hijackers gained access to the cockpit; FAA rules required that the doors remain closed and locked during flight. Ong speculated that they had "jammed their way" in. Perhaps the terrorists stabbed the flight attendants to get a cockpit key, to force one of them to open the cockpit door, or to lure the captain or first officer out of the cockpit. [1, p. 5]

At the same time or shortly thereafter, Atta--the only terrorist on board trained to fly a jet--would have moved to the cockpit from his business-class seat, possibly accompanied by Omari. As this was happening, passenger Daniel Lewin, who was seated in the row just behind Atta and Omari, was stabbed by one of the hijackers--probably Satam al Suqami, who was seated directly behind Lewin. Lewin had served four years as an officer in the Israeli military. He may have made an attempt to stop the hijackers in front of him, not realizing that another was sitting behind him. [1, p. 5]

The hijackers quickly gained control and sprayed Mace, pepper spray, or some other irritant in the first-class cabin, in order to for the passengers and flight attendants toward the rear of the plane. They claimed they had a bomb. [1, p. 5]

About five minutes after the hijacking began, Betty Ong contacted the American Airlines Southeastern Reservations Office in Cary, North Carolina, via an AT&T airphone to report an emergency aboard the flight. The emergency call lasted approximately 25 minutes, as Ong calmly and professionally relayed information about events taking place aboard the airplane to authorities on the ground. [1, p. 5]

At 8:19, Ong reported: "The cockpit is not answering, somebody's stabbed in business class--and I think there's Mace--that we can't breathe--I don't know, I think we're getting hijacked." She then told of the stabbings of the two flight attendants. [1, p. 5]

At 8:46:40, American 11 crashed into the North Tower of the World Trade Center in New York City. All on board, along with an unknown number of people in the tower, were killed instantly.

American's Southeastern Reservations Office quickly contacted the American Airlines operations center in Fort Worth, Texas, who soon contacted the FAA's Boston Air Traffic Control Center. Boston Center knew of a problem on the flight in part because just before 8:25 the hijackers had attempted to communicate with the passengers. The microphone was keyed, and immediately one of the hijackers said, "Nobody move. Everything will be okay. If you try to make any moves, you'll endanger yourself and the airplane. Just stay quiet." Air traffic controllers heard the transmission; Ong did not. The hijackers probably did not know how to operate the cockpit radio communication system correctly, and thus inadvertently broadcast their message over the air traffic control channel instead of the cabin public-address channel. Also at 8:25, and again at 8:29, Amy Sweeney got through to the American Flight Services Office in Boston but was cut off after she reported someone was hurt aboard the flight. Three minutes later, Sweeney was reconnected to the office and began relaying updates to her manager. [1, pp. 5-6]

At 8:26, Ong reported that the plane was "flying erratically." A minute later, Flight 11 turned south. American also began getting identifications of the hijackers, as Ong and then Sweeney passed on some of the seat numbers of those who had gained unauthorized access to the cockpit. [1, p. 6]

At 8:41 Sweeney reported that passengers in coach were under the impression there was a routine medical emergency in first class. Other flight attendants were busy at duties such as getting medical supplies while Ong and Sweeney were reporting events. [1, p. 6]

At 8:41, American's operations center learned that air traffic controllers had declared Flight 11 a hijacking, and thought it was headed toward Kennedy airport in New York City. Air traffic control was busy moving other flights out of the way as they tracked Flight 11 on primary radar, which seemed to show the aircraft descending. [1, p. 6]

At 8:44 contact was lost with Betty Ong. About this time Sweeney reported "Something is wrong. We are in a rapid descent... we are all over the place." When asked to look out the window, Sweeney reported "We are flying low. We are flying very, very low. We are flying way too low." Seconds later she said, "Oh my God we are way too low." The phone call ended. [1, p. 7]

At 8:46:40, American 11 crashed into the North Tower of the World Trade Center in New York City. All on board, along with an unknown number of people in the tower, were killed instantly. [1, p. 7]

The Hijacking of United 175

United Airlines Flight 175 was scheduled to depart for Los Angeles at 8:00. Captain Victor Saracini and First Officer Michael Horrocks piloted the Boeing767, which had seven flight attendants. Fifty-six passengers boarded the flight. [1, p. 7]

United 175 pushed back from its gate at 7:58 and departed Logan Airport at 8:14. By 8:33, it had reached its assigned cruising altitude of 31,000 feet. The flight attendants would have begun their cabin service. [1, p. 7]

The hijackers attacked sometime between 8:42 and 8:46. They used knives, Mace, and the threat of a bomb. They stabbed members of the flight crew. Both pilots had been killed. The eyewitness accounts came from calls made from the rear of the plane, from passengers originally seated further forward in the cabin, a sign that passengers and perhaps crew had been moved to the back of the aircraft. [1, p. 7]

The first operational evidence that something was abnormal on United 175 came at 8:47 when the aircraft changed beacon codes twice within a minute. At 8:51, the flight deviated from its assigned altitude, and a minute later New York air traffic controllers began repeatedly and unsuccessfully trying to contact it.

The first operational evidence that something was abnormal on United 175 came at 8:47 when the aircraft changed beacon codes twice within a minute. At 8:51, the flight deviated from its assigned altitude, and a minute later New York air traffic controllers began repeatedly and unsuccessfully trying to contact it. [1, p. 7]

At 8:52, in Easton, Connecticut, a man named Lee Hanson received a phone call from his son Peter, a passenger on United 175. His son told him: "I think they've taken over the cockpit--an attendant has been stabbed--and someone else up front may have been killed. The plane is making strange moves. Call United Airlines--Tell them it's Flight 175, Boston to LA." Lee Hansen then called the Easton Police Department and relayed what he had heard. [1, p. 7]

Also at 8:52, a male flight attendant called a United office in San Francisco. The flight attendant reported that the flight had been hijacked, both pilots killed, a flight attendant stabbed, and the hijackers were probably flying the plane. The call lasted about two minutes. [1, pp. 7-8]

At 8:58, the flight took a heading toward New York City. At 8:59, Flight 175 passenger Brian David Sweeney tried to call his wife, Julie. He left a message on their home answering machine that the plane had been hijacked. He then called his mother, Luise Sweeney, told her the flight had been hijacked, and added that the passengers were thinking about storming the cockpit to take control of the plane away from the hijackers. [1, p. 8]

At 9:03:11, United Airlines Flight 175 struck the South Tower of the World Trade Center. All on board, along with an unknown number of people in the tower, were killed instantly.

At 9:00, Lee Hanson received a second call from his son Peter: It's getting bad, Dad--A stewardess was stabbed--They seem to have knives and Mace--They said they have a bomb--It's getting very bad on the plane--Passengers are throwing up and getting sick--The plane is making jerky movements--I don't think the pilot is flying the plane--I think we are going down--I think they intend to go to Chicago or someplace and fly into a building--Don't worry Dad--If it happens, it'll be very fast--My God, my God. [1, p. 8]

The call ended abruptly. Lee Hanson had heard a woman scream just before it cut off. He turned on a television, and in her home so did Luise Sweeney. Both then saw the second aircraft hit the World Trade Center. [1, p. 8]

At 9:03:11, United Airlines Flight 175 struck the South Tower of the World Trade Center. All on board, along with an unknown number of people in the tower, were killed instantly. [1, p. 8]

The Hijacking of American 77

American Airlines Flight 77 was scheduled to depart from Washington Dulles for Los Angeles at 8:10. The aircraft was a Boeing 757 piloted by Captain Charles F. Burlingame and First Officer David Charlebois. There were four flight attendants. On September 11, the flight carried 58 passengers. [1, p. 8]

American 77 pushed back from its gate at 8:09 and took off at 8:20. At 8:46, the flight reached its assigned cruising altitude of 35,000 feet. Cabin service would have begun. At 8:51, American 77 transmitted its last routine radio communication. The hijacking began between 8:51 and 8:54. As on American 11 and United 175, the hijackers used knives and moved all the passengers to the rear of the aircraft. Unlike the earlier flights, the Flight 77 hijackers were reported by a passenger to have box cutters. Finally, a passenger reported that an announcement had been made by the "pilot" that the plane had been hijacked. Neither of the firsthand accounts mentioned any stabbings or the threat or use of either a bomb or Mace, though both witnesses began the flight in the first-class cabin. [1, p. 8]

At 8:54, American 77 deviated from its assigned course, turning south. Two minutes later the transponder was turned off and even primary radar contact with the aircraft was lost. The Indianapolis Air Traffic Control Center repeatedly tried and failed to contact the aircraft. American Airlines dispatchers also tried, without success.

At 8:54, the aircraft deviated from its assigned course, turning south. Two minutes later the transponder was turned off and even primary radar contact with the aircraft was lost. The Indianapolis Air Traffic Control Center repeatedly tried and failed to contact the aircraft. American Airlines dispatchers also tried, without success. [1, p. 9]

At 9:00, American Airlines Executive Vice President Gerard Arpey learned that communications had been lost with American 77. This was now the second American aircraft in trouble. He ordered all American Airlines flights in the Northeast that had not taken off to remain on the ground. After learning that United Airlines was missing a plane, American Airlines headquarters extended the ground stop nationwide. [1, p. 9]

At 9:12, Renee May called her mother, Nancy May, in Las Vegas. She said her flight was being hijacked by six individuals who had moved them to the rear of the plane. She asked her mother to alert American Airlines. Nancy May and her husband promptly did so. [1, p. 9]

As some point between 9:16 and 9:26, Barbara Olson called her husband, Ted Olson, the solicitor general of the United States. She reported that the flight had been hijacked, and the hijackers had knives and box cutters. She further indicated that the hijackers were not aware of her phone call, and that they had put all the passengers in the back of the plane. About a minute into the conversation the call was cut off. [1, p. 9]

Shortly after the first call, Barbara Olson reached her husband again. She reported that the pilot had announced that the flight had been hijacked, and she asked her husband what she should tell the captain to do. Ted Olson asked for her location and she replied that the aircraft was then flying over houses. Another passenger told her they were traveling northeast. The Solicitor General then informed his wife of the two previous hijackings and crashes. She did not display signs of panic and did not indicate any awareness of an impending crash. At that point the second call was cut off. [1, p. 9]

At 9:37:46, American Airlines Flight 77 crashed into the Pentagon, traveling at approximately 530 miles per hour. All on board, as well as many civilian and military personnel in the building, were killed.

At 9:20, the autopilot on American 77 was disengaged; the aircraft was at 7,000 feet and approximately 38 miles west of the Pentagon. At 9:32, controllers at the Dulles Terminal Radar Approach Control "observed a primary radar target tracking eastbound at a high rate of speed." This was later determined to have been Flight 77. [1, p. 9]

At 9:34, Ronald Reagan Washington National Airport advised the Secret Service of an unknown aircraft heading in the direction of the White House. American 77 was then 5 miles west-southwest of the Pentagon and began a 330 degree turn. At the end of the turn, it was descending through 2,200 feet, pointed toward the Pentagon and downtown Washington. The hijacker pilot then advanced the throttles to maximum power an dove toward the Pentagon. [1, p. 9]

At 9:37:46, American Airlines Flight 77 crashed into the Pentagon, traveling at approximately 530 miles per hour. All on board, as well as many civilian and military personnel in the building, were killed. [1, p. 10]

The Battle for United 93

At 8:42, United Airlines Flight 93 took off from Newark (New Jersey) Liberty International Airport bound for San Francisco. The aircraft was piloted by Captain Jason Dahl and First Officer Leroy Homer, and there were five flight attendants. Thirty-seven passengers, including the hijackers, boarded the plane. Scheduled to depart the gate at 8:00, the Boeing 757's takeoff was delayed because of the airport's typically heavy morning traffic. [1, p. 10]

As United 93 left Newark, the flight's crew members were unaware of the hijacking of American 11. Around 9:00, the FAA, American, and United were facing the staggering realization of apparent multiple hijackings. At 9:03, they would see another aircraft strike the World Trade Center. Crisis managers at the FAA and the airlines did not yet act to warn other aircraft. At the same time, Boston Center realized that a message transmitted just before 8:25 by the hijacker pilot of American 11 included the phrase, "We have some planes." [1, p. 10]

The hijackers attacked at 9:28. While traveling 35,000 feet above eastern Ohio, United 93 suddenly dropped 700 feet. Eleven seconds into the descent, the FAA's air traffic control center in Cleveland received the first of two radio transmissions from the aircraft. During the first broadcast, the captain or first officer could be heard declaring "Mayday" amid the sounds of a physical struggle in the cockpit. The second radio transmission, 35 seconds later, indicated that the fight was continuing. The captain or first officer could be heard shouting: "Hey get out of here--get out of here--get out of here." [1, p. 11]

At 9:32, a hijacker, probably Jarrah, made or attempted to make the following announcement to the passengers of Flight 93: "Ladies and Gentlemen: Here the captain, please sit down keep remaining sitting. We have a bomb on board. So, sit." The flight data recorder (also recovered) indicates that Jarrah then instructed the plane's autopilot to turn the aircraft around and head east. [1, p. 11]

Aboard United 93, five calls described the intent of passengers and surviving crew members to revolt against the hijackers. According to one call, they voted on whether to rush the terrorists in an attempt to retake the plane. They decided, and acted.

The cockpit voice recorder data indicate that a woman, most likely a flight attendant, was being held captive in the cockpit. She struggled with one of the hijackers who killed or otherwise silenced her. [1, p. 12]

Shortly thereafter, the passengers and flight crew began a series of calls from GTE airphones and cellular phones. The calls between family, friends, and colleagues took place until the end of the flight and provided those on the ground with firsthand accounts. They enabled the passengers to gain critical information, including the news that two aircraft had slammed into the World Trade Center. [1, p. 12]

Five calls described the intent of passengers and surviving crew members to revolt against the hijackers. According to one call, they voted on whether to rush the terrorists in an attempt to retake the plane. They decided, and acted. [1, p. 13]

At 9:57, the passenger assault began. Several passengers had terminated phone calls with loved ones in order to join the revolt. One of the callers ended her message as follows: "Everyone's running up to first class. I've got to go. Bye." [1, p. 13]

The cockpit voice recorder captured the sounds of the passenger assault muffled by the intervening cockpit door. Some family members who listened to the recording report that they can hear the voice of a loved one among the din. We cannot identify whose voices can be heard. But the assault was sustained. [1, p. 13]

In response, Jarrah immediately began to roll the airplane to the left and right, attempting to knock the passengers off balance. At 9:58:57, Jarrah told another hijacker in the cockpit to block the door. Jarrah continued to roll the airplane sharply left and right, but the assault continued. At 9:59:52, Jarrah changed tactics and pitched the nose of the airplane up and down to disrupt the assault. The recorder captured the sounds of loud thumps, crashes, shouts, and breaking glasses and plates. At 10:00:03, Jarrah stabilized the airplane. [1, pp. 13-14]

At 10:02:23, with the sounds of the passenger counterattack continuing, United 93 plowed into an empty field in Shanksville, Pennsylvania, at 580 miles per hour, about 20 minutes flying time from Washington, D.C.

Five seconds later, Jarrah asked, "Is that it? Shall we finish it off?" A hijacker responded, "No. Not yet. When they all come, we finish it off." The sounds of fighting continued outside the cockpit. Again, Jarrah pitched the nose of the aircraft up and down. At 10:00:26, a passenger in the background said, "In the cockpit. If we don't we'll die!" Sixteen seconds later, a passenger yelled, "Roll it!" Jarrah stopped the violent maneuvers about 10:01:00 and said, "Allah is the greatest! Allah is the greatest!" He then asked another hijacker in the cockpit. "Is that it? I mean, shall we put it down?" To which the other replied, "Yes, put it in it, and pull it down." [1, p. 14]

The passengers continued their assault and at 10:02:23, a hijacker said, "Pull it down! Pull it down!" The hijackers remained at the controls but must have judged that the passengers were only seconds from overcoming them. The airplane headed down; the control wheel was turned hard to the right. The airplane rolled onto its back, and one of the hijackers began shouting "Allah is the greatest. Allah is the greatest." With the sounds of the passenger counterattack continuing, the aircraft plowed into an empty field in Shanksville, Pennsylvania, at 580 miles per hour, about 20 minutes flying time from Washington, D.C. [1, p. 14]

Jarrah's objective was to crash his airliner into symbols of the American Republic, the Capitol or the White House. He was defeated by the alerted, unarmed passengers of United 93. [1, p. 14]

Table 3-2: 9/11 Timeline

11 Sep 01	Flt.	Events
07:59	AA 11	Takeoff from Boston Logan
08:14	UA 175	Takeoff from Boston Logan
08:19	AA 11	Report of Onboard Trouble
08:20	AA 77	Takeoff from Dulles
08:41	AA 11	Declared Hijacking
08:42	UA 175	Suspected Time of Attack
08:42	UA 93	Takeoff from Newark
08:46	AA 11	Crashes into WTC North Tower
08:47	UA 175	Aircraft Beacon Codes Changed
08:51	AA 77	Suspected Time of Attack
08:54	AA 77	Aircraft Deviates from Course
09:03	UA 175	Crashes into WTC South Tower
09:28	UA 93	Suspected Time of Attack
09:32	AA 77	Tracked Inbound to DC
09:37	AA 77	Crashes into Pentagon
09:57	UA 93	Passengers Assault Hijackers
10:03	UA 93	Crashes in Shanksville, PA

Conclusion

More than 2,600 people died at the World Trade Center; 125 died at the Pentagon; 256 died on the four planes. The death toll surpassed that at Pearl Harbor in December 1941. This immeasurable pain was inflicted by 19 young Arabs acting at the behest of Islamist extremists headquartered in distant Afghanistan. Some had been in the United States for more than a year, mixing with the rest of the population. Though four had training as pilots, most were not well-educated. Most spoke English poorly, some hardly at all. In groups of four or five, carrying with them only small knives, box cutters, and cans of Mace or pepper spray, they had hijacked the four planes and turned them into deadly guided missiles.

Challenge Your Understanding

The following questions are designed to challenge your understanding of the material presented in this chapter. Some questions may require additional research outside this book in order to provide a complete answer.

1. Who was responsible for airport security on 9/11?
2. Describe three airport security measures the 19 hijackers defeated on 9/11.
3. What was the purpose of hijacking transcontinental passenger jets?
4. Describe three different methods the hijackers used to subdue aircraft cabin and crew.
5. How were the hijackers able to evade FAA tracking?
6. Why do you suppose the Twin Towers and Pentagon were selected as targets?
7. What do you suppose was the target of the fourth aircraft?
8. Why do you suppose the passengers of the first three aircraft didn't mount a collective resistance?
9. Identify five similarities between 9/11 and the 1995 Tokyo subway attacks.
10. Do you think a similar attack would be successful today? Explain your answer.

Chapter 4

And They Saved Many

Learning Outcomes

Careful study of this chapter will help a student do the following:

- Describe emergency response efforts in New York City on 9/11.
- Evaluate emergency response efforts in New York City on 9/11.
- Appreciate the dedication and effectiveness of first responders on 9/11.

"That day we lost 2,752 people at the World Trade Center; 343 were firefighters. But we also saved 25,000 people. And that's what people should remember because firefighters and rescuers went in and they knew it was dangerous, but they went in to save people. And they saved many."

- 9/11 Commission Staff Statement No. 13, 2004

Introduction

Unlike most of America, both New York City and the World Trade Center had been the target of terrorist attacks before 9/11. On February 26, 1993, a 1,500-pound bomb stashed in a rental van was detonated on a parking garage ramp beneath the Twin Towers. The explosion killed six people, injured 1,000 more, and exposed vulnerabilities in the World Trade Center's and the City's emergency preparedness. The towers lost power and communications capability. Generators had to be shut down to assure safety. Elevators stopped. The public address system and emergency lighting systems failed. The unlit stairwells filled with smoke and were so dark as to be impassable. Rescue efforts by the Fire Department of New York were hampered by the inability of its radios to function in buildings as large as the Twin Towers. The 9-1-1 emergency call system was overwhelmed. [1, p. 3] Despite a $100 million overhaul to the WTC, including fire safety enhancements, many of the same problems plagued the WTC response on 9/11. This chapter reviews the emergency response to the 9/11 attacks in New York City, and examines compounding factors that contributed to the largest loss of life of any emergency response agency in U.S. history.

The WTC actually consisted of seven buildings spread across 16 acres, connected by an underground mall. The Twin Towers were the signature structures, containing 10.4 million square feet of office space. On any given work day up to 50,000 office workers occupied the towers, and 40,000 visitors passed through the complex.

The World Trade Center

The World Trade Center (WTC) complex was built for the Port Authority of New York and New Jersey. Construction began in 1967, and tenants began to occupy its space in 1970. The Twin Towers came to occupy a unique and symbolic place in the culture of New York City and America. [1, p. 2]

The WTC actually consisted of seven buildings, including one hotel, spread across 16 acres of land. The buildings were connected by an underground mall one level below the plaza area. The Twin Towers ("1 WTC" or the "North Tower," and "2 WTC" or the "South Tower") were the signature structures, containing 10.4 million square feet of office space. On any given work day up to 50,000 office workers occupied the towers, and 40,000 visitors passed through the complex. [1, p. 2]

The Twin Towers

Both towers had 110 stories and were about 1,350 feet high. Both were square; each wall measured 208 feet in length. The outside of each tower was covered by a frame of 14- inch-wide steel columns; the centers of the steel columns were 40 inches apart. These exterior walls bore the majority of the weight of the building. [1, p. 2]

The interior core of the buildings was a hollow steel shaft, in which elevators and stairwells were grouped. Each tower contained three central stairwells, which ran essentially from top to bottom, and 99 elevators. Generally, elevators originating in the lobby ran to "sky lobbies" on upper floors, where further elevators carried passengers to the tops of the buildings. [1, p. 2]

Stairwells A and C ran from the 110th floor to the mezzanine level and Stairwell B ran from the 107th floor to level B6. All three stairwells ran essentially straight up and down, except for two deviations in Stairwells A and C where the staircase jutted out toward the perimeter of the building. These deviations were necessary because of the placement of heavy elevators and machine rooms. These areas were located between the 42nd and 48th floors and the 76th and 82nd floors in both towers. [1, p. 2]

On the upper and lower boundaries of these deviations were "transfer" hallways contained within the stairwell proper. Each hallway contained "smoke doors" to prevent smoke from rising from lower to upper portions of the building. Smoke doors were kept closed but not locked. Other than these slight deviations in Stairwells A and C, the stairs ran straight up and down. [1, p. 2]

Doors leading to the roof were kept locked. The Port Authority told us that this was because of structural and radiation hazards, and for security reasons. To access the roof in either towers required passing through three doors: one leading from the stairwell onto the 110th floor, and two leading from the floor onto the roof itself. There was no rooftop evacuation plan. The roof was a cluttered surface that would be a challenging helipad even in good conditions and, in a fire, smoke from the building would travel upward. [1, pp. 2-3]

Emergency Preparedness

To address the problems encountered during the response to the 1993 bombing, the Port Authority implemented $100 million in physical, structural, and technological changes to the WTC. In addition, the Port Authority enhanced its fire safety plan. [1, p. 3]

The Port Authority added battery-powered emergency lighting to the stairwells and backup power to its alarm system. Other upgrades included glow-in-the-dark signs and markings. Upgrades to the elevator system included a redesign of each building's lobby command board to enable it to monitor all of the elevators. [1, p. 3]

To aid communications the Port Authority installed a "repeater system" for use by the Fire Department of New York. The "repeater" used an antenna on the top of 5 WTC to "repeat" and greatly amplify the wave strength of radio communications, so they could be heard more effectively by firefighters operating many floors apart. [1, p. 3]

Civilians were not informed that rooftop evacuations were not part of the Port Authority's evacuation plan. They were not informed that access to the roof required a key. The Port Authority acknowledges that it had no protocol for rescuing people trapped above a fire in the towers.

The Port Authority also sought to prepare civilians better for future emergencies. Deputy fire safety directors conducted biannual fire drills, with advance notice to tenants. During a fire drill, designated fire wardens were instructed to lead people in their respective areas to the center of the floor where they would use an emergency intercom phone to obtain specific information on how to proceed. [1, p. 3]

Civilians were taught basic procedures such as to evacuate by the stairs and to check doors for heat before proceeding. Civilians who evacuated in both 1993 and 2001 have told us that they were better prepared in 2001. [1, p. 3]

Civilians were not, however, directed into the stairwells during these drills. Civilians were not provided information about the configuration of the stairwells and the existence of transfer hallways or smoke doors. Neither full nor partial evacuation drills were held. Participation in the drills that were held, moreover, varied greatly from tenant to tenant. [1, pp. 3-4]

Civilians were never instructed not to evacuate up. The standard fire drill instructions advised participants that in the event of an actual emergency, they would be directed to descend to at least two floors below the fire. Most civilians recall simply being taught to await instructions which would be provided at the time of an emergency. [1, p. 4]

Civilians were not informed that rooftop evacuations were not part of the Port Authority's evacuation plan. They were not informed that access to the roof required a key. The Port Authority acknowledges that it had no protocol for rescuing people trapped above a fire in the towers. [1, p. 4]

First Responders

On 9/11, the principal first responders were from the Fire Department of New York (FDNY), the New York Police Department (NYPD), the Port Authority Police Department (PAPD), and the Mayor's Office of Emergency Management (OEM). [1, p. 4]

NYPD

The 40,000-officer New York Police Department consisted of three primary divisions: operations, intelligence, and administration. The Special Operations Division supervised units critical in responding to a major event. This division included the aviation unit, which provided helicopters for the purpose of survey and/or rescue, and the Emergency Service Units (ESU), or rescue teams, which carried out specialized missions. [1, p. 4]

On 9/11, the principal first responders were from the Fire Department of New York (FDNY), the New York Police Department (NYPD), the Port Authority Police Department (PAPD), and the Mayor's Office of Emergency Management (OEM).

The NYPD had standard operating procedures for the dispatch of officers to an incident. Gradations in response were called "mobilization" levels and went from 1 (lowest) to 4 (highest). Level 3 and 4 mobilizations could not be ordered by someone below the rank of captain. [1, p. 4]

The NYPD ran the City's 9-1-1 emergency call center. 9-1-1 operators were civilians trained in the rudiments of emergency response. Fire emergencies were transferred to the FDNY dispatch center. [1, p. 4]

FDNY

The 11,000-member Fire Department of New York was headed by a Fire Commissioner, who, unlike the Police Commissioner, lacked operational authority. Operations were controlled by the Chief of the Fire Department. The logistics of fire operations were coordinated by Fire Dispatch Operations division. 9-1-1 calls concerning fire emergencies were transferred to this division. [1, p. 4]

Basic operating units included ladder companies, to conduct standard rescue operations, and engine companies, to put out fires. The Department's Specialized Operations Command contained specialized units, including five rescue companies, to perform specialized and highly risky rescue operations, and one HAZMAT team. [1, p. 4]

Alarm levels escalated from first (lowest) to fifth (highest) with a pre-established number of units associated with each. Prior to 9/11, it was common FDNY practice for units to arrive with extra personnel, and for off-duty firefighters to respond to major incidents. . [1, p. 5]

The years leading up to 9/11 were successful ones for the FDNY. In 2000, fewer people died from fires in New York City—107—than in any year since 1946. Firefighter deaths—22 during the 1990s—compared favorably with the best periods in FDNY history. The FDNY had fought 153,000 fires in 1976; in 1999, that number had been reduced to 60,000. [1, p. 5]

The Mayor's creation of the Office of Emergency Management and the issuance of his Incident Command Directive were attempts to address the long-standing rivalry between the NYPD and the FDNY.

Emergency Operations

In July 2001, Mayor Rudolph Giuliani signed a directive entitled "Direction and Control of Emergencies in the City of New York." Its purpose was "to ensure the optimum use of agency resources while ... eliminating potential conflict among responding agencies which may have areas of overlapping expertise and responsibility." [1, p. 5]

The directive designated, for different types of emergencies, an appropriate agency as "Incident Commander." The Incident Commander would be "responsible for the management of the City's response to the emergency." The role of the Mayor's Office of Emergency Management was supportive, to "coordinate the participation of all city agencies in resolving the event," and to "assist the Incident Commander in his/her efforts in the development and implementation of the strategy for resolving the event." [1, p. 5]

The Mayor's creation of the Office of Emergency Management and the issuance of his Incident Command Directive were attempts to address the long-standing rivalry between the NYPD and the FDNY. This rivalry has been acknowledged by every witness we have asked about it. Some characterized the more extreme manifestations of the rivalry—fistfights at the scenes of emergencies, for instance—as the actions of "a few knuckleheads." Some described the rivalry as the result of healthy organizational pride and competition. Others told us that the problem has escalated over time and has hampered the ability of the City to respond well in emergency situations. [1, p. 5]

The NYPD and the FDNY were two of the preeminent emergency response organizations in the United States. But each considered itself operationally autonomous. Each was accustomed to responding independently to emergencies. By September 11 neither had demonstrated the readiness to respond to an "Incident Commander" if that commander was an official outside of their Department. The Mayor's Office of Emergency Management had not overcome this problem. [1, p. 5]

September 11, 2001

At 8:46:40 a.m. the hijacked American Airlines Flight 11 flew into the upper portion of the North Tower. [1, p. 6]

A jet fuel fireball erupted upon impact, and shot down at least one bank of elevators. The fireball exploded onto numerous lower floors, including the 77th, 50th, 22nd, West Street lobby level, and the B4 level, four stories below ground. The burning jet fuel immediately created thick, black smoke which enveloped the upper floors and roof of the North Tower. The roof of the South Tower was also engulfed in smoke because of prevailing light winds from the north. [1, p. 6]

At 8:46:40 a.m. the hijacked American Airlines Flight 11 flew into the upper portion of the North Tower. The first response came from private firms and individuals—the people and companies in the building. Everything that would happen to them during the next few minutes would turn on their circumstances and their preparedness, assisted by building personnel on site.

Within minutes, New York City's 9-1-1 system was flooded with eyewitness accounts of the event. Most callers correctly identified the target of the attack. Some identified the plane as a commercial airliner. [1, p. 6]

The first response came from private firms and individuals—the people and companies in the building. Everything that would happen to them during the next few minutes would turn on their circumstances and their preparedness, assisted by building personnel on site. [1, p. 6]

Trapped

Because all of the building's stairwells were destroyed in the impact zone, the hundreds of survivors trapped on or above the 92nd floor gathered in large and small groups, primarily between the 103rd and 106th floors. A large group was reported on the 92nd floor, technically below the impact but trapped by debris. Civilians were also reported trapped below the impact zone, mostly on floors in the eighties, though also on at least the 47th and 22nd floors, as well as in a number of elevators. [1, p. 6]

Because of damage to the building's systems, civilians did not receive instructions on how to proceed over the public address system. Many were unable to use the emergency intercom phones as instructed in fire drills. Many called 9-1-1. [1, p. 6]

9-1-1 operators and FDNY dispatchers had no information about either the location or magnitude of the impact zone and were therefore unable to provide information as fundamental as whether callers were above or below the fire. 9-1-1 operators were also not given any information about the feasibility of rooftop rescues. In most instances, 9-1- 1 operators and FDNY dispatchers, to whom the 9-1-1 calls were transferred, therefore relied on standard operating procedure for high-rise fires. Those procedures are to advise civilians to stay low, remain where they are, and wait for emergency personnel to reach them. This advice was given to callers from the North Tower for locations both above and below the impact. [1, pp. 6-7]

Although the default guidance to stay in place seemed understandable in cases of conventional fire, all the emergency officials that morning quickly judged that the North Tower should be evacuated. The acting fire safety director in the North Tower immediately ordered everyone to evacuate that building, but the public address system was damaged and no one apparently heard the announcement.

The protocol of advising against evacuation, of telling people to stay where they were, was one of the lessons learned from the 1993 bombing. Fire chiefs told us that the evacuation of tens of thousands of people from skyscrapers can create many new problems, especially for disabled individuals or those in poor health. Many of the injuries after the 1993 bombing occurred during the evacuation. Evacuees also may complicate the movements and work of firefighters and other emergency workers. [1, p. 7]

Although the default guidance to stay in place may seem understandable in cases of conventional high rise fires, all the emergency officials that morning quickly judged that the North Tower should be evacuated. The acting fire safety director in the North Tower immediately ordered everyone to evacuate that building, but the public address system was damaged and no one apparently heard the announcement. [1, p. 7]

Hence, one of the few ways to communicate to people in the building was through calls to the 9-1-1 or other emergency operators. We found no protocol for communicating updated evacuation guidance to the 9-1-1 operators who were receiving calls for help. Improvising as they learned information from callers, some operators advised callers that they could break windows. Some operators were advising callers to evacuate if they could. [1, p. 7]

Evacuation

Below the impact zone in the North Tower, those civilians who could began evacuating down the stairs almost immediately. [1, p. 7]

Civilians who called the Port Authority police desk at 5 WTC were advised to leave if they could. Most civilians began evacuating without waiting to obtain instructions over the intercom system. Some had trouble reaching the exits because of damage caused by the impact. While evacuating, they were confused by deviations in the increasingly crowded stairwells, and impeded by doors which were locked or jammed as a result of the impact. Despite these obstacles, the evacuation was relatively calm and orderly. [1, p. 7]

Within ten minutes of impact, smoke was beginning to rise to the upper floors in debilitating volumes and isolated fires were reported, although there were some pockets of refuge. Faced with insufferable heat, smoke, and fire, and no prospect for relief, some jumped or fell from the building. [1, p. 8]

Within ten minutes of impact, smoke was beginning to rise to the upper floors in debilitating volumes and isolated fires were reported, although there were some pockets of refuge. Faced with insufferable heat, smoke, and fire, and no prospect for relief, some jumped or fell from the building.

Confusion Next Door

Many civilians in the South Tower were unaware initially of what happened in the other tower. Many people decided to leave. Some were advised to do so by fire wardens. In addition, some entire companies, including Morgan Stanley, which occupied over 20 floors of the South Tower, were evacuated by company security officials. [1, p. 8]

The evacuation standard operating procedures did not provide a specific protocol for when to evacuate one tower in the event of a major explosion in the other. At 8:49 a.m. the deputy fire safety director in the North Tower spoke with his counterpart in the South Tower. They agreed to wait for the FDNY to arrive before determining whether to evacuate the South Tower. According to one fire chief, it was unimaginable, "beyond our consciousness," that another plane might hit the adjacent tower. [1, p. 8]

In the meantime, an announcement came over the public address system in the South Tower urging people to stay in place. Indeed, evacuees in the sky lobbies and the main lobby were advised by building personnel to return to their offices. The Port Authority told us that the advice may have been prompted by the safety hazard posed by falling debris and victims outside the building. Similar advice was given by security officials in the sky lobby of the South Tower. We do not know the reason for this advice, in part because the on-duty deputy fire safety director in charge of the South Tower perished in the tower's collapse. As a result of the announcement, many civilians in the South Tower remained on their floors. Others reversed their evacuation and went back up. The Port Authority Police desk in 5 WTC gave conflicting advice to people in the South Tower about whether to evacuate. [1, pp. 8-9]

FDNY Response

The FDNY response began immediately after the crash. Chief Pfeifer, Deputy Assistant Chief, FDNY and four companies arrived at about 8:52 a.m. As they entered the lobby, they immediately encountered badly burned civilians who had been caught in the path of the fireball. [1, p. 9=10]

Peter Hayden, Assistant Chief, FDNY, and Chief Pfeifer, the initial FDNY incident commanders were briefed on building systems by building personnel. Units began mobilizing in the increasingly crowded lobby. It was challenging for the chiefs to keep track of arriving units. They were frustrated by the absence of working building systems and elevators. [1, p. 10]

The FDNY response began immediately after the crash. Chief Pfeifer, Deputy Assistant Chief, FDNY and four companies arrived at about 8:52 a.m. Shortly before 9:00 a.m., FDNY chiefs advised building personnel and a Port Authority Police Department officer to evacuate the adjacent South Tower. Impressed by the magnitude of the catastrophe, fire chiefs had decided to clear the whole WTC complex.

Shortly before 9:00 a.m., FDNY chiefs advised building personnel and a Port Authority Police Department officer to evacuate the adjacent South Tower. Impressed by the magnitude of the catastrophe, fire chiefs had decided to clear the whole WTC complex, including the South Tower. [1, p. 11]

By 9:00 a.m., many senior FDNY leaders, including seven of the eleven most highly ranked chiefs in the department, had begun responding from headquarters in Brooklyn. The Chief of Department and the Chief of Operations called a 5th alarm, which would bring additional engine and ladder companies; they also called two more FDNY Rescue teams. The Chief of Department arrived at approximately 9:00 a.m. He established an overall Incident Command Post on the median of the West Side Highway. [1, p. 11]

Emergency Medical Service (EMS) personnel were directed to one of four triage areas around the perimeter of the WTC. In addition, many private hospital ambulances were rushing to the WTC complex. [1, p. 11]

In the North Tower lobby, the chiefs quickly made the decision that the fire in the North Tower could not be fought. The chiefs decided to concentrate on evacuating civilians from the North Tower, although they held various views about whether anyone at or above the impact zone could be saved. [1, p. 11]

As of 9:00 a.m., if only those units dispatched had responded, and if those dispatched units were not "riding heavy" with extra men, 235 firefighters would be at the scene or enroute. The vast majority of these would be expected to enter the North Tower. [1, p. 11]

NYPD Response

The NYPD response also began seconds after the crash. At 8:47 a.m. the NYPD ordered a Level 3 Mobilization. An initial mobilization point for patrol officers was established on the west side of the intersection of West and Liberty Streets. NYPD rescue teams were directed to mobilize at the intersection of Church and Vesey Streets. The first of these officers arrived at Church and Vesey at 8:56 a.m. At 8:50 a.m., the aviation unit of the NYPD dispatched two helicopters to the WTC to report on conditions and assess the feasibility of a rooftop landing or special rescue operations. [1, p. 12]

Within ten minutes of the crash, NYPD and Port Authority Police personnel were assisting with the evacuation of civilians. [1, p. 12]

The NYPD response also began seconds after the crash. At 8:47 a.m. the NYPD ordered a Level 3 Mobilization. At 8:58 a.m., the NYPD Chief raised the department's mobilization to Level 4—its highest level—which would result in the dispatch of approximately 30 lieutenants, 100 sergeants, and 800 police officers, in addition to rescue teams, which were already at the scene.

At 8:58 a.m., a helicopter pilot reported on rooftop conditions for the possibility of rooftop extraction. They didn't see anybody up on the roof. Even so, the heat and the smoke from the building interfered with the rotor system, making it difficult to hold position. [1, p. 12]

At 8:58 a.m., while enroute, the Chief of the NYPD raised the department's mobilization to Level 4—its highest level—which would result in the dispatch of approximately 30 lieutenants, 100 sergeants, and 800 police officers, in addition to rescue teams, which were already at the scene. The Chief of Department arrived at Church and Vesey at 9:00 a.m. [1, p. 12]

At 9:01 a.m., the NYPD patrol mobilization point at West and Liberty was moved to West and Vesey, in order to handle the greater number of patrol officers who would be responding to the Level 4 mobilization. These officers would be stationed around the perimeter of the complex to assist with evacuation and crowd control. [1, p. 13]

Around the city, the NYPD cleared routes along major thoroughfares for emergency vehicles responding to the WTC. The NYPD and Port Authority police coordinated the closing of bridges, subways, PATH trains, and tunnels into Manhattan. [1, p. 13]

Port Authority Response

The Port Authority's on-site commanding police officer was standing in the concourse when a fireball exploded out of the North Tower lobby, causing him to dive for cover. Within minutes of impact Port Authority police from bridge, tunnel, and airport commands began responding to the WTC. Officers from the WTC command began assisting in evacuating civilians. The Port Authority Police Department lacked clear standard operating procedures to guide personnel responding from one command to another during a major incident. [1, p. 13]

The Port Authority's on-site commanding police officer was standing in the concourse when a fireball exploded out of the North Tower lobby, causing him to dive for cover. Within minutes of impact Port Authority police from bridge, tunnel, and airport commands began responding to the WTC. Officers from the WTC command began assisting in evacuating civilians.

The fire safety director in charge of the complex arrived in the North Tower lobby at approximately 8:52 a.m. and was informed by the deputy fire safety director there that evacuation instructions had been announced over the public address system within one minute of impact. As mentioned earlier, to our knowledge, because the public address system had been damaged upon impact, no civilians heard that announcement. [1, p. 13]

At 9:00 a.m., the Port Authority Police commanding officer ordered an evacuation of civilians in the World Trade Center complex because of the danger posed by highly flammable jet fuel from Flight 11. The order was issued, however, over a radio channel which could be heard only by officers on the Port Authority WTC command channel. There is no evidence that this order was communicated to officers in other Port Authority Police commands or to members of other responding agencies. At 9:00 a.m., the Port Authority Police Superintendent and Chief of Department arrived together at the WTC complex, and made their way to the North Tower lobby. Some Port Authority officers immediately began climbing the stairs and assisting civilians. [1, p. 13]

OEM Response

Officials in the Office of Emergency Management's headquarters at 7 WTC began to activate its emergency operation center immediately after the North Tower was hit. At approximately 8:50 a.m. a senior representative from that office arrived in the lobby of the North Tower and began to act as its field responder. [1, p. 13]

In the 17-minute period between 8:46 a.m. and 9:03 a.m. on September 11, New York City and the Port Authority of New York and New Jersey had mobilized the largest rescue operation in the City's history. Well over one thousand first responders had been deployed, evacuations had begun, and the critical decision that the fire could not be fought had been made. [1, p. 14]

The decision was made to evacuate the South Tower as well. At 9:02 a.m., a further announcement in the South Tower advised civilians to begin an orderly evacuation if conditions warranted. [1, p. 14]

One minute later, a plane hit the South Tower. [1, p. 14]

Second Crash

At 9:03 a.m., the hijacked United Airlines Flight 175 hit 2 WTC (the South Tower) from the south, crashing through the 78th to 84th floors. What had been the largest and most complicated rescue operation in city history instantly doubled in magnitude. [1, p. 14]

In the 17-minute period between 8:46 a.m. and 9:03 a.m. on September 11, New York City and the Port Authority of New York and New Jersey had mobilized the largest rescue operation in the City's history. Well over one thousand first responders had been deployed, evacuations had begun, and the critical decision that the fire could not be fought had been made.

The plane banked as it hit the building, leaving portions of the building undamaged on impact floors. As a consequence—and in contrast to the situation in the North Tower—one of the stairwells (Stairwell A) initially remained passable from top to bottom. [1, p. 14]

At the lowest point of impact, the 78th floor sky lobby, hundreds had been waiting to evacuate when the plane hit. Many were killed or injured severely; others were relatively unaffected. We know of at least one civilian who seized the initiative and shouted that anyone who could walk should walk to the stairs, and anyone who could help should help others in need of assistance. At least two small groups of civilians descended from that floor. [1, p. 14]

Others remained alive in the impact zone above the 78th floor, though conditions on these floors began to deteriorate within ten minutes. [1, p. 14]

Repeat Nightmare

As in the North Tower, civilians became first responders. Some civilians ascended the stairs and others remained on affected floors to assist colleagues. Although Stairwell A in the South Tower remained passable from above the impact zone to the lobby, conditions were difficult and deteriorating. [1, p. 15]

Many ascended in search of clearer air or to attempt to reach the roof. Those attempting to reach the roof were thwarted by locked doors. Others attempting to descend were frustrated by jammed or locked doors in stairwells or confused by the structure of the stairwell deviations. [1, p. 16]

By 9:35 a.m., the West Street lobby level of the South Tower was becoming overwhelmed by injured who had descended to the lobby but were having difficulty continuing. [1, p. 16]

Within 15 minutes of the impact, debilitating smoke had reached at least one location on the 100th floor, and severe smoke conditions were reported throughout floors in the nineties and hundreds over the course of the following half hour. By 9:30 a.m. a number of civilians who had failed to reach the roof and could not descend because of intensifying smoke became trapped on the 105th floor. There were reports of tremendous smoke in most areas of that floor, but at least one area remained less affected until shortly before the building collapsed. [1, p. 16]

In the North Tower, evacuation generally continued. Thousands of civilians continued to descend in an orderly manner. On the 91st floor, the highest floor with stairway access, all but one were uninjured and able to descend.

Still, there were several areas between the impact zone and the uppermost floors where conditions were better. At least a hundred people remained alive on the 88th and 89th floors, in some cases calling 9-1-1 for direction. The 9-1-1 system remained plagued by the operators' lack of awareness of what was occurring and by the sheer volume of emergency calls. [1, p. 16]

No one in the first responder community knew that Stairwell A remained potentially passable. No callers were advised that helicopter rescues were not feasible. Civilians below the impact were also generally advised to remain where they were by 9-1-1 or FDNY dispatch operators. [1, p. 17]

North Tower

Back in the North Tower, evacuation generally continued. Thousands of civilians continued to descend in an orderly manner. On the 91st floor, the highest floor with stairway access, all but one were uninjured and able to descend. At 9:11 a.m., Port Authority workers at the 64th floor of the North Tower were told by the Port Authority Police desk in Jersey City to stay near the stairwells and wait for assistance. These workers eventually began to descend anyway, but most of them died in the collapse of the North Tower. [1, p. 17]

Those who descended Stairwell B of the North Tower exited between the elevator banks in the lobby. Those who descended the Stairwells A and C exited at the raised mezzanine level, where the smoky air was causing respiratory problems. All civilians were directed into the concourse at lobby level. Officers from the Port Authority and New York Police Departments continued to assist with the evacuation of civilians, for example, guiding them through the concourse in order to shelter the evacuees from falling debris and victims. [1, p. 17]

By 9:55 a.m., those few civilians who were still evacuating consisted primarily of injured, handicapped, elderly, or severely overweight individuals. [1, p. 17]

Calls to 9-1-1 reflect that others remained alive above and below the impact zone, reporting increasingly desperate conditions. [1, p. 17]

Double Trouble

Immediately after the second plane hit, the FDNY Chief of Department called a second 5th alarm. While nine Brooklyn units had been staged on the Brooklyn side of the Brooklyn Battery tunnel at 8:53 a.m., these units were not dispatched to the scene at this time. Instead, units from further away were dispatched. [1, p. 17]

Just after the South Tower impact, chiefs in the North Tower lobby huddled to discuss strategy for the operations and communication in the two towers.

Just after the South Tower impact, chiefs in the North Tower lobby huddled to discuss strategy for the operations and communication in the two towers. [1, p. 18]

At 9:05 a.m., two FDNY chiefs tested the WTC complex's repeater system. This was the system installed after the 1993 bombing in order to enable firefighters operating on upper floors to maintain consistent radio communication with the lobby command. The system had been activated for use on portable radios at 8:54 a.m., but a second button which would have enabled the master hand-set was not activated at that time. The chief testing the master handset at 9:05 a.m. did not realize that the master handset had not been activated. When he could not communicate, he concluded that the system was down. The system was working, however, and was used subsequently by firefighters in the South Tower. [1, p. 18]

The FDNY Chief of Safety agreed with the consensus that the only choice was to let the fires "burn up and out." The chiefs in the North Tower were forced to make decisions based on little or no information. [1, p. 18]

Climbing up the stairwells carrying heavy equipment was a laborious task even for physically fit firefighters. Though the lobby command post did not know it, one battalion chief in the North Tower found a working elevator, which he took to the 16th floor before beginning to climb. Just prior to 10:00 a.m., about an hour after firefighters first began streaming into the North Tower, at least two companies of firefighters had climbed to the sky lobby on the 44th floor of the North Tower. Numerous units were located between the 5th and 37th floors in the North Tower. [1, p. 18]

South Tower

At approximately 9:07 a.m., two chiefs commenced operations in the South Tower lobby. Almost immediately they were joined by an Office of Emergency Management field responder. They were not immediately joined by a sizable number of fire companies, as most, if not all units which had been in the North Tower lobby remained there. One chief and a ladder company found a working elevator to the 40th floor. From there they proceeded to climb Stairwell B. One member of the ladder company stayed behind to operate the elevator. [1, pp. 18-19]

Poor Communications

At approximately 9:07 a.m., two FDNY chiefs commenced operations in the South Tower lobby. Unlike the commanders in the North Tower lobby, these chiefs in the South Tower kept their radios on the repeater channel. Because they were unaware of the repeater channel, chiefs in the North Tower lobby and outside were unable to reach the South Tower lobby command post initially.

Unlike the commanders in the North Tower lobby, these chiefs in the South Tower kept their radios on the repeater channel. For the first 15 minutes of the operations in the South Tower, communications among them and the ladder company which ascended with the chief worked well. Upon learning from a company security official that the impact zone began at the 78th floor, a ladder company transmitted this information, and the chief directed an engine company on the 40th floor to attempt to find an elevator to reach that upper level. [1, p. 19]

Unfortunately, no FDNY chiefs outside the South Tower realized that the repeater channel was functioning and being used by units in the South Tower. Chiefs in the North Tower lobby and outside were unable to reach the South Tower lobby command post initially. [1, p. 19]

Communications also began to break down within the South Tower. Those units responding to the South Tower were advised to use tactical channel 3. From approximately 9:21 a.m. on, the ascending chief was unable to reach the South Tower lobby command post. The lobby chief ceased to transmit on repeater channel 7 at that time. [1, p. 19]

The first FDNY fatality of the day occurred at approximately 9:25 a.m. when a civilian landed on a fireman on West Street. [1, p. 19]

Confusion

By 9:30 a.m., few of the units dispatched to the South Tower had arrived at their staging area. Many units were unfamiliar with the complex and could not enter the South Tower because of the danger of victims and debris falling on Liberty Street. Some units entered the Marriott Hotel and were given assignments there; others mistakenly responded to the North Tower. An additional 2nd alarm was requested at 9:37 a.m. because so few units had reported. At this time, units which had been staged on the Brooklyn side of the Brooklyn Battery Tunnel were sent, and many of them arrived at the WTC by 9:55 a.m. [1, p. 19]

At 9:50 a.m., a ladder company had made its way up to the 70th floor of the South Tower. There they encountered many seriously injured people. At 9:53 a.m. a group of civilians were found trapped in an elevator on the 78th floor sky lobby. By 9:58 a.m., the ascending chief had reached the 78th floor on Stairwell A, and reported that it looked open to the 79th floor. He reported numerous civilian fatalities in the area. A ladder company on the 78th floor was preparing to use hoses to fight the fire when the South Tower collapsed. [1, p. 19]

By 9:30 a.m., few of the units dispatched to the South Tower had arrived at their staging area. Many units were unfamiliar with the complex and could not enter the South Tower because of the danger of victims and debris falling on Liberty Street. Some units entered the Marriott Hotel and were given assignments there; others mistakenly responded to the North Tower.

Incident Command

The overall incident command was just outside the WTC complex. At approximately 9:10 a.m., because of the danger of falling debris, this command post was moved from the middle of West Street to its western edge by the parking garage in front of 2 World Financial Center. The overall command post's ability to track all FDNY units was extremely limited. [1, pp. 19-20]

At approximately 9:20 a.m., the Mayor and the NYPD Commissioner reached the FDNY overall command post. The FDNY Chief of Department briefed the Mayor on operations and stated that this was a rescue mission of civilians. He stated that he believed they could save everyone below the impact zones. He also advised that, in his opinion, rooftop rescue operations would be impossible. None of the chiefs present believed a total collapse of either tower was possible. Later, after the Mayor had left, one senior chief present did articulate his concern that upper floors could begin to collapse in a few hours, and so he said that firefighters thus should not ascend above floors in the sixties. [1, p. 20]

Surge

By 9:20 a.m., significantly more firemen than were dispatched were at the WTC complex or enroute. Many off-duty firemen were given permission by company officers to "ride heavy." Others found alternative transportation and responded. In one case an entire company of off-duty firefighters managed to congregate and come to the WTC as a complete team, in addition to the on-duty team which already had been dispatched to the scene. Numerous fire marshals also reported to the WTC. [1, p. 20]

At 9:46 a.m., the Chief of Department called a third 5th alarm. This meant that over one third of all of the FDNY units in New York City were at or enroute to the WTC. [1, p. 20]

By 9:20 a.m., significantly more firemen than were dispatched were at the WTC complex or enroute. Many off-duty firemen were given permission by company officers to "ride heavy." Others found alternative transportation and responded. In one case an entire company of off-duty firefighters managed to congregate and come to the WTC as a complete team.

The Police Department was also responding massively after the attack on the South Tower. Almost 2,000 officers had been called to the scene. In addition, the Chief of the Department called for Operation Omega, to evacuate and secure sensitive locations around the city. At 9:06 a.m. the NYPD Chief of Department instructed that no units were to land on the roof of either tower. [1, p. 20]

An NYPD rescue team in the North Tower lobby prepared to climb at approximately 9:15 a.m. They attempted to check in with the FDNY chiefs present, but were rebuffed. Office of Emergency Management personnel present did not intercede. The team went to work anyway, climbing Stairwell B in order to set up a triage center on upper floors for victims who could not walk. Later, a second rescue team arrived in the North Tower and did not attempt to check-in with the FDNY command post. [1, p. 20]

NYPD rescue teams also entered the South Tower. The Office of Emergency Management field responder present ensured that they check-in with the lobby chief. In this case, both agreed that the rescue team would ascend in support of FDNY personnel. By 9:15 a.m., two more of these teams were preparing to leave the Church and Vesey mobilization point in order to enter the towers. [1, p. 20]

At approximately 9:30 a.m. one of the helicopters present advised that a rooftop evacuation still would not be possible. [1, p. 20]

Structural Failure

At 9:37 a.m., a civilian on the 106th floor of the South Tower reported to a 9-1-1 operator that a lower floor—"90-something floor"—was collapsing. This information was conveyed incorrectly by the 9-1-1 operator to an NYPD dispatcher. The NYPD dispatcher further confused the substance of the 9-1-1 call in conveying at 9:52 a.m. to NYPD officers that "the 106th floor is crumbling." [1, p. 21]

By 9:58 a.m., there were two NYPD rescue teams in each of the two towers, another approaching the North Tower, and approximately ten other NYPD officers climbing in the towers. [1, p. 21]

The Port Authority Police Department lacked clear standard operating procedures for coordinating a multi -command response to the same incident. It also lacked a radio channel that all commands could access. Many officers remained on their local command channels, which did not work once they were outside the immediate geographic area of their respective commands.

In addition, there were numerous NYPD officers on the ground floors throughout the complex, assisting with evacuation, and patrolling and securing the WTC perimeter. A greater number of NYPD officers were staged throughout lower Manhattan, assisting in civilian evacuation, keeping roads clear, and conducting other operations in response to the attacks. [1, p. 21]

Prior to 9:59 a.m., no NYPD helicopter transmission predicted that either tower would collapse. [1, p. 21]

Agency Coordination

Initial responders from outside Port Authority Police commands proceeded to the police desk in 5 WTC or to the fire safety desk in the North Tower lobby. Officers were assigned to assist in stairwell evacuations and to expedite evacuation in the plaza, concourse, and PATH station. As reports of trapped civilians were received, Port Authority Police officers also started climbing stairs for rescue efforts. Others, including the Port Authority Police Superintendent, began climbing toward the impact zone in the North Tower. The Port Authority Police Chief and other senior officers began climbing in the North Tower with the purpose of reaching the Windows of the World restaurant on the 106th floor, where there were at least 100 people trapped. [1, p. 21]

The Port Authority Police Department lacked clear standard operating procedures for coordinating a multi-command response to the same incident. It also lacked a radio channel that all commands could access. Many officers remained on their local command channels, which did not work once they were outside the immediate geographic area of their respective commands. [1, pp. 21-22]

Many Port Authority Police officers from different commands responded on their own initiative. By 9:30 a.m. the Port Authority's central police desk requested that responding officers meet at West and Vesey and await further instructions. In the absence of predetermined leadership roles for an incident of this magnitude, a number of Port Authority inspectors, captains, and lieutenants stepped forward at West and Vesey to formulate an on-site response plan. They were hampered by not knowing how many officers were responding to the site and where those officers were operating. Many of the officers who responded to this command post lacked suitable protective equipment to enter the complex. [1, p. 22]

At 9:59 a.m., the South Tower collapsed in ten seconds. It is believed that all of the people still inside the tower were killed, as well as a number of individuals—both first responders and civilians—in the concourse, the Marriott, and on neighboring streets.

By 9:58 a.m., one Port Authority Police officer had reached the sky lobby on the 44th floor of the North Tower. Also in the North Tower, two Port Authority teams had reached floors in the upper and lower twenties. Numerous officers also were climbing in the South Tower, including the Port Authority rescue team. Many also were on the ground floors of the complex assisting with evacuation, manning the Port Authority Police desk in 5 WTC, or supporting lobby command posts. [1, p. 22]

The emergency response effort escalated with the crash of United 175 into the South Tower. With that escalation, communications and command-and-control became increasingly critical and increasingly difficult. First responders assisted thousands of civilians in evacuating the towers, even as incident commanders from responding agencies lacked knowledge of what other agencies and, in some cases, their own responders were doing. [1, p. 22]

Then the South Tower collapsed. [1, p. 22]

South Tower Collapse

At 9:59 a.m., the South Tower collapsed in ten seconds. It is believed that all of the people still inside the tower were killed, as well as a number of individuals—both first responders and civilians—in the concourse, the Marriott, and on neighboring streets. [1, pp. 22-23]

The next emergency issue was to decide what to do in the North Tower, once the South Tower had collapsed. In the North Tower, 9-1-1 calls placed from above the impact zone grew increasingly desperate. The only civilians still evacuating above the 10th floor were those who were injured or handicapped. First responders were assisting those people in evacuating. [1, p. 23]

Every FDNY command post ceased to operate upon the collapse of the South Tower. Lacking awareness of the South Tower's collapse, the chiefs in the North Tower nonetheless ordered an evacuation of the building. [1, p. 23]

An FDNY marine unit radioed immediately that the South Tower had collapsed. To our knowledge, this information did not reach the chiefs at the scene. [1, p. 23]

Within minutes some firefighters began to hear evacuation orders over tactical 1, the channel being used in the North Tower. Some FDNY personnel also gave the evacuation instruction on command channel 2, which was much less crowded, as only chiefs were using it. Two battalion chiefs on upper floors heard the instruction on Command 2 and repeated it to everyone they encountered. At least one of them also repeated the evacuation order on tactical 1. [1, p. 23]

None of the evacuation orders given to FDNY units in the North Tower followed the specific protocols to be given for the most urgent building evacuation. None of the evacuation orders mentioned that the South Tower had collapsed. Firefighters who received these orders lacked a uniform sense of urgency in their evacuation.

Other firefighters did not receive the transmissions. The reasons varied. Some FDNY radios may not have picked up the transmission in the difficult high-rise environment. The difficulty of that environment was compounded by the numerous communications all attempted on tactical 1 after the South Tower collapsed; the channel was overwhelmed, and evacuation orders may have been lost. Some of the firefighters in the North Tower were among those who had responded even though they were off-duty, and they did not have their radios. Finally, some of the firefighters in the North Tower were supposed to have gone to the South Tower and were using the tactical channel assigned to that Tower. [1, p. 24]

Many firefighters who did receive the evacuation order delayed their evacuation in order to assist victims who could not move on their own. Many perished. [1, p. 24]

Many chiefs on the scene were unaware that the South Tower collapsed. To our knowledge, none of the evacuation orders given to units in the North Tower followed the specific protocols—which would include stating "mayday, mayday, mayday"—to be given for the most urgent building evacuation. To our knowledge none of the evacuation orders mentioned that the South Tower had collapsed. Firefighters who received these orders lacked a uniform sense of urgency in their evacuation. [1, p. 24]

The Police Department had a better understanding of the situation. The South Tower's collapse disrupted the NYPD rescue team command post at Church and Vesey. Nonetheless, the NYPD command structure gave vital help to its units. [1, p. 24]

Many NYPD radio frequencies became overwhelmed with transmissions relating to injured, trapped, or missing officers. By 10:10 a.m., the NYPD rescue team advised that they were moving their command post north and began moving vehicles in that direction. [1, p. 25]

The Police Department had a better understanding of the situation. The South Tower's collapse disrupted the NYPD rescue team command post at Church and Vesey. Nonetheless, the NYPD command structure gave vital help to its units.

NYPD Aviation radioed in immediately that the South Tower had collapsed. At 10:08 a.m., an aviation helicopter pilot advised that he did not believe the North Tower would last much longer. There was no ready way to relay this information to the fire chiefs in the North Tower. [1, p. 25]

Both NYPD rescue teams in the North Tower knew that the South Tower had collapsed and evacuated the building. One remained in the complex near 5 and 6 WTC in order to keep searching for people who needed help. A majority of these officers died. [1, p. 25]

At the time of the South Tower's collapse, a number of NYPD and Port Authority Police officers, as well as some FDNY personnel, were operating in different groups in the North Tower mezzanine, the WTC plaza, and the concourse, as well as on the neighboring streets. Many of these officers were thrown into the air and were enveloped in the total darkness of the debris cloud. Within minutes of the South Tower collapse, these officers began to regroup in the darkness and to lead the remaining civilians and injured officers out of the complex. Many of these officers continued rescue operations in the immediate vicinity of the North Tower and remained there until the North Tower collapsed. Many lost their lives. [1, p. 25]

The collapse of the South Tower also forced the evacuation of the Port Authority Police command post on West and Vesey, forcing its officers to move north. There is no evidence that Port Authority Police officers from outside the WTC command ever heard an evacuation order on their radios. Some of these officers in the North Tower determined to evacuate, either on their own, or in consultation with other first responders they came across. One Port Authority Police officer from the WTC command reported that he heard an urgent evacuation instruction on his radio soon after the South Tower collapsed. Other Port Authority police stayed in the WTC complex, assisting with the evacuation. [1, pp. 25-26]

North Tower Collapse

The FDNY Chief of Department and the Port Authority Police Department Superintendent and many of their senior staff were killed. The Fire Department of New York suffered 343 casualties, the largest loss of life of any emergency response agency in U.S. history. The Port Authority Police Department suffered 37 casualties, the largest loss of life of any American police force in history. The New York Police Department suffered 23 casualties, the second largest loss of life of any police force in U.S. history, exceeded only by the loss of Port Authority police the same day. [1, p. 26]

On 9/11, 403 officers from FDNY, NYPD, and PAPD lost their lives. They were part of the 2,752 killed at the World Trade Center that day. The nation suffered the largest loss of civilian life on its soil as a result of a domestic attack in its history. [1, p. 26]

On 9/11, 403 officers from FDNY, NYPD, and PAPD lost their lives. They were part of the 2,752 killed at the World Trade Center that day. The nation suffered the largest loss of civilian life on its soil as a result of a domestic attack in its history.

Conclusion

Because of its experience in 1993, New York City was seen as the best prepared city in the nation ready to contend with catastrophic terrorism. The events of 9/11 proved otherwise. And if New York City wasn't ready, how did that bode for the rest of the nation? These concerns would weigh heavily in the shaping of U.S. homeland security policy.

Challenge Your Understanding

The following questions are designed to challenge your understanding of the material presented in this chapter. Some questions may require additional research outside this book in order to provide a complete answer.

1. Which tower was first hit, and which tower was first to collapse on 9/11?
2. Why do you suppose the standing guidance was to remain in place during an emergency?
3. What options were available to those whose offices were located above the crash sites?
4. What options were available to those whose offices were located below the crash sites?
5. Identify the three agencies who led emergency response efforts at the World Trade Center.
6. Summarize the overall emergency response plan devised by the first responders.
7. Describe the problems with first responder coordination and communication at the World Trade Center.
8. Identify two reasons why self -dispatching units would complicate an emergency response?
9. Identify two ways that first responders significantly reduced the death toll at the World Trade Center.
10. If you had been mayor of New York City, what would you have done different on 9/11?

Chapter 5

Not By Chance

Learning Outcomes

Careful study of this chapter will help a student do the following:

- Describe emergency response efforts at the Pentagon on 9/11.
- Evaluate emergency response efforts at the Pentagon on 9/11.
- Appreciate the dedication and effectiveness of first responders on 9/11.
- Compare emergency operations at the Pentagon to emergency operations at the World Trade Center.

"The success of the ACFD response to the terrorist attack on the Pentagon did not happen by chance."

- Arlington County After Action Report, 2002

Introduction

On any other day, the disaster at the Pentagon would be remembered as a singular challenge, an extraordinary national story. Yet the calamity at the World Trade Center included catastrophic damage 1,000 feet above the ground that instantly imperiled tens of thousands of people. The two experiences are not comparable. Nonetheless, broader lessons in integrating multiagency response efforts are apparent in analyzing the Pentagon response. [1, p. 4]

On September 11, 2001, exactly 60 years after the Pentagon's construction began, American Airlines Flight 77 was hijacked and flown into the Western side of the building, killing 189 people including the five hijackers. It was the first significant foreign attack on the capital's governmental facilities since the burning of Washington during the War of 1812.

The Pentagon

The Pentagon is the headquarters of the United States Department of Defense, located in Arlington County, Virginia. [2] It has served for more than 70 years as a symbol of power in defense of the United States. Ironically, the groundbreaking ceremony for construction of the Pentagon took place on September 11, 1941, less than 3 months before the U.S. entry into World War II. Built on a site previously known as Arlington Farms, the five surrounding roadways dictated its pentagonal shape. The Pentagon's placement was personally approved by President Franklin Roosevelt to avoid obstructing the view of the U.S. Capitol from Arlington National Cemetery. The 380,000 tons of sand dredged from the Potomac River produced the reinforced concrete used to construct the building and the 41,492 concrete piles that support it. This innovative use of concrete saved enough steel to build an additional aircraft carrier for the War Department. Construction of the Pentagon was completed in just 16 months at a cost of $83 million. [3, p. 7]

The Pentagon is a massive structure. The building covers 29 acres of land, with a floor area of almost 7 million square feet. Almost 18 miles of corridors connect the 5 floors of office space housing some 23,000 employees. The heating and refrigeration plant alone covers a full acre and more than 100,000 miles of telephone cables run through the building. Although the network of corridors, escalators, elevators, and stairwells is designed to speed movement from place to place, to the uninitiated, maneuvering through the Pentagon can be daunting. [3, p. 7]

On September 11, 2001, exactly 60 years after the building's construction began, American Airlines Flight 77 was hijacked and flown into the Western side of the building, killing 189 people including the five hijackers. It was the first significant foreign attack on the capital's governmental facilities since the burning of Washington during the War of 1812. [2]

Emergency Preparedness

In the event of a fire, even one of significant size, the issue of "who's in charge" is usually straightforward. The fire department that owns the jurisdiction owns the scene until the fire is extinguished or brought under control. All other organizations support and are under the tactical control of the fire department's designated Incident Commander. Once the fire is out, command might be transferred to a law enforcement agency if, for example, arson or some other criminal act is suspected. The fire scene would then become a crime scene. [3, pp. A-20]

While the Pentagon resided firmly within the jurisdiction of the Arlington County Fire Department (ACFD), many unique aspects about the facility combined to create overlapping areas of authority. To begin with, the Pentagon is a U.S. military facility under direct control of the Secretary of Defense. Building entry is restricted and controlled by its own law enforcement organization, the Defense Protective Service (DPS). The fire station at the Pentagon heliport is operated by the Fort Myer Fire Department. [3, pp. A-20] The responsibility for contingency operations at Department of Defense (DoD) facilities in the Washington Metropolitan Area, including the Pentagon, belong to the Commanding General of the Military District of Washington (MDW). [3, p. 8]

While the Pentagon resided firmly within the jurisdiction of the Arlington County Fire Department (ACFD), many unique aspects about the facility combined to create overlapping areas of authority. Fortunately, in March 2001, the Washington area Council of Governments adopted the National Incident Management System (NIMS) and Incident Command System (ICS) model.

Another complication was the nature of the incident itself. Following on the heels of the attacks on the World Trade Center in New York, it was clear this was a terrorist act. Under the terms of Presidential Decision Directive (PDD)-39, acts of terrorism are the exclusive domain of the Department of Justice (DOJ) and the FBI. This major fire incident, the jurisdictional responsibility of the ACFD, occurred because of a terrorist attack, thereby rendering the site a crime scene, the responsibility of the FBI. These complex jurisdictional and organizational relationships tested the coordination and relationships of everyone involved. [3, pp. A-20]

Fortunately, in March 2001, the Washington area Council of Governments adopted the National Incident Management System (NIMS) and Incident Command System (ICS) model. Thus, there was a common understanding of basic working relationships among local jurisdictions. However, establishing and maintaining command of the response to the Pentagon attack was daunting. There were thousands of people and hundreds of pieces of equipment from more than a dozen different jurisdictions, as well as many Federal, State, and Arlington County government agencies, and scores of volunteer organizations, businesses, and individuals. This understandably challenged the leadership of a fire department that usually directs the efforts of some 260 uniformed personnel. Although the ACFD performed well in responding to the terrorist attack on the Pentagon, the actual experience of coordinating the multifaceted response proved significantly more challenging than previously envisioned. [3, pp. A-20]

September 11, 2001

The only thing special about the morning of September 11, 2001, was the spectacular fall weather across the Washington Metropolitan Area. In Arlington County, the 67 firefighters and emergency medical technicians of the fire department's "B" shift were staffing the county's 10 neighborhood fire stations. By 8:30 a.m., training classes at the Arlington County Fire Training Academy were in full swing. Other ACFD personnel were engaged in meetings in the District of Columbia, preparing for the upcoming International Monetary Fund (IMF) conference. Several Arlington County chief officers were at a county sponsored management class at the Fairlington Community Center. At 8:45 a.m., when American Airlines Flight #11 slammed into the north tower of New York City's World Trade Center, it was abundantly clear this would be a day like no other. At 9:06 a.m., United Airlines Flight #175 crashed into the World Trade Center's south tower, revealing the true nature of the unprecedented horror. A brutal, mind-numbing terrorist attack was under way against the United States. [3, pp. A-4]

At 9:37 a.m., in Arlington County, Captain Steve McCoy and the crew of ACFD Engine 101 were enroute to a training session in Crystal City, traveling north on Interstate 395. Their conversation about the World Trade Center attack earlier that morning was interrupted by the sight and sound of a commercial airliner in steep descent, banking sharply to its right before disappearing beyond the horizon. At the same time, Arlington County Police on patrol in south Arlington County, saw a large American Airlines aircraft in a steep dive and on a collision course with the Pentagon. [3, p. 9]

At 9:38 a.m., American Airlines Flight #77 crashed into the west side of the Pentagon, just beyond the heliport. It was traveling at a speed of about 400 miles per hour, accelerating with close to its full complement of fuel at the time of impact. [3, p. 9]

The destruction caused by the attack was immediate and catastrophic. The 270,000 pounds of metal and jet fuel hurtling into the solid mass of the Pentagon was the equivalent in weight of a diesel train locomotive, except it was traveling at more than 400 miles per hour. More than 600,000 airframe bolts and rivets and 60 miles of wire were instantly transformed into white-hot shrapnel. The resulting impact, penetration, and burning fuel had catastrophic effects to the five floors and three rings in and around Pentagon Corridors 4 and 5. [3, p. 9]

All 64 people aboard the airliner were killed, as were 125 people inside the Pentagon (70 civilians and 55 military service members). [1, p. 5]

Emergency Response

At 9:38 a.m., shortly after American Airlines Flight #77 disappeared from sight, a tremendous explosion preceded a massive plume of smoke and fire. Unable to pinpoint the precise location, Captain McCoy aboard Engine 101 immediately radioed the Arlington County Emergency Communications Center (ECC), reporting an airplane crash in the vicinity of the 14th Street Bridge or in Crystal City. Aware of the World Trade Center attack, Captain McCoy also advised that the Federal Bureau of Investigation should be notified, since this was a possible terrorist attack. Hearing the radio message, fire and rescue units from Arlington County and elsewhere began to respond, self-dispatching from stations or diverting from other destinations. [3, pp. A-4]

At 9:38 a.m., shortly after American Airlines Flight #77 disappeared from sight, a tremendous explosion preceded a massive plume of smoke and fire. Unable to pinpoint the precise location, Captain McCoy aboard Engine 101 immediately radioed the Arlington County Emergency Communications Center (ECC), reporting an airplane crash in the vicinity of the 14th Street Bridge or in Crystal City.

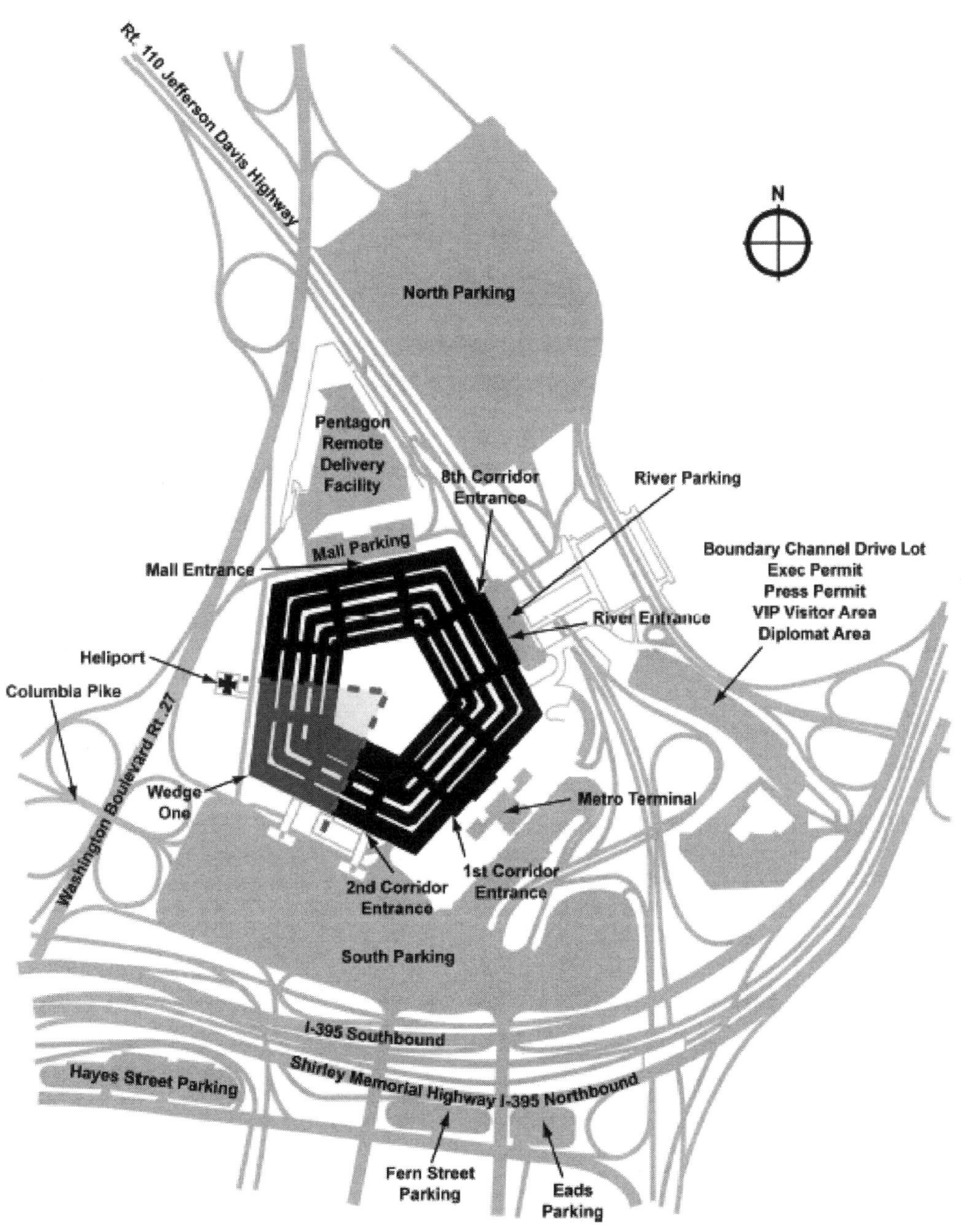

Figure 5-1: Pentagon Crash Site [3, p. 8]

At 9:38 a.m. on September 11, only one fire crew, Foam 161 of the Fort Myer Fire Department, knew the exact location of the crash site. Captain Dennis Gilroy and his team were already on station at the Pentagon when Flight #77 slammed into it, just beyond the heliport. Foam 161 caught fire and suffered a flat tire from flying debris. Firefighters Mark Skipper and Alan Wallace were outside the vehicle at impact and received burns and lacerations. Recovering from the initial shock, they began helping victims climb out of the Pentagon's first floor windows. Captain Gilroy called the Fort Myer Fire Department, reporting for the first time the actual location of the crash. [3, pp. A-4]

Help was already on the way from several directions as units sped toward the source of the smoke plume, not toward a specific street address. ACFD Truck 105 reached the scene first, followed shortly by fire and medical units from several Arlington County stations.

Help was already on the way from several directions as units sped toward the source of the smoke plume, not toward a specific street address. ACFD Truck 105 reached the scene first, followed shortly by fire and medical units from several Arlington County stations. [3, pp. A-5]

At the FBI Washington Field Office (WFO), Special Agent-in-Charge (SAC) Arthur Eberhart was putting in motion the steps necessary to support New York City. Of WFO's four senior leaders, he was the only one present at headquarters that morning. Upon learning of the World Trade Center crashes, SAC Eberhart activated the WFO Command Center. Members of the WFO National Capital Response Squad (NCRS) were paged and instructed to report immediately to headquarters. Supervisory Special Agent (SSA) Jim Rice, the NCRS leader, was at the FBI WFO Command Center on the telephone with Mr. Larry Cirutti of the Military District of Washington at the Pentagon when a monitored District of Columbia police radio transmission reported an explosion at the Pentagon. Mr. Cirutti told SSA Rice a helicopter must have "slid off the helipad" into the building. Special Agent Chris Combs, the NCRS Fire Service Liaison, was teaching a class at the District of Columbia Fire Academy when he received his page. While enroute to the WFO Headquarters, he heard a news report of the Pentagon attack and proceeded directly to the Pentagon. [3, pp. A-6]

Meanwhile, at the Metropolitan Washington Airports Authority (MWAA) Fire Department at Ronald Reagan Washington National Airport, Captain Michael Defina was investigating an incident at Terminal B when he heard the impact and saw the smoke rising in the distance. He called Fire Communications and was advised of a report of a Boeing 757 crash off the end of Runway 1-19. That was quickly amended, identifying the Pentagon as the crash site. The MWAA contacted the Arlington ECC and was directed to respond to the Pentagon. They did so with substantial resources: a rescue engine, two foam units, two mass casualty units, a mini-pumper, and a command vehicle. Because MWAA had authority to respond automatically to an airplane crash within 5 miles of the airport, two heavy rescue units had already self-dispatched to the Pentagon. [3, pp. A-6]

ACFD's Training Officer Captain Chuck Gibbs reached the incident site within the first 3 minutes, followed by Battalion Chief Bob Cornwell, who assumed initial Incident Command responsibilities. Those duties were quickly assumed by Assistant Fire Chief for Operations James Schwartz, who assigned Battalion Chief Cornwell, a 35-year veteran firefighter, to lead fire suppression efforts inside the building. Captain Gibbs commanded the River Division. Special Agent Combs arrived moments after Chief Schwartz. The partnership between Chief Schwartz and Special Agent Combs, who served as FBI agency representative to the Incident Commander, proved invaluable in the days ahead. [3, pp. A-6]

Incident Command

When ACFD Chief Edward Plaugher arrived at the Pentagon shortly after the attack, he chose not to assume Incident Command, but let it remain delegated to Chief Schwartz. Chief Plaugher recognized he would be more valuable as a free agent, buffering the command structure from outside distractions, such as the media, and directing his attention to support requiring his personal intervention. This proved to be a fortuitous decision. [3, pp. A-21]

A tiered command structure quickly evolved in the first hours of the incident. Chief Schwartz directed fire and rescue operations from the Incident Command Post (ICP). Around midday, he established an ICS Operations Section at the Pentagon heliport, from which day-to-day firefighting and rescue efforts were planned and executed.

A tiered command structure quickly evolved in the first hours of the incident. Chief Schwartz directed fire and rescue operations from the Incident Command Post (ICP). Around midday, he established an ICS Operations Section at the Pentagon heliport, from which day-to-day firefighting and rescue efforts were planned and executed. Chief Gray, a second-generation ACFD Firefighter, led the Operations Section supported by Chief Cornwell and Captain Gibbs. Battalion Chief Tom Hurlihy, from the District of Columbia, was later added to the operations team. [3, pp. A-21]

Away from the incident scene, Battalion Chief George Lyon designated Fire Station 1 as a Field Operations Center. It was there that replacement personnel and equipment were organized and dispatched to the Pentagon. [3, pp. A-21]

At about 1:00 p.m., Chief Schwartz learned that a task force led by Loudoun County Chief Jack Brown had arrived at Fire Station 1. He asked Chief Brown, formerly with the Fairfax County Fire and Rescue Department and a long-time colleague, to report to the ICP and lead the Planning Section. When the Fairfax County Urban Search and Rescue (US&R) Team deployed by the Federal Emergency Management Agency (FEMA) arrived about 2:00 p.m., the Incident Commander recognized that these very special resources would require considerable attention and asked Chief Brown to serve as their liaison. A Logistics Section was added later that day. It ramped up and was fully operational on the morning of September 12. Functional branches were established for fire suppression at the impact area (River Division), the Center Courtyard (A-E Division), and medical treatment (South Parking Lot). [3, pp. A-21]

The Incident Command also interfaced with the Arlington County Emergency Operations Center (EOC), located in the county government complex. The EOC was responsible for policy guidance and resource support. EOC personnel and equipment were assembled by 10:30 a.m. and, at 12:30 p.m., County Manager Ron Carlee convened the first Emergency Management Team meeting. [3, pp. A-22]

The FBI deployed both the Joint Terrorism Task Force (JTTF) and the National Capital Response Squad. Special Agent Combs established the FBI initial command presence with the ACFD Incident Command. The collaboration and cooperation between the FBI and ACFD was remarkable. The FBI Evidence Recovery Team began arriving before 10:00 a.m. and set up in a grassy area a short distance from the heliport. Because of the extremely congested traffic conditions, it took several hours for the entire FBI contingent to negotiate the route from the District of Columbia to the Pentagon. [3, pp. A-22]

The FBI had more than one role. It was responsible for the entire crime scene operation, including evidence gathering and body recovery. That operation engaged more than 700 FBI agents at the Pentagon, assisted by hundreds of people from other organizations. It was also responsible for organizing and operating the Federal interagency Joint Operations Center (JOC) as the Federal agency "coordination" center. The FBI was also responsible for investigating the hijacking at Washington Dulles International Airport. [3, pp. A-23]

Thus, the Pentagon attack required a fully coordinated response by the ACFD Incident Commander, the FBI On-Scene Commander, and the Commanding General of the MDW representing the DoD. From the moment Special Agent Combs reported to Chief Schwartz as the FBI representative and initial FBI On-Scene Commander, the collaboration and cooperation between the FBI and ACFD was under way. The FBI carefully respected the command primacy of the ACFD while it retrieved evidence during the 10-day fire and rescue phase. The FBI assumed command of the scene from the ACFD on September 21. The foundation for this relationship had formed long before the attack on the Pentagon. Special Agent Combs, a former New York firefighter, had worked routinely with every Washington Metropolitan Area fire department. He had taught classes at area fire academies and met regularly with the fire community leadership. Similarly, Major General James Jackson of the MDW placed his formidable resources in support of the ACFD Incident Command and the FBI until control was returned to the DoD on September 28. [3, pp. A-20]

Thus, the Pentagon attack required a fully coordinated response by the ACFD Incident Commander, the FBI On-Scene Commander, and the Commanding General of the MDW representing the DoD. From the moment Special Agent Combs reported to Chief Schwartz as the FBI representative and initial FBI On-Scene Commander, the collaboration and cooperation between the FBI and ACFD was under way.

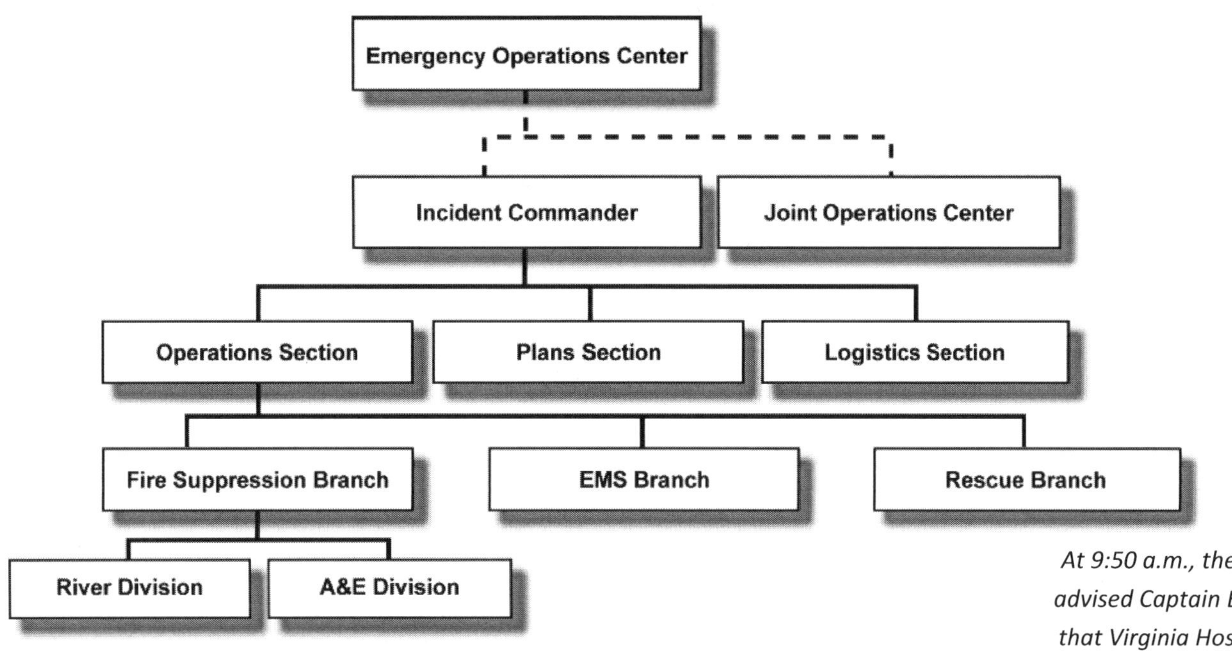

Figure 5-2: ACFD Incident Command on 9/11 [3, pp. A-23]

At 9:50 a.m., the ECC advised Captain Blunt that Virginia Hospital Center - Arlington, Inova Fairfax Hospital, and Washington Hospital Center were prepared to accept as many victims as needed.

Emergency Medical Services

ACFD Captain Edward Blunt also arrived at the Pentagon within minutes of the crash and assumed control of Emergency Medical Services (EMS). Captain Blunt immediately contacted the Arlington County Emergency Communications Center and requested and immediately received a separate EMS operations channel. He also asked for 20 medic units, 2 buses, and a command vehicle (EMS Supervisor Vehicle 112) to support the EMS response. Captain Blunt designated the field adjacent to Washington Boulevard (Route 27) as the treatment area, and asked the Arlington County Police Department (ACPD) patrol units on-scene to clear Washington Boulevard to create north and south access for emergency response traffic. Captain Alan Dorn arrived shortly after Captain Blunt, and was assigned as Triage Officer. Together, Captains Blunt and Dorn began working with military medical personnel who volunteered to help set up triage areas. [3, pp. A-6 - A-7]

Initially, medical units staged in the Pentagon South Parking Lot, adjacent to Route 110, until called forward to the EMS sector on Route 27. By 9:50 a.m., six ACFD EMS units had already arrived at the incident site (M-102, M-104, M-105, M-106, M-109, and M-110). M-101, Engine 103, and an ACFD Reserve Medic Unit quickly joined them. Two additional ACFD Reserve Medic Units (RM-111 and RM-112) arrived next and were directed to provide EMS support at the Pentagon's Center Courtyard. [3, pp. A-7]

At 9:50 a.m., the ECC advised Captain Blunt that Virginia Hospital Center - Arlington, Inova Fairfax Hospital, and Washington Hospital Center were prepared to accept as many victims as needed. [3, pp. A-7]

Sizing Up

The massive size of the Pentagon and the complexity of its various rings, corridors, and floors compounded the challenge of the response force. First of all, it distorted the perception of the task at hand. It is true that fire damage was contained to a relatively small area, but it was a relatively small area in one of the largest business complexes in the world. This was office space built to accommodate a substantial workforce, with all the accompanying common space, meeting and conference rooms, and other support facilities. [3, pp. A-7]

The gash created by the Boeing 757 airliner was large, but it affected a specific area of only two of the Pentagon's five Wedges. Neither the depth of the incursion nor the massive devastation inside the building was readily apparent as flames burned behind blast-proof windows. Huge heaps of rubble and burning debris littered with the bodies and body parts of 188 victims covered an area the size of a

To those watching on television, or even from the Pentagon's South Parking Lot, the gash created by the Boeing 757 airliner was large, but it affected a specific area of only two of the Pentagon's five Wedges. Neither the depth of the incursion nor the massive devastation inside the building was readily apparent as flames burned behind blast-proof windows. Huge heaps of rubble and burning debris littered with the bodies and body parts of 188 victims covered an area the size of a modern shopping mall. Flight #77 penetrated the outer wall of the Pentagon's E Ring and the damage extended all the way through the inner wall of the C Ring, a distance of approximately 285 feet. [3, pp. A-8]

Furthermore, the unique design of the Pentagon hid from view activities at the Center Courtyard in the middle of the complex. Battalion Chief Jerome Smith was assigned responsibility for fire suppression from the Center Courtyard, with units from the District of Columbia and ACFD. His mission was to prevent the fire from breaching the B Ring. Upon reaching the Center Courtyard, Battalion Chief Smith found the area in turmoil. More than 400 building occupants crowded the Center Courtyard. Others leapt from the upper floors, as colleagues armed with fire extinguishers attempted to extinguish the flames consuming burning comrades. [3, pp. A-10 - A-11]

Dispatching Units

Although self-dispatching quickened the arrival of a substantial number of fire, rescue, and medical units, many arrived haphazardly. The occupants of those vehicles were singularly intent on saving victims and attacking the fire. Police engaged in area traffic control were understandably reluctant to delay emergency vehicles descending on the scene with lights flashing and sirens blaring. [3, pp. A-10]

Deploying EMS units from other jurisdictions, particularly self-dispatched units, found it easy to bypass the staging area and proceed directly to the response site. Some victims flagged down EMS units before they reached the staging area. The crew from one Alexandria unit reported that it independently performed triage and treatment in the Pentagon South Parking Lot to assist five severely burned victims. [3, pp. A-10]

As a result, although the ACFD instituted Incident Command procedures very early on, they still faced the monumental challenge of gaining control of the resources already onsite and those arriving minute-by-minute. [3, pp. A-10]

Unit Accountability

Captain Jeff Liebold, working at the Incident Command Post, was tasked to determine what units were onsite and where they were working. Because radio communications were overloaded and ineffective, Captain Liebold sent two firefighters on foot to record the identification number and location of every piece of equipment on the Pentagon grounds. In the first few hours, foot messengers at times proved to be the most reliable means of communicating. [3, pp. A-10]

At 10:15 a.m., Chief Schwartz ordered the immediate evacuation of the incident site. The FBI had warned him that a second hijacked airliner was flying on a course toward the Pentagon and was 20 minutes away.

The uncontrolled influx of fire and rescue personnel had important accountability implications. had there been a second attack, as occurred at the World Trade Center, it would have been virtually impossible for the Incident Commander to assess the impact to response operations. [3, pp. A-10]

As it was, at 10:15 a.m., Chief Schwartz ordered the immediate evacuation of the incident site. The FBI had warned him that a second hijacked airliner was flying on a course toward the Pentagon and was 20 minutes away. [3, pp. A-13]

Triage

At approximately 9:55 a.m., Assistant Chief John White arrived and was directed by Chief Schwartz to command the EMS Branch. Chief Schwartz advised him that Captains Dorn and Blunt were assessing and establishing mass triage sites at the traffic circle area of Washington Boulevard and westbound Columbia Pike. Captain Dorn organized responders and military volunteers, while Captain Blunt performed forward assessment. [3, pp. A-12]

Chief White instructed Captain Dorn to continue making preparations for casualties in the designated triage and treatment areas and to use the EMS units located along Route 27. ACFD triage and treatment sectors were established using ACFD assets, mutual-aid responders and military emergency medical technicians, nurses, and physicians. The military participants were receptive to direction and readily deferred to EMS officers. A military nurse equipped with a radio was able to communicate with the Defense Protective Service and aid stations in the Pentagon. [3, pp. A-13]

Chief White then met with Captain Blunt along Route 27 adjacent to the Pentagon heliport for a forward assessment report. Chief White asked him for a count of the casualties in his area by triage designators: red (IMMEDIATE: Life Threatening Injury); yellow (DELAYED: Serious, Not Life Threatening); and green (MINOR: Ambulatory). [3, pp. A-13]

After Chief Schwartz issued the 10:15 a.m. evacuation order, Chief White instructed Captain Blunt to "load and go," transporting as many patients as possible out of the area. The first wave of patients was enroute to area hospitals within 10 minutes of the evacuation notice and all other personnel were relocated to the Columbia Pike underpass at the South Parking Lot. Medivac helicopters that had responded to the Pentagon incident scene were relocated to a safer place. [3, pp. A-13]

At the underpass, Chief White, in coordination with EMS officers and military medical volunteers, made plans to reestablish triage in that area. He designated Captain Dorn as Triage Officer, Captain Blunt as Forward Triage Officer, Chief Glen Butler from the MWAA as Treatment Officer, and Firefighter Paramedic David Hehr as Transportation and Disposition Officer. [3, pp. A-14]

Dr. James Vafier, the Alexandria EMS Medical Director, accompanied an EMS unit to the incident site and was assigned a forward assessment role with a position on the sidewalk between Corridors 3 and 4. The plan was for military stretcher bearers to carry victims extracted by firefighters to Dr. Vafier's position for preliminary assessment. He would then assign them to the appropriate triage and treatment area. [3, pp. A-14]

After the all clear was sounded and site evacuation ended, EMS and military responders implemented Chief White's operations plan. [3, pp. A-14]

Fire Suppression

During the first 24 hours, it was necessary to evacuate the Pentagon on four separate occasions because of the risk of structural collapse or the threat of additional terrorist attacks. It is difficult to measure the full impact of repeated building evacuations, but it was clearly negative and significant. Each time an evacuation was ordered, firefighters interrupted operations, abandoned equipment, shut off hoses, and ran several hundred yards to protected areas. From there, they had to watch as flames reclaimed the parts of the Pentagon they had just evacuated. [3, pp. A-16] Firefighting was also hampered by unique aspects of the Pentagon itself.

Teams of firefighters assigned suppression work on the Pentagon roof had difficulty finding access points from the fifth floor. Neither building engineers nor detailed structural drawings were available to assist them at that location. Captain Robert Swarthout, Incident Safety Officer at the ICP, was in contact with a Pentagon engineer, but that resource was not accessible at the point of fire attack. Firefighters eventually climbed onto a ledge from a fifth-floor window then hoisted themselves onto the roof. [3, pp. A-16]

Attacking the fire on the roof was particularly difficult. The thick wood-plank inner layer burned out of control, protected by a layer of concrete below and a thick slate roof above. Firefighters cut trenches across the slate roof. It was physically demanding and involved a certain degree of guesswork to breach the roof ahead of a fire that could not be seen. On the second day, September 12, a military representative pointed out to Battalion Chief Randy Gray, the Incident Command Operations Section Chief, the locations of two key communications and operations facilities threatened by the roof fire. The fire was stopped short of those facilities. [3, pp. A-16]

Height restrictions limited equipment access along A-E Drive into the Center Courtyard. Eventually, the tiller cab had to be cut off of an ACFD ladder truck so it could support the fire attack from inside the Center Courtyard. [3, pp. A-16]

Despite these difficulties, fire suppression in the first 12 hours was able to contain the damage without interrupting critical worldwide military command and control during a major national security emergency. Despite the magnitude, complexity, and duration of operations, there were no fatalities or serious injuries among fire and rescue personnel. This can be attributed in large part to the skill level in core competencies, professionalism, training, and teamwork of ACFD personnel and their counterparts in supporting jurisdictions. [3, pp. A-17]

Communications

Communication at the scene was challenging. Radio traffic overwhelmed the system to the extent that foot messengers became the most reliable means of communicating. Fortunately, there was a growing surplus of people onsite and available to serve in that capacity. [3, pp. A-36]

Radio communications inside the Pentagon were, for the most part, impossible. Where line of sight could be achieved, "talk around" was minimally effective. Initially, as calls jammed local towers, cellular telephones were not useful. No priority was assigned to emergency services. Nextel telephones with the 2-way radio capability were somewhat more reliable. [3, pp. A-36]

There was not a clearinghouse hospital designated. Thus, EMS Control did not have a single communications point of contact among hospitals and clinics. [3, pp. A-36]

Some mutual-aid jurisdictions arrived without handheld radios. Others used equipment incompatible with the ACFD or preprogrammed in ways that limited communications. [3, pp. A-37]

Beginning on September 12, the Incident Command Operations Section organized the fire suppression units into four divisions, each led by a chief officer from the preeminent jurisdiction (Division A – Arlington, Division B – the District of Columbia, Division C – Alexandria, and Division D – Fairfax). They were instructed to use the assigned home jurisdiction radio channel for communicating. This facilitated "talk around" within each division. However, in one instance, a DCFD replacement crew worked on one portion of the roof of the Pentagon while an ACFD team worked on a different portion. The two units had no way to communicate with each other in case either team needed help. [3, pp. A-37]

Crime Scene Investigation

The FBI began collecting evidence immediately after arriving at the Pentagon incident site on September 11. As fire and rescue efforts proceeded, FBI activity involving evidence recovery and removal of bodies and body parts became a 24-hour operation. Special Agent Adams directed this phase of the criminal investigation during the day shift, with Special Agent Thomas O'Connor taking over at night. The FBI worked closely with FEMA US&R teams and the fire department Technical Rescue Teams (TRTs). Special Agent Adams and Special Agent O'Connor attended the preshift briefings by the US&R Incident Support Team (IST) coordinator. US&R and TRT members would first shore up an area to ensure it was reasonably safe, then begin hunting through the debris, searching primarily for surviving victims buried in the rubble. [3, pp. C-54]

The FBI began collecting evidence immediately after arriving at the Pentagon incident site on September 11. As fire and rescue efforts proceeded, FBI activity involving evidence recovery and removal of bodies and body parts became a 24-hour operation.

As they encountered bodies, parts of bodies, and other evidence linked to the crime, they called forward the FBI contingent assigned to each team. Each item was photographed, numbered, and tagged. This information, along with a diagram showing where the evidence was found, was given to one of the soldiers from the Army's Old Guard, the 3rd Infantry Regiment from Fort Myer, VA, who transported the human remains to the FBI's temporary morgue at the North Parking Lot loading dock. Sixty soldiers supported the FBI on each 12-hour shift. [3, pp. C-54]

SSA Jim Rice assigned Special Agent Tara Bloesch to set up and manage the temporary morgue. Special Agent Bloesch had previous experience establishing morgue operations during FBI overseas operations in Kosovo and other overseas locations. She determined that the North Parking Lot loading dock was a suitable site. The doors remained closed except when receiving remains, and a large tarp was hung to safeguard the privacy of the morgue. The DPS, the FBI Critical Incident Response Group (CIRG), the ACPD SWAT team, the U.S. Marshals Service, and military police from MDW provided security at different times throughout the operation. [3, pp. C-55]

Summary

The first ACFD personnel arrived at the Pentagon within 2 minutes of the attack. ACFD and mutual-aid medical personnel began aiding victims immediately. Within 4 minutes of the attack, the ACFD had established its command presence. MWAA fire and medical units were on the scene and the first contingent of the FBI's NCRS had arrived within 5 minutes of impact. Three major Washington Metropolitan Area hospitals were ready to receive injured victims 12 minutes after the attack. By 10:00 a.m. on September 11, most of the ACFD duty shift was engaged at the Pentagon. [3, pp. A-7]

The first ACFD personnel arrived at the Pentagon within 2 minutes of the attack. ACFD and mutual-aid medical personnel began aiding victims immediately. Within 4 minutes of the attack, the ACFD had established its command presence.

All 64 aboard Flight #77 were killed when the Boeing 757 crashed into the Pentagon. Damage and debris penetrated halfway into the five-story building, about 285 feet, killing an additional 125 personnel including 70 civilians and 55 service members. Approximately 110 people were seriously injured and transported to area hospitals. [1, pp. 4-5] Only 42 injured victims received on-site medical care. An estimated 100 additional victims were treated for minor injuries. [3, pp. A-14] Because of the quick response and triage of ACFD EMS and supporting units, all of them survived. [3, pp. A-8]

By September 13, all surviving victims had been treated or transported from the Pentagon, and the EMS branch stood down. Eight days later, ten days after arriving on scene, the Arlington County Fire Department also stood down, and on September 21 turned over Incident Command to the FBI. [3, pp. A-27]

Conclusion

To be sure, several factors facilitated the response to the Pentagon and distinguish it from the response to the World Trade Center: 1) there was a single incident; 2) the incident site was relatively easy to secure and contain; 3) there were no other buildings in the immediate area; and 4) there was no collateral damage beyond the Pentagon. [1, p. 5] To be fair, the Pentagon response encountered problems similar to those at the WTC, including 1) difficulties accounting for self-dispatched units, and 2) overwhelmed and incompatible radio communications. [1, pp. 9-10] Even so, while no emergency response is flawless, the response to the 9/11 terrorist attack on the Pentagon was mainly a success for three reasons: 1) strong professional relationships and trust established among emergency responders; 2) the pursuit of a regional approach to response, and 3) the adoption of the Incident Command System. [1, p. 5] As a result, following 9/11 a consensus emerged among the First Responder community that a clear Incident Command System should be required of all response agencies. [1, p. 6]

Challenge Your Understanding

The following questions are designed to challenge your understanding of the material presented in this chapter. Some questions may require additional research outside this book in order to provide a complete answer.

1. List the response agencies having jurisdictional authority at the Pentagon on 9/11.
2. How did Incident Command facilitate emergency operations at the Pentagon on 9/11?
3. What was the advantage of having a single Incident Command Post at the Pentagon on 9/11?
4. Describe the circumstances behind the order to evacuate first responders from the Pentagon.
5. How was the order to evacuate first responders from the Pentagon different from the order to evacuate first responder from the South Tower on 9/11?
6. Why was it important for Incident Command to notify area hospitals of pending casualties?
7. Why is it important for Incident Command to account for first responders on scene of an incident?
8. At what point, as Incident Commander, do you let crime scene investigators take control of the site?
9. Explain how emergency operations at the Pentagon were similar to emergency operations at the World Trade Center on 9/11.
10. Explain how emergency operations at the Pentagon were different to emergency operations at the World Trade Center on 9/11.

Chapter 6

Surpassing Disproportion

Learning Outcomes

Careful study of this chapter will help a student do the following:

- Explain the distinguishing characteristic of the 9/11 attacks.
- Explain how critical infrastructure makes the nation vulnerable to domestic catastrophic attack.
- Describe the relationship between critical infrastructure protection and cyber security.
- Separate motive from action; differentiate terrorism from domestic catastrophic attack.

"The 9/11 attack was an event of surpassing disproportion."

- 2004 9/11 Commission Report

Introduction

The 9/11 attacks killed 2,973 people and caused more than $41.5B in damages. [1, pp. CRS-2 - CRS-3] On September 11th, 2001, nineteen hijackers inflicted more damage on the United States than the Imperial Japanese Navy on December 7th, 1941. [2, p. 2] According to the 9/11 Commission, the attacks were distinguished by their "surpassing disproportion". They were carried out by a tiny group of people dispatched from one of the poorest, most remote, and least industrialized countries on earth. Measured on a governmental scale, the resources behind it were trivial. [3, pp. 339-340] Altogether, the attacks cost no more than $500,000 to execute. [3, p. 172] The hijackers were able to achieve this level of destruction not by employing weapons of mass destruction, but by subverting the nation's transportation infrastructure, turning passenger jets into guided missiles. This chapter will explore the new, unprecedented threat unveiled by 9/11: the threat of domestic catastrophic attack by non-state actors preying on the nation's critical infrastructure.

According to the 9/11 Commission, the attacks were distinguished by their "surpassing disproportion".

Critical Infrastructure

According to Title 42, Section 5195c of United States Code, "critical infrastructure" is "systems and assets, whether physical or virtual, so vital to the United States that the incapacity or destruction of such systems and assets would have a debilitating impact on security, national economic security, national public health or safety, or any combination of those matters." The nation's health, wealth, and security rely on the production and distribution of certain goods and services. The array of physical assets, functions, and systems across which these goods and services move is called critical infrastructure. [4, p. 2] Critical infrastructure is a network of independent, mostly privately-owned, man-made systems and processes that function collaboratively and synergistically to produce and distribute a continuous flow of essential goods and services. [5, p. 3]

The transportation infrastructure moves goods and people within and beyond our borders, and makes it possible for the United States to play a leading role in the global economy. [5, p. 3]

The oil and gas production and storage infrastructure fuels transportation services, manufacturing operations, and home utilities. [5, p. 3]

The water supply infrastructure assures a steady flow of water for agriculture, industry (including various manufacturing processes, power generation, and cooling), business, firefighting, and our homes. [5, p. 4]

The emergency services infrastructure in communities across the country responds to urgent police, fire, and medical needs, saving lives and preserving property. [5, p. 4]

The government services infrastructure consists of federal, state, and local agencies that provide essential services to the public, promoting the general welfare. [5, p. 4]

The hijackers were able to achieve this level of destruction not by employing weapons of mass destruction, but by subverting the nation's transportation infrastructure, turning passenger jets into guided missiles.

The banking and finance infrastructure manages trillions of dollars, from deposit of our individual paychecks to the transfer of huge amounts in support of major global enterprises. [5, p. 4]

The electrical power infrastructure consists of generation, transmission, and distribution systems that are essential to all other infrastructures and every aspect of our economy. Without electricity, our factories would cease production, our televisions would fade to black, and our radios would fall silent (even a battery-powered receiver depends on an electric-powered transmitter). Our street intersections would suddenly be dangerous. Our homes and businesses would go dark. Our computers and our telecommunications would no longer operate. [5, p. 4]

The telecommunications infrastructure has been revolutionized by advances in information technology to form an information and communications infrastructure, consisting of the Public Telecommunications Network (PTN), the Internet, and the many millions of computers in home, commercial, academic, and government use. Taking advantage of the speed, efficiency and effectiveness of computers and digital communications, all the critical infrastructures are increasingly connected to networks, particularly the Internet. Thus, they are connected to one another. Networking enables the electronic transfer of funds, the distribution of electrical power, and the control of gas and oil pipeline systems. Networking is essential to a service economy as well as to competitive manufacturing and efficient delivery of raw materials and finished goods. The information and communications infrastructure is basic to responsive emergency services. It is the backbone of our military command and control system. And it is becoming the core of our educational system. [5, p. 4]

Disruption of any infrastructure is always inconvenient and can be costly and even life threatening. Major disruptions could lead to major losses and affect national security, the economy, and the public good. Mutual dependence and the interconnectedness made possible by the information and communications infrastructure lead to the possibility that our infrastructures may be vulnerable in ways they never have been before. Intentional exploitation of these new vulnerabilities could have severe consequences for our economy, security, and way of life. [5, p. 4]

Domestic Catastrophic Attack

Mutual dependence and the interconnectedness made possible by the information and communications infrastructure lead to the possibility that our infrastructures may be vulnerable in ways they never have been before. Intentional exploitation of these new vulnerabilities could have severe consequences for our economy, security, and way of life.

In terms of fatalities, 9/11 ranks fourth among the top ten disasters in the United States. [6] Suppose you are a member of a small militant group and you want to surpass this record, how do you do it? You can't do it with traditional firearms. The Virginia Tech shooting on April 16, 2007, the single deadliest U.S. incident by a lone gunman killed 32 people and wounded 17 others. [7] What about multiple shooters? Unlikely. In November 2008, 10 members of Lashkar-e Taiba mounted coordinated attacks on six separate locations in Mumbai India. They killed 164 people and wounded at least 308. [8] Since the 1999 shooting at Columbine High School in Colorado, U.S. police are trained to respond to active shooters as quickly as possible, making it unlikely that a similar attack would last four days as it did in Mumbai. [9, pp. 1-2] So what about explosives? On April 19, 1995, Timothy McVeigh detonated a truck bomb that killed 168 people and injured more than 680 others in the Alfred P. Murrah Federal Building in Oklahoma City. It would be difficult to replicate this attack since ammonium nitrate, which comprised the main component of the bomb, is much more closely controlled. [10] Furthermore, a similar bomb failed to topple the World Trade Center in 1993. [11] Conventional weapons might suit conventional crime, but they are unsuited to domestic catastrophic attack.

The single largest incident of manmade destruction was the atomic bombing of Hiroshima Japan on August 6, 1945. The estimated toll from the blast was 70,000 casualties, plus the utter destruction of the city. [12] However, creating mass-casualty weapons capable of killing thousands or even tens of thousands of people requires advanced knowledge, significant financial resources, and access to unique equipment. Stealing one presents equally challenging options as the materials and weapons are kept under the tightest security. Even if one could be acquired, it would still entail tremendous difficulties in transportation and deployment. [13, pp. 20-38] Just as the 1995 Tokyo subway attacks demonstrate the feasibility of employing WMD, they also demonstrate the difficulty of employing WMD.

Unlike WMD which are sequestered under lock-and-key, critical infrastructure is inherently accessible to the public. Millions depend on it to sustain their lives, and millions are at risk should it go wrong. On April 26, 1986, the meltdown of the Chernobyl Nuclear Power Plant in Ukraine killed 31 personnel, forced the evacuation and resettlement of 350,400 residents, and exposed an estimated 530,000 recovery workers to higher levels of radiation. While experts debate how this exposure might affect future cancer rates, they have taken the precaution of establishing a "zone of alienation" 19 miles in all directions from the plant (187 mi^2). Ukrainian officials estimate the area will not be safe for human life again for another 20,000 years. [14] Most infrastructure failure is the result of accident, not only Chernobyl, but also Bhopal India, where in December 1984, 2,259 people were killed overnight when methyl isocyanate accidentally vented from a nearby Union Carbide pesticide plant. [15]

But as demonstrated on 9/11, infrastructure may also be purposely subverted. The essential vulnerability of today's critical infrastructure is that little of it was centrally planned or designed, and virtually none of it was built to withstand deliberate attack. The result is that millions of lives depend on networks that are not fully understood, riddled with weaknesses, and susceptible to malicious tampering. And while physical exploitation of physical vulnerabilities, such as happened on 9/11, remain worrisome, the greater concern is virtual exploitation of cyber vulnerabilities through the Internet. [5, p. 5]

Without a great deal of thought about security, the nation shifted control of essential processes in manufacturing, utilities, banking, and communications to networked computers. Today's processes are more efficient, but they lack the redundant characteristics that gave their predecessors more resilience. They are also susceptible to cyber attack.

Cyber Vulnerability

The information technology revolution of the 1990s-2000s changed the way U.S. business and government operate. Without a great deal of thought about security, the nation shifted control of essential processes in manufacturing, utilities, banking, and communications to networked computers. As a result, the cost of doing business dropped and productivity skyrocketed. [16, p. 5] But at the same time, the proliferation of networks blurred ownership boundaries diffusing accountability, decreasing "end-to -end" or system-wide analysis and responsibility, reducing investment in research and development, and reserve capacity. Today's processes are more efficient, but they lack the redundant characteristics that gave their predecessors more resilience. They are also susceptible to cyber attack. [5, pp. 8-10]

Technologies and techniques that have fueled major improvements in the performance of our infrastructures can also be used to disrupt them. The United States, where close to half of all computer capacity and 60 percent of Internet assets reside, is at once the world's most advanced and most dependent user of information technology. More than any other country, we rely on a set of increasingly accessible and technologically reliable infrastructures, which in turn have a growing collective dependence on domestic and global networks. This provides great opportunity, but it also presents new vulnerabilities that can be exploited. It heightens risk of cascading technological failure, and therefore of cascading disruption in the flow of essential goods and services. [5, pp. 4-5] A cyber attack against the national electric grid is a particularly unsettling prospect.

Electric utilities rely on supervisory control and data acquisition (SCADA) systems to manage the nation's power generation, transmission, and distribution networks. While generally protected from intrusion, SCADA systems operate over the Internet. The move to SCADA boosts efficiency at utilities because it allows workers to operate equipment remotely. But this access to the Internet exposes these once-closed systems to cyber attacks. Project Aurora in 2006 demonstrated how a generator could be remotely commanded over the Internet to physically self-destruct [11, p. 21]. Physical damage to generators and other critical components on a large scale could result in a prolonged outage as procurement for these components range from months to years [12, p. 12]. Of potential concern is a cyber attack causing an extended outage across a significant portion of the North American Grid. In August 2003, an extended blackout affected 50 million people in the northeastern United States and Canada, causing an estimated $4-$10 billion in economic losses. Though it lasted only a week, the outage resulted in a 0.7% drop in Canada's gross domestic product [9, p. 2]. A John Hopkins study determined that New York City experienced a 122% increase in accidental deaths and 25% increase in disease-related deaths, and that ninety people died as a direct result of the power outage [10]. Depending on the timing of the attack, the death toll could be significant. In 1995, 739 people died from heat exhaustion in Chicago. Most of the victims were elderly poor residents who could not afford air conditioning. [17] In 2003, 14,802 French citizens died from heat-related ailments because most homes did not have air conditioning. [18] An attack on the North American Grid knocking out electricity over an extended region for an extended period in summer could potentially dwarf the damage suffered on 9/11.

Cyber attacks against SCADA systems controlling oil refineries, or oil and gas pipeline networks could be equally devastating, depriving large metropolitan areas of critical fuel for extended periods. A cyber attack disrupting the Federal Reserve system would have profound implications for the U.S. economy. [5, p. 12]

9/11 was a "wake-up call" to the catastrophic potential of critical infrastructure. [19, p. 5] The rapid assimilation of the Internet, originally designed to facilitate collaboration among trusted colleagues, makes that same infrastructure vulnerable to hostile agents. [16, p. viii] Together, the expansion and integration of the Internet with infrastructure has fundamentally changed national security.

9/11 was a "wake-up call" to the catastrophic potential of critical infrastructure.. The rapid assimilation of the Internet, originally designed to facilitate collaboration among trusted colleagues, makes that same infrastructure vulnerable to hostile agents. Together, the expansion and integration of the Internet with infrastructure has fundamentally

Changing Geography

Few enemies of the United States have ever had the means to seriously threaten our heartland. Even in the darkest early days of World War II, just after Pearl Harbor, no enemy had the shipping, landing craft, or forces to invade the continental U.S., or aircraft with the range to reach the mainland and return. For most of our history we never had to worry much about being attacked at home; broad oceans east and west and peaceable neighbors north and south gave us all the protection needed. [5, p. 7]

In the early 1950s, the geography that kept us safe was overcome by Soviet long-range bombers and intercontinental ballistic missiles aimed not only at our military capabilities, but also at the industries and institutions that give our nation its character. We had to learn to think differently about our safety and security. We built backyard bomb shelters, and whole generations practiced diving beneath their school desks at the sound of a siren. The fear of surprise nuclear attack slowly faded as we developed satellites and other early warning capabilities that enabled us to overcome geography and detect a Soviet missile launch in time to launch our own missiles— thus ensuring the credibility of the deterrent policy of Mutual Assured Destruction. [5, p. 7]

The demise of the Soviet Union, "detargeting" of nuclear missiles, and strategic arms reductions appeared to leave America once more relatively invulnerable to physical attack by foreign nations. However, as the threat of a nuclear war has diminished, new technologies have appeared that render physical geography less relevant and our domestic sanctuary less secure. Today, a computer can cause switches or valves to open and close, move funds from one account to another, or convey a military order almost as quickly over thousands of miles as it can from next door, and just as easily from an unauthorized computer as an authorized one. A false or malicious computer message can traverse multiple national borders, leaping from jurisdiction to jurisdiction to avoid identification, complicate lawful pursuit, or escape retribution. [5, p. 7]

In short, the global reach of the Internet coupled with the catastrophic potential of critical infrastructure, eliminates the protective advantage the U.S. has enjoyed most of its history.

In short, the global reach of the Internet coupled with the catastrophic potential of critical infrastructure, eliminates the protective advantage the U.S. has enjoyed most of its history. The Internet makes it possible for an enemy to attack us from a distance, using cyber tools, without first confronting our military power and with a good chance of going undetected. The new geography is a borderless cyber geography whose major topographical features are technology and change. [5, p. 7] Taking advantage of this new geography is a new threat, that of the non-state actor.

Changing Threat

A threat is traditionally defined as a capability linked to hostile intent. Linking capability to intent works well when malefactors are clearly discernible and U.S. intelligence agencies can focus collection efforts to determine what capabilities they possess or are trying to acquire. During the Cold War, for example, weapons with potential to threaten the United States took years to develop, involved huge industrial complexes, and were on frequent display in large military exercises. Today, however, malefactors are no longer necessarily nation-states, and expensive weapons of war are joined by means that are easier to acquire, harder to detect, and have legitimate peacetime applications. [5, p. 14] The ability of non-state actors to wield destruction on a scale previously reserved to nation-states represents an historic shift in national security affairs.

Previously, national security entailed protecting U.S. interests from other nations. Among the community of nations where each state is a sovereign entity unbound by the laws of another nation, relations are maintained by diplomacy, commerce, and when necessary, military force. Thus, for example, after a string of attacks in the early 1980s were linked to the Libyan government of Muammar Gaddafi, the U.S. applied diplomacy, economic sanctions, and eventually military force to put an end to the country's malfeasance. [20] Al Qaeda, on the other hand, was not a sovereign entity, nor bin Laden a head of state. Though they operated from Afghanistan they were not Afghan, nor did they conduct their attacks at the behest of the Taliban government. In fact, bin Laden could claim no country for his own, having had his Saudi citizenship revoked in 1994. [3, p. 63] As private individuals, bin Laden and members of al Qaeda were subject to law. Following the 1998 attack on the U.S. embassies in Tanzania and Kenya, bin Laden was placed on the FBI's list of Ten Most Wanted Fugitives. [21] Following 9/11, bin Laden was indicted for terrorism and placed on the FBI's list of Most Wanted Terrorists. [22]

Title 18, Section 2331 of United States Code defines terrorism as "acts dangerous to human life that are a violation of the criminal laws of the United States or any State intended to i) intimidate or coerce a civilian population; ii) influence the policy of a government by intimidation or coercion; or iii) affect the conduct of a government by mass destruction, assassination, or kidnapping within the territorial jurisdiction of the United States." Without doubt, the 9/11 attacks were terrorist acts, motivated as they were by bin Laden's 1998 fatwa declaring war on America. [3, p. 47] However, in protecting the nation from future such attacks, focusing on "terrorism" as a motive for hostile intent is very limiting. Narcotics trafficking and economic crime may also serve as motivating factors for hostile intent in attacking the nation's infrastructure. [5, p. 8] In fact, the potential number of motives that might stoke hostile intent are innumerable, making threat identification problematic at best.

Since 9/11, much attention has been devoted to the foreign terrorist threat. While certainly a concern, it is only one possibility among an infinite variety. The inherent vulnerability of critical infrastructure to physical and cyber attack means that the perpetrator need not be foreign, and the motive need not be terrorism. Whatever the motive, assault of any size is a crime under U.S. law. Together with motive, means and opportunity are required to commit a crime. While infrastructure remains vulnerable to various means of attack, and motives are impossible to count, perhaps the best means of preventing another 9/11-type attack is to reduce the window of opportunity by protecting critical infrastructure. This is precisely what was decided in the months following 9/11, and why critical infrastructure protection became a cornerstone of subsequent homeland security policy.

Since 9/11, much attention has been devoted to the foreign terrorist threat. While certainly a concern, it is only one possibility among an infinite variety. The inherent vulnerability of critical infrastructure to physical and cyber attack means that the perpetrator need not be foreign, and the motive need not be terrorism. Whatever the motive, assault of any size is a crime

Conclusion

9/11 exposed the vulnerability of critical infrastructure for abetting domestic catastrophic attack by small groups or individuals. Overnight, the historical protection afforded by vast oceans and friendly neighbors vanished. The instruments of destruction were woven into the fabric of our society. Non-state actors had usurped a power of devastation that was once reserved to nation-states. Our national security posture was shattered. Whereas before we could count and specifically identify our enemies and deter their actions, our enemies were now uncountable and more difficult to identify. Though terrorism remains a likely threat indicator, it is but one of an unlimited number of potential motives. Given a vast array of means and motives, restricting a criminal's opportunity seems the most efficient strategy for preventing a similar crime. Thus, critical infrastructure protection became a cornerstone of the nation's homeland security policy.

Challenge Your Understanding

The following questions are designed to challenge your understanding of the material presented in this chapter. Some questions may require additional research outside this book in order to provide a complete answer.

1. According to the 9/11 Commission, what was the distinguishing characteristic of the 9/11 attacks?
2. How did the 9/11 hijackers achieve WMD effects without using WMD?
3. Why is critical infrastructure critical?
4. Why is critical infrastructure vulnerable?
5. What is the relationship between critical infrastructure protection and cyber security?
6. Was 9/11 an act of terrorism? Explain your answer.
7. Was the Oklahoma City bombing an act of terrorism? Explain your answer.
8. Is terrorism the only motive that might precipitate catastrophic attack? Explain your answer.
9. Was 9/11 a criminal act or an act of war? Explain your answer.
10. Can we prevent another domestic catastrophic attack? Explain your answer.

Chapter 7

Failure of Imagination

Learning Outcomes

Careful study of this chapter will help a student do the following:

- Explain the respective failures that precipitated the 9/11 tragedy.
- Describe what changes might have prevented 9/11.
- Discuss the need to improve post - attack emergency response.
- Explain the need to undertake the largest reorganization of U.S. government since the end of World War II.

"We believe the 9/11 attacks revealed four kinds of failures: in imagination, policy, capabilities, and management."

- 2004 9/11 Commission Report

Introduction

While the 9/11 attacks ushered in a new threat to the nation's security, they also tested those institutions that were established at the end of World War II to prevent another "Pearl Harbor". The 9/11 Commission found those institutions sorely lacking, and enumerated their failures of imagination, policy, capabilities, and management. And despite the heroic efforts of First Responders at the World Trade Center, the 9/11 Commission could not help but wonder if better coordination might have kept more of them alive. This chapter presents those findings from the 9/11 Commission Report that would result in profound changes to American institutions and significantly shape subsequent homeland security policy.

Before 9/11, al Qaeda and its affiliates had killed fewer than 50 Americans, including the East Africa embassy bombings and the Cole attack. The U.S. government took the threat seriously, but not in the sense of mustering anything like the kind of effort that would be gathered to confront an enemy of the first, second, or even third rank.

Failure of Imagination

Before 9/11, al Qaeda and its affiliates had killed fewer than 50 Americans, including the East Africa embassy bombings and the Cole attack. The U.S. government took the threat seriously, but not in the sense of mustering anything like the kind of effort that would be gathered to confront an enemy of the first, second, or even third rank. The modest national effort exerted to contain Serbia and its depredations in the Balkans between 1995 and 1999, for example, was orders of magnitude larger than that devoted to al Qaeda. [1, p. 340]

Beneath the acknowledgment that Bin Laden and al Qaeda presented serious dangers, there was uncertainty among senior officials about whether this was just a new and especially venomous version of the ordinary terrorist threat America had lived with for decades, or was radically new, posing a threat beyond any yet experienced. [1, p. 343]

Both Presidents Bill Clinton and George Bush and their top advisers understood Bin Laden was a danger. But given the character and pace of their policy efforts, it is not clear they fully understood just how many people al Qaeda might kill, and how soon it might do it. [1, pp. 342-343]

In late 1998, reports came in of a possible al Qaeda plan to hijack a plane. One, a December 4 Presidential Daily Briefing for President Clinton, brought the focus back to more traditional hostage taking; it reported Bin Laden's involvement in planning a hijack operation to free prisoners such as the "Blind Sheikh," Omar Abdel Rahman, convicted in the 1993 World Trade Center bombing. Threat reports also mentioned the possibility of using an aircraft filled with explosives. The most prominent of these mentioned a possible plot to fly an explosives-laden aircraft into a U.S. city. [1, p. 344] The possibility of a suicide hijacking emerged following the crash of a Boeing 767 off the coast of Massachusetts, EgyptAir Flight 990 on October 31, 1999. The most plausible explanation was that one of the pilots had gone berserk, seized the controls, and flown the aircraft into the sea. President Clinton's counter-terrorism advisor, Richard Clarke, later testified he thought that warning about the possibility of a suicide hijacking would have been just one more speculative theory among a thousand others, probably hundreds of thousands. Yet the possibility was imaginable, and had been imagined. [1, p. 345]

In early August 1999, the Federal Aviation Administration's (FAA's) Civil Aviation Security intelligence office summarized the Bin Laden hijacking threat. After a solid recitation of all the information available on the topic, the paper identified a few principal scenarios, one of which was a "suicide hijacking operation." The FAA analysts judged such an operation unlikely, because "it does not offer an opportunity for dialogue to achieve the key goal of obtaining Rahman and other key captive extremists. . . . A suicide hijacking is assessed to be an option of last resort." [1, p. 345]

In citing a "failure of imagination", the 9/11 Commission Report draws parallels between the 9/11 attacks and the 1941 attack on Pearl Harbor. In both cases, the evidence leading up to the attacks was clear and obvious in hindsight. The 9/11 Commission Report makes the argument, though, that the "clear signal" that emerges in hindsight might have been equally evident in foresight had those responsible given stronger consideration to scenarios they dismissed as implausible.

The North American Aerospace Defense Command (NORAD) imagined the possible use of aircraft as weapons, too, and developed exercises to counter such a threat—from planes coming to the United States from overseas, perhaps carrying a weapon of mass destruction. None of this speculation was based on actual intelligence of such a threat. One idea, intended to test command and control plans and NORAD's readiness, postulated a hijacked airliner coming from overseas and crashing into the Pentagon. The idea was put aside in the early planning of the exercise as too much of a distraction from the main focus (war in Korea), and as too unrealistic. [1, p. 346]

In citing a "failure of imagination", the 9/11 Commission Report draws parallels between the 9/11 attacks and the 1941 attack on Pearl Harbor. In both cases, the evidence leading up to the attacks was clear and obvious in hindsight. The 9/11 Commission Report makes the argument, though, that the "clear signal" that emerges in hindsight might have been equally evident in foresight had those responsible given stronger consideration to scenarios they dismissed as implausible. The failure of imagination was the failure to consider not only what had been, but also what could be. If more concerted attention had been given to the suicide hijacking scenario conceived by some agencies, then indicators and warnings could have been devised, emerging evidence matched against them, and counteraction prepared in advance. This was nothing new. Such procedures had been painstakingly developed by the Intelligence Community in the decades after Pearl Harbor. In this case, they were not employed to analyze an enemy that, as the twentieth century closed, was most likely to launch a surprise attack directly against the United States. [1, pp. 344-348]

Failure of Policy

The road to 9/11 again illustrates how the large, unwieldy U.S. government tended to underestimate a threat that grew ever greater. The terrorism fostered by Bin Laden and al Qaeda was different from anything the government had faced before. The existing mechanisms for handling terrorist acts had been trial and punishment for acts committed by individuals; sanction, reprisal, deterrence, or war for acts by hostile governments. The actions of al Qaeda fit neither category. Its crimes were on a scale approaching acts of war, but they were committed by a loose, far-flung, nebulous conspiracy with no territories or citizens or assets that could be readily threatened, overwhelmed, or destroyed. [1, p. 348]

The road to 9/11 again illustrates how the large, unwieldy U.S. government tended to underestimate a threat that grew ever greater.

The U.S. policy response to al Qaeda before 9/11 was essentially defined following the embassy bombings of August 1998. The tragedy of the embassy bombings provided an opportunity for a full examination, across the government, of the national security threat that bin Laden posed. Such an examination could have made clear to all that issues were at stake that were much larger than the domestic politics of the moment. But the major policy agencies of the government did not meet the threat. [1, p. 349]

The diplomatic efforts of the Department of State were largely ineffective. Al Qaeda and terrorism was just one more priority added to already-crowded agendas with countries like Pakistan and Saudi Arabia. After 9/11 that changed. [1, p. 349]

Policymakers turned principally to the CIA and covert action to implement policy. Before 9/11, no agency had more responsibility—or did more—to attack al Qaeda, working day and night, than the CIA. But there were limits to what the CIA was able to achieve in its energetic worldwide efforts to disrupt terrorist activities or use proxies to try to capture or kill bin Laden and his lieutenants. As early as mid-1997, one CIA officer wrote to his supervisor: "All we're doing is holding the ring until the cavalry gets here." [1, p. 349]

Military measures failed or were not applied. Before 9/11 the Department of Defense was not given the mission of ending al Qaeda's sanctuary in Afghanistan. Officials in both the Clinton and Bush administrations regarded a full U.S. invasion of Afghanistan as practically inconceivable before 9/11. It was never the subject of formal interagency deliberation. [1, p. 349]

Lesser forms of intervention could also have been considered. One would have been the deployment of U.S. military or intelligence personnel, or special strike forces, to Afghanistan itself or nearby—openly, clandestinely (secretly), or covertly (with their connection to the United States hidden). Then the United States would no longer have been dependent on proxies to gather actionable intelligence. However, it would have needed to secure basing and overflight support from neighboring countries. A significant political, military, and intelligence effort would have been required, extending over months and perhaps years, with associated costs and risks. Given how hard it later proved to locate bin Laden even with substantial ground forces in Afghanistan, the odds of success before 9/11 are hard to calculate. There is no indication that President Clinton was offered such an intermediate choice, or that this option was given any more consideration than the idea of invasion. [1, p. 349]

These policy challenges are linked to the problem of imagination. Since both President Clinton and President Bush were genuinely concerned about the danger posed by al Qaeda, approaches involving more direct intervention against the sanctuary in Afghanistan apparently must have seemed—if they were considered at all—to be disproportionate to the threat. [1, p. 349]

Failures in Capability

Before 9/11, the United States tried to solve the al Qaeda problem with the same government institutions and capabilities it had used in the last stages of the Cold War and its immediate aftermath. These capabilities were insufficient, but little was done to expand or reform them. [1, pp. 350-351]

Before 9/11, the United States tried to solve the al Qaeda problem with the same government institutions and capabilities it had used in the last stages of the Cold War and its immediate aftermath. These capabilities were insufficient, but little was done to expand or reform them.

For covert action, of course, the White House depended on the Counterterrorist Center and the CIA's Directorate of Operations. Though some officers, particularly in the bin Laden unit, were eager for the mission, most were not. The higher management of the directorate was unenthusiastic. The CIA's capacity to conduct paramilitary operations with its own personnel was not large, and the Agency did not seek a large-scale general expansion of these capabilities before 9/11. James Pavitt, the head of this directorate, remembered that covert action, promoted by the White House, had gotten the Clandestine Service into trouble in the past. He had no desire to see this happen again. He thought, not unreasonably, that a truly serious counterterrorism campaign against an enemy of this magnitude would be business primarily for the military, not the Clandestine Service. [1, p. 351]

At no point before 9/11 was the Department of Defense fully engaged in the mission of countering al Qaeda, though this was perhaps the most dangerous foreign enemy then threatening the United States. The Clinton administration effectively relied on the CIA to take the lead in preparing long-term offensive plans against an enemy sanctuary. The Bush administration adopted this approach, although its emerging new strategy envisioned some yet undefined further role for the military in addressing the problem. Within Defense, both Secretary Cohen and Secretary Donald Rumsfeld gave their principal attention to other challenges. [1, pp. 351-352]

America's homeland defenders faced outward. NORAD itself was barely able to retain any alert bases. Its planning scenarios occasionally considered the danger of hijacked aircraft being guided to American targets, but only aircraft that were coming from overseas. It would have been a tough sell to make a costly change in NORAD's defense posture to deal with the danger of suicide hijackers before such a threat had ever actually been realized. But NORAD did not canvass available intelligence and try to make the case. [1, p. 352]

The most serious weaknesses in agency capabilities were in the domestic arena. [1, p. 352]

The most serious weaknesses in agency capabilities were in the domestic arena. America's homeland defenders faced outward.

The FBI did not have the capability to link the collective knowledge of agents in the field to national priorities. The acting director of the FBI did not learn of his Bureau's hunt for two possible al Qaeda operatives in the United States or about his Bureau's arrest of an Islamic extremist taking flight training until September 11. The director of central intelligence knew about the FBI's Moussaoui investigation weeks before word of it made its way even to the FBI's own assistant director for counterterrorism. [1, p. 352]

The FAA's capabilities to take aggressive, anticipatory security measures were especially weak. Any serious policy examination of a suicide hijacking scenario, critiquing each of the layers of the security system, could have suggested changes to fix glaring vulnerabilities—expanding no-fly lists, searching passengers identified by the CAPPS screening system, deploying Federal Air Marshals domestically, hardening cockpit doors, alerting air crew to a different kind of hijacking than what they had been trained to expect, or adjusting the training of controllers and managers in the FAA and NORAD. [1, p. 352]

Furthermore, the FAA set and enforced aviation security rules, which airlines and airports were required to implement. The rules were supposed to produce a "layered" system of defense. This meant that the failure of any one layer of security would not be fatal, because additional layers would provide backup security. But each layer relevant to hijackings—intelligence, passenger prescreening, checkpoint screening, and onboard security—was seriously flawed prior to 9/11.Taken together, they did not stop any of the 9/11 hijackers from getting on board four different aircraft at three different airports. [1, p. 83]

In 2001, the Immigration and Naturalization Service (INS) was overwhelmed by the challenges posed by illegal entry over the southwest border, criminal aliens, and a growing backlog of applications for naturalizing immigrants. [1, p. 80] The immigration system as a whole was widely viewed as increasingly dysfunctional and badly in need of reform. [1, p. 384] The system was in such poor state that the 9/11 hijackers had little trouble exploiting it to their advantage. Beginning in 1997, the 19 hijackers submitted 24 applications and received 23 visas. They entered the United States a total of 33 times. They arrived through ten different airports, though more than half came in through Miami, JFK, or Newark. When applying for a visa, the application was checked against a "consular lookout" database called CLASS, which included a substantial watchlist of known and suspected terrorists called TIPOFF. Upon entering the country, passports were again checked against terrorist watchlists and criminal databases. Despite these measures, known al Qaeda operatives were able to secure U.S. visas using detectable false statements, and enter the country with passports manipulated in a fraudulent manner. Those operatives who were flagged for secondary screening were still able to gain entry by making false statements to INS officials. Moreover, six of the 9/11 hijackers violated immigration laws after arriving in country. None of these violations were detected or acted upon by INS inspectors or agents. [2] The 9/11 Commission found that closer examination of the operatives' travel documents and more effective use of the watchlists might have exposed 15 of the 19 hijackers. The central problems were 1) lack of well-developed counterterrorism measures, and 2) the inability of the system to deliver on its basic commitments. [1, p. 384]

In the events leading up to 9/11, many opportunities were lost to thwart the plot. Information was not shared, sometimes inadvertently or because of legal misunderstandings. Analysis was not pooled. Effective operations were not launched. Often the handoffs of information were lost across the divide separating the foreign and domestic agencies of the government.

Failures in Management

In the events leading up to 9/11, many opportunities were lost to thwart the plot. Information was not shared, sometimes inadvertently or because of legal misunderstandings. Analysis was not pooled. Effective operations were not launched. Often the handoffs of information were lost across the divide separating the foreign and domestic agencies of the government. [1, p. 353]

However the specific problems are labeled, they appear to be symptoms of the government's broader inability to adapt how it manages problems to the new challenges of the twenty-first century. The agencies are like a set of specialists in a hospital, each ordering tests, looking for symptoms, and prescribing medications. What is missing is the attending physician who makes sure they work as a team. [1, p. 353]

One missing element was effective management of transnational operations. Action officers should have drawn on all available knowledge in the government. This management should have ensured that information was shared and duties were clearly assigned across agencies, and across the foreign-domestic divide. [1, p. 353]

Consider, for example, the case of Khalid al Mihdhar and Nawaf al Hazmi, and their January 2000 trip to Kuala Lumpur. In late 1999, the National Security Agency (NSA) analyzed communications associated with a man named Khalid, a man named Nawaf, and a man named Salem. They correctly concluded that "Nawaf" and "Khalid" might be part of "an operational cadre" and that "something nefarious might be afoot." The NSA did not pursue these leads however. It saw itself as an agency to support intelligence consumers, such as CIA. It did not initiate actions, but it waited to be asked. Since nobody asked, nobody was informed. If this information had been made available to the CIA al Qaeda unit, a case officer might have checked with the State Department and learned that U.S. visas had been issued to two gentlemen with the same names on the same day in Jeddah, Saudi Arabia. Armed with this information, the CIA could have notified the Immigration and Naturalization Service (INS) and FBI to be on the look for the two suspects when they entered the country. As it was, no such contact was made and the two entered the country without notice. [1, pp. 353-354]

Even if watchlisting had prevented or at least alerted U.S. officials to the entry of Hazmi and Mihdhar, it is unlikely that watchlisting, by itself, would have prevented the 9/11 attacks. Al Qaeda adapted to the failure of some of its operatives to gain entry into the United States. None of these future hijackers was a pilot. Alternatively, had they been permitted entry and monitored, some larger results might have been possible had the FBI been watching. [1, p. 354]

The details of this case illuminate real management challenges, past and future. The U.S. government must find a way of pooling intelligence and using it to guide the planning of and assignment of responsibilities for joint operations involving organizations as disparate as the CIA, the FBI, the State Department, the military, and the agencies involved in homeland security. [1, p. 357]

Beyond those day-to-day tasks of bridging the foreign-domestic divide and matching intelligence with plans, the challenges include broader management issues pertaining to how the top leaders of the government set priorities and allocate resources. [1, p. 357]

On December 4, 1998, DCI Tenet issued a directive to several CIA officials and his deputy for community management, stating: "We are at war. I want no resources or people spared in this effort, either inside CIA or the Community."38 The memorandum had little overall effect on mobilizing the CIA or the intelligence community. [1, p. 357]

The episode indicates some of the limitations of the DCI's authority over the direction and priorities of the intelligence community, especially its elements within the Department of Defense. The DCI had to direct agencies without controlling them. He did not receive an appropriation for their activities, and therefore did not control their purse strings. He had little insight into how they spent their resources. U.S. intelligence was not a coordinated effort. [1, p. 357]

Failure to Coordinate

The National Institute of Standards and Technology estimates that between 16,400 and 18,800 civilians were in the World Trade Center complex when American Airlines Flight 11 slammed into the North Tower at 8:46 am, September 11. At most, 2,152 individuals died at the WTC who were not on the aircraft or were not First Responders. Some 1,942 are thought to have worked or were attending meetings above the respective impact zones in the Twin Towers. Only 110, or 5.36% of those who died worked below the impact zone. It is impossible to measure how many more civilians would have died without the assistance of the FDNY, PAPD, and NYPD. It is impossible to measure the calming influence that ascending firefighters had on descending civilians that might otherwise have turned into a panicked and dangerous mob. But the positive impact of the First Responders on the evacuation came at a tremendous cost in lives. [1, pp. 316-317] Given the contrast to the Pentagon response, it is not unreasonable to speculate whether more First Responders would have been spared if there had been better coordination between agencies.

It is impossible to measure how many more civilians would have died without the assistance of the FDNY, PAPD, and NYPD. But the positive impact of the First Responders on the evacuation came at a tremendous cost in lives. It is also clear, however, that the response operations lacked the kind of integrated communications of a unified command .

To some degree, on 9/11 First Responders followed Mayor Giuliani's directive for incident command issued in July. It was clear that the lead response agency was the FDNY, and that the other responding agencies acted in a supporting role. There was a tacit understanding that FDNY personnel would have primary responsibility for evacuating civilians who were above the ground floors of the Twin Towers, while NYPD and PAPD personnel would be in charge of evacuating civilians from the WTC complex once they reached ground level. The NYPD also greatly assisted responding FDNY units by clearing emergency lanes to the WTC. In addition, coordination occurred at high levels of command. For example, the Mayor and Police Commissioner consulted with the Chief of the Department of the FDNY at approximately 9:20. There were other instances of coordination at operational levels, and information was shared on an ad hoc basis. For example, an NYPD Emergency Service Unit passed the news of their evacuation order to firefighters in the North Tower. It is also clear, however, that the response operations lacked the kind of integrated communications and unified command contemplated in the directive. These problems existed both within and among individual responding agencies. [1, p. 319]

For a unified incident management system to succeed, each participant must have command and control of its own units and adequate internal communications. This was not always the case at the WTC on 9/11. FDNY was lacking command and control as it proved incapable of coordinating the number of units dispatched to different points within the 16-acre complex. As a result, numerous units were congregating in the undamaged Marriott Hotel and at the overall command post on West Street by 9:30, while chiefs in charge of the South Tower still were in desperate need of units. With better understanding of the resources already available, additional units might not have been dispatched to the South Tower at 9:37. The situation was rendered even more difficult by internal communications breakdowns resulting from the limited capabilities of radios in the high-rise environment of the WTC, and from confusion over which personnel were assigned to which frequency. Furthermore, when the South Tower collapsed the overall FDNY command post ceased to operate, which compromised the FDNY's ability to understand the situation; an FDNY marine unit's immediate radio communication to FDNY dispatch that the South Tower had fully collapsed was not conveyed to chiefs at the scene. The FDNY's inability to coordinate and account for the different radio channels that would be used in an emergency of this scale contributed to the early lack of units in the South Tower, whose lobby chief initially could not communicate with anyone outside that tower. Though almost no one at 9:50 on September 11 was contemplating an imminent total collapse of the Twin Towers, many First Responders and civilians were contemplating the possibility of imminent additional terrorist attacks throughout New York City. Had any such attacks occurred, the FDNY's response would have been severely compromised by the concentration of so many of its off-duty personnel, particularly its elite personnel, at the WTC. [1, pp. 319-320]

Any attempt to establish a unified command on 9/11 would have been further frustrated by the lack of communication and coordination among responding agencies. Certainly, the FDNY was not positioned to be "responsible for the management of the City's response to the emergency," as the Mayor's directive would have required. Agency command posts were in different locations, and OEM headquarters, which could have served as a focal point for information sharing, did not play an integrating role in ensuring that information was shared among agencies on 9/11, even prior to its evacuation. There was a lack of comprehensive coordination between FDNY, NYPD, and PAPD personnel climbing above the ground floors in the Twin Towers. Information that was critical to informed decision making was not shared among agencies. FDNY chiefs in leadership roles that morning were hampered by a lack of information from NYPD aviation. At 9:51 A.M., a helicopter pilot cautioned that "large pieces" of the South Tower appeared to be about to fall and could pose a danger to those below. Immediately after the tower's collapse, a helicopter pilot radioed that news. This transmission was followed by communications at 10:08, 10:15, and 10:22 that called into question the condition of the North Tower. The FDNY chiefs would have benefited greatly had they been able to communicate with personnel in a helicopter. Moreover, FDNY, PAPD, and NYPD did not coordinate their units that were searching the WTC complex for civilians. In many cases, redundant searches of specific floors and areas were conducted. It is unclear whether fewer first responders in the aggregate would have been in the Twin Towers if there had been an integrated response, or what impact, if any, redundant searches had on the total number of first responder fatalities. [1, p. 320]

Whether the lack of coordination between the FDNY and NYPD on September 11 had a catastrophic effect has been the subject of controversy. It is clear, however, that the Incident Command System did not function to integrate awareness among agencies or to facilitate interagency response [1, p. 320]

Conclusion

The 9/11 attacks were the culmination of many failures on the part of America's national security apparatus; too many failures for the 9/11 Commission to assess specific blame, but sufficient to suggest that 9/11 might have been thwarted at any number of opportunities if things had gone only slightly different. Emphasizing a "failure of imagination" was the Commission's way of pointing out a systemic problem that stifled innovation and agility, and was absent accountability. Accordingly, the appropriate solution was a systemic change to America's national security apparatus, adding justification to establishing a new Department of Homeland Security. The new Department would bridge the gaps and provide accountability against this new threat to national security. While attention was focused against these new manmade threats, the nation was blindsided by a catastrophic natural hazard.

Challenge Your Understanding

The following questions are designed to challenge your understanding of the material presented in this chapter. Some questions may require additional research outside this book in order to provide a complete answer.

1. List three different attacks on U.S. service members overseas in the years before the attack on the USS Cole.
2. Identify three differences and three similarities between the attacks you listed and the attack on the USS Cole.
3. Compared to the other three attacks, would you have thought al Qaeda a major threat in December 2000? Explain.
4. Describe the failed efforts by the CIA and DoD to capture or kill Osama bin Laden before 9/11.
5. Explain why the FBI failed to arrest known al Qaeda operatives in the U.S. as they trained for the 9/11 attacks.
6. Explain how FAA regulations abetted the 9/11 hijackers even after they were flagged by CAPPS.
7. Describe the U.S. air defense posture on 9/11.
8. Explain what the 9/11 Commission meant by a "failure of imagination".
9. Even if the CIA and FBI had coordinated better, how might they have still failed to prevent 9/11? Explain.
10. Discuss the possible repercussions if NORAD had shot down the hijacked aircraft before they crashed into the South Tower and Pentagon on 9/11.

Chapter 8

Failure of Initiative

Learning Outcomes

Careful study of this chapter will help a student do the following:

- Describe events that contributed to the deaths of 1,464 New Orleans residents.
- Discuss breakdowns between City, State, and Federal officials that frustrated emergency response.
- Assess the consequences and difficulties of evacuating a major U.S. city.

"If 9/11 was a failure of imagination, then Katrina was a failure of initiative. It was a failure of leadership."

- 2005 House Committee Report

Introduction

No matter how secure the country is made from malicious acts, it will remain susceptible to acts of nature. When a natural disaster overwhelms local emergency management, an intricate choreography is required to engage State and Federal support, and efficiently coordinate the combined response to maximize lifesaving efforts within the first critical 72 hours of a disaster. The deaths and breakdown of civil order in New Orleans as a result of Hurricane Katrina are a cautionary tale of what happens when this choreography breaks down, and emergency aid is neither swift nor efficient because of a leadership failure of initiative.

First responders — local fire, police, and emergency medical personnel who respond to all manner of incidents such as earthquakes, storms, and floods — have the lead responsibility for carrying out emergency management efforts. Their role is to prevent, protect against, respond to, and assist in the recovery from emergencies, including

Local Disaster Response

First responders — local fire, police, and emergency medical personnel who respond to all manner of incidents such as earthquakes, storms, and floods — have the lead responsibility for carrying out emergency management efforts. Their role is to prevent, protect against, respond to, and assist in the recovery from emergencies, including natural disasters. Typically, first responders are trained and equipped to arrive first at the scene of an incident and take action immediately, including entering the scene, setting up a command center, evacuating those at the scene, tending to the injured, redirecting traffic, and removing debris. [1, p. 45]

Local governments — cities, towns, counties or parishes — and the officials who lead them are responsible for developing the emergency operations and response plans by which their communities respond to disasters and other emergencies, including terrorist attacks. Local emergency management directors are also generally responsible for providing training to prepare for disaster response and seek assistance from their state emergency management agencies when the situation exceeds or exhausts local capabilities. In many states, they may also negotiate and enter into Mutual Aid Agreements (MAAs) with other jurisdictions to share resources when, for example, nearby jurisdictions are unaffected by the emergency and are able to provide some assistance. [1, p. 46]

State Disaster Response

As the state's chief executive, the Governor is responsible for the public safety and welfare of the state's citizens and generally has wide-ranging emergency management responsibilities. Governors are responsible for coordinating state resources to address the full range of actions necessary to prevent, prepare for, and respond to incidents such as natural disasters. [1, p. 46]

Upon their declaration of an emergency or disaster, governors typically assume a variety of emergency powers, including authority to control access to an affected area and provide temporary shelter. Also, in most cases, states generally authorize their governors to order and enforce the evacuation of residents in disaster and emergency situations. [1, p. 46]

As the state's chief executive, the Governor is responsible for the public safety and welfare of the state's citizens and generally has wide-ranging emergency management responsibilities.

Governors also serve as the commanders-in-chief of their state military forces, specifically, the National Guard when in state active duty or Title 32 status. In state active duty — to which governors can call the Guard in response to disasters and other emergencies — National Guard personnel operate under the control of the governor, are paid according to state law, and can perform typical disaster relief tasks, such as search and rescue, debris removal, and law enforcement. Most governors have the authority to implement mutual aid agreements with other states to share resources with one another during disasters or emergencies when, for example, others (particularly nearby states) are unaffected by the emergency and able to provide assistance. Most states request and provide this assistance through the Emergency Management Assistance Compact (EMAC). If all these resources are not fast enough or sufficient, then the Governor may petition the President for support. [1, p. 46]

Federal Disaster Support

When an incident overwhelms, or is likely to overwhelm, state and local resources, the Stafford Act (Title 42 USC Ch. 68) authorizes the President, in response to a request from the Governor of the affected state, to issue two types of declarations—emergency or major disaster. An emergency is "any occasion or instance for which, in the determination of the President, federal assistance is needed to supplement state and local efforts and capabilities to save lives and to protect property and public health and safety, or to lessen or avert the threat of a catastrophe in any part of the United

States." A major disaster is "any natural catastrophe (including any hurricane, tornado, storm, high water, wind-driven water, tidal wave, tsunami, earthquake, volcanic eruption, landslide, mudslide, snowstorm, or drought), or, regardless of cause, any fire, flood, or explosion, in any part of the United States, which in the determination of the President causes damage of sufficient severity and magnitude to warrant major disaster assistance under this chapter to supplement the efforts and available resources of States, local governments, and disaster relief organizations in alleviating the damage, loss, hardship, or suffering caused thereby." [1, p. 31]

If the President approves an emergency or major disaster declaration, then the Federal Emergency Management Agency (FEMA) will setup a Joint Field Office (JFO) in proximity to the State Emergency Operations Center (SEOC), and a FEMA Federal Coordinating Officer (FCO) will begin working with the designated State Coordinating Officer (SCO) to deliver requested federal assistance.

If the President approves an emergency or major disaster declaration, then the Federal Emergency Management Agency (FEMA) will setup a Joint Field Office (JFO) in proximity to the State Emergency Operations Center (SEOC), and a FEMA Federal Coordinating Officer (FCO) will begin working with the designated State Coordinating Officer (SCO) to deliver requested federal assistance. [1, p. 38]

The federal government typically responds to most natural disasters after the affected states request support. In practice, states may make these requests before disasters strike because of the near certainty that federal assistance will be necessary after such an event (e.g., with hurricanes) or, afterwards, once they have conducted preliminary damage assessments and determined that their response capabilities are overwhelmed. In either case, the resources the federal government provides in any disaster response are intended to supplement state and local government resources devoted to the ongoing disaster relief and recovery effort. This system in use for most disasters — providing federal assistance in response to requests of the states (or local governments via the states) — is often referred to as a "pull" system in that it relies on states to know what they need and to be able to request it from the federal government. [1, pp. 30-31]

In certain instances, however, the federal response may also be considered a "push" system, in which federal assistance is provided and/or moved into the affected area prior to a disaster or without waiting for specific requests from the state or local governments. [1, p. 31] The "push" system can be risky, especially if resulting damages are less than expected and the expended federal resources are not needed by the State. The "push" system has the distinct advantage, though, of reducing delays and expediting delivery of federal aid to the disaster. Much of the criticism leveled at the federal government was that it relied on a "pull" system when it should have initiated a "push" system in response to Hurricane Katrina.

Hurricane Katrina

Hurricane Katrina was the costliest natural disaster, as well as one of the five deadliest hurricanes in the history of the United States. The storm ranks third behind the 1935 Labor Day hurricane and Hurricane Camille in 1969. Overall, at least 1,500 people died in the hurricane and subsequent floods, making it the deadliest United States hurricane since the 1928 Okeechobee hurricane. Total property damage was estimated at $108 billion. [2]

The tropical depression that became Hurricane Katrina formed over the Bahamas on August 23, 2005. Early the following day, the new depression intensified into Tropical Storm Katrina. The cyclone headed generally westward toward Florida and strengthened into a hurricane only two hours before making landfall between Hallandale Beach and Aventura on Thursday morning, August 25. The storm weakened as it crossed over Florida, but regained hurricane strength shortly after emerging into the Gulf of Mexico on Friday, August 26. The storm strengthened to a Category 5 hurricane over the warm waters of the Gulf of Mexico, but weakened before making its second landfall as a Category 3 hurricane in southeast Louisiana in the early morning hours of Monday, August 29. [2]

Hurricane Katrina was the costliest natural disaster, as well as one of the five deadliest hurricanes in the history of the United States. The storm ranks third behind the 1935 Labor Day hurricane and Hurricane Camille in 1969.

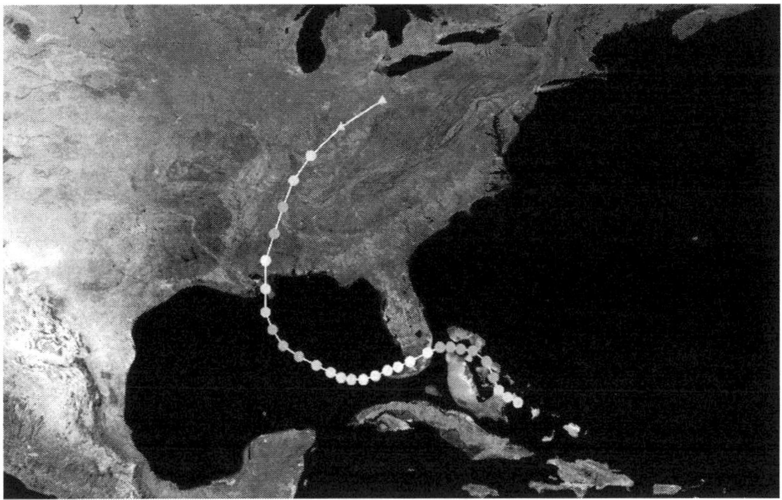

Figure 8-1: Track of Hurricane Katrina [2]

Katrina caused severe destruction along the Gulf coast from central Florida to Texas, much of it due to high winds and flooding. Florida suffered twice, first when the storm crossed over South Florida August 25, and a second time August 29 when Katrina drove ashore in Louisiana, grazing the Florida Panhandle. Twelve deaths were blamed on the storm in South Florida. It also left 1.45 million people without power and caused $523 million in damages, most of it to crops. Two more deaths were attributed to the storm as it grazed the Florida Panhandle, leaving another 77,000 people without power, and causing an additional $100 million in damages. Overall, the hurricane killed 14 people and caused $623 million in damages to Florida. Alabama was also hit by winds and floods as Katrina made landfall. Sustained winds of 67 mph left 600,000 people without power. A 12-foot storm surge caused significant flooding several miles inland along Mobile Bay. The combined winds and high waters washed ships, oil rigs, boats, and fishing piers ashore along Mobile Bay. Four tornadoes were spawned inland. Two deaths were attributed to the storm. Twenty-two Alabama counties were declared disaster areas. In its second landfall, Katrina's powerful right-front quadrant passed over the west and central Mississippi coast, causing a 27-foot storm surge to penetrate 6 miles inland, and up to 12 miles along bays and rivers. Together with the storm surge, the state was battered by heavy winds and torrential rains. The combination proved devastating, destroying 90% of all structures within a half mile of the coastline. The storm destroyed bridges, barges, boats, piers, houses, and cars. Eighty-two counties were declared disaster areas. Some 900,000 people were left without power; 238 people were left dead. Mississippi might have been the center of national attention, except for what happened in New Orleans. [2]

New Orleans was at particular risk. Though about half the city actually lies above sea level, its average elevation is about six feet below sea level–and it is completely surrounded by water.

New Orleans

New Orleans was at particular risk. Though about half the city actually lies above sea level, its average elevation is about six feet below sea level–and it is completely surrounded by water. Over the course of the 20th century, the Army Corps of Engineers had built a system of levees and seawalls to keep the city from flooding. The levees along the Mississippi River were strong and sturdy, but the ones built to hold back Lake Pontchartrain, Lake Borgne and the waterlogged swamps and marshes to the city's east and west were much less reliable. Even before the storm, officials worried that those levees, jerry-built atop sandy, porous, erodible soil, might not withstand a massive storm surge. Neighborhoods that sat below sea level, many of which housed the city's poorest and most vulnerable people, were at great risk of flooding. [3]

The day before Katrina hit, New Orleans Mayor Ray Nagin issued the city's first-ever mandatory evacuation order. [3] Between 80 and 90 percent of the residents of New Orleans were evacuated safely in time before the hurricane struck. Despite this, about 100,000 remained in the city, mainly those who did not have access to personal vehicles. [2] To assist those left behind, Mayor Nagin opened the Superdome as a "shelter of last resort". The stadium was situated on relatively high ground near downtown. It had been used as a shelter during previous storms, including Hurricane Georges in 1998. The Superdome had been estimated to withstand winds up to 200 miles per hour, and water levels of 35 feet. By the evening of August 28, the night before Hurricane Katrina hit, some 20,000 people had taken shelter in the Superdome under the care of 300 Louisiana National Guard. [4]

At 3 a.m. on August 29, Hurricane Katrina made landfall near Buras-Triumph, Louisiana as a strong Category 3 storm with 125 mph winds. It brought a 14-foot storm surge and 8-10 inches of rain. These raised the level of Lake Pontchartrain causing significant flooding along its northeastern shore. Several bridges were destroyed, including the I-10 Twin Span Bridge connecting New Orleans to Slidell. Most of the roads traveling into and out of the city were damaged. The only routes out of the city were the westbound Crescent City Connection and Lake Pontchartrain Causeway, which was restricted to emergency traffic. Power went out. High winds blew out the windows of many high-rise buildings, and peeled back the waterproof membrane of the Superdome. However, by mid-day as the eye of the hurricane passed east of the city, it seemed New Orleans had been spared the worst of the storm. Despite the heavy winds and rain, most buildings appeared to be structurally intact. But then the levees began to break. [4]

Katrina's storm surge overwhelmed the city's levees and drainage canals. The Mississippi River Gulf Outlet breached its levees in 20 places, flooding much of east New Orleans, most of Saint Bernard Parish, and the East Bank of Plaquemines Parish. The federally built levee system protecting metro New Orleans breached in 53 places

Katrina's storm surge overwhelmed the city's levees and drainage canals. The Mississippi River Gulf Outlet breached its levees in 20 places, flooding much of east New Orleans, most of Saint Bernard Parish, and the East Bank of Plaquemines Parish. The federally built levee system protecting metro New Orleans breached in 53 places, including the 17th Street Canal, London Avenue Canal, and the Industrial Canal. By August 31, 2005, 80% of New Orleans was flooded, with some parts under 15 feet of water. [4]

The extensive flooding stranded many residents in their homes. Many chopped their way onto their roofs with hatchets and sledge hammers, which residents had been urged to store in their attics in case of such events. House tops across the city were dotted with survivors. Some were trapped inside their attics, unable to escape. Trapped in their homes, many families awaited rescue, without power, without water, without food. [4]

The first deaths were reported shortly before midnight on August 28, as three nursing home patients died during an evacuation to Baton Rouge. By 11:00 pm on August 29, Mayor Nagin described the loss of life as "significant" with reports of bodies floating on the water throughout the city, though primarily in the eastern portions. The National Guard began setting up temporary morgues in select locations. [4]

After the storm passed, on August 30, as flood waters continued to rise, the media reported rampant arson and looting across the city. Atrocities were reported at the Superdome. Later investigations proved most of the reports greatly exaggerated. Still, there was a breakdown in civil order, spurred, in part, by desertions within the New Orleans Police Department. On August 31, Mayor Nagin imposed a curfew and ordered the NOPD to abandon search and rescue missions in order to restore civil order. The same day, Governor Blanco ordered in 6500 National Guard. Relief efforts were disrupted by violence. Charity Hospital was forced to halt patient evacuations after coming under gunfire. On September 2, Governor Blanco requested an additional 40,000 National Guard for assistance in evacuation and security. [4]

The situation was indeed miserable at the Superdome. On August 29, as Katrina passed over New Orleans it ripped two holes into the roof. The scene inside the building was described as chaotic; reports of rampant drug use, fights, rape, and filthy living conditions were widespread. Despite increasingly squalid conditions, the population inside continued to grow as many more arrived hoping to find food, water, and maybe transportation out of town. On August 31, Governor Blanco ordered the Superdome evacuated, and sent in 68 school buses to relocate civilians to the Houston Astrodome. By September 4, the Superdome was completely evacuated. [4]

Final reports indicate that the official death toll, according to the Louisiana Department of Health, was 1,464 people. Investigations following the hurricane decried many of the deaths as "preventable". Furthermore, they determined that the suffering in the days and weeks after the storm was unnecessarily prolonged.

As rescue operations commenced on August 29, rescuers began dropping people off outside the Convention Center. It was meant to be a transit point to shelter. The problem was, no transportation was sent. By the afternoon of the 29th, a crowd of about 1,000 people had begun to gather outside the Convention Center. After being told the facility had no food, water, or services, the crowd nonetheless broke in and took refuge. The next day, a contingent of 250 National Guard engineers arrived and began working from the facility. The engineers were never given orders to control the crowd, nor were they prepared for the task. Still, the number of people at the Convention Center continued to grow over the next three days; some sent there from the Superdome, some dropped off after being rescued from their roof, and some arriving of their own volition. There was nobody in charge; nobody to provide for the evacuees' care and safety. Reports of robberies, murder, and rape began to surface. A large cache of alcohol was stolen. People died, and their bodies left where they passed. Finally, on September 2, a sizable contingent of National Guard arrived to establish order and provide essential provisions. On September 3, buses began arriving and refugees evacuated. By September 4, the Convention Center was completely evacuated. [4]

Final reports indicate that the official death toll, according to the Louisiana Department of Health, was 1,464 people. [4] Investigations following the hurricane decried many of the deaths as "preventable". [1, p. 2] Furthermore, they determined that the suffering in the days and weeks after the storm was unnecessarily prolonged, and even exacerbated by the failure of government at all levels to plan, prepare, and respond aggressively to the storm. [5, p. 2]

Table 8-1: Hurricane Katrina New Orleans Timeline

Date	Description
Wed. 24 Aug 05	• First alerts of a tropical storm stirring in Caribbean
Fri. 26 Aug 05	• Most residents work a full day and take "wait and see" approach • 5 pm warnings from National Weather Service show Hurricane Katrina turning • New Orleans potentially within range
Sat. 27 Aug 05	• Saturday morning most residents learn that Katrina's path is set for New Orleans • Metro-area evacuations begin en masse clogging all outbound arteries of the city for 48 hours • St. Tammany, St. Charles, Plaquemines Parishes announce mandatory evacuations • Orleans and Jefferson Parish both announce voluntary evacuations • Governor Blanco sends "State of Emergency" letter to President Bush • Louisiana State University scientists issue a projected storm surge map
Sun. 28 Aug 05	• At 9:30 am Orleans Parish issues first-ever mandatory evacuation • At 10 am Katrina becomes a Category 5 storm with winds of 175 mph • At 11:30 am, President Bush vows to help those affected by the storm • State puts contra-flow plan into effect on interstates • Superdome designated city's "refuge of last resort" • Director of the National Hurricane Center warns Times-Picayune of a "worst-case scenario" • Tropical storm-force winds close down emergency services in metro area • At 9 pm, Times-Picayune building loses power, generators power up
Mon. 29 Aug 05	• At 3 am, Katrina makes landfall as a Category 3 hurricane • Metro-area emergency officials hold status meeting • At 6 am, 317,000 households are without power • At 7 am, water reported coming over the levee in the 9th Ward • At 8:45 am, six to eight-foot flood waters reported in Lower 9th Ward • At 9 am, winds rip hole in roof of Superdome • At 9 am, eye of the storm passes to the east of New Orleans central business district. • Windows in high-rise buildings blow out • 11 am, National Weather Service reports a breach in the Industrial Canal levee, emptying Lake Pontchartrain into the neighborhoods of Eastern New Orleans, the Lower Ninth Ward in Orleans Parish and all of St. Bernard Parish • 2 pm, breach in the 17th Street Canal is confirmed; Lakeview, Mid-City, Broodmoor, Gentilly flooded over next 48 hours. • 2 pm, flood waters in the Lower Ninth Ward reach 12 feet in some areas • Flood waters continue to rise and it becomes apparent that it is a worst-case scenario
Tue. 30 Aug 05	• 9 am, Times-Picayune employees evacuate building in delivery trucks as water rises a foot an hour • Local media reports that Martial Law is declared in Orleans, Jefferson and Plaquemines Parish • Looting reports go national presenting • Flood waters continue to rise throughout city
Wed. 31 Aug 05	• Flood waters reach an equilibrium as the "bowl" of the city is now even with Lake Ponchartrain • Some neighborhoods under as much as 20 feet of water • Hellish scenes reported from those stranded in the Superdome: assaults, rape and suicide reported though later most dismissed • Estimates of 30 days before city can be pumped out • Thousands stranded in houses, on roofs • Approximately one million people without power in metro area • Media reports that thousands are stranded in the New Orleans Convention Center without food or water as a steady stream of people, many from the flooded Central City neighborhood, trickled first toward Lee Circle and then to the Convention Center, hoping to be saved from increasingly desperate straits

Date	Description
Thu. 1 Sep 05	• Corps of Engineers begins to build dam to stop levee breach at the 17th Street Canal • More than 10,000 people have been rescued in St. Bernard Parish • Times-Picayune asks, "Where is the Cavalry?"; No federal help arrived • Governor Blanco demands "no less than 40,000 troops" • Mayor Nagin lambasts federal officials in a tirade for their lack of effective response • First 5,000 of approximately 23,000 evacuees arrive at Houston Astrodome by bus • Bush seeks $10.5 billion storm-relief package
Fri. 2 Sep 05	• 7,000 soldiers move in on the Convention Center; they confront 15,000 angry refugees and a boulevard littered with putrefying corpses • Fires break out in various warehouses across the city • Bush tours area, says what is wrong "we're going to make right" • Mayor Nagin predicts electricity to be out in city for three months • Airport becomes way station for refugees • Thousands of refugees still in Superdome, Convention Center and I-10
Sat. 3 Sep 05	• FEMA says storm overwhelmed agency; outrage grows in Washington • Authorities begin to regain grip on city with military's aid • President Bush orders 7,200 additional active duty troops to the region, for a total of 30,000 • Rape, gunfire reported at Convention Center • Law enforcement agencies fielded about 1,000 distress 911 calls Saturday • St. Bernard rescuers find 31 dead in nursing home • Death toll expected to be in thousands, though nothing official yet • Last of evacuees taken from Superdome and Convention Center • Jefferson Parish President Aaron Broussard breaks down on "Meet the Press" and tells how a colleague's elderly mother died in her home Friday after waiting four days for rescuers that never arrived • Rescuers continue to pluck residents from hellish waters
Sun. 4 Sep 05	• Estimated 2,000 people, many of them with serious medical problems, were still housed inside Louis Armstrong International Airport
Mon. 5 Sep 05	• 16,000 National Guard troops dedicated to search and rescue mission • Jefferson Parish residents allowed home to survey damage • Agencies begin trying to save stranded pets • Corps of Engineers shifts work to damning London Avenue Canal • Mayor Nagin says more than 10,000 could be dead • Makeshift morgue set up in St. Gabriel, La. to handle 140 bodies per day [6]

Failure Analysis

According to the Senate investigation of Hurricane Katrina, government failure was pervasive in that 1) long-term warnings went unheeded and government officials neglected their duties to prepare for a forewarned catastrophe; 2) government officials took insufficient actions or made poor decisions in the days immediately before and after landfall; 3) systems on which officials relied on to support their response efforts failed, and 4) government officials at all levels failed to provide effective leadership. The results were tragic loss of life and human suffering on a massive scale, and an undermining of confidence in the governments' ability to plan, prepare for, and respond to national catastrophes. [5, p. 2]

Unheeded Warnings

The potentially devastating threat of a catastrophic hurricane to the Gulf region has been known for forty years: New Orleans experienced flooding in some areas of remarkably similar proportions from Hurricane Betsy in 1965, and Hurricane Camille devastated the Gulf Coast in 1969. More recently, numerous experts and governmental officials had been anticipating an increase in violent hurricanes, and

New Orleans' special and growing vulnerability to catastrophic flooding due to changing geological and other conditions was widely described in both technical and popular media. [5, p. 4]

Hurricane Georges hit the Gulf in 1998, spurring the state of Louisiana to ask FEMA for assistance with catastrophic hurricane planning. Little was accomplished for the next six years. Between 2000 and 2003, state authorities, an emergency-preparedness contractor, and FEMA's own regional staff repeatedly advised FEMA headquarters in Washington that planning for evacuation and shelter for the "New Orleans scenario" was incomplete and inadequate, but FEMA failed to approach other federal agencies for help with transportation and shelter or to ensure that the City and State had the matters in hand. [5, p. 4]

According to the Senate investigation of Hurricane Katrina, government failure was pervasive in that 1) long-term warnings went unheeded ; 2) government officials took insufficient actions; 3) systems on which officials relied on to support their response efforts failed, and 4) government officials at all levels failed to provide effective leadership.

Then, in 2004, after a White House aide received a briefing on the catastrophic consequences of a Category 3 hurricane hitting New Orleans, the federal government sponsored a planning exercise, with participation from federal, state, and local officials, based on a scenario whose characteristics foreshadowed most of Katrina's impacts. While this hypothetical "Hurricane Pam" exercise resulted in draft plans beginning in early 2005, they were incomplete when Katrina hit. Nonetheless, some officials took the initiative to use concepts developed in the drafts, with mixed success in the critical aspects of the Katrina response. However, many of its admonitory lessons were either ignored or inadequately applied. [5, p. 4]

During the Pam exercise, officials determined that massive flooding from a catastrophic storm in New Orleans could threaten the lives of 60,000 people and trap hundreds of thousands more, while incapacitating local resources for weeks to months. The Pam exercise gave all levels of government a reminder that the "New Orleans scenario" required more forethought, preparation, and investment than a "typical" storm. Also, it reinforced the importance of coordination both within and among federal, state, and local governments for an effective response. [5, p. 5]

The specific danger that Katrina posed to the Gulf Coast became clear on the afternoon of Friday, August 26, when forecasters at the National Hurricane Center and the National Weather Service saw that the storm was turning west. First in phone calls to Louisiana emergency management officials and then in their 5 p.m. EDT Katrina forecast and accompanying briefings, they alerted both Louisiana and Mississippi that the track of the storm was now expected to shift significantly to the west of its original track to the Florida panhandle. The National Hurricane Center warned that Katrina could be a Category 4 or even a 5 by landfall. By the next morning, Weather Service Officials directly confirmed to the Governor of Louisiana and other state and local officials that New Orleans was squarely at risk. [5, p. 5]

Over the weekend, there was a drumbeat of warnings: FEMA held video-teleconferences on both days, where the danger of Katrina and the particular risks to New Orleans were discussed; Max Mayfield of the Hurricane Center called the governors of the affected states, something he had only done once before in his 33 year career; President Bush took the unusual step of declaring in advance an emergency for the states in the impact zone; numerous media reports noted that New Orleans was a "bowl" and could be left submerged by the storm; the Department of Homeland Security's Simulation and Analysis group generated a report stating that the levees protecting New Orleans were at risk of breaching and overtopping; internal FEMA slides stated that the projected impacts of Katrina could be worse than those in the Hurricane Pam exercise. The warnings were as widespread as they were dire. [5, p. 5]

While Katrina's destructive force could not be denied, state and local officials did not marshal enough of the resources at their disposal.

Insufficient Preparation

While the State of Louisiana and the City of New Orleans undertook unprecedented measures to prepare ahead of the storm, ineffective leadership, poor advance planning and an unwillingness to devote sufficient resources to emergency management over the long term doomed them to fail when Katrina struck. Despite the understanding of the Gulf Coast's particular vulnerability to hurricane devastation, officials braced for Katrina with full awareness of critical deficiencies in their plans and gaping holes in their resources. While Katrina's destructive force could not be denied, state and local officials did not marshal enough of the resources at their disposal. [5, p. 6]

For example, while Governor Blanco stated in a letter to President Bush two days before landfall that she anticipated the resources of the state would be overwhelmed, she made no specific request for assistance in evacuating the known tens of thousands of people without means of transportation, and a senior state official identified no unmet needs in response to a federal offer of assistance the following day. The state's transportation secretary also ignored his responsibilities under the state's emergency operations plan, leaving no arm of the state government prepared to obtain and deliver additional transportation to those in New Orleans who lacked it, when Katrina struck. In view of the long-standing role of requests as a trigger for action by higher levels of government, the state bears responsibility for not signaling its needs to the federal government more clearly. [5, p. 6]

Compounded by leadership failures of its own, the federal government bears responsibility for not preparing effectively for its role in the post storm response. [5, p. 6]

FEMA was unprepared for a catastrophic event of the scale of Katrina. Established in 1979 to consolidate emergency management functions previously dispersed throughout federal government, FEMA had not developed – nor had it been designed to develop – response capabilities sufficient for a catastrophe the size of Katrina. Nor had it developed the capacity to mobilize sufficient resources from other federal agencies, and the private and nonprofit sectors. [5, p. 6]

Moreover, FEMA's Director, Michael Brown, lacked the leadership skills that were needed. Before landfall, Brown did not direct the adequate pre-positioning of critical personnel and equipment, and willfully failed to communicate with his boss, Secretary Chertoff. Earlier in the hurricane season, FEMA had pre-positioned an unprecedented amount of relief supplies in the region. But the supplies were not enough. Similarly, while both FEMA and the Department of Health and Human Services made efforts to activate the federal emergency health capabilities of the National Disaster Medical System (NDMS) and the U.S. Public Health Service, only a limited number of federal medical teams were actually in position prior to landfall to deploy into the affected area. Only one such team was in a position to provide immediate medical care in the aftermath of the storm. [5, p. 7]

More broadly, the newly created Department of Homeland Security, charged with preparing for and responding to domestic incidents, failed to effectively lead the federal response to Hurricane Katrina.

More broadly, the newly created Department of Homeland Security, charged with preparing for and responding to domestic incidents, failed to effectively lead the federal response to Hurricane Katrina. DHS leadership failed to bring a sense of urgency to the federal government's preparation for Hurricane Katrina, and Secretary Chertoff himself should have been more engaged in preparations over the weekend before landfall. Secretary Chertoff made only top-level inquiries into the state of preparations, and accepted uncritically the reassurances he received. He did not appear to reach out to the other Cabinet Secretaries to make sure that they were readying their departments to provide whatever assistance DHS – and the people of the Gulf – might need. [5, p. 7]

Similarly, had he invoked the Catastrophic Incident Annex (CIA) of the NRP, Secretary Chertoff could have helped remove uncertainty about the federal government's need and authority to take initiative before landfall and signaled that all federal government agencies were expected to think – and act – proactively in preparing for and responding to Katrina. The Secretary's activation of the National Response Plan (NRP) CIA could have increased the urgency of the federal response and led the federal government to respond more proactively rather than waiting for formal requests from overwhelmed state and local officials. Understanding that delay may preclude meaningful assistance and that state and local resources could be quickly overwhelmed and incapacitated, the NRP CIA directed federal agencies to pre-position resources without awaiting requests from the state and local governments. Even then, the NRP CIA held these resources at mobilization sites until requested by state and local officials, except in certain prescribed circumstances. [5, p. 7]

The military also had a role to play, and ultimately, the National Guard and active duty military troops and assets deployed during Katrina constituted the largest domestic deployment of military forces since the Civil War. And while the Department of Defense took additional steps to prepare for Katrina beyond those it had taken for prior civil support missions, its preparations were not sufficient for a storm of Katrina's magnitude. Individual commanders took actions that later helped improve the response, but these actions were not coordinated by the Department. The Department's preparations were consistent with how DOD interpreted its role under the National Response Plan, which was to provide support in response to requests for assistance from FEMA. However, additional preparations in advance of specific requests for support could have enabled a more rapid response. [5, pp. 7-8]

The military also had a role to play, and ultimately, the National Guard and active duty military troops and assets deployed during Katrina constituted the largest domestic deployment of military forces since the Civil War.

In addition, the White House shared responsibility for the inadequate pre-landfall preparations. To be sure, President Bush, at the request of FEMA Director Michael Brown, did take the initiative to personally call Governor Blanco to urge a mandatory evacuation. He also took the unusual step of declaring an emergency in the Gulf States prior to Katrina making landfall. On the other hand, the President did not leave his Texas ranch to return to Washington until two days after landfall, and only then convened his Cabinet as well as a White House task force to oversee federal response efforts. [5, p. 8]

The effect of the long-term failures at every level of government to plan and prepare adequately for a catastrophic hurricane in the Gulf was evident in the inadequate preparations before Katrina's landfall and then again in the initial response to the storm. [5, p. 8]

Inadequate Response

Flooding in New Orleans drove thousands of survivors to attics and rooftops to await rescue. Infrastructure damage complicated the organization and conduct of search-and -rescue missions. Destruction of communications towers and equipment in particular limited the ability of crews to communicate with one another, undermining coordination and efficiency. Rescuers also had to contend with weapons fire, debris, and polluted water. [5, p. 8]

Planning for search and rescue was also insufficient. FEMA, for instance, failed to provide boats for its search and rescue teams even though flooding had been confirmed by Tuesday. Moreover, interagency coordination was inadequate at both the state and federal levels. While the Louisiana Department of Fisheries and Wildlife and FEMA are responsible for interagency search and rescue coordination at the state and federal levels respectively, neither developed adequate plans for this mission. Staggeringly, the City of New Orleans Fire Department owned no boats, and the New Orleans Police Department owned five. Meanwhile, widespread communications failures in Louisiana and Mississippi were so bad that many officers reverted to either physically running messages from one person to another, or passing messages along a daisy chain of officers using radios with limited range. [5, p. 9]

The Department of Defense also was slow to acquire information regarding the extent of the storm's devastation. DOD officials relied primarily on media reports for their information.

While authorities recognized the need to begin search-and-rescue missions even before the hurricane winds fully subsided, other aspects of the response were hindered by a failure to quickly recognize the dimensions of the disaster. On the day after landfall, DHS officials were still struggling to determine the "ground truth" about the extent of the flooding despite the many reports it had received about the catastrophe; key officials did not grasp the need to act on the less-than-complete information that is to be expected in a disaster. DHS leaders did not become fully engaged in recovery efforts until Thursday, September 1, two days after Hurricane Katrina hit New Orleans. But this effort should have begun sooner. [5, p. 9]

FEMA Director Michael Brown, then in Louisiana, contributed to the problem by refusing to communicate with Secretary Chertoff opting instead to pass information directly to White House staff. Moreover, even though senior DHS officials did receive on the day of landfall numerous reports that should have led to an understanding of the increasingly dire situation in New Orleans, many indicated they were not aware of the crisis until sometime Tuesday morning, August 30, the day after landfall. [5, p. 9]

The Department of Defense also was slow to acquire information regarding the extent of the storm's devastation. DOD officials relied primarily on media reports for their information. Many senior DOD officials did not learn that the levees had breached until Tuesday; some did not learn until Wednesday, August 31, two days after Katrina made landfall. As DOD waited for DHS to provide information about the scope of the damage, it also waited for the lead federal agency, FEMA, to identify the support needed from DOD. The lack of situational awareness during this phase appears to have been a major reason for DOD's belated adoption of the forward-looking posture necessary in a catastrophic incident. [5, p. 10]

While large numbers of active-duty troops did not arrive until the end of the first week following landfall, the Department of Defense contributed in other important ways during that period. Early in the week, DOD ordered its military commanders to push available assets to the Gulf Coast. They also streamlined their ordinarily bureaucratic processes for handling FEMA requests for assistance and emphasized movement based on vocal commands with the paperwork to follow, though some FEMA officials believe that DOD's approval process continued to take too long. They provided significant support to search-and-rescue missions, evacuee airlifts, logistics management of buses arriving in the State for evacuation, and other matters. [5, p. 11]

Without effective law enforcement, real or imagined safety threats interrupted virtually every aspect of the response.

Toward the end of the week, with its own resources stretched thin, FEMA turned to DOD to take over logistics for all commodity movements. The Department of Defense acceded to the request, and provided some logistics assistance to FEMA. However, it did not undertake the complete logistical take-over initially requested by FEMA because that was not needed. [5, p. 12] On Wednesday, August 31, the National Guard Bureau began calling on state Adjutants General to deploy National Guard forces. This process quickly resulted in the largest National Guard deployment in U.S. history, with 50,000 troops and supporting equipment arriving from 49 states and four territories within two weeks. [5, p. 11] These forces brought in relief supplies provided by FEMA, established law and order, and assisted with evacuations. [5, p. 12]

Law Enforcement

Law enforcement outside the Superdome and the Convention Center was a problem, and was fueled by several contributing factors, including erroneous statements by top city officials inflaming the public's perception of the lawlessness in New Orleans. [5, p. 12]

Without effective law enforcement, real or imagined safety threats interrupted virtually every aspect of the response. Fearing for their personal safety, medical and search and rescue teams withdrew from their missions. FEMA and commercial vendors of critical supplies often refused to make deliveries until military escorts could be arranged. In fact, there was some lawlessness, yet for every actual act there were rumors of dozens more, leading to widespread and inaccurate reporting that severely complicated a desperate situation. Unfortunately, local, state, and federal officials did little to stanch this rumor flow. Police presence on the streets was inadequate, in part because in a matter of hours Katrina turned the New Orleans police department from protectors of the public to victims of the storm. Nonetheless, most New Orleans police officers appear to have reported for duty, many setting aside fears about the safety of their families or the status of their homes. [5, p. 12]

Even so, the ability of the officers who remained to perform their duties was significantly hampered by the lack of basic supplies. While supplies such as weapons and ammunition were lost to flooding, the NOPD leadership did not provide its officers with basic necessities such as food; nor did the department have logistics in place to handle supplies. Members of the NOPD also identified the lack of a unified command for this incident as a major problem; eight members of the Command Staff were extremely critical of the lack of leadership from the city's Office of Emergency Preparedness (OEP). The department's rank and file were unfamiliar with both the department's and the city's emergency-operations manuals and other hurricane emergency procedures. Deficiencies in the NOPD's manual, lack of training on this manual, lack of familiarity with it, or a combination of the three resulted in inadequate protection of department resources. [5, p. 13]

Federal law-enforcement assistance was too slow in coming, in large part because the two federal departments charged with providing such assistance – DHS and the Department of Justice (DOJ) – had done almost no pre-storm planning.

Federal law-enforcement assistance was too slow in coming, in large part because the two federal departments charged with providing such assistance – DHS and the Department of Justice (DOJ) – had done almost no pre-storm planning. In fact, they failed to determine even well into the post-landfall period which of the two departments would assume the lead for federal law enforcement. As a result, later in the week, as federal law-enforcement officers did arrive, some were distracted by a pointless "turf war" between DHS and DOJ over which agency was in the lead. In the end, federal assistance was crucial, but should have arrived much sooner. [5, p. 13]

Health Care

Medical teams had to triage more than 70,000 evacuees and provide acute care to the sick and wounded. While officials used plans developed in Hurricane Pam as a helpful framework for managing this process, existing emergency-room facilities were overwhelmed by the volume of patients. Local and state officials quickly set up temporary field hospitals at a sports arena and a K-mart in Baton Rouge to supplement hospital capacity. [5, p. 14]

New Orleans had a large population of "special needs patients," individuals living at home who required ongoing medical assistance. Before Katrina struck, the City Health Department activated a plan to establish a care facility for this population within the Superdome and provided transportation to evacuate several hundred patients and their caregivers to Baton Rouge. While Superdome facilities proved useful in treating special needs patients who remained behind, they had to contend with shortages of supplies, physical damage to the facility necessitating a post-landfall relocation of patients and equipment to an area adjacent to the Dome, and a population of more than 20,000 people using the Superdome as a refuge of last resort. Also, FEMA's

Disaster Medical Assistance Teams which provide the invaluable resources of pharmacies and hospital equipment, arrived at the Superdome on the night following landfall, but left temporarily on Thursday, before the evacuation of the Superdome's special needs population was completed, because of security concerns. [5, p. 14]

In Louisiana, hospitals had to evacuate after landfall on short notice principally due to loss of electrical power. While hospitals had evacuated some of their patients before landfall, they had retained others thought to be too frail for transport, and believed by staying open they would be available to serve hurricane victims. Their strategy became untenable after landfall when power was lost, and their backup generators were rendered inoperable by flooding and fuel shortages. The Louisiana Department of Health and Hospitals stepped in to arrange for their evacuation; while successful, it had to compete with search and rescue teams for helicopters and other needed resources. [5, p. 14]

The City of New Orleans, with primary responsibility for evacuation of its citizens, had language in its plan stating the city's intent to assist those who needed transportation for pre-storm evacuation, but had no actual plan provisions to implement that intent.

Many nursing homes in and around New Orleans lacked adequate evacuation plans. While they were required to have plans on file with local government, there was no process to ensure that there were sufficient resources to evacuate all the nursing homes at once, and dozens of patients who were not evacuated died. When evacuation became necessary, some sent their patients to the Superdome, where officials struggling to handle the volume of patients already there were obliged to accept still more. [5, p. 14]

Evacuations

The City of New Orleans, with primary responsibility for evacuation of its citizens, had language in its plan stating the city's intent to assist those who needed transportation for pre-storm evacuation, but had no actual plan provisions to implement that intent. In late 2004 and 2005, city officials negotiated contracts with Amtrak, riverboat owners and others to pre-arrange transportation alternatives, but received inadequate support from the city's Director of Homeland Security and Emergency Preparedness, and contracts were not in place when Katrina struck. As Katrina approached, notwithstanding the city's evacuation plans on paper, the best solution New Orleans had for people without transportation was a private-citizen volunteer carpool initiative called Operation Brothers' Keepers and transit buses taking people – not out of the city, but to the Superdome. [5, p. 16]

The Louisiana Department of Transportation and Development, whose Secretary had personally accepted departmental responsibility under the state's emergency operations plan to arrange for transportation for evacuation in emergencies, had done nothing to prepare for that responsibility prior to Katrina. Had his department identified available buses or other means of transport for evacuation within the state in the months before the hurricane, at a minimum the State would have been prepared to evacuate people stranded in New Orleans after landfall more quickly than it did. [5, p. 16]

While the Superdome provided shelter from the devastating winds and water, conditions there deteriorated quickly. Katrina's "near miss" ripped the covering off the roof, caused leaking, and knocked out the power, rendering the plumbing, air conditioning, and public announcement system totally useless. [5, p. 16] By Tuesday afternoon, the New Orleans Superdome had become overcrowded, leading officials to turn additional refugees away. Mayor Nagin directed evacuees be sent to the Convention Center, but communicated his decision to state and federal officials poorly, if at all. That failure, in addition to the delay of shipments due to security concerns and DHS's own independent lack of awareness of the situation, contributed to the paucity of food, water, security or medical care at the Convention Center, as a population of approximately 19,000 gathered there. [5, p. 12]

The Louisiana Department of Transportation and Development, whose Secretary had personally accepted departmental responsibility under the state's emergency operations plan to arrange for transportation for evacuation in emergencies, had done nothing to prepare for that responsibility prior to Katrina.

On Monday, August 29, as Katrina passed over New Orleans, Governor Blanco asked FEMA Director Michael Brown for buses. Brown assured the state the same day that 500 buses were enroute to assist in the evacuation of New Orleans and would arrive within hours. In spite of Brown's assurances and the state's continued requests over the course of the next two days, FEMA did not direct the U.S. Department of Transportation to send buses until very early on Wednesday, August 31, two days after landfall. Still, the buses did not begin to arrive until Wednesday evening and not in significant numbers until the next day, four days after landfall. Concerned over FEMA's delay in providing buses – and handicapped by the Louisiana Department of Transportation and Development's utter failure to make any preparation to carry out its lead role for evacuation under the state's emergency plan – Governor Blanco directed members of her office to begin locating buses on Tuesday and approved an effort to commandeer school buses for evacuation on Wednesday. But these efforts were too little, too late. Tens of thousands of people were forced to wait in unspeakably horrible conditions until as late as Saturday, September 4, to be evacuated. [5, p. 13]

Conclusion

Effective response to mass emergencies is a critical role of every level of government. It is a role that requires a substantial amount of planning, coordination and dispatch among governments' diverse units. Following the terrorist attacks of 9/11, the nation underwent one of the most sweeping reorganizations of federal government in history. While driven primarily by concerns of terrorism, the reorganization was designed to strengthen our nation's ability to address the consequences of both natural and man-made disasters. In its first major test, this reorganized system failed. [5, p. 2]

Challenge Your Understanding

The following questions are designed to challenge your understanding of the material presented in this chapter. Some questions may require additional research outside this book in order to provide a complete answer.

1. Why wasn't New Orleans completely evacuated in advance of the storm?
2. How did City and State emergency managers fail to assist the evacuation?
3. How did City and State emergency managers fail to provide adequate shelter?
4. How did the breakdown in local law enforcement contribute to the disaster?
5. Describe the breakdown in communications between the Governor and President.
6. Describe the breakdown in communications within the new Department of Homeland Security.
7. Describe the breakdown in communications between the responding military forces.
8. Explain why the House Report characterized the response to Hurricane Katrina as a "failure of initiative".
9. If you were mayor of New Orleans, why would you wait to evacuate your city?
10. If you were mayor of New Orleans, how would you expedite your city's evacuation?

Part II: HS, DHS, & HS Enterprise

This section examines the purpose, formation, evolution, and performance of the Department of Homeland Security, and its role within the Homeland Security Enterprise. We begin by examining the definition of homeland security. Unfortunately, the official definition as listed in the 2010 Quadrennial Homeland Security Review, and affirmed in the 2014 QHSR, is completely inadequate. If terrorism and natural disasters are indeed the primary homeland security concerns as indicated, then a Department of Homeland Security would've been created decades earlier following any number of terrorist incidents or natural disasters. In order to cut through the confusion we offer our own working definition of homeland security: "To safeguard the United States from domestic catastrophic destruction." This definition makes clear that the homeland security concern is domestic catastrophic destruction, no matter what the motive or cause. And because there are no guaranteed safeguards, homeland security must encompass missions across the spectrum of prevent, protect, mitigate, respond, and recover. In the prevent and protect mission areas, DHS is nationally responsible for aviation security, maritime security, surface transportation security, border security, and immigration enforcement. In the mitigation mission area, DHS works together in partnership with public and private agencies to reduce critical infrastructure vulnerability to attack, especially cyber attack. And in the respond and recover mission areas, DHS leads national efforts to enhance interoperability and capability within the First Responder community. Under authorities provided in the Homeland Security Act, and at the explicit direction of Congress, DHS has evolved since it was established to better meet its mission requirements. In 2010, at the direction of Congress, DHS instituted the QHSR process to continuously and systematically review their mission and organization to ensure they continue to do the right thing, and that they continue to do it right. And while DHS has filled important gaps exposed by 9/11, homeland security remains a team sport, requiring cooperation not just among Federal agencies, but also among State, Local, and Tribal governments as part of the Homeland Security Enterprise. For some missions, like critical infrastructure protection, DHS is the primary agency and leads efforts with help from many supporting agencies, including infrastructure owners and operators. For other missions, like counterterrorism, DHS is a supporting agency to the FBI, forwarding actionable leads developed by its many components and partners. Though DHS' progress has not been without significant challenges, and they still have substantial ground to gain, it can be confidently stated that the nation is better prepared to deal with catastrophic destruction than at any time before 9/11 or Hurricane Katrina.

Chapter 9

Homeland Security

Learning Outcomes

Careful study of this chapter will help a student do the following:

- Discuss the evolving definition of "homeland security".
- Evaluate the various definitions of "homeland security".
- Explain why the U.S. invaded Afghanistan in October 2001.

Con·flate /kən'flāt/ Verb. To combine two or more ideas into one.

- Dictionary.com

Introduction

The 1995 Tokyo subway attack was a turning point in American national security policy when non-state actors bearing weapons of mass destruction became a credible threat to the United States. [1] After the 1993 World Trade Center bombing and 1995 Oklahoma City bombing, two terrorist-motivated attacks on U.S. soil, three separate government commissions were established to investigate terrorist attacks employing WMD in the United States. As 9/11 would prove, the commissions found the nation unprepared to respond let alone thwart a catastrophic attack, and ultimately recommended the establishment of a homeland security agency to address such threats. [2, p. vi] In the process, they also conflated the concepts of "terrorism" and "domestic catastrophic attack", consequently confusing the concept of "homeland security". The purpose of this chapter is to examine the definition of "homeland security", and make a clear understanding of what it is, and what it is not.

"A direct attack against American citizens on American soil is likely over the next quarter century."

- Hart-Rudman Commission, February 2001

Pre-9/11

The Hart-Rudman Commission was chartered by Secretary of Defense William Cohen in 1998 to provide a comprehensive review of U.S. national security requirements for the 21st century. The U.S. Commission on National Security/21st Century was tasked "to analyze the emerging international security environment; to develop a U.S. national security strategy appropriate to that environment; and to assess the various security institutions for their current relevance to the effective and efficient implementation of that strategy, and to recommend adjustments as necessary". [3] Phase I concluded in September 1999 with the publication of "New World Coming: American Security in the 21st Century". Phase II produced the April 2000 publication, "Seeking a National Strategy: A Concert for Preserving Security and Promoting Freedom". Phase III, presented in February 2001 was titled "Road Map for National Security: Imperative for Change". [2, pp. v-vi]

Six months before 9/11, the Hart-Rudman Commission summarized its previous findings with this chilling prediction:

> "The combination of unconventional weapons proliferation with the persistence of international terrorism will end the relative invulnerability of the U.S. homeland to catastrophic attack. A direct attack against American citizens on American soil is likely over the next quarter century. The risk is not only death and destruction but also a demoralization that could undermine U.S. global leadership. In the face of this threat, our nation has no coherent or integrated governmental structures." [2, p. viii]

In recognition of this perceived threat, the Commission Phase III report recommended establishing an independent National Homeland Security Agency "with responsibility for planning, coordinating, and integrating various U.S. government activities involved in homeland security." The report went on to recommend building the proposed new agency on the foundation of the Federal Emergency Management Agency and incorporating the Coast Guard, Customs Service, and Border Patrol. Additionally, the agency would have responsibility for protecting the nation's critical infrastructure. [2, p. viii]

The Phase III report is interesting for what it does: 1) it accurately predicts a catastrophic attack on the U.S., 2) it proposes a cabinet-level agency foreshadowing establishment of the Department of Homeland Security, and 3) it anticipates the composition and functions of the future DHS. The report is also interesting for what it does not do: it doesn't define "homeland security". The Hart-Rudman Commission first makes reference to homeland security in its Phase II report, yet does not define it there either. [4, p. 14] While the Commission fails to give an outright definition of "homeland security", it does make it clear that it is about domestic catastrophic attack involving weapons of mass destruction or disruption employed by non-state actors. Because the expected target was U.S. territory, the Commission saw homeland security as central to national security, not peripheral to it. [2, p. 10] It also saw that homeland security was a mission too broad for any single agency, but requiring the coordination of many agencies at the Federal, State, and Local levels. [2, pp. 11-22]

The first definition of homeland security is found in the 2002 National Strategy for Homeland Security.

Post-9/11

The first definition of "homeland security" appeared after 9/11. On October 8, 2001, only weeks after the 9/11 attacks, President Bush issued Executive Order 13228 establishing an Office of Homeland Security (OHS) within the White House. The purpose of OHS was to coordinate the executive branch's efforts to "detect, prepare for, prevent, protect against, respond to, and recover from terrorist attacks within the United States." One of OHS' first priorities was to develop "a comprehensive national strategy to secure the United States from terrorist attacks." [5] It is in this document that the first definition of homeland security was published:

"Homeland security is a concerted national effort to prevent terrorist attacks within the United States, reduce America's vulnerability to terrorism, and minimize the damage and recover from attacks that do occur."

- 2002 National Strategy for Homeland Security

Terrorism is defined in 18 USC S2331, as ""Acts dangerous to human life that are a violation of the criminal laws of the United States or of any State, that appear to be intended to intimidate or coerce a civilian population; influence the policy of a government by intimidation or coercion; or to affect the conduct of a government by mass destruction, assassination, or kidnapping." Terrorism is a specific crime distinguished by a specific motive, that of intimidating or coercing the U.S. government. Though it may not be the only motive that might prompt domestic catastrophic attack, it was certainly the motive behind the 9/11 attacks. Thus, given its directive, OHS defined homeland security in terms of terrorism. This definition was retained in the 2007 update to homeland security strategy, [6, p. 3] but was changed in 2010 as a result of Hurricane Katrina.

The second and reigning definition of homeland security was advanced in the 2010 QHSR, and affirmed (though not stated) in the 2014 QHSR.

In recognition that homeland security is an integral part of national security, in 2010 the Obama Administration merged homeland security strategy with national security strategy. Unlike the previous homeland security strategies, the 2010 National Security Strategy did not define homeland security but described its functions instead. [7, p. 15] Similarly, the 2015 National Security Strategy did not define homeland security either. [8] The task of defining homeland security had been removed by Congress from strategy formulation to mission formulation. In August 2007, Congress passed Public Law 110-53, "Implementing Recommendations of the 9/11 Commission Act". Among its provisions, the law required DHS to conduct a comprehensive examination of the nation's homeland security strategy every four years starting in fiscal year 2009. In February 2010, DHS released its first Quadrennial Homeland Security Review (QHSR) defining homeland security. [9, p. 13] The same definition was not included, but affirmed in the 2014 QHSR. [10, p. 94]

"Homeland security is a concerted national effort to ensure a homeland that is safe, secure, and resilient against terrorism and other hazards where American interests, aspirations, and way of life can thrive."

- 2010 Quadrennial Homeland Security Review

Analysis

While the focus on "terrorism" is understandable, it is also dangerously misleading because it is peripheral to the problem that launched three separate government commission investigations: domestic catastrophic destruction. The Gilmore Commission was established to investigate the potential for "mass destruction" or "mass casualties" as the result of domestic employment of WMD. [1, pp. i-xi] The Hart-Rudman Commission independently came to this conclusion when it determined that "America will become increasingly vulnerable to hostile attack on our homeland, and our military superiority will not entirely protect us." [11, p. 4] The Bremer Commission was also motivated by concerns of "mass casualties". [12, p. iv] Yet, the three commissions investigated domestic catastrophic destruction in connection with terrorism, which is how the two concepts became conflated. As defined in 18 USC S2331, terrorism is a crime distinguished by a specific motive to affect change in U.S. government actions. In the universe of potential motives for causing domestic catastrophic destruction, terrorism is but one possibility among countless others. In fact, the destruction caused by Hurricane Katrina proved that no motive is necessary at all.

The current definition of homeland security is also incomplete. The current definition is focused on initiators of catastrophic destruction related to terrorist motive, natural means, and accidental opportunity. It does not address other motives, cyber means, or infrastructure opportunities. Certainly they could be included, but this would be cumbersome and also incomplete. Instead of trying to enumerate all possible "initiators" of the problem, why not focus on the problem itself? Why not make the definition about the effect, regardless of the cause? Why not make a more clear and concise definition of homeland security?

The current definition confuses causes with effects. Consequently, we offer a working definition of homeland security focusing on effect to eliminate such confusion: "Safeguard the U.S. from domestic catastrophic destruction."

Working Definition

It is good to know the official definition of homeland security as promulgated by the U.S. government. Unfortunately, knowing this definition is not helpful to understanding homeland security. As such, the following working definition is offered to help guide study in this textbook:

"Safeguard the United States from domestic catastrophic destruction."

The stated working definition is as insightful as it is direct. It is direct because it directly identifies "domestic catastrophic destruction" as the central concern of homeland security. Yet, it is not restricted by specifying either the cause or scale of destruction. Because it's unspecified, the destruction may be measured either in terms of deaths or damages, or a combination of both. Moreover, the destruction is not confined to first-order effects, but may include second- or third-order effects resulting from mass disruption. The ultimate determinant is the impact on society, which is clearly "catastrophic", distinguishing the destruction from other incidents by its magnitude. Similarly, because the cause of destruction is not specified, it can encompass all means, motives, and opportunities that might result in catastrophic destruction. These include both natural and manmade means, as well as terrorist and other motives, and accidental as well as intentional opportunities.

Regarding manmade means, the working definition is insightful as to the relationship between homeland security and national security. If the threat is a sovereign state, then the homeland security concern is addressed by national security measures. If the threat is a non-state actor, then the homeland security concern is addressed by legal measures under U.S. law. In both circumstances, the threat remains a homeland security concern.

The word "safeguard" was chosen in recognition of the fact that no defense is invulnerable, and you can't stop natural disasters.

The word "safeguard" was also carefully chosen. It was chosen in recognition of the fact that no defense is invulnerable to a determined attacker, and you can't stop natural disasters. Consequently, the word "safeguard" encompasses actions during the four phases of any catastrophe: 1) prevent, 2) protect, 3) respond, and 4) recover. Prevention measures necessarily include detection, and deterrence and interception in the case of manmade threats, and mitigation and sheltering in the case of natural hazards. Protection measures may be similar for both manmade threats and natural hazards, including isolation, hardening, redundancy, and a host of other actions. Prevention and protection measures are typically implemented before an incident. Response and recovery measures are typically implemented after an incident. Response measures include resources and actions necessary to save lives and protect property. Recovery measures include resources and actions necessary to restore living conditions to their pre-incident status or better. Most importantly, the word "safeguard" means that nothing is ever completely safe. Everything is a matter of risk, and all measures taken before and after an incident are about risk management.

Understanding the working definition provides a lens through which you can gain insight and perspective on homeland security. We will now use this lens to examine events following 9/11.

Ultimatum

By late in the evening of September 11, the President had addressed the nation on the terrible events of the day. The long day was not yet over. When the larger meeting that included his domestic department heads broke up, President Bush chaired a smaller meeting of top advisers, a group he would later call his "war council." This group usually included Vice President Cheney, Secretary of State Powell, Secretary of Defense Donald Rumsfeld, General Hugh Shelton, Vice Chairman of the Joint Chiefs (later to become chairman) General Myers, Director of Central Intelligence (DCI) George Tenet, Attorney General Ashcroft, and FBI Director Robert Mueller. From the White House staff, National Security Advisor Condoleezza Rice and Chief of Staff Card were part of the core group, often joined by their deputies, Stephen Hadley and Joshua Bolten. In this restricted National Security Council meeting, the President said it was a time for self-defense. The United States would punish not just the perpetrators of the attacks, but also those who harbored them. [13, p. 330]

A cross check of the 9/11 flight manifests implicated al Qaeda in the attacks. On September 13, The State Department proposed delivering an ultimatum to the Taliban: produce bin Laden and his deputies and shut down al Qaeda camps within 24 to 48 hours, or the United States will use all necessary means to destroy the terrorist infrastructure. The State Department did not expect the Taliban to comply. President Bush recalled that he quickly realized that the administration would have to invade Afghanistan with ground troops. [13, p. 332]

The State and Defense departments would have to build an international coalition to go into Afghanistan. Both departments would consult with NATO and other allies and request intelligence, basing, and other support from countries, according to their capabilities and resources. All these diplomatic and military plans were reviewed over the weekend of September 15–16, as President Bush convened his war council at Camp David. After hearing from his senior advisers, President Bush discussed with Rice the contents of the directives he would issue to set all the plans into motion. Rice prepared a paper that President Bush then considered with principals on Monday morning, September 17. "The purpose of this meeting," he recalled saying," is to assign tasks for the first wave of the war against terrorism. It starts today." [13, p. 333]

9/11 was a criminal act. Any assault against U.S. citizens or territory is a crime, no matter what the nationality of the perpetrator. Osama bin Laden was guilty of planning and committing murder on U.S. soil.

In a speech before Congress on September 21, President Bush delivered the U.S. ultimatum to the Taliban: "Deliver to U.S. authorities all the leaders of al Qaeda... or share in their fate." He said: "Either you are with us, or you are with the terrorists." The terms were non-negotiable. [14] That same day, the Taliban ambassador to Pakistan, Abdul Salam Zaeef, insisted his country would not hand over Osama bin Laden. He told a news conference in the capital, Islamabad: "Our position on this is that if America has proof, we are ready for the trial of Osama bin Laden in light of the evidence." Asked if he was ready to hand Bin Laden over, he replied: "No." [15]

On September 22, the United Arab Emirates, and later Saudi Arabia, withdrew recognition of the Taliban as Afghanistan's legal government, leaving neighboring Pakistan as the only remaining country with diplomatic ties. On October 4, the Taliban agreed to turn bin Laden over to Pakistan for trial in an international tribunal that operated according to Islamic Sharia law, but Pakistan blocked the offer as it was not possible to guarantee his safety. On October 7, the Taliban ambassador to Pakistan offered to detain bin Laden and try him under Islamic law if the U.S. made a formal request and presented the Taliban with evidence. The offer was rejected on grounds there would be no negotiating. Plus, the U.S. had begun military operations in Afghanistan. [16]

Enduring Freedom

President Bush approved military plans to attack Afghanistan in meetings with Central Command's General Tommy Franks and other advisers on September 21 and October 2. Originally titled "Infinite Justice," the operation's code word was changed—to avoid the sensibilities of Muslims who associate the power of infinite justice with God alone—to "Enduring Freedom." [13, p. 337]

On October 7, less than one month after the September 11 attacks, the U.S., aided by the United Kingdom, Canada, and other countries including several from the NATO alliance, initiated military action, bombing Taliban and Al-Qaeda-related camps. The stated intent of military operations was to remove the Taliban from power, and prevent the use of Afghanistan as a terrorist base of operations. [16]

When the Taliban government of Afghanistan refused to extradite Osama bin Laden and turn him over to the FBI, President Bush sent in the U.S. military to take down the Taliban government for abetting terrorism, and capture or kill Osama bin Laden.

The CIA's elite Special Activities Division (SAD) units were the first U.S. forces to enter Afghanistan. They joined with the Afghan United Front, also known as the Northern Alliance, to prepare for the subsequent arrival of U.S. Special Operations forces. [16] The CIA provided intelligence, experience, cash, covert action capabilities, and liaison with tribal allies. In turn, the U.S. military offered combat expertise, firepower, logistics, and communications. [13, p. 338] Together, the Northern Alliance and SAD and Special Forces combined to overthrow the Taliban with minimal coalition casualties, and without the use of international conventional ground forces. [16]

On October 14, the Taliban offered to discuss handing over Osama bin Laden to a neutral country in return for a bombing halt, but only if the Taliban were given evidence of bin Laden's involvement. The U.S. rejected this offer, and continued military operations. Mazar-i-Sharif fell to United Front troops of Ustad Atta Mohammad Noor and Abdul Rashid Dostum on November 9, triggering a cascade of provinces falling with minimal resistance. [16]

On the night of November 12, the Taliban retreated south from Kabul. On November 15, they released eight Western aid workers after three months in captivity. By November 13, the Taliban had withdrawn from both Kabul and Jalalabad. Finally, in early December, the Taliban gave up Kandahar, their last stronghold, dispersing without surrendering. [16]

Within about two months of the start of combat operations, several hundred CIA operatives and Special Forces soldiers, backed by the striking power of U.S. aircraft and a much larger infrastructure of intelligence and support efforts, had combined with Afghan militias and a small number of other coalition soldiers to destroy the Taliban regime and disrupt al Qaeda. They had killed or captured about a quarter of the enemy's known leaders. Mohammed Atef, al Qaeda's military commander and a principal figure in the 9/11 plot, had been killed by a U.S. air strike. [13, p. 338]

At the Bonn Conference in December 2001, Hamid Karzai was selected to head the Afghan Interim Administration, which after a 2002 loya jirga in Kabul became the Afghan Transitional Administration. In the popular elections of 2004, Karzai was elected president of the country, now named the Islamic Republic of Afghanistan. [17]

In less than two months, the U.S. military succeeded in toppling the Taliban. However, in the midst of action, both the Taliban leader, Mohammed Omar, and Osama bin Laden managed to escape and evade capture.

Escape

The U.S. and its allies drove the Taliban from power and built military bases near major cities across the country. Most al-Qaeda and Taliban, however, were not captured, escaping to neighboring Pakistan or retreating to rural or remote mountainous regions. [17] Among the escapees was Osama bin Laden.

In December 2001, Afghan forces, with limited U.S. support, engaged al Qaeda elements in a cave complex called Tora Bora. It was later determined that bin Laden was present, and the failure by the United States to commit enough ground troops allowed him to escape. [18]

In March 2002, the largest engagement of the war was fought, in the mountainous Shah-i-Kot area south of Gardez, against a large force of al Qaeda jihadists. Almost all remaining al Qaeda forces fled across the border and took refuge in Pakistan's equally mountainous and lightly governed frontier provinces. [13, p. 338]

As the U.S. turned its attention to Iraq, the Taliban began to reorganize under their former leader Mohammed Omar, and in 2003 launched an insurgency against the newly established Afghan government and its supporting allies. The insurgency drew the United States into its longest lasting military engagement in history. After 13 years, the United States officially ended combat operations in Afghanistan on October 26, 2014. Despite Mohammed Omar's death in April 2013, the insurgency continued. As of 2015, U.S. forces still maintained a presence in Afghanistan and supported the Afghan military with air strikes and Special Operations raids. [17]

Captured or Killed

Beginning on September 11, Immigration and Naturalization Service agents working in cooperation with the FBI began arresting individuals for immigration violations. Eventually, 768 aliens were arrested as "special interest" detainees. Some, such as Zacarias Moussaoui, were already in INS custody before 9/11. [13, p. 327] Moussaoui had been arrested by the FBI for immigration violation in August 2001 after arousing suspicion over his flight training courses in Eagan, Minnesota. On December 11, 2001, Moussaoui was indicted by a federal grand jury in United States District Court for the Eastern District of Virginia on six felony charges: conspiracy to commit acts of terrorism transcending national boundaries, conspiracy to commit aircraft piracy, conspiracy to destroy aircraft, conspiracy to use weapons of mass destruction, conspiracy to murder United States employees, and conspiracy to destroy property. Moussaoui was alleged by federal prosecutors to have been a replacement for the "first" 20th hijacker, possibly Ramzi bin al-Shibh who was denied a visa. Moussaoui pleaded guilty in federal court for which he was found guilty in May 2006. As a result of his conviction, he is serving six life sentences without parole at the Federal Supermax prison in Florence, Colorado. [19]

After bin Laden fled Tora Bora in 2001, numerous speculative press reports were issued about his whereabouts or even death. In April 2011, various intelligence outlets pinpointed bin Laden's suspected location near Abbottabad, Pakistan.

On March 1, 2003, Khalid Sheikh Mohammed, the mastermind behind the 9/11 plot, was captured in hiding in Rawalpindi, Pakistan, by a combined force from the CIA and Pakistan Inter-Services Intelligence (ISI) agency. Over the next several years, KSM was interrogated by the CIA in secret prison camps located in Europe. In 2006 he was transferred to military custody and Guantanamo Bay detention camp in Cuba. In February 2008, KSM was charged with war crimes and murder by a U.S. military commission. He remains in Guantanamo awaiting trial. [20]

After bin Laden fled Tora Bora in 2001, numerous speculative press reports were issued about his whereabouts or even death. Some placed bin Laden in different locations during overlapping time periods. None were ever definitively proven. After military offensives in Afghanistan failed to uncover his whereabouts, Pakistan was regularly identified as his suspected hiding place. [18]

In April 2011, various intelligence outlets pinpointed bin Laden's suspected location near Abbottabad, Pakistan. It was previously believed that bin Laden was hiding near the border between Afghanistan and Pakistan's Federally Administered Tribal Areas, but he was found 100 miles away in a three-story mansion in Abbottabad, less than a mile from the Pakistan Military Academy. [18]

On April 29, 2011, President Obama authorized a team of Navy SEALs to raid the compound in Abbottabad. On May 2, 2011, Operation NEPTUNE SPEAR launched from Afghanistan into Pakistan aboard specially modified stealth helicopters. They were supported by multiple additional aircraft, including Air Force fighters and drones. As the helicopters maneuvered to discharge the SEALs, one lost lift and crash landed inside the compound. None of the team was seriously injured, and they quickly regained their composure. The other helicopter landed outside the compound and the SEALs scaled the walls to get inside. The SEALs then advanced into the house, breaching walls and doors with explosives. The interior was pitch dark because CIA operatives had cut the power to the neighborhood. However, the SEALs wore night vision goggles. They made their way to the third floor where bin Laden lived with his family. Bin Laden peered through his bedroom door at the Americans advancing up the stairs, and then retreated into the room as the lead SEAL fired a shot at him, which either missed or hit him in the side. Bounding into the room, they found bin Laden with one of his wives. Bin Laden was shot twice in the forehead, and once more as he crumpled to the floor. He was dead. The SEAL team leader radioed, "For God and country—Geronimo, Geronimo, Geronimo", using a call sign to confirm they had found bin Laden. After being prompted for confirmation, the SEAL team leader announced "Geronimo E.K.I.A.", military-speak for “enemy killed in action”. Watching the operation in the White House Situation Room, Obama said, "We got him." [18]

"For God and country—Geronimo, Geronimo, Geronimo."

From entry to exit, the SEALS spent no more than 38 minutes in the Abbottabad compound. The helicopter damaged in the crash was destroyed to safeguard its classified equipment. A standby Chinook was sent in to pick up the SEALS together with bin Laden’s body and evidence gathered in the raid. The team flew back to Afghanistan where bin Laden’s body was transferred to a waiting V-22 Osprey and flown out to the aircraft carrier Carl Vinson. Muslim religious rites were performed and the body wrapped in a white sheet and placed in a weighted plastic bag. At approximately 11:00 am, bin Laden’s body was buried at sea, to be gone forever. [18]

But the threat did not end with him.

Conclusion

Homeland security is about safeguarding the United States from domestic catastrophic destruction. Osama bin Laden was indicted by the FBI for capital crimes related to the 1998 embassy bombings and 9/11 attacks. When the Taliban government of Afghanistan refused to extradite him, the United States initiated military action to remove the Taliban and capture bin Laden. In the confusion of battle, both bin Laden and Mohammed Omar managed to escape and become fugitives. Mohammed Omar instigated the Taliban insurgency which continued after his death in 2013. Osama bin Laden was eventually located inside Pakistan, and killed in a special operations raid in 2011. The U.S. remains engaged in Afghanistan as part of U.S. national security strategy to prevent that country from again harboring agents who would pose a homeland security threat. By the same token, the U.S. federal government undertook sweeping changes to close the gaps exposed by 9/11, and establish homeland security as an essential component of national security.

Challenge Your Understanding

The following questions are designed to challenge your understanding of the material presented in this chapter. Some questions may require additional research outside this book in order to provide a complete answer.

1. When and where did the term "homeland security" originate?
2. What was the first definition of "homeland security"?
3. What was the second definition of "homeland security"?
4. What are the basic differences between the first and second definitions?
5. What precipitated the change in definitions?
6. Which of the following incidents would be considered a homeland security concern by the first definition? Explain.

    a. 9/11 Attacks

    b. Hurricane Katrina

    c. 2003 Northeast Blackout
7. Which of the previous incidents would be a homeland security concern by the second definition? Explain.
8. Which of the previous incidents would be a homeland security concern by the working definition? Explain.
9. Why are the 9/11 attacks considered a crime, but not the 1941 attacks on Pearl Harbor?
10. What is the relationship between Osama bin Laden and the U.S. invasion of Afghanistan in October 2001?

Chapter 10

DHS Formation

Learning Outcomes

Careful study of this chapter will help a student do the following:

- Explain why Congress was already considering homeland security legislation before 9/11.
- Describe measures taken by the White House to coordinate homeland security immediately after 9/11.
- Explain why the White House advocated an executive department for homeland security after 9/11.
- Assess the organization and mission of the new Department of Homeland Security.

"The combination of unconventional weapons proliferation with the persistence of international terrorism will end the relative invulnerability of the U.S. homeland to catastrophic attack. We therefore recommend the creation of an independent National Homeland Security Agency with responsibility for planning, coordinating, and integrating various U.S. government activities involved in homeland security."

- Phase III Report of the Hart-Rudman Commission, February 15, 2001

Introduction

The United States Department of Homeland Security (DHS) is a Cabinet department of the Federal government of the United States that is concerned with protecting the American homeland and the safety of American citizens. The department was created from a conglomeration of twenty-two existing federal agencies in response to the terrorist attacks of September 11th, 2001. It was established on November 25th, 2002, by the Homeland Security Act and officially began operation on January 24th, 2003. The formation of the Department of Homeland Security was the largest government reorganization in 50 years since the establishment of the Department of Defense in 1947.

Organizing for Homeland Security

In the immediate aftermath of 9/11, White House Deputy chief of Staff, Joshua Bolten, chaired a temporary "domestic consequences" group to address problems of how to help victims and stanch the flowing losses to the American economy stemming from the closure of American airspace and the stock market. The very process of reviewing these issues underscored the absence of an effective government organization dedicated to assessing vulnerabilities and handling problems of protection and preparedness. Though a number of agencies had some part of the task, none had security as its primary mission. [1, p. 327]

By September 14, Vice President Cheney had decided to recommend, at least as a first step, a new White House entity to coordinate all the relevant agencies rather than tackle the challenge of combining them in a new department. This new White House entity would be a homeland security adviser and Homeland Security Council—paralleling the National Security Council system. Vice President Cheney reviewed the proposal with President Bush and other advisers. President Bush announced the new post and its first occupant— Pennsylvania governor Tom Ridge— in his address to a joint session of Congress on September 20. [1, p. 327]

Office of Homeland Security

On October 8, 2001, President Bush issued Executive Order 13228 establishing both an Office of Homeland Security and Homeland Security Council. Both would be headed by the Assistant to the President for Homeland Security. The mission of the Office was to develop and implement a comprehensive national strategy to secure the United States from terrorist attacks. To fulfill its mission, OHS was assigned functions necessary to detect, prepare for, prevent, protect against, respond to, and recovery from terrorist attacks within the United States. [2]

Detection. The Homeland Security Advisor was to work with the National Security Advisor in setting priorities for collection of intelligence outside the United States regarding threats of terrorism inside the United States. Furthermore, the Homeland Security Advisor was to facilitate collection from State and Local government of information pertaining to terrorist threats or activities within the United States, and ensure that such information was legally disseminated among all appropriate and necessary law enforcement agencies. [2]

On October 8, 2001, President Bush issued Executive Order 13228 establishing both an Office of Homeland Security and Homeland Security Council.

Preparedness. The Office of Homeland Security was to coordinate national efforts to prepare for and mitigate the consequences of terrorist attacks within the United States. This meant updating federal emergency response plans, developing a national exercise program, reviewing vaccination policies (for biological attack), and lending federal assistance to State and Local governments to help them prepare for and respond to terrorist attacks. [2]

Prevention. The Office of Homeland Security was to coordinate national efforts to prevent terrorist attacks within the United States. To facilitate this, the Homeland Security Advisor was to strengthen border security to prevent entry of terrorists and terrorist materials and supplies into the United States. All suspected terrorists already in the United States were to be removed, and monitoring and surveillance increased along the land, air, and sea approaches. [2]

Protection. Office of Homeland Security was to coordinate efforts to protect the United States and its critical infrastructure from terrorist attack. This included strengthening measures for protecting high-value assets, services, and events; developing plans for protecting critical infrastructure; and preventing unauthorized access to, development of, and unlawful importation into the United States, of chemical, biological, radiological, nuclear, explosive, or other related materials that have the potential to be used in terrorist attacks. [2]

Response and Recovery. The Office of Homeland Security was to coordinate efforts to respond to and recover from terrorist attacks within the United States. This included working with Federal, State, and Local governments, and private entities as appropriate to rapidly restore essential services following an attack. The Office was to develop plans and programs to provide medical, financial, and other assistance to victims and their families. The Office was also to coordinate the containment and removal of chemical, biological, radiological, explosive, or other hazardous materials resulting from a terrorist attack. [2]

Additionally, EO 13228 designated the Homeland Security Advisor the primary official responsible for coordinating the federal response to domestic attack, and ensuring continuity of the Federal government following an attack. [2]

The Office of Homeland Security was formed as a matter of expediency to assist the President with the urgent task of securing the nation immediately following 9/11. Congress, in the meantime, began debating the necessity of fundamentally restructuring the Federal government to assure a more permanent solution.

The Office of Homeland Security was formed as a matter of expediency to assist the President with the urgent task of securing the nation immediately following 9/11. Congress, in the meantime, began debating the necessity of fundamentally restructuring the Federal government to assure a more permanent solution.

Department of Homeland Security

Congress's deliberations on reorganizing the government's homeland security functions were largely built on the recommendations of the U.S. Commission on National Security for the 21st Century (Hart-Rudman Commission), which submitted its last report to Congress in February 2001. This commission proposed creating a new federal agency by consolidating the Coast Guard, the Customs Service, the Immigration and Naturalization Service (INS), and FEMA into a new National Homeland Security Agency. [3]

In April 2001, Representative William (Mac) Thornberry (R-TX) introduced H.R. 1158 to create that agency. Shortly after September 11, Senator Joseph Lieberman (D-CT) proposed similar legislation (S. 1534) to create a National Homeland Security Department (NHSD). Other Members, such as Representative Alcee Hastings (D-FL) and Senator Bob Graham (D-FL), promoted the findings of the Advisory Panel to Assess Domestic Response Capabilities for Terrorism Involving Weapons of Mass Destruction (Gilmore Commission) in H.R. 3078. The Gilmore Commission had concluded that a White House office with detailed statutory authority, modeled after the Office of National Drug Control Policy (ONDCP), would be best situated to solve the federal government's coordination problems. [3]

After the introduction of H.R. 1158 and S. 1534, Representative Thornberry and Senator Lieberman refined their proposals to gain the support of more Members of Congress, and in May 2002 introduced the National Homeland Security and Combating Terrorism Act of 2002 (H.R. 4660). Before debate could proceed much further, on June 6, 2002, the White House issued a presidential proposal for a new cabinet-level Department of Homeland Security. [3]

In the eight months after its creation, the Office of Homeland Security was hindered by the fragmentation of responsibilities among federal agencies, as well overlapping authorities and insufficient resources within agencies. [3] According to the White House, responsibilities for homeland security were dispersed among more than 100 different government organizations. No one single government agency had homeland security as its primary mission. [4] The President's initiative called for consolidating most federal agencies with homeland security missions in one department to focus the government's resources more efficiently and effectively on domestic security. The President's plan built on the recommendations of various national commissions as well as some of the legislative proposals placed before Congress. Creating a Department of Homeland Security would solve such organizational problems and facilitate the OHS' coordination role. [3]

On June 24, 2002, Representative Richard Armey (R-TX) submitted House Resolution 5005 (H.R. 5005) calling for the establishment of a Department of Homeland Security.

The President's proposal combined existing federal agencies and offices with homeland security responsibilities under one authority. For example, the proposal transferred Transportation Security Administration and the Coast Guard to the DHS, removing all direct homeland security duties from the U.S. Department of Transportation. The proposal also folded the Federal Emergency Management Agency (FEMA) and the Department of Agriculture's Animal and Plant Health Inspection Service (APHIS) into DHS. The functions of the offices relocated to the DHS would be distributed among four major divisions:

1. Border and Transportation Security;
2. Emergency Preparedness and Response;
3. Chemical, Biological, Radiological and Nuclear Countermeasures; and
4. Information Analysis and Infrastructure Protection. [3]

Acting on the President's proposal, on June 24, 2002, Representative Richard Armey (R -TX) submitted House Resolution 5005 (H.R. 5005) calling for the establishment of a Department of Homeland Security. HR 5005 incorporated most of the provisions set forth in H.R. 4660. H.R. 5005 passed the House July 26, 2002, and was handed over to the Senate on July 30th. [5] H.R. 5005 wasn't without its detractors, and stalled in the Senate.

Controversy centered on whether the Federal Bureau of Investigation and the Central Intelligence Agency should be incorporated in part or in whole (neither were included). The bill itself was also controversial for the presence of unrelated "riders", as well as for eliminating standard civil service and labor protections for department employees. Without these protections, employees could be expeditiously reassigned or dismissed on grounds of security, incompetence or insubordination. [6]

The impasse was broken when both the House and Senate agreed to a compromise resolution, H.R. 5710 incorporating provisions by Senator Joseph Lieberman authorizing the President to bypass traditional civil service procedures provided he first consult with Congress and mediate with the federal employees union. [7]

On November 25, 2002, President Bush signed into law the Homeland Security Act establishing the Department of Homeland Security. Tom Ridge, the former governor of Pennsylvania, was appointed the first Secretary of Homeland Security.

On November 20, 2002, the Senate passed H.R. 5005 by a vote of 90-9 authorizing the creation of a Department of Homeland Security consolidating twenty-two federal agencies under a single executive department. President Bush signed the bill into law, Public Law 107-296, the Homeland Security Act, on November 25, 2002. Tom Ridge was made secretary of the new department.

Pulling It Together

Pursuant to section 1502 of the of the Homeland Security Act, on November 25, 2002, the White House submitted to the House of Representatives a Reorganization Plan for the Department of Homeland Security. The plan identified what agencies would be transferred to the new Department, and how and when they would be transferred. [8] According to the plan, all transfers were to be completed no later than March 1, 2003. [9] Approximately 169,000 personnel were transferred to the Department of Homeland Security from the organizations shown in Table 1. [10]

Organizing Concept

The organization of the Department of Homeland Security was designed to realign the previous patchwork of government activities into a single department with the primary mission to protect the homeland. [11, p. 1] The Department of Homeland Security would make the country safer because the nation would have:

- One department whose primary mission is to protect the American homeland;
- One department to secure borders, the transportation sector, ports, and critical infrastructure;
- One department to synthesize and analyze homeland security intelligence from multiple sources;
- One department to coordinate communications with state and local governments, private industry, and the American people about threats and preparedness;

Table 10-1: Organizations Transferred to DHS [10]

	DHS Directorate	Transferred Organization	Transferring Agency
1	Border & Transportation Security	U.S. Customs Service	Treasury
2		Immigration and Naturalization Service	Justice
3		Federal Protective Service	
4		Transportation Security Administration	Transportation
5		Federal Law Enforcement Training Center	Treasury
6		Animal and Plant Health Inspection Service	Agriculture
7		Office for Domestic Preparedness	Justice
8	Emergency Preparedness & Response	FEMA	FEMA
9		Strategic National Stockpile & National Disaster Medical System	HHS
10		Nuclear Incident Response Team	Energy
11		Domestic Emergency Support Teams	Justice
12		National Domestic Preparedness Office	FBI
13	Science & Technology Directorate	CBRN Countermeasures Programs	Energy
14		Environmental Measurements Laboratory	Energy
15		National BW Defense Analysis Center	Defense
16		Plum Island Animal Disease Center	Agriculture
17	Information Analysis & Infrastructure Protection	Federal Computer Incident Response Center	GSA
18		National Communications System	Defense
19		National Infrastructure Protection Center	FBI
20		Energy Security and Assurance Program	Energy
21	U.S. Secret Service	U.S. Secret Service	Treasury
22	U.S. Coast Guard	U.S. Coast Guard	Transportation

- One department to coordinate efforts to protect the American people against bioterrorism and other weapons of mass destruction;
- One department to help train and equip for first responders;
- One department to manage federal emergency response activities; and
- More security officers in the field working to stop terrorists and fewer resources in Washington managing duplicative and redundant activities that drain critical homeland security resources. [11, p. 1]

DHS Organization

In the final version of H.R. 5005 signed into law as the Homeland Security Act, the Department of Homeland Security would be comprised of five directorates:

1. Border and Transportation Security;
2. Emergency Preparedness and Response;
3. Information Analysis and Infrastructure Protection;
4. Science and Technology; and
5. Management [12]

Border and Transportation Security Directorate. BTS was designed to ensure the security of the nation's borders and transportation systems. Its first priority was to prevent the entry of terrorists and the instruments of terrorism while simultaneously ensuring the efficient flow of lawful traffic and commerce. BTS managed and coordinated port of entry activities and led efforts to create borders that feature greater security through better intelligence, coordinated national efforts and international cooperation against terrorists and the instruments of terrorism and other international threats. BTS was comprised of the Customs and Border Protection (CBP), Immigration and Customs Enforcement (ICE), the Transportation Security Administration (TSA), Federal Law Enforcement Training Center (FLETC), and the Office of Domestic Preparedness (ODP). [8, p. 8]

The same day President Bush signed the Homeland Security Act, he submitted a Reorganization Plan for the Department of Homeland Security, identifying what agencies would be transferred to the new Department, and how and when they would be transferred. All transfers were to be completed no later than March 1, 2003.

U.S. Customs and Border Protection provided security at the borders and ports of entry as well as extending the zone of security beyond physical borders so that they are the last line of defense, not the first. CBP was also responsible for apprehending individuals attempting to enter the United States illegally, stemming the flow of illegal drugs and other contraband; protecting the nation's agricultural and economic interests from harmful pests and diseases; protecting American businesses from theft of intellectual property; regulating and facilitating international trade; collecting import duties; and enforcing United States trade laws. [8, p. 8]

U.S. Immigration and Customs Enforcement enforced federal immigration, customs and air security laws. ICE's primary mission was to detect vulnerabilities and prevent violations that threatened national security. ICE was the largest investigative arm of the new department. ICE deterred, interdicted and investigated threats arising from the movement of people and goods into and out of the United States; and by policing and securing federal government facilities across the Nation. [8, p. 8]

The Transportation Security Administration was a new government agency created in the wake of 9/11 because airline security screeners had failed to spot weapons carried by the hijackers. Congress moved quickly to pass the Aviation and Transportation Security Act in November 2001 creating the Transportation Security Administration mandating a federalized workforce of security screeners to inspect airline passengers and their baggage. The act gave the TSA broad authority to assess vulnerabilities in aviation security and take steps to mitigate these risks. [8, p. 8] [13, p. iii]

Federal Law Enforcement Training Center (FLETC) was the Federal Government's leader for law enforcement training. FLETC prepared new and experienced law enforcement professionals to fulfill their responsibilities safely and at the highest level of proficiency. [8, p. 9]

Office of Domestic Preparedness ensured the United States was prepared for acts of terrorism by providing training and funds for the purchase of equipment, support for the planning and execution of exercises, and technical assistance and other support to assist State and Local jurisdictions in preventing, planning for, and responding to acts of terrorism. [8, p. 9]

Emergency Preparedness and Response. EP&R was designed to ensure that the nation was prepared for, and able to recover from terrorist attacks and natural disasters. EP&R provided domestic disaster preparedness training and coordinated government disaster response. The core of emergency preparedness was the Federal Emergency Management Agency, responsible for reducing the loss of life and property and protecting our nation's institutions from all types of hazards through a comprehensive, emergency management program of preparedness, prevention, response and recovery. [8, p. 9]

The Department of Homeland Security was formed from the consolidation of twenty-two Federal agencies and transfer of approximately 169,000 personnel.

Information Analysis and Infrastructure Protection. IAIP was designed to identify and assesses a broad range of intelligence information concerning threats to the homeland, issue timely warnings and take appropriate preventive and protective action. Information Analysis was meant to provide actionable intelligence for preventing acts of terrorism and, with timely and thorough analysis and dissemination of information about terrorists and their activities, improve the government's ability to disrupt and prevent terrorist acts and to provide useful warning to state and local government, the private sector and citizens. Infrastructure Protection was meant to coordinate national efforts to secure America's critical infrastructure, including vulnerability assessments, strategic planning efforts and exercises. Protecting America's critical infrastructure was the shared responsibility of federal, state and local governments, in active partnership with the private sector, the owners and operators of the majority of the nation's critical infrastructure. [8, p. 8]

Science and Technology Directorate. S&T provided federal, state and local operators with the technology and capabilities needed to protect the nation from catastrophic terrorist attacks, including threats from weapons of mass destruction. The S&T Directorate would develop and deploy state-of-the-art, high performance, low operating cost systems to detect and rapidly mitigate the consequences of terrorist attacks, including those that may use chemical, biological, radiological and nuclear materials. [8, p. 9]

The Management Directorate oversaw the budget; appropriations; expenditure of funds; accounting and finance; procurement; human resources and personnel; information technology systems; facilities, property, equipment and other material resources; and identification and tracking of performance measures aligned with the mission of the Department. The Chief Financial Officer, Chief Information Officer, Chief Human Capital Officer, Chief Procurement Officer and the Chief of Administrative Services reported to the Undersecretary for Management as allowed by the Homeland Security Act of 2002. [8, p. 9]

In addition to the five major directorates, the Department of Homeland Security was in charge of the United States Coast Guard (USCG), United States Secret Service (USSS), and U.S. Citizenship and Immigration Services (USCIS). [8, p. 9]

The establishment of the Department of Homeland Security was the largest reorganization of Federal government since the 1947 National Security Act created the National Security Council, Department of Defense, and Central Intelligence Agency.

The United States Coast Guard ensured maritime safety, mobility and security and protected natural marine resources. Its mission was to protect the public, the environment and the United States economic interests in the nation's ports and waterways, along the coast, on international waters, or in any maritime region as required to support national security. The Coast Guard also prevented maritime terrorist attacks; halted the flow of illegal drugs and contraband; prevented individuals from entering the United States illegally; and prevented illegal incursion into exclusive economic zones. The Coast Guard had dual responsibility. Upon declaration of war, or when the President so directed, the USCG would operate as an element of the Department of Defense. [8, p. 9]

The United States Secret Service protected the President and Vice President, their families, heads of state and other designated individuals; investigated threats against these protectees; protected designated buildings within Washington, D.C.; and planned and implemented security for designated National Special Security Events. The USSS also investigated violations of laws relating to counterfeiting and financial crimes, including computer fraud and computer-based attacks on the nation's financial, banking, and telecommunications infrastructure. [8, p. 9]

The U.S. Citizenship and Immigration Services directed the nation's immigration system and promoted citizenship values by providing immigration services such as immigrant and nonimmigrant sponsorship; adjustment of status; work authorization and other permits; naturalization of qualified applicants for United States citizenship; and asylum or refugee processing. USCIS made certain that America continues to welcome visitors and those who seek opportunity while excluding terrorists and their supporters. [8, p. 9]

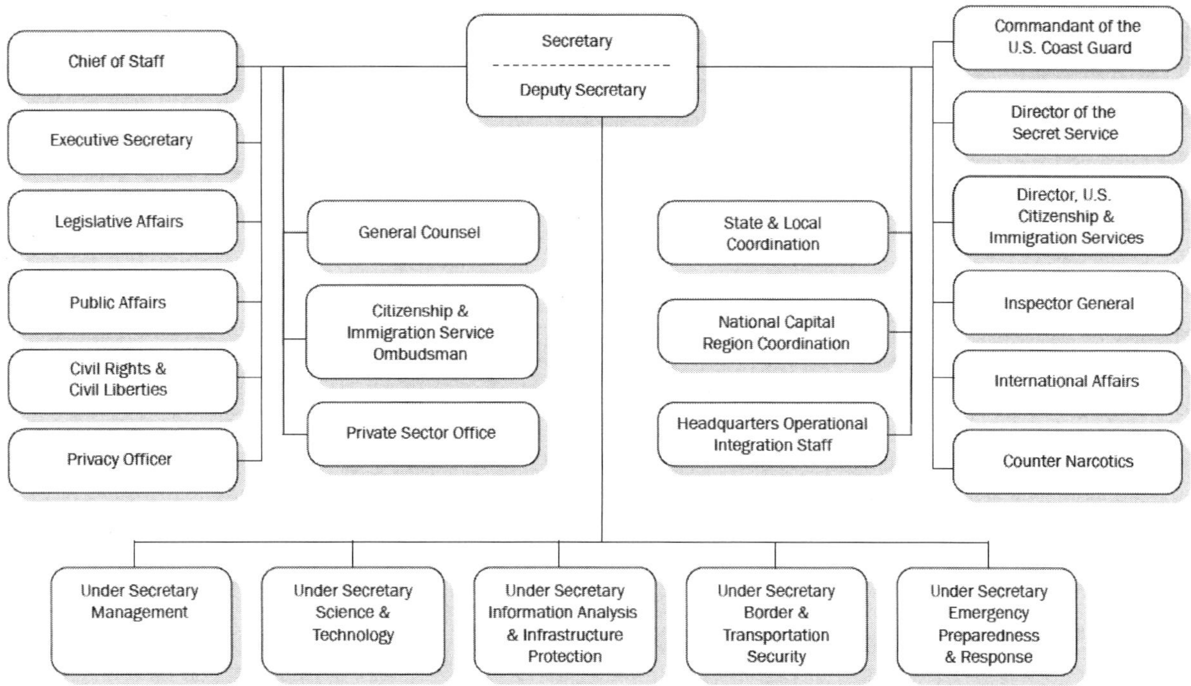

Figure 10-1: DHS Organization [8, p. 10]

Where is the Department of Homeland Security Located?

DHS personnel are currently located in 50 different offices across the Washington DC metropolitan area. Headquarters is located at 3801 Nebraska Avenue, NW, Washington, DC. The Nebraska Avenue Complex (NAC) is a 37-acre site with 30 buildings and 653,400 square feet of office space. The campus is a secure facility with an established security perimeter and on-site generators. Unfortunately, the NAC only accommodates about 2,390 of the 28,000 employees in the DC region. [7, p. i] It also wastes millions of dollars in leased office space and transportation costs. According to former DHS Secretary Michael Chertoff, the attendant logistical difficulties of a dispersed workforce slowed the government response to Hurricane Katrina in 2005, and a terrorist plot to blow up transatlantic airliners with liquid explosives in 2006. Chertoff recalled "People were shuttling back and forth in those critical days after the plot was exposed, and that just made it much more difficult and time-consuming," he said. Calling it urgent, Chertoff released a plan in 2006 to begin construction of a new centralized headquarters to be completed by 2015. The new headquarters would cost about $3 billion and accommodate 14,000 DHS employees. With the exception of the new Coast Guard building, little progress has been made, while cost estimates have risen to $4.5 billion and completion pushed out to 2026. One of the main reasons for the cost overruns and schedule delays is that the chosen site for DHS headquarters is the former St. Elizabeth's Hospital, a national historic landmark. Built in 1852 on a 176-acre hilltop site east of the Anacostia River, St. Elizabeth's was the first federal psychiatric institution. Its grounds were once home to patients like Ezra Pound, the poet, and John Hinckley Jr., the attempted assassin of President Reagan. St. Elizabeth's was among 14 possibilities because it was the only location that met size and security requirements. More than 50 historic buildings would need to be renovated and new ones erected for DHS' new home. Even before costs began to soar, planners were aware they would face millions of dollars in outlays for historic preservation and rehabilitation of antiquated utilities and infrastructure. A decade after work began, St. Elizabeth's venture – the capital region's largest planned construction project since the Pentagon – has become a monumental example of Washington inefficiency and drift. [8]

Conclusion

In the immediate aftermath of 9/11, on October 8, 2001, President Bush issued E.O. 13228 establishing an Office of Homeland Security and Homeland Security Council under the direction of a new Assistant to the President for Homeland Security. Former Pennsylvania Governor, Tom Ridge, was appointed the first Homeland Security Advisor. OHS was responsible for developing and coordinating the implementation of a comprehensive national strategy to secure the United States from terrorist attacks. HSC was responsible for advising and assisting the President with respect to all aspects of homeland security. In his June 2002 proposal for a Department of Homeland Security, President Bush appeared to anticipate the continued operation of both OHS and HSC. When the Homeland Security Act was signed into law November 25, 2002, it created the Department of Homeland Security and rechartered the HSC as an agency within the Executive Office of the President [14, pp. CRS-1] Tom Ridge was appointed the new Secretary of Homeland Security. Many of the functions of the Office of Homeland Security transferred to the new Department together with the new Secretary. [15, p. 9] OHS was closed and the remnants transferred to HSC. [14, pp. CRS-3] The Department of Homeland Security was formed by realigning the previous patchwork of twenty-two government activities into a single department with the primary mission to protect the homeland. President Bush signed Executive Order 13284 activating the Department of Homeland Security effective January 23rd, 2003.

Challenge Your Understanding

The following questions are designed to challenge your understanding of the material presented in this chapter. Some questions may require additional research outside this book in order to provide a complete answer.

1. What findings from the Hart-Rudman Commission report prompted a bill to be submitted before Congress in April 2001 to form a National Homeland Security Department?
2. List and describe the two organizations created immediately after 9/11 to assist the President with developing and managing homeland security policy.
3. Why did the White House feel the need to propose an executive department for homeland security?
4. Make two arguments for, and two arguments against creating a Department of Homeland Security.
5. What was the primary mission proposed by the White House for the Department of Homeland Security?
6. How was the new Department of Homeland Security going to improve domestic security?
7. Do you think it would've been a good idea to integrate either or both the CIA and FBI within DHS? Explain.
8. What do you notice when you compare DHS' original organization to the Critical Mission Areas listed in the 2002 National Strategy for Homeland Security (written before DHS was formed)?
9. Which DHS directorate do you think had the most important mission? Explain your answer.
10. Where did FEMA fit into the new Department of Homeland Security?

Chapter 11

DHS Evolution

Learning Outcomes

Careful study of this chapter will help a student do the following:

- Explain how and why the DHS mission and organization were oriented when it was created in 2003.
- Explain how and why the DHS mission and organization significantly changed after Hurricane Katrina.
- Describe both internal and external initiatives that re - oriented DHS' mission between 2005 and 2007.
- Evaluate the evolution of the DHS cybersecurity mission between 2003 and 2010.
- Debate the merits of merging homeland security strategy and national security strategy.
- Discuss the purpose and value of the Quadrennial Homeland Security Review.

"The most serious mistakes are not being made as a result of wrong answers. The true dangerous thing is asking the wrong question."

- Peter F. Drucker

Introduction

Peter Drucker is hailed as "the man who invented management". His writings are highly regarded for predicting major business trends and influencing successful corporations through much of the 20th century. [1] Among his key insights was the need to continually reassess core assumptions and ensure that an organization's missions are properly aligned with their objectives. Accordingly, the Department of Homeland Security's mission and organization have evolved since it first became operational, January 23, 2003. This chapter examines the evolution of DHS' mission and organization, and the factors that influenced that change.

The 2002 National Strategy for Homeland Security defined homeland security as "a concerted national effort to prevent terrorist attacks within the United States, reduce America's vulnerability to terrorism, and minimize the damage and recover from attacks that do occur."

2002 Homeland Security Strategy

On October 8, 2001, President Bush issued Executive Order 13228 establishing the Office of Homeland Security within the Executive Office of the President. The mission of the office was to develop and implement a comprehensive national strategy to secure the United States from terrorist attacks. [2]

In July 2002, the Office of Homeland Security released the first National Strategy for Homeland Security. The 2002 Strategy set the stage by defining homeland security, and explaining its terms:

"Homeland security is a concerted national effort to prevent terrorist attacks within the United States, reduce America's vulnerability to terrorism, and minimize the damage and recover from attacks that do occur."

- 2002 National Strategy for Homeland Security [3, p. 2]

The 2002 Strategy explained that a "concerted national effort" meant that homeland security was not just the job of the anticipated new Department of Homeland Security, but the shared responsibility of all branches at all levels of government, and the private sector. The fact that DHS could not accomplish the mission alone would lead to the concept of a "homeland security enterprise" presented later in this book. The 2002 Strategy explained that "prevention" is the first priority, obviously to avoid the consequences of a domestic catastrophic attack. It noted that "detection" is an essential precondition for "prevention", suggesting the need for intelligence surveillance both at home and abroad. In explaining the definition of homeland security, the 2002 Strategy made it clear that the central risk was "mass casualties, massive property loss, and immense social disruption." It further identified the potential means for inflicting domestic catastrophic destruction in the form of "weapons of mass destruction, strategic information warfare, attacks on critical infrastructure, and attacks on the highest leadership of government." These are the types of attacks homeland security seeks to prevent by terrorists. Additionally, the 2002 Strategy defined "terrorist attacks" as "any premeditated, unlawful act dangerous to human life or public welfare that is intended to intimidate or coerce civilian populations or governments." According to the 2002 Strategy, this definition covered kidnappings; hijackings; shootings; conventional bombings; attacks involving chemical, biological, radiological, or nuclear weapons; cyber attacks; and any number of other forms of malicious violence. The 2002 Strategy also noted that terrorists could be U.S. citizens or foreigners, acting in concert with others, on their own, or on behalf of a hostile state. Detection was again singled out as a method of reducing the nation's vulnerability to terrorist attack. But the 2002 Strategy also noted the specific vulnerability of critical infrastructure, as exposed by 9/11, and prescribed the need for the government to work with the private sector to identify and protect it. The difficulty of reducing vulnerabilities, as noted in the 2002 Strategy, is that it requires an imprecise and constant adjusting of the balance between safety and security, and cost and liberty. The 2002 Strategy was also insightful, noting that as defenses are shored up in one area, terrorists might exploit vulnerabilities in others. By this observation the 2002 Strategy tacitly acknowledged the impossibility of preventing all terrorist attacks. Thus, the definition also addressed minimizing damages and quickly recovering from attacks that do occur. To minimize damages, the 2002 Strategy proposed improving coordination and helping prepare First Responders for catastrophic incidents. Similarly, rapid recovery was deemed necessary to restoring economic growth and public confidence. [3, pp. 2-3]

The corresponding objectives from the 2002 National Strategy for Homeland Security were:

1. *Prevent terrorist attacks within the U.S.;*
2. *Reduce America's Vulnerability to terrorism; and*
3. *Minimize the damage and recovery from attacks that do occur.*

The 2002 Strategy further explained that homeland security is an exceedingly complex mission. It involves efforts both at home and abroad, and demands a range of government and private sector capabilities. It also calls for coordinated and focused effort from many agencies who are not otherwise required to work together and for whom security is not always a primary mission. In order to provide clear direction amidst this confusion, the 2002 Strategy recast the definition of homeland security into a set of three objectives to help prioritize actions:

1. Prevent terrorist attacks within the United States;
2. Reduce America's vulnerability to terrorism; and
3. Minimize the damage and recover from attacks that do occur. [3, p. 3]

From the preceding definition of homeland security, the 2002 Strategy also derived six critical mission areas for aligning and focusing homeland security functions: this is what the new Department was expected to do:

1. Intelligence & Warning
2. Border & Transportation Security
3. Domestic Counterterrorism
4. Protecting Critical Infrastructure
5. Defending Against Catastrophic Terrorism
6. Emergency Preparedness and Response [3, p. viii]

From the 2002 definition and objectives for homeland security were derived six critical mission areas:

1. *Intelligence & Warning*
2. *Border & Transportation Security*
3. *Domestic Counterterrorism*
4. *Protecting Critical Infrastructure*
5. *Defending Against Catastrophic Terrorism*
6. *Emergency Preparedness & Response*

The first three mission areas focus primarily on preventing terrorist attacks (objective #1); the next two on reducing the nation's vulnerabilities (objective #2); and the final one on minimizing the damage and recovering from attacks that do occur (objective #3).

Intelligence & Warning. The essential function of I&W is to detect terrorist activity before it manifests itself into an attack so that proper preemptive, preventative, and protective action can be taken. The 2002 Strategy identified five major initiatives in this area:

1. Enhance the analytic capabilities of the FBI for domestic intelligence;
2. Conduct vulnerability assessments and risk analysis of critical infrastructure;
3. Implement a Homeland Security Advisory System;
4. Cross reference and correlate terrorist activity with "dual -use" items;
5. Employ "red team" techniques. [3, p. viii]

Border & Transportation Security. The essential function of BTS is to promote the efficient and reliable flow of people, goods, and services across borders while keeping out terrorists and terrorist weapons. The 2002 Strategy identified six major initiatives in this area:

1. Ensure accountability in border and transportation security;
2. Create "smart borders" through better intelligence and coordination;
3. Increase security of international shipping containers;
4. Implement the Aviation and Transportation Security Act of 2001;
5. Recapitalize the U.S. Coast Guard; and
6. Reform immigration services. . [3, p. viii]

Domestic Counterterrorism. While law enforcement agencies will continue to investigate and prosecute criminal activity, they should now assign priority to preventing and interdicting terrorist activity within the United States. All legal means—both traditional and nontraditional—will be used to identify, halt, and, prosecute terrorists in the United States. The 2002 Strategy identified six major initiatives under this area:

1. Improve intergovernmental law enforcement coordination;
2. Facilitate apprehension of potential terrorists;
3. Continue ongoing investigations and prosecutions;
4. Complete FBI restructuring to emphasize prevention of terrorist attacks;
5. Target and attack terrorist financing; and
6. Track foreign terrorists and bring them to justice. [3, p. ix]

Protecting Critical Infrastructure. This function seeks to improve protection of the individual pieces and interconnecting systems that make up our critical infrastructure. The 2002 Strategy identified eight major initiatives under this area:

1. Unify America's infrastructure protection effort in the Department of Homeland Security;
2. Build and maintain a complete and accurate assessment of America's critical infrastructure and key assets;
3. Enable effective partnership with state and local governments and the private sector;
4. Develop a national infrastructure protection plan;
5. Secure cyberspace;
6. Harness the best analytic and modeling tools to develop effective protective solutions;
7. Guard America's critical infrastructure and key assets against "inside" threats; and
8. Partner with the international community to protect our transnational infrastructure. [3, p. ix]

Defending Against Catastrophic Threats. This function seeks a unified approach to preventing, preparing, responding, and recovering from the deployment of chemical, biological, radiological, or nuclear weapons in the United States. The 2002 Strategy identified six major initiatives in this area:

1. Prevent terrorist use of nuclear weapons through better sensors and procedures;
2. Detect chemical and biological materials and attacks;
3. Improve chemical sensors and decontamination techniques;
4. Develop broad spectrum vaccines, antimicrobials, and antidotes;
5. Harness the scientific knowledge and tools to counter terrorism; and
6. Maintain the Select Agent Program regulating the shipment of hazardous biological organisms and toxins. [3, p. ix]

Emergency Preparedness and Response. The EP&R function seeks to build a comprehensive national system to bring together and coordinate all necessary response assets quickly and effectively. This function also includes planning, equipping, training, and exercising First Responders to mobilize without warning for any emergency. The 2002 Strategy identified twelve major initiatives in this area:

1. Integrate separate federal response plans into a single all-discipline incident management plan;
2. Create a national incident management system;
3. Improve tactical counterterrorist capabilities;
4. Enable seamless communication among all responders;
5. Prepare health care providers for catastrophic terrorism;
6. Augment America's pharmaceutical and vaccine stockpiles;
7. Prepare for chemical, biological, radiological, and nuclear decontamination;
8. Plan for military support to civil authorities;
9. Build the Citizen Corps;
10. Implement the First Responder Initiative of the Fiscal Year 2003 Budget;
11. Build a national training and evaluation system; and
12. Enhance the victim support system.

DHS Formation

The Department of Homeland Security was established by the Homeland Security Act, signed by President Bush November 25, 2002. Former Pennsylvania Governor Tom Ridge relinquished his position as Homeland Security Advisor to become the first Secretary of Homeland Security. Between November 2002 and January 2003, Secretary Ridge consolidated 180,000 personnel from twenty-two federal agencies to form the new Department of Homeland Security. On January 23, 2003, President Bush issued Executive Order 13284 activating the new Department. [4, p. 7]

When it began operations, DHS was largely organized like a hand — the palm being the office of the Secretary/Deputy Secretary with the thumb and fingers being individual directorates for (1) Management, (2) Science and technology, (3) information Analysis and Infrastructure protection, (4) Border and Transportation Security, and (5) Emergency preparedness and response. In addition, however, approximately two dozen other units within the department, but not located within one of the directorates, reported directly to the Secretary. These included program entities, such as the United States Coast Guard and United States Secret Service, and units within the office of the Secretary, such as the Office of International Affairs and Office of State and Local Government Coordination, as well as some Assistant Secretaries. At the time of its creation, only 18,000 DHS employees worked in the Washington, DC, area, indicating that the new department had a considerable field organization. [5, pp. CRS-2]

On January 23, 2003, President Bush issued Executive Order 13284 activating the new Department.

As the former director of the Office of Homeland Security responsible for developing the 2002 National Strategy for Homeland Security, Secretary Ridge strove to implement the critical mission initiatives within the new Department. But the 2002 Strategy was based on the President's proposed organization for DHS, and the actual organization as stipulated in the 2002 Homeland Security Act was slightly different as shown in Table 1.

Table 11-1: DHS Initial Operating Organization

	President's Proposal, June 24, 2002 [6, p. 2]	**Homeland Security Act, November 25, 2002**
1.	Border & Transportation Security	Border & Transportation Security
2.	Emergency Preparedness & Response	Emergency Preparedness & Response
3.	CBRN Countermeasures	Science & Technology
4.	Information Analysis & Infrastructure Protection	Information Analysis & Infrastructure Protection
5.	U.S. Coast Guard	U.S. Coast Guard
6.	U.S. Secret Service	U.S. Secret Service
7.	Office of State & Local Coordination	Office of State & Local Coordination
8.		U.S. Citizenship & Immigration Services

The most significant difference between the President's proposed structure for DHS and the organization resulting from the Homeland Security Act was replacement of the CBRN Countermeasures Directorate with the Science and Technology Directorate. The President's proposed CBRN Countermeasures Directorate would have led the federal government's efforts in preparing for and responding to the full range of threats involving weapons of mass destruction. According to the President's proposal, this would have required setting national policy and establishing guidelines for State and Local governments. It would direct exercises and drills for Federal, State, and Local CBRN response teams and plans. [6, p. 2] The Homeland Security Act conceived a greater role for the Science & Technology Directorate. In addition to formulating national policy and plans to prepare and respond to WMD, S&T would also develop countermeasures for CBRN agents. Moreover, it would support basic and applied research to develop, demonstrate, test, and evaluate activities relevant to any or all elements of the Department. [4]

The Department of Homeland Security, as initially established, was designed to have a clear and efficient relationship between its organization and function. [6, p. 2]

The most significant difference between the President's proposed structure for DHS and the organization resulting from the Homeland Security Act was replacement of the CBRN Countermeasures Directorate with the Science and Technology Directorate.

Table 11-2: Mapping DHS Organization & Critical Mission Areas

	DHS Agency	Assigned Critical Mission Areas
1.	Border & Transportation Security	Border & Transportation Security
2.	Emergency Preparedness & Response	Emergency Preparedness & Response
3.	Science & Technology	Defending Against Catastrophic Threats
4.	Information Analysis & Infrastructure Protection	Intelligence & Warning Domestic Counterterrorism Protecting Critical Infrastructure
5.	U.S. Coast Guard	Border & Transportation Security Protecting Critical Infrastructure
6.	U.S. Secret Service	Domestic Counterterrorism Protecting Critical Infrastructure
7.	Office of State & Local Coordination	Domestic Counterterrorism Emergency Preparedness & Response
8.	U.S. Citizenship & Immigration Services	Border & Transportation Security

2003 Reorganization Plan

Although Section 442 of the Homeland Security Act established a Bureau of Border Security within the Border and Transportation Security Directorate, it did not fully delineate its responsibilities. On January 30, 2003, President Bush submitted a modification to the November 2002 reorganization plan that established and described new organizational units in the Border and Transportation Security Directorate. [9, p. 12]

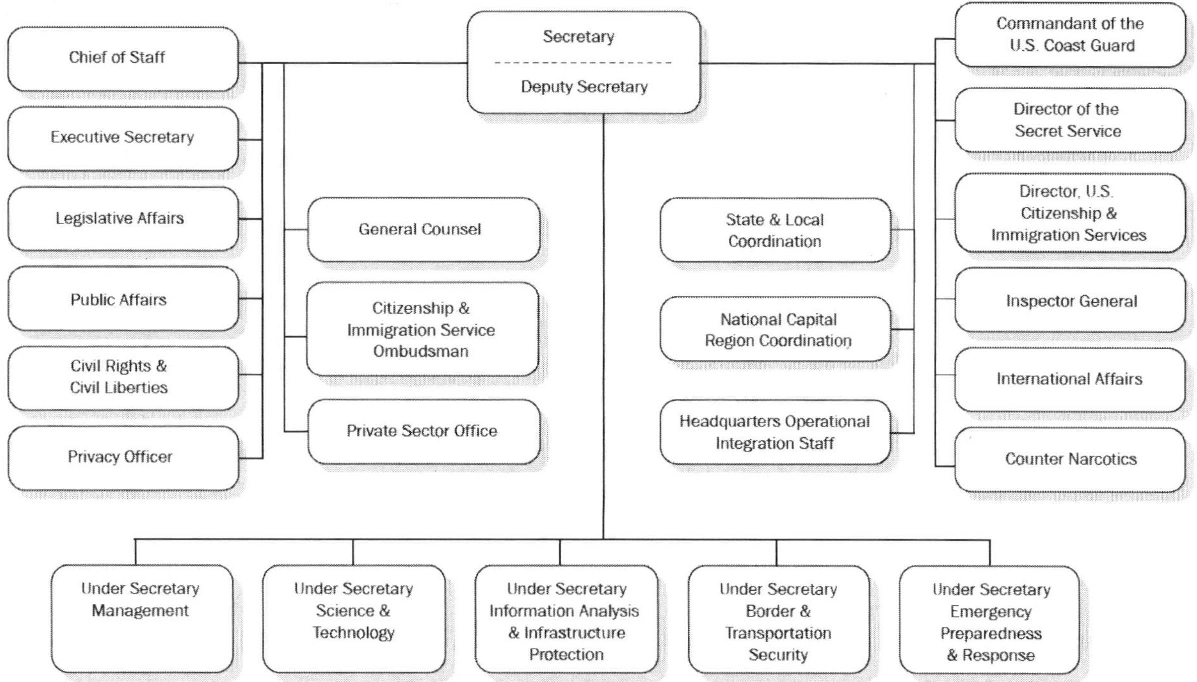

Figure 11-1: 2003 DHS Organization [4, p. 10]

The Department of Homeland Security, as initially established, maintained clear alignment between its missions and organization.

The January 2003 Plan renamed the Bureau of Border Security as the Bureau of Immigration and Customs Enforcement, incorporating parts of the Immigration and Naturalization Service (INS), the Customs Service, and the Federal Protective Service (FPS) and outlined its functions: to enforce immigration and customs laws within the interior of the United States and to protect specified federal buildings. [9, p. 12]

The January 2003 plan also renamed the U.S. Customs Service as the Bureau of Customs and Border Protection (now known as U.S. Customs and Border Protection, or CBP). The new Bureau incorporated the border and ports of entry functions of the Customs Service, inspection responsibilities and the Border Patrol from INS, and agricultural inspection functions from the Department of Agriculture. [9, p. 12]

These changes were made after the Department became operational, but before marking its official inception date of March 1, 2003. On that date, the majority of the previously existing agencies, such as the Federal Emergency Management Agency, the Transportation Security Administration, the Coast Guard, the Customs Service, and the United States Secret Service transferred to the new Department. [9, p. 12]

2004 Adjustments

In 2004, Secretary Ridge exercised his authority under Section 872 of the 2002 Homeland Security Act to adjust the Department's organization [10], adding two new reports to the Secretary: The Headquarters Operational Integration Staff (I-Staff) and the Office of State and Local Government Coordination and Preparedness (SGLCP). [9, p. 14]

On March 26, 2004, the Department consolidated the Office for Domestic Preparedness and the Office of State and Local Government Coordination to form the Office of State and Local Government Coordination and Preparedness, reporting directly to the Secretary. [9, p. 14]

Within provisions authorized in the 2002 Homeland Security Act, Secretary Ridge continued until the end of his term to make minor adjustments to the Department's organization.

On January 15, 2004, the I-Staff was formed to assist DHS leadership with coordinating and Department missions and operational activities, including threat response and preparedness, within DHS Headquarters. I-Staff also took the lead on drafting the National Response Plan (NRP) and National Incident Management System (NIMS) and implementing coordination between Headquarters and field offices as part of the Regions plan. I-Staff activities were discontinued with the implementation of the Second Stage Review (2SR) reorganization in October 2005. [9, p. 14]

2005 Second Stage Review

Tom Ridge was Secretary of Homeland Security for two years before resigning on November 30, 2004. [11] In January 2005, President Bush nominated Michael Chertoff to replace Tom Ridge as Secretary of Homeland Security. Michael Chertoff was a distinguished attorney who was serving as a Judge on the U.S. Court of Appeals when Secretary Ridge resigned. [12] Secretary Chertoff took office on February 15, 2005, and launched the Second Stage Review, or 2SR, a systematic evaluation of the department's operations, policies, and structures. [9, p. 16]

More than 250 members of the department, formed into 18 action teams, participated. The teams also consulted with public and private partners at the federal, state, local, tribal, and international levels. Based on the findings, on July 13, 2005, Secretary Chertoff proposed to Congress the following six point agenda: [9, p. 16]

1. Increase preparedness, with particular focus on catastrophic events.
2. Strengthen border security and interior enforcement and reform immigration processes.
3. Harden transportation security without sacrificing mobility.

4. Enhance information sharing with our partners, particularly with state, local and tribal governments and the private sector.

5. Improve DHS stewardship, particularly with stronger financial, human resource, procurement and information technology management.

6. Re - align the DHS organization to maximize mission performance. [5, pp. CRS-3]

Spurred in part by the flawed response to Hurricane Katrina, Congress formally approved the 2SR recommendations October 18, 2005. [13, p. 259] The subsequent reorganization abolished the Directorates for Border and Transportation Security, Information Analysis and Infrastructure Protection, and Emergency Response and Preparedness. With the abolition of these Directorates, the Director of the Federal Emergency Management Agency (FEMA), the Commissioner of Customs and Border Protection, the Assistant Secretary for the Transportation Security Administration, Director of Operations Coordination, Assistant Secretary for Intelligence and Analysis and the Assistant Secretary for Immigration and Customs Enforcement now reported directly to the Secretary. [9, p. 16]

Shortly after assuming office in February 2005, Secretary Chertoff announced his intention to reorganize DHS according to a plan he called the Second Stage Review (2SR).

The reorganization created two new directorates. The Policy Directorate took on most of the policy responsibilities from the former Assistant Secretary for Policy and Planning in the Border and Transportation Security Directorate, as well as newly created Assistant Secretaries for Legislative and Intergovernmental Affairs, Strategic Plans, the Private Sector, and International Affairs. The Preparedness Directorate consisted of preparedness functions transferred from FEMA and also included the U.S. Fire Administration, the Office of National Capitol Region, the Office of Infrastructure Preparedness, functions of the Office of State and Local Government Coordination, and the new offices of the Assistant Secretary for Grants and Training and the Chief Medical Officer. [9, p. 16]

The reorganization also created four new offices. The Office of Policy was created to serve as the primary Department-wide coordinator for policies, regulations, and other initiatives. These functions were previously performed under the Border and Transportation Security Directorate. The Office of Intelligence and Analysis was created to gather, analyze, and report information from relevant field operations and information from other parts of the intelligence community. These functions were previously performed, in part, under the Information Analysis and Infrastructure Protection Directorate. The Office of Operations Coordination was established to conduct joint operations across the Department, coordinate incident management and the management of the Homeland Security Operations Center. The Office of Legislative and Intergovernmental Affairs was created to merge similar functions previously provided by the Office of Legislative Affairs and the Office of State and Local Government Coordination. [13, p. 259]

2006 Post-Katrina Reform Act

Hurricane Katrina struck Florida and the Gulf Coast states in the last days of August 2005, followed within weeks by Hurricanes Rita and Wilma. These disasters will long be remembered for disrupting families, changing and ending lives, and forcing Americans to rethink vulnerability and risk assumptions. In addition to these impacts, the hurricanes served as catalysts for significant changes in federal policy and the organization of responsible federal entities, notably within the Department of Homeland Security. [14, p. 1]

As a result of the flawed response to Hurricane Katrina, Congress approved the 2SR reorganization and added its own adjustments with the 2006 Post-Katrina Emergency Reform Act.

Reports issued by committees of the 109th Congress, the White House, federal offices of Inspector General, and the Government Accountability Office (GAO), among others, concluded that the losses caused by Hurricane Katrina were due, in part, to deficiencies such as questionable leadership decisions and capabilities, organizational failures, overwhelmed preparation and communication systems, and inadequate statutory authorities. As a result, the 109th Congress revised federal emergency management policies vested in the President; reorganized the Federal Emergency Management Agency; and enhanced and clarified the mission, functions, and authorities of the agency, as well as those of its parent, the Department of Homeland Security. [14, p. i]

After FEMA was established in 1979, it was charged with carrying out activities to enable Federal, State, and Local governments to address a broad spectrum of emergency management functions. In carrying out its mission, FEMA 1) funded and coordinated emergency preparedness activities, 2) provided and coordinated immediate federal response to save lives and property, 3) funded the reconstruction of damaged homes and infrastructure to help stricken families and communities recover, and 4) supported hazard mitigation activities to ensure that future disasters do not recur, or are less destructive in the future. These four elements of preparedness, response, recovery, and hazard mitigation constitute what has been generally referred to as the Comprehensive Emergency Management (CEM) system. [14, p. 3]

When the Homeland Security Act transferred FEMA to DHS in 2003, some CEM responsibilities were transferred to the Border and Transportation Security Directorate. As part of the Second Stage Review, CEM functions were further divided between FEMA and the new Preparedness Directorate. As part of its investigation into Hurricane Katrina, Congress concluded that these mission and organizational shifts deteriorated FEMA's capabilities as functions, resources, and responsibilities moved to other DHS units. Others argued that an emphasis on terrorist-caused incidents within DHS dominated planning and allocation decisions and contributed to FEMA's diminished capabilities for all hazards. These findings led to congressional enactment of significant revisions to FEMA's structure and mission in the Post-Katrina Act. [14, pp. 3-4]

One of the most significant changes brought about by the Post-Katrina Reform Act was that it expanded and elevated FEMA as a distinct entity within the Department of Homeland Security.

On October 4, 2006, as part of the Homeland Security FY2007 Appropriations Bill (Public Law 109-295), the President signed into law the Post-Katrina Emergency Reform Act. The Act established new leadership positions within the Department, brought additional functions into the Federal Emergency Management Agency (FEMA), and created and reallocated functions within the Department. [9, p. 25]

The Post-Katrina Emergency Management Reform Act of 2006 established new leadership positions and position requirements within the Federal Emergency Management Agency, brought new missions into FEMA and restored some that had previously been removed, and enhanced the agency's authority by directing the FEMA Administrator to undertake a broad range of activities before and after disasters occur. The Post-Katrina Act contained provisions that set out new law, amended the Homeland Security Act, and modified the Robert T. Stafford Disaster Relief and Emergency Assistance Act (the Stafford Act). [14, p. 1]

Specifically, the Act renamed the Under Secretary for Federal Emergency Management as the Administrator of FEMA and elevated the position to the deputy secretary level. The Administrator was designated the principal advisor to the President, the Homeland Security Council, and the Secretary for all matters relating to emergency management and can be designated by the President to serve as a member of the Cabinet in the event of disasters. FEMA was legislatively protected as a distinct entity in the Department and is subject to reorganization only by statute. [9, p. 25]

The Post-Katrina Emergency Management Reform Act transferred to FEMA all functions of the Preparedness Directorate, including the Office of Grants and Training, the United States Fire Administration (USFA), and the Office of National Capital Region Coordination. The Office of Infrastructure Protection, the National Communications System, the National Cybersecurity Division, and the Office of the Chief Medical Officer remained in the Preparedness Directorate. [9, p. 25]

The Post-Katrina Act reorganized DHS with a reconfigured FEMA with consolidated emergency management functions, elevated status within the department, and enhanced organizational autonomy. Effective March 31, 2007, the Post-Katrina Act restored to FEMA the responsibility to lead and support efforts to reduce the loss of life and property and protect the nation from all hazards through a risk-based system that focuses on expanded CEM components. The statute also added a fifth component—protection—to the four CEM components, but did not define the term. [14, pp. 5-6]

The 2006 SAFE Port Act completed the reorganization of FEMA, and authorized the creation of a Domestic Nuclear Detection Office. After the Post-Katrina Emergency Reform Act transferred many functions to FEMA, the Preparedness Directorate was renamed the National Protection and Programs Directorate (NPPD).

2006 SAFE Port Act

On October 13, 2006, Congress passed the Security Accountability for Every Port Act, or SAFE Port Act of 2006 (Public Law 109-347). The act authorized the Domestic Nuclear Detection Office (DNDO) and completed the reorganization of FEMA, transferring the Radiological Preparedness Program and the Chemical Stockpile Emergency Preparedness Program to FEMA. [9, p. 25]

To implement and complement the changes in FEMA mandated by the Post-Katrina Management Reform Act of 2006 and the SAFE Port Act of 2006, the Department reorganized FEMA and made other organizational changes. [9, p. 25]

After the Post-Katrina Emergency Reform Act transferred many functions to FEMA, the Preparedness Directorate was renamed the National Protection and Programs Directorate (NPPD) and retained some Preparedness elements not transferred to FEMA, including the Office of Infrastructure Protection; the Office of Cyber Security and Telecommunications combined with National Communications System and new Office of Emergency Communications and renamed the Office of Cyber Security and Communications; and the Office for State and Local Government Coordination, renamed the Office of Intergovernmental Programs. Additionally the new Directorate contained US-VISIT and the Office of Risk Management and Analysis, formerly a part of the Office of Infrastructure Protection. An Office of Health Affairs was also established within NPPD, led by an Assistant Secretary/Chief Medical Officer. These changes became effective March 21, 2007. [9, pp. 25-26]

2007 National Strategy for Homeland Security

Hurricane Katrina resulted in a fundamental change to homeland security strategy, adding natural disasters to the list of domestic catastrophic threats together with manmade disasters. This change was reflected in the 2007 National Strategy for Homeland Security. In addition to hurricanes, the 2007 Strategy identified earthquakes, floods, tornadoes, wildfires, and infectious disease as significant hazards. [15, p. 10] While this recognition did not change the definition of homeland security according to the 2007 Strategy, [15, p. 3] it did lead to the introduction of a new term, that of "all-hazards". [15, p. 32] FEMA defines "all-hazards" as: "Any incident or event, natural or human caused, that requires an organized response... in order to protect life, public health, and safety... and to minimize any disruption to governmental, social, and economic services." [16] Accordingly, to accommodate this expanded mission set, the 2007 Strategy identifies four primary goals of homeland security:

1. Prevent and disrupt terrorist attacks;
2. Protect the American people, our critical infrastructure, and key resources;
3. Respond and recover from incidents that do occur;
4. Continue to strengthen the foundation to ensure our long - term success. [15, p. 1]

The second National Strategy for Homeland Security released in 2007 adjusted its homeland security objectives, now called "goals", to accommodate lessons learned from Hurricane Katrina and encompass "all hazards", not just terrorist threats.

As shown in Table 3, the 2007 Strategy Objectives compare very similar to the 2002 Strategy Objectives. The primary difference is subtle word changes that shift the focus away from the exclusive concern over terrorism. Objective #2 in the 2007 Strategy is still concerned with reducing vulnerability, but it replaces the threat to vulnerability with the targets of vulnerability, allowing broader interpretation beyond just terrorism. Objective #3 replaces "attacks" with "incidents" so it too can encompass a broader range of threats and hazards besides terrorism.

Table 11-3: Comparison of Strategy Objectives

	2007 Strategy	2002 Strategy
1.	Prevent and disrupt terrorist attacks	Prevent terrorist attacks within the U.S.
2.	Protect the American people, & CI/KR	Reduce America's vulnerability to terrorism
3.	Respond and recover from incidents that do occur	Minimize the damage and recover from attacks that do occur
4.	Continue to strengthen the foundation to ensure our long-term success	

Similar to the 2002 Strategy Objectives, the first three objectives of the 2007 Strategy were designed to organize and prioritize national efforts. Objective #4 of the 2007 Strategy was different in that it was aimed at creating and transforming homeland security principles, systems, structures, and institutions. This included applying a comprehensive approach to risk management, building a culture of preparedness, improving incident management, better utilizing science and technology, and leveraging all instruments of national power and influence. [15, p. 1] In short, Objective #4 was meant to put the Department on a path of continuous and systematic improvement. That objective was met when Congress passed and the President signed the Implementing Recommendations of the 9/11 Commission Act of 2007.

The Implementing Recommendations of the 9/11 Commission Act of 2007 further empowered FEMA, elevated Intelligence and Analysis within the Department, and directed the Secretary to systematically examine its mission and organization in a Quadrennial Homeland Security Review (QHSR).

Implementing Recommendations of the 9/11 Commission Act of 2007

Months after the 9/11 Commission had officially issued its seminal report and ceased its functions, Chairman Kean and other commissioners toured the country to draw attention to the recommendations of the commission for reducing the terror risk, claiming that some of their recommendations were being ignored. Co-chairs Kean and Hamilton wrote a book about the constraints they faced as commissioners titled Without Precedent: The Inside Story of the 9/11 Commission. The book was released August 15, 2006 and chronicled the work of Kean (Commission Chairman) and Hamilton (Commission Vice-Chairman) of the 9/11 Commission. [17] Congress responded in January 2007 by introducing a bill titled "Implementing Recommendations of the 9/11 Commission Act". The bill was finally approved and signed into law (PL 110-53) on August 3, 2007. [18] The Act built on the Post-Katrina Emergency Management Reform Act of 2006, focusing on the reorganization of the grant process as administered by FEMA. The Act also reorganized intelligence operations at the Department, elevating the Assistant Secretary for Intelligence and Analysis to the Under Secretary level, requiring Senate confirmation. [9, p. 30] Among the many provisions impacting DHS programs and organization, Section 707 required the Department to conduct a comprehensive examination of its mission and organization every four years starting in 2009. These periodic introspectives were designated the Quadrennial Homeland Security Review (QHSR). [19]

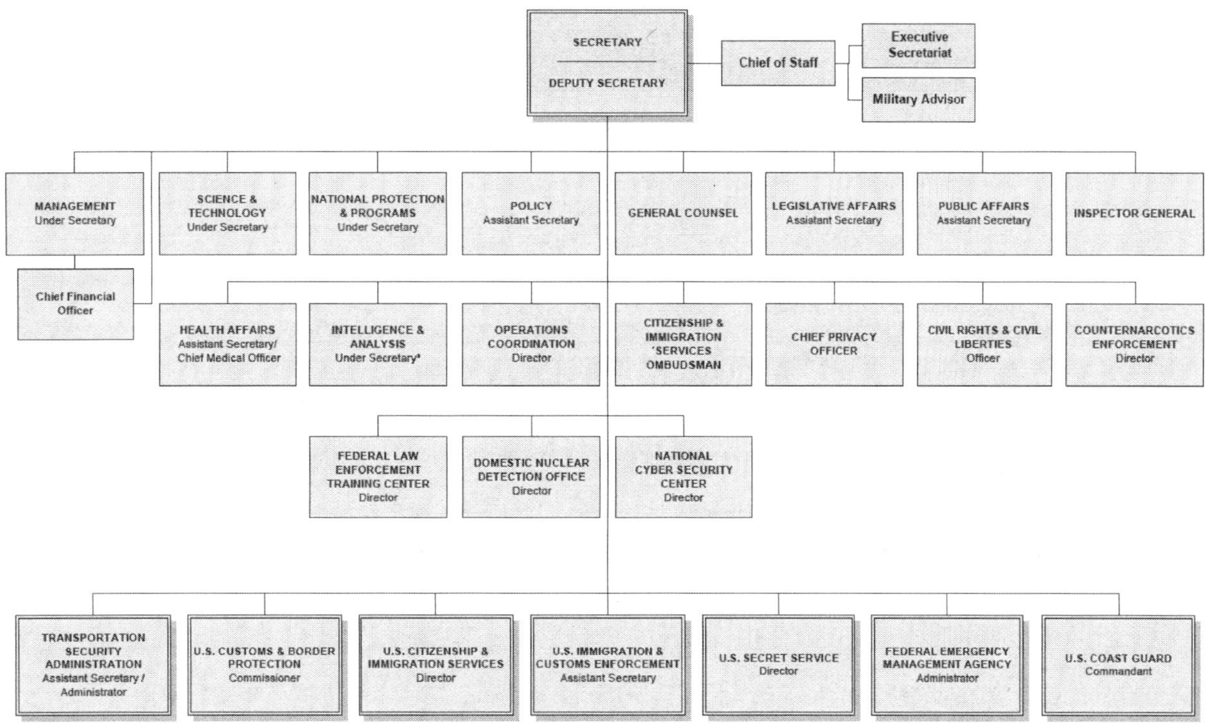

Figure 11-2: 2008 DHS Organization [20]

Quadrennial Homeland Security Review

In 2009, DHS conducted its first Quadrennial Homeland Security Review under the auspices of its new Secretary, Janet Napolitano. Former Governor of Arizona, Janet Napolitano was appointed by the incoming Obama Administration and later confirmed by Congress as Secretary of Homeland Security on January 20, 2009. [21] The first QHSR was released in February 2010. The QHSR was a comprehensive examination of the homeland security strategy of the nation and included recommendations regarding the long-term strategy and priorities of the nation for homeland security. The QHSR Report included the results of the QHSR, a national homeland security strategy, a description of the critical homeland security missions of the nation, and an explanation of the underlying assumptions used in conducting the review. [22, p. v]

The 2010 QHSR revised the definition of homeland security first established in the 2002 National Strategy for Homeland Security. The new definition of homeland security according to the 2010 QHSR:

> "Homeland security is a concerted national effort to ensure a homeland that is safe, secure, and resilient against terrorism and other hazards where American interests, aspirations, and way of life can thrive."
>
> - 2010 Quadrennial Homeland Security Review [23, p. 13]

Table 11-4: QHSR Missions & Goals [23, p. x]

Mission 1: Preventing Terrorism and Enhancing Security
Goal 1.1: Prevent Terrorist Attacks
Goal 1.2: Prevent the Unauthorized Acquisition or Use of CBRN Materials and Capabilities
Goal 1.3: Manage Risks to Critical Infrastructure, Key Leadership, and Events
Mission 2: Securing and Managing Our Borders
Goal 2.1: Effectively Control U.S. Air, Land, and Sea Borders
Goal 2.2: Safeguard Lawful Trade and Travel
Goal 2.3: Disrupt and Dismantle Transnational Criminal Organizations
Mission 3: Enforcing and Administering Our Immigration Laws
Goal 3.1: Strengthen and Effectively Administer the Immigration System
Goal 3.2: Prevent Unlawful Immigration
Mission 4: Safeguarding and Securing Cyberspace
Goal 4.1: Create a Safe, Secure, and Resilient Cyber Environment
Goal 4.2: Promote Cybersecurity Knowledge and Innovation
Mission 5: Ensuring Resilience to Disasters
Goal 5.1: Mitigate Hazards
Goal 5.2: Enhance Preparedness
Goal 5.3: Ensure Effective Emergency Response
Goal 5.4: Rapidly Recover

The first QHSR conducted in 2010 under Secretary Napolitano provided a new definition of homeland security and reformulation of missions. The most notable difference between the QHSR and 2002 and 2007 homeland security strategy mission sets was the elevation of Cybersecurity.

From this new definition, the 2010 QHSR derived five homeland security missions and associated goals listed in Table 4.

The most notable difference between the QHSR and 2002 and 2007 homeland security strategy mission sets was the elevation of Cybersecurity. Cybersecurity is defined as "The activity or process, ability or capability, or state whereby information and communications systems and the information contained therein are protected from and/or defended against damage, unauthorized use or modification, or exploitation." [24] The potential for using the Internet as an avenue for attacking the nation's critical infrastructure was first raised by the President's Commission on Critical Infrastructure Protection in October 1997. [25] This concern was not forgotten even though the 9/11 attacks were precipitated through physical subversion of the nation's critical infrastructure. Even so, cybersecurity was subordinated as a function of critical infrastructure protection in both the 2002 and 2007 Strategies, [3, p. ix] [15, p. 27] although a separate National Strategy to Secure Cyberspace was issued in February 2003. [26] By the time the QHSR was conducted in 2009, the U.S. had been subject to cyber attacks of increasing frequency and severity [27]. Because much of the nation's critical infrastructure was interconnected through the Internet, safeguarding and securing it became one of homeland security's most important missions. [23, p. 29]

The elevation of the cybersecurity mission in the 2010 QHSR was preceded by the establishment of the National Cyber Security Center (NCSC) in DHS. On January 8, 2008, President Bush issued Homeland Security Presidential Directive 23 (HSPD-23), creating NCSC, making it responsible for coordinating cybersecurity efforts and improving situational awareness and information sharing across the Federal government. [9, p. 32]

As a result of the findings from the QHSR, DHS initiated a bottom-up review (BUR) in November 2009. The BUR included an assessment of the organizational alignment of the Department with the homeland security missions set forth in the QHSR, including the Department's organizational structure, management systems, procurement systems, and physical and technical infrastructure. The BUR also included a review and assessment of the effectiveness of the mechanisms of the Department for turning the requirements developed in the QHSR into an acquisition strategy and expenditure plan within the Department. [22, p. v]

The BUR resulted in a comprehensive catalogue of DHS activities across the homeland security missions, as well as a list of over 300 potential initiatives and enhancements. The resulting report detailed the results of the analysis, describing the alignment of the Department with the homeland security missions, and setting forth the Department's priority initiatives and enhancements to increase mission performance, improve Departmental management, and increase accountability over the next four years. The BUR Report also included recommendations for improving the organizational alignment of the Department and enhancing its business processes. DHS subsequently included these recommended changes in its FY 2012 budget request to Congress. [22, p. v]

As a result of the findings from the QHSR, DHS initiated a bottom-up review (BUR) in November 2009. The BUR included an assessment of the organizational alignment of the Department with the homeland security missions set forth in the QHSR.

In 2014, DHS conducted its second QHSR under the auspices of its fourth Secretary Jeh Charles Johnson. Jeh Johnson was serving as General Counsel for the Department of Defense when he was nominated by President Obama to replace Secretary Napolitano after she resigned in August 2013. Secretary Johnson was confirmed by the Senate on December 16, 2013. [28] The 2014 QHSR built upon the 2010 QHSR to provide an updated view of the nation's homeland security mission goals and objectives. While the missions remained unchanged, the 2014 QHSR introduced five strategic priorities impacting them:

1. An updated posture to address the increasingly decentralized terrorist threat;
2. A strengthened path forward for cybersecurity that acknowledges the increasing interdependencies among critical systems and networks;
3. A homeland security strategy to manage the urgent and growing risk of biological threats and hazards;
4. A risk segmentation approach to securing and managing flows of people and goods into and out of the United States; and
5. A new framework for improving the efficiency and effectiveness of DHS mission execution through public-private partnerships. [29, p. 16]

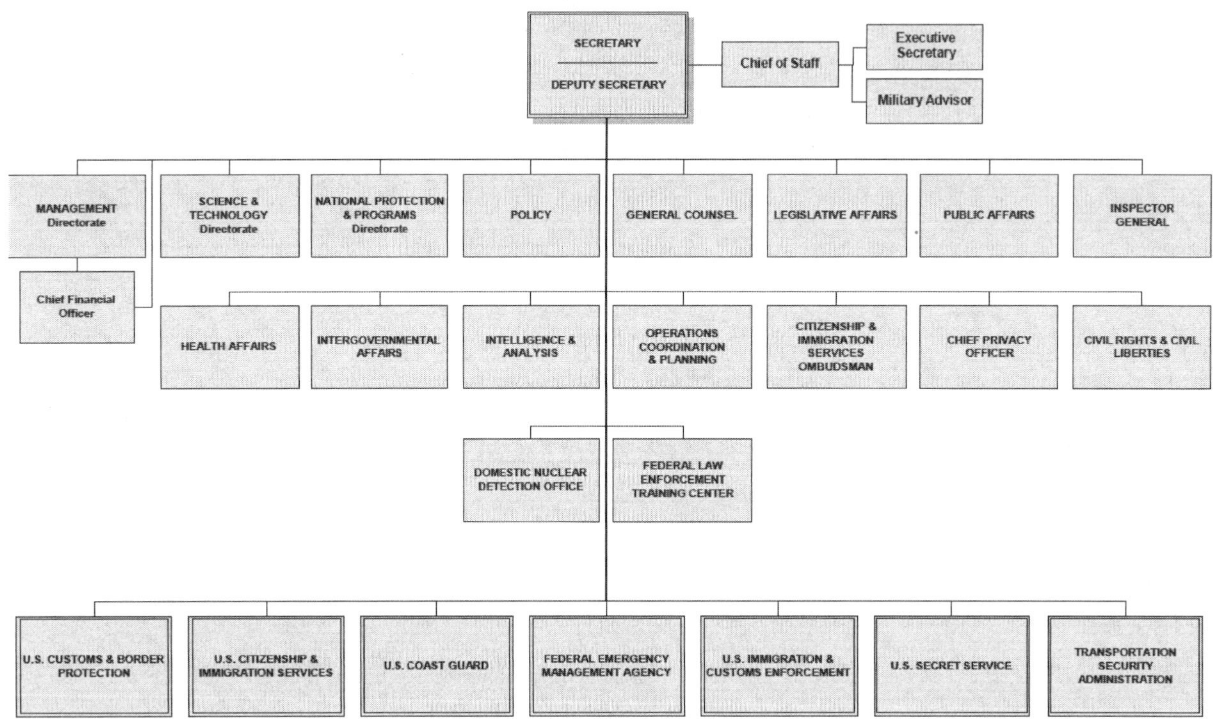

Figure 11-3: 2015 DHS Organization [30]

The second QHSR, conducted under Secretary Johnson in 2014, introduced "strategic priorities" giving precedence to the missions and goals formulated under the 2010 QHSR.

Beyond these strategic priorities, the 2014 QHSR also highlighted ongoing areas of priority and renewed areas of emphasis based on risk and other considerations—countering nuclear threats, strengthening the immigration system, and enhancing national resilience. [29, p. 16] The Department's current organization is depicted in Figure 3.

Homeland Security Strategy

In order to be effective, an organization must not only be aligned internally, but externally as well. In the case of the Department of Homeland Security, its missions and organization must align with nationally promulgated homeland security strategy. Strategy, in general, is defined as a plan of action design to achieve a particular aim. [31] The 2002 National Strategy for Homeland Security articulated five critical mission areas to attain the strategic objectives of 1) Prevent terrorist attacks within the United States; 2) Reduce America's vulnerability to terrorism; and 3) Minimize the damage and recover from attacks that do occur. [3, p. vii] Following Hurricane Katrina in 2005, homeland security strategy was adjusted to account for natural as well as manmade disasters. The 2007 National Strategy for Homeland Security revised the previous strategy objectives to 1) Prevent and disrupt terrorist attacks; 2) Protect the American People, critical infrastructure, and key resources; and 3) Respond to and recover from incidents that do occur. [15, p. 13]

Both the 2002 and 2007 homeland security strategies were crafted separate from national security strategy. The 2002 Strategy was written by the Office of Homeland Security before the Department of Homeland Security was established. The 2007 Strategy was written by the Homeland Security Council after the Department was established. The Homeland Security Council was established shortly after 9/11 to advise the President and coordinate homeland security actions among Federal agencies. While homeland security was always recognized as a part of national security, [3, p. 5] the split in staff raised concerns about effective coordination. Shortly after assuming office, on February 23, 2009 President Obama launched a 60-day organizational review of White House staff. Based on this review, on May 26, 2009, President Obama announced the merging of the Homeland Security Council with the National Security Council. [32] As a result, homeland security strategy was incorporated into the Obama Administration's 2010 National Security Strategy. Section 603 of the 1986 Goldwater-Nichols Act (P.L. 99-433) requires the President to submit a report of national security strategy annually to Congress. [33] The 2010 National Security Strategy recast homeland security strategy objectives as shared efforts to 1) identify and interdict threats; 2) deny hostile actors the ability to operate within our borders; 3) maintain effective control of our physical borders; 4) safeguard lawful trade and travel into and out of the United States; 5) disrupt and dismantle transnational terrorist, and criminal organizations; and 6) ensure national resilience in the face of the threat and hazards. [34, p. 15]

After 9/11, President Bush created a separate Homeland Security Council and separate homeland security strategy to ensure dedicated treatment to the mission. In 2009 President Obama re-integrated the HSC into the NSC, and in 2010 he merged homeland security into national security strategy to ensure both missions were interlocked and aligned.

In February 2015, the Obama Administration issued a revised National Security Strategy. In a highly abbreviated form, the 2015 National Security Strategy essentially affirmed the strategic objectives enumerated in the 2010 National Security Strategy. [35, p. 8] Perhaps most notably, the 2015 National Security Strategy addressed the threat of catastrophic terrorist attack, [35, p. 9] spread and use of Weapons of Mass Destruction, [35, p. 11] and cybersecurity [35, p. 12] outside the confines of homeland security, together with more traditional national security objectives. The changes mark the most intensive attempt yet to integrate homeland security strategy and national security strategy.

Conclusion

According to the management guru Peter Drucker, the hallmark of an effective organization is when its people and policies are aligned with its mission. The mission of the Department of Homeland Security has evolved since it was first founded in January 2003. The original mission set was founded on a definition of which, in turn, was shaped by the events of 9/11. Thus, when it was first founded DHS was primarily focused on the threat of domestic catastrophic damage resulting from manmade actions associated with terrorist motives. The Department's flawed response to Hurricane Katrina in August 2005 prompted a fundamental change in its focus, adding natural disasters to the list of threats that could create domestic catastrophic damage. Between 2005 and 2007, DHS underwent a number changes, initiated both internally and externally to re-align its mission sets accordingly. Included in these changes was a mandate by Congress for the Department to periodically review its missions and organization. The first Quadrennial Homeland Security Review in 2010 revised the definition of homeland security to include both natural and manmade threats. Both the Department's organization and mission support the nation's overall homeland security strategy. Initially, homeland security strategy was devised by the Homeland Security Council established after 9/11. In 2009, the Homeland Security Council was absorbed into the National Security Council. Since 2010, homeland security strategy has been combined and published as part of National Security Strategy. In one sense, the effectiveness of the Department of Homeland Security may be measured by alignment of its organization to mission, strategy, and definition of homeland security. Another measure of the Department's effectiveness is by what is has accomplished.

Challenge Your Understanding

The following questions are designed to challenge your understanding of the material presented in this chapter. Some questions may require additional research outside this book in order to provide a complete answer.

1. How did the 2002 National Strategy for Homeland Security influence DHS organization and missions?
2. Identify three significant changes the Second Stage Review made to DHS.
3. Identify the single most significant change the 2006 Post -Katrina Reform Act made to DHS.
4. Identify the single most significant change the 2006 Safe Port Act made to DHS.
5. Describe the motivation behind the 2007 Implementing Recommendations of the 9/11 Commission Act.
6. What was the major difference between the 2002 and 2007 homeland security strategies?
7. Summarize the Department's change in mission and organization between 2003 and 2008.
8. What is the purpose of the Quadrennial Homeland Security Review?
9. Why was homeland security strategy merged into national security strategy in 2009?
10. Summarize how the cybersecurity mission evolved from 2003 to 2010.

Chapter 12

DHS Progress

Learning Outcomes

Careful study of this chapter will help a student do the following:

- Describe the findings from the 2007 GAO Assessment of DHS performance.
- Describe the findings from the 2011 GAO Assessment of DHS performance.
- Evaluate the collective findings from the 2007 and 2011 GAO assessments.
- Assess for yourself whether you think DHS has made the nation safer.

"Measurement is the first step that leads to control and eventually to improvement. If you can't measure something, you can't understand it. If you can't understand it, you can't control it. If you can't control it, you can't improve it."

- H. James Harrington

Introduction

The Department of Homeland Security was formed from 22 different federal agencies to consolidate many separate homeland security activities under a single agency. Since DHS began operations in March 2003, it has implemented various policies and programs to meet its mission requirements and taken actions to integrate its management functions and to transform its component agencies into an effective cabinet department. [1, p. 2] Often it takes years for the consolidated functions in new organizations to effectively build on their combined strengths, and it is not uncommon for management challenges to remain for decades. For example, the 1947 legislation creating the Department of Defense was amended by Congress in 1949, 1953, 1958, and 1986 to improve the department's structural effectiveness. Despite these and other changes made by DOD, sixty years after its establishment, DOD continues to face a number of serious management challenges. [1, p. 1] Thus the Government Accountability Office (GAO) designated the implementation and transformation of DHS as high-risk because it represented an enormous undertaking that would require time to achieve in an effective and efficient manner. Additionally, the components merged into DHS already faced a wide array of existing challenges, and any DHS failure to effectively carry out its mission would expose the nation to potentially serious consequences. Accordingly, DHS has remained on GAO's high-risk list since 2003. [1, p. 2] In the meantime, GAO has conducted periodic assessments of DHS' progress. This chapter examines DHS' progress in performing assigned homeland security missions by way of reviewing findings from GAO's assessments.

2007 GAO Assessment

In November 2002, the Homeland Security Act of 2002 was enacted into law, creating DHS. This act defined the department's missions to include preventing terrorist attacks within the United States; reducing U.S. vulnerability to terrorism; and minimizing the damages, and assisting in the recovery from, attacks that occur within the United States. The act also specified major responsibilities for the department, including analyzing information and protecting infrastructure; developing countermeasures against chemical, biological, radiological, and nuclear, and other emerging terrorist threats; securing U.S. borders and transportation systems; and organizing emergency preparedness and response efforts. DHS officially began operations on March 1, 2003. [1, pp. 6-7]

Based on the notion it takes 5 to 7 years to complete a successful merger, GAO performed a comprehensive assessment of DHS' progress four years after the Department was activated. [1, p. ii] The 2007 GAO investigation examined DHS progress across 14 areas:

1. Border Security
2. Immigration Enforcement
3. Immigration Services
4. Aviation Security
5. Surface Transportation Security
6. Maritime Security
7. Emergency Preparedness and Response
8. Critical Infrastructure Protection
9. Science and Technology
10. Acquisition Management
11. Financial Management
12. Human Capital Management
13. Information Technology Management
14. Real Property Management [1, p. 8]

For each mission and management area, GAO identified performance expectations and vetted them with DHS officials. Performance expectations were a composite of the responsibilities or functions—derived from legislation, homeland security presidential directives and executive orders, DHS planning documents, and other sources—that the department was to achieve. GAO analysts and subject matter experts reviewed prior GAO work, DHS Inspector General work, and evidence DHS provided between March and July 2007, including DHS officials' assertions when supported by documentation. On the basis of this analysis and expert judgment, GAO then assessed the extent to which DHS had achieved each of the expectations identified. If DHS generally achieved more than 75 percent of the identified performance expectations, GAO identified its overall progress as substantial. When the number achieved was more than 50 percent but 75 percent or less, GAO identified its overall progress as moderate. If DHS generally achieved more than 25 percent but 50 percent or less, GAO identified its overall progress as modest. For mission and management areas in which DHS generally achieved 25 percent or less of the performance expectations, GAO identified overall progress as limited. [1, pp. 9-10]

For each mission and management area, GAO identified performance expectations and vetted them with DHS officials. GAO then assessed the extent to which DHS had achieved each of the expectations identified.

Border Security. This mission includes detecting and preventing terrorists and terrorist weapons from entering the United States; facilitating the orderly and efficient flow of legitimate trade and travel; interdicting illegal drugs and other contraband; apprehending individuals who are attempting to enter the United States illegally; inspecting inbound and outbound people, vehicles, and cargo; and enforcing laws of the United States at the border. GAO identified 12 performance expectations for DHS in the area of border security and found that DHS generally achieved 5 of them and generally did not achieve 7 others. [1, p. 12]

Table 12-1: 2007 GAO Assessment of Border Security [1, p. 12]

Performance expectation	Total
Generally achieved	**5**
Implement a biometric entry system to prevent unauthorized border crossers from entering the United States through ports of entry	
Develop a program to detect and identify illegal border crossings between ports of entry	
Develop a strategy to detect and interdict illegal flows of cargo, drugs, and other items into the United States	
Provide adequate training for all border-related employees	
Develop staffing plans for hiring and allocating human capital resources to fulfill the agency's border security mission	
Generally not achieved	**7**
Implement a biometric exit system to collect information on border crossers leaving the United States through ports of entry	
Implement a program to detect and identify illegal border crossings between ports of entry	
Implement a strategy to detect and interdict illegal flows of cargo, drugs, and other items into the United States	
Implement effective security measures in the visa issuance process	
Implement initiatives related to the security of certain documents used to enter the United States	
Ensure adequate infrastructure and facilities	
Leverage technology, personnel, and information to secure the border	
Overall assessment of progress	**Modest**

Immigration Enforcement. This mission includes apprehending, detaining, and removing criminal and illegal aliens; disrupting and dismantling organized smuggling of humans and contraband as well as human trafficking; investigating and prosecuting those who engage in benefit and document fraud; blocking and removing employers' access to undocumented workers; and enforcing compliance with programs to monitor visitors. GAO identified 16 performance expectations for DHS in the area of immigration enforcement and found that DHS has generally achieved 8 of them and generally did not achieve 4 others. For performance expectations, GAO could not make an assessment. [1, pp. 12-13]

Table 12-2: 2007 GAO Assessment of Immigration Enforcement [1, p. 13]

Performance expectation	Total
Generally achieved	8
Develop a program to ensure the timely identification and removal of noncriminal aliens subject to removal from the United States	
Assess and prioritize the use of alien detention resources to prevent the release of aliens subject to removal	
Develop a program to allow for the secure alternative detention of noncriminal aliens	
Develop a prioritized worksite enforcement strategy to ensure that only authorized workers are employed	
Develop a comprehensive strategy to interdict and prevent trafficking and smuggling of aliens into the United States	
Develop a law enforcement strategy to combat criminal alien gangs in the United States and cross-border criminal activity	
Develop a program to screen and respond to local law enforcement and community complaints about aliens who many be subject to removal	
Develop staffing plans for hiring and allocating human capital resources to fulfill the agency's immigration enforcement mission	
Generally not achieved	4
Implement a program to ensure the timely identification and removal of noncriminal aliens subject to removal from the United States	
Ensure the removal of criminal aliens	
Implement a prioritized worksite enforcement strategy to ensure that only authorized workers are employed	
Implement a comprehensive strategy to interdict and prevent trafficking and smuggling of aliens into the United States	
No assessment made	4
Implement a program to allow for the secure alternative detention of noncriminal aliens	
Implement a law enforcement strategy to combat criminal alien gangs in the United States and cross-border criminal activity	
Disrupt and dismantle mechanisms for money laundering and financial crimes	
Provide training, including foreign language training, and equipment for all immigration enforcement personnel to fulfill the agency's mission	
Overall assessment of progress	**Moderate**

Immigration Services. This mission includes administering immigration benefits and working to reduce immigration benefit fraud. GAO identified 14 performance expectations for DHS in the area of immigration services and found that DHS generally achieved 5 of them and generally did not achieve 9 others. [1, p. 13]

Table 12-3: 2007 GAO Assessment of Immigration Services [1, p. 14]

Performance expectation	Total
Generally achieved	**5**
Institute process and staffing reforms to improve application processes	
Establish online access to status information about benefit applications	
Establish revised immigration application fees based on a comprehensive fee study	
Communicate immigration-related information to other relevant agencies	
Create an office to reduce immigration benefit fraud	
Generally not achieved	**9**
Eliminate the benefit application backlog and reduce application completion times to 6 months	
Establish a timetable for reviewing the program rules, business processes, and procedures for immigration benefit applications	
Institute a case management system to manage applications and provide management information	
Develop new programs to prevent future backlogs from developing	
Establish online filing for benefit applications	
Capture biometric information on all benefits applicants	
Implement an automated background check system to track and store all requests for applications	
Establish training programs to reduce fraud in the benefits process	
Implement a fraud assessment program to reduce benefit fraud	
Overall assessment of progress	**Modest**

Aviation Security. This mission includes strengthening airport security; providing and training a screening workforce; prescreening passengers against terrorist watch lists; and screening passengers, baggage, and cargo. GAO identified 24 performance expectations for DHS in the area of aviation security and found that DHS generally achieved 17 of them and generally did not achieve 7 others. [1, p. 14]

Table 12-4: 2007 GAO Assessment of Aviation Security [1, p. 15]

Performance expectation	Total
Generally achieved	**17**
Implement a strategic approach for aviation security functions	
Ensure the screening of airport employees against terrorist watch lists	
Hire and deploy a federal screening workforce	
Develop standards for determining aviation security staffing at airports	
Establish standards for training and testing the performance of airport screener staff	
Establish a program and requirements to allow eligible airports to use a private screening workforce	
Train and deploy federal air marshals on high-risk flights	
Establish standards for training flight and cabin crews	
Establish a program to allow authorized flight deck officers to use firearms to defend against any terrorist or criminal acts	
Establish policies and procedures to ensure that individuals known to pose, or suspected of posing, a risk or threat to security are identified and subjected to appropriate action	
Develop and implement processes and procedures for physically screening passengers at airport checkpoints	
Develop and test checkpoint technologies to address vulnerabilities	
Deploy explosive detection systems (EDS) and explosive trace detection (ETD) systems to screen checked baggage for explosives	
Develop a plan to deploy in-line baggage screening equipment at airports	
Pursue the deployment and use of in-line baggage screening equipment at airports	
Develop a plan for air cargo security	
Develop and implement procedures to screen air cargo	
Generally not achieved	**7**
Establish standards and procedures for effective airport perimeter security	
Establish standards and procedures to effectively control access to airport secured areas	
Establish procedures for implementing biometric identifier systems for airport secured areas access control	
Develop and implement an advanced prescreening system to allow DHS to compare domestic passenger information to the Selectee List and No Fly List	
Develop and implement an international passenger prescreening process to compare passenger information to terrorist watch lists before aircraft departure	
Deploy checkpoint technologies to address vulnerabilities	
Develop and implement technologies to screen air cargo	
Overall assessment of progress	**Moderate**

Surface Transportation Security. This mission includes establishing security standards and conducting assessments and inspections of surface transportation modes, which include passenger and freight rail; mass transit; highways, including commercial vehicles; and pipelines. GAO identified 5 performance expectations for DHS in the area of surface transportation security and found that DHS generally achieved 3 of them and generally did not achieve 2. [1, pp. 15-16]

Table 12-5: 2007 GAO Assessment of Surface Transportation Security [1, p. 16]

Performance expectation	Total
Generally achieved	**3**
Develop and adopt a strategic approach for implementing surface transportation security functions	
Conduct threat, criticality, and vulnerability assessments of surface transportation assets	
Administer grant programs for surface transportation security	
Generally not achieved	**2**
Issue standards for securing surface transportation modes	
Conduct compliance inspections for surface transportation systems	
Overall assessment of progress	**Moderate**

Maritime Security. This mission includes port and vessel security, maritime intelligence, and maritime supply chain security. GAO identified 23 performance expectations for DHS in the area of maritime security and found that DHS generally achieved 17 of them and generally did not achieve 4 others. For 2 performance expectations, GAO could not make an assessment. [1, p. 16]

Table 12-6: 2007 GAO Assessment of Maritime Security [1, p. 17]

Performance expectation	Total
Generally achieved	**17**
Develop national plans for maritime security	
Develop national plans for maritime response	
Develop national plans for maritime recovery	
Develop regional (port-specific) plans for security	
Develop regional (port-specific) plans for response	
Ensure port facilities have completed vulnerability assessments and developed security plans	
Ensure that vessels have completed vulnerability assessments and developed security plans	
Exercise security, response, and recovery plans with key maritime stakeholders to enhance security, response, and recovery efforts	
Implement a port security grant program to help facilities improve their security capabilities	
Establish operational centers to monitor threats and fuse intelligence and operations at the regional/port level	
Collect information on incoming ships to assess risks and threats	
Develop a vessel-tracking system to improve intelligence and maritime domain awareness on vessels in U.S. waters	
Collect information on arriving cargo for screening purposes	
Develop a system for screening and inspecting cargo for illegal contraband	
Develop a program to work with foreign governments to inspect suspicious cargo before it leaves for U.S. ports	
Develop a program to work with the private sector to improve and validate supply chain security	
Develop an international port security program to assess security at foreign ports	
Generally not achieved	**4**
Develop regional (port-specific) plans for recovery	
Implement a national facility access control system for port secured areas	
Develop a long-range vessel-tracking system to improve maritime domain awareness	
Develop a program to screen incoming cargo for radiation	
No assessment made	**2**
Develop a national plan to establish and improve maritime intelligence	
Develop standards for cargo containers to ensure their physical security	
Overall assessment of progress	**Substantial**

Emergency Preparedness and Response. This mission includes preparing to minimize the damage and recover from terrorist attacks and disasters; helping to plan, equip, train, and practice needed skills of first responders; and consolidating federal response plans and activities to build a national, coordinated system for incident management. GAO identified 24 performance expectations for DHS in the area of emergency preparedness and response and found that DHS generally achieved 5 of them and generally did not achieve 18 others. For 1 performance expectation, GAO could not make an assessment. [1, pp. 17-18]

Table 12-7: 2007 GAO Assessment of Emergency Preparedness & Response [1, p. 18]

Performance expectation	Total
Generally achieved	5
Establish a program for conducting emergency preparedness exercises	
Develop a national incident management system	
Provide grant funding to first responders in developing and implementing interoperable communications capabilities	
Administer a program for providing grants and assistance to state and local governments and first responders	
Allocate grants based on assessment factors that account for population, critical infrastructure, and other risk factors	
Generally not achieved	18
Establish a comprehensive training program for national preparedness	
Conduct and support risk assessments and risk management capabilities for emergency preparedness	
Ensure the capacity and readiness of disaster response teams	
Coordinate implementation of a national incident management system	
Establish a single, all-hazards national response plan	
Coordinate implementation of a single, all-hazards response plan	
Develop a complete inventory of federal response capabilities	
Develop a national, all-hazards preparedness goal	
Develop plans and capabilities to strengthen nationwide recovery efforts	
Develop the capacity to provide needed emergency assistance and services in a timely manner	
Provide timely assistance and services to individuals and communities in response to emergency events	
Implement a program to improve interoperable communications among federal, state, and local agencies	
Implement procedures and capabilities for effective interoperable communications	
Increase the development and adoption of interoperability communications standards	
Develop performance goals and measures to assess progress in developing interoperability	
Provide guidance and technical assistance to first responders in developing and implementing interoperable communications capabilities	
Provide assistance to state and local governments to develop all-hazards plans and capabilities	
Develop a system for collecting and disseminating lessons learned and best practices to emergency responders	
No assessment made	1
Support citizen participation in national preparedness efforts	
Overall assessment of progress	Limited

Critical Infrastructure Protection. This mission includes developing and coordinating implementation of a comprehensive national plan for critical infrastructure protection, developing partnerships with stakeholders and information sharing and warning capabilities, and identifying and reducing threats and vulnerabilities. GAO identified 7 performance expectations for DHS in the area of critical infrastructure and key resources protection and found that DHS generally achieved 4 of them and generally did not achieve 3 others. [1, p. 19]

Table 12-8: 2007 GAO Assessment of Critical Infrastructure Protection [1, p. 19]

Performance expectation	Total
Generally achieved	**4**
Develop a comprehensive national plan for critical infrastructure protection	
Develop partnerships and coordinate with other federal agencies, state and local governments, and the private sector	
Identify and assess threats and vulnerabilities for critical infrastructure	
Support efforts to reduce threats and vulnerabilities for critical infrastructure	
Generally not achieved	**3**
Improve and enhance public/private information sharing involving attacks, threats, and vulnerabilities	
Develop and enhance national analysis and warning capabilities for critical infrastructure	
Provide and coordinate incident response and recovery planning efforts for critical infrastructure	
Overall assessment of progress	**Moderate**

Science and Technology. This mission includes coordinating the federal government's civilian efforts to identify and develop countermeasures to chemical, biological, radiological, nuclear, and other emerging terrorist threats. GAO identified 6 performance expectations for DHS in the area of science and technology and found that DHS generally achieved 1 of them and generally did not achieve 5 others. [1, p. 19]

Table 12-9: 2007 GAO Assessment of Science and Technology [1, p. 20]

Performance expectation	Total
Generally achieved	**1**
Coordinate with and share homeland security technologies with federal, state, local, and private sector entities	
Generally not achieved	**5**
Develop a plan for departmental research, development, testing, and evaluation activities	
Assess emerging chemical, biological, radiological, and nuclear threats and homeland security vulnerabilities	
Coordinate research, development, and testing efforts to identify and develop countermeasures to address chemical, biological, radiological, nuclear, and other emerging terrorist threats	
Coordinate deployment of nuclear, biological, chemical, and radiological detection capabilities and other countermeasures	
Assess and evaluate nuclear, biological, chemical, and radiological detection capabilities and other countermeasures	
Overall assessment of progress	**Limited**

Overall, the 2007 GAO report determined that DHS made more progress in its mission areas than in its management areas, reflecting an understandable focus on implementing efforts to secure the nation.

Overall, the 2007 GAO report determined that DHS made more progress in its mission areas than in its management areas, reflecting an understandable focus on implementing efforts to secure the nation. Even so, GAO concluded that while DHS made progress in developing plans and programs, it faced difficulties in implementing them. [1, p. 2] GAO acknowledged that DHS had to undertake its missions while also working to transform itself into a fully functioning cabinet department—a difficult task for any organization. Still, GAO noted the importance for the Department to continue to develop more measurable goals to guide implementation efforts and to enable better accountability. GAO also urged DHS to continually reassess its mission and management goals, measures, and milestones to evaluate progress made, identify past and emerging obstacles, and examine alternatives to effectively address those obstacles.

2011 GAO Assessment

Ten years after 9/11, GAO took another look at DHS' progress. By 2011, DHS had grown to become the third-largest Federal department, with more than 200,000 employees and an annual budget of more than $50 billion. [2, p. 2] In February 2010, DHS issued its first Quadrennial Homeland Security Review (QHSR). The report identified five homeland security missions—Preventing Terrorism and Enhancing Security; Securing and Managing Our Borders; Enforcing and Administering Our Immigration Laws; Safeguarding and Securing Cyberspace; and Ensuring Resilience to Disasters—and goals and objectives to be achieved within each mission. The ensuing Bottom-Up Review (BUR) made recommendations to align DHS's programs and organization with missions and goals identified in the QHSR. [2, pp. 4-5]

Since the 2007 GAO assessment, DHS continued to take action to strengthen its operations and the management of the department, including enhancing its performance measurement efforts. In 2011, GAO was again asked to review the progress made by DHS in implementing its homeland security missions since its creation. Accordingly, the 2011 assessment was based on past GAO reviews plus DHS Inspector General reports, but with an emphasis on work completed since 2008. GAO drew their 2011 mission areas from the 2010 QHSR. With the exception of Science and Technology, the 2011 assessment addresses all the mission areas from the 2007 assessment, plus CBRN Threats and Cybersecurity. [2, pp. 6-7]

The 2011 assessment was based on past GAO reviews plus DHS Inspector General reports, but with an emphasis on work completed since 2008.

Table 12-10: Comparison of 2011 & 2007 GAO Mission Area Assessments

2010 GAO Mission Area Assessments	2007 GAO Mission Area Assessments
1. Aviation Security	4. Aviation Security
2. CBRN Threats	
3. Critical Infrastructure Protection – Physical	8. Critical Infrastructure Protection
4. Surface Transportation Security	5. Surface Transportation Security
5. Border Security	1. Border Security
6. Maritime Security	6. Maritime Security
7. Immigration Enforcement	2. Immigration Enforcement
8. Immigration Services	3. Immigration Services
9. Critical Infrastructure Protection – Cyber Assets	
10. Emergency Preparedness and Response	7. Emergency Preparedness & Response
	9. Science and Technology

For the 2011 assessment, GAO began with the expectations identified in the August 2007 report, and updated or added to them by analyzing requirements and plans set forth in homeland security-related laws, presidential directives and executive orders, national strategies related to homeland security, and DHS's and components' strategic plans and documents. The 2011 assessment further grouped the expectations into "sub areas" to account for criteria that pertained to more than one mission area. Otherwise, the analysis was conducted similar to the 2007 assessment, from April to September 2011. Unlike the 2007 assessment, however, the 2011 assessment does not assign a measure of progress, such as "substantial", "moderate", "modest", or "limited". Instead, the 2011 assessment provides a narrative description of what progress DHS made in implementing a given mission function since operations began, together with a narrative description of what work, if any, remains. [2, pp. 7-9] Consequently, it is difficult to compare progress between the 2007 and 2011 assessments. Perhaps a direct comparison between the two assessments would be fruitless, given that DHS mission and performance have always been subject to change by external influencing factors. Figure 1 identifies some of the significant influencing factors affecting DHS in the first ten years following 9/11.

The 2011 GAO Assessment began with the expectations identified in the 2007 GAO Assessment. Unlike the 2007 GAO Assessment, however, the 2011 GAO Assessment does not assign a measure of progress.

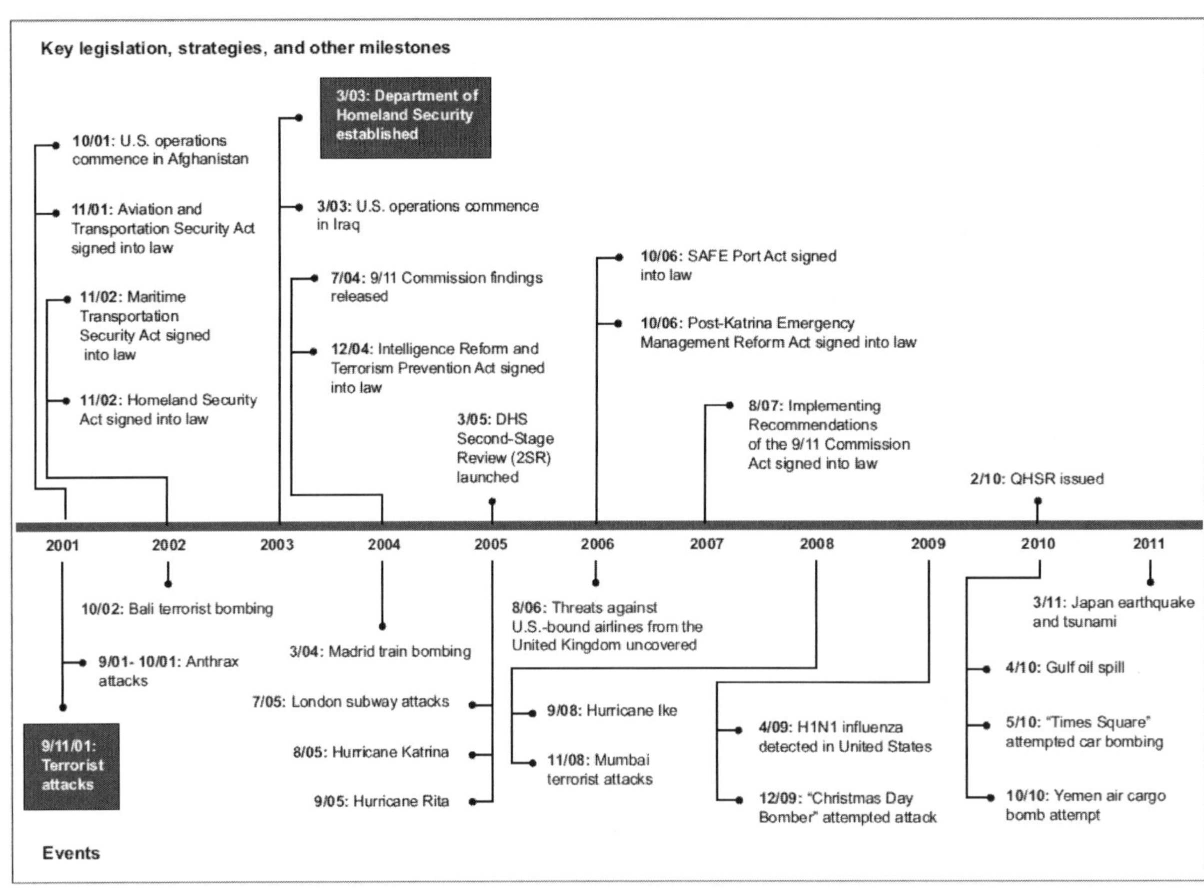

Figure 12-1: Selected Factors Influencing DHS Mission and Performance Ten Years Following 9/11 [2, p. 15]

Aviation Security. DHS developed and implemented Secure Flight, a program for screening airline passengers against terrorist watchlist records. DHS also developed new programs and technologies to screen passengers, checked baggage, and air cargo. However, DHS does not yet have a plan for deploying checked baggage screening technologies to meet recently enhanced explosive detection requirements, a mechanism to verify the accuracy of data to help ensure that air cargo screening is being conducted at reported levels, or approved technology to screen cargo once it is loaded onto a pallet or container. [2, p. ii]

Key Progress: DHS has enhanced aviation security in key areas related to the aviation security workforce, passenger prescreening, passenger checkpoint screening, checked baggage security, air cargo screening, and security of airports. For example, DHS developed and implemented Secure Flight, a passenger prescreening program through which the federal government now screens all passengers on all domestic and international commercial flights to, from, and within the United States. DHS also deployed technology to screen passengers and checked baggage at airports. For example, in response to the December 25, 2009, attempted attack on Northwest flight 253, DHS revised the advanced imaging technology procurement and deployment strategy, increasing the planned deployment of advanced imaging technology from 878 to between 1,350 and 1,800 units. Further, DHS is screening passengers using staff trained in behavior detection principles and has deployed about 3,000 Behavior Detection Officers to 161 airports as part of its Screening of Passengers by Observation Techniques program. Moreover, DHS reported, as of August 2010, that it had established a system to screen 100 percent of domestic air cargo (cargo transported within and outbound from the United States) transported on passenger aircraft by, among other things, creating a voluntary program to facilitate screening throughout the air cargo supply chain and taking steps to test technologies for screening air cargo. [2, p. 19]

Remaining Work: DHS should take additional action to strengthen its aviation security efforts. For example, a risk-based strategy and a cost/benefit analysis of airport checkpoint technologies would improve passenger checkpoint screening. TSA's strategic plan to guide research, development, and deployment of passenger checkpoint screening technologies was not risk-based and did not reflect some of the key risk management principles, such as conducting a risk assessment based on the three elements of risk— threat, vulnerability, and consequence—and including a cost-benefit analysis and performance measures. Further, in March 2010, GAO reported that it was unclear whether the advanced imaging technology would have detected the weapon used in the December 25, 2009, attempted terrorist attack based on the preliminary testing information received. DHS also had not validated the science supporting its Screening of Passengers by Observation Techniques program, or determined if behavior detection techniques could be successfully used across the aviation system to detect threats before deploying the program. DHS completed a program validation study in April 2011 which found that the program was more effective than random screening, but that more work was needed to determine whether the science could be used for counterterrorism purposes in the aviation environment. Moreover, DHS does not yet have a plan and schedule for deploying checked baggage screening technologies to meet recently enhanced explosive detection requirements. In addition, DHS does not yet have a mechanism to verify the accuracy of domestic and inbound air cargo screening data to help ensure that screening is being conducted at reported levels, and DHS does not yet have approved technology to screen cargo once it is loaded onto a pallet or container—both of which are common means of transporting air cargo on passenger aircraft, thus requiring that screening occur before incorporation into pallets and containers. [2, p. 19]

Table 12-11: 2011 GAO Expectations for Aviation Security [2, pp. 40-41]

Functional Mission Area: Aviation Security
Sub Area #1: Security Workforce
1a: Ensure the screening of airport workers against terrorist watchlist records
1b: Hire and deploy a federal screening workforce
1c: Develop standards for determining aviation security staffing at airports
1d: Establish standards for training and testing the performance of airport screener staff
1e: Establish a program and requirements to allow eligible airports to use a private screening workforce
1f: Train and deploy federal air marshals on high-risk flights
1g: Establish standards for training flight and cabin crews
1h: Establish a program to allow authorized flight deck officers to use firearms to defend against any terrorist or criminal acts
1i: Establish policies and procedures to ensure that individuals known to pose, or suspected of posing, a risk or threat to security are identified and subjected to appropriate action
Sub Area #2: Passenger Prescreening
2a: Develop and implement an advanced prescreening system to allow DHS to compare domestic passenger information to the Selectee List and No Fly List[a]
2b: Develop and implement an international passenger prescreening process to compare passenger information to terrorist watchlists before aircraft departure
Sub Area #3: Checkpoint Screening
3a: Develop and implement processes and procedures for physically screening passengers at airport checkpoints
3b: Develop and test checkpoint technologies to address vulnerabilities
3c: Deploy checkpoint technologies to address vulnerabilities
3d: Establish a program for armed law enforcement officers traveling by commercial aircraft
3e. Utilize behavioral and appearance indicators to identify persons who pose a risk to aviation security
Sub Area #4: Checked Baggage Screening
4a: Deploy explosive detection systems and explosive trace detection systems to screen checked baggage for explosives
4b: Develop a plan to deploy in-line and other optimal baggage screening systems at airports, as appropriate
4c: Pursue the deployment and use of in-line or other optimal baggage screening systems at airports, as appropriate
Sub Area #5: Air Cargo Security
5a: Develop a plan for air cargo security
5b: Develop and implement procedures to screen domestic and in-bound international air cargo
5c: Develop and implement technologies to screen air cargo
Sub Area #6: Security of Airports
6a: Establish standards and procedures for effective airport perimeter security
6b: Establish standards and procedures to effectively control access to secured airport areas
6c: Establish procedures for implementing biometric identifier systems for secured airport areas access control

CBRN Threats. DHS assessed risks posed by CBRN threats and deployed capabilities to detect CBRN threats. However, DHS should work to improve its coordination of CBRN risk assessments, and identify monitoring mechanisms for determining progress made in implementing the global nuclear detection strategy. [2, p. iii]

Key Progress: DHS made progress in assessing risks posed by CBRN threats, developing CBRN detection capabilities, and planning for nuclear detection. For example, DHS develops risk assessments of CBRN threats and has issued seven classified CBRN risk assessments since 2006.b DHS also assessed the threat posed by specific CBRN agents in order to determine which of those agents pose a material threat to the United States, known as material threat assessments. With regard to CBRN detection capabilities, DHS implemented the BioWatch program in more than 30 metropolitan areas to detect specific airborne biological threat agents. Further, DHS established the National Biosurveillance Integration Center to enhance the federal government's capability to identify and track biological events of national concern. In addition, DHS coordinated the development of a strategic plan for the global nuclear detection architecture—a multidepartment effort to protect against terrorist attacks using nuclear and radiological materials through coordinated activities—and has deployed radiation detection equipment. [2, p. 20]

Remaining Work: More work remains for DHS to strengthen its CBRN assessment, detection, and mitigation capabilities. For example, DHS should better coordinate with the Department of Health and Human Services in conducting CBRN risk assessments by developing written policies and procedures governing development of the assessments. Moreover, the National Biosurveillance Integration Center lacks resources necessary for operations, such as data and personnel from its partner agencies. Additionally, work remains for DHS in its implementation of the global nuclear detection architecture. Specifically, the strategic plan for the architecture did not include some key components, such as funding needed to achieve the strategic plan's objectives, or monitoring mechanisms for determining programmatic progress and identifying needed improvements. DHS officials told us that they will address these missing elements in an implementation plan, which they plan to issue by the end of 2011. [2, p. 20]

Table 12-12: 2011 GAO Expectations for CBRN Threats [2, p. 41]

Functional Mission Area: Chemical, Biological, Radiological, and Nuclear Threats
Sub Area #1: Assessment
1a: Assess emerging chemical, biological, radiological, and nuclear threats and homeland security vulnerabilities
Sub Area #2: Detection and Mitigation
2a: Coordinate deployment of chemical, biological, radiological, and nuclear detection and other mitigation capabilities
2b: Assess and evaluate chemical, biological, radiological, and nuclear detection capabilities and other countermeasures

Critical Infrastructure Protection of Physical Assets.

Key Progress: DHS expanded its efforts to conduct risk assessments and planning, provide for protection and resiliency, and implement partnerships and coordination mechanisms for physical critical assets. For example, DHS updated the National Infrastructure Protection Plan to include an emphasis on resiliency (the capacity to resist, absorb, or successfully adapt, respond to, or recover from disasters), and an enhanced discussion about DHS risk management. Moreover, DHS components with responsibility for critical infrastructure sectors, such as transportation security, have begun to use risk based assessments in their critical infrastructure related planning and protection efforts. Further, DHS has various voluntary programs in place to conduct vulnerability assessments and security surveys at and across facilities from the 18 critical infrastructure sectors, and uses these assessments to develop and disseminate information on steps asset owners and operators can take to protect their facilities. In addition, DHS coordinated with critical infrastructure stakeholders, including other federal regulatory authorities to identify overlaps and gaps in critical infrastructure security activities. [2, p. 20]

Remaining Work: Additional actions are needed for DHS to strengthen its critical infrastructure protection programs and efforts. For example, DHS has not fully implemented an approach to measure its effectiveness in working with critical asset owners and operators in their efforts to take actions to mitigate resiliency gaps identified during various vulnerability assessments. Moreover, DHS components have faced difficulties in incorporating risk-based assessments in critical infrastructure planning and protection efforts, such as in planning for security in surface transportation modes like highway infrastructure. Further, DHS should determine the feasibility of developing an approach to disseminating information on resiliency practices to its critical infrastructure partners to better position itself to help asset owners and operators consider and adopt resiliency strategies, and provide them with information on potential security investments. [2, p. 21]

Table 12-13: 2011 GAO Expectations for CIP of Physical Assets [2, p. 41]

Functional Mission Area: Critical Infrastructure Protection—Physical Assets
Sub Area #1: Risk Assessment and Planning
1a: Develop a comprehensive national plan for critical infrastructure protection
1b: Establish and maintain a national database of critical systems and assets
1c: Identify and assess risks to critical infrastructure
Sub Area #2: Protection and Resiliency
2a: Provide and coordinate incident response and recovery planning efforts for critical infrastructure
2b: Support efforts to reduce risks to critical infrastructure
Sub Area #3 Partnerships and Coordination Mechanisms
3a: Improve and enhance public/private information sharing involving attacks and risks
3b: Develop partnerships and coordinate with other federal agencies, state and local governments, and the private sector
3c: Develop and enhance national analysis and warning capabilities for critical infrastructure

Surface Transportation Security.

Key Progress: DHS expanded its efforts in key surface transportation security areas, such as risk assessments and strategic planning; the surface transportation inspector workforce; and information sharing. For example, DHS conducted risk assessments of surface transportation modes and developed a transportation sector security risk assessment that assessed risk within and across the various modes. Further, DHS more than doubled its surface transportation inspector workforce and, as of July 2011, reported that its surface inspectors had conducted over 1,300 site visits to mass transit and passenger rail stations to complete station profiles, among other things. Moreover, DHS allocates transit grant funding based on risk assessments and has taken steps to measure performance of its Transit Security Grant Program, which provides funds to owners and operators of mass transit and passenger rail systems. In addition, DHS expanded its sharing of surface transportation security information by, among other things, establishing information networks. [2, p. 21]

Remaining Work: DHS should take further action to strengthen its surface transportation security programs and operations. For example, DHS's efforts to improve elements of risk assessments of surface transportation modes are in the early stages of implementation. Moreover, DHS noted limitations in its transportation sector security risk assessment—such as the exclusion of threats from lone wolf operators—that could limit its usefulness in guiding investment decisions across the transportation sector as a whole. Further, DHS has not yet completed a long-term workforce plan that identifies future needs for its surface transportation inspector workforce. It also has not yet issued regulations for a training program for mass transit, rail, and bus employees, as required by the Implementing Recommendations of the 9/11 Commission Act of 2007. Additionally, DHS's information sharing efforts would benefit from improved streamlining, coordination, and assessment of the effectiveness of information sharing mechanisms. [2, p. 21]

Table 12-14: 2011 GAO Expectations for Surface Transportation Security [2, pp. 41-42]

Functional Mission Area: Surface Transportation Security
Sub Area #1: Risk Assessment and Planning
1a: Develop and adopt a strategic approach for implementing surface transportation security functions
1b: Conduct threat, criticality, and vulnerability assessments of surface transportation assets
Sub Area #2: Standards, Inspections, and Training
2a: Issue standards for securing surface transportation modes
2b: Conduct inspections of surface transportation systems
2c: Develop programs to detect contraband and undeclared passengers entering the United States by rail and for tracking the shipment of security-sensitive materials
2d: Provide surface transportation security training
2e: Train and deploy explosives detection canine teams
Sub Area #3: Grants
3a: Administer grant programs for surface transportation security
Sub Area #4: Information Sharing
4a: Share information with stakeholders to enhance surface transportation security

Border Security. DHS implemented the U.S. Visitor and Immigrant Status Indicator Technology program to verify the identities of foreign visitors entering and exiting the country by processing biometric and biographic information. However, DHS has not yet determined how to implement a biometric exit capability and has taken action to address a small portion of the estimated overstay population in the United States (individuals who legally entered the country but then overstayed their authorized periods of admission). DHS also deployed infrastructure to secure the border between ports of entry, including more than 600 miles of fencing. However, DHS experienced schedule delays and performance problems with the Secure Border Initiative Network, which led to the cancellation of this information technology program. [2, p. ii]

Key Progress: DHS expanded its efforts in key border security areas, such as inspection of travelers and cargo at ports of entry, security of the border between ports of entry, visa adjudication security, and collaboration with stakeholders. Specifically, DHS has undertaken efforts to keep terrorists and other dangerous people from entering the country. For example, DHS implemented the US-VISIT program to verify the identities of foreign visitors entering and exiting the United States by storing and processing biometric and biographic information. DHS established plans for, and had begun to interact with and involve stakeholders in, developing an exit capability. DHS deployed technologies and other infrastructure to secure the border between ports of entry, including more than 600 miles of tactical infrastructure, such as fencing, along the border. DHS also improved programs designed to enhance the security of documents used to enter the United States. For example, DHS deployed the Visa Security Program, in which DHS personnel review visa applications to help prevent individuals who pose a threat from entering the United States, to 19 posts in 15 countries, and developed a 5-year expansion plan for the program. In addition, DHS improved collaboration with federal, state, local, tribal, and international partners on northern border security efforts through, among other things, the establishment of interagency forums. [2, p. 22]

Remaining Work: More work remains for DHS to strengthen its border security programs and operations. For example, although it has developed a plan, DHS has not yet adopted an integrated approach to scheduling, executing, and tracking the work needed to deliver a comprehensive biometric exit solution as part of the US-VISIT program. Further, DHS experienced schedule delays and performance problems with its information technology program for securing the border between ports of entry—the Secure Border Initiative Network—which led to its cancellation. Because of the program's decreased scope, uncertain timing, unclear costs, and limited life cycle management, it was unclear whether DHS's pursuit of the program was cost-effective. DHS is transitioning to a new approach for border technology, which GAO is assessing. With regard to the Visa Security Program, DHS did not fully follow or update its 5-year expansion plan. For instance, it did not establish 9 posts identified for expansion in 2009 and 2010, and had not taken steps to address visa risk at posts that did not have a Visa Security Program presence. Additionally, DHS should strengthen its oversight of interagency forums operating along the northern border. [2, p. 22]

Table 12-15: 2011 GAO Expectations for Border Security [2, p. 42]

Functional Mission Area: Border Security
Sub Area #1: Inspection of Individuals at Ports of Entry
1a: Implement a biometric entry system to prevent unauthorized border crossers from entering the United States through ports of entry
1b: Implement a biometric exit system to collect information on border crossers leaving the United States through ports of entry
Sub Area #2: Inspection of Cargo and Goods at Ports of Entry while Facilitating Commerce
2a: Develop and implement strategies to detect and interdict illegal flows of cargo, drugs, and other items into and out of the United States while facilitating legitimate commerce
Sub Area #3: Securing the Border between Ports of Entry
3a: Develop and implement programs to detect and identify illegal border crossings between ports of entry
3b: Leverage technology, infrastructure, personnel, and information to secure the border between ports of entry
Sub Area #4: Enhancing Security in the Visa Issuance and Travel Documentation Process
4a: Enhance security measures in the visa issuance process
4b: Enhance the security of certain documents used to enter the United States
Sub Area #5: Collaborating on Border Security Efforts
5a: Enhance collaboration with international, federal, state, local, and tribal law enforcement as well as community groups and the private sector to increase border security, exchange relevant information, and facilitate commerce
Sub Area #6: Border Security Resources
6a: Ensure adequate assets and facilities (at ports of entry for moving people and cargo)
6b: Provide adequate training and equipment for all border-related employees
6c: Develop and implement staffing plans for hiring and allocating human capital resources to fulfill the agency's border security mission

Maritime Security.

Key Progress: DHS expanded its efforts in key maritime security areas, such as port facility and vessel security, maritime security domain awareness and information sharing, and international supply chain security. For example, DHS strengthened risk management through the development of a risk assessment model, and addressed risks to port facilities through annual inspections in which DHS identified and corrected deficiencies, such as facilities failing to follow security plans for access control. Further, DHS took action to address risks posed by foreign seafarers entering U.S. seaports by, for example, conducting advance screening before the arrival of vessels at U.S. ports, inspections, and enforcement operations. DHS developed the Transportation Worker Identification Credential program to manage the access of unescorted maritime workers to secure areas of regulated maritime facilities. DHS also implemented measures to help secure passenger vessels including cruise ships, ferries, and energy commodity vessels such as tankers, including assessing risks to these types of vessels. Moreover, for tracking vessels at sea, the Coast Guard uses a long-range identification and tracking system, and a commercially provided long-range automatic identification system. For tracking vessels in U.S. coastal areas, inland waterways, and ports, the Coast Guard operates a land-based automatic identification system, and also either operates, or has access to, radar and cameras in some ports. DHS also developed a layered security strategy for cargo container security, including deploying screening technologies and partnering with foreign governments. [2, p. 23]

Remaining Work: DHS should take additional action to strengthen its maritime security efforts. For example, because of a lack of technology capability, DHS does not electronically verify identity and immigration status of foreign seafarers, as part of its onboard admissibility inspections of cargo vessels, thus limiting the assurance that fraud could be identified among documents presented by them. In addition, the Transportation Worker Identification Credential program's controls were not designed to provide reasonable assurance that only qualified applicants acquire credentials. For example, during covert tests of the Transportation Worker Identification Credential at several selected ports, their investigators were successful in accessing ports using counterfeit credentials and authentic credentials acquired through fraudulent means. Moreover, DHS has not assessed the costs and benefits of requiring cruise lines to provide passenger reservation data for screening, which could help improve identification and targeting of potential terrorists. Further, the vessel tracking systems used in U.S. coastal areas, inland waterways, and ports had more difficulty tracking smaller and noncommercial vessels because these vessels were not generally required to carry automatic identification system equipment, and because of the technical limitations of radar and cameras. In addition, DHS has made limited progress in scanning containers at the initial ports participating in the Secure Freight Initiative, a program at selected ports with the intent of scanning 100 percent of U.S.-bound container cargo for nuclear and radiological materials overseas, leaving the feasibility of 100 percent scanning largely unproven. CBP has not yet developed a plan for full implementation of a statutory requirement that 100 percent of U.S.-bound container cargo be scanned by 2012. [2, p. 23]

Table 12-16: 2011 GAO Expectations for Maritime Security [2, pp. 42-43]

Functional Mission Area: Maritime Security
Sub Area #1: Port Facility and Vessel Security
1a: Develop regional (port-specific) plans for security
1b: Develop regional (port-specific) plans for response
1c: Develop regional (port-specific) plans for recovery
1d: Develop, update, and coordinate protocols for resuming trade after a transportation security disruption or incident
1e: Ensure port facilities have completed vulnerability assessments and developed and implemented security plans
1f: Implement a port security grant program to help facilities improve their security capabilities
1g: Implement a national facility access control system for port secured areas
1h: Ensure that vessels have completed vulnerability assessments and developed and implemented security plans
1i: Exercise security, response, and recovery plans with key maritime stakeholders to enhance security, response, and recovery efforts
Sub Area #2: Maritime Domain Awareness and Information Sharing
2a: Develop a national plan to establish and improve maritime intelligence
2b: Establish operational centers to monitor threats and fuse intelligence and operations at the regional/port level
2c: Collect and analyze information on incoming vessels to assess risks and threats
2d: Develop and implement a vessel-tracking system to improve intelligence and maritime domain awareness on vessels in U.S. waters
2e: Develop and implement a long-range vessel tracking system to improve maritime domain awareness
2f: Identify and address homeland security needs in the Arctic
2g: Develop and implement an international port security program to assess security at foreign ports
Sub Area #3: International Supply Chain Security
3a: Collect and analyze information on arriving cargo for screening purposes
3b: Develop and implement a system for screening and inspecting cargo for illegal contraband and radiation
3c: Develop and implement a program to work with foreign governments to inspect suspicious cargo before it leaves for U.S. ports
3d: Develop and implement a program to work with the private sector to improve and validate supply chain security
3e: Develop standards for cargo containers to ensure their physical security
Sub Area #4: National Planning
4a: Develop national plans for maritime security
4b: Develop national plans for maritime response
4c: Develop national plans for maritime recovery

Immigration Enforcement.

Key Progress. DHS expanded its immigration and customs enforcement programs and activities in key areas such as overstay enforcement, compliance with workplace immigration laws, alien smuggling, and firearms trafficking. For example, DHS increased its resources for investigating overstays (unauthorized immigrants who entered the United States legally on a temporary basis then overstayed their authorized periods of admission) and alien smuggling operations, and deployed border enforcement task forces to investigate illicit smuggling of people and goods, including firearms. In addition, DHS took action to improve the E-Verify program, which provides employers a voluntary tool for verifying an employee's authorization to work in the United States, by, for example, increasing the program's accuracy by expanding the number of databases it can query. Further, DHS expanded its programs and activities to identify and remove criminal aliens in federal, state, and local custody who are eligible for removal from the United States by, for example, entering into agreements with state and local law enforcement agencies to train officers to assist in identifying those individuals who are in the United States illegally. [2, p. 24]

Remaining Work: Key weaknesses remain in DHS's immigration and customs enforcement efforts. For example, DHS took action to address a small portion of the estimated overstay population in the United States, and lacks measures for assessing its progress in addressing overstays. In particular, DHS field offices had closed about 34,700 overstay investigations assigned to them from fiscal year 2004 through 2010, as of October 2010; these cases resulted in approximately 8,100 arrests, relative to a total estimated overstay population of 4 million to 5.5 million. Additionally, GAO reported that since fiscal year 2006, U.S. Immigration and Customs Enforcement within DHS allocated about 3 percent of its investigative work hours to overstay investigations. Moreover, DHS should better leverage opportunities to strengthen its alien smuggling enforcement efforts by assessing the possible use of various investigative techniques, such as those that follow cash transactions flowing through money transmitters that serve as the primary method of payment to those individuals responsible for smuggling aliens. Further, weaknesses with the E-Verify program, including challenges in accurately estimating E-Verify costs, put DHS at an increased risk of not making informed investment decisions. [2, p. 24]

Table 12-17: 2011 GAO Expectations for Immigration Enforcement [2, pp. 43-44]

Functional Mission Area: Immigration Enforcement
Sub Area #1: Investigations of Immigration Offenses
1a: Develop and implement strategies and programs to enforce immigration laws at the workplace
1b: Develop and implement a comprehensive strategy to interdict and prevent trafficking and smuggling of aliens into the United States
1c: Develop and implement a law enforcement strategy to combat criminal alien gangs in the United States and cross-border criminal activity
Sub Area #2: Investigations of Customs Offenses
2a: Disrupt and dismantle cross-border mechanisms for money laundering and financial crimes
2b: Investigate illegal imports and exports that threaten public safety, including illicit commodities, weapons, and drugs
Sub Area #3: Identification, Detention, and Removal of Aliens Subject to Removal
3a: Develop and implement programs to ensure the timely identification, prioritization, and removal of noncriminal aliens subject to removal from the United States
3b: Develop and implement a program to screen and respond to local law enforcement and community reports of aliens who may be subject to removal from the United States
3c: Ensure the identification, prioritization, and removal of criminal aliens subject to removal from the United States
3d: Assess and prioritize the use of alien detention resources to prevent the release of aliens subject to removal
3e: Develop and implement a program to allow for the secure alternative detention of noncriminal aliens subject to removal
Sub Area #4: Management and Training of Immigration Enforcement Human Capital
4a: Develop staffing plans for hiring and allocating human capital resources to fulfill the agency's immigration enforcement mission
4b: Provide training, including foreign language training, and equipment for all immigration enforcement personnel to fulfill the agency's mission

Immigration Services.

Key Progress: DHS improved the quality and efficiency of the immigration benefit administration process, and expanded its efforts to detect and deter immigration fraud. For example, DHS initiated efforts to modernize its immigration benefit administration infrastructure; improve the efficiency and timeliness of its application intake process; and ensure quality in its benefit adjudication processes. Further, DHS designed training programs and quality reviews to help ensure the integrity of asylum adjudications. Moreover, in 2004 DHS established the Office of Fraud Detection and National Security, now a directorate, to lead immigration fraud detection and deterrence efforts, and this directorate has since developed and implemented strategies for this purpose. [2, p. 24]

Remaining Work: More work remains in DHS's efforts to improve its administration of immigration benefits. For example, DHS's program for transforming its immigration benefit processing infrastructure and business practices from paper-based to digital systems missed its planned milestones by more than 2 years, and has been hampered by management challenges, such as insufficient planning and not adhering to DHS acquisition guidance before selecting a contractor to assist with implementation of the transformation program. Additionally, while the Fraud Detection and National Security Directorate put in place strategies for detecting and deterring immigration fraud, DHS should take additional action to address vulnerabilities identified in its assessments intended to determine the extent and nature of fraud in certain applications. Further, despite mechanisms DHS had designed to help asylum officers assess the authenticity of asylum claims, such as identity and security checks and fraud prevention teams, asylum officers surveyed cited challenges in identifying fraud as a key factor affecting their adjudications. For example, 73 percent of asylum officer survey respondents reported it was moderately or very difficult to identify document fraud. [2, p. 25]

Table 12-18: 2011 GAO Expectations for Immigration Services [2, p. 44]

Functional Mission Area: Immigration Services
Sub Area #1: Administration of Immigration Benefits
1a: Institute process and staffing reforms to improve application processes
1b: Eliminate the benefit application backlog and reduce application completion times to 6 months
1c: Implement programs to prevent future backlogs from developing
1d: Establish revised immigration application fees based on a comprehensive fee study
1e: Capture biometric information on all benefits applicants
1f: Implement an automated background check system to track and store all requests for immigration benefits
1g: Establish online access to status information about benefit applications
1h: Establish online filing for benefit applications
1i: Communicate immigration-related information to other relevant agencies
1j: Establish a timetable for reviewing the program rules, business processes, and procedures for immigration benefit applications
1k: Institute a case management system to manage applications and provide management information
Sub Area #2: Immigration Benefit Fraud
2a: Create and maintain an office to reduce immigration benefit fraud
2b: Establish and enhance training programs to reduce fraud in the benefits process
2c: Implement a fraud assessment program to reduce benefit fraud
Sub Area #3: Immigrant Integration
3a: Promote immigrant integration by enhancing understanding of U.S. citizenship and providing support to immigrants through the naturalization process

Critical Infrastructure Protection of Cyber Assets.

Key Progress: DHS expanded its efforts to conduct cybersecurity risk assessments and planning, provide for the protection and resilience of cyber assets, and implement cybersecurity partnerships and coordination mechanisms. For example, DHS developed the first National Cyber Incident Response Plan in September 2010 to coordinate the response of multiple federal agencies, state and local governments, and hundreds of private firms, to incidents at all levels. DHS also took steps to secure external network connections in use by the federal government by establishing the National Cybersecurity Protection System, operationally known as Einstein, to analyze computer network traffic information to and from agencies. In 2008, DHS developed Einstein 2, which incorporated network intrusion detection technology into the capabilities of the initial version of the system. Additionally, the department made progress in enhancing its cyber analysis and incident warning capabilities through the establishment of the U.S. Computer Emergency Readiness Team, which, among other things, coordinates the nation's efforts to prepare for, prevent, and respond to cyber threats to systems and communications networks. Moreover, since conducting a major cyber attack exercise, called Cyber Storm, DHS demonstrated progress in addressing lessons it had learned from this exercise to strengthen public and private incident response capabilities. [2, p. 25]

Remaining Work: Key challenges remain in DHS's cybersecurity efforts. For example, to expand its protection and resiliency efforts, DHS needs to lead a concerted effort to consolidate and better secure Internet connections at federal agencies. Further, DHS faced challenges regarding deploying Einstein 2, including understanding the extent to which its objective was being met because the department lacked performance measures that addressed whether agencies report whether the alerts represent actual incidents. DHS also faces challenges in fully establishing a comprehensive national cyber analysis and warning capability. For example, the U.S. Computer Emergency Readiness Team did not fully address 15 key attributes of cyber analysis and warning capabilities. These attributes are related to (1) monitoring network activity to detect anomalies, (2) analyzing information and investigating anomalies to determine whether they are threats, (3) warning appropriate officials with timely and actionable threat and mitigation information, and (4) responding to the threat. For instance, the U.S. Computer Emergency Readiness Team provided warnings by developing and distributing a wide array of notifications; however, these notifications were not consistently actionable or timely. Additionally, expectations of private sector stakeholders are not being met by their federal partners in areas related to sharing information about cyber-based threats to critical infrastructure. [2, p. 26]

Table 12-19: 2011 GAO Expectations for CIP of Cyber Assets [2, p. 44]

Functional Mission Area: Critical Infrastructure Protection—Cyber Assets
Sub Area #1: Risk Assessment and Planning
1a: Develop a comprehensive national plan for critical infrastructure protection
1b: Establish and maintain a national database of critical systems and assets
1c: Identify and assess risks to critical infrastructure
Sub Area #2: Protection and Resiliency
2a: Provide and coordinate incident response and recovery planning efforts for critical infrastructure
2b: Support efforts to reduce risks to critical infrastructure
Sub Area #3: Partnerships and Coordination Mechanisms
3a: Improve and enhance public/private information sharing involving attacks and risks
3b: Develop partnerships and coordinate with other federal agencies, state and local governments, and the private sector
3c: Develop and enhance national analysis and warning capabilities for critical infrastructure

Emergency Preparedness and Response. DHS issued the National Preparedness Guidelines that describe a national framework for capabilities- based preparedness, and a Target Capabilities List to provide a national-level generic model of capabilities defining all-hazards preparedness. DHS is also finalizing a National Disaster Recovery Framework, and awards preparedness grants based on a reasonable risk methodology. However, DHS needs to strengthen its efforts to assess capabilities for all-hazards preparedness, and develop a long-term recovery structure to better align timing and involvement with state and local governments' capacity. DHS should also improve the efficacy of the grant application process by mitigating duplication or redundancy within the various preparedness grant programs. [2, pp. ii-iii]

Key Progress: DHS expanded its efforts to improve national emergency preparedness and response planning; improved its emergency assistance services; and enhanced emergency communications. For example, DHS developed various plans for disaster preparedness and response. In particular, in 2004 DHS issued the National Response Plan and subsequently made revisions to it, culminating in the issuance of the National Response Framework in January 2008, which outlines the guiding principles and major roles and responsibilities of government, nongovernmental organizations, and private sector entities for response to disasters of all sizes and causes. Further, DHS issued the National Preparedness Guidelines that describe a national framework for capabilities-based preparedness, and a Target Capabilities List, designed to provide a national-level generic model of capabilities defining all-hazards preparedness. DHS also assisted local communities with developing long-term disaster recovery plans as part of its post-disaster assistance. For example, DHS assisted Iowa City's recovery from major floods in 2008 by, among other things, identifying possible federal funding sources for specific projects in the city's recovery plan, and advising the city on how to prepare effective project proposals. DHS is also finalizing a National Disaster Recovery Framework, intended to provide a model to identify and address challenges that arise during the disaster recovery process. Moreover, DHS issued the National Emergency Communications Plan—the first strategic document for improving emergency communications nationwide. [2, p. 26]

Remaining Work: More work remains in DHS's efforts to assess capabilities for all-hazards preparedness and provide long-term disaster recovery assistance. For example, DHS has not yet developed national preparedness capability requirements based on established metrics to provide a framework for assessing preparedness. Further, the data DHS collected to measure national preparedness were limited by reliability and measurement issues related to the lack of standardization. Until a framework for assessing preparedness is in place, DHS will not have a basis on which to operationalize and implement its conceptual approach for assessing local, state, and federal preparedness capabilities against capability requirements and identify capability gaps for prioritizing investments in national preparedness. Moreover, with regard to long-term disaster recovery assistance, DHS's criteria for when to provide the assistance were vague, and, in some cases, DHS provided assistance before state and local governments had the capacity to work effectively with DHS. Additionally, DHS should improve the efficacy of the grant application and review process by mitigating duplication or redundancy within the various preparedness grant programs. Until DHS evaluates grant applications across grant programs, DHS cannot ascertain whether or to what extent multiple funding requests are being submitted for similar purposes. [2, p. 27]

Table 12-20: 2011 GAO Expectations for Emergency Preparedness and Response [2, pp. 45-46]

Functional Mission Area: Emergency Preparedness and Response
Sub Area #1: National Emergency Preparedness and Response Planning
1a: Develop a national incident management system
1b: Coordinate implementation of a national incident management system
1c: Establish and implement an all-hazards national response framework
1d: Coordinate implementation of an all-hazards response framework
1e: Develop a complete inventory of federal response capabilities
1f: Develop a national, all-hazards preparedness goal
1g: Develop a national preparedness system
1h: Develop a national preparedness report
1i: Support citizen participation in national preparedness efforts
1j: Develop plans and capabilities to strengthen nationwide recovery efforts
1k: Conduct and support risk assessments and risk management capabilities for emergency preparedness
1l: Establish a comprehensive preparedness assessment system
Sub Area #2: Provision of Emergency Assistance and Services
2a: Develop the capacity to provide needed emergency assistance and services in a timely manner
2b: Provide timely assistance and services to individuals and communities in response to emergency events
2c: Provide oversight of emergency response contracts
Sub Area #3: Emergency and Interoperable Communications
3a: Implement a program to improve interoperable communications among federal, state, and local agencies
3b: Implement procedures and capabilities for effective interoperable communications
3c: Increase the development and adoption of interoperability communications standards
3d: Develop and implement performance goals and measures to assess progress in developing interoperability
3e: Provide grant funding to first responders in developing and implementing interoperable communications capabilities
3f: Provide guidance and technical assistance to first responders in developing and implementing interoperable communications capabilities
3g: Coordinate research, development, and testing efforts to identify and develop technologies to facilitate sharing of emergency alerts and threat-related information
Sub Area #4: Support to State and Local Partners
4a: Provide assistance to state and local governments to develop all-hazards plans and capabilities
4b: Administer a program for providing grants and assistance to state and local governments and first responders
4c: Allocate grants based on assessment factors that account for population, critical infrastructure, and other risk factors
Sub Area #5: Emergency Preparedness Best Practices and Training and Exercise Programs
5a: Develop a system for collecting and disseminating lessons learned, best practices, and threat information to emergency responders and other relevant stakeholders
5b: Establish a comprehensive training program for national preparedness
5c: Establish a program for conducting emergency preparedness exercises
Sub Area #6: Emergency Preparedness Human Capital Management
6a: Develop and implement a strategic human capital plan, including filling vacancies and standards for credentialing personnel
6b: Ensure the capacity and readiness of disaster response teams

Overall, the 2011 GAO assessment found that since it began operations in 2003, DHS has implemented key homeland security operations and achieved important goals and milestones in many areas to create and strengthen a foundation to reach its potential. As it continues to mature, however, more work remains for DHS to address gaps and weaknesses in its current operational and implementation efforts, and to strengthen the efficiency and effectiveness of those efforts to achieve its full potential. DHS's accomplishments include developing strategic and operational plans; deploying workforces; and establishing new, or expanding existing, offices and programs. Such accomplishments are noteworthy given that DHS has had to work to transform itself into a fully functioning department while implementing its missions—a difficult undertaking that can take years to achieve. While DHS has made progress, its transformation remains high risk due to its management challenges. [2, p. ii]

Overall, the 2011 GAO Assessment found that since it began operations in 2003, DHS has implemented key homeland security operations and achieved important goals and milestones in many areas to create and strengthen a foundation to reach its potential.

2015 GAO Assessment

By 2015, DHS had grown to 240,000 employees and approximately $60 billion in budget authority. [3, p. 1] In 2003, GAO designated implementing and transforming DHS as high risk because DHS had to transform 22 agencies into one department, and failure to address associated risks could have serious consequences for U.S. national and economic security. As a result, in its 2013 high-risk update, GAO narrowed the scope of the high-risk area to focus on strengthening and integrating DHS management functions (human capital, acquisition, financial, and information technology). At the request of Congress, in February 2015 GAO took another look at DHS's progress and actions remaining in strengthening and integrating its management functions. [3, p. ii]

Key to addressing the department's management challenges is DHS demonstrating the ability to achieve sustained progress across 30 actions and outcomes that GAO identified and DHS agreed were needed to address the high-risk area. GAO found in its 2015 high-risk update report that DHS fully addressed 9 of these actions and outcomes, while work remains to fully address the remaining 21. Of the 9 actions and outcomes that DHS has addressed, 5 have been sustained as fully implemented for at least 2 years. For example, DHS fully met 1 outcome for the first time by obtaining a clean opinion on its financial statements for 2 consecutive years. DHS has also mostly addressed an additional 5 actions and outcomes, meaning that a small amount of work remains to fully address them. However, DHS has partially addressed 12 and initiated 4 of the remaining actions and outcomes. For example, DHS does not have modernized financial management systems, a fact that affects its ability to have ready access to reliable information for informed decision making. Addressing some of these actions and outcomes, such as modernizing the department's financial management systems and improving employee morale, are significant undertakings that will likely require multiyear efforts. In GAO's 2015 high-risk update report, GAO concluded that in the coming years, DHS needs to continue to show measurable, sustainable progress in implementing its key management initiatives and achieving the remaining 21 actions and outcomes. [3, p. ii]

While challenges remain for DHS across its range of missions, it has made considerable progress. DHS efforts to strengthen and integrate its management functions have resulted in the Department meeting two and partially meeting three of GAO's criteria for removal from the high-risk list. [3, p. ii]

Table 12-21: 2015 GAO Assessment of DHS Management Functions [3, p. ii]

Table 1: Assessment of Department of Homeland Security (DHS) Progress in Addressing the Strengthening *DHS Management Functions* High-Risk Area, as of February 2015

Criterion for removal from high-risk list	Met[a]	Partially met[b]	Not met[c]
Leadership commitment	X		
Corrective action plan	X		
Capacity		X	
Framework to monitor progress		X	
Demonstrated, sustained progress		X	
Total	**2**	**3**	**0**

Source: GAO analysis of DHS documents, interviews, and prior GAO reports. | GAO 15-388T

[a]"Met":There are no significant actions that need to be taken to further address this criterion.

[b]"Partially met": Some but not all actions necessary to generally meet the criterion have been taken.

[c]"Not met": Few, if any, actions toward meeting the criterion have been taken.

Conclusion

Since DHS' activation in March 2003, the General Accountability Office, the "watch dog" arm of U.S. government, has made approximately 2,200 recommendations to DHS to strengthen program management, performance measurement efforts, and management processes, among other things. DHS has implemented more than 69 percent of these recommendations and has actions under way to address others. [3, p. 1] As generally acknowledged, DHS remains a "work in progress". The key question, "are we safer" is undoubtedly a resounding "yes". Unfortunately, the nature of the threat makes it impossible to ever be completely safe, leading to the ultimate question about homeland security: "how safe at what cost?" The answer at present is unknown, and likely will never be answered conclusively.

Challenge Your Understanding

The following questions are designed to challenge your understanding of the material presented in this chapter. Some questions may require additional research outside this book in order to provide a complete answer.

1. What was the focus of the 2007 GAO Assessment?
2. According to the 2007 GAO Assessment, which DHS mission demonstrated the most progress?
3. According to the 2007 GAO Assessment, which DHS mission demonstrated the least progress?
4. Given the broad changes in organization and mission between 2003and 2007, do you think the GAO Assessment was accurate? Explain your answer.
5. How did the 2011 GAO Assessment differ from the 2007 GAO Assessment?
6. How did the highest performing mission in the 2007 GAO Assessment compare in the 2011 GAO Assessment?
7. How did the lowest performing mission in the 2007 GAO Assessment compare in the 2011 GAO Assessment?
8. Given the less expansive changes in organization and mission between 2007 and 2011, do you think the GAO Assessment was accurate? Explain your answer.
9. Do you think a member of Congress, trying to assess the return on taxpayer investment, would find the GAO assessments useful? Explain your answer.
10. Do you think yourself that the GAO assessments answer the question, "are we safer?"

Chapter 13

HS Enterprise

Learning Outcomes

Careful study of this chapter will help a student do the following:

- Explain the purpose of the homeland security enterprise.
- Describe the role of DHS with respect to the homeland security enterprise.
- Identify the roles and responsibilities of different members of the homeland security enterprise.

"This Nation can protect itself. But we must all play a role—and in the commitment of each, we will secure the homeland for all."

- 2010 Quadrennial Homeland Security Review

Introduction

9/11 marked a watershed in national security. 9/11 demonstrated the ability of small groups to wreak destructive power on a scale once only wielded by the military might of nations. Whereas national security was focused on protecting United States sovereignty among the community of nations, homeland security became necessary to protect United States citizens from the catastrophic designs of non-state actors, both foreign and domestic. This required an unprecedented level of cooperation between Federal, State, and Local law enforcement and the national security apparatus. With the addition of natural disasters to the list of catastrophic agents following Hurricane Katrina, it also required an unprecedented level of integration with the emergency response community. In order to safeguard the nation from domestic catastrophic incidents, the Department of Homeland Security must work together in close coordination with other Federal, State, and Local public and private agencies comprising the Homeland Security Enterprise.

Whereas national security was focused on protecting United States sovereignty among the community of nations, homeland security became necessary to protect United States citizens from the catastrophic designs of non-state actors, both foreign and domestic.

Homeland Security Enterprise

The Department of Homeland Security is one among many components of the Homeland Security Enterprise. In some areas, like securing borders or managing the immigration system, the Department possesses unique capabilities and, hence, responsibilities. In other areas, such as critical infrastructure protection or emergency management, the Department's role is largely one of leadership and stewardship on behalf of those who have the capabilities to get the job done. In still other areas, such as counterterrorism, defense, and diplomacy, other Federal departments and agencies have critical roles and responsibilities, including the Departments of Justice, Defense, and State, the Federal Bureau of Investigation, and the National Counterterrorism Center. Homeland security can only be optimized when the distributed and decentralized nature of the enterprise is oriented in pursuit of common goals. [1, p. iii]

The term "enterprise" refers to the collective efforts and shared responsibilities of Federal, State, Local, Tribal, Territorial, nongovernmental, and private-sector partners—as well as individuals, families, and communities—to maintain critical homeland security capabilities. It connotes a broad-based community with a common interest in the public safety and well-being of America and American society and is composed of multiple partners and stakeholders whose roles and responsibilities are distributed and shared. Yet it is important to remember that these partners and stakeholders face diverse risks, needs, and priorities. The challenge for the enterprise, then, is to balance these diverse needs and priorities, while focusing on shared interests and responsibilities to collectively secure the homeland. [1, p. 12]

With the establishment of homeland security, and the linking of domestic security concerns to broader national security interests and institutions, there is a temptation to view homeland security so broadly as to encompass all national security and domestic policy activities. This is not the case. Homeland security is deeply rooted in the security and resilience of the nation, and facilitating lawful interchange with the world. As such, it intersects with many other functions of government. Homeland security is built upon critical law enforcement functions, but is not about preventing all crimes or administering our Nation's judicial system. It is deeply embedded in trade activities, but is neither trade nor economic policy. It requires international engagement, but is not responsible for foreign affairs. Rather, homeland security is meant to connote a concerted, shared effort to ensure a homeland that is safe, secure, and resilient against terrorism and other hazards where American interests, aspirations, and way of life can thrive. [1, p. 13]

Homeland security spans the authorities and responsibilities of Federal departments and agencies, State, Local, Tribal and Territorial governments, the private sector, as well as private citizens and communities. For this reason, coordination and cooperation are essential to successfully carrying out and accomplishing the homeland security missions.

Homeland security spans the authorities and responsibilities of Federal departments and agencies, State, Local, Tribal and Territorial governments, the private sector, as well as private citizens and communities. For this reason, coordination and cooperation are essential to successfully carrying out and accomplishing the homeland security missions. Documents such as the National Infrastructure Protection Plan (NIPP) and National Response Framework (NRF), as well as documents produced by the National Counterterrorism Center, spell out roles and responsibilities for various aspects of homeland security. The following discussion highlights key current roles and responsibilities of the many actors across the Homeland Security Enterprise. They are derived largely from statutes, Presidential directives, and other authorities, as well as from the NIPP and NRF. [1, pp. A-1]

President of the United States

The President of the United States is the Commander in Chief and the leader of the Executive Branch of the Federal Government. The President, through the National Security Council and the National Security Staff, provides overall homeland security policy direction and coordination. [1, pp. A-1]

Secretary of Homeland Security

The Secretary of Homeland Security leads the Federal agency as defined by statute charged with homeland security: preventing terrorism and managing risks to critical infrastructure; securing and managing the border; enforcing and administering immigration laws; safeguarding and securing cyberspace; and ensuring resilience to disasters. [1, pp. A-1]

United States Attorney General

The Attorney General has lead responsibility for criminal investigations of terrorist acts or terrorist threats by individuals or groups inside the United States, or directed at United States citizens or institutions abroad, as well as for related intelligence collection activities within the United States. Following a terrorist threat or an actual incident that falls within the criminal jurisdiction of the United States, the Attorney General identifies the perpetrators and brings them to justice. The Attorney General leads the Department of Justice, which also includes the Federal Bureau of Investigation, Drug Enforcement Administration, and Bureau of Alcohol, Tobacco, Firearms, and Explosives, each of which has key homeland security responsibilities. [1, pp. A-1]

Secretary of State

The Secretary of State has the responsibility to coordinate activities with foreign governments and international organizations related to the prevention, preparation, response, and recovery from a domestic incident, and for the protection of U.S. citizens and U.S. interests overseas. The Department of State also adjudicates and screens visa applications abroad. [1, pp. A-1]

Secretary of Defense

The Secretary of Defense leads the Department of Defense, whose military services, defense agencies, and geographic and functional commands defend the United States from direct attack, deter potential adversaries, foster regional stability, secure and assure access to sea, air, space, and cyberspace, and build the security capacity of key partners. DOD also provides a wide range of support to civil authorities at the direction of the Secretary of Defense or the President when the capabilities of State and Local authorities to respond effectively to an event are overwhelmed. [1, pp. A-2]

Secretary of Health and Human Services

The Secretary of Health and Human Services leads the coordination of all functions relevant to Public Health Emergency Preparedness and Disaster Medical Response. Additionally, the Department of Health and Human Services (HHS) incorporates steady-state and incident-specific activities as described in the National Health Security Strategy. HHS is the coordinator and primary agency for Emergency Support Function (ESF) #8 – Public Health and Medical Services, providing the mechanism for coordinated Federal assistance to supplement State, local, tribal, and territorial resources in response to a public health and medical disaster, potential or actual incident requiring a coordinated Federal response, and/or during a developing potential health and medical emergency. HHS is also the Sector-Specific Agency for the Healthcare and Public Health Sector. [1, pp. A-2]

Secretary of the Treasury

The Secretary of the Treasury works to safeguard the U.S. financial system, combat financial crimes, and cut off financial support to terrorists, WMD proliferators, drug traffickers, and other national security threats. [1, pp. A-2]

Secretary of Agriculture

The Secretary of Agriculture provides leadership on food, agriculture, natural resources, rural development, and related issues based on sound public policy, the best available science, and efficient management. The Department of Agriculture (USDA) is the Sector-Specific Agency for the Food and Agriculture Sector, a responsibility shared with the Food and Drug Administration with respect to food safety and defense. In addition, USDA is the coordinator and primary agency for two Emergency Support Functions: ESF #4 – Firefighting and ESF #11 – Agriculture and Natural Resources. USDA, together with the Department of the Interior, also operates the National Interagency Fire Center. [1, pp. A-2]

Director of National Intelligence

The Director of National Intelligence serves as the head of the Intelligence Community (IC), acts as the principal advisor to the President and National Security Council for intelligence matters relating to national security, and oversees and directs implementation of the National Intelligence Program. The IC, composed of 16 elements across the U.S. Government, functions consistent with law, Executive order, regulations, and policy to support the national security-related missions of the U.S. Government. It provides a range of analytic products that assess threats to the homeland and inform planning, capability development, and operational activities of homeland security enterprise partners and stakeholders. In addition to IC elements with specific homeland security missions, the Office of the Director of National Intelligence maintains a number of mission and support centers that provide unique capabilities for homeland security partners, including the National Counterterrorism Center (NCTC), National Counterproliferation Center, and National Counterintelligence Executive. NCTC serves as the primary U.S. government organization for analyzing and integrating all intelligence pertaining to terrorism and counterterrorism, and conducts strategic operational planning for integrated counterterrorism activities. [1, pp. A-3]

Secretary of Commerce

The Secretary of Commerce, supportive of national economic security interests and responsive to Public Law and Executive direction, is responsible for promulgating Federal information technology and cybersecurity standards; regulating export of security technologies; representing U.S. industry on international trade policy and commercial data flow matters; security and privacy policies that apply to the Internet's domain name system; protecting intellectual property; conducting cybersecurity research and development; and assuring timely availability of industrial products, materials, and services to meet homeland security requirements. [1, pp. A-3]

Secretary of Education

The Secretary of Education oversees discretionary grants and technical assistance to help schools plan for and respond to emergencies that disrupt teaching and learning. The Department of Education is a supporting Federal agency in the response and management of emergencies under the National Response Framework. [1, pp. A-3]

Secretary of Energy

The Secretary of Energy maintains stewardship of vital national security capabilities, from nuclear weapons to leading edge research and development programs. The Department of Energy (DOE) is the designated Federal agency to provide a unifying structure for the integration of Federal critical infrastructure and key resources protection efforts specifically for the Energy Sector. It is also responsible for maintaining continuous and reliable energy supplies for the United States through preventive measures and restoration and recovery actions. DOE is the coordinator and primary agency for ESF #12 – Energy when incidents require a coordinated Federal response to facilitate the restoration of damaged energy systems and components. [1, pp. A-3]

Environmental Protection Agency

The Administrator of the Environmental Protection Agency (EPA) leads the EPA, which is charged with protecting human health and the environment. For certain incidents, EPA is the coordinator and primary agency for ESF #10 – Oil and Hazardous Materials Response, in response to an actual or potential discharge and/or uncontrolled release of oil or hazardous materials. EPA is the Sector-Specific Agency for securing the Water Sector. [1, pp. A-4]

Secretary of Housing and Urban Development

The Secretary of Housing and Urban Development is the coordinator and primary agency for ESF #14 – Long-Term Community Recovery, which provides a mechanism for coordinating Federal support to State, tribal, regional, and local governments, nongovernmental organizations (NGOs), and the private sector to enable community recovery from the long-term consequences of extraordinary disasters.

Secretary of the Interior

The Secretary of the Interior develops policies and procedures for all types of hazards and emergencies that impact Federal lands, facilities, infrastructure, and resources; tribal lands; and insular areas. The Department of the Interior (DOI) is also a primary agency for ESF #9 – Search and Rescue, providing specialized lifesaving assistance to State, tribal, and local authorities when activated for incidents or potential incidents requiring a coordinated Federal response. DOI, together with the Department of Agriculture, also operates the National Interagency Fire Center. [1, pp. A-4]

Secretary of Transportation

The Secretary of Transportation collaborates with DHS on all matters relating to transportation security and transportation infrastructure protection and in regulating the transportation of hazardous materials by all modes (including pipelines). The Secretary of Transportation is responsible for operating the national airspace system. [1, pp. A-4]

Other Federal Agencies

Other Federal Agencies are also part of the homeland security enterprise and contribute to the homeland security mission in a variety of ways. This includes agencies with responsibilities for regulating elements of the Nation's critical infrastructure to assure public health, safety, and the common defense, developing and implementing pertinent public policy, supporting efforts to assure a resilient homeland, and collaborating with those departments and agencies noted above in their efforts to secure the homeland. [1, pp. A-4]

Critical Infrastructure Owners and Operators

Critical Infrastructure and Key Resource (CIKR) Owners and Operators develop protective programs and measures to ensure that systems and assets, whether physical or virtual, are secure from and resilient to cascading, disruptive impacts. Protection includes actions to mitigate the overall risk to CIKR assets, systems, networks, functions, or their interconnecting links, including actions to deter the threat, mitigate vulnerabilities, or minimize the consequences associated with a terrorist attack or other incident. CIKR owners and operators also prepare business continuity plans and ensure their own ability to sustain essential services and functions. [1, pp. A-5]

Major and Multinational Corporations

Major and Multinational Corporations operate in all sectors of trade and commerce that foster the American way of life and support the operation, security, and resilience of global movement systems. They take action to support risk management planning and investments in security as a necessary component of prudent business planning and operations. They contribute to developing the ideas, science, and technology that underlie innovation in homeland security. During times of disaster, they provide response resources (donated or compensated)—including specialized teams, essential service providers, equipment, and advanced technologies—through public-private emergency plans/partnerships or mutual aid and assistance agreements, or in response to requests from government and nongovernmental-volunteer initiatives. [1, pp. A-5]

Small Business

Small Businesses contribute to all aspects of homeland security and employ more than half of all private-sector workers. They support response efforts by developing contingency plans and working with local planners to ensure that their plans are consistent with pertinent response procedures. When small businesses can survive and quickly recover from disasters, the Nation and economy are more secure and more resilient. They perform research and development, catalyze new thinking, and serve as engines of innovation for development of new solutions to key challenges in homeland security. [1, pp. A-5]

Governors

Governors are responsible for overseeing their State's threat prevention activities as well the State's response to any emergency or disaster, and take an active role in ensuring that other State officials and agencies address the range of homeland security threats, hazards, and challenges. During an emergency, Governors will play a number of roles, including the State's chief communicator Critical Infrastructure and Key Resource (CIKR) Owners and Operators develop protective programs and measures to ensure that systems and assets, whether physical or virtual, are secure from and resilient to cascading, disruptive impacts. Protection includes actions to mitigate the overall risk to CIKR assets, systems, networks, functions, or their interconnecting links, including actions to deter the threat, mitigate vulnerabilities, or minimize the consequences associated with a terrorist attack or other incident. CIKR owners and operators also prepare business continuity plans and ensure their own ability to sustain essential services and functions. [1, pp. A-5]

State and Territorial Governments

State and Territorial Governments coordinate the activity of cities, counties, and intrastate regions. States administer Federal homeland security grants to local and tribal (in certain grant programs) governments, allocating key resources to bolster their prevention and preparedness capabilities. State agencies conduct law enforcement and security activities, protect the Governor and other executive leadership, and administer State programs that address the range of homeland security threats, hazards, and challenges. States government officials lead statewide disaster and mitigation planning. During response, States coordinate resources and capabilities throughout the State and are responsible for requesting and obtaining resources and capabilities from surrounding States. States often mobilize these substantive resources and capabilities to supplement the local efforts before, during, and after incidents. [1, pp. A-6]

Tribal Leaders

Tribal Leaders are responsible for the public safety and welfare of their membership. They can serve as both key decision makers and trusted sources of public information during incidents. [1, pp. A-6]

Tribal Governments

Tribal Governments, which have a special status under Federal laws and treaties, ensure the provision of essential services to members within their communities, and are responsible for developing emergency response and mitigation plans. Tribal governments may coordinate resources and capabilities with neighboring jurisdictions, and establish mutual aid agreements with other tribal governments, local jurisdictions, and State governments. Depending on location, land base, and resources, tribal governments provide law enforcement, fire, and emergency services as well as public safety to their members. [1, pp. A-6]

Mayors and Other Elected Officials

Mayors and other local elected and appointed officials (such as city managers) are responsible for ensuring the public safety and welfare of their residents, serving as their jurisdiction's chief communicator and a primary source of information for homeland security-related information, and ensuring their governments are able to carry out emergency response activities. They serve as both key decision makers and trusted sources of public information during incidents. [1, pp. A-6]

Local Governments

Local Governments provide front-line leadership for local law enforcement, fire, public safety, environmental response, public health, and emergency medical services for all manner of hazards and emergencies. Through the Urban Areas Security Initiative (UASI) program, cities (along with counties in many cases) address multijurisdictional planning and operations, equipment support and purchasing, and training and exercises in support of high-threat, high-density urban areas. UASI grants assist local governments in building and sustaining homeland security capabilities. Local governments coordinate resources and capabilities during disasters with neighboring jurisdictions, NGOs, the State, and the private sector. [1, pp. A-7]

County Leaders

County Leaders serve as chief operating officers of county governments, both rural and urban. This includes supporting and enabling the county governments to fulfill their responsibilities to constituents, including public safety and security. In some States, elected county officials such as sheriffs or judges also serve as emergency managers, search and rescue officials, and chief law enforcement officers. [1, pp. A-7]

County Governments

County Governments provide front-line leadership for local law enforcement, fire, public safety, environmental response, public health, and emergency medical services for all manner of hazards and emergencies. In many cases, county government officials participate in UASIs with other urban jurisdictions to assist local governments in building and sustaining capabilities to prevent, protect against, respond to, and recover from threats or acts of terrorism. County governments coordinate resources and capabilities during disasters with neighboring jurisdictions, NGOs, the State, and the private sector. [1, pp. A-7]

American Red Cross

The American Red Cross is a supporting agency to the mass care functions of ESF #6 – Mass Care, Emergency Assistance, Housing, and Human Services under the NRF. As the Nation's largest mass care service provider, the American Red Cross provides sheltering, feeding, bulk distribution of needed items, basic first aid, welfare information, and casework, among other services, at the local level as needed. In its role as a service provider, the American Red Cross works closely with local, tribal, and State governments to provide mass care services to victims of every disaster, large and small, in an affected area. [1, pp. A-7]

Voluntary Organizations Active in Disaster

National Voluntary Organizations Active in Disaster (National VOAD) is a consortium of approximately 50 national organizations and 55 State and territory equivalents that typically send representatives to the Federal Emergency Management Agency's National Response Coordination Center to represent the voluntary organizations and assist in response coordination. Members of National VOAD form a coalition of nonprofit organizations that respond to disasters as part of their overall mission. [1, pp. A-8]

Nongovernmental Organizations

Nongovernmental Organizations (NGOs) provide sheltering, emergency food supplies, counseling services, and other vital support services to support response and promote the recovery of disaster victims. They often provide specialized services that help individuals with special needs, including those with disabilities, and provide resettlement assistance and services to arriving refugees. NGOs also play key roles in engaging communities to integrate lawful immigrants into American society and reduce the marginalization or radicalization of these groups. [1, pp. A-8]

Community Organizations

Communities and community organizations foster the development of organizations and organizational capacity that act toward a common goal (such as Neighborhood Watch, Community Emergency Response Teams, or providing emergency food or shelter). These groups may possess the knowledge and understanding of the threats, local response capabilities, and special needs within their jurisdictions and have the capacity necessary to alert authorities of those threats, capabilities, or needs. Additionally, during an incident these groups may be critical in passing along vital incident communications to individuals and families, and to supporting critical response activities in the initial stages of a crisis. [1, pp. A-8]

Individuals and Families

Individuals and Families take the basic steps to prepare themselves for emergencies, including understanding the threats and hazards that they may face, reducing hazards in and around their homes, preparing an emergency supply kit and household emergency plans (that include care for pets and service animals), monitoring emergency communications carefully, volunteering with established organizations, mobilizing or helping to ensure community preparedness, enrolling in training courses, and practicing what to do in an emergency. These individual and family preparedness activities strengthen community resilience and mitigate the impact of disasters. In addition, individual vigilance and awareness can help communities remain safer and bolster prevention efforts. [1, pp. A-8]

Conclusion

In order to safeguard the nation from domestic catastrophic incidents requires the collective and coordinated efforts of many agencies, organizations, and individuals. While the nation looks to the Department of Homeland Security to lead the way, homeland security is an enterprise. Each of us—government, business, and individual alike—has a role to play in contributing to the collective strength of this country. [1, p. 78]

Challenge Your Understanding

The following questions are designed to challenge your understanding of the material presented in this chapter. Some questions may require additional research outside this book in order to provide a complete answer.

1. Why is a homeland security "enterprise" necessary?
2. What are the essential elements required to make the homeland security enterprise work?
3. Which member of the enterprise is responsible for overseeing their State's threat prevention activities as well the State's response to any emergency or disaster?
4. Which member of the enterprise serves as the head of the Intelligence Community, acts as the principal advisor to the President and National Security Council for intelligence matters relating to national security?
5. Which member of the enterprise provides sheltering, emergency food supplies, counseling services, and other vital services to support response and promote the recovery of disaster victims?
6. Which member of the enterprise provides front-line leadership for local law enforcement, fire, public safety, environmental response, public health, and emergency medical services for all manner of hazards and emergencies?
7. Which member of the enterprise is responsible for criminal investigations of terrorist acts inside the United States, or directed at United States citizens or institutions abroad, as well as for related intelligence collection activities within the United States?
8. Which member of the enterprise defends the United States from direct attack, deters potential adversaries, fosters regional stability, secures and assures access to sea, air, space, and cyberspace?
9. Which member of the enterprise is responsible for taking basic steps to prepare themselves for emergencies and understanding the threats and hazards that they may face?
10. Which member of the enterprise is the coordinator and primary agency in response to an actual or potential discharge and/or uncontrolled release of oil or hazardous materials?

Part III: Mission Areas

In this section we will examine the missions performed by the Department of Homeland Security to safeguard the U.S. from domestic catastrophic destruction. These missions are defined in the 2014 Quadrennial Homeland Security Review and are re-evaluated every four years under the QHSR process. As was seen in Chapter 11, these missions have evolved since DHS' activation in 2003. Still, they remain grounded in the strategic implications and tactical lessons learned from 9/11. From a strategic standpoint, they address the means for committing domestic catastrophic destruction by protecting critical infrastructure, countering weapons of mass destruction, and securing cyberspace. From a tactical perspective, they seek to plug the holes exposed on 9/11, and subsequent attacks in Madrid (2004) and London (2007), by rooting out those with malicious intent, preventing them from entering the country or otherwise smuggling in WMD, and tightening security within our mass transit systems. However, because no defense is invulnerable and we cannot stop the destructive forces of nature, the ability to mount a coordinated response and recovery remains critical to saving lives and alleviating suffering. In order to facilitate understanding, each chapter is organized to 1) describe the problem, 2) explain what's being done to address it, 3) what has been accomplished and, 4) what remains to be done.

Chapter 14

Critical Infrastructure Protection

Learning Outcomes

Careful study of this chapter will help a student do the following:

- Explain how the importance of critical infrastructure protection was realized before 9/11.
- Describe how critical infrastructure protection has been shaped and evolved since PDD - 63.
- Explain the role of the Federal government in critical infrastructure protection.
- Assess the importance of various steps in the Risk Management Framework.

"We did find widespread capability to exploit infrastructure vulnerabilities. The capability to do harm—particularly through information networks—is real; it is growing at an alarming rate; and we have little defense against it."

- 1997 President's Commission on Critical Infrastructure Protection

Introduction

In July 1996, President Clinton appointed a Commission on Critical Infrastructure Protection to report on the scope and nature of vulnerabilities and threats to the nation's critical infrastructure. The Commission found concern for cyber attack. As a result, in May 1998, President Clinton issued PDD-63 setting a national goal to protect the nation's critical infrastructure from intentional attack.

9/11 thrust critical infrastructure protection to the forefront of US security concerns. Previously, in July 1996 President Clinton appointed a Commission on Critical Infrastructure Protection to report the scope and nature of vulnerabilities and threats to the nation's critical infrastructure, and recommend a comprehensive national plan for protecting them including any necessary regulatory changes. The Commission was chartered in response to growing concerns stemming from the 1993 attack on the World Trade Center in New York City, 1995 bombing of the Murrah Federal Building in Oklahoma City, and 1996 bombing of the Khobar Towers US military barracks in Dhahran Saudi Arabia. Examining both the physical and cyber vulnerabilities, the Commission found no immediate crisis threatening the nation's infrastructures. However, it did find reason to take action, especially in the area of cybersecurity. The rapid growth of a computer-literate population (implying a greater pool of potential hackers), the inherent vulnerabilities of common protocols in computer networks, the easy availability of hacker "tools" (available on many websites), and the fact that the basic tools of the hacker (computer, modem, telephone line) were the same essential technologies used by the general population indicated to the Commission that both threat and vulnerability exist. The Commission Report, released in October 1997, led to Presidential Decision Directive No. 63 (PDD-63) issued in May 1998. PDD-63 set as a national goal the ability to protect the nation's critical infrastructure from intentional attacks (both physical and cyber) by the year 2003. According to the PDD, any interruptions in the ability of these infrastructures to provide their goods and services must be "brief, infrequent, manageable, geographically isolated, and minimally detrimental to the welfare of the United States". [1, p. 4]

PDD-63

PDD-63 identified a set of twelve infrastructure "sectors" whose assets should be protected: information and communications; banking and finance; water supply; aviation, highways, mass transit, pipelines, rail, and waterborne commerce; emergency and law enforcement services; emergency, fire, and continuity of government services; public health services; electric power, oil and gas production, and storage. A federal Lead Agency (LA) was assigned to each of these "sectors". Each Lead Agency was directed to appoint a Sector Liaison Official to interact with appropriate private sector organizations. The private sector was encouraged to select a Sector Coordinator to work with the agency's sector liaison official. Together, the liaison official, sector coordinator, and all affected parties were to contribute to a Sector Security Plan (SSP) which was to be integrated into a National Infrastructure Assurance Plan. [1, p. 4]

Following the attacks of September 11, 2001, critical infrastructure protection became a high priority. On October 16, 2001, President Bush signed Executive Order (EO) 13231 stating that it is US policy "to protect against the disruption of the operation of information systems for critical infrastructure ... and to ensure that any disruptions that occur are infrequent, of minimal duration, and manageable, and cause the least damage possible." On October 26, 2001, President Bush signed into law the USA PATRIOT Act, defining critical infrastructure as "systems and assets, whether physical or virtual, so vital to the United States that the incapacity or destruction of such systems and assets would have a debilitating impact on security, national economic security, national public health or safety, or any combination of those matters". In July 2002, the Office of Homeland Security released the first National Strategy for Homeland Security. It identified protecting the nation's critical infrastructures and key assets as one of six critical mission areas. The Strategy also expanded upon the list of sectors considered to comprise critical infrastructure to include public health, the chemical industry and hazardous materials, postal and shipping, the defense industrial base, and agriculture and food. Key assets were defined later to include national monuments and other historic attractions, dams, nuclear facilities, and large commercial centers, including office buildings and sport stadiums, where large numbers of people congregate to conduct business, personal transactions, or enjoy recreational activities. Then on December 17, 2003, the Bush Administration released Homeland Security Presidential Directive No. 7 (HSPD-7). HSPD-7 essentially updated the policy of the United States and the roles and responsibilities of various agencies in regard to critical infrastructure protection as outlined in previous documents, national strategies, and the Homeland Security Act of 2002. For example, the Directive reiterated the Secretary of Homeland Security's role in coordinating the overall national effort to protect critical infrastructure. It also reiterated the role of Sector-Specific Agencies (formerly "Lead Agencies") to work with their sectors to identify, prioritize, and coordinate protective measures. The Directive captured the expanded set of critical infrastructures and key assets and Sector-Specific Agencies assignments made in the National Strategy for Homeland Security. One major difference between PDD-63 and the Bush Administration's efforts was a shift in focus. PDD-63 focused on cybersecurity. While the post-September 11 effort was still concerned with cybersecurity, its focus on physical threats, especially those that might cause mass casualties, was greater than the pre-September 11 effort. [1, p. 12]

In December 2003, President Bush issued HSPD-7 updating national policy on critical infrastructure protection, following the same pattern established in PDD-63. Because 9/11 had succeeded in subverting critical infrastructure in a physical attack, HSPD-7 gave greater emphasis to physical protection compared to PDD-63's emphasis on cybersecurity.

HSPD-7

HSPD-7 directed development of a National Plan for Critical Infrastructure and Key Resources Protection to outline national goals, objectives, milestones, and key initiatives. Previously, PDD-63 had called for development of a National Infrastructure Assurance Plan. The corresponding focus on cybersecurity resulted in the National Plan for Information Systems Protection released in January 2000. While this plan formed the basis for the 2003 National Strategy to Secure Cyberspace, it did not support the revised focus on physical security stemming from 9/11. After two furtive

Table 14-1: CIP Directives, Strategies, & Plans

HS Law	HS Directives	HS Strategies	CIP Plans
2002 HSA	1998 PDD-63	2002 NSHS	2005 Interim NIPP
	2003 HSPD-7	2007 NSHS	2005 Draft NIPP
	2013 PPD-21	2010 NSS	2006 NIPP
		2015 NSS	2009 NIPP
			2013 NIPP

In February 2013, President Obama issue PPD-21 again updating national policy on critical infrastructure protection. PPD-21 restored emphasis on cybersecurity, and introduced the concept of resilience.

attempts in 2005, the Department of Homeland Security (DHS) released the National Infrastructure Protection Plan (NIPP) in June 2006. The NIPP identified and integrated specific processes to guide an integrated national risk management effort. It defined and standardized, across all sectors, a Risk Management Framework (RMF) process for identifying and selecting assets for further analysis, identifying threats and conducting threat assessments, assessing vulnerabilities to those threats, analyzing consequences, determining risks, identifying potential risk mitigation activities, and prioritizing those activities based on cost effectiveness. The NIPP also called for implementation plans for these risk reduction activities, with timelines and responsibilities identified, and tied to resources. Each Sector-Specific Agency (SSA) was to work with its sector to generate Sector Specific Plans, utilizing the processes outlined in the NIPP. DHS was to use these same processes to integrate the sector specific plans into a national plan identifying those assets and risk reduction plans that require national level attention because of the risk the incapacitation of those assets pose to the nation as a whole. The NIPP was updated in 2009 to adopt an "all-hazards" approach to risk management, and again in 2013 to emphasize the importance of resilience. [1, p. 24]

PPD-21

In February 2013, the Obama Administration issued Presidential Policy Directive No. 21 (PPD-21), Critical Infrastructure Security and Resilience, superseding HSPD-7. PPD-21 made no major changes in policy, roles and responsibilities, or programs, but did order an evaluation of the existing public-private partnership model, the identification of baseline data and system requirements for efficient information exchange, and the development of a situational awareness capability (a continuous policy objective since President Clinton's PDD- 63). PPD-21 reflected an increased interest in resilience and all-hazard approach that has evolved in critical infrastructure policy over the years. It also updated sector designations, but made no major changes in Sector-Specific Agency designations. However, PPD-21 did give the energy and communications sectors a higher profile, due to the Administration's assessment of their importance to the operations of the other infrastructures. To date, the Obama Administration has kept or slowly evolved the policies, organizational structures, and programs governing physical security of critical infrastructure assets. It has focused much more effort to expand upon the cybersecurity policies and programs associated with critical infrastructure protection. [1, pp. 13-14]

Table 14-2: Infrastructure Sectors and Lead/Sector-Specific Agencies

1998 PDD-63			2003 HSPD-7			2013 PPD-21		
#	Sector	LA	#	Sector	SSA	#	Sector	SSA
1.	Intelligence	CIA	1.	Chemical	DHS	1.	Chemical	DHS
2.	Information & Communications	DOC	2.	Commercial Facilities	DHS	2.	Commercial Facilities	DHS
3.	National Defense	DOD	3.	Communications	DHS	3.	Communications	DHS
4.	Electric, Power, Gas, & Oil	DOE	4.	Critical Manufacturing	DHS	4.	Critical Manufacturing	DHS
5.	Emergency Law Enforcement	DOJ	5.	Dams	DHS	5.	Dams	DHS
6.	Law Enforcement & Internal Security	DOJ	6.	Emergency Services	DHS	6.	Emergency Services	DHS
7.	Foreign Affairs	DOS	7.	Government Facilities	DHS	7.	Information Technology	DHS
8.	Transportation	DOT	8.	Information Technology	DHS	8.	Nuclear Reactors, Materials, & Waste	DHS
9.	Water	EPA	9.	Nuclear Reactors, Materials, & Waste	DHS	9.	Transportation Systems	DHS & DOT
10.	Emergency Fire Service	FEMA	10.	Postal & Shipping	DHS	10.	Government Facilities	DHS & GSA
11.	Emergency Medicine	HHS	11.	Defense Industrial Base	DOD	11.	Defense Industrial Base	DOD
12.	Banking & Finance	TREAS	12.	Energy	DOE	12.	Energy	DOE
			13.	National Monuments & Icons	DOI	13.	Water & Wastewater Systems	EPA
			14.	Transportation Systems	DHS & DOT	14.	Healthcare & Public Health	HHS
			15.	Water	EPA	15.	Financial Services	TREAS
			16.	Healthcare & Public Health	HHS	16.	Food & Agriculture	USDA
			17.	Banking & Finance	TREAS			
			18.	Agriculture & Food	USDA			

Risk Management Framework

The Risk Management Framework has evolved since it was first introduced in the 2005 Interim National Infrastructure Protection Plan. [2, p. 8] Yet it remains, as currently prescribed in the 2013 National Infrastructure Protection Plan, a continuous process for incrementally reducing vulnerability within critical infrastructure. The Risk Management Framework is conducted in voluntary cooperation between the Department of Homeland Security and public and private partners organized into Sector Coordinating Councils representing the sixteen infrastructure sectors listed in Table 2. [3, pp. 10-11] The Risk Management Framework is conducted in five steps comprised of 1) Set Goals and Objectives, 2) Identify Infrastructure, 3) Assess and Analyze Risks, 4) Implement Risk Management Activities, and 5) Measure Effectiveness. [3, p. 15]

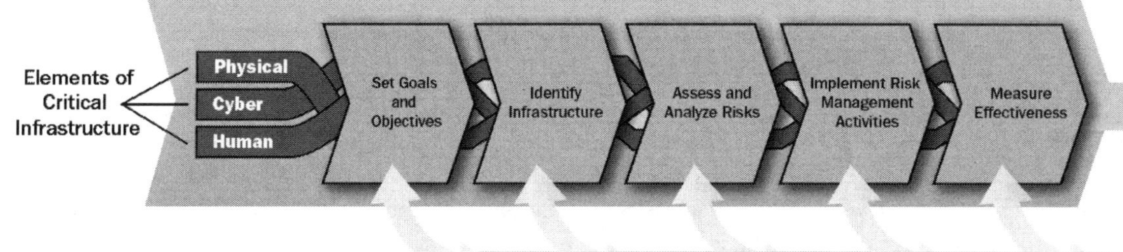

Figure 14-1: 2013 NIPP Risk Management Framework [3, p. 15]

The DHS Risk Management Framework is the implementing procedure of the National Infrastructure Protection Plan.

RMF Step 1: Set Goals and Objectives. The risk reduction priorities for each sector are established in Sector Specific Plans (SSPs). [3, p. 16] The first SSPs were released in May 2007, after the first official National Infrastructure Protection Plan was issued in 2006. Of the 17 plans drafted, 7 were made available to the public. The other 11 plans were designated "For Official Use Only" and withheld from public release. A review by the Government Accountability Office found that while all the plans complied, more or less, with NIPP requirements, some were more developed and comprehensive than others. The Sector Security Plans were revised in 2010 after the NIPP was revised in 2009. HSPD-7 stipulated that the SSPs should be updated annually. However, in 2010, DHS and its sector partners decided that a four-year cycle was sufficient for updating the SSPs. [1, pp. 23-24] As of 2015, the SSPs had yet to be updated and the most recent versions were dated 2010.

RMF Step 2: Identify Infrastructure. Despite the definition in the USA PATRIOT Act, critical infrastructure identification has been fraught with difficulties. While the National Infrastructure Protection Plan was still under development, the Department of Homeland Security undertook Operation Liberty Shield to catalog the nation's critical infrastructure in advance of the U.S. invasion of Iraq. Over the summer of 2003, DHS personnel cataloged 160 assets across various sectors it determined needed additional protection or mitigation against potential attack. Under pressure from Congress, the list was expanded to 1,849 assets and called the Protected Measures Target list (PMTL). At the same time it was conducting Operation Liberty Shield, DHS issued a grant asking states to conduct a critical infrastructure self-assessment. The resulting data call added another 26,359 assets to the PMTL, including zoos, festivals, shopping centers, and other "out-of-place" assets. [4, p. 6] The dubious results were attributed to "minimal guidance" given to the states. Accordingly, in July 2004 DHS issued a second data call to correct the problems from the 2003 data call. The 2004 data call included more precise instructions in the form of separate Guidelines for Identifying National Level Critical Infrastructure and Key Resources. States responded by submitting 47,701 additional assets to the PMTL. Together, the combined data from Operation Liberty Shield and 2003 and 2004 data calls comprised 77,069 assets of what DHS called the National Asset Database (NADB). Still, the DHS Inspector General noted that the list contained too many "out-of-place" assets, making subsequent prioritization difficult. [4, pp. 8-10] Congress intervened with the Implementing Recommendations of the 9/11 Commission Act which mandated the establishment of a second database containing a prioritized list of assets. [5] DHS complied with Congress by initiating the National Critical Infrastructure Prioritization Program (NCIPP) working with public and private partners to identify and classify critical infrastructure as either Level 1 or Level 2 priority based on the consequences associated with the asset's disruption or destruction. [6, p. 4] In 2006, the NADB was replaced by the Infrastructure Information Collection System (IICS) available from the DHS Infrastructure Protection Gateway. [7] According to the 2013 NIPP, the National Critical Infrastructure Prioritization Program remains the primary program for prioritizing critical infrastructure at the national level. [6, p. 17] The number and identity of assets collected by NCIPP is protected information unavailable to the public.

The Risk Management Framework is a risk-based methodology for prioritizing allocation of scarce national resources to reducing vulnerabilities among critical infrastructure.

RMF Step 3: Assess and Analyze Risks. DHS Protective Security Advisors (PSAs) located in all fifty States and Puerto Rico conduct Security Surveys and Resilience Assessments under the Enhanced Critical Infrastructure Protection (ECIP) and Regional Resiliency Assessment Program (RRAP). [8] According to DHS guidance, PSAs are to conduct Site Assistance Visits (SAVs) with infrastructure owners and operators within their districts giving priority to Level 1 assets. PSAs use an Infrastructure Survey Tool to gather information on 1,500 variables covering six major components and forty-two subcomponents. The results are compiled by Argonne National Laboratory into a "dashboard" indicating the asset's overall protective measure score and compare it with the scores of similar assets that have previously undergone a Security Survey. The interactive dashboard allows owners to consider alternative security upgrades and see how they affect the overall security of the asset as shown in Figure 2. PSA Security Surveys are done in voluntary cooperation with infrastructure owner/operators. [9, pp. 9-10] Out of 2,195 Security Surveys and 655 Vulnerability Assessments conducted during fiscal years 2009 through 2011, GAO identified a total of 135 Security Surveys and 44 Vulnerability Assessments that matched assets on the NCIPP list of high-priority assets. GAO also identified an additional 106 Security Surveys and 23 Vulnerability Assessments that were potential matches with assets on the NCIPP lists of priority assets, but could not be certain that the assets were the same because of inconsistencies in the way the data were recorded in the two different databases. All told, GAO determined that in two years DHS had conducted 241 Security Surveys and 67 Vulnerability Assessments on high-priority assets listed in the NCIPP database. [9, pp. 15-17]

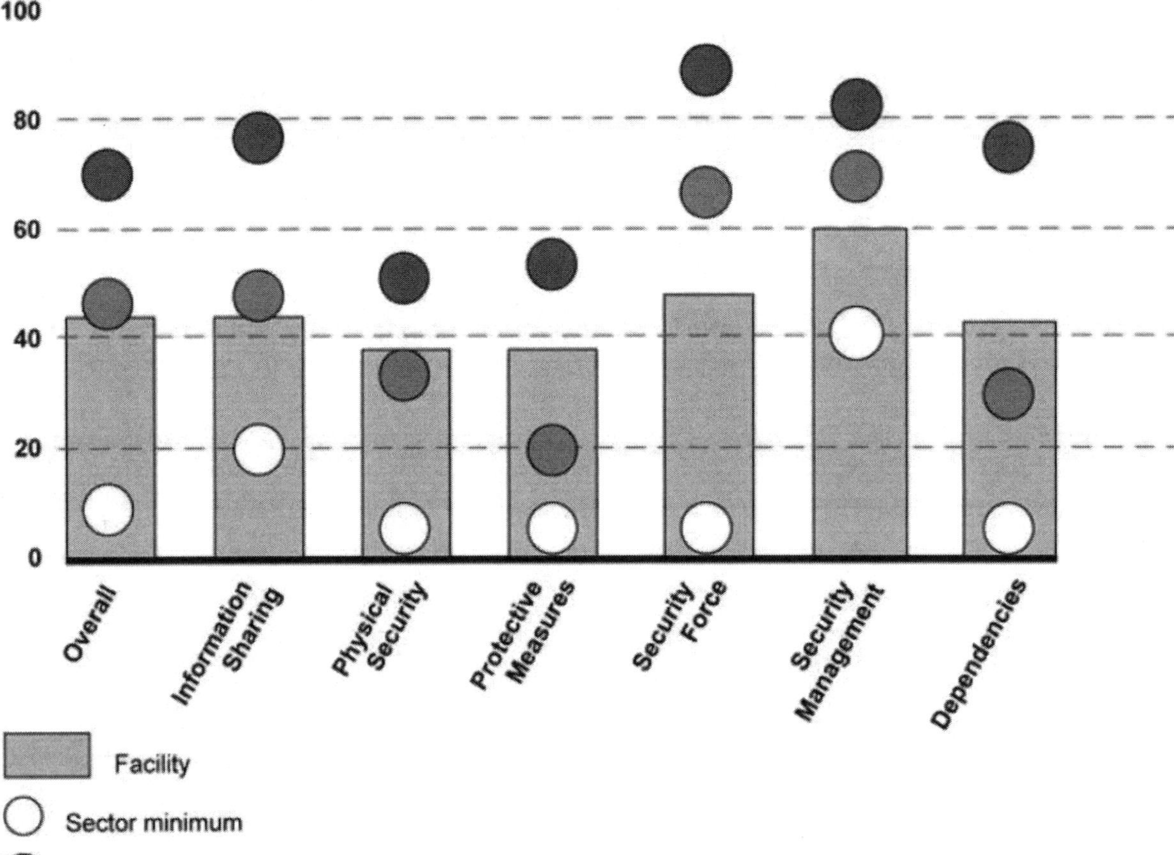

Figure 14-2: PSA Security Survey Example "Dashboard" Results

The Infrastructure Survey Tool is but one method for performing risk analysis on critical infrastructure. Over the years, each sector has developed its own set of risk analysis tools. The 2010 Sector Security Plan for Water identifies three assessment tools: 1) Risk Assessment Methodology-Water (RAM-W), 2) Security and Environmental Management System (SEMS); and 3) Vulnerability Self-Assessment Tool (VSAT). [10, p. 27] Similarly, the 2010 Transportation Systems Sector Specific Plan cites the use of the Aviation Modal Risk Assessment (AMRA) as part of a broader Transportation Systems Sector Security Risk Assessment (TSSRA) program. [11, pp. 135-136] The PSA Site Assistance Visit is listed as the method for conducting risk assessments in the 2010 Sector Specific Plan for Energy. [12, p. 32] Originally, DHS intended for every sector to use the same risk analysis tool in order to facilitate risk comparison across not only infrastructure assets, but also across infrastructure sectors. In the 2006 National Infrastructure Protection Plan DHS announced it was sponsoring development of a suite of tools based on the Risk Analysis and Management for Critical Asset Protection (RAMCAP). [13, p. 36] RAMCAP was developed at the request of the White House by the American Society of Mechanical Engineers (ASME). [14, p. xiii] The 2006 NIPP deemed RAMCAP to satisfy the "baseline criteria for risk assessment". This "baseline criteria" assessed risk as a function of consequence, vulnerability, and threat, expressed as R=f(C,V,T). [13, pp. 35-36] The 2013 NIPP affirmed this formulation as part of Step 3 in the Risk Management Framework, [3, p. 17] but RAMCAP was no longer the preferred method. It was not mentioned in either the 2009 or 2013 National Infrastructure Protection Plans. It did survive, however, as the American Water Works Association (AWWA) J100-10 standard for Risk and Resilience Management of Water and Wastewater Systems. [14]

The Risk Management Framework has proven problematic at every step. DHS has yet to make the system work as envisioned. Until these problems are solved, the nation's critical infrastructure will remain vulnerable to malicious attack.

RMF Step 4: Implement Risk Management Activities. As a result of risk analysis, owners/operators are expected to take actions to increase resilience and reduce their vulnerability to potential consequences. [3, p. 18] However, infrastructure owner/ operators are very sensitive to costs, in many instances regulated, and cannot afford to take all measures on their own. Accordingly, DHS may lend assistance through the FEMA Grants Program Directorate State and Local Grant Programs. Specific grant programs include the State Homeland Security Formula-based Grants, the Urban Area Security Initiative (UASI) Grants (both of which primarily support first responder needs, but include certain infrastructure protection expenditures), Port Security Grants, Rail and Transit Security Grants, Intercity Bus Security Grants, and Highway (Trucking) Security Grants, and Buffer Zone Protection Plan. [1, pp. 27-28] Ostensibly, the results from risk analysis are included in a Critical Infrastructure National Annual Report [3, p. 26] submitted each year with the DHS budget to the Executive Office of the President. [15, p. 2]

RMF Step 5: Measure Effectiveness. The 1993 Government Performance and Results Act, as amended, requires all Federal programs to develop "outcome measures" and report them annually to Congress to guide and assess effective investment of taxpayer funds. [16] The Risk Management Framework incorporates this principle in Step 5, before starting all over again with Step 1 in an incremental, continuous improvement process. [3, p. 20]

Conclusion

While supporting aspects of the National Infrastructure Protection Plan including Information Sharing and Analysis Centers (ISACs) and Sector Coordinating Councils have increased awareness and security among participating infrastructure sectors, the core of the plan, the Risk Management Framework, has yet to live up to expectations. Various GAO reports detail fundamental problems with each step of the process including 1) inability to adequately identify infrastructure assets (mobile assets, such as aircraft, are not included in NCIPP criteria), 2) matching PSA Site Assistance Visits with priority assets listed on NCIPP, 3) deploying a standard formulation to uniformly assess risk across all infrastructure sectors, 4) applying risk results to determine Federal grant priorities, and 5) providing an objective risk measure to guide and assess taxpayer investments. While these problems remain, the nation will remain vulnerable to the potential catastrophic effects inherent in critical infrastructure as demonstrated on 9/11.

Challenge Your Understanding

The following questions are designed to challenge your understanding of the material presented in this chapter. Some questions may require additional research outside this book in order to provide a complete answer.

1. What is the scope and authority of a presidential executive order or directive?
2. What was the finding by the Commission on Critical Infrastructure Protection that prompted President Clinton to issue PDD-63?
3. How did HSPD-7 issued by President Bush change the emphasis on critical infrastructure protection from PDD-63?
4. How did PPD-21 issued by President Obama again change the emphasis on critical infrastructure protection from HSPD-7?
5. Why can't owners/operators protect their own infrastructure?
6. What is the purpose of the Risk Management Framework?
7. How does it affect the RMF if you can't correctly identify critical infrastructure?
8. How does it affect the RMF if you can't assess risk uniformly across different infrastructures?
9. As a member of Congress, what would be your priority in allocating funding to protect critical infrastructure?
10. What do you suppose might be a moral hazard of funding infrastructure protection programs?

Chapter 15

Counter WMD Strategy

Learning Outcomes

Careful study of this chapter will help a student do the following:

- Describe the various prohibitions against WMD agents.
- Explain how the 1995 Tokyo subway attack changed the WMD threat.
- Explain the different roles of agencies in national counter WMD strategy.

"The potential proliferation of weapons of mass destruction, particularly nuclear weapons, poses a grave risk. Even as we have decimated al-Qa'ida's core leadership, more diffuse networks of al-Qa'ida, ISIL, and affiliated groups threaten U.S. citizens, interests, allies, and partners."

- 2015 National Security Strategy

Introduction

WMD agents are prohibited under Title 18 USC, S2332a, and international conventions, including the 1968 (nuclear) Non-Proliferation Treaty, 1975 Biological Weapons Convention, and 1997 Chemical Weapons Convention.

The history of human warfare may be characterized as an escalating development of tactics and weapons designed to kill more people more quickly. As the industrial revolution accelerated the production and refinement of weapons on an unprecedented scale, the Geneva Conventions were begun in 1864 to contain the carnage and bound the limits of warfare [1]. Similar attempts were made with the Hague Conventions to place limits on the types of weapons that could be employed. As early as 1899, the Hague Conventions sought to outlaw the use of chemical weapons by warring nations. [2] After Germany breached this agreement in 1915, the British retaliated in kind, and every major belligerent was guilty of employing chemical weapons by the end of World War I. [3] After the war, nations continued to maintain and expand their stocks of chemical weapons as a deterrent to their future use. It wasn't until the Chemical Weapons Convention of 1997 that nations agreed to destroy their stocks, but the task is only 85% complete as nations remain wary of relinquishing their deterrent capability against the possibility of hidden caches. [4] The prohibition against chemical weapons came after a similar agreement prohibiting the development, production, and stockpiling of biological weapons in the 1975 Biological Weapons Convention. [5] This was preceded by the 1968 Non-Proliferation Treaty in which nations agreed to prevent the spread of nuclear weapons and weapons technology. [6] The most difficult problem with all these treaties is enforcement. Despite monitoring and surveillance provisions written into them, the ultimate guarantor of compliance is the threat of retaliation by similar means. While this threat may work on nations, it does not work as well on individuals. The 1995 Tokyo subway attacks demonstrated the ability of non-state actors to employ weapons of mass destruction. And while Title 18 U.S. Code Section 2332a makes it illegal to use, threaten, attempt, or conspire to use a weapon of mass destruction in the United States, arresting the perpetrator after the fact is too little too late. Thus the nation's security today relies on an unprecedented cooperation between military, intelligence, and law enforcement agencies, between Federal, State, and Local governments to combat weapons of mass destruction (CWMD).

Combating WMD

The Department of Homeland Security is member of the Counterproliferation Program Review Committee (CPRC) together with the Department of Defense (DoD), Department of Energy (DoE), Department of State (DoS), Office of the Director of National Intelligence (ODNI), and Office of the Chairman of the Joint Chiefs of Staff (CJCS). Together, they represent the primary Federal agencies responsible for safeguarding the U.S. from WMD attack. In 1994, Congress commissioned the CPRC to report on their combined efforts to combat WMD and its means of delivery. [7, p. 1]

The missions and objectives of CPRC members are guided by the 2002 National Strategy to Combat Weapons of Mass Destruction. The 2002 Strategy prescribes three primary mission areas: 1) Nonproliferation (NP), 2) Counterproliferation (CP), and 3) Consequence Management (CM). [7, p. 3] Nonproliferation seeks to dissuade or impede both state and non-state actors from acquiring chemical, biological, radiological, and nuclear (CBRN) weapons. Counterproliferation seeks to develop both active and passive measures to deter and defend against the employment of CBRN weapons. Consequence management seeks to develop measures to quickly respond and recover against a domestic CBRN attack. [8, p. 2] This basic strategy is further refined by supplemental guidance listed in Table 1. These assist departments and agencies with developing goals and objectives, identifying capability requirements, and ultimately providing material and nonmaterial solutions for combating weapons of mass destruction. [9, p. 2]

The Department of Defense, Department of Energy, Department of State, and Office of the Director of National Intelligence together represent the primary Federal agencies responsible for safeguarding the U.S from WMD attack.

Table 15-1: CWMD Guidance Documents [9, p. 2]

2012 Sustaining U.S. Global Leadership: Priorities for 21st Century Defense
2012 National Strategy for Biosurveillance
2011 National Strategy for Counterterrorism
2010 Nuclear Posture Review
2009 National Strategy for Countering Biological Threats
2006 National Strategy for Strategic Interdiction
2002 National Strategy to Combat Weapons of Mass Destruction

Department of Defense

DoDD 2060.2 establishes policy, assigns responsibilities, and formalizes relationships among DoD components to combat weapons of mass destruction. [9, p. 15] DODD 2060.2 refers to CWMD mission areas described in the 2006 National Military Strategy to Combat WMD. [10, p. 2] This was replaced in 2014 by the Defense Strategy to

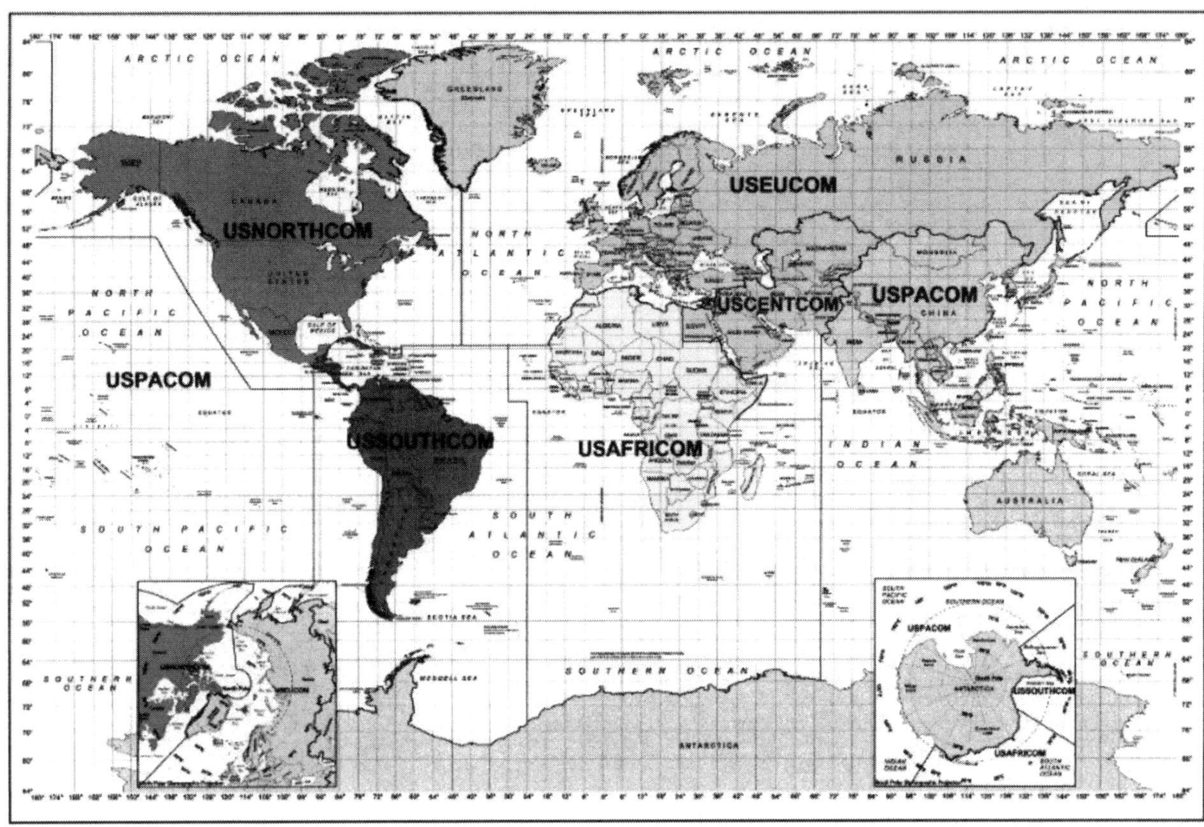

Figure 15-1: DoD Geographic Combatant Commands [12]

According to the 2014 Defense Strategy, DoD works to 1) prevent acquisition of WMD (nonproliferation), 2) contain and reduce the threat of WMD employment (counterproliferation), and 3) respond to crises (consequence management).

Combat WMD. According to the 2014 Defense Strategy, DoD works towards three CWMD end states: 1) no new WMD possession (NP), 2) no WMD use (CP), and 3) minimization of WMD effects (CM). The end states are pursued through three main lines of effort: 1) Prevent Acquisition, 2) Contain and Reduce Threats, and 3) Respond to Crises. According to this strategy, DoD will seek to dissuade those who do not possess WMD from acquiring them by promoting transparency, security, and disarmament; convincing aspirants that their activities will be detected, attributed, and mitigated; taking action to delay, disrupt, or complicate WMD acquisition; and when necessary, undertake direct actions to prevent WMD acquisition. DoD will contain and reduce threats by supporting arms control initiatives; working with partners to guard against accidental or unintentional WMD employment; maintaining an effective defense and retaliatory deterrent; and when necessary, undertaking operations to secure, exploit, and destroy WMD. DoD will also remain prepared to locate, disrupt, disable neutralize, or destroy an adversary's WMD assets before they can be used; however, if employed, DoD is prepared to support civil authorities with CBRN response capabilities to mitigate consequences. [11, pp. 9-12] DoD capabilities supporting CWMD policy reside with DoD agencies, commands, and components. The Defense Threat Reduction Agency (DTRA) leads the Department's nonproliferation efforts by implementing provisions of the Nunn-Lugar Global Cooperation Program and promoting arms control. United States Strategic Command directs the nation's air, land, and sea based nuclear forces. [9, pp. 15-17] United States Northern Command maintains defense of the nation's air, land, sea, and space approaches. United States Special Operations Command is prepared to undertake precise missions around the world. The remaining geographic combatant commands, Southern Command, Central Command, European Command, Pacific Command, and Africa Command, maintain stabilizing relations within their areas of responsibility, but are prepared to conduct military operations with assigned Army, Navy, Marine, and Air Force units when directed by the President. [12] In the event WMD is employed within the U.S., the National Guard maintains 10 regional Homeland Response Forces (HRFs) that may be tasked to a State governor to assist with CBRN mitigation. [13]

Department of Energy

DOE contributes to national CWMD efforts by ensuring energy security, producing and maintaining the nation's nuclear stockpile, promoting nuclear nonproliferation, providing specialized nuclear and radiological emergency response, assisting nuclear and radiological counterterrorism and counterproliferation efforts, and fostering fundamental science, advanced computing, and technological innovation. [14, pp. III-10] DOE supports CWMD missions through its nuclear proliferation prevention and counter-terrorism activities as well as through access to the many sites engaged by its scientific cadre. DOE plays a critical role, through its core nuclear work, in addressing inspection and monitoring activities of arms control agreements and regimes; protection of WMD and WMD-related materials and components; detection and tracking of these materials and components; removal of materials from compliant nation states; export control activities; and responding to nuclear and radiological emergencies in the United States and abroad. DOE works closely with DoD, DHS, DOS, and the Intelligence Community to detect, characterize, and defeat WMD and WMD-related facilities. [7, p. 18] Within DOE, the National Nuclear Security Administration (NNSA) is responsible for performing these missions. The NNSA works together with the Group of Eight (G8) Global Partnership and the International Atomic Energy Agency to perform its missions abroad. Within the NNSA, responsibility for countering nuclear terrorism resides principally with the Office of Counterterrorism and Counterproliferation, designated NA-80. NA-80's purpose is to advance government's technical understanding of the terrorist nuclear threat and advocate for technically informed policies across Federal agencies. [9, p. 18] The NNSA also maintains Nuclear Emergency Response Teams (NERTs) capable of 1) searching for radiological devices, 2) rendering them safe, and 3) mapping radiological contamination that might be spread. [15]

DOE contributes to national CWMD efforts by ensuring energy security, producing and maintaining the nation's nuclear stockpile, promoting nuclear nonproliferation, providing specialized nuclear and radiological emergency response, assisting nuclear and radiological counterterrorism and counterproliferation efforts, and fostering fundamental science, advanced computing, and technological innovation.

Department of State

Central to DOS's responsibility for diplomatic engagement on international security, DOS aims to build international consensus on arms control and nonproliferation based on common concern and shared responsibility. The Under Secretary for Arms Control and International Security leads interagency policy development on nonproliferation and manages global US security policy, principally in the areas of nonproliferation, arms control, regional security and defense relations, and arms transfers and security assistance. This entails overseeing the negotiation, implementation, and verification of international agreements in arms control and international security. Other specific responsibilities include directing and coordinating export control policies and policies to prevent missile, nuclear, chemical, biological, and conventional weapons proliferation. All of these contribute to the DOS's strategic goal of countering threats to the US and the international order. DOS CWMD responsibilities are primarily planned and executed via: the Bureau of Arms Control, Verification, and Compliance (AVC); the Bureau of International Security and Nonproliferation (ISN); and the Bureau of Political-Military Affairs (PM); all of which report to the Under Secretary for Arms Control and International Security. [14, pp. III-7]

ODNI directs the activities of the Intelligence Community to provide high-value intelligence supporting U.S. policies and actions to discourage, prevent, rollback, deter, and mitigate the consequences of WMD.

Office of the Director of National Intelligence

ODNI directs the activities of the Intelligence Community to provide high-value intelligence supporting U.S. policies and actions to discourage, prevent, rollback, deter, and mitigate the consequences of WMD. ODNI leads the nation's CWMD intelligence efforts through various interagency groups and centers: [9, p. 20]

CBRN Counterterrorism Group (CCTG). ODNI manages the CCTG formed by the merger of the Central Intelligence Agency's (CIA's) Counterterrorism Center and National Counterterrorism Center's CBRN analysis group. The CCTG pools analytical experts from CIA, NCTC, the Defense Intelligence Agency (DIA), FBI, and other U.S. Government organizations to support a wide range of intelligence activities focused on CWMD. [9, p. 20]

National Counterproliferation Center (NCPC). The NCPC helps the U.S counter threats caused by the development and spread of WMD. NCPC works with the Intelligence Community to identify critical gaps in WMD knowledge resulting from shortfalls in collection, analysis, or exploitation and then develop solutions to reduce or close these gaps. The NCPC does this by analyzing, integrating, and disseminating comprehensive all-source WMD proliferation intelligence; providing all-source intelligence support needed for the execution of counterproliferation plans or activities; and performing independent WMD proliferation analyses. It may also play a role in the nuclear attribution process by fusing law enforcement and intelligence information with nuclear forensics conclusions provided by national technical nuclear forensics center. The NCPC also provides WMD briefs and analyses to the President, Congress, and the appropriate Federal departments and agencies, as required. The majority of the NCPC staff are detailees from the intelligence community, as well as DoD and the DOE national laboratories. [14, pp. III-6 - III-7]

National Counterterrorism Center (NCTC). The NCTC is the primary organization in the U.S. Government that integrates and analyzes intelligence pertaining to terrorism and counterterrorism, including all intelligence related to terrorist use of WMD. The CT community lead for identifying critical intelligence problems, key knowledge gaps, and major resource constraints is the NCTC. The NCTC combines intelligence, military, law enforcement, and homeland security networks to facilitate information sharing across government departments and agencies. In addition to its information sharing role, the NCTC provides a strategic-level operational planning function for CT activities and is responsible for integrating all elements of national power toward successful implementation of the national CT strategy. [14, pp. III-6]

Department of Homeland Security

The Department of Homeland Security also plays a role in national CWMD strategy by: 1) Preventing Terrorism and Enhancing Security; 2) Securing and Managing Borders; and 3) Ensuring Resilience to Disasters.

The 2010 Quadrennial Homeland Security Review identified three CWMD-related mission areas: 1) Preventing Terrorism and Enhancing Security; 2) Securing and Managing Borders; and 3) Ensuring Resilience to Disasters. [9, pp. 18-19] DHS also maintains the National Response Framework (NRF) for guiding how U.S. Government departments and agencies should work together to prepare for and respond to WMD events. DHS agencies, along with the Federal Bureau of Investigation (FBI), DOE, the Department of the Treasury (TREAS), the Department of Commerce (DOC), and the intelligence community, play a vital role in supporting national CWMD efforts. Agencies within the DHS that contribute to the CWMD mission include: [14, pp. III-8]

United States Coast Guard (USCG). The USCG may play an integral role in WMD interdiction operations by protecting US economic and security interests in maritime regions, including international waters, U.S. coastal regions, ports, and waterways. USCG personnel can be used to enforce U.S. laws anywhere in the world, with certain restrictions, and can participate in regular DoD-led interdiction operations under their Title 14, USC authorities, even if assigned DoD forces. [14, pp. III-8]

Customs and Border Protection (CBP). To prevent WMD smuggling, the CBP works through existing partnerships with customs and law enforcement agencies in partner nations to protect U.S. borders, ports of entry, and screen admissibility of persons, cargo, and vessels arriving into U.S. ports. CBP also supports a National Targeting Center and operates the Container Security Initiative with the DOE. [14, pp. III-8]

Federal Emergency Management Agency. The Federal Emergency Management Agency provides support to our nation's critical infrastructure in response to CBRN hazards through comprehensive emergency management programs including risk reduction, preparedness, response, and recovery. [14, pp. III-8]

Domestic Nuclear Detection Office (DNDO). DNDO improves the Nation's ability to detect and report transportation of nuclear or radiological material. Additionally, DNDO operates the National Technical Nuclear Forensics Center, which has two primary missions. The first provides centralized planning, integration, assessment, and stewardship of the nation's nuclear forensics capabilities to ensure a ready, robust, and enduring capability in coordination with other U.S. Government departments and agencies who have assigned responsibilities for national technical nuclear forensics. These include the Department of Justice and FBI, who is the lead federal agency responsible for the criminal investigation of terrorist events and the nuclear forensic investigation of planned or actual attack; DoD, DOE, DOS, ODNI, and DHS. The second mission is to advance the capability to perform nuclear forensics on nuclear and radiological materials in a pre-detonation (intact) state. [14, pp. III-8]

Immigration and Customs Enforcement (ICE). ICE enforces US immigration and customs regulations. One of its highest priorities is to prevent illicit procurement networks, terrorist groups, and hostile nations from illegally obtaining U.S. military products, sensitive dual-use technology, WMD, or CBRN materials. The ICE homeland security investigation's counterproliferation investigations program oversees a broad range of investigative activities related to such violations. The counterproliferation investigations program enforces US laws involving the export of military items, controlled dual-use goods, firearms, and ammunition, as well as exports to sanctioned or embargoed countries. [14, pp. III-9]

Conclusion

The effects of U.S. CWMD policy range from the mundane to the profound. Patients of nuclear medicine are routinely pulled aside after tripping Radiation Portal Monitors installed in airports and other major U.S. ports of entry. [16] Citing the need to disarm Iraq of suspected caches of WMD, President Bush in March 2003 launched the U.S.-led invasion of Iraq. The invasion and subsequent eight-year occupation cost the nation $1.7 trillion, 4,488 U.S. casualties, and 32,223 U.S. wounded. Iraq itself suffered an estimated 189,000 casualties and counting as it continues to struggle with internal strife. [17] No definitive caches of WMD were found.

Challenge Your Understanding

The following questions are designed to challenge your understanding of the material presented in this chapter. Some questions may require additional research outside this book in order to provide a complete answer.

1. Which WMD agent was first used in warfare?
2. Which WMD agent emerged during World War One?
3. Which WMD agent emerged during World War Two?
4. How did the 1995 Tokyo subway attacks change the WMD threat?
5. What is DoD's role in national counter WMD strategy?
6. What is DOS's role in national counter WMD strategy?
7. What s DOE's role in national counter WMD strategy?
8. What is ODNI's role in national counter WMD strategy?
9. What is DHS's role in national counter WMD strategy?
10. Which WMD agent do you think is easiest to obtain? Explain your answer.

Chapter 16

Cybersecurity

Learning Outcomes

Careful study of this chapter will help a student do the following:

- Explain the relationship between cybersecurity and critical infrastructure protections.
- Explain why cyber attack holds so much destructive potential.
- Describe Internet ownership and management relationships.
- Identify key components of the Internet.
- Discuss potential Internet vulnerabilities.
- Evaluate computer crime.
- Describe DHS's cybersecurity roles and responsibilities.

"Because our economy is increasingly reliant upon interdependent cyber-supported infrastructures, non-traditional attacks on our infrastructure and information systems may be capable of significantly harming both our military power and our economy."

- 1998 Presidential Decision Directive No. 63

Introduction

Cybersecurity goes hand-in-hand with critical infrastructure protection, because 1) cyberspace provides an avenue for attacking critical infrastructure from anywhere around the world; 2) cyber components make critical infrastructure susceptible to subversion, disruption, or destruction; and 3) cyberspace itself is a critical infrastructure on which many other critical infrastructures depend. What keeps the experts awake at night is the knowledge that the potential consequences of a coordinated cyber attack could dwarf any previous disaster in U.S. history, either natural or manmade. This chapter will take a look at some of those nightmare scenarios and examine what the Department of Homeland Security is doing to keep them from becoming reality.

Cybersecurity Concerns: 1) cyberspace provides an avenue for attacking critical infrastructure from anywhere around the world; 2) cyber components make critical infrastructure susceptible to subversion, disruption, or destruction; and 3) cyberspace itself is a critical infrastructure on which many other critical infrastructures depend.

Worst Case Scenarios

The worst disaster in U.S. history was the 1900 hurricane that hit Galveston Texas; as many as 12,000 people are thought to have perished in that disaster. The worst manmade disaster in U.S. history was 9/11 in which 3,000 people lost their lives. [1] Yet the death and damages resulting from these disasters might pale in comparison to the destruction that could conceivably be wrought by a coordinated cyber attack on selected infrastructure. We present just three plausible scenarios that have been considered, at one time or another, at the highest levels of U.S. leadership.

Shutdown the North American Electric Grid.

In August 2003, an electricity blackout affected 50 million people in the northeastern United States and Canada, causing an estimated $4-$10 billion in economic losses. Though it lasted only a week, the outage resulted in a 0.7% drop in Canada's gross domestic product. [2, p. 2] A John Hopkins study determined that New York City experienced a 122% increase in accidental deaths and 25% increase in disease-related deaths, and that ninety people died as a direct result of the power outage. [3] Though the 2003 outage was an accident, it raised concerns whether an even wider outage could be induced deliberately. In 2006, DHS and the Department of Energy conducted a joint experiment named Project Aurora. In this experiment, researchers proved that a generator could be remotely commanded over the Internet to physically self-destruct. [4, p. 21] The implications were shocking because the time necessary to replace a generator can range from months to years. [5, p. 12] Of course the North American electric grid is designed and monitored to sustain service in the event a given component fails. It is not designed, however, to sustain large-scale damages that might result from a coordinated attack. If such an attack was successful, a significant portion of the United States could lose power for periods lasting months, not weeks. Unlike the aftermath of Hurricane Katrina, there would be no "islands of power" from which to stage recovery or seek refuge. The affected regions would go dark, and their supporting infrastructure would collapse. The cascading effects would be disastrous. No doubt the nation would survive, but it would be deeply wounded as no other experience since the Civil War.

Multiple Simultaneous Meltdowns.

In March 1979, a series of incidents almost resulted in a meltdown of reactor number two at the Three Mile Island nuclear power plant in Dauphin County Pennsylvania. Though a meltdown was averted, and only a slight amount of radiation released, 140,000 people were evacuated from a 20-mile radius before the situation was contained. [6] By comparison, the residents of Pripyat in the Ukraine were not so lucky when in April 1986, reactor number four at the Chernobyl Nuclear Power Plant exploded. Though a different design than the plant at Three Mile Island, the Chernobyl nuclear accident amply demonstrates the dangers of a nuclear meltdown: 350,400 people were permanently evacuated from a radius extending 19-miles in all directions from the plant. Radiation from the fallout is so intense inside the "zone of alienation" that it will remain unsafe for human habitation for another 20,000 years (though a stalwart contingent of 300 residents refuse to leave and remain in the area). [7] Again, these were accidents, but as the Stuxnet attack in 2010 proved, they could conceivably become deliberate. In 2010, the Iranian nuclear program was set back due to production losses at the Natanz uranium enrichment facility. The problem was eventually traced to a piece of malware inserted in Siemens equipment controlling the separation centrifuges. Later called Stuxnet, the malware was extraordinary not only for the damage it caused, but also for how it was implanted. The equipment was not connected to the Internet. The malware had been introduced in the supply chain, somewhere between manufacture and delivery. [8] Stuxnet demonstrates how a similar virus could be concealed inside critical components and timed to initiate a simultaneous meltdown at multiple nuclear power plants. It certainly wouldn't be easy, but it's certainly not improbable.

The death and damages resulting from past national disasters might pale in comparison to the destruction that could conceivably be wrought by a coordinated cyber attack on selected infrastructure.

Shutting Down the Federal Reserve.

The Federal Reserve is the central banking system of the United States. The system is comprised of a Board of Governors, a Federal Open Market Committee, and twelve regional Federal Reserve Banks located in major cities throughout the nation. The Federal Reserve was established in 1913 in response to the financial crisis of 1907 in which payments were disrupted across the country because many banks refused to clear checks drawn on other banks, eventually leading to their failure. To preclude similar panics, the Federal Reserve was formed as a "banker's bank" to facilitate transactions between commercial institutions. Through its actions, the Federal

Reserve influences the availability of money and credit, transacting trillions of dollars underpinning the U.S. economy. [9] The vast majority of these transactions are conducted electronically, between the Reserve Banks and their corporate clients. The system is mostly closed and very well protected, but no defense is invulnerable. Conceivably it could be compromised through a Stuxnet-like attack or by an "insider" attack. An "insider" attack is perpetrated by someone with legitimate access conducting unauthorized actions. Alternatively, a "phishing" attack might trick an authorized user into divulging their access codes to a criminal agent. This last approach is particularly disconcerting because it means system security is only as strong as the weakest person in the chain (of course the computer system has internal as well as external access controls, but accomplished hackers will use their initial access to gain higher authorizations). The potential consequences of a hostile agent shutting down the Federal Reserve are too broad to contemplate. Like electricity, monetary transactions pervade every aspect of society, from ordering a latte to paying the mortgage. What would happen if all forms of electronic payment halted? While you might not be evicted for missing a mortgage payment, you also could not buy that latte, or more importantly, buy gas for your car or groceries for your family. How long would the Federal Reserve have to be down before panic ensued? Not long at all. Again, it's not easy, but it's not impossible.

The Internet is a connected graph of links and routers. What is fundamentally important to the Internet is that each component is independently owned and operated by different public and private agencies: the Internet does not belong to any single entity.

Cyberspace

As explained in the introduction, cyberspace serves as both an avenue of attack and a means of support for other critical infrastructure. Understanding what it is, therefore, is an important precondition to protecting it. According to the DHS Glossary of Common Cybersecurity Terminology, cyberspace is "the interdependent network of information technology infrastructures, that includes the Internet, telecommunications networks, computer systems, and embedded processors and controllers." [10] Essentially "cyberspace" is a broad term encompassing the Internet and everything connected to it. So what is the Internet? By definition the Internet is a "network of networks". The key enabling technologies are links, standards, protocols, and routers. A link is a physical communications path between two points. A link may be wired (copper or fiber) or wireless (light or radio), depending on required cost, distance, and bandwidth. A link serves to transmit electronic data packets conforming to the Open System Interconnection (OSI) standard. The source and destination of each data packet are internally encoded in a globally unique Internet Protocol (IP) address. A link may terminate at a router, which, in turn, may be connected to two or more links. A router examines the destination address of each arriving packet and forwards it on to another link to convey it closer or quicker to its final destination. It may require many packets to transmit a single text, graphic, sound, or video object. The Transmission Control Protocol (TCP) ensures that all packets are properly re-assembled into the

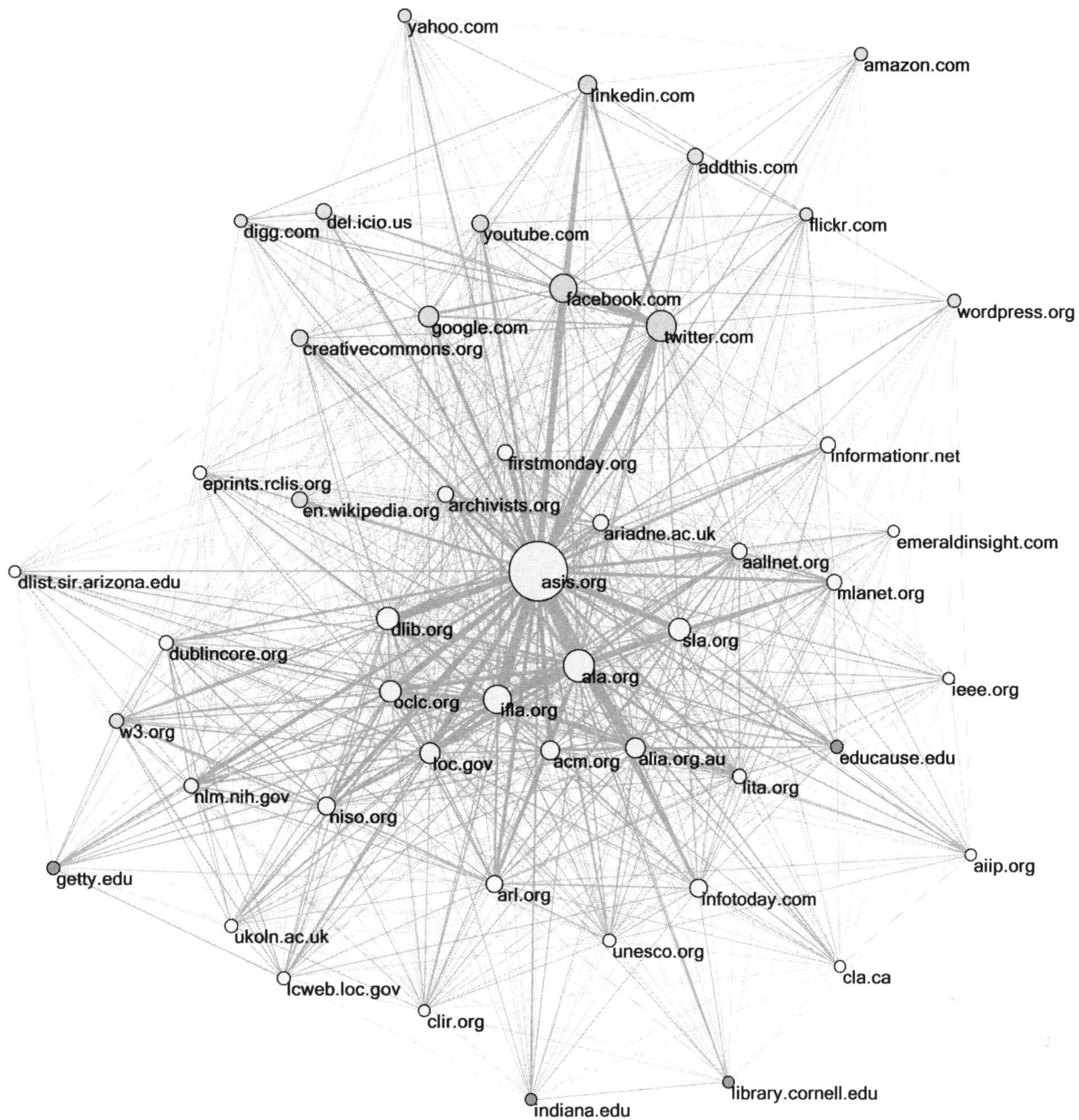

Figure 16-1: Schematic Representation of a Portion of the Internet

original object at their intended destination[1]. While greatly simplified and highly abstract, the preceding description provides a physical conception of the Internet, which may be schematically represented as shown in Figure 1.

As shown in Figure 1, the Internet is a connected graph of links and routers. What is not shown, and what is fundamentally important to the Internet, is that each component is independently owned and operated by different public and private agencies: the Internet does not belong to any single entity. It is a collection of diverse

[1]A "message" may be digitized text, graphics, sound, or video. Sound and video packets may be transmitted using the User Datagram Protocol (UDP) which trades speed for reliability compared to TCP. A few lost sound or video packets will not be discernable to the human ear or eye.

components conforming to an agreed set of engineering standards. The individual owners are collectively called Internet Service Providers (ISPs). The Internet is built and grows as ISPs join their networks with those of other ISPs.

The individual owners are collectively called Internet Service Providers (ISPs). The Internet is built and grows as ISPs join their networks with those of other ISPs.

ISPs are unofficially classified into "Tiers" based on the size of their networks and how they connect with other ISPs. ISPs connect to each other through either a "peering" or "transit" agreement. Peering is when a pair of ISPs establish a reciprocal agreement to connect with each other and exchange traffic without charge. On the other hand, a transit relationship requires some form of fee based on the amount of traffic shared between the ISPs. [11] Accordingly, ISPs are classified as Tier 1, Tier 2, or Tier 3. Tier 1 ISPs are the largest, and peer with other Tier 1 ISPs to reach every other ISP on the Internet without purchasing transit. Table 1 lists the seven U.S. Tier 1 ISPs. Tier 2 ISPs peer with some ISPs, but purchase transit to reach at least some portion of the Internet. Examples of Tier 2 ISPs are major cable, Digital Service Link (DSL), and mobile providers. Tier 3 ISPs must purchase transit from other ISPs to access the Internet. Examples of Tier 3 ISPs are small regional providers, small mobile providers, and university networks. [12]

Table 16-1: U.S. Tier 1 ISPs [13]

1.	AT&T	5.	Level 3
2.	Verizon	6.	NTT/Verio
3.	Spring	7.	Cogent
4.	Century Link		

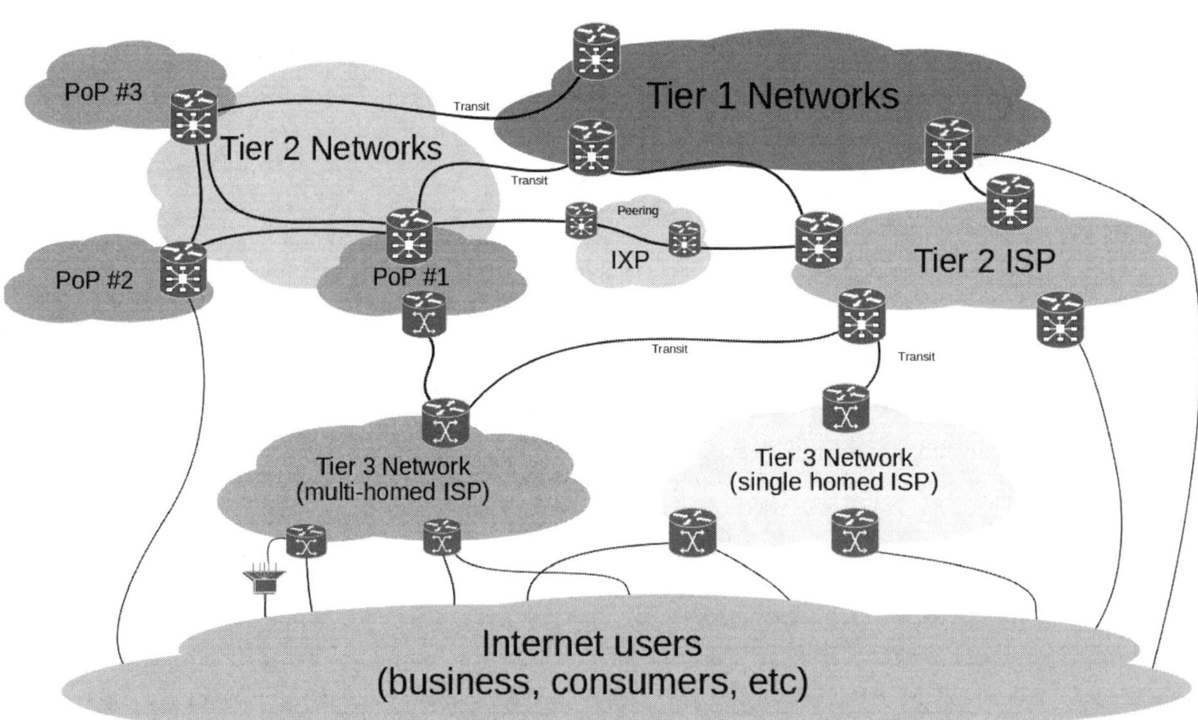

Figure 16-2: Internet ISP Tiers

Transiting and peering between ISPs is facilitated by Internet Exchange Points (IXPs). The primary role of an IXP is to keep local traffic local and reduce the costs associated with traffic exchange between Internet providers. IXPs are a vital part of the Internet. Without them, the Internet would not function efficiently because the different networks that make up the Internet would need to directly interconnect with every other network in order to be able to exchange traffic with each other. [15]

The compelling benefits of IXPs spurred their rapid global growth. As of 2012, there were 350 IXPs operational worldwide. The US has about 86 IXPs strategically located across the country. Other countries with more than 10 IXPs are: Australia (11), Brazil (19), France (15), Germany (14), Japan (16), Russia (14), Sweden (12), and United Kingdom (12). [15]

Internet Exchange Points (IXPs) are a vital part of the Internet. Without them, the Internet would not function efficiently because the different networks that make up the Internet would need to directly interconnect with every other network in order to be able to exchange traffic with each other.

As mentioned previously, the Internet is not owned by any single entity, however, it does rely on central services to ensure unique Internet Protocol addresses for each component connected to it. IP addresses are controlled by the Internet Corporation for Assigned Names and Numbers (ICANN). ICANN is a global non-profit agency operating out of Los Angeles California. IP addresses come in two forms: 1) human-readable, i.e., "alias", and 2) machine-readable, i.e., "numeric". While the human-readable address is easier for people to remember (e.g., facebook.com, Google.com, Amazon.com), the machine-readable address is the form required by routers (e.g., 173.252.120.6, 74.125.70.102, 72.21.215.232). Accordingly, the Internet relies on

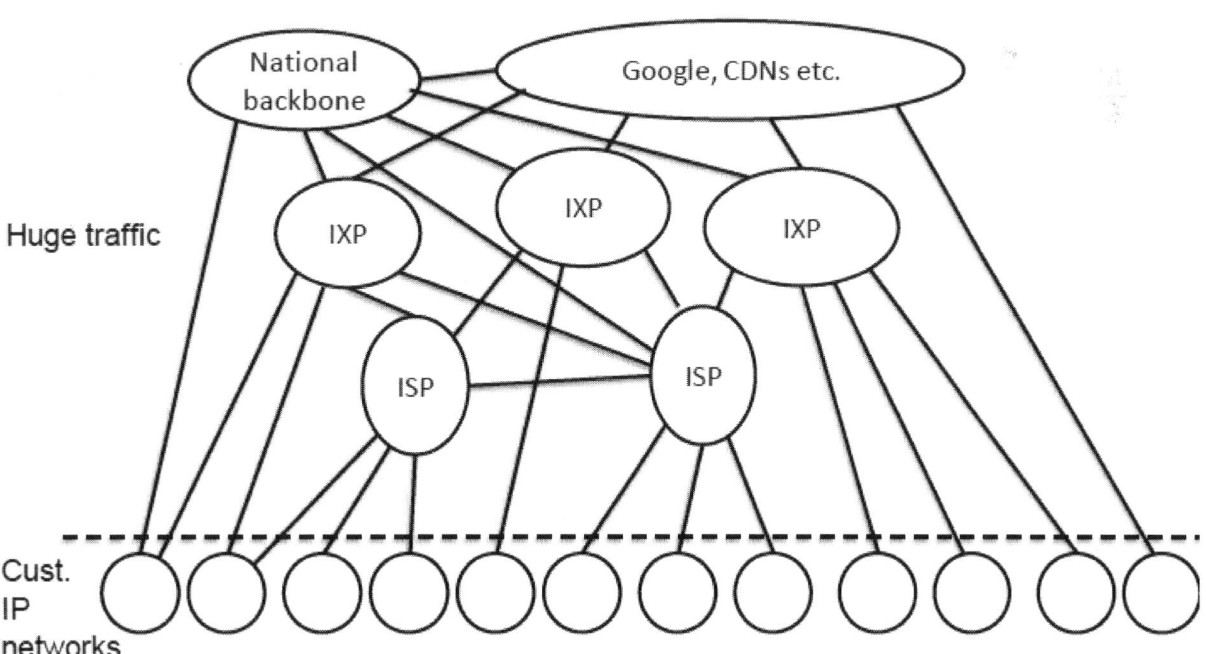

Figure 16-3: IXP Role in Today's Internet [16]

Domain Name Services (DNS) to translate one form of IP address into another and help route traffic along the Internet. DNS is maintained by a department of ICANN called the Internet Assigned Numbers Authority (IANA). IANA operates and maintains DNS services provided by hundreds of computers known as root servers located in many countries in every region of the world. Root servers contain the IP addresses of all the Top-Level Domain (TLD) registry name servers; e.g., ".com" and ".de". Root servers "translate" aliases into numbers. They perform a critical if somewhat "back-office" role in ensuring the continuity and therefore reliability of the Internet. [17]

Cyber Attack

The 1984 Counterfeit Access Device and Computer Fraud & Abuse Act (18 USC S1030) prohibits unauthorized access to computers used by the Federal government, banks, and otherwise used for interstate or international commerce. Due to the inter-state nature of the Internet, the law is interpreted to mean most all computers including cell phones.

The 1984 Counterfeit Access Device and Computer Fraud & Abuse Act (18 USC S1030) prohibits unauthorized access to computers used by the Federal government, banks, and otherwise used for interstate or international commerce. Due to the inter-state nature of the Internet, the law is interpreted to mean most all computers including cell phones. A 1986 amendment further criminalized the distribution of malicious code, trafficking in passwords, and denial of service attacks. [18] According to the U.S. National Research Council, a cyber attack is any "deliberate action to alter, disrupt, deceive, degrade, or destroy computer systems or networks or the information and /or programs resident in or transiting these systems or networks." [19, p. 9] There are many different ways to mount a cyber attack as illustrated in Figure 4. According to a 2014 report by the Center for Strategic and International Studies, the two most common attack methods are social engineering and vulnerability exploitation. According to the Center, social engineering is where an attacker tricks a user into granting access, and vulnerability exploitation is where an attacker takes advantage of a programming or implementation failure to gain access. [20, p. 10] According to the report, cybercrime is a growth industry because the returns are great and the risks are low. The Center estimates that the annual cost to the global economy is more than $400 billion, yet most cybercrime goes unreported, and few cybercriminals are caught or even identified. [20, p. 2&4]

Cyber Security

The DHS Glossary of Common Cybersecurity Terminology defines cybersecurity as "the activity or process, ability or capability, or state whereby information and communications systems and the information contained therein are protected from and/or defended against damage, unauthorized use or modification, or exploitation. [10] Cybersecurity is also a growth industry. According to the Center for Strategic and International Studies, the global market for cybersecurity products and services is $58 billion and growing annually. [20, p. 17] In concept, cybersecurity is very simple. All you have to do is ensure the confidentiality, integrity, and availability of the computer system and its data. Confidentiality ensures the system and data are not accessed by an unauthorized agent. Integrity ensures that the system and data are not corrupted by an unauthorized agent. Availability ensures that the system and data are always

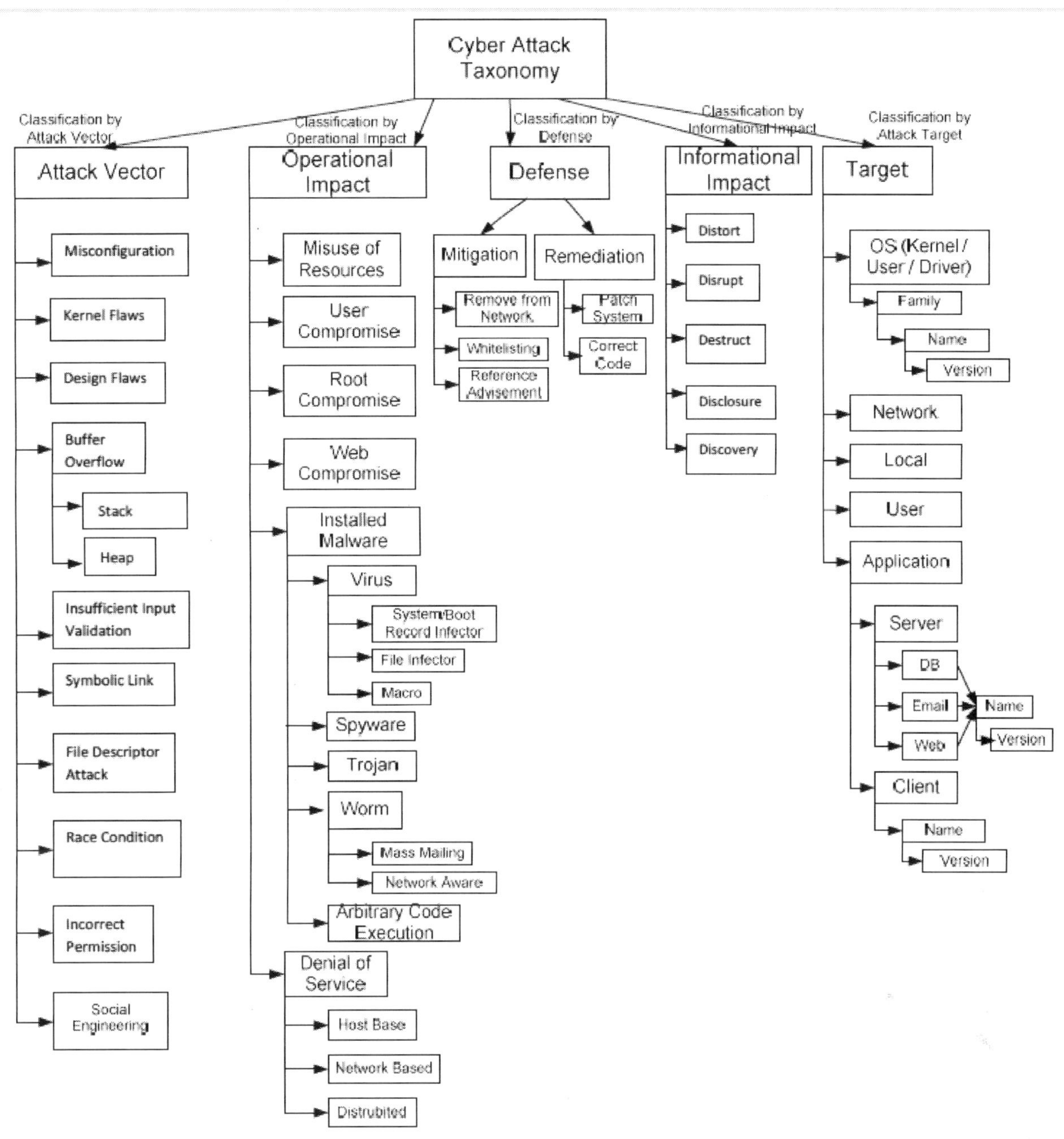

Figure 16-4: AVOIDIT Cyber Attack Taxonomy [23]

accessible when needed. [21, pp. 1-2] These seemingly simple goals, however, are very difficult to attain because computers are inherently stupid and fragile. Computers are stupid, because unlike humans, computers are incapable of making value judgments regarding their actions and will perform as directed regardless of outcome, even if the consequences are catastrophic. Computers are also fragile; a single wrong character can disrupt millions of lines of code, compared to buildings which do not collapse because one brick fails. Finding such flaws is impossible. Even a small 100-line program with some nested paths and a single loop executing less than twenty times may contain 100 trillion paths. Assuming each path could be evaluated in a millisecond (one-thousandth of a second), testing would take 3170 years. [22] The cumulative effect makes computers inherently vulnerable to diversion from their intended purpose, either through oversight or tampering.

Protecting Cyberspace

Section 103 of the Homeland Security Act made the Department of Homeland Security responsible for cybersecurity at the same time it made it responsible for critical infrastructure protection. [24] As an infrastructure, the Internet underpins the functioning of most other infrastructures, making it essential to the economy and security of the United States. [25, p. 1] Although the Internet is comprised of billions of components globally, it depends on only a thousand to maintain proper functioning, offering a relatively small set of lucrative targets capable of incapacitating the Internet. These include the Internet Exchange Points and DNS Root Servers. Any number of attacks could possibly be launched and some have already been attempted against these high-value assets. In October 2002, a Distributed Denial of Service (DDoS) attack succeeded in affecting 9 of 13 root servers, and at least two root servers "suffered badly" from another attack in February 2007. [26] Because IXPs are designed to manage large traffic loads, a specific type of DDoS attack called a Cross-Plane Session Termination (CXPST) attack employing about 250,000 "bots" would be needed. It is surmised that a well targeted and well timed attack could take down significant parts of the Internet. [16, p. 48]

Although the Internet is comprised of billions of components globally, it depends on only a thousand to maintain proper functioning, offering a relatively small set of lucrative targets capable of incapacitating the Internet. These include the Internet Exchange Points and DNS Root Servers.

As an infrastructure, the Internet is included in the DHS National Infrastructure Protection Plan (NIPP). The DHS National Cyber Security Division (NCSD) under the Office of Cybersecurity and Communications (CS&C) is the Sector Specific Agency (SSA) for the Information Technology (IT) Sector. DHS has no regulatory authority over the IT sector. NCSD, therefore, works in voluntary cooperation with private partners in the Sector Coordinating Council (SCC), including some Tier 1 Internet Service Providers listed in Table 1. As part of the NIPP, DHS supports an IT Information Sharing and Analysis Center (IT-ISAC) to promote the exchange of threat and security information among SCC partners. Private organizations may also report cyber incidents to the DHS National Incident Coordinating Center (NICC). In 2010, NCSD worked with sector partners to produce the IT Sector Specific Plan (IT-SSP). The 2010 IT-SSP reported the results of a 2008-2009 IT Sector Baseline Risk Assessment (ITSRA), noting concerns about DNS root services. [27] ITSRA appears to be a one-off study, conducted as the NIPP Risk Management Framework (RMF) was still gaining traction. In May 2013, DHS noted the use of an NCSD-developed Cyber Assessment Risk Management Approach (CARMA) for conducting risk assessment of cyber assets in conjunction with the NIPP Risk Management Framework. [28]

The basic problem of the Internet is that it is a victim of its own success. Originally designed as a research tool for a trusted community of researchers, the Internet has expanded well beyond its original design specifications and must today operate in an environment that cannot be trusted.

Protecting Infrastructure from Cyberspace

Many critical infrastructures including electricity transmission systems, gas pipelines, and water distribution systems rely on Industrial Control Systems (ICSs) to monitor and control physical objects and devices, such as switches and valves that are often located in remote locations. Industrial Control Systems include Supervisory Control and Data Acquisition (SCADA) systems, Distributed Control Systems (DCSs), Programmable Logic Controllers (PLCs), and General-Purpose Controllers (GPCs). Most ICSs began as proprietary, stand-alone systems that were separated from the rest of the world and isolated from most external sources. Today, widely available software applications, Internet-enabled devices and other nonproprietary information technology offerings have been integrated into most ICSs. This connectivity has delivered many benefits, but it also has increased the vulnerability of these systems to malicious attacks, equipment failures, and other threats. ICS disruptions or failure can result in death or injury, property damage, and loss of critical services. [29]

In 2004, the Department of Homeland Security's National Cybersecurity Division established the Control Systems Security Program (CSSP), which was chartered to work with control systems security stakeholders through awareness and outreach programs that encourage and support coordinated control systems security enhancement efforts. In 2009, the CSSP established the Industrial Control System Joint Working Group (ICSJWG) as a coordination body to facilitate the collaboration of control system stakeholders and to encourage the design, development and deployment of enhanced security for control systems. In 2011, the ICSJWG released a Cross-Sector Roadmap for Cybersecurity. [29]

Industrial Control Systems present a particularly worrisome problem as a coordinated attack might result in some form of worst case scenario. Accordingly, in 2010 DHS released a National Cyber Incident Response Plan (NCIRP) describing how it would prepare for, respond to, and begin to coordinate recovery from a significant cyber incident.

Industrial Control Systems present a particularly worrisome problem as a coordinated attack might result in some form of worst case scenario examined at the beginning of this chapter. Accordingly, in 2010 DHS released a National Cyber Incident Response Plan (NCIRP) describing how it would prepare for, respond to, and begin to coordinate recovery from a significant cyber incident. A significant cyber incident is classified as a Level 2, "substantial" incident on the National Cyber Risk Alert Level (NCRAL) shown in Table 2. Threat levels are monitored at the DHS National Cybersecurity and Communications Integration Center (NCCIC), a 24-hour operations center ready to coordinate a national cyber incident response. Among its assets, the NCCIC has access to both the US-CERT and ICS-CERT. [30]

Table 16-2: DHS National Cyber Risk Alert Levels

Level	Label	Risk	Response
1	Severe	Highly disruptive levels of consequences are occurring or imminent	Response functions are overwhelmed, and top-level national executive authorities and engagements are essential. Exercise of mutual aid agreements and Federal/non-Federal assistance is essential
2	Substantial	Observed or imminent degradation of critical functions with moderate to significant level of consequences, possibly coupled with indicators of higher levels of consequences impending	Surged posture becomes indefinitely necessary, rather than only temporarily. The DHS Secretary is engaged, and appropriate designation of authorities and activation of Federal capabilities such as the Cyber Unified Command Group take place. Other similar non-Federal incident response mechanisms are engaged
3	Elevated	Early indications of, or the potential for but no indicators of, moderate to severe levels of consequences	Upward shift in precautionary measures occurs. Responding entities are capable of managing incidents/events within the parameters of normal, or slight enhanced, operational posture
4	Guarded	Baseline of risk acceptance	Baseline operations, regular information sharing, exercise of processes and procedures, reporting, and mitigation strategy continue without undue disruption or resource allocation

U.S. Computer Emergency Readiness Team (US-CERT). US-CERT is a partnership between DHS and the public and private sectors. US-CERT is charged with providing response support and defense against cyber attacks for the Federal Civil Executive Branch (.gov) and information sharing and collaboration among State, Local, Tribal and Territorial governments, industry, and international partners. US-CERT interacts with Federal agencies, industry, the research community, State, Local, Tribal and Territorial governments, and other entities to disseminate reasoned and actionable cybersecurity information to the public. US-CERT also provides a way for citizens, businesses, and other institutions to communicate and coordinate directly with the U.S. Government about cybersecurity. [30, pp. N-2]

Industrial Control Systems Cyber Emergency Response Team (ICS-CERT). ICS-CERT provides focused operational capabilities for defending control system environments against emerging cyber threats. ICS-CERT provides efficient coordination of control systems-related security incidents and information sharing with Federal, State, Local, Tribal and Territorial agencies and organizations; the Intelligence Community (IC); private sector constituents, including vendors, owners, and operators; and international and private sector CERTs. ICS-CERT leads this effort by responding to and analyzing control systems-related incidents, conducting vulnerability and malware analysis, providing onsite support for forensic investigations, and providing situational awareness in the form of actionable intelligence and reports. [30, pp. N-2]

The DHS NCCIC primarily serves as a warning and alerting system. While the US-CERT and ICS-CERT may provide analysis and recommendations, DHS does not have deployable cyber units that will show up onsite and fix your cyber problems. The closest such capability is being built by the Department of Defense (DoD) as part of their National Cyber Mission Force (CMF) promulgated under the DoD's Cyber Strategy. The DoD Cyber Strategy has three missions: 1) defend DoD networks, systems, and information; 2) defend the U.S. homeland and U.S. national interests against cyber attacks of significant consequence; and 3) provide cyber support to military operational and contingency plans. Towards this end, DoD will develop 68 Cyber Protection Teams (CPTs) to perform the first mission; 13 National Mission Teams (NMTs) for the second mission; 27 Combat Mission Teams (CMTs) for the third mission; and 25 National Support Teams (NSTs) to assist them all. [31]

The DHS National Cybersecurity and Communications Integration Center (NCCIC) primarily serves as a warning and alerting system. While the US-CERT and ICS-CERT may provide analysis and recommendations, DHS does not have deployable cyber units that will show up onsite and fix your cyber problems.

The 13 National Mission Teams comprising the National Mission Force (NMF) will be supported by 8 NSTs (also called Direct Support Teams), and will be designed to defend the nation against strategic cyber attacks on U.S. interests. Reportedly, the NMTs will employ counter-cyber force to stop cyber attacks and malicious cyber activity of significant consequences against the nation. [32, p. 9]

While details remain sketchy, it appears the NMTs will only be employed in the case of foreign cyber attack. Attribution is a thorny problem when it comes to cyber attack. As was already mentioned, few cyber criminals are identified let alone caught. The implication is that NMTs will have very limited domestic utility, and there will be no cyber cavalry coming to the rescue in the event of a significant domestic cyber attack. Ultimately, infrastructure owners/operators must rely on their own devices to protect their assets.

Protecting Cyber Assets

In February 2013, President Obama signed EO 13636, Improving Critical Infrastructure Cybersecurity, assigning the National Institute of Standards and Technology (NIST) responsibility for developing a Cybersecurity Framework. The framework was to form the basis for a Voluntary Critical Infrastructure Cybersecurity Program that would encourage critical infrastructure owners and operators to improve the security of their information networks. NIST released Version 1.0 of the Framework February 12, 2014. [33, p. 13]

EO 13636 also required those agencies with regulatory authority over certain critical infrastructure owner and operators to evaluate whether "the agency has clear authority to establish requirements... to sufficiently address current and project cyber risks to critical infrastructure." Although DHS has no regulatory authority over Internet Service Providers, as the Sector Specific Agency DHS recommended voluntary application of cybersecurity measures for the Information Technology sector. [34]

The NIST Cybersecurity Framework is a risk-based approach to managing cybersecurity risk, and is composed of three parts: the Framework Core, the Framework Implementation Tiers, and the Framework Profiles. Each Framework component reinforces the connection between business drivers and cybersecurity activities. [35]

In February 2013, President Obama signed EO 13636 directing the National Institute of Standards and Technology (NIST) to develop a Cybersecurity Framework. A year later, NIST released v1.0 of a framework that was to form the basis of a Voluntary Cybersecurity Program encouraging critical infrastructure owners and operators to improve the

The Framework Core is a set of cybersecurity activities, desired outcomes, and applicable references that are common across critical infrastructure sectors. The Core presents industry standards, guidelines, and practices in a manner that allows for communication of cybersecurity activities and outcomes across the organization from the executive level to the implementation/operations level. The Framework Core consists of five concurrent and continuous Functions—Identify, Protect, Detect, Respond, Recover. When considered together, these Functions provide a high-level, strategic view of the lifecycle of an organization's management of cybersecurity risk. The Framework Core then identifies underlying key Categories and Subcategories for each Function, and matches them with example Informative References such as existing standards, guidelines, and practices for each Subcategory. [35]

Framework Implementation Tiers ("Tiers") provide context on how an organization views cybersecurity risk and the processes in place to manage that risk. Tiers describe the degree to which an organization's cybersecurity risk management practices exhibit the characteristics defined in the Framework (e.g., risk and threat aware, repeatable, and adaptive). The Tiers characterize an organization's practices over a range, from Partial (Tier 1) to Adaptive (Tier 4). These Tiers reflect a progression from informal, reactive responses to approaches that are agile and risk-informed. During the Tier selection process, an organization should consider its current risk management practices, threat environment, legal and regulatory requirements, business/mission objectives, and organizational constraints. [35]

A Framework Profile ("Profile") represents the outcomes based on business needs that an organization has selected from the Framework Categories and Subcategories. The Profile can be characterized as the alignment of standards, guidelines, and practices to the Framework Core in a particular implementation scenario. Profiles can be used to identify opportunities for improving cybersecurity posture by comparing a "Current" Profile (the "as is" state) with a "Target" Profile (the "to be" state). To develop a Profile, an organization can review all of the Categories and Subcategories and, based on business drivers and a risk assessment, determine which are most important; they can add Categories and Subcategories as needed to address the organization's risks. The Current Profile can then be used to support prioritization and measurement of progress toward the Target Profile, while factoring in other business needs including cost-effectiveness and innovation. Profiles can be used to conduct self-assessments and communicate within an organization or between organizations. [35]

While the NIST Cybersecurity Framework doesn't explain how, it is assumed that an asset's profile can be mapped to a tier level. Presumably the higher the tier level, the more secure the asset. But this is all about risk management, so there are no guarantees.

Conclusion

Cybersecurity as a mission of homeland security has come full circle. Recognizing that the growing use of the Internet portended a potential avenue of attack, the 1997 Report of the President's Commission on Critical Infrastructure can be considered the beginning of homeland security. PDD-63 laid the foundation for the critical infrastructure protection mission. Whereas PDD-63 was focused on cyber threats to infrastructure, HSPD-7 understandably gave priority to physical threats after the example of 9/11. In response to the growing frequency and ferocity of cyber attacks on the nation, PPD-21 restored the primacy of cybersecurity to homeland security. Cybersecurity and critical infrastructure protection are inseparable. Aware of the potential worst case scenarios, today we remain an ever vigilant nation against cyber attack.

Challenge Your Understanding

The following questions are designed to challenge your understanding of the material presented in this chapter. Some questions may require additional research outside this book in order to provide a complete answer.

1. How is cybersecurity related to critical infrastructure protection?
2. Why does cyber attack hold so much destructive potential?
3. Of the possible worst case scenarios, which do you think would be most devastating? Explain.
4. Of the possible worst case scenarios, which do you think would be most long lasting? Explain.
5. Who owns the Internet?
6. Who manages the Internet?
7. According to the 1984 Counterfeit Access Device and Computer Fraud & Abuse Act, which of the following actions constitute a crime?
    a. Accessing a computer without the owner's consent.
    b. Probing a network to assess its security measures.
    c. Disconnecting the Internet to contain a virus.
8. List and describe two potential targets that could shutdown the Internet.
9. What is DHS's role in cybersecurity?
10. How many cyber teams does DHS have ready to deploy in the event of a national emergency?

Chapter 17

Counterterrorism

Learning Outcomes

Careful study of this chapter will help a student do the following:

- Explain how terrorism uniquely distinguishes the crime of assault.
- Explain why Islamic extremism is considered a terrorist threat.
- Evaluate the 2011 National Strategy for Counterterrorism.
- Assess the different roles of the FBI and DHS under PDD - 39/HSPD-5.
- Discuss the primary means for dealing with known terrorists, foreign or domestic.
- Compare different options for dealing with foreign terrorists.

"Those who would give up essential Liberty, to purchase a little temporary Safety, deserve neither Liberty nor Safety."

- Benjamin Franklin, November 11, 1755

Introduction

9/11 was largely seen as a failure of coordination between Law Enforcement and the Intelligence Community. While debating the role and structure of the new Department of Homeland Security, Congress briefly considered subordinating the Intelligence Community under the direction of the new Department. Concerns over potential abuses infringing on civil liberties, however, quickly ended this consideration. Instead, DHS was assigned a role of bridging the gap between the Law Enforcement and Intelligence Communities to prevent future such attacks. While the Department of Homeland Security plays an integral role filling the gaps exposed by 9/11, primary responsibility for counterterrorism remains with the Federal Bureau of Investigation. This chapter will briefly examine the threat, the roles and relationships of the responsible Federal agencies, and what they're doing to counter it.

Assault of any type is generally illegal. What distinguishes terrorism is the motive behind the assault; an intention to intimidate or coerce the U.S. population or government.

Terrorism

As has already been seen, terrorism is a crime distinguished by motive. Terrorism is defined in Title 18 United States Code, Section 2331, as "Acts dangerous to human life that are a violation of the criminal laws of the United States or of any State, that appear to be intended to intimidate or coerce a civilian population; influence the policy of a government by intimidation or coercion; or to affect the conduct of a government by mass destruction, assassination, or kidnapping." The particular crime is assault. There are many different types of assault, all of them generally illegal. What distinguishes terrorism is the motive behind the assault; an intention to intimidate or coerce the U.S. population or government.

Terrorists, accordingly, are people guilty of the crime of terrorism. They need not execute the crime to be guilty of it. Merely planning the crime makes them guilty of criminal conspiracy, which makes the planners terrorists. Similarly, even though terrorism is a crime under U.S. law, it does not just apply to U.S. citizens. Anybody guilty of planning or committing a crime on U.S. territory is subject to U.S. law, and may therefore be brought before U.S. justice.

Terrorism, as a motive, is a homeland security concern. Unfortunately, terrorism and homeland security have become synonymous. It is important to understand the difference. Certainly the 9/11 hijackers were terrorists by every means of the definition. So was Timothy McVeigh, the criminal behind the 1995 Oklahoma City Bombing. While terrorism is a concern for homeland security, it is not the homeland security concern. As has been shown, the homeland security concern is about domestic catastrophic destruction. While terrorism may be one motivating factor, it is not the only motivating factor. As Hurricane Katrina demonstrated, homeland security threats need have no motive whatsoever.

A similar confusion seems to relate terrorism to mass murder. The two are not the same. The act of "mass killing" is defined by the 2012 Investigative Assistance for Violent Crimes Act (28 USC 530C) as "three or more killings in a single incident". Thus the 1999 shootings that killed 13 at Columbine High School CO, 2012 shootings that killed 26 at Sandy Hook Elementary School CT, and 2007 shootings that killed 32 at Virginia Technical University, VA may be labeled "mass killings", but no evidence indicates that the shooters harbored terrorist motives. They were not terrorist incidents.

Terrorism is a crime under Title 18 USC, S2331. Anybody guilty of planning or committing a terrorist act on U.S. territory, or against a U.S. citizen anywhere , is subject to U.S. law and may be brought before U.S. justice.

The Terrorist Threat

From a legal standpoint, the terrorist threat is nothing more than criminal assault undertaken for the purpose of extorting the U.S. government. Of course all crime is to be discouraged, but what makes this particular class of crime a national priority? The short answer is 9/11; Oklahoma City too. In both cases, terrorist motives drove the perpetrators to extreme measures. Their crimes were shocking in both their magnitudes and proportions. It is concern about preventing another 9/11 that distinguishes terrorism. And because of their anti-government sentiment, domestic militias and radical Islamists are a particular concern.

The militia movement is a relatively new right-wing extremist movement consisting of armed paramilitary groups, both formal and informal, with an anti-government, conspiracy-oriented ideology. Militia groups began to form not long after the deadly standoff at Waco, Texas, in 1993; by the spring of 1995, they had spread to almost every state. Many members of militia groups have been arrested since then, usually on weapons, explosives and conspiracy charges. Although the militia movement has declined in strength from its peak in early 1996, it remains an active movement, especially in the Midwest, and continues to cause a number of problems for law enforcement and the communities in which militia groups are active. [1]

Radical Islamists, also known as Fundamental Islamists, Islamic Extremists, and Militant Islamists, came to be represented by Osama bin Laden's organization, al Qaeda, following the 9/11 attacks. Al Qaeda became a rallying point for disaffected Muslims who sought to strike at the United States directly during operations in Iraq and Afghanistan. Founded on the writings of Sayyid Qutb, Al Qaeda fought to restore Islam by establishing "true Islamic states", implementing sharia, and eliminating non-Muslim influences and the enemies of Islam, which in their view the United States figured prominently. [2] The al Qaeda movement continued long after bin Laden went into hiding and was eventually killed. Then in 2013, al Qaeda was eclipsed by the Islamic State (IS). The movement consolidated various opposition forces, including elements of al Qaeda, to support armed insurgencies in Iraq and Syria. Two years after U.S. troops withdrew from Iraq in 2011, IS forces overran western Iraq and parts of Syria and claimed the territory as part of a new Islamic Caliphate. IS became notorious for broadcasting executions of captured western prisoners. IS also claimed responsibility for the November 2015 attacks that killed 130 people in Paris. [3] The U.S. accordingly renewed its commitment of military support to assist Iraq in driving back IS, and similarly strengthened military operations against IS in Syria. Given their past records of attack and avowed enmity towards the United States, the prevailing concern is that either al Qaeda or IS might seek to mount another 9/11 or similar attack against the U.S.

Because of their anti-government sentiment, domestic militias and radical Islamists are a particular terrorist concern.

Counterterrorism

Following the Tokyo Subway and Oklahoma City attacks, on June 21 1995 President Clinton issued Presidential Decision Directive No. 39 (PDD-39) stating U.S. Policy on Counterterrorism: "The United States regards all such terrorism as a potential threat to national security as well as a criminal act and will apply all appropriate means to combat it. In doing so, the U.S. shall pursue vigorously efforts to deter and preempt, apprehend and prosecute, or assist other governments to prosecute, individuals who perpetrate or plan to perpetrate such attacks." [4] The shorthand description for these activities is "counterterrorism", abbreviated "CT". Counterterrorism is defined in Joint Publication 3-26 as "Activities and operations taken to neutralize terrorists and their organizations and networks in order to render them incapable of using violence to instill fear and coerce governments or societies to achieve their goals." [5, pp. GL-3]

National Strategy for Counterterrorism

The 2011 National Strategy for Counterterrorism articulates the U.S. Government's approach to countering terrorism and identifies the range of tools employed by the strategy. Though specifically directed against the threat of al Qaeda, the same approach applies to IS. [6, p. 2] The 2011 Strategy identified eight overarching goals:

1. Protect the American People, Homeland, and American Interests. The most solemn responsibility of the President and the United States Government is to protect the American people, both at home and abroad. This includes eliminating threats to their physical safety, countering threats to global peace and security, and promoting and protecting U.S. interests around the globe. [6, p. 8]

2. Disrupt, Degrade, Dismantle, and Defeat al-Qa'ida and Its Affiliates and Adherents. The American people and interests will not be secure from attacks until this threat is eliminated—its primary individuals and groups rendered powerless, and its message relegated to irrelevance. [6, p. 8]

3. Prevent Terrorist Development, Acquisition, and Use of Weapons of Mass Destruction. The danger of nuclear terrorism is the greatest threat to global security. Terrorist organizations, including al-Qa'ida, have engaged in efforts to develop and acquire weapons of mass destruction (WMD)—and if successful, they are likely to use them. Therefore, the United States will work with partners around the world to deter WMD theft, smuggling, and terrorist use; target and disrupt terrorist networks that engage in WMD-related activities; secure nuclear, biological, and chemical materials; prevent illicit trafficking of WMD-related materiel; provide multilateral nonproliferation organizations with the resources, capabilities, and authorities they need to be effective; and deepen international cooperation and strengthen institutions and partnerships that prevent WMD and nuclear materials from falling into the hands of terrorists. Success will require us to work with the international community in each of these areas while establishing security measures commensurate with the threat, reinforcing counter-smuggling measures, and ensuring that all of these efforts are sustained over time. [6, pp. 8-9]

Radical Islamists, also known as Fundamental Islamists, Islamic Extremists, and Militant Islamists, came to be represented by al Qaeda. Founded on the writings of Sayyid Qutb, Al Qaeda fought to restore Islam by establishing "true Islamic states", implementing sharia, and eliminating non-Muslim influences and the enemies of Islam, which in their view the United States figured prominently.

4. Eliminate Safehavens. Al-Qa'ida and its affiliates and adherents rely on the physical sanctuary of ungoverned or poorly governed territories, where the absence of state control permits terrorists to travel, train, and engage in plotting. In close coordination with foreign partners, the United States will continue to contest and diminish al-Qa'ida's operating space through mutually reinforcing efforts designed to prevent al-Qa'ida from taking advantage of these ungoverned spaces. We will also build the will and capacity of states whose weaknesses al-Qa'ida exploits. Persistent insecurity and chaos in some regions can undermine efforts to increase political engagement and build capacity and provide assistance, thereby exacerbating chaos and insecurity. Our challenge is to break this cycle of state failure to constrict the space available to terrorist networks. [6, p. 9]

5. Build Enduring Counterterrorism Partnerships and Capabilities. Foreign partners are essential to the success of our CT efforts; these states are often themselves the target of—and on the front lines in countering—terrorist threats. The United States will continue to rely on and leverage the capabilities of its foreign partners even as it looks to contribute to their capacity and bolster their will. To achieve our objectives, partners must demonstrate the willingness and ability to operate independently, augmenting and complementing U.S. CT efforts with their unique insights and capabilities in their countries and regions. Building strong enduring partnerships based on shared understandings of the threat and common objectives is essential to every one of our overarching CT objectives. Assisting partners to improve and expand governance in select instances is also critical, including strengthening the rule of law so that suspected terrorists can be brought

to justice within a respected and transparent system. Success will depend on our ability to work with partners bilaterally, through efforts to achieve greater regional integration, and through multilateral and international institutions. [6, p. 9]

6. Degrade Links between al-Qa'ida and its Affiliates and Adherents. Al-Qa'ida senior leaders in Pakistan continue to leverage local and regional affiliates and adherents worldwide through formal and informal alliances to advance their global agenda. Al-Qa'ida exploits local grievances to bolster recruitment, expand its operational reach, destabilize local governments, and reinforce safehavens from which it and potentially other terrorist groups can operate and attack the United States. Together with our partners, we will degrade the capabilities of al-Qa'ida's local and regional affiliates and adherents, monitor their communications with al-Qa'ida leaders, drive fissures between these groups and their bases of support, and isolate al-Qa'ida from local and regional affiliates and adherents who can augment its capabilities and further its agenda. [6, p. 9]

The 2011 National Strategy for Counterterrorism articulates the U.S. Government's approach to countering terrorism and identifies the range of tools employed by the strategy. Though specifically directed against the threat of al Qaeda, the same approach applies to Islamic State (IS).

7. Counter al-Qa'ida Ideology and Its Resonance and Diminish the Specific Drivers of Violence that al-Qa'ida Exploits. This Strategy prioritizes U.S. and partner efforts to undercut al-Qa'ida's fabricated legitimization of violence and its efforts to spread its ideology. As we have seen in the Middle East and North Africa, al-Qa'ida's calls for perpetual violence to address longstanding grievances have met a devastating rebuke in the face of nonviolent mass movements that seek solutions through expanded individual rights. Along with the majority of people across all religious and cultural traditions, we aim for a world in which al-Qa'ida is openly and widely rejected by all audiences as irrelevant to their aspirations and concerns, a world where al-Qa'ida's ideology does not shape perceptions of world and local events, inspire violence, or serve as a recruiting tool for the group or its adherents. Although achieving this objective is likely to require a concerted long-term effort, we must retain a focus on addressing the near-term challenge of preventing those individuals already on the brink from embracing al-Qa'ida ideology and resorting to violence. We will work closely with local and global partners, inside and outside governments, to discredit al-Qa'ida ideology and reduce its resonance. We will put forward a positive vision of engagement with foreign publics and support for universal rights that demonstrates that the United States aims to build while al-Qa'ida would only destroy. We will apply focused foreign and development assistance abroad. At the same time, we will continue to assist, engage, and connect communities to increase their collective resilience abroad and at home. These efforts strengthen bulwarks against radicalization, recruitment, and mobilization to violence in the name of al-Qa'ida and will focus in particular on those drivers that we know al-Qa'ida exploits. [6, pp. 9-10]

8. Deprive Terrorists of their Enabling Means. Al-Qa'ida and its affiliates and adherents continue to derive significant financial support from donors in the Persian Gulf region and elsewhere through kidnapping for ransom and from exploitation of or control over lucrative elements of the local economy. Terrorist facilitation extends beyond the financial arena to those who enable travel of recruits and operatives; acquisition and movement of materiel; and electronic and non-electronic communication. The United States will collaborate with partner nations around the world to increase our collective capacity to identify terrorist operatives and prevent their travel and movement of supplies across national borders and within states. We will continue to expand and enhance efforts aimed at blocking the flow of financial resources to and among terrorist groups and to disrupt terrorist facilitation and support activities, imposing sanctions or pursuing prosecutions to enforce violations and dissuade others. We will also continue our focus on countering kidnapping for ransom, which is an increasingly important funding source for al-Qa'ida and its affiliates and adherents. Through our diplomatic outreach, we will continue to encourage countries—especially those in Europe—to adopt a policy against making concessions to kidnappers while using tailored messages unilaterally and with our partners to delegitimize the taking of hostages. Mass media and the Internet in particular have emerged as enablers for terrorist planning, facilitation, and communication, and we will continue to counter terrorists' ability to exploit them. [6, p. 10]

PDD-39 made the FBI responsible for preventing and responding to domestic terrorist attacks. In 2003, after establishment of the Department of Homeland Security, HSPD-5 amended PDD-39 making DHS responsible for coordinating the Federal response to domestic incidents, including terrorist attacks.

Counterterrorism Responsibilities

PDD-39 placed responsibility for U.S. counterterrorism efforts with the Department of Justice (DOJ) and the Department of State (DOS). PDD-39 made the Federal Bureau of Investigation (FBI) under DOJ responsible for preventing and responding to domestic terrorist attacks. Conversely, PDD-39 made the State Department responsible through its ambassadors for coordinating response to attacks on U.S. interests overseas. [4] Following 9/11, Homeland Security Presidential Directive No. 5 modified these roles making the Department of Homeland Security responsible for coordinating the Federal response to domestic incidents, including terrorist attacks. Otherwise, HSPD-5 preserved the FBI's role with investigating and prosecuting acts of terrorism, and DOS retained its role of protecting U.S. interests overseas. [7]

FBI Counterterrorism

The FBI is the lead federal law enforcement agency charged with counterterrorism investigations. This includes terrorist acts committed within and outside U.S. national boundaries. Since the 9/11 attacks, the FBI has implemented a series of reforms intended to transform itself from a largely reactive law enforcement agency focused on investigations of criminal activity into a more proactive, agile, flexible, and intelligence-driven agency that can prevent acts of terrorism. [8, p. ii] The FBI's post-9/11 transformation is particularly evident in four areas: The USA PATRIOT Act provided the FBI additional authorities and enhanced investigative tools. The FBI and DOJ altered the way the Bureau investigated terrorism with the 2008 revision of The Attorney General's Guidelines for Domestic FBI Operations. The FBI expanded operationally via a proliferation of Joint Terrorism Task Forces (JTTFs) across the United States. In so doing, it also increased its cooperation with state, local, and federal agencies. Finally, watershed changes were made in the Bureau's intelligence program. [8, p. 3]

Since the 9/11 attacks, the FBI has implemented a series of reforms intended to transform itself from a largely reactive law enforcement agency focused on investigations of criminal activity into a more proactive, agile, flexible, and intelligence-driven agency that can prevent acts of terrorism.

Historically, there have been differences between electronic surveillance (wiretaps) conducted for intelligence and for law enforcement purposes. Among these is the protection of the constitutional rights of persons under criminal investigation. The Foreign Intelligence Surveillance Act (FISA) regulates intelligence collection directed at foreign powers and agents of foreign powers in the United States to include those engaged in international terrorism. FISA required the government to certify that "the purpose" of surveillance was to gather foreign intelligence information. Prior to the USA PATRIOT Act, DOJ turned the "primary purpose" standard into written policy that had the effect of limiting the coordination between intelligence and criminal investigators. This came to be known as "the Wall" between intelligence and law enforcement and the "unfortunate consequences" of this barrier to information sharing were noted by the 9/11 Commission in its report on the 9/11 attacks. Section 218 of the USA PATRIOT Act amended FISA to replace the phrase "the purpose" with the phrase "a significant purpose." As one legal scholar described it, by moving the FISA requirement from the purpose to a significant purpose, the USA PATRIOT Act "knocked out the foundation for 'the Wall.'" This removed impediments to the exchange of information about terrorism or other national security threats between intelligence and law enforcement personnel. [8, pp. 3-4]

The FBI and DOJ also emphasized their forward-leaning approach with the September 29, 2008, revision of the Attorney General's Guidelines for Domestic FBI Operations, which they claim "make the FBI's operations in the United States more effective by providing simpler, clearer, and more uniform standards and procedures." Referred to as the "Mukasey Guidelines" after Michael B. Mukasey, who was Attorney General at the time of their release, this is the latest in a series of guidelines stretching back to 1976 that govern the FBI's investigative activities. The Mukasey Guidelines went into effect on December 1, 2008. In large part, these guidelines sprang from the post-9/11 national security context, in which the FBI surmised that it could not simply react to crimes. It had to preemptively search for criminal, counterintelligence, and terrorist threats to the homeland. The most prominent changes in the Mukasey Guidelines concern "assessments." Agents and analysts may now use assessments outside of the more traditional preliminary and full investigations, which require some level of factual predication. Preliminary investigations can be opened with "any 'allegation or information' indicative of possible criminal activity or threats to the national security." Opening a full investigation requires an "'articulable factual basis' of possible criminal or national threat activity." On the other hand, opening an assessment does not require particular factual predication. Assessments are not to be "pursued for frivolous or improper purposes and are not based solely on First Amendment activity or on the race, ethnicity, national origin, or religion of the subject of the assessment, or a combination of only such factors." Assessments offer terrorism investigators a variety of techniques, including public surveillance and the use of confidential informants to penetrate conspiracies. The Bureau has incorporated assessments into its investigative processes. According to numbers made publicly available in March 2011, the FBI initiated 11,667 assessments to check leads on individuals, activities, groups, or organizations between December 2008 and March 2009. These, in turn, led to 427 preliminary or full investigations. Officials noted that about one-third of the assessments resulted from vague tips. Reportedly, between March 2009 and March 2011, the Bureau opened 82,325 assessments. About half of the assessments from this time frame focused on determining whether specific groups or individuals were spies or terrorists. This pool of 42,888 assessments produced just under 2,000 full or preliminary investigations. [8, pp. 11-12]

The FBI's post-9/11 transformation was facilitated by 1) enhanced authorities provided under the USA PATRIOT Act; 2) new General Guidelines making it easier to develop a terrorist case; 3) expansion of Joint Terrorism Task Forces (JTTFs) increasing cooperation with State and Local law enforcement; and 4) watershed changes to the Bureau's intelligence program.

JTTFs are locally based, multi-agency teams of investigators, analysts, linguists, SWAT experts, and other specialists who investigate terrorism and terrorism-related crimes. Seventy-one of the more than 100 JTTFs operated by DOJ and the FBI were created since 9/11. Over 4,400 federal, state, and local law enforcement officers and agents—more than four times the pre-9/11 total— work in them. These officers and agents come from more than 600 state and local agencies and 50 federal agencies. The FBI considers the JTTFs "the nation's front line on terrorism." They "investigate acts of terrorism that affect the U.S., its interests, property and citizens, including those employed by the U.S. and military personnel overseas." As this suggests, their operations are highly tactical and focus on investigations, developing human sources (informants), and gathering intelligence to thwart terrorist plots. JTTFs also offer an important conduit for the sharing of intelligence developed from FBI-led counterterrorism investigations with outside agencies and state and local law enforcement. To help facilitate this, especially as the threat of homegrown jihadists has emerged, the number of top-secret security clearances issued to local police working on JTTFs has increased from 125 to 878 between 2007 and 2009. There is also a National JTTF, which was established in July 2002 to serve as a coordinating mechanism with the FBI's partners. Some 40 agencies are now represented in the National JTTF, which has become a focal point for information sharing and the management of large-scale projects that involve multiple partners. [8, pp. 13-14]

DOS Counterterrorism

The Department of State has six regional bureaus that address foreign policy considerations on a regional basis. The assistant secretaries of the regional bureaus are key actors in CT activities and operations policy in their assigned regions. Furthermore, the DOS Bureau of Counterterrorism publishes an annual country report on terrorism and manages US policy for a whole-of-government approach to CT. The DOS Bureau of Counterterrorism maintains the Foreign Terrorist Organizations List that provides justification for the President to block or freeze tangible property and freeze financial accounts of individuals or terrorist organizations pursuant to Executive Order 13224, Blocking Property and Prohibiting Transactions With Persons Who Commit, Threaten to Commit, or Support Terrorism. This tool is designed to sever terrorists' organizations logistics and resources. These efforts are worked through Partner Nations (PNs) where the United States maintains country teams under the leadership of the local ambassador, technically known as the Chief of Mission (COM). [5, pp. III-2]

DHS does not generally engage in traditional foreign intelligence collection activities such as imagery intelligence, signals intelligence, human intelligence, measurement and signatures intelligence, and foreign open source intelligence.

The COM is the personal representative of the President and the official U.S. Government (USG) representative in the host country. The COM is responsible for the conduct of relations with the host government and is the primary channel for communications with that government. The COM directs, coordinates, and supervises all USG executive branch employees in that effort, except those under the command of a U.S. military commander. CT activities and operations conducted by the Department of Defense (DoD) and other USG departments and agencies require COM concurrence prior to execution, unless otherwise directed by the President. [5, pp. III-2]

The FBI, in coordination with the Secretary of State and the COM, will assume lead responsibility for law enforcement investigation of terrorist or WMD incidents abroad. The FBI's tasks may include taking custody of suspected terrorists, lawful transfer of custody of suspected terrorists, forensic examination of material collected of possible intelligence or criminal prosecution value, and hostage negotiation support. [5, pp. III-2]

DHS Counterterrorism

The 2002 Homeland Security Act made it the mission of the Department of Homeland Security to "prevent terrorist attacks within the United States." [9] Since its inception in 2003, DHS has had an intelligence component to support this mission and has been a member of the U.S. Intelligence Community (IC). The Homeland Security Act of 2002, assigned the original DHS intelligence component—the Directorate of Information

Analysis and Infrastructure Protection—with responsibility to receive, analyze, and integrate law enforcement and intelligence information in order to— "(A) identify and assess the nature and scope of terrorist threats to the homeland; (B) detect and identify threats of terrorism against the United States; and (C) understand such threats in light of actual and potential vulnerabilities of the homeland." [10, pp. ii-1]

Following the Second Stage Review (2SR) in July 2005, former Secretary of Homeland Security, Michael Chertoff established a strengthened Office of Intelligence and Analysis (I&A) and made the Assistant Secretary for Information Analysis the Chief Intelligence Officer (CINT) for the Department. He also tasked I&A with ensuring that intelligence is coordinated, fused, and analyzed within the Department to provide a common operational picture; provide a primary connection between DHS and the IC as a whole; and to act as a primary source of information for state, local and private sector partners. [10, p. ii]

DHS I&A combines the unique information collected by DHS components as part of their operational activities (e.g., at airports, seaports, and the border) with foreign intelligence from the Intelligence Community; law enforcement information from Federal, state, local, and tribal sources; private sector data about critical infrastructure and key resources; and information from domestic open sources to develop homeland security intelligence.

Today, the DHS Intelligence Enterprise (DHS IE) consists of those elements within DHS that have an intelligence mission. These include I&A, the Office of Cyber and Infrastructure Analysis (OCIA), and the Intelligence Division of the Office of Operations Coordination and Planning (all located at DHS headquarters), and the intelligence elements of six DHS operational components: U.S. Customs and Border Protection (CBP), U.S. Immigration and Customs Enforcement (ICE), U.S. Citizenship and Immigration Services (USCIS), the Transportation Security Administration (TSA), U.S. Coast Guard (USCG), and U.S. Secret Service (USSS). [10, p. 3]

The heads of the DHS intelligence components do not report to the I&A Under Secretary, but to their respective component chiefs. However, pursuant to the Implementing Recommendations of the 9/11 Commission Act of 2007, they are required to advise and coordinate closely with the Under Secretary on their activities in support of the intelligence mission of the Department. In order to provide senior-level direction for Department-wide intelligence activities, a Homeland Security Intelligence Council (HSIC) was formed. The HSIC is comprised of the key intelligence officials from applicable DHS components. [10, p. 7]

DHS does not generally engage in traditional foreign intelligence collection activities such as imagery intelligence, signals intelligence, human intelligence, measurement and signatures intelligence, and foreign open source intelligence. I&A combines the unique information collected by DHS components as part of their operational activities (e.g., at airports, seaports, and the border) with foreign intelligence from the Intelligence Community; law enforcement information from Federal, state, local, and tribal sources; private sector data about critical infrastructure and key resources; and information from domestic open sources to develop homeland security intelligence.

This encompasses a broad range of homeland security threats. It includes border security information to counter human smuggling and trafficking, cargo data to prevent the introduction of dangerous items, information to protect critical infrastructure against all hazards, information about infectious diseases, and demographic data and other research about 'violent radicalization.' [10, p. 5]

Nevertheless, I&A is a full partner within the Intelligence Community and represents DHS on several IC committees. The Under Secretary, for example, is a member of the Director of National Intelligence (DNI) Executive Committee. I&A contributes analytic staff to the National Counterterrorism Center (NCTC). The office also contributes items to the President's Daily Brief providing a unique homeland security perspective on terrorism and other threats to the United States to the nation's leaders. [10, p. 6]

As terrorism is a crime, the first order of action is to apprehend and arrest those suspected of planning or executing such crimes and prosecuting them under State and Federal law.

I&A produces numerous intelligence products including the Homeland Security Threat Assessment, an annual report identifying major threats to the homeland. I&A also produces Intelligence Notes, Intelligence Warnings, Homeland Security Assessments, etc. I&A makes the products of its analysis available to state and local officials through the Homeland Security Information Network (HSIN), a web-based platform that facilitates Sensitive But Unclassified information sharing and collaboration between federal, state, local, tribal, private sector, and international partners. HSIN provides real-time, interactive connectivity between states and major urban areas and the DHS National Operations Center (NOC). [10, pp. 9-10]

Congress made information sharing a top priority of the Department's intelligence component in the Homeland Security Act of 2002 and underscored its importance through the Intelligence Reform and Terrorism Prevention Act of 2004. Since the 2SR reorganization, Congress imposed additional requirements for intelligence analysis; information sharing; department-wide intelligence integration; and support to state, local, tribal governments, and the private sector through the Implementing Recommendations of the 9/11 Commission Act of 2007. [10, p. ii]

In an effort to strengthen intelligence and information sharing and analysis capabilities with states and major urban areas, DHS established intelligence fusion centers. Congress defines fusion centers as a "collaborative effort of two or more Federal, state, local, or tribal government agencies that combines resources, expertise, or information with the goal of maximizing the ability of such agencies to detect, prevent, investigate, apprehend, and respond to criminal or terrorist activity." At the end of 2009, there were 72 DHS/FBI designated state and Urban Area Security Initiative (UASI) fusion centers. I&A supports these centers by providing operational, analytic, reporting, and management advice and assistance; training; information technology systems and connectivity; and intelligence officers and analysts. [10, pp. 11-12]

Direct Actions

As terrorism is a crime, the first order of action is to apprehend and arrest those suspected of planning or executing such crimes and prosecuting them under State and Federal law. For suspects beyond our borders, the Attorney General will attempt to extradite them and render them to U.S. justice. In the case that a foreign government refuses to surrender a suspect, the U.S. might conduct a rendition essentially kidnapping the suspect and forcefully taking them into custody. In the case where a foreign government is incapable of surrendering or otherwise controlling a terrorist menace, the U.S. might employ military force to remove or eliminate the threat.

Persons suspected of criminal or terrorist activity may be transferred from one State (i.e., country) to another for arrest, detention, and/or interrogation. Commonly, this is done through extradition, by which one State surrenders a person within its jurisdiction to a requesting State via a formal legal process, typically established by treaty. Far less often, such transfers are effectuated through a process known as "extraordinary rendition" or "irregular rendition." These terms have often been used to refer to the extrajudicial transfer of a person from one State to another. [11, p. ii] The first well-known rendition case involved the Achille Lauro hijackers in 1985: after they were given a plane and were enroute in international air space, they were forced by United States Navy fighter planes to land at the Naval Air Station Sigonella, an Italian military base in Sicily used by the US Navy and NATO. [12] Following the attacks of September 11, 2001, however, what had been a limited program expanded dramatically, with some experts estimating that 150 foreign nationals taken by the CIA. Foreign nationals suspected of terrorism have been transported to detention and interrogation facilities in Jordan, Iraq, Egypt, Diego Garcia, Afghanistan, Guantánamo, and elsewhere. [13] Suspects were reportedly arrested, blindfolded, shackled, and sedated, or otherwise kidnapped, and transported by private jet or other means to the destination country. [12] The practice became controversial during the Bush Administration because the destination countries were known to employ harsh interrogation techniques rising to the level of torture, purportedly with the knowledge or acquiescence of the United States. In January 2009, President Obama issued an Executive Order creating a special task force to review U.S. transfer policies, including the practice of rendition, to ensure compliance with applicable legal requirements. [11, p. ii]

For suspects beyond our borders, the Attorney General will attempt to extradite them and render them to U.S. justice. In the case that a foreign government refuses to surrender a suspect, the U.S. might conduct a rendition essentially kidnapping the suspect and forcefully taking them into custody. In the case where a foreign government is incapable of surrendering or otherwise controlling a terrorist menace, the U.S. might employ military force to remove or eliminate the threat.

Terrorist suspects beyond the reach of rendition may be subject to U.S. military force. In November 2002, Qaed Salim Sinan al-Harethi, an al-Qaeda operative and Yemeni citizen suspected of involvement in the October 2000 bombing of the USS Cole, was killed by the CIA using a Predator drone firing a Hellfire missile. The attack was controversial because it also killed Kamal Derwish, a U.S. citizen accompanying al-Harethi. The Bush Administration defended the action citing a presidential finding that permitted worldwide covert actions against members of al-Qaeda. Despite the controversy, the use of Predators to kill suspected terrorists has become common practice. [14]

Military force may be delivered in all shapes and sizes, and not just by the Department of Defense. The CIA has an extensive paramilitary capability of its own.

Military force may be delivered in all shapes and sizes, and not just by the Department of Defense. The CIA has an extensive paramilitary capability of its own. By DoD definition, paramilitary forces are distinct from the regular armed forces of any country, but resembling them in organization, equipment, training or mission. In addition to providing intelligence support US military operations from the Korean War era to Iraq today, the CIA has also worked closely alongside DoD personnel in military operations. The CIA typically takes on missions that must be clandestine or covert to avoid directly implicating the U.S. Government. Examples of CIA covert operations include the 1961 Bay of Pigs invasion of Cuba, and interdiction missions along the Ho Chi Minh Trail in Laos, a neutral country during the Vietnam conflict. Despite these mixed results, the CIA is credited with helping depose the Taliban government after they refused to surrender Bin Laden following 9/11. [15, p. 1] Units from the CIA's Special Activities Division (SAD) were the first U.S. forces to enter Afghanistan in September 2001. They joined with the Afghan United Front (Northern Alliance) to prepare for the subsequent arrival of U.S. Special Operations Forces (SOF). Together, the United Front, SAD, and SOF combined to overthrow the Taliban by November. The campaign was noted for its minimal use of conventional military force and correspondingly low casualty count among allies. [16] The CIA was also instrumental in developing the Predator drone, which saw its first combat use in Afghanistan. Today, the Predator is employed extensively to target suspected terrorist leaders around the world. [17]

The DoD employs Special Operations Forces to deliver military capability in hostile, denied, or politically sensitive areas of the world. Special operations are distinguished from regular military operations by degree of physical and political risk, operational techniques, and mode of employment. DoD special operations are frequently clandestine, designed in such a say to conceal them, but not necessarily covert, that is, designed to conceal the identity of the sponsor. [15, p. 1] SOF teams helped provide the Afghan United Front with airpower during the early months of Operation ENDURING FREEDOM. Joint Terminal Attack Controllers (JTACs) using laser range finders helped direct precision guided munitions dropped from orbiting U.S. Air Force B -1 and B-52 bombers onto Taliban targets. This use of airpower proved instrumental in helping the United Front capture the northern city of Mazar-e-Sharif in November 2001. [18] Supported by CIA operatives on the ground, Navy SEALs mounted the raid into Pakistan that succeeded in killing Osama bin Laden on May 2, 2011. [19]

Interagency Coordination

Interagency coordination for counterterrorism operations is accomplished through the National Counterterrorism Center (NCTC). The National Counterterrorism Center was established in 2004 to ensure that information from any source about potential terrorist acts against the U.S. could be made available to analysts and that appropriate responses could be planned. According to the NCTC Charter (P.S. 108-458), the NCTC serves as the principal advisor to the Director of National Intelligence (DNI) on intelligence operations relating to terrorism, and provides strategic operational plans for military and civilian counterterrorism efforts and for effective integration of counterterrorism intelligence and operations across agency boundaries within and outside the United States. The NCTC Director is appointed by the President of the United States. And though the Director reports to the DNI, in practice Director works through the National Security Council and the White House staff. [20]

Interagency coordination for counterterrorism operations is accomplished through the National Counterterrorism Center (NCTC). Interagency coordination for counterterrorism policy is orchestrated by the National Security Council (NSC).

Interagency coordination for counterterrorism policy is orchestrated by the National Security Council. The National Security Council is the key integrator of the President's whole-of-government CT policy and strategies, which requires interagency coordination at the Principals Committee, Deputies Committee, and supporting interagency policy committees, and the efforts of the National Security Council Staff. The key interagency policy committee for CT is the Counterterrorist Security Group, which is led by the Assistant to the President for Homeland Security and Counterterrorism (i.e., the former Homeland Security Advisor). [5, pp. III-1]

Conclusion

The basic difficulty in capturing or killing terrorists is finding them, preferably before they strike. The first problem is identifying potential terrorists. Psychological studies have found no common factors among the profiles of past terrorists: they can be anybody. Attempts by the National Security Agency to identify terrorists by studying their contacts and communications also proved fruitless as well as illegal. And even if they are identified, terrorists are not easy to locate: it took ten years to locate Bin Laden even with a $25 million bounty on his head. The unspoken fact of the matter is that the terrorist threat can never be eliminated. Given this realization, the question arises whether it is more effective to pursue terrorists, or deny them the means for inflicting catastrophic damage?

Challenge Your Understanding

The following questions are designed to challenge your understanding of the material presented in this chapter. Some questions may require additional research outside this book in order to provide a complete answer.

1. How does terrorism uniquely distinguish the crime of assault?
2. Why does al Qaeda remain a terrorist threat after Osama bin Laden's death?
3. Looking at the 2011 National Strategy for Counterterrorism, which short-term goal do you think most effective? Explain.
4. Looking at the 2011 National Strategy for Counterterrorism, which long-term goal do you think most effective? Explain.
5. According to PDD -39/HSPD-5, what is the counterterrorism role of the FBI?
6. According to HSPD -5, what is the counterterrorism role of DHS?
7. How did the USA PATRIOT Act improve the FBI's ability to investigate terrorism?
8. What is the primary means for dealing with known terrorists, foreign or domestic?
9. Describe two options available to the President if foreign governments are unwilling or unable to render unto justice terrorist elements within their country that threaten the United States.
10. As the Director of the National Counterterrorism Center, what circumstances might move you to recommend CIA paramilitary forces over DoD special forces to perform a particular overseas counterterrorism mission?

Chapter 18

Emergency Preparedness & Response

Learning Outcomes

Careful study of this chapter will help a student do the following:

- Explain the responsibility of State Governors to their citizens.
- Explain why 9/11 raised concern about State and Local emergency preparedness.
- Describe Stafford Act authorities to grant Federal disaster assistance to States.
- Describe the FEMA process and means for delivering assistance to States.
- Describe the considerable means available to States for responding to emergencies.
- Evaluate the Incident Commander's role and means for directing emergency response.
- Evaluate the role of exercises for improving emergency preparedness.

"We must prepare to minimize the damage and recover from any future terrorist attacks that may occur despite our best efforts at prevention."

- 2002 National Strategy for Homeland Security

Introduction

9/11 forced the realization that the nation was unprepared to respond to a WMD attack. While FEMA had been established in 1979 to streamline Federal support to natural disasters, it had no corresponding capabilities to integrate Federal support to manmade catastrophes. Moreover, the contrast between the local response at the World Trade Center and the local response at the Pentagon on 9/11 proved that the structured integration of responding agencies through the Incident Command System saved lives. Accordingly, the Department of Homeland Security was commissioned by Congress to begin strengthening the response capabilities of the nation, and make sure they were integrated from the bottom-up through the Local, State, and Federal levels of government.

Following 9/11, the President and Congress sought to improve the nation's ability to respond and recover to domestic catastrophic attack. Of particular concern was the potential employment of WMD.

Integrating the Federal Response

Following 9/11, the President and Congress sought to improve the nation's ability to respond and recover to domestic catastrophic attack. Of particular concern was the potential employment of WMD. In 2002, few parts of the country had the ability to respond to a WMD attack. Even the best prepared states and localities didn't have adequate resources to respond to the full range of potential threats exposed by 9/11. Many did not have in place mutual aid agreements to facilitate cooperation with their neighbors in time of emergency. The Federal government had done relatively little to remedy the situation. What few domestic preparedness programs that existed were spread across eight different Federal departments and agencies, and provided money under a tangled web of grant programs. Accordingly, one of the first objectives for the new Department of Homeland Security was to create a fully integrated national emergency response system capable of dealing with most any catastrophe, both natural and manmade. [1, p. 42]

The first order of business was consolidation. The 2002 Homeland Security Act authorized the establishment of an Emergency Preparedness and Response Directorate within the new Department of Homeland Security. [2] The new directorate incorporated the Strategic National Stockpile and National Disaster Medical System from Health and Human Services, the Nuclear Incident Response Team from the Department of Energy, and the Domestic Emergency Support Teams from the Department of Justice. [3] The Homeland Security Act also allowed the Federal Emergency Management Agency to be incorporated as an independent agency under the new directorate. With FEMA came the authority to distribute grants under the Homeland Security Grant Program. [2]

After consolidation, the next order of business was establishing clear lines of responsibility and authority. On February 28, 2003, HSPD-5 was issued making the Secretary of Homeland Security the Principal Federal Official (PFO) for domestic incident management. It was the Secretary's responsibility to see that executive agencies were prepared to respond and to coordinate their response when Federal assistance was needed in a disaster. HSPD-5 also directed the Secretary to develop a National Response Plan (NRP) detailing how the Federal government would marshal its resources for a disaster, and a National Incident Management System (NIMS) detailing how those resources would be integrated into a local disaster response. [4]

The NIMS provides a standard command and management structure for coordinating a multi-agency response to disaster. Much of NIMS is built upon the Incident Command System (ICS), which was developed by Federal, State, and local wildland fire agencies during the 1970s. ICS is a management system designed to enable effective incident management by integrating a combination of facilities, equipment, personnel, procedures and communications operating within a common organizational structure. [5, pp. 48-49] To facilitate coordination between Federal, State, and Local agencies responding to a disaster, HSPD-5 mandated NIMS for all Federal agencies starting in 2003, and made it a prerequisite for State and Local governments to receive Homeland Security Grant Program funds starting in 2005. [4]

HSPD-5 issued in February 2003 directed the Secretary to develop a National Response Plan (NRP) detailing how the Federal government would marshal its resources for a disaster, and a National Incident Management System (NIMS) detailing how those resources would be integrated into a local disaster response.

The Homeland Security Act mandated the creation of a National Response Plan to replace the previous Federal Response Plan. [2] HSPD-5 assigned the task to the DHS Secretary and provided further guidance on its preparation. [4] The subsequent NRP was released in December 2004. It was a large document comprised of some 426 pages. It provided the basic plan how the Federal government would prepare and respond to disaster at the request of State and Local government. The underlying principle of the plan was that Federal capabilities would be packaged into fifteen Emergency Support Functions (ESFs). Various Federal agencies were assigned responsibility for preparing, maintaining, and providing these ESF capabilities when requested. The Secretary of Homeland Security, under the authority of HSDP-5, was responsible for seeing that the ESFs were ready and available when needed. [6, p. xi] Because it was so big, the problem with the NRP was that few people were familiar with it, let alone had read it by the time Hurricane Katrina struck in August 2005. The flawed response to Hurricane Katrina was attributed, in part, to a failure to follow the NRP. Congress acted by passing the 2006 Post-Katrina Emergency Management Reform Act which elevated FEMA to report directly to the Secretary, and mandated changes to the NRP. [7, pp. CRS-3-CRS-4] As a result, in January 2008, DHS issued the National Response Framework (NRF) which remains the nation's plan for responding to disaster.

Requesting Federal Assistance

Federal disaster assistance is provided upon request of the State Governor. Such a request is made under the authority of the Robert T. Stafford Disaster Relief and Emergency Assistance Act (P.L. 93-288, as amended, hereinafter "the Stafford Act"). To request Federal assistance, the Governor must declare either a State emergency or major disaster. Emergency declarations are made to protect property and public health and safety and to lessen or avert the threat of a major disaster or catastrophe. Emergency declarations are often made when a threat is recognized (such as emergency declarations for hurricanes which may be made prior to landfall) and are intended to supplement and coordinate local and state efforts prior to the event. Emergency declarations are also made to provide direct federal assistance to protect lives and property. This aids activities such as evacuations and the protection of public assets. In contrast, a major disaster declaration is made as a result of the disaster or catastrophic event and constitutes a broader authority that helps states and local communities, as well as families and individuals, respond and recover from the damage caused by the event. [8, pp. ii-1]

Federal disaster assistance is provided upon request of the State Governor. Such a request is made under the authority of the Robert T. Stafford Disaster Relief and Emergency Assistance Act.

Ordinarily, only a Governor can initiate a request for a Presidential emergency or major disaster declaration. In extraordinary circumstances, the President may unilaterally declare a major disaster or emergency. This request is made through the FEMA Regional Administrator and based on a finding that the disaster is of such severity and magnitude that effective response is beyond the capabilities of the State and affected local governments, and that Federal assistance is necessary. [5, p. 41]

The completed request, addressed to the President, is submitted through the FEMA Regional Administrator, who evaluates the damage and requirements for Federal assistance and makes a recommendation to the FEMA Administrator. The FEMA Administrator, acting through the Secretary of Homeland Security, may then recommend a course of action to the President. [5, p. 42] If the Governor's request is accepted, the President, in turn, will issue a corresponding declaration of emergency or major disaster. This Presidential declaration triggers the release of funds from the President's Disaster Relief Fund, managed by FEMA under the Stafford Act. The Presidential declaration will also activate disaster aid programs from other Federal departments and agencies. A Presidential major disaster declaration triggers long-term Federal recovery programs, some of which are matched by State programs, and designed to help disaster victims, businesses, and public entities. An emergency declaration is more limited in scope and without the long-term Federal recovery programs of a major disaster declaration. Generally, Federal assistance and funding are provided to meet a specific emergency need or to help prevent a major disaster from occurring. [5, pp. 40-42]

In many cases, assistance may be obtained from the Federal Government without a Presidential declaration. For example, FEMA places liaisons in State EOCs and moves commodities near incident sites that may require Federal assistance prior to a Presidential declaration. Additionally, some types of assistance, such as Fire Management Assistance Grants – which provide support to States experiencing severe wildfires – are performed by Federal departments or agencies under their own authorities and do not require Presidential approval. Finally, Federal departments and agencies may provide immediate lifesaving assistance to States under their own statutory authorities without a formal Presidential declaration. [5, p. 42]

Responding Federal departments and agencies respect the sovereignty and responsibilities of local, tribal, and State governments while rendering assistance. The intention of the Federal Government in these situations is not to command the response, but rather to support the affected local, tribal, and/or State governments. [5, p. 40]

If the Governor's request is accepted, the President, in turn, will issue a corresponding declaration of emergency or major disaster. This Presidential declaration triggers the release of funds from the President's Disaster Relief Fund, managed by FEMA under the Stafford Act.

NRF Response

The DHS National Operations Center (NOC) serves as the national fusion center, collecting and synthesizing all-source information, including information from State fusion centers, across all-threats and all-hazards information covering the spectrum of homeland security partners. Federal departments and agencies report information regarding actual or potential incidents requiring a coordinated Federal response to the NOC. [5, p. 33]

When notified of a threat or an incident that potentially requires a coordinated Federal response, the NOC evaluates the information and notifies appropriate senior Federal officials and Federal operations centers: the FEMA National Response Coordination Center (NRCC), the FBI Strategic Information Operations Center (SIOC), the National Counterterrorism Center (NCTC), and the National Military Command Center (NMCC). The NOC serves as the primary coordinating center for these and other operations centers. [5, p. 34]

After being notified, departments and agencies should:

- Identify and mobilize staff to fulfill their department's or agency's responsibilities, including identifying appropriate subject-matter experts and other staff to support department operations centers.

- Identify staff for deployment to the NOC, the NRCC, FEMA Regional Response Coordination Centers (RRCCs), or other operations centers as needed, such as the FBI's Joint Operations Center. These organizations have standard procedures and call-down lists, and will notify department or agency points of contact if deployment is necessary.
- Identify staff that can be dispatched to the Joint Field Office (JFO), including Federal officials representing those departments and agencies with specific authorities, lead personnel for the JFO Sections (Operations, Planning, Logistics, and Administration and Finance) and the ESFs.
- Begin activating and staging Federal teams and other resources in support of the Federal response as requested by DHS or in accordance with department or agency authorities.
- Execute pre-scripted mission assignments and readiness contracts, as directed by DHS. [5, p. 36]

Once a Presidential declaration is issued, FEMA will establish a Joint Field Office (JFO) in proximity to the State Emergency Operations Center (SEOC), and send a Federal Coordinating Officer (FCO) to assist the State Coordinating Officer (SCO) with ordering Federal resources.

The FEMA Regional Administrator deploys a liaison to the State Emergency Operations Center (SEOC) to provide technical assistance and also activates the Regional Response Coordination Center. Federal department and agency personnel, including Emergency Support Function primary and support agency personnel, staff the RRCC as required. The RRCCs:

- Coordinate initial regional and field activities.
- In coordination with State, tribal, and local officials, deploy regional teams to assess the impact of the event, gauge immediate State needs, and make preliminary arrangements to set up operational field facilities.
- Coordinate Federal support until a Joint Field Office (JFO) is established.
- Establish a Joint Information Center (JIC) to provide a central point for coordinating emergency public information activities. [5, p. 44]

In coordination with the RRCC and the State, FEMA may deploy an Incident Management Assistance Team (IMAT). IMATs are interagency teams composed of subject-matter experts and incident management professionals. IMAT personnel may be drawn from national or regional Federal department and agency staff according to established protocols. IMAT teams make preliminary arrangements to set up Federal field facilities and initiate establishment of the Joint Field Office. [5, p. 44]

Emergency Support Functions

FEMA coordinates response support from across the Federal Government and certain NGOs by calling up, as needed, one or more of fifteen Emergency Support Functions. The ESFs are coordinated by FEMA through its NRCC. During a response, ESFs are a critical mechanism to coordinate functional capabilities and resources provided by Federal departments and agencies, along with certain private-sector and nongovernmental organizations. They represent an effective way to bundle and funnel resources and capabilities to local, tribal, State, and other responders. These functions are coordinated by a single agency but may rely on several agencies that provide resources for each functional area. The mission of the ESFs is to provide the greatest possible access to capabilities of the Federal Government regardless of which agency has those capabilities.

FEMA coordinates response support from across the Federal Government and certain NGOs by calling up, as needed, one or more of fifteen Emergency Support Functions.

ESF #1 - Transportation

ESF #2 - Communications

ESF #3 - Public Works and Engineering

ESF #4 - Firefighting

ESF #5 - Emergency Management

ESF #6 - Mass Care, Emergency Assistance, Housing, and Human Services

ESF #7 - Logistics Management and Resource Support

ESF #8 - Public Health and Medical Services

ESF #9 - Search and Rescue

ESF #10 - Oil and Hazardous Materials Response

ESF #11 - Agriculture and Natural Resources

ESF #12 - Energy

ESF #13 - Public Safety and Security

ESF #14 - Long-Term Community Recovery

ESF #15 - External Affairs [5, p. 57]

ESFs may be selectively activated for both Stafford Act and non-Stafford Act incidents under circumstances as defined in HSPD-5. Not all incidents requiring Federal support result in the activation of ESFs. FEMA can deploy assets and capabilities through ESFs into an area in anticipation of an approaching storm or event that is expected to cause a significant impact and result. This coordination through ESFs allows FEMA to position Federal support for a quick response, though actual assistance cannot normally be provided until the Governor requests and receives a Presidential major disaster or emergency declaration. Many States have also organized an ESF structure along this approach. [5, p. 57]

When ESFs are activated, they may have a headquarters, regional, and field presence. At FEMA headquarters, the ESFs support decision making and coordination of field operations within the NRCC. The ESFs deliver a broad range of technical support and other services at the regional level in the Regional Response Coordination Centers, and in the Joint Field Office and Incident Command Posts, as required by the incident. At all levels, FEMA issues mission assignments to obtain resources and capabilities from across the ESFs in support of the State. [5, p. 57]

All ESF support is directed to the local Incident Commander operating under the Incident Command System.

All ESF support is directed to the local Incident Commander operating under the Incident Command System. The incident command structure enables the ESFs to work collaboratively. For example, if a State requests assistance with a mass evacuation, the Joint Field Office would request personnel from ESF #1 (Transportation), ESF #6 (Mass Care, Emergency Assistance, Housing, and Human Services), and ESF #8 (Public Health and Medical Services). These would then be integrated into a single branch or group within the ICS Operations Section to ensure effective coordination of evacuation services. [5, p. 57]

Bottom-Up Support

All disasters are local. Under the United States federal system of government, State, County, Municipal, and Tribal governments are responsible for the safety and security of the citizens within their jurisdiction. This separation of authorities is manifested in Article X of the Constitution, which stipulates that "The powers not delegated to the United States by the Constitution, nor prohibited by it to the States, are reserved to the States respectively, or to the people." From a more practical standpoint, local jurisdictions are best suited to respond to incidents by virtue of their proximity. Hence, the National Response Framework is a bottom-up system, designed to provide assistance only when State and Local resources have been overwhelmed or exhausted.

Most jurisdictions maintain sufficient capability to respond to most incidents. However, when an incident exceeds the capacity of the local jurisdiction, it may request assistance from a neighboring or higher jurisdiction. This determination typically originates with the on-scene Incident Commander (IC).

The Incident Commander is the individual responsible for all response activities, including the development of strategies and tactics and the ordering and release of resources. The Incident Commander has overall authority and responsibility for conducting incident operations and is responsible for the management of all incident operations at the incident site. The Incident Commander directs incident response operations from an Incident Command Post (ICP). [5, p. 50]

If the Incident Commander determines that additional resources or capabilities are needed, he or she will contact the local Emergency Operations Center (EOC) and relay requirements to the local Emergency Manager (EM). Local EOCs are the physical locations where multiagency coordination occurs. EOCs help form a common operating picture of the incident, relieve on-scene command of the burden of external coordination, and secure additional resources. The core functions of an EOC include coordination, communications, resource allocation and tracking, and information collection, analysis, and dissemination. During an incident, the local Emergency Manager ensures the EOC is staffed to support the Incident Command Post and arranges needed resources. Resources may be provided in the form of Emergency Support Functions, similar to the NRF. The EOC also serves to update and advise elected or appointed officials so they may provide policy direction as needed to support the incident response. [5, pp. 50-51]

If the Incident Commander determines that additional resources are needed, he or she will contact the local Emergency Operations Center (EOC) and relay requirements to the local Emergency Manager (EM). In turn, the EOC might request additional resources from neighboring jurisdictions through a Mutual Aid Agreement (MAA).

The EOC might request additional resources from neighboring jurisdictions through a Mutual Aid Agreement (MAA). An MAA is formed between neighboring jurisdictions specifying the conditions under which assistance will be provided, and the terms for remuneration. Because of the financial obligations involved with an MAA, the EOC might first have to consult with fiduciary officials before invoking such an agreement. Of course, time is most precious during an incident.

When multiple agencies become involved in the incident, as determined by the type of incident or by invoking an MAA, then the Incident Commander might form a Unified Command with other officials having legal authority over the responding assets. Operating from the Incident Command Post, the Unified Command will exercise direction and control over tactical operations through corresponding officials acting in concert from a single Incident Action Plan (IAP). Under a Unified Command, each participating agency retains its authority, responsibility and accountability for assigned assets. [5, p. 48]

If the incident is of such magnitude or complexity that it exceed Local response capacity, the EOC might have to defer to the State Emergency Operations Center (SEOC) to request additional resources. In some cases, this might require the local elected official to issue a declaration of emergency or disaster to gain access to State funds or resources. The SEOC, in turn, might marshal resources under Mutual Aid Agreements with other jurisdictions or even direct the use of the National Guard. All responding assets report to the on-scene Incident Command Post and take direction according to the Incident Action Plan.

If State resources prove insufficient to the task, the Governor might request assistance from neighboring states under the Emergency Management Assistance Compact (EMAC). Under the terms of the EMAC, neighboring States can provide civilian resources and National Guard support under the direction of the local Incident Command Post. [5, p. 6]

If the combined resources of the States are insufficient, or additional funds or special capabilities are needed to contend with the incident, the Governor may appeal for Federal assistance. The Governor may appoint a State Coordinating Officer (SCO) to work with the local FEMA region official to prepare the corresponding declarations of emergency or major disaster to request Stafford Act support. Upon the recommendation of the FEMA Administrator and the Secretary of Homeland Security, the President will appoint a Federal Coordinating Officer (FCO) to deploy to the SEOC. [5, p. 67]

If the incident exceeds Local response capacity, the EOC might defer to the State Emergency Operations Center to request additional resources. States can marshal resources under Mutual Aid Agreements with other jurisdictions or even direct the use of the National Guard. All responding assets report to the on-scene Incident Command Post (ICP) and take

The FCO is a senior FEMA official trained, certified, and well experienced in emergency management, and specifically appointed to coordinate Federal support in the response to and recovery from emergencies and major disasters. The FCO executes Stafford Act authorities, including commitment of FEMA resources and the mission assignment of other Federal departments or agencies via ESFs. If a major disaster or emergency declaration covers a geographic area that spans all or parts of more than one State, the President may decide to appoint a single FCO for the entire incident, with other individuals as needed serving as Deputy FCOs. [5, p. 67]

In all cases, the FCO represents the FEMA Administrator in the field to discharge all FEMA responsibilities for the response and recovery efforts underway. For Stafford Act events, the FCO is the primary Federal representative with whom the SCO and other State, Tribal, and Local response officials interface to determine the most urgent needs and set objectives for an effective response. [5, p. 67]

Strengthening Local Response

In 2003, FEMA initiated the State Homeland Security Grant Program (SHSGP) to strengthen State and Local response capabilities, particularly in regard to WMD and other terrorist incidents. It authorized purchase of specialized equipment to enhance State and Local agencies' capabilities in preventing and responding to WMD incidents and other terrorist incidents, and provided funds for protecting critical infrastructure of national importance. SHSGP provided funds for designing, developing, conducting, and evaluating terrorism response exercises; developing and conducting counter-terrorism training programs; and updating and implementing each state's Homeland Security Strategy (SHSS). SHSGP funds could also be used to plan, design, develop, conduct, and evaluate exercises to train First Responders, and to assess the readiness of State and Local jurisdictions to prevent and respond to terrorist attacks. Exercises had to be threat- and performance-based, in accordance with FEMA's Homeland Security Exercise and Evaluation Program (HSEEP). [9, pp. CRS-4]

To help guide the incremental buildup of State and Local response capacity to WMD and terrorist incidents, in December 2003 the Bush Administration issued HSPD-8 directing DHS to develop a National Preparedness Goal (NPG) establishing preparedness objectives, measures, and priorities. In December 2005, DHS issued a draft National Preparedness Goal as follows:

> "To achieve and sustain capabilities that enable the nation to collaborate in successfully preventing terrorist attacks on the homeland, and rapidly and effectively responding to and recovering from any terrorist attack, major disaster, or other emergency that does occur to minimize the impact on lives, property, and the economy. This state of national preparedness will be achieved by reaching risk-based target levels of capability, and sustained by measuring readiness and directing resources to areas of greatest risk and need." [10, pp. CRS-3]

If State resources prove insufficient to the task, the Governor might request assistance from neighboring states under the Emergency Management Assistance Compact (EMAC). Under the terms of the EMAC, neighboring States can provide civilian resources and National Guard support under the direction of the local Incident Command Post.

To help attain the NPG, DHS began work on a National Preparedness System (NPS). The NPS began with identifying fifteen National Planning Scenarios providing examples of potential catastrophic incidents. From these fifteen incidents, DHS worked with Federal, State, and Local agencies to derive a Universal Task List (UTL). The UTL identifies the operations and tasks expected to be performed in order to respond to events similar to those set out in the National Planning Scenarios. The UTL was comprised of hundreds of individual tasks set across four mission areas: 1) prevent, 2) protect, 3) respond, and 4) recover. From the Universal Task List DHS then derived the Target Capability List (TCL). The TCL identifies thirty-six areas in which responding agencies would be expected to be proficient in order to meet the expectations set out in the UTL. The National Preparedness System also included the National Response Plan and National Incident Management System as the means for implementing these capabilities. Starting in 2005, States had to demonstrate how they were meeting UTL and TCL requirements in order to receive State Homeland Security Grant Program funding. [10]

In March 2011, the Obama Administration issued PPD-8 calling for a new National Preparedness Goal based on core capabilities. [11] In September 2011, DHS release its new National Preparedness Goal as follows:

> "A secure and resilient Nation with the capabilities required across the whole community to prevent, protect against, mitigate, respond to, and recover from the threats and hazards that pose the greatest risk." [12, p. 1]

The 2011 NPG replaced the 36 Target Capabilities with 35 Core Capabilities. The revised National Preparedness System issued in November 2011 now required States to link HSGP funding requests towards achieving the Core Capabilities. They would demonstrate this by annually conducting a Threat and Hazard Identification and Risk Assessment (THIRA). [13]

The 2011 National Preparedness System also introduced the National Planning Framework. Just as the NRP and NIMS were considered part of the 2005 National Preparedness System, the National Planning Framework provided a family of plans, not only updating the National Response Framework, and also adding a National Prevention Framework, National Protection Framework, National Mitigation Framework, and National Disaster Recovery Framework. [14, p. 1]

First Responders may apply to the FEMA Homeland Security Grant Program (HSGP) to obtain funding for equipment and training. Funding needs are determined by the Threat and Hazard Identification and Risk Assessment (THIRA) program that requires States to assess their readiness against a set of Core Capabilities. The idea is to achieve the National Preparedness Goal through incremental improvement.

In September 2015, DHS issued a second National Preparedness Goal under the Obama Administration. The 2015 version did not change the NPG itself, however, it did revise the Core Capabilities, reducing their number from 35 to 32. Otherwise, the Disaster Preparedness System remained unchanged. [15]

Homeland Security Exercises

To validate existing Core Capabilities, the 2011 National Preparedness System advocates the use of homeland security exercises. [13, p. 5] In 2007, DHS issued guidance in four volumes for conducting homeland security exercise in the form of the Homeland Security Exercise and Evaluation Program. HSEEP offered a systematic method for planning, executing, and documenting homeland security exercises. [16] In 2013, the four HSEEP volumes were slimmed down to one. [17] Otherwise, not much had changed. The ultimate objective of HSEEP exercises is to identify deficiencies and take actions to correct them. State and Local government may request funding to conduct HSEEP exercises under the FEMA Homeland Security Grant Program.

At the Federal level, homeland security exercises are conducted more formally under the National Exercise Program (NEP). In December 2003, the Bush Administration issued HSPD-8 authorizing a National Exercise Program to train and test national decision makers across multiple Federal departments. [18] The 2006 Post-Katrina Emergency Management Reform Act required NEP to conform to HSEEP. NEP exercises are planned and executed by the FEMA National Exercise Division under the guidance and coordination of the White House Domestic Readiness Group. Prior to 2013, the NEP consisted of two types of exercises: 1) National Level Exercises (NLEs), and 2) Principal Level Exercises (PLEs). An NLE was an operations-based exercise conducted annually addressing potential catastrophic scenarios involving Federal, State, and Local agencies. A PLE was a quarterly discussion-based exercise designed to assist senior policy makers with evaluating emerging threats. [19] Starting in 2013, the NEP began a two-year exercise cycle. Each NEP cycle includes various types of exercises at the Federal, State, and Local levels, culminating in a capstone NLE at the end of the cycle. The sequence of exercises is designed to become increasingly more complex during the course of the NEP cycle. Some exercises may be classified. The number of exercises executed during each cycle depend on the Principal Objectives recommended by the White House Domestic Readiness Group and approved by the National Security Council Principal's Committee. Lessons learned during the exercise are evaluated and disseminated to respective agencies to take appropriate corrective action as necessary. [20]

The first series of national homeland security exercises were called TOPOFF, short for TOP OFFICIALS. TOPOFF exercises were conducted from 2000 to 2009.

Exercises are a part of the National Preparedness System which establishes a continuous cycle of equipping, training, exercising, and evaluating. At the national level, Federal agencies participate in the National Exercise Program (NEP) that now culminate in a two-year capstone National Level Exercise (NLE).

- TOPOFF 1, May 2000, simulated biological and chemical attacks in Denver CO and Portsmouth NH.
- TOPOFF 2, May 2003, simulated WMD attacks in Chicago IL and Seattle WA.
- TOPOFF 3, April 2005, simulated biological and chemical attacks in Connecticut and New Jersey.
- TOPOFF 4, October 2007, simulated dirty bomb attacks in Guam, Phoenix AZ, and Portland OR. [21]

TOPOFF exercises were replaced by NLEs starting in 2009. Then in 2013, NLEs became Capstone exercises ending the two-year NEP cycle.

- NLE 09, July 2009, simulated terrorist attempts to enter U.S. after major overseas attack.
- NLE 10, May 2010, simulated terrorist attack using Improvised Nuclear Device (IND).
- NLE 11, May 2011, simulated earthquake along the New Madrid Seismic Zone (NMSZ).
- NLE 12, multiple exercises simulating cyber attacks on critical infrastructure.
- NLE 14, multiple exercises simulating nuclear weapon accident in Alaska.
- NLE 15, multiple exercises simulating earthquakes, nuclear accidents, and chemical attacks. [21]

Conclusion

Since 2003, the Department of Homeland Security has led efforts to integrate and strengthen the nation's ability to respond to catastrophic incidents. The failure of Hurricane Katrina intensified those efforts. As a result, responding agencies across the country have adopted the Incident Command System and acquired new capabilities particularly with respect to WMD attack. Since hurricane Katrina, it is fair to say that the nation has become proficient at responding to natural disasters. And though the nation has mercifully not been put to the test, it may also be said that it is much better prepared than it was on 9/11. This is a DHS success.

Challenge Your Understanding

The following questions are designed to challenge your understanding of the material presented in this chapter. Some questions may require additional research outside this book in order to provide a complete answer.

1. What is the responsibility of the State Governor?
2. How did 9/11 prompt Federal support for State and Local first responders?
3. List and describe the two major emergency response initiatives introduced by HSPD -5.
4. Under what authority may the President grant Federal assistance to State Governors?
5. Who does the FCO represent and who do they work with to coordinate Federal assistance?
6. In what form is Federal assistance provided to the States?
7. When Federal assistance arrives on -scene to the disaster, who do they work for?
8. How does the Incident Commander direct all elements towards a common objective?
9. What agreement allows States to request assistance from each other?
10. How do exercise programs help improve emergency preparedness?

Chapter 19

Aviation Security

Learning Outcomes

Careful study of this chapter will help a student do the following:

- Describe aviation security changes since 9/11.
- Explain ongoing aviation security challenges.
- Evaluate different aviation security measures.
- Assess different aviation security priorities.

"The security and economic prosperity of the United States depend significantly upon the secure operation of its Aviation Transportation System and safe use of the world's airspace."

- 2010 Transportation Sector-Specific Plan

Introduction

In the aftermath of 9/11, the Federal government moved swiftly to plug the security gaps exposed in the nation's Aviation Transportation System. The chapter describes the security apparatus entrusted with protecting the aviation subsector, and ensuing programs and concerns that have evolved since 9/11.

The National Airspace System (NAS) is comprised of more than 690 Air Traffic Control (ATC) facilities; more than 19,800 general aviation and commercial aviation airports; and over 11,000 air navigation facilities.

Aviation Infrastructure

The aviation infrastructure is a subsector of the transportation infrastructure sector, one of sixteen national critical infrastructure sectors identified in Presidential Policy Directive No. 21. Aviation is one of seven subsectors in the Transportation Sector as listed in Table 1. As such, the aviation subsector is covered under the Department of Homeland Security National Infrastructure Protection Plan (NIPP). As part of the NIPP, aviation security is coordinated through a Sector Coordinating Council (SCC) guided by a U.S. Government Sector-Specific Agency (SSA). The Transportation Security Administration (TSA), part of DHS, is the SSA for the overall transportation sector. However, TSA works in conjunction with the Federal Aviation Administration (FAA) which has regulatory authority over the aviation subsector. Under the NIPP, the SSA works with the SCC to produce and periodically update a corresponding Sector-Specific Plan (SSP). The first Transportation Systems SSP was produced in 2007. The Transportation Systems SSP was last updated in 2010. Annex A to the 2010 SSP addresses security measures undertaken within the aviation subsector. [1]

Table 19-1: Transportation Subsectors

1	Aviation	5.	Mass Transit
2.	Freight Rail	6.	Passenger Rail
3.	Highway	7.	Pipelines
4.	Maritime		

According to Annex A, the aviation subsector is formally identified as the Aviation Transportation System (ATS). Furthermore, the ATS is said to be comprised of the National Airspace System (NAS). The NAS, in turn, is comprised of more than 690 air traffic control (ATC) facilities with associated systems and equipment to provide radar and communication services; more than 19,800 general aviation and commercial aviation airports capable of accommodating an array of aircraft operations; and volumes of procedural and safety information necessary for users to operate in the system. In addition, the NAS includes over 11,000 air navigation facilities and approximately 13,000 flight procedures. [1, p. 129]

Under Title 49 of the Code of Federal Regulations (CFR), the FAA has regulatory authority over aircraft operators, air cargo, foreign air carriers, indirect air carriers, commercial airports, general aviation, and flight schools. Extensive rules and regulations apply to aircraft operations in national airspace and around the globe. U.S. security rules are also extended to those foreign airports and air carriers that fly to the United States. [1, p. 130]

Aviation Security Partners

Aviation security and protection functions apply to non-travelers, travelers and their carry-on items, checked baggage, cargo, and aviation industry personnel, including staff, vendors, tenants, and flight crews. They impact the operation of foreign and domestic airlines, airports, and the air cargo supply chain. Because various agencies have jurisdictional authority over different components, aviation security entails a complex choreography among both public and private stakeholders. [1, p. 131]

The Transportation Security Administration (TSA) screens passengers and checked baggage; deploys Federal Air Marshals (FAMs); assesses security at domestic and foreign airports; and performs vulnerability assessments of aviation assets.

The Transportation Security Administration screens passengers and checked baggage; deploys Federal Air Marshals (FAMs); assesses security at domestic and foreign airports; performs vulnerability assessments of aviation assets; and provides training, public education, and information sharing to enhance the protection of passengers, cargo, and infrastructure. Additionally, TSA inspectors audit air carriers for compliance with security programs, standards, and regulations. Furthermore, TSA deploys aviation security specialists in response to high-threat situations and global security challenges. TSA operations are monitored and coordinated nationally from the Transportation Security Operations Center in Herndon, VA. [1, p. 132]

Customs and Border Protection (CBP) agents are law enforcement officers with legal authority to arrest and apprehend unlawful travelers. CBP further maintains the Air and Marine Operations Surveillance System (AMOSS) supporting counterterrorism and counter-narcotics missions focused on general aviation aircraft. CBP coordinates these actions nationally from its Air and Marine Operations Center (AMOC) in Riverside CA. [1, p. 132]

The Federal Aviation Administration within the Department of Transportation (DOT) is responsible for securing NAS facilities and systems supporting air navigation. The FAA also monitors safe air transit from its National Operations Control Center (NOCC) in Herndon, VA. [1, p. 132]

The Federal Bureau of Investigation (FBI) within the Department of Justice (DOJ) is responsible for the ground-based tactical response to hijacking, air piracy, or other terrorist threats; the investigation, enforcement, and prosecution of criminal law violations within its jurisdiction that occur in the ATS; coordinating the law enforcement community; and intelligence collection, counterintelligence, and foreign intelligence sharing. [1, p. 132]

The Department of Defense (DoD) is responsible for deterring, defending against, and defeating aviation threats to the United States and its global interests; airborne response and resolution of nation-state threats within the ATS; and the operational response to actual or potential airborne threats in U.S. airspace or the approaches to the United States and the threat has either been resolved for defeated. [1, p. 132]

DoD is responsible for deterring, defending against, and defeating aviation threats to the United States; It provides airborne response and resolution of nation-state threats within the Air Transportation System (ATS); and it responds to actual or potential airborne threats in U.S. airspace or the approaches to our territory.

The Department of State (DOS) is responsible for coordinating U.S. Government initiatives that involve foreign governments and international organizations, including regional aviation security cooperation. [1, p. 132]

The Department of Commerce (DOC) is responsible for providing aviation industry and trade policy expertise in both interagency policy efforts and international negotiations. [1, p. 132]

Federal departments and agencies represent a segment of the aviation security community. The large volume of cargo and number of passengers flying into the United States from overseas increases the importance of strong partnerships at the Federal level and with international and domestic aviation partners. Foreign governments, State and Local law enforcement, and passengers play key roles in the multi-layered protective posture that has been put in place since 9/11.

Post-9/11 Aviation Security

Following the 9/11 terrorist attacks, Congress took swift action to create the Transportation Security Administration, federalizing all airline passenger and baggage screening functions and deploying significantly increased numbers of armed air marshals on commercial passenger flights. To this day, the federalization of airport screening remains controversial. Some in Congress contended that, in hindsight, the decision to create TSA as a federal agency functionally responsible for passenger and baggage screening was a "big mistake," and that frontline screening responsibilities should have been left in the hands of private security companies. While airports have the option of opting out of federal screening, alternative private screening under TSA contracts has been limited to 21 airports out of approximately 450 commercial passenger airports where passenger screening is required. While Congress has sought to ensure that optional private screening remains available for those airports that want to pursue this option, proposals seeking more extensive reforms of passenger screening have not been extensively debated. Rather, the aviation security legislation in the aftermath of the 9/11 attacks has largely focused on specific mandates to comprehensively screen for explosives and carry out background checks and threat assessments. [2, pp. 1-2]

Despite the extensive focus on aviation security for more than a decade, a number of challenges remain, including

- effectively screening passengers, baggage, and cargo for explosives threats;
- developing effective risk-based methods for screening passengers and others with access to aircraft and sensitive areas;
- exploiting available intelligence information and watchlists to identify individuals who pose potential threats to civil aviation;
- effectively responding to security threats at airports and screening checkpoints;
- developing effective strategies for addressing aircraft vulnerabilities to shoulder fired missiles and other standoff weapons; and
- addressing the potential security implications of unmanned aircraft operations in domestic airspace. [2, p. 2]

Despite the extensive focus on aviation security for more than a decade, a number of challenges remain.

Explosives Screening Strategy

Prior to the 9/11 attacks, explosives screening was limited in scope and focused on selective screening of checked baggage placed on international passenger flights. Immediately following the 9/11 attacks, the Aviation and Transportation Security Act (ATSA; P.L. 107-71) mandated 100% screening of all checked baggage placed on domestic passenger flights and on international passenger flights to and from the United States. [2, p. 2]

In addition, the Implementing the 9/11 Commission Recommendations Act of 2007 (P.L. 110-53) mandated the physical screening of all cargo placed on passenger flights. Unlike passenger and checked baggage screening, TSA does not routinely perform physical inspections of air cargo. Rather, TSA satisfies this mandate through the Certified Cargo Screening Program. Under the program, manufacturers, warehouses, distributors, freight forwarders, and shippers carry out screening inspections using TSA -approved technologies and procedures both at airports and at off-airport facilities in concert with certified supply-chain security measures and chain of custody standards. Internationally, TSA works with other governments, international trade organizations, and industry to assure that all U.S.-bound and domestic cargo carried aboard passenger aircraft meet the requirements of the mandate. [2, p. 2]

Additionally, TSA works closely with Customs and Border Protection (CBP) to carry out risk-based targeting of cargo shipments, including use of the CBP Advance Targeting System-Cargo (ATS-C), which assigns risk-based scores to inbound air cargo shipments to identify shipments of elevated risk. Originally designed to combat drug smuggling, ATS-C has evolved and adapted over the years, particularly in response to the October 2010 cargo aircraft bomb plot that originated in Yemen, to assess shipments for explosives threats or other terrorism-related activities. [2, pp. 2-3]

Given the focus on the threats to aviation posed by explosives, a significant focus of TSA acquisition efforts has been on explosives screening technologies.

Given the focus on the threats to aviation posed by explosives, a significant focus of TSA acquisition efforts has been on explosives screening technologies. However, in 2014, Congress found that TSA has continued to face numerous challenges in meeting key performance requirements set for explosives detection, has only recently developed a technology investment plan, and has not consistently implemented Department of Homeland Security policy and best practices for procurement. The Transportation Security Acquisition Reform Act (P.L. 113- 245) seeks to address these concerns by requiring a five-year technology investment plan, and to increase accountability for acquisitions through formal justifications and certifications that technology investments are cost-beneficial. The act also requires tighter inventory controls and processes to ensure efficient utilization of procured technologies, as well as improvements in setting and attaining goals for small-business contracting opportunities. [2, p. 3]

A major thrust of TSA's acquisition and technology deployment strategy is improving the capability to detect concealed explosives and bomb-making components carried by airline passengers. On December 25, 2009, a passenger attempted to detonate an explosive device concealed in his underwear aboard Northwest Airlines flight 253 during its approach to Detroit, MI. Al Qaeda in the Arabian Peninsula claimed responsibility. Al Qaeda and its various factions have maintained a particular interest in attacking U.S.-bound airliners. Since 9/11, Al Qaeda has also been linked to the Richard Reid shoe bombing incident aboard American Airlines flight 63 enroute from Paris to Miami on December 22, 2001, a plot to bomb several trans-Atlantic flights departing the United Kingdom for North America in 2006, and the October 2010 plot to detonate explosives concealed in air cargo shipments bound for the United States. [2, p. 3]

In response to the Northwest Airlines flight 253 incident, the Obama Administration accelerated deployment of Advanced Imaging Technology (AIT) whole body imaging (WBI) screening devices and other technologies at passenger screening checkpoints. This deployment responds to the 9/11 commission recommendation to improve the detection of explosives on passengers. In addition to AIT, next generation screening technologies for airport screening checkpoints include advanced technology X-ray systems for screening carry-on baggage, bottled liquids scanners, cast and prosthesis imagers, shoe scanning devices, and portable explosives trace detection equipment. [2, p. 3]

The use of AIT has raised a number of policy questions. Privacy advocates have objected to the intrusiveness of AIT, particularly if used for primary screening. To allay privacy concerns, TSA eliminated the use of human analysis of AIT images, and does not store imagery. In place of human image analysts, TSA has deployed automated threat detection capabilities using automated targeting recognition (ATR) software. Another concern raised about AIT centered on the potential medical risks posed by backscatter X-ray systems, but those systems are no longer in use for airport screening, and current millimeter wave systems emit nonionizing millimeter waves not considered harmful. [2, pp. 3-4]

In 2010, the Obama Administration accelerated deployment of Advanced Imaging Technology (AIT) whole body imaging (WBI) screening devices and other technologies at passenger screening checkpoints. This deployment responds to the 9/11 commission recommendation to improve the detection of explosives on passengers.

Some have advocated for risk-based use of AIT. Past legislative proposals have specifically sought to prohibit the use of WBI technology for primary screening, although primary screening using AIT is now commonplace, at least at larger airports. Checkpoints at many smaller airports, however, have not been furnished with AIT equipment and other advanced checkpoint detection technologies. This raises questions about TSA's long-range plans to expand AIT to ensure more uniform approaches to explosives screening across all categories of airports. Through FY2014, TSA had deployed about 750 AIT units, roughly 86% of its projected full operating capability of 870 units. Full operating capability, once achieved, will still leave many smaller airports without this capability. TSA plans to manage this risk to a large extent through risk-based passenger screening measures, primarily through increased use of voluntary passenger background checks under the PreCheck trusted traveler program. However, this program, likewise, has not been rolled out at many smaller airports: currently, the program's incentive of expedited screening is offered at less than one-third of all commercial passenger airports. [2, p. 4]

Risk-Based Passenger Screening

TSA has initiated a number of risk-based screening initiatives to focus its resources and apply directed measures based on intelligence-driven assessments of security risk. These include a trusted traveler program called PreCheck, modified screening procedures for children 12 and under, and a program for expedited screening of known flight crew and cabin crew members. Programs have also been developed for modified screening of elderly passengers similar to those procedures put in place for children. [2, p. 4]

A cornerstone of TSA's risk-based initiatives is the PreCheck program. Participants vetted through a background check process, as well as other passengers randomly selected and deemed to be low-risk under a process known as "managed inclusion," are processed through expedited screening lanes where they can keep shoes on and keep liquids and laptops inside carry-on bags.

A cornerstone of TSA's risk-based initiatives is the PreCheck program. PreCheck is TSA's latest version of a trusted traveler program that has been modeled after CBP programs such as Global Entry, SENTRI, and NEXUS. Under the PreCheck program, participants vetted through a background check process, as well as other passengers randomly selected and deemed to be low-risk under a process known as "managed inclusion," are processed through expedited screening lanes where they can keep shoes on and keep liquids and laptops inside carry-on bags. As of March 2015, PreCheck expedited screening lanes were available at more than 130 airports. The cost of background checks under the PreCheck program is recovered through application fees of $85 per passenger for a five-year membership. TSA's goal is to process 50% of passengers through PreCheck expedited screening lanes, thus reducing the need for standard security screening lanes. [2, p. 4]

A predecessor test program, called the Registered Traveler program, which involved private vendors that issued and scanned participants' biometric credentials, was scrapped by TSA in 2009 because it failed to show a demonstrable security benefit. Although initial evaluations and consumer response have suggested that PreCheck offers an effective, streamlined screening process, some questions remain regarding whether PreCheck is fully effective in directing security resources to unknown or elevated-risk travelers. While questions remain regarding the security effectiveness of risk-based screening measures like PreCheck, these approaches have demonstrated improved screening efficiency, resulting in cost savings for TSA. TSA estimates annual savings in screener workforce costs totaling $110 million as a result of risk-based screening efficiencies. [2, pp. 4-5]

One concern raised over PreCheck, and the passenger screening process in general, is the public dissemination of instructions, posted on Internet sites, detailing how to decipher boarding passes to determine whether a passenger has been selected for expedited screening, standard screening, or more thorough secondary screening. The lack of encryption and the limited capability TSA has to authenticate boarding passes and travel documents could be exploited to attempt to avoid detection of threat items by more extensive security measures. Other concerns raised over the PreCheck program include the lack of biometric identity authentication and the extensive use of managed inclusion to route travelers not enrolled in or vetted through the PreCheck program through designated PreCheck expedited screening lanes based on random selection or observations by Behavior Detection Officers (BDOs), canine explosives detection teams, or explosives trace detection equipment. The Government Accountability Office (GAO) found that TSA had not fully tested its managed inclusion practices, and recommended that TSA take steps to ensure and document that testing of the program adheres to established evaluation design practices. [2, p. 5]

In addition to passenger screening, TSA, in coordination with participating airlines and labor organizations representing airline pilots, has developed a known crewmember program to expedite security screening of airline flight crews. In July 2012, TSA expanded the program to include flight attendants. [2, p. 5]

TSA has also developed a passenger behavior detection program to identify potential threats based on observed behavioral characteristics. TSA initiated early tests of its Screening Passengers by Observational Techniques (SPOT) program in 2003. By FY2012, the program deployed almost 3,000 BDOs at 176 airports, at an annual cost of about $200 million. Despite its significant expansion, questions remain regarding the effectiveness of the behavioral detection program, and privacy advocates have cautioned that it could devolve into racial or ethnic profiling of passengers despite concerted efforts to focus solely on behaviors rather than individual passenger traits or characteristics. While some Members of Congress have sought to shutter the program, Congress has not moved to do so. For example, House Amendment 127 (113th Congress), an amendment to the FY2014 DHS appropriations measure that sought to eliminate funding for the program, failed to pass a floor vote. Congress also has not taken specific action to revamp the program, despite the concerns raised by GAO and the DHS Office of Inspector General. [2, p. 5]

TSA has also developed a passenger behavior detection program to identify potential threats based on observed behavioral characteristics. TSA initiated early tests of its Screening Passengers by Observational Techniques (SPOT) program in 2003. By FY2012, the program deployed almost 3,000 BDOs at 176 airports.

Terrorist Watchlists

The failed bombing attempt of Northwest Airlines flight 253 on December 25, 2009, raised policy questions regarding the effective use of terrorist watchlists and intelligence information to identify individuals who may pose a threat to aviation. Specific failings to include the bomber on either the no-fly or selectee list, despite intelligence information suggesting that he posed a security threat, prompted reviews of the intelligence analysis and terrorist watchlisting processes. Adding to these concerns, on the evening of May 3, 2010, Faisal Shazad, a suspect in an attempted car bombing in New York's Times Square, was permitted to board an Emirates Airline flight to Dubai at John F. Kennedy International airport, even though his name had been added to the no-fly list earlier in the day. He was subsequently identified, removed from the aircraft, and arrested after the airline forwarded the final passenger manifest to CBP's National Targeting Center just prior to departure. Subsequently, TSA modified security directives to require airlines to check passenger names against the no-fly list within two hours of being electronically notified of an urgent update, instead of allowing 24 hours to recheck the list. The event also accelerated the transfer of watchlist checks from the airlines to TSA under the Secure Flight program. [2, p. 6]

By the end of November 2010, DHS announced that 100% of passengers flying to or from U.S. airports are being vetted using the Secure Flight system. Secure Flight continues the no-fly and selectee list practices of vetting passenger name records against a subset of the Terrorist Screening Database (TSDB). On international flights, Secure Flight operates in coordination with the use of watchlists by CBP's National Targeting Center - Passenger, which relies on the Advance Passenger Information System (APIS) and other tools to vet both inbound and outbound passenger manifests. In addition to these systems, TSA also relies on risk-based analysis of passenger data carried out by the airlines through use of the Computer-Assisted Passenger Prescreening System (CAPPS). In January 2015, TSA gave notification that it would start incorporating the results of CAPPS assessments, but not the underlying data used to make such assessments, into Secure Flight, along with each passenger's full name, date of birth and PreCheck traveler number (if applicable). These data are used within the Secure Flight system to perform risk-based analyses to determine whether passengers receive expedited, standard, or enhanced screening at airport checkpoints. [2, p. 6]

By the end of November 2010, DHS announced that 100% of passengers flying to or from U.S. airports are being vetted using the Secure Flight system. Secure Flight continues the no-fly and selectee list practices of vetting passenger name records against a subset of the Terrorist Screening Database (TSDB).

Central issues surrounding the use of terrorist watchlists include the speed with which watchlists are updated as new intelligence information becomes available; the extent to which all information available to the federal government is exploited to assess possible threats among passengers and airline and airport workers; the ability to detect identity fraud or other attempts to circumvent terrorist watchlist checks; the adequacy of established protocols for providing redress to individuals improperly identified as potential threats; and the adequacy of coordination with international partners. [2, p. 7]

Security Response to Incidents at Screening Checkpoints

On November 1, 2013, a lone gunman targeting TSA employees fired several shots at a screening checkpoint at Los Angeles International Airport (LAX), killing one TSA screener and injuring two other screeners and one airline passenger. The incident raised concerns about the ability of TSA and airport security officials to mitigate and respond to such threats. In a detailed post-incident action report, TSA identified several proposed actions to improve checkpoint security, including enhanced active shooter incident training for screeners; better coordination and dissemination of information regarding incidents; expansion and routine testing of alert notification capabilities; and expanded law enforcement presence at checkpoints during peak times. TSA did not recommend mandatory law enforcement presence at checkpoints, and did not support proposals to arm certain TSA employees or provide screeners with bulletproof vests. [2, p. 7]

The Gerardo Hernandez Airport Security Act of 2015 (H.R. 720), named in honor of the TSA screener killed in the LAX incident, addresses security incident response at airports. It would mandate airports to put in place working plans for responding to security incidents including terrorist attacks, active shooters, and incidents targeting passenger checkpoints. Such plans would be required to include details on evacuation, unified incident command, testing and evaluation of communications, time frames for law enforcement response, and joint exercises and training at airports. Additionally, the bill would require TSA to create a mechanism for sharing information among airports regarding best practices for airport security incident planning, management, and training. The bill also would require TSA to identify ways to expand the availability of funding for checkpoint screening law enforcement support through cost savings from improved efficiencies. [2, p. 7]

Mitigating the Threat of Shoulder-Fired Missiles to Civilian Aircraft

The threat to civilian aircraft posed by shoulder-fired missiles or other standoff weapons capable of downing an airliner remains a vexing concern for aviation security specialists and policymakers. The State Department has estimated that, since the 1970s, over 40 civilian aircraft have been hit by shoulder-fired missiles, causing 25 crashes and more than 600 deaths. Most of these incidents involved small aircraft operated at low altitudes in areas of ongoing armed conflicts, although some larger jets have also been destroyed. Notably, on April 6, 1994, an executive jet carrying the presidents of Rwanda and Burundi was shot down while on approach to Kigali, Rwanda, and on October 10, 1998, a Boeing 727 was destroyed by rebels in the Democratic Republic of Congo. The dangers of operating civil aircraft in and near regions of armed conflict has recently been a topic of particular concern following the July 17, 2014, downing of Malaysia Airlines Flight 17, a Boeing 777, over eastern Ukraine after being struck by a much larger surface-to-air missile. [2, pp. 7-8]

The threat to civilian aircraft posed by shoulder-fired missiles or other standoff weapons capable of downing an airliner remains a vexing concern for aviation security specialists and policymakers. The State Department has estimated that, since the 1970s, over 40 civilian aircraft have been hit by shoulder-fired missiles, causing 25 crashes and more than 600 deaths.

The terrorist threat posed by small man-portable shoulder-fired missiles was brought into the spotlight soon after the 9/11 terrorist attacks by the November 2002 attempted downing of a chartered Israeli airliner in Mombasa, Kenya, the first time such an event took place outside of a conflict zone. In 2003, then Secretary of State Colin Powell remarked that there was “no threat more serious to aviation.” Since then, Department of State and military initiatives seeking bilateral cooperation and voluntary reductions of man-portable air defense systems (MANPADS) stockpiles have reduced worldwide inventories by at least 32,500 missiles. Despite this progress, such weapons may still be in the hands of potential terrorists. This threat, combined with the limited capability to improve security beyond airport perimeters and to modify flight paths, leaves civil aircraft vulnerable to missile attacks. [2, p. 8]

The most visible DHS initiative to address the threat was the multiyear Counter-MANPADS program carried out by the DHS Science & Technology Directorate. The program concluded in 2009 with extensive operational and live-fire testing along with Federal Aviation Administration certification of two systems capable of protecting airliners against heat-seeking missiles. The systems have not been operationally deployed on commercial airliners, however, due largely to high acquisition and life-cycle costs. Some critics have also pointed out that the units do not protect against the full range of potential weapons that pose a potential threat to civil airliners. Proponents, however, argue that the systems do appear to provide effective protection against what is likely the most menacing standoff threat to civil airliners: heat-seeking MANPADS. Nonetheless, the airlines have not voluntarily invested in these systems for operational use, and argue that the costs for such systems should be borne, at least in part, by the federal government. Policy discussions have focused mostly on whether to fund the acquisition of limited numbers of the units for use by the Civil Reserve Aviation Fleet, civilian airliners that can be called up to transport troops and supplies for the military. Other approaches to protecting aircraft, including ground-based missile countermeasures and escort planes or drones equipped with antimissile technology, have been considered on a more limited basis, but these options face operational challenges that may limit their effectiveness. [2, p. 8]

The DHS Counter-MANPADS program concluded in 2009 with extensive operational and live-fire testing along with Federal Aviation Administration certification of two systems capable of protecting airliners against heat-seeking missiles. The systems have not been operationally deployed on commercial airliners, however, due largely to high acquisition and life-cycle costs.

While MANPADS are mainly seen as a security threat to civil aviation overseas, a MANPADS attack in the United States could have a considerable, long-lasting impact on the airline industry. At the airport level, improving security and reducing the vulnerability of flight paths to potential MANPADS attacks continues to pose unique challenges. While major U.S. airports have conducted vulnerability studies, and many have partnered with federal, state, and local law enforcement agencies to reduce vulnerabilities to some degree, these efforts face significant challenges because of limited resources and large geographic areas where aircraft are vulnerable to attack. While considerable attention has been given to this issue in years past, considerable vulnerabilities remain, and any terrorist attempts to exploit those vulnerabilities could quickly escalate the threat of shoulder-fired missiles to a major national security priority. [2, pp. 8-9]

Cybersecurity

While much attention has been focused on physical security, there is a growing concern about the emerging threat from cyber attack. New generation electronic-enabled (e-enabled) aircraft (such as the Boeing 787, Airbus A380, Airbus A350, Bombardier C-Series, Gulfstream 650, and others) and retrofitted legacy aircraft implement an unprecedented amount of new technologies such as IP-enabled networks, commercial-off-the shelf (COTS) components, wireless connectivity (e.g., Bluetooth®), and global positioning systems (GPSs). Aircraft/avionics manufacturers are implementing "wireless" systems to reduce the amount of wiring within an aircraft.

The reduction in weight helps an aircraft achieve lower fuel consumption and can also reduce support costs by simplifying aircraft configurations; however, these wireless systems are vulnerable to cybersecurity threats. [3, p. 12]

With the introduction of new generation e-enabled aircraft, a new era has begun where aircraft navigation and communication functions are transitioning from operating as isolated and independent system to being integrated into a centralized network system that is dependent on exchanging digital information between the e-enabled aircraft and external networks located on the ground and on other e-enabled aircraft. Current aircraft systems architectures are relying heavily on IP-based networks that interconnect aircraft systems such as flight controls, displays, avionics, engine, and cabin systems. While providing unprecedented global connectivity, these e-enabled aircraft technologies and COTS components introduce many access points to aircraft networks; as a result, e-enabled security vulnerabilities not present in past aircraft designs have the potential to significantly impact current aircraft safety. [3, p. 12]

The introduction of new e-enabled aircraft is centralizing aircraft navigation and communication functions into a network system capable of exchanging data with the ground and other e-enabled aircraft. This technology is creating security vulnerabilities not present in past aircraft designs, and has the potential to significantly impact current aircraft safety.

At the same time, unprecedented access to aircraft systems and networks from external systems—including GateLink, wireless local area networks (WLANs), Avionics Full Duplex Switched Ethernet (AFDX) Networking, engine health and usage monitoring systems (HUMSs), and electronic flight bags (EFBs)—are being introduced. While these connections allow for the convenience of two-way transfer of critical information to and from the airplane, this two-way information transfer makes it easier for inaccurate information to be transferred—either by mistake or through malicious intent—to and from the airplane. [3, pp. 12-13]

In April 2015, a passenger was removed from a United Airlines flight after tweeting a joke about hacking the plane's Inflight Entertainment System (IFE). In a deposition to the FBI the passenger claimed he was able to access the Thrust Management Computer (TMC) through the IFE. The TMC works with the autopilot to calculate the optimum power setting for the engines. According to the affidavit, the passenger was able to issue a "climb command", which "caused one of the airplane engines to climb resulting in a lateral or sideways movement of the plane." Boeing and independent aviation experts asserted that what the FBI affidavit described was technically impossible. Whether the passenger hacked the plane or not, it is clear they were able to gain access and prod where they shouldn't. United Airlines took the precaution of banning the passenger from subsequent flights. [4]

Table 19-2: Cyber Attack Vectors [5]

#	Attack Vector
1.	Remote Connections from Aircraft to Ground Websites • Anything traversing the internet is exposed to attack
2.	Network Connections between Aircraft Systems and Vulnerable Equipment • Vulnerable due to external connections • Inherent vulnerabilities of laptops, tablets, & USB devices
3.	Corrupted Services • Command Radio • Global Positioning System (GPS) • Aircraft Communications Addressing and Reporting System (ACARS) • Automatic Dependent Surveillance – Broadcast (ADS-B) • Digital Weather • Broadband Satellite • WiFi/Cellular Connections

In 2004, the Department of Homeland Security's National Cybersecurity Division (NCSD) established the Control Systems Security Program (CSSP), which was chartered to work with control systems security stakeholders through awareness and outreach programs that encourage and support coordinated control systems security enhancement efforts.

Whatever the true circumstances of the previous incident, the implications are clear: newer aircraft are becoming increasingly vulnerable to cyber threats. Some potential attack vectors against aircraft are listed in Table 2, and some potential forms of cyber attack listed in Table 3. [5]

In 2004, the Department of Homeland Security's National Cybersecurity Division (NCSD) established the Control Systems Security Program (CSSP), which was chartered to work with control systems security stakeholders through awareness and outreach programs that encourage and support coordinated control systems security enhancement efforts. In 2009, the CSSP established the Industrial Control System Joint Working Group (ICSJWG) as a coordination body to facilitate the collaboration of control system stakeholders and to encourage the design, development and deployment of enhanced security for control systems. In 2011, the ICSJWG released a Cross-Sector Roadmap for Cybersecurity. Roadmaps develop near, mid, and long-term perspectives to guide industry efforts toward common goals. Based on the ICSJWG effort, in 2012, the Transportation Sector Working Group (TSWG) released its own Roadmap to Secure Control Systems in the Transportation Sector. The TSWG Roadmap describes a plan for voluntarily improving Industrial Control Systems cybersecurity across all transportation modes, including aviation. [3, pp. 1-5]

Table 19-3: Potential Types of Aircraft Cyber Attacks [6]

#	Attack Type	Examples
1.	Spoofing • Modifying data that otherwise appears to be from a legitimate source • Uses protocol weaknesses, compromised security data or ground systems	• Flight Plans • GPS Navigation Data
2.	Exploiting • Using a digital connection to execute malicious instructions on installed equipment • Uses software vulnerabilities such as buffer overflows	• Bots • Automated Sabotage
3.	Denial of Service • Using a digital connection to disrupt service • Often uses inherent protocol features	• Flooding • ARP Poisoning
4.	Counterfeiting • Inserting malicious content into a legitimate part, software component, or database	• Trojan Horse • Backdoor • RootKit

The TSWG Roadmap established four goals:

1. Build a Culture of Cybersecurity. End State: Cybersecurity and ICS are viewed as inseparable and integrated throughout the Transportation Sector.
2. Assess and Monitor Risk. End State. The Transportation Sector has a robust portfolio of ICS-recommended security analysis tools to effectively assess and monitor ICS cybersecurity risk.
3. Develop and Implement Risk Reduction and Mitigation Measures. End State: Security solutions for legacy systems, new architectural designs, and secured communication systems in the Transportation Sector are readily available and deployed across the Sector.
4. Manage Incidents. The Transportation Sector is quickly alerted of cybersecurity ICS incidents, and sophisticated, effective, and efficient mitigation strategies are implemented in operation. [3, p. 30]

In 2012, the Transportation Sector Working Group (TSWG) released its own Roadmap to Secure Control Systems in the Transportation Sector. The TSWG Roadmap describes a plan for voluntarily improving Industrial Control Systems cybersecurity across all transportation modes, including aviation.

When viewed together, the four goals are intended to capture the full spectrum of activities needed for transportation control systems cybersecurity. To achieve these goals within a ten-year timeframe, the TSWG Roadmap identifies subordinate objectives with near-term (0-2 years), mid-term (2-5 years), and long-term (5-10 years) milestones. The Transportation Roadmap milestones and metrics provide broad quantification information that can be used to determine progress as a whole towards achieving the corresponding objectives, and are presumably monitored under the auspices of the corresponding National Infrastructure Protection Plan Sector Coordinating Council and Sector-Specific Plan. [3, p. 30]

Conclusion

Despite much progress, many holes remain in securing the nation's Aviation Transportation System. From a physical standpoint, given that current security measures are imperfect, the question remains "how much security at what price"? And while TSA continues to search for the right balance, the emerging threat from cyber attack may render most physical security measures meaningless. In the absence of any specific solutions, the Department of Homeland Security can only do what it's already doing, and that's to navigate a protective course guided by risk management.

Challenge Your Understanding

The following questions are designed to challenge your understanding of the material presented in this chapter. Some questions may require additional research outside this book in order to provide a complete answer.

1. Why was the Transportation Security Administration created immediately following 9/11?
2. What are the respective roles of the FAA and DoD with regard to the National Airspace System?
3. Explain the challenge to preventing explosives from being smuggled aboard aircraft?
4. Explain the advantages and disadvantages to screening passengers with Advanced Imaging Technology.
5. List and describe two means TSA uses to keep potential hijackers from boarding aircraft.
6. Why was the DHS Counter -MANPADS program cancelled in 2009?
7. Why is cyber attack a potentially bigger concern than hijacking?
8. What is DHS doing to reduce the risk from cyber attack against aircraft?
9. Do you think all the airport security changes since 9/11 were worth the investment? Explain your answer.
10. If you were the TSA administrator, what would be your priority research project? Explain your answer.

Chapter 20

Maritime Security

Learning Outcomes

Careful study of this chapter will help a student do the following:

- Explain why U.S. ports and navigable waterways are critical to the national economy.
- Describe how the USCG protects U.S. ports and waterways.
- Identify maritime patrol forces according to their respective capabilities.
- Explain the USCG "security in - depth" strategy.
- Evaluate both the importance and difficulty of screening shipping containers.

"The security of the MTS is paramount for protecting the Nation and its economy; however, it presents daunting and unique challenges for managers of the maritime mode."

- 2010 Transportation Sector-Specific Plan

Introduction

Ships plying the maritime domain are the primary mode of transportation for world trade, carrying more than 80 percent of the world's trade by volume. U.S. maritime trade is integral to the global economy, representing 10.68 percent of global trade generated in 2008. From a system-of-systems perspective, the Maritime Transportation System (MTS) is a network of maritime operations interfacing with shoreside operations at intermodal connections and is part of global supply chains and domestic commercial operations. Through the MTS, the maritime mode is the primary transportation mode providing connectivity between the United States and global economies; 99% of overseas trade by volume enters or leaves the United States by ship. The nation's economic and military security fundamentally relies upon the health and functionality of the MTS. [1, p. 171]

The Maritime Transportation System (MTS) includes 361 ports and 12,000 miles of inland navigable waters. The MTS serves 10 million passengers on 4,200 cruises annually; 147 million ferry passengers; 7,100 commercial ships making approximately 60,000 port calls; and 2.3 billion metric tons of domestic and foreign trade goods annually.

Maritime Infrastructure

The maritime infrastructure is a subsector of the transportation infrastructure sector, one of sixteen national critical infrastructure sectors identified in Presidential Policy Directive No. 21. The maritime subsector is one of seven in the Transportation Sector as listed in Table 1. As such, the maritime subsector is covered under the Department of Homeland Security National Infrastructure Protection Plan (NIPP). As part of the NIPP, maritime security is coordinated through a Sector Coordinating Council (SCC) guided by a U.S. Government Sector-Specific Agency (SSA). The Transportation Security Administration (TSA), part of DHS, is the SSA for the overall transportation sector. However, the United States Coast Guard (USCG) is the designated SSA for maritime security. Under the NIPP, the SSA works with the SCC to produce and periodically update a corresponding Sector-Specific Plan (SSP). The first Transportation Systems SSP was produced in 2007. The Transportation Systems SSP was last updated in 2010. Annex B to the 2010 SSP addresses security measures undertaken within the maritime subsector. [1]

Table 20-1: Transportation Subsectors

1	Aviation	5.	Mass Transit
2.	Freight Rail	6.	Passenger Rail
3.	Highway	7.	Pipelines
4.	Maritime		

According to Annex B, the maritime subsector is formally identified as the Maritime Transportation System. [1, p. 176] The MTS includes 95,000 miles of coastline and 361 ports, from the largest mega-ports to the smallest fishing harbors and marinas. The MTS also includes the system of interconnected inland rivers and the Intracoastal Waterway (ICW), which consists of 12,000 miles of navigable waters connecting inland metropolitan areas, industrial complexes, and the agricultural heartland of the country. The MTS includes the Great Lakes, along 6,700 miles of U.S. coastline and 1,500 miles of international maritime border with Canada, that connect the industrial north and northern population centers of the Midwest through the St. Lawrence Seaway System to the Atlantic Ocean. [2, p. 9] The MTS services 10 million passengers on 4,200 cruises annually; 147 million ferry passengers; 7,100 commercial ships making approximately 60,000 port calls; and 2.3 billion metric tons of domestic and foreign trade goods. Forty-eight percent of U.S. foreign trade is transported by ship. [1, p. 176]

The U.S. Coast Guard (USCG) is responsible for protecting the MTS. Under its Title 14 authorities, the USCG conducts maritime security, performing four main missions: 1) Ports, Waterways, and Coastal Security; 2) Drug Interdiction; 3) Migrant Interdiction; and 4) Defense Readiness.

United States Coast Guard

The USCG is responsible for protecting the U.S. Maritime Transportation System. [3, p. 5] Title 14 of the U.S. Code specifies that the Coast Guard is a military service and a branch of the Armed Forces of the United States at all times, not just in wartime or when the President directs. Coast Guard cutters are warships of the United States. This status affords certain rights under international conventions and practice, such as the right to approach any vessel to ascertain its identity and country of origin. It gives USCG vessels sovereign immunity from other countries' laws. The USCG is the only branch of the Armed Forces of the United States to which Posse Comitatus, preventing the other military services from acting as law enforcement agents on U.S. soil, in U.S. territorial waters, or against U.S. citizens under most circumstances, has not been applied. The USCG possesses the authority to board any vessel subject to U.S. jurisdiction, or to the operation of any U.S. law, to make inquiries, examinations, inspections, searches, seizures, and arrests upon the high seas and waters over which the U.S. has jurisdiction. [3, p. 11]

Under its Title 14 authorities, the United States Coast Guard conducts maritime security, protecting the U.S. from threats delivered by sea. Within this role, the USCG performs four main missions: 1) Ports, Waterways, and Coastal Security; 2) Drug Interdiction; 3) Migrant Interdiction; and 4) Defense Readiness. [2, p. 8]

Ports, Waterways, and Coastal Security (PWCS). Under this mission, USCG conducts harbor patrols, vulnerability assessments, enforces security zones, approves vessel and facility security compliance, develops Area Maritime Security Plans, conducts risk assessments, assesses foreign port antiterrorism measures, and other activities to prevent terrorist attacks and minimize the damage from attacks that occur. [2, p. 8]

Drug Interdiction. The USCG deploys cutters, aircraft and deployable specialized forces to conduct patrols, interdict and seize maritime drug trafficking vessels. [2, p. 8] The Coast Guard is the designated lead agency for maritime interdiction under the National Drug Control Strategy and the co-lead agency for air interdiction operations with U.S. Customs and Border Protection. USCG cutters and aircraft have forward deployed off Central and South America in drug transit zones. They have disrupted trans-national terrorist and criminal organizations by intercepting thousands of tons of contraband that otherwise would have found its way to America's streets, apprehending thousands of suspected narco-terrorists and smugglers, and supporting successful prosecutions in the United States and in many other countries. [3, pp. 11-12]

The Coast Guard had three defined geographic operational areas: 1) Offshore, anywhere around the world from 50 miles seaward of the U.S. coast; 2) Coastal, from the beach to 50 miles out from U.S. territory; and 3) Inland, all waters shoreward from the U.S. coast.

Migrant Interdiction. The USCG deploys cutters and aircraft to prevent, disrupt and interdict maritime smuggling and maritime migration by undocumented migrants to the U.S.

Defense Readiness. The USCG provides forces to the Department of Defense (DoD) to perform joint military operations worldwide. It deploys cutters, boats, aircraft and specialized forces in and around harbors to protect DoD force mobilization operations in the U.S. and expeditionary operations overseas. [2, p. 8]

USCG Operational Areas

The Coast Guard has defined three geographic operational areas:

1. Offshore. The offshore operational area extends seaward from 50 nautical miles (nm) seaward of the U.S. baseline to the far reaches of the sea, including foreign waters, when authorized. It also includes international operations, including land-based forces deployed to foreign territory, when authorized. This area also includes the polar regions, defined as north of 60° N latitude (Arctic) and areas south of 60° S latitude (Antarctic), but does not include the U.S. coastal operational areas along Alaska.
2. Coastal. The coastal operational area includes waters extending from the U.S. baseline seaward to a distance of 50 miles offshore, including the territorial sea, contiguous zone, and that part of the U.S. Economic Exclusion Zone (EEZ) extending seaward to 50 miles from the baseline. This area includes the waters seaward of the baseline on the U.S. side of the international boundary on the Great Lakes.
3. Inland. The inland operational area includes all waters shoreward of the U.S. baseline that are subject to the jurisdiction of the U.S., including the Western Rivers System. This area does not include those waters on the U.S. side of the international boundary on the Great Lakes that are seaward of (extending out from) the baseline. [2, p. 9]

USCG Operating Forces

Coast Guard forces are organized into the Coast Guard Maritime Trident of Forces: (1) Shore-based Forces, (2) Maritime Patrol Forces, and (3) Deployable Specialized Forces. [2, p. 19]

Shore-based Forces

Shore-based Forces are comprised of Sector commands and specific subordinate units that operate in ports, waterways, and coastal regions of the U.S. and its territories. Sector commands include a command and control element and staff (with organic mission support and intelligence functions), and prevention and response elements. Prevention elements conduct marine inspections, waterways management and marine investigations activities (e.g., aids-to-navigation, issuing safety and security zones, inspecting regulated vessels and facilities, investigating marine casualties). Response elements conduct incident management and enforcement activities (e.g., SAR, pollution investigation, security patrols, vessel boardings). [2, p. 19]

Coast Guard forces are organized into the Coast Guard Maritime Trident of Forces: (1) Shore-based Forces, (2) Maritime Patrol Forces, and (3) Deployable Specialized Forces.

Shore-based Forces execute the broad legal authorities and roles of the Sector Commander, which include Captain of the Port, Officer in Charge of Marine Inspection, Federal On-Scene Coordinator, Federal Maritime Security Coordinator, and SAR Mission Coordinator. [2, p. 20]

Shore-based Forces include the following subordinate units:

- Boat Stations. These fixed response units conduct operations in inland and coastal areas using motor life boats, response boats, and special purpose craft.
- Aids to Navigation Team (ANT). These mobile prevention units conduct operations in inland and coastal areas using aids to navigation boats.
- Marine Safety Unit (MSU) and Marine Safety Detachment (MSD). These fixed prevention units, located geographically distant from the Sector headquarters and staff, conduct operations through a range of prevention activities, including inspections, investigations and waterways management in support of the Sector.
- Vessel Traffic Services (VTS). These fixed prevention units conduct operations to facilitate the safe and efficient transit of commercial vessel traffic along high-density routes in inland and coastal areas. VTS coordinates commercial vessel movement through specified areas using command and control, communications and surveillance, and supports Coast Guard operations by providing domain awareness.
- River, Construction, and Inland Buoy Tenders. These cutters conduct operations to maintain aids to navigation in inland areas. They also conduct other prevention and response activities (e.g., assisting with flood recovery operations).

- Harbor and Icebreaking Tugs. These cutters conduct operations to break ice in inland areas, including the Great Lakes, to keep the MTS open for commerce. They also conduct other prevention and response activities (e.g., SAR, maritime security patrols). [2, p. 20]

Although Coast Guard Air Stations are shore-based commands, all fixed-wing and rotary-wing aircraft that deploy from Air Stations are categorized as Maritime Patrol Forces because of their capabilities and employment. [2, p. 20]

Maritime Patrol Forces

Maritime Patrol Forces are comprised of Coast Guard cutters and aircraft, and their crews. These assets deploy primarily in coastal and offshore areas to conduct prevention and response operations through patrol, presence, and at-sea operations (e.g., interdiction, boarding, enforcement, search and rescue).

Maritime Patrol Forces are comprised of Coast Guard cutters and aircraft, and their crews. These assets deploy primarily in coastal and offshore areas to conduct prevention and response operations through patrol, presence, and at-sea operations (e.g., interdiction, boarding, enforcement, search and rescue). Cutters provide armed, persistent presence and command and control capabilities throughout the maritime domain. In addition to conducting Coast Guard operations, cutters project U.S. presence and protect U.S. sovereignty. These forces provide unique capabilities to DoD for joint operations, including warfighting under combatant commander operational control. Cutters also include the polar icebreakers, the nation's only capability for providing access to polar regions when restricted by ice. [2, p. 20]

Maritime Patrol Forces also conduct Intelligence, Surveillance, and Reconnaissance (ISR) activities in support of Coast Guard and national requirements. [2, p. 20]

Maritime Patrol Forces can also operate in inland areas when required, such as performing mobile command and control, prevention and response operations following a disaster or disruption to normal Sector operations, or when Sectors require augmenting forces. Maritime Patrol Forces include:

- Major Cutters. These large oceangoing cutters conduct the full range of Coast Guard operations, except for icebreaking, primarily in the offshore operational area. Superior endurance and sea keeping capabilities provide the ability to maintain persistent presence in a range of environmental conditions. Major cutters include national security cutters (NSC), high (WHEC) and medium endurance (WMEC) cutters, and the planned offshore patrol cutters (OPC). Major cutters have assigned small boats and routinely deploy with embarked rotary wing aircraft.

- Patrol Boats. These smaller cutters conduct the full range of Coast Guard operations, except for icebreaking, primarily in the coastal operational area. Patrol Boats include fast response cutters (FRC), patrol boats (WPB), and coastal patrol boats (CPB). They are designed for rapid response, patrol, and interdiction. They may also deploy overseas in support of the combatant commanders for foreign coastal interdiction operations in the offshore operational area.

- Polar and Great Lakes Icebreakers. These cutters assure access to the polar regions and U.S. ports and navigational channels in the Great Lakes. They are specifically designed with reinforced and tailored hulls for open-water icebreaking.

    - Polar Icebreakers. These cutters protect U.S. sovereignty in the polar regions, support science and research, supply remote stations, and perform other operations across the Coast Guard mission spectrum. They are the only means of providing assured surface access in support of polar maritime security, national defense, and sea control requirements.

    - Great Lakes Icebreaker. This cutter assists in keeping channels and harbors open to commercial navigation on the Great Lakes to ensure a regular navigation season on the Great Lakes and St. Lawrence Seaway.

Coast Guard icebreakers assure access to the polar regions and U.S. ports and navigational channels in the Great Lakes.

- Oceangoing and Coastal Buoy Tenders. These cutters maintain aids to navigation in inland and coastal operational areas. They also conduct operations across the Coast Guard mission spectrum. Certain oceangoing buoy tenders may carry an organic dive team as part of the crew to support aids to navigation operations.

- Fixed-Wing Aircraft. These all-weather aircraft deploy primarily from land-based Coast Guard Air Stations to conduct airborne operations. They consist of Long Range Surveillance (LRS) and Medium Range Surveillance (MRS) aircraft. These aircraft conduct operations supporting all Coast Guard missions and perform mission support activities (e.g., logistics/transport flights).

- Rotary-Wing Aircraft. These aircraft deploy primarily from land-based Coast Guard Air Stations or underway cutters to conduct airborne operations supporting all Coast Guard missions. They consist of Medium Range Response (MRR) and Short Range Response (SRR) helicopters. These aircraft conduct operations supporting all Coast Guard missions and perform mission support activities (e.g., logistics/transport flights). [2, p. 21]

Deployable Specialized Forces

Deployable Specialized Forces (DSF) are teams of readily available and globally deployable personnel and assets with specialized capabilities, organized into unit types by specialty function and capabilities. DSF conduct operations across a range of Coast Guard missions where their unique capabilities are required. DSF includes:

- Maritime Safety and Security Team (MSST). These units consist of law enforcement teams with boat forces and deployable boats that conduct waterborne operations and limited shoreside security operations across Coast Guard mission areas. MSSTs have specialized capabilities to conduct maritime security and response operations. MSSTs operate primarily in the inland operational area.
- Maritime Security Response Team (MSRT). This unit consists of advanced tactical teams with specialized capabilities for conducting law enforcement and counterterrorism operations through advanced interdiction, boarding, and enforcement activities. MSRT has specialized capabilities to conduct maritime security and response operations, including chemical, biological, radiological, nuclear, and high-yield explosive (CBRNE) detection and response. MSRT operates in all operational areas.
- Tactical Law Enforcement Team (TACLET). These units consist of deployable Law Enforcement Detachments (LEDETs). LEDETs primarily deploy aboard and operate from U.S. Navy or allied vessels to conduct law enforcement operations through interdiction, boarding, and enforcement activities. LEDETs operate primarily in the offshore areas.
- Port Security Unit (PSU). These units consist of a command element, security forces, and boat forces with deployable boats and organic mission support capabilities. PSUs conduct expeditionary operations through coastal and port security activities in support of combatant commander requirements. PSUs operate primarily in the offshore operational area.
- The National Strike Force (NSF). This unit consists of the National Strike Force Coordination Center and three National Strike Teams that provide high-end pollution and hazardous materials response. NSF has specialized capabilities to detect and respond to CBRNE incidents. NSF operates in all operational areas.
- Regional Dive Locker (RDL). These units conduct military diving operations in support of PWCS, Aids to Navigation (ATON), and Polar Operations missions. Coast Guard divers also conduct underwater ship husbandry and underwater search and recovery in support of other operations and mission support requirements. This does not include explosive ordnance disposal capabilities. [2, p. 22]

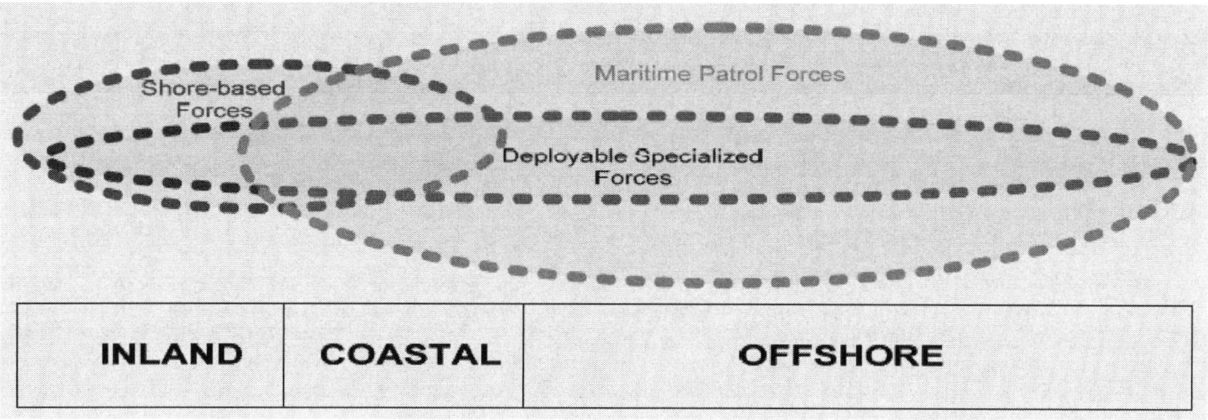

Figure 20-1: USCG Security In-Depth [2]

Security-in-Depth

The Coast Guard employs security-in-depth to conduct operations. Personnel and assets are deployed and stationed in layers in the offshore, coastal, and inland operational areas to prevent and respond to threats well before they reach U.S. waters and the MTS. Coast Guard forces reduce the risk of security incidents by identifying and addressing vulnerabilities to threats, then detecting, interdicting and defeating threats before they approach U.S. shores. When an incident occurs, Coast Guard forces remain ready to conduct response operations and assist with initial recovery. [2, p. 28]

The Coast Guard employs security-in-depth to conduct operations. Personnel and assets are deployed and stationed in layers in the offshore, coastal, and inland operational areas to prevent and respond to threats well before they reach U.S. waters and the MTS.

This layered security regime begins in foreign countries, where Coast Guard personnel conduct foreign port assessments under the International Port Security Program to assess effectiveness of foreign port security and antiterrorism measures. Also, Coast Guard personnel are posted as attachés, liaisons, and maritime advisors with many U.S. embassies around the world. The International Mobile Training Branch (MTB) temporarily deploys to foreign countries under Department of State direction to conduct international engagement with foreign partners. [2, p. 29]

In the offshore operational area, Maritime Patrol Forces and DSF (when embarked on cutters, U.S. Navy or allied ships) provide persistent presence and deterrence in areas of potential threats primarily by patrolling, conducting ISR, and response operations through detection, interdiction, boarding, and enforcement. [2, p. 29]

In the coastal operational area, Maritime Patrol Forces, Shore-based Forces, and DSF conduct operations through a combination of scheduled prevention operations, patrols, and response operations. Coast Guard forces maintain high states of readiness to enable immediate or rapid response to threats or incidents. [2, p. 29]

In the inland operational area, Shore-based Forces, DSF, and aviation forces conduct prevention and response operations and maintain high states of readiness to enable immediate or rapid response to threats or incidents. [2, p. 29]

Security-in-depth demands that Coast Guard operations be synchronized with other U.S. and international operations to respond to maritime threats with unity of effort. The Coast Guard relies on the National Response Framework (NRF), Incident Command System (ICS), and Maritime Operational Threat Response (MOTR) Plan and Protocols to synchronize U.S. response to maritime threats and incidents, including coordination with foreign governments. [2, p. 29]

Because the bulk of U.S. overseas trade is carried by ships, the economic consequences of a maritime terrorist attack could be significant. A key concern is smuggling an Improvised Nuclear Device (IND) into the country or detonating one while at port.

Maritime Security Concerns

Because the bulk of U.S. overseas trade is carried by ships, the economic consequences of a maritime terrorist attack could be significant. [4, p. 14] A key concern is smuggling an Improvised Nuclear Device (IND) into the country or detonating one while at port.

In September 2002, high radiation levels were detected on the container ship PALERMO SENATOR during a routine boarding in Newark, NJ. USCGC ESCANABA escorted the container ship back out to sea and then detained the vessel offshore while a multi-agency boarding was conducted to determine the source of the initial radiation detection. The PALERMO SENATOR was eventually cleared to return to port; it had been a false alarm. [2, p. 32]

A key challenge for U.S. policymakers is prioritizing maritime security activities among a virtually unlimited number of potential attack scenarios. There are far more potential attack scenarios than likely ones, and far more than could be meaningfully addressed with limited counter-terrorism resources. Two port security initiatives are the 100% container scanning requirement and the port worker security card system. [4, p. 14]

Container Scanning Requirement

Section 1701 of the Implementing Recommendations of the 9/11 Commission Act of 2007 (P.L. 110-53) requires that all imported marine containers be scanned by nonintrusive imaging equipment and radiation detection equipment at a foreign loading port by July 1, 2012, unless DHS can demonstrate it is not feasible, in which case the deadline can be extended by two years on a port-by-port basis. DHS has sought a blanket extension for all ports, citing numerous challenges to implementing the 100% scanning requirement at overseas ports. In a letter requesting renewal of the two-year extension, DHS Secretary Jeh Johnson stated:

"I have personally reviewed our current port security and DHS's short term and long term ability to comply with 100% scanning requirement. Following this review, I must report, in all candor, that DHS's ability to fully comply with this unfunded mandate of 100% scanning, even in the long term, is highly improbable, hugely expensive, and in our judgment, not the best use of taxpayer resources to meet this country's port security and homeland security needs." [4, p. 14]

Major U.S. trading partners oppose 100% scanning. The European Commission has determined that 100% scanning is the wrong approach, favoring a multilayered risk management approach to inspecting cargo. DHS Customs and Border Protection (CBP) has tested the feasibility of scanning all U.S.-bound containers at several overseas ports and identified numerous operational, technical, logistical, financial, and diplomatic obstacles, including opposition from host government officials. One-hundred percent scanning conflicts with DHS's general approach to risk management, which seeks to focus scarce inspection resources on the highest-risk containers. By scanning a smaller number of containers, DHS may be able to devote additional resources to each individual scan. This consideration is important because reviewing the scans is labor-intensive, and scanning fewer containers may allow DHS to subject individual scans to greater scrutiny, and to maintain a lower threshold for opening containers with questionable scanning images. [4, pp. 14-15]

Section 1701 of the Implementing Recommendations of the 9/11 Commission Act of 2007 requires that all imported marine containers be scanned at a foreign loading port by July 1, 2012. In 2014, Secretary Johnson wrote to Congress saying that the mandate was "highly improbable, hugely expensive, and in our judgment, not the best use of taxpayer resources".

If illicit cargo is estimated to be limited to less than 1% of incoming containers, as CBP believes to be the case, focusing enforcement on the likeliest containers may be the most effective enforcement strategy. This approach would emphasize risk-based scanning along with investment in CBP intelligence to improve targeting, and/or increase CBP personnel, which would allow ports to conduct a larger number of targeted special enforcement operations. [4, p. 15]

Transportation Worker Identification Credential (TWIC)

In January 2007, TSA and the Coast Guard issued a final rule implementing the Transportation Worker Identification Credential (TWIC) at U.S. ports. Longshoremen, port truck drivers, railroad workers, merchant mariners, and other workers at a port must apply for a TWIC card to obtain unescorted access to secure areas of port facilities or vessels. The card was authorized under the Maritime Transportation Security Act of 2002 (MTSA; §102 of P.L. 107-295). Since October 2007, when TSA began issuing TWICs, about 2.9 million maritime workers have obtained a card. The card must be renewed every five years. [4, p. 15]

TSA conducts a security threat assessment of each worker before issuing a card. The security threat assessment uses the same procedures and standards established by TSA for truck drivers carrying hazardous materials, including examination of the applicant's criminal history, immigration status, and possible links to terrorist activity to determine whether a worker poses a security threat. A worker pays a fee of about $130 that is intended to cover the cost of administering the cards. The card uses biometric technology for positive identification. Terminal operators were to deploy card readers at the gates to their facilities, so that a worker's fingerprint template would be scanned each time he enters the port area and matched to the data on the card. [4, p. 15]

Finding a card reader that worked reliably in a harsh marine environment proved difficult. In March 2013, the Coast Guard issued a notice of proposed rulemaking (NPRM) in which it proposed requiring card readers only for facilities or vessels handling dangerous bulk commodities (including barge fleeting areas) or facilities handling more than 1,000 passengers at a time, as these are the areas the Coast Guard considers to be of higher risk. The Coast Guard estimated that 38 U.S.-flag vessels and 352 facilities would be required to have card readers, which equates to about 0.3% of the vessels and 16% of the facilities it regulates under MTSA. Other vessels and facilities, including those handling containerized cargo, would continue to use the TWIC as a "flash pass," but the biometric data on the card would not be used to positively identify the worker. Currently, the Coast Guard performs spot checks with hand-held biometric readers while conducting port security inspections. [4, p. 15]

GAO audits have been highly critical of how the TWIC has been implemented. A 2013 audit found that the results of a pilot test of card readers should not be relied upon for developing regulations on card reader requirements because they were incomplete, inaccurate, and unreliable. Another 2013 GAO audit examined TSA's Adjudication Center (which performs security threat assessments on TWIC applicants and other transportation workers), and recommended steps the agency could take to better measure the center's performance. A 2011 audit found internal control weaknesses in the enrollment, background checking, and use of the TWIC card at ports, which were said to undermine the effectiveness of the credential in screening out unqualified individuals from obtaining access to port facilities. [4, p. 16]

Conclusion

The Maritime Transportation System is critical to the health and functioning of the U.S. economy. The United States Coast Guard maintains security in-depth to prevent malicious agents and WMD from entering the country. The problem is the volume of goods and people transiting the MTS are just too large to effectively screen. Despite mandates to secure ship containers and the people who work with them, the programs have proved ineffective, and the nation remains vulnerable to this potential avenue of attack.

Challenge Your Understanding

The following questions are designed to challenge your understanding of the material presented in this chapter. Some questions may require additional research outside this book in order to provide a complete answer.

1. What makes U.S. ports and navigable waterways such important assets?
2. List and describe three measures the USCG employs to protect ports and waterways.
3. Which type of USCG maritime patrol force has specifically designed and reinforced hulls to assure access to the polar regions and U.S. ports and navigational channels in the Great Lakes?
4. Which type of USCG maritime patrol force has superior endurance and sea keeping capabilities allowing it to maintain persistent presence under a range of environmental conditions in the offshore operational area?
5. Which type of USCG maritime patrol force designed for rapid response, patrol, and interdiction operates primarily in the coastal operational area?
6. Which type of USCG maritime patrol force comes in two forms and is highly versatile at supporting all types of USCG missions?
7. In what operational area do USCG maritime patrol forces primarily conduct intelligence, surveillance, reconnaissance, response operations, interdiction, boarding, and law enforcement?
8. In what operational area do USCG maritime patrol forces primarily maintain high states of readiness to enable immediate or rapid response to threats or incidents?
9. What is considered the most significant threat to the Maritime Transportation System?
10. Why is container security so important, yet so difficult?

Chapter 21

Surface Transportation Security

Learning Outcomes

Careful study of this chapter will help a student do the following:

- Differentiate between the various types of surface transportation.
- Compare the relative vulnerabilities and significance of each type of surface transportation.
- Discuss the merits of different protection strategies being applied to surface transportation.

"Passenger rail systems—primarily subway systems—in the United States carry about five times as many passengers each day as do airlines, over many thousands of miles of track, serving stations that are designed primarily for easy access."

- 2015 Congressional Research Service Report

Introduction

Surface transportation networks are essential to the economic vitality of the nation. They also afford opportunities for mass disruption and death through natural and manmade causes. Protecting them is problematic due to their vastness and volume. Protection is further complicated by the necessity to facilitate the free-flow of traffic. This chapter examines how the Department of Homeland Security works with both public and private partners to manage risks to this critical infrastructure.

The surface transportation sector encompasses freight rail, highway, mass transit, and passenger rail infrastructure subsectors.

Surface Transportation Infrastructure

The surface transportation infrastructure comprises multiple subsectors of the transportation infrastructure sector, one of sixteen national critical infrastructure sectors identified in Presidential Policy Directive No. 21. Surface transportation encompasses the freight rail, highway, mass transit, and passenger rail subsectors in the Transportation Sector as listed in Table 1. As such, surface transportation is covered under the Department of Homeland Security National Infrastructure Protection Plan (NIPP). As part of the NIPP, surface transportation security is coordinated through a Sector Coordinating Council (SCC) guided by a U.S. Government Sector-Specific Agency (SSA). The Transportation Security Administration (TSA), part of DHS, is the SSA for surface transportation modes. Under the NIPP, the SSA works with corresponding SCCs to produce and periodically update a corresponding Sector-Specific Plan (SSP). The first Transportation Systems SSP was produced in 2007. The Transportation Systems SSP was last updated in 2010. Annexes C, D, and E to the 2010 SSP addresses security measures undertaken within the surface transportation subsector. [1]

Table 21-1: Transportation Subsectors

1	Aviation	5.	Mass Transit
2.	Freight Rail	6.	Passenger Rail
3.	Highway	7.	Pipelines
4.	Maritime		

Mass Transit and Passenger Rail

The mass transit and passenger rail mode includes service by buses, rail transit (commuter rail, heavy rail – also known as subways or metros, and light rail, including trolleys and streetcars), long-distance rail – namely Amtrak and Alaska railroad, and other, less common types of service (cable cars, inclined planes, funiculars, and automated guideway systems). It also includes demand response services for seniors and persons with disabilities as well as vanpool/rideshare programs and taxi services operated under contract with a public transportation agency. The mass transit and passenger rail mode does not include over-the-road motorcoach operators, school bus systems, or private shuttle system operators. [1, p. 216]

The mass transit and passenger rail mode includes service by buses, rail transit (commuter rail, heavy rail – also known as subways or metros, and light rail, including trolleys and streetcars), long-distance rail – namely Amtrak and Alaska railroad, and other, less common types of service (cable cars, inclined planes, funiculars, and automated guideway systems).

Approximately 6000 transit service providers, commuter railroads, and long distance passenger railroad providers operate in the United States. The majority of these agencies operate more than one type of service. About 2,000 agencies provide bus services; 5,300 agencies operate demand response services; and 150 agencies operate other forms of transportation such as inclined planes or water-borne services. There are 565 transit systems that operate in urban areas with a population greater than 50,000 persons. Amtrak operates the nation's primary intercity passenger rail service over a 22,000-mile network, primarily over leased freight railroad tracks, serving more than 500 stations in 46 states and the District of Columbia. In fiscal year 2008, 28.7 million passengers traveled aboard Amtrak. About two-thirds of this ridership is concentrated in the "Northeast Corridor," between Boston and Washington DC. Additionally, Amtrak operates commuter rail services in certain jurisdictions on behalf of State and regional transportation authorities. Since 1995, the transit and commuter ridership in the United States has grown by 38% due to rising fuel prices and increasing road congestion. In 2008, Americans took 10.7 billion trips using mass transit and passenger rail. The American Public Transportation Association (APTA) estimates that about 35 million trips are taken each weekday in the United States. [1, p. 216]

The mass transit and passenger rail mode includes thousands of employees, operational and maintenance facilities, construction sites, utilities, administrative facilities, and thousands of computerized networks, which facilitate operations and ensure efficient and reliable service. [1, p. 216]

Securing the mass transit and passenger rail infrastructure is a shared responsibility between the Transportation Security Administration, Federal Transit Administration (FTA), and Federal Railroad Administration (FRA).

TSA is specifically empowered to develop policies, strategies, and plans for dealing with threats to transportation. TSA is responsible for assessing intelligence and other information to identify individuals who pose a threat to transportation security and to coordinate countermeasures with other Federal agencies to address such threats. TSA also is to enforce security-related regulations and requirements, oversee the implementation and ensure the adequacy of security measures at transportation facilities, and carry out other appropriate duties relating to transportation security. Under the broad regulatory authorities assigned by the 2001 Aviation and Transportation Security Act (ATSA), TSA may issue, rescind, and revise such regulations as are necessary to carry out TSA functions, including issuing regulations and security directives without notice or comment or prior approval of the Secretary of Homeland Security if determined necessary to protect transportation security. TSA is also charged with serving as the primary liaison for transportation security to the intelligence and law enforcement communities. [1, p. 217]

TSA is specifically empowered to develop policies, strategies, and plans for dealing with threats to transportation.

The Federal Transit Administration is an agency within the U.S. Department of Transportation (DOT) that provides financial and technical assistance to local public transit systems. The FTA is one of ten modal administrations within the DOT. [2] FTA promotes safety and security through its grant-making authority. FTA stipulates conditions of grants, such as safety and security statutory and regulatory requirements, and may withhold funds for noncompliance. The FTA enforces 49 CFR Part 659 requiring transit system operators to conduct an annual review of their security plans, and regularly update and assess their effectiveness. [1, pp. 218-219]

The Federal Railroad Administration (FRA) is also an agency within the U.S. Department of Transportation. The FRA maintains regulatory authority for rail safety over commuter rail operators and Amtrak. The agency employs a force of several hundred rail inspectors that monitor the implementation of safety and emergency preparedness plans required under 49 CFR Part 239. [1, p. 219]

Active deterrence is a strategic priority for the mass transit and passenger rail subsectors. TSA support implementation of random, unpredictable security activities designed to create changing layers of security through multiple means. [1, p. 213]

Visible Intermodal Prevention and Response (VIPR) team deployments augment security capabilities for random patrols and surges, behavior detection, and explosives detection. More than 900 VIPR operations were conducted in mass transit and passenger rail systems between 2005 and 2010. [1, p. 213]

Eighty-two TSA-certified explosives detection canine teams also support random patrols and security surges. The most extensive demonstration of this effort occurred when law enforcement officers from 150 departments participated in surge operations along the Northeast Corridor at passenger rail stations from Fredericksburg, VA, to Portland ME. Similar deterrence operations are conducted in metropolitan areas across the country with mass transit and passenger rail agencies and local law enforcement departments simultaneously collaborating in random patrols and surges. [1, p. 213]

Interagency coordination and collaboration help place limited resources where they are most needed. The TSA Office of Intelligence (TSA-OI) works with the FBI Joint Terrorism Task Force (JTTF) and participates in the Public Transit Information Sharing and Analysis Center (PT-ISAC) to make most effective use of deterrence measures. TSA Transportation Security Inspectors (TSIs) help facilitate this process, and also conduct inspections to ensure carrier compliance with applicable security regulations. [1, pp. 212-213]

Active deterrence is a strategic priority for the mass transit and passenger rail subsectors. TSA support implementation of random, unpredictable security activities designed to create changing layers of security through multiple means.

Highway Infrastructure and Motor Carriers

The nation's highway network includes nearly 4 million miles of roadway, 600,000 bridges, and 400 tunnels. Although most of the highway infrastructure is funded and maintained by the public sector, it is local governments who own and operate more than 75% of the nearly 4 million miles of roadway, and over half of the nearly 600,000 bridges. Furthermore, most of the vehicles used on these roads are owned and operated by private individuals and firms. Thus, protecting the nation's highway network is a shared responsibility between State and Local transportation and law enforcement agencies, Federal transportation agencies, the private sector, and the public, all of whom travel over 3 billion vehicle highway miles annually. [1, pp. 253-254]

The motorcoach industry is comprised of approximately 3,137 for-profit companies operating some 29,325 buses and employing over 118,000 people in full and part-time jobs. These companies engage primarily in interstate operations that include wholly-owned bus terminals, shared terminals with other transportation modes such as passenger rail, charter group determined pick-up and drop-off locations, or form their own company property. Motorcoaches carry approximately 751 million passengers annually to millions of destinations in the United States, Canada, and Mexico. [1, p. 255]

The school transportation industry is a network that ensures the safe and secure transportation of 23 million students to approximately 80,000 different schools within 15,000 school districts. The assets of this system include 460,000 school buses, approximately 15,000 parking and maintenance locations, and more than 500,000 drivers, maintenance personnel, and staff officials. For the most part, each school district is an independent entity working within the boundaries of State and Federal rules and statutes. Approximately 70% of school transportation assets are owned and operated by the individual school districts, and approximately 30% of school transportation assets are privately owned by for-profit companies. [1, p. 255]

Destruction of key tunnels or bridges would have significant impact on local economies in the United States. Measureable economic impacts would result from the closure of main arteries due not only to manmade incidents, but also natural disasters such as floods, fires, earthquakes, and hurricanes.

There are more than 214,000 for-hire motor carriers and an additional 27,600 private trucking fleets engaged in interstate commerce. Additionally, there are 89,000 other registered trucking fleets, including some that engage only in intrastate commerce. These fleets operate over 29 million trucks, hauling more than 10 billion tons of freight annually. Among motor carriers, 96% operate 20 trucks or less, while 87% operate 6 trucks or less. The trucking industry employs 8.9 million people, of whom nearly 3.5 million are drivers. In 2007, trucks hauled $325 billion in goods representing over 58% of total trade with Canada, the United States largest trading partner. In that same year, trucks hauled $230 billion worth of goods representing over 66% of total trade with Mexico the United States' third-largest trading partner. Nearly every good consumed in the United States is put on a truck at some point. The industry hauls 69% of all freight in the United States, by weight, and 83% of all freight by value. [1, p. 256]

That the Highway Infrastructure and Motor Carrier (HMC) subsector is at risk is evidenced by the 1993 attack against the World Trade Center in New York, and the 1995 bombing of the Alfred P. Murrah Federal Building in Oklahoma City. That the HMC remains susceptible is further demonstrated by the use of improvised explosive devices (IEDs) placed on or near highways in Iraq and Afghanistan. Destruction of key tunnels or bridges would have significant impact on local economies in the United States. Measureable economic impacts would result from the closure of main arteries due not only to manmade incidents, but also natural disasters such as floods, fires, earthquakes, and hurricanes. [1, p. 257]

State, Local, and Tribal governments manage protection efforts for the highway sector assets, systems, and networks within their jurisdiction. They serve as crucial coordination hubs, bringing together prevention, protection, response, and recovery authorities, capabilities, and resources of the various jurisdictions. State, Local, and Tribal agencies are often the first on the scene of a transportation security incident, either natural or manmade. Federal agencies work closely with these partners to coordinate protection efforts and collaborate with transportation system owners and operators. This cooperation is formally facilitated through the National Infrastructure Protection Plan partnership councils, and actively through the Highway Information Sharing and Analysis Center. [1, pp. 258-260]

State, Local, and Tribal governments manage protection efforts for the highway sector assets, systems, and networks within their jurisdiction. Federal agencies work closely with these partners to coordinate protection efforts. This cooperation is formally facilitated through the National Infrastructure Protection Plan partnership councils, and actively through the Highway Information Sharing and Analysis Center.

HMC protection is also pursued through Risk Mitigation Activities (RMAs). The Federal Highway Administration (FHWA) conducts workshops to promote awareness of vehicle -borne improvised explosive devices (VBIED) threats to bridge and tunnel components of the HMC. FHWA developed the Component Level Risk Management Methodology to assist engineers and managers with developing cost-effective risk management plans. FHWA also developed online training to enhance risk awareness among freight transportation and planning professionals. FHWA worked together with the American Association of State and Highway Transportation Officials (AASHTO) to develop a Costing Asset Protection Guide (CAPTA) to assist transportation agencies with managing and reducing risks relevant to specific threats and hazards. [1, p. 264]

Other Risk Mitigation Activities are targeted to specific components of the HMC. The Intercity Bus Security Grant Program (IBSGP) facilitates training and programs to protect motorcoaches from explosive and non-conventional threats that could cause major loss of life. Working with the National School Transportation Association (NSTA), the Transportation Security Administration developed a voluntary list of security actions for school transportation industry administrators and employees. TSA also works with the U.S. DOT Federal Motor Carrier Safety Administration (FMCSA) and Pipeline Hazardous Materials Safety Administration (PHMSA) to ensure HAZMAT shipments are transported according to Hazardous Materials Transportation Security Requirements (HM-232). Industry also contributes to Risk Mitigation Activities such as the American Chemistry Council which operates the Chemical Transportation Emergency Center (CHEMTREC) providing round-the-clock immediate emergency response information for accidental chemical releases. [1, pp. 265-266]

Freight Rail

There are approximately 140,000 miles of active railroad track in the United States. A total of 565 common carrier freight railroads use these tracks, and they earned $63 billion in revenue in 2008. Of the common carrier freight railroads, there are 7 Class I freight railroads that generate a minimum operating revenue of $401 million. Though they comprise only 1 percent of all railroads, Class I carriers operate on over 94,000 miles of track, representing 67% of the total track in the United States. Of the approximately 180,000 railroad employees, Class I railroads employ over 164,000 and generate over $59 billion or 93% of the total industry revenue. Class I railroads operate over large areas, in multiple States, and concentrate on the long-haul, high-density, intercity traffic lines. The remaining 558 carriers are commonly referred to as regional and short line railroads, or otherwise classified as Class II and Class III carriers. Regional railroads operate on at least 350 miles of active lines and have revenues between $40 and $400 million. Freight railroads serve nearly every industrial, wholesale, retail, and resource-based sector of the U.S. economy. In 2007, freight railroads generated $91.5 billion in U.S. trade with Canada and Mexico. [1, p. 284]

Freight rail is especially important to the energy sector. Coal generates half of America's electricity. Freight railroads transport more than 70% of all coal shipments, amounting to 7.7 million carloads in 2008. Of more concern are the approximately 101,000 shipments of Toxic Inhalation Hazard (TIH) materials transported by rail each year. Ninety percent of that volume comes from six chemicals: 1) anhydrous ammonia, 2) chlorine, 3) ethylene oxide, 4) anhydrous hydrogen fluoride, 5) sulfur dioxide, and 6) anhydrous hydrogen chloride. Chlorine and anhydrous ammonia are the most frequently transported and constitute 78% of all TIH rail shipments. These materials are essential to making motor fuels, purifying drinking water, providing air conditioning, and supporting farming, medicine, and industrial processes. In January 2005, 9 people were killed and 5,400 evacuated due to a derailment releasing 56.3 tons of chlorine. This and other accidents demonstrate the potential impact of an intentional large-scale release of TIH materials. [1, p. 284]

Freight rail is especially important to the energy sector. Coal generates half of America's electricity. Freight railroads transport more than 70% of all coal shipments, amounting to 7.7 million carloads in 2008. Of more concern are the approximately 101,000 shipments of Toxic Inhalation Hazard (TIH) materials transported by rail each year.

Federal law requires freight railroads to carry all shipments (including TIH) that are tendered in accordance with DOT regulations. Radioactive materials, which are classified as hazardous materials, are also transported by rail. The Nuclear Regulatory Commission and the Department of Energy have primary security oversight for these shipments. [1, p. 284]

The TSA Freight Rail Security Division (TSA-FRSD) maintains oversight of the freight rail subsector. TSA-FRSD manages oversight through the Rail Security Coordinator Network (RSCN), the primary means for sharing security information among public and private freight rail partners. Under TSA regulations (73 FR 72130), operators who ship Rail Security-Sensitive Materials (RSSM) in proximity to a High Threat Urban Area (HTUA) are required to appoint a Rail Security Coordinator (RSC). RSCs serve as the primary contact for intelligence information and security-related activities, and are the primary liaison between freight rail operators and TSA through the RSCN. [1, pp. 288-289]

Since 2001, the Association of American Railroads (AAR) Security Operations Center has provided 24/7 security support to include threat warning and incident reporting. The AAR security operations center supports the Railroad Alert Network (RAN), and provides oversight and direction to the Surface Transportation ISAC (ST-ISAC). The ST-ISAC provides the means for sharing threat and vulnerability information between stakeholders. [1, p. 289]

Since 2001, the Association of American Railroads (AAR) Security Operations Center has provided 24/7 security support to include threat warning and incident reporting. The AAR security operations center supports the Railroad Alert Network (RAN), and provides oversight and direction to the Surface Transportation ISAC (ST-ISAC).

TSA also manages the Toxic Inhalation Hazard Risk Reduction Program. As part of this program, TSA together with DOT developed a list of best practices called Security Action Items (SAIs). In June 2006, 24 SAIs were issued as voluntary security guidelines to rail carriers and Federal partners. These SAIs covered a broad range of security practices at both the corporate and field operational levels and addressed three general areas: system security, access control, and enroute security. In November 2006, TSA issued supplemental SAI guidance addressing 1) expedited movement of TIH materials through HTUAs; 2) reduced occurrences of unattended TIH cars; 3) providing secure storage areas for TIH cars; and 4) limiting movement of TIH materials near public venues during National Special Security Events (e.g. the Super Bowl). [1, p. 294]

Surface Transportation Security Concerns

Bombings of passenger trains in Europe and Asia have illustrated the vulnerability of passenger rail systems to terrorist attacks. Passenger rail systems—primarily subway systems—in the United States carry about five times as many passengers each day as do airlines, over many thousands of miles of track, serving stations that are designed primarily for easy access. The increased security efforts around air travel have led to concerns that terrorists may turn their attention to “softer” targets, such as transit or passenger rail. A key challenge is balancing the desire for increased rail passenger security with the efficient functioning of transit systems, with the potential costs and damages of an attack, and with other federal priorities. [3, p. 11]

The volume of ridership and number of access points make it impractical to subject all rail passengers to the type of screening all airline passengers undergo. Consequently, transit security measures tend to emphasize managing the consequences of an attack. Nevertheless, steps have been taken to try to reduce the risks, as well as the consequences, of an attack. These include vulnerability assessments; emergency planning; emergency response training and drilling of transit personnel (ideally in coordination with police, fire, and emergency medical personnel); increasing the number of transit security personnel, installing video surveillance equipment in vehicles and stations; and conducting random inspections of bags, platforms, and trains. [3, p. 11]

The volume of ridership and number of access points make it impractical to subject all rail passengers to the type of screening all airline passengers undergo. Consequently, transit security measures tend to emphasize managing the consequences of an attack.

The challenges of securing rail passengers are dwarfed by the challenge of securing bus passengers. There are some 76,000 buses carrying 19 million passengers each weekday in the United States. Some transit systems have installed video cameras on their buses, but the number and operation characteristics of transit buses make them all but impossible to secure. [3, p. 11]

The Implementing Recommendations of the 9/11 Commission Act of 2007 (P.L. 110-53), passed by Congress on July 27, 2007, included provisions on passenger rail and transit security and authorized $3.5 billion for FY2008-FY2011 for grants for public transportation security. The act required public transportation agencies and railroads considered to be high-risk targets by DHS to have security plans approved by DHS (§1405 and §1512). Other provisions required DHS to conduct a name-based security background check and an immigration status check on all public transportation and railroad frontline employees (§1414 and §1522), and gave DHS the authority to regulate rail and transit employee security training standards (§1408 and §1517). [3, p. 11]

Conclusion

The bitter irony of protecting the transportation infrastructure from potential security risks is that it poses one of the nation's greatest safety hazards. In 2013 alone, 32,719 Americans were killed in motor vehicle accidents. This is more people than have ever been killed in any single natural disaster and all acts of terrorism combined. Only the annual death toll from disease is greater. If homeland security is about trying to prevent the preventable, why then is there a seeming absence of similar concern about national highway safety? The contradiction appears to support a notion of "acceptable loss". If this is the case regarding safety, why would it not be so regarding security?

Since 2001, the Association of American Railroads (AAR) Security Operations Center has provided 24/7 security support to include threat warning and incident reporting. The AAR security operations center supports the Railroad Alert Network (RAN), and provides oversight and direction to the Surface Transportation ISAC (ST-ISAC).

Challenge Your Understanding

The following questions are designed to challenge your understanding of the material presented in this chapter. Some questions may require additional research outside this book in order to provide a complete answer.

1. Which type of surface transportation includes service by buses, subways, trolleys and streetcars?
2. Which type of surface transportation is provided by a single carrier?
3. Which type of surface transportation is primarily maintained by State, Local, and Tribal governments?
4. Which type of surface transportation is essential to baseline electricity generation?
5. What is TSA's general strategy for protecting the surface transportation subsector?
6. Identify two potential types of highway transportation targets, and explain how their loss could be critical.
7. Why does the freight rail system pose a potentially lethal target?
8. How does information sharing between carriers enhance surface transportation security?
9. Does it make sense to screen rail passengers the same as aviation passengers? Explain your answer.
10. What is the difference between the 3,000 deaths on 9/11 and the 30,000+ annual deaths on the nation's roads?

Chapter 22

Border Security

Learning Outcomes

Careful study of this chapter will help a student do the following:

- Describe the purpose of border security.
- Explain the competing priorities of customs and border agents.
- Assess the particular difficulties of securing the nation's borders.
- Discuss trends and influences on illegal border crossings.

"Who knows what evil lurks in the hearts of men?"

- 1930s "The Shadow" Radio Program

Introduction

The ease in which the 9/11 attackers had in traversing the nation's borders made border protection a priority mission for the Department of Homeland Security. This chapter examines how border security has been strengthened since 9/11.

Border Security Threats

At their roots, border-related threats are closely linked to the flow of people (travelers) and goods (cargo) from one country to another. Any smuggled item or individual hidden among the legitimate flows potentially constitutes a threat to U.S. security or interests.

The United States confronts a wide array of threats at U.S. borders, ranging from terrorists who may have weapons of mass destruction, to transnational criminals smuggling drugs or counterfeit goods, to unauthorized migrants intending to live and work in the United States. Understanding border risks begins with identifying key threats. At their roots, border-related threats are closely linked to the flow of people (travelers) and goods (cargo) from one country to another. Any smuggled item or individual hidden among the legitimate flows potentially constitutes a threat to U.S. security or interests. [1, p. ii]

The intentions and actions of unauthorized travelers separate them into different threat categories, including terrorists, transnational criminals, and other illegal migrants. [1, p. ii]

Illegal goods are distinguished by their inherent legitimacy or illegitimacy. Certain weapons, illegal drugs, and counterfeit goods are always illegal and categorically prohibited, while other goods are legal under most circumstances, but become illegitimate if they are smuggled to avoid enforcement of specific laws, taxes, or regulations. [1, p. ii]

Border Security Agencies

After the massive reorganization of federal agencies precipitated by the creation of the Department of Homeland Security, there are four main federal agencies charged with securing the United States' borders: the U.S. Customs and Border Protection (CBP), which patrols the border and conducts immigrations, customs, and agricultural inspections at ports of entry; the U.S. Immigrations and Customs Enforcement (ICE), which investigates immigrations and customs violations in the interior of the country; the United States Coast Guard, which provides maritime and port security; and the Transportation Security Administration (TSA), which is responsible for securing the nation's land, rail, and air transportation networks. [2, p. ii]

U.S. Customs and Border Protection combined portions of the previous border law enforcement agencies under one administrative umbrella. This involved absorbing employees from the Immigration and Naturalization Service (INS), the Border Patrol, the Customs Service, and the Department of Agriculture. CBP's mission is to prevent terrorists and terrorist weapons from entering the country, provide security at U.S. borders and ports of entry, apprehend illegal immigrants, stem the flow of illegal drugs, and protect American agricultural and economic interests from harmful pests and diseases. As it performs its official missions, CBP maintains two overarching and sometimes conflicting goals: increasing security while facilitating legitimate trade and travel. [2, p. 2]

Between official ports of entry, the U.S. Border Patrol (USBP)—a component of CBP—enforces U.S. immigration law and other federal laws along the border. As currently comprised, the USBP is the uniformed law enforcement arm of the Department of Homeland Security. Its primary mission is to detect and prevent the entry of terrorists, weapons of mass destruction, and unauthorized aliens into the country, and to interdict drug smugglers and other criminals. In the course of discharging its duties the USBP patrols over 8,000 miles of international border with Mexico and Canada and the coastal waters around Florida and Puerto Rico. [2, p. 2]

As it performs its official missions, DHS Customs and Border Protection (CBP) maintains two overarching and sometimes conflicting goals: increasing security while facilitating legitimate trade and travel.

At official ports of entry, CBP officers are responsible for conducting immigrations, customs, and agricultural inspections on entering aliens. As a result of the "one face at the border" initiative, CBP inspectors are being cross-trained to perform all three types of inspections in order to streamline the border crossing process. This initiative unifies the prior inspections processes, providing entering aliens with one primary inspector who is trained to determine whether a more detailed secondary inspection is required. [2, p. 2]

CBP inspectors enforce immigration law by examining and verifying the travel documents of incoming international travelers to ensure they have a legal right to enter the country. On the customs side, CBP inspectors ensure that all imports and exports comply with U.S. laws and regulations, collect and protect U.S. revenues, and guard against the smuggling of contraband. Additionally, CBP is responsible for conducting agricultural inspections at ports of entry in order to enforce a wide array of animal and plant protection laws. In order to carry out these varied functions, CBP inspectors have a broad range of powers to inspect all persons, vehicles, conveyances, merchandise, and baggage entering the United States from a foreign country. [2, p. 2]

Immigrations and Customs Enforcement merged the investigative functions of the former INS and the Customs Service, the INS detention and removal functions, most INS intelligence operations, and the Federal Protective Service (FPS). This makes ICE the principal investigative arm for DHS. ICE's mission is to detect and prevent terrorist and criminal acts by targeting the people, money, and materials that support terrorist and criminal networks. Unlike CBP, whose jurisdiction is confined to law enforcement activities along the border, ICE special agents investigate immigrations and customs violations in the interior of the United States. ICE's mandate includes uncovering national security threats such as weapons of mass destruction or potential terrorists, identifying criminal aliens for removal, probing immigration-related document and benefit fraud, investigating work-site immigration violations, exposing alien and contraband smuggling operations, interdicting narcotics shipments, and detaining illegal immigrants and ensuring their departure (or removal) from the United States. ICE is also responsible for the collection, analysis and dissemination of strategic and tactical intelligence data pertaining to homeland security, infrastructure protection, and the illegal movement of people, money, and cargo within the United States. [2, p. 3]

About 362 million travelers (citizens and non-citizens) entered the United States in FY2013, including about 102 million air passengers and crew, 18 million sea passengers and crew, and 242 million land travelers. At the same time about 205,000 aliens were denied admission at ports of entry (POEs); and about 24,000 persons were arrested at POEs on criminal warrants.

Border Security at Ports of Entry

About 362 million travelers (citizens and non-citizens) entered the United States in FY2013, including about 102 million air passengers and crew, 18 million sea passengers and crew, and 242 million land travelers. At the same time about 205,000 aliens were denied admission at ports of entry (POEs); and about 24,000 persons were arrested at POEs on criminal warrants. [3, p. ii]

Within the Department of Homeland Security, U.S. Customs and Border Protection's Office of Field Operations (OFO) is responsible for conducting immigration inspections at America's 329 POEs. CBP's primary immigration enforcement mission at ports of entry is to confirm that travelers are eligible to enter the United States and to exclude inadmissible aliens. Yet strict enforcement is in tension with a second core mission: to facilitate the flow of lawful travelers, who are the vast majority of persons seeking admission. A fundamental question for DHS is how to balance these competing concerns. [3, p. ii]

In general, DHS and CBP rely on "risk management" to strike this balance. One part of the risk management strategy is to conduct screening at multiple points in the immigration process, beginning well before travelers arrive at U.S. POEs. DHS and other departments involved in the inspections process use a number of screening tools to distinguish between known, low-risk travelers and lesser-known, higher-risk travelers. Low-risk travelers may be eligible for expedited admissions processing, while higher-risk travelers are usually subject to more extensive secondary inspections. [3, p. ii]

As part of its dual mission and in support of its broader mandate to manage the U.S. immigration system, DHS also is responsible for implementing an electronic entry-exit system at POEs. Congress required DHS' predecessor to develop an entry-exit system beginning in 1996, but the implementation of a fully automated, biometric system has proven to be an elusive goal. The current system collects and stores biographic entry data (e.g., name, date of birth, travel history) from almost all non-citizens entering the United States, but only collects biometric data (e.g., fingerprints and digital photographs) from non-citizens entering at air or seaports, and from a subset of land travelers that excludes most Mexican and Canadian visitors. With respect to exit data, the current system relies on information sharing agreements with air and sea carriers and with Canada to collect biographic data from air and sea travelers and from certain non-citizens exiting through northern border land ports; but the system does not collect data from persons exiting by southern border land ports and does not collect any biometric exit data. The primary concern is DHS' ability to use existing entry-exit data to identify and apprehend visa overstayers. [3, p. ii]

In addition to securing its 329 official Ports of Entry, the U.S. Customs and Border Protection is also responsible for securing 101,900 miles of border, including 8,000 shared land miles with Mexico and Canada.

The inspections process and entry-exit system continue to be perennial concern for DHS and a number of questions persist. Moreover, the scope of illegal migration through ports of entry, and how DHS can minimize such flows without unduly slowing legal travel continue to challenge policymakers and agency officials. [3, p. ii]

Border Security Between Ports of Entry

In addition to securing its 329 official Ports of Entry, the U.S. Customs and Border Protection is also responsible for securing 101,900 miles of border, including 8,000 shared land miles with Mexico and Canada. [4, p. ii] Border enforcement has been an ongoing subject of congressional interest since the 1970s, when illegal immigration to the United States first registered as a serious national problem; and border security has received additional attention in the years since the terrorist attacks of 2001. [5, p. ii]

Congress created the U.S. Border Patrol (USBP) within the Department of Commerce and Labor by an appropriations act in 1924, two days after passing the first permanent numeric immigration restrictions. Numerical limits only applied to the Eastern Hemisphere, barring most Asian immigration; and the Border Patrol's initial focus was on preventing the entry of Chinese migrants, as well as combating gun trafficking and alcohol imports during prohibition. The majority of agents were stationed on the northern border. The Border Patrol became part of the new Immigration and Naturalization Service (INS) in 1933, and the INS moved from the Department of Labor to the Department of Justice in 1940. The Border Patrol's focus shifted to the Southwest border during World War II, but preventing illegal migration across the Southwest border remained a low priority during most of the 20th century. [5, p. 2]

Illegal migration from Mexico increased after 1965 as legislative changes restricted legal Mexican immigration at the same time that social and economic changes caused stronger migration "pushes" in Mexico (e.g., inadequate employment opportunities) and stronger "pulls" in the United States (e.g., employment opportunities, links to migrant communities in Mexico). Congress held hearings on illegal immigration beginning in 1971, and after more than a decade of debate passed the Immigration Reform and Control Act of 1986 (IRCA, P.L. 99-603), which described border enforcement as an "essential element" of immigration control and authorized a 50% increase in funding for the Border Patrol, among other provisions. Congress passed at least 11 additional laws addressing illegal immigration over the next two decades, 7 of which included provisions related to the border. [5, p. 2]

Seventy years after it began operations, the Border Patrol developed its first formal national border control strategy in 1994. The National Strategic Plan (NSP) was developed in response to a widespread perception that the Southwest border was being overrun by unauthorized immigration and drug smuggling, and to respond to a study commissioned by the Office of National Drug Control Policy. The study recommended that the INS change its approach from arresting unauthorized immigrants after they enter the United States, as had previously been the case, to focus instead on preventing their entry. Under the new approach, the INS would place personnel, surveillance technology, fencing, and other infrastructure directly on the border to discourage illegal flows, a strategy that became known as "prevention through deterrence." According to the 1994 INS plan, "the prediction is that with traditional entry and smuggling routes disrupted, illegal traffic will be deterred, or forced over more hostile terrain, less suited for crossing and more suited for enforcement." [5, p. 3]

As predicted, apprehensions within the San Diego and El Paso sectors fell sharply beginning in 1994-1995, and traffic patterns shifted, primarily to the Tucson and South Texas (Rio Grande Valley) sectors. A 1997 General Accounting Office (GAO) report was cautiously optimistic about the strategy. [5, p. 4]

Congress supported the prevention through deterrence approach. In 1996, House and Senate appropriators directed the INS to hire new agents and to reallocate personnel from the interior to front line duty. And the Illegal Immigration Reform and Immigrant Responsibility Act of 1996 (P.L. 104-208) expressly authorized the construction and improvement of fencing and other barriers along the Southwest border and required the completion of a triple-layered fence along 14 miles of the border near San Diego where the INS had begun to install fencing in 1990. [5, p. 4]

In the wake of the September 11, 2001, terrorist attacks, the USBP refocused its priorities on preventing terrorist penetration, while remaining committed to its traditional duties of preventing the illicit trafficking of people and contraband between official ports of entry. Shortly after the creation of DHS, the USBP was directed to formulate a new National Border Patrol Strategy (NBPS) that would better reflect the realities of the post-9/11 security landscape. In March 2004, the Border Patrol unveiled the National Border Patrol Strategy, which placed greater emphasis on interdicting terrorists and featured five main objectives:

1. Establishing the substantial probability of apprehending terrorists and their weapons as they attempt to enter illegally between the ports of entry;
2. Deterring illegal entries through improved enforcement;
3. Detecting, apprehending, and deterring smugglers of humans, drugs, and other contraband;
4. Leveraging "Smart Border" technology to multiply the deterrent and enforcement effect of agents; and
5. Reducing crime in border communities, thereby improving the quality of life and economic vitality of those areas. [5, p. 5]

The NBPS was an attempt to lay the foundation for achieving "operational control" over the border, defined by the Border Patrol as "the ability to detect, respond, and interdict border penetrations in areas deemed as high priority for threat potential or other national security objectives." The strategy emphasized a hierarchical and vertical command structure, featuring a direct chain of command from headquarters to the field. The document emphasized the use of tactical, operational, and strategic intelligence and sophisticated surveillance systems to assess risk and target enforcement efforts; and the rapid deployment of USBP agents to respond to emerging threats. Additionally, the plan called for the Border Patrol to coordinate closely with CBP's Office of Intelligence and other federal intelligence agencies. [5, p. 5]

In November 2005, the Department of Homeland Security launched the Secure Border Initiative (SBI). Under SBI, DHS announced plans to obtain operational control of the northern and southern borders within five years.

In November 2005, the Department of Homeland Security launched the Secure Border Initiative (SBI). SBI provided the program structure for implementing the National Border Patrol Strategy. Under SBI, DHS announced plans to obtain operational control of the northern and southern borders within five years. The centerpiece of the plan was SBInet. [5, p. 5]

SBInet was to provide an electronic frontier for detecting and capturing unlawful entries into the country. SBInet was to be comprised of a network of remote video surveillance (RVS) systems (including cameras and infrared systems), and sensors (including seismic, magnetic, and thermal detectors), linked into a computer network, known as the Integrated Computer Assisted Detection (ICAD) database. The system was intended to ensure seamless coverage of the border by combining the feeds from multiple cameras and sensors into one remote-controlled system linked to a central communications control room at a USBP station or sector headquarters. USBP personnel monitoring ICAD screens would direct RVS cameras toward locations where sensor alarms were tripped. Control room personnel were then to alert field agents to the intrusion and coordinate the response. [5, p. 18]

CBP awarded the SBInet contract to Boeing who began work in September 2006. The initial 28-mile prototype began operating in the Arizona desert in February 2008, following months of delays and technical glitches. Initial plans developed in 2005 and 2006 called for SBInet to extend across the entire U.S.-Mexico land border. After completing only 53 miles at a cost of $1 billion, the program was cancelled in January 2011. [6] SBInet had struggled to meet deployment timelines and failed to satisfy delivery requirements. DHS had also faced criticism for non-competitive contracting, inadequate oversight, and cost overruns. In announcing the cancellation, Secretary Napolitano cited continuing cost overruns and technical problems indicating the program would never perform to expectations. [5, p. 18]

Nearly half of all arrests of illegal aliens occur along the 387-mile Arizona border with Mexico. After the cancellation of SBInet, CPB developed the Arizona Border Surveillance Technology Plan (ABSTP). [7] Under this plan, the Border Patrol will deploy a mix of different surveillance technologies designed to meet the specific needs of different border regions. As of November 2012, deployed assets included 337 Remote Video Surveillance Systems (RVSS) consisting of fixed daylight and infrared cameras that transmit images to a central location (up from 269 in 2006), 198 short and medium range Mobile Vehicle Surveillance Systems (MVSS) mounted on trucks and monitored in the truck's passenger compartment (up from zero in 2005) and 41 long range Mobile Surveillance Systems (MSS, up from zero in 2005), 12 hand-held agent portable medium range surveillance systems (APSS, up from zero in 2005), 15 Integrated Fixed Towers that were developed as part of the SBInet system (up from zero in 2005), and 13,406 unattended ground sensors (up from about 11,200 in 2005). According to CBP officials, the department's acquisitions strategy emphasizes flexible equipment and mobile technology that permits USBP to surge surveillance capacity in a particular region, and off-the shelf technology in order to hold down costs and get resources on the ground more quickly. [5, pp. 18-19]

After completing only 53 miles at a cost of $1 billion, SBI was cancelled in January 2011. SBI struggled to meet deployment timelines and failed to satisfy delivery requirements. DHS was criticized for non-competitive contracting, inadequate oversight, and cost overruns. In cancelling SBI, Secretary Napolitano cited continuing cost overruns and technical problems indicating the program would never perform to expectations.

In addition to these ground-based surveillance assets, CBP deploys manned and unmanned aircraft as well as marine vessels to conduct surveillance. Air and marine vessels patrol regions of the border that are inaccessible to other surveillance assets, with unmanned aerial systems (UAS) deployed in areas considered too high-risk for manned aircraft or personnel on the ground. In FY2012, CBP's Office of Air and Marine deployed 19 types of aircraft and three classes of marine vessels, for a total of 269 aircraft and 293 marine vessels operating from over 70 locations. The agency reported 81,045 flight hours and 47,742 underway hours in marine vessels. As of November 2012, CBP operated a total of 10 UAS up from zero in 2006, including 2 UAS on the Northern border, 5 on the Southwest border, and 3 in the Gulf of Mexico. UAS accounted for 5,737 flight hours in FY2012, up from 4,406 hours in FY2011. [5, p. 19]

While much attention has been focused on high-tech surveillance capabilities, border security also relies on the low-tech capabilities of fences. The former INS installed the first fencing along the U.S.-Mexican border beginning in 1990 east of the Pacific Ocean near San Diego. Congress expressly authorized the construction and improvement of fencing and other barriers under Section 102(a) of the Illegal Immigration Reform and Immigrant Responsibility Act of 1996 (IIRIRA), which also required the completion of a triple-layered fence along the original 14-mile border segment near San Diego. The Secure Fence Act of 2006 amended IIRIRA with a requirement for double-layered fencing along five segments of the Southwest border, totaling about 850 miles. IIRIRA was amended again by the Consolidated Appropriations Act, FY2008. Under that amendment, the Secretary of Homeland Security was directed to construct reinforced fencing "along not less than 700 miles of the southwest border where fencing would be most practical and effective and provide for the installation of additional physical barriers, roads, lighting, cameras, and sensors to gain operational control of the southwest border." The act further specified, however, that the Secretary of Homeland Security is not required to install fencing "in a particular location along the international border of the United States if the Secretary determines that the use or placement of such resources is not the most appropriate means to achieve and maintain operational control over the international border at such location." [5, p. 16]

As of October 2014, DHS installed 352.7 miles of primary pedestrian fencing, 299 miles of vehicle fencing (total of 651 miles), and 36.3 miles of secondary fencing. The Border Patrol reportedly had identified a total of 653 miles of the border as appropriate for fencing and barriers (i.e., 2 additional miles). [5, p. 17]

In 2006 Congress passed the Secure Fence Act funding installation of a more conventional, double-layered fence along 850 miles of the Southwest border. As of October 2014, DHS installed 352.7 miles of primary pedestrian fencing, 299 miles of vehicle fencing (total of 651 miles), and 36.3 miles of secondary fencing.

By themselves, fences are a very poor deterrent. They only serve to slow, not stop unlawful border crossings. USBP agents are authorized under Federal regulations to enforce section 287 of the Immigration and Nationality Act (INA), which allows them to search, interrogate, and arrest unauthorized aliens and all others who violate immigration laws. Federal regulations allow USBP agents to exercise their authority within 100 air miles of the border. This distance may be increased under special circumstances. Additionally, federal regulations state that Border Patrol agents have the right to interrogate suspected illegal aliens anywhere inside or outside the United States. [8, p. 3 & 30]

Congress has passed at least four laws since 1986 authorizing increased Border Patrol personnel. USBP staffing roughly doubled in the decade after 1986, doubled again between 1996 and the 9/11 attacks, and doubled again in the decade after 9/11. As of September 20, 2014, the USBP had 20,863 agents, including 18,156 posted at the Southwest border. [5, p. 14]

The USBP may also be augmented by the National Guard. National Guard troops were first deployed to the border on a pilot basis in 1988, when about 100 soldiers assisted the U.S. Customs Service at several Southwest border locations, and National Guard and active military units provided targeted support for the USBP's surveillance programs throughout the following decade. The first large-scale deployment of the National Guard to the border occurred in 2006-2008, when over 30,000 troops provided engineering, aviation, identification, technical, logistical, and administrative support to CBP as part of "Operation Jump Start." President Obama announced an additional deployment of up to 1,200 National Guard troops to the Southwest border on May 25, 2010, with the National Guard supporting the Border Patrol, by providing intelligence work and drug and human trafficking interdiction. The 2010 deployment was originally scheduled to end in June 2011, but the full deployment was extended twice (in June and September 2011). The Administration announced in December 2011 that the deployment would be reduced to fewer than 300 troops beginning in January 2012, with National Guard efforts focused on supporting DHS's aerial surveillance operations. In December 2012, DHS and the Department of Defense announced that the National Guard deployment would be extended through December 2013. [5, pp. 15 -16]

For 90 years, the Border Patrol has recorded the number of deportable aliens apprehended in the United States; and alien apprehensions remain the agency's primary indicator of immigration enforcement. The overwhelming majority of apprehensions take place along the Southwest border. In FY2014, the Border Patrol apprehended 479,377 aliens along this border, an increase of 64,980 from the previous year. The majority of these apprehensions occurred in the Rio Grande Valley Sector. Falling apprehensions in San Diego and El Paso during the late 1990s initially were more than offset by rising apprehensions in the Tucson, AZ, sector and other border locations, including the Laredo and Del Rio, TX, sectors. Since FY2011, apprehensions in Tucson have fallen back to their lowest level since 1993, but apprehensions in the Rio Grande Valley have increased, and now account for more than a quarter of Southwest border apprehensions. Thus, since the initiation of the prevention through deterrence approach in the mid-1990s, it appears that success in San Diego and El Paso may have come at the expense of Tucson and other sectors. [5, p. 20 & 22]

By themselves, fences are a very poor deterrent. They only serve to slow, not stop unlawful border crossings.

Apprehensions data are imperfect indicators of illegal flows because they exclude two important groups when it comes to unauthorized migration: aliens who successfully enter and remain in the United States (i.e., enforcement failures) and aliens who are deterred from entering the United States (i.e., certain enforcement successes). Thus, analysts do not know if a decline in apprehensions is an indicator of successful enforcement, because fewer people are attempting to enter, or of enforcement failures, because more of them are succeeding. A further limitation to apprehensions data is that they count events, not unique individuals, so the same person may appear multiple times in the dataset after multiple entry attempts. [5, p. 28]

Arguably the most well-developed approach to measuring unauthorized migration focuses on the number of unauthorized migrants residing in the United States. For many years, analysts within DHS and other social scientists have used the so-called "residual method" to estimate this number. In essence, the method involves using legal admissions data to estimate the legal, foreign-born population, and then subtracting this number from the overall count of foreign-born residents based on U.S. census data. [5, p. 29]

The residual method provides limited information about the border per se because many unauthorized residents enter the United States through ports of entry, lawfully or otherwise. Nonetheless, estimates of the size of the unauthorized population may offer several advantages over other border metrics. First, for many people, how many unauthorized aliens reside within the United States ultimately is a more important question than how many cross the border. After all, if illegal border flows fall to zero, but many people continue to enter illegally through ports of entry or by overstaying nonimmigrant visas, many people would consider such an outcome problematic. Second, for this reason, the size of the unauthorized population more comprehensively reflects how well immigration policy and immigration enforcement function, including for example the effectiveness of worksite and other interior enforcement efforts as well as how well visas meet employer and family demands. Third, estimates of the unauthorized population offer the advantage of a nearly 30-year track record and a relatively uncontroversial methodology. [5, p. 29]

While no single metric accurately and reliably describes border security, most analysts agree, based on available data, that the number of illegal border crossers fell sharply between about 2005 and 2011.

While no single metric accurately and reliably describes border security, most analysts agree, based on available data, that the number of illegal border crossers fell sharply between about 2005 and 2011, with some rise in illegal flows in 2012. This conclusion is supported by key Border Patrol enforcement data, including the drop in total apprehensions. [5, p. 32]

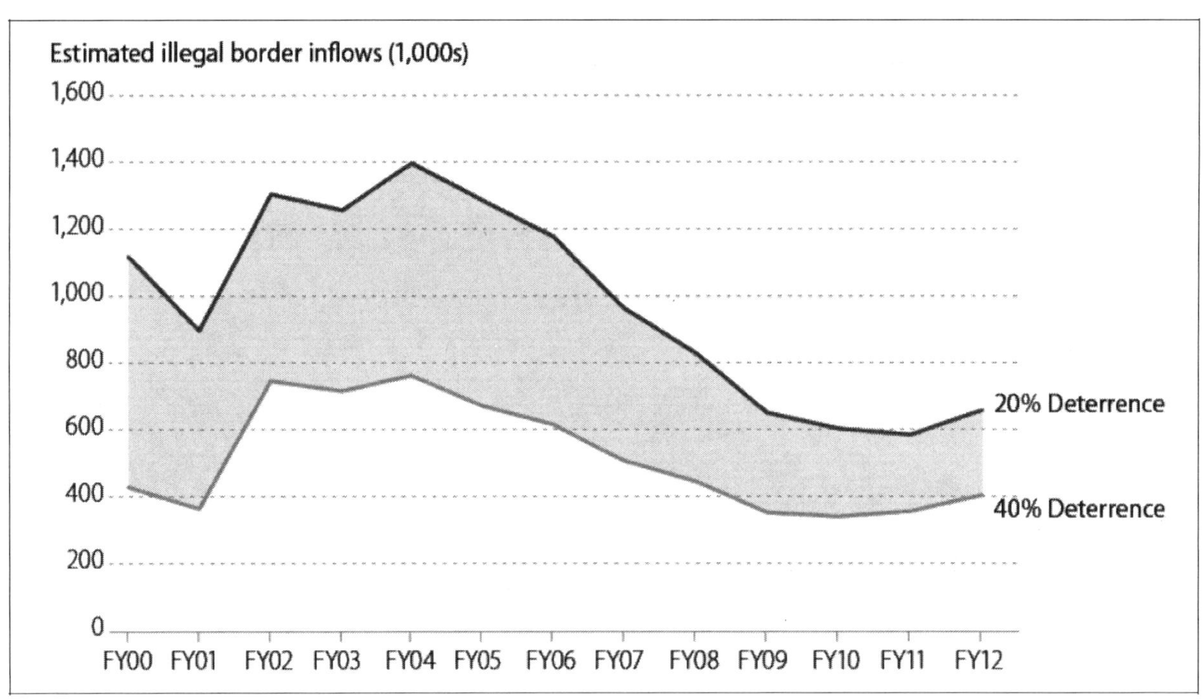

Figure 22-1: Total Estimated Illegal Border Inflows, FY2000-FY2012 [5, p. 34]

Based on available data, the estimated deterrence rates in 2000-2012 were between 20% and 40%. As depicted in Figure 1, total estimated illegal inflows fell from a high of between 760,000 and 1.4 million in 2004 to a low of between 340,000 and 580,000 in 2009-2010. The model estimates that total illegal inflows were between 400,000 and 660,000 in 2012. Apprehension levels and survey data from the 1980s and 1990s suggest that total illegal inflows likely were lower in 2007-2012 than at any other point in the last three decades. [5, p. 33]

Conclusion

The embarrassing fact is that despite the best efforts to tighten control over illegal entry into the United States, hundreds of thousands of people still manage to remain illicitly each year. Even a cursory cost-benefit analysis would argue for an alternative solution. If a loaded gun sits on a table in a room full of people, does it make more sense to remove the people or remove the gun? It seems that the time and expense of sifting through the millions who come peaceably to this country each year might be better allocated towards a more attainable goal.

Challenge Your Understanding

The following questions are designed to challenge your understanding of the material presented in this chapter. Some questions may require additional research outside this book in order to provide a complete answer.

1. What are the two things that customs and border agents are trying to keep from entering the country?
2. What are the two conflicting priorities in screening travelers and cargo?
3. What is the primary difficulty with preventing illegal border crossings?
4. Where has DHS positioned the majority of its border agents?
5. Why did the Secure Border Initiative fail?
6. Why is a conventional chain -linked fence a poor measure for stopping illegal border crossings?
7. How did the trend in illegal border crossings fare between 2005 and 2011?
8. Do you think the Great Recession from 2007 -2009 helped reduce illegal border crossings? Explain.
9. Do malicious agents need to smuggle weapons into the U.S. to mount a catastrophic attack? Explain.
10. Do malicious agents necessarily have to enter the U.S. to mount a catastrophic attack? Explain.

Chapter 23

Immigration Enforcement

Learning Outcomes

Careful study of this chapter will help a student do the following:

- Describe how immigration has shaped the United States.
- Explain how immigration is controlled in the United States.
- Discuss how people may illegally remain in the United States.
- Assess the difficulty of making an accurate count of illegal immigrants.

"We're Americans, with a capital 'A', huh? You know what that means? Do ya? That means that our forefathers were kicked out of every decent country in the world. We are the wretched refuse. We're the underdog. We're mutts!"

- 1981 Bill Murray, Stripes

Introduction

We are a nation of immigrants. Thomas Jefferson thought it would take 300 years to populate the vast interior of the American continent; it took less than 100. Throughout the 19th century, America welcomed immigrants without question. Then, in the early 20th century, the United States began imposing quotas on who and how many could enter. Immigration trailed off accordingly. However, in the first decade of the 21st century the nation is experiencing a resurgent trend; at 40 million, the number of foreign-born residents is the highest in U.S. history. This chapter will examine immigration by the numbers, and explain who we are, where we come from, and how we got here as a nation.

Historical Trends

The Immigration and Nationality Act (INA), which was first codified in 1952, contains the provisions detailing the requirements for admission (permanent and temporary) of foreign nationals, grounds for exclusion and removal of foreign nationals, document and entry-exit controls for U.S. citizens and foreign nationals, and eligibility rules for the naturalization of foreign nationals.

The Immigration and Nationality Act (INA), which was first codified in 1952, contains the provisions detailing the requirements for admission (permanent and temporary) of foreign nationals, grounds for exclusion and removal of foreign nationals, document and entry-exit controls for U.S. citizens and foreign nationals, and eligibility rules for the naturalization of foreign nationals. Congress has significantly amended the INA several times since 1952, most notably by the Immigration Amendments of 1965, the Refugee Act of 1980, the Immigration Reform and Control Act (IRCA) of 1986, the Immigration Act of 1990, and the Illegal Immigration Reform and Immigrant Responsibility Act (IIRIRA) of 1996. [1, p. 1]

As shown in Figure 1, legal immigration encompasses permanent admissions (e.g., employment-based or family-based legal permanent residents) and temporary admissions (e.g., guest workers, foreign students). Immigration control encompasses an array of enforcement tools, policies, and practices to secure the border and to prevent and investigate violations of immigration laws. [1, p. 1]

Immigration to the United States was peaking at the beginning of the 20th century. In 1910, foreign-born residents made up 14.8% of the U.S. population. Immigration dropped as a result of the numerical limits and national origins quotas imposed by the Immigration Acts in 1921 and 1924. Levels fell further during the Great Depression and World War II. The annual number of settled immigrants, typically referred to as legal permanent residents (LPRs), rose gradually after World War II. In 1952, the INA was codified and, as amended, remains the governing statute. [1, p. 2]

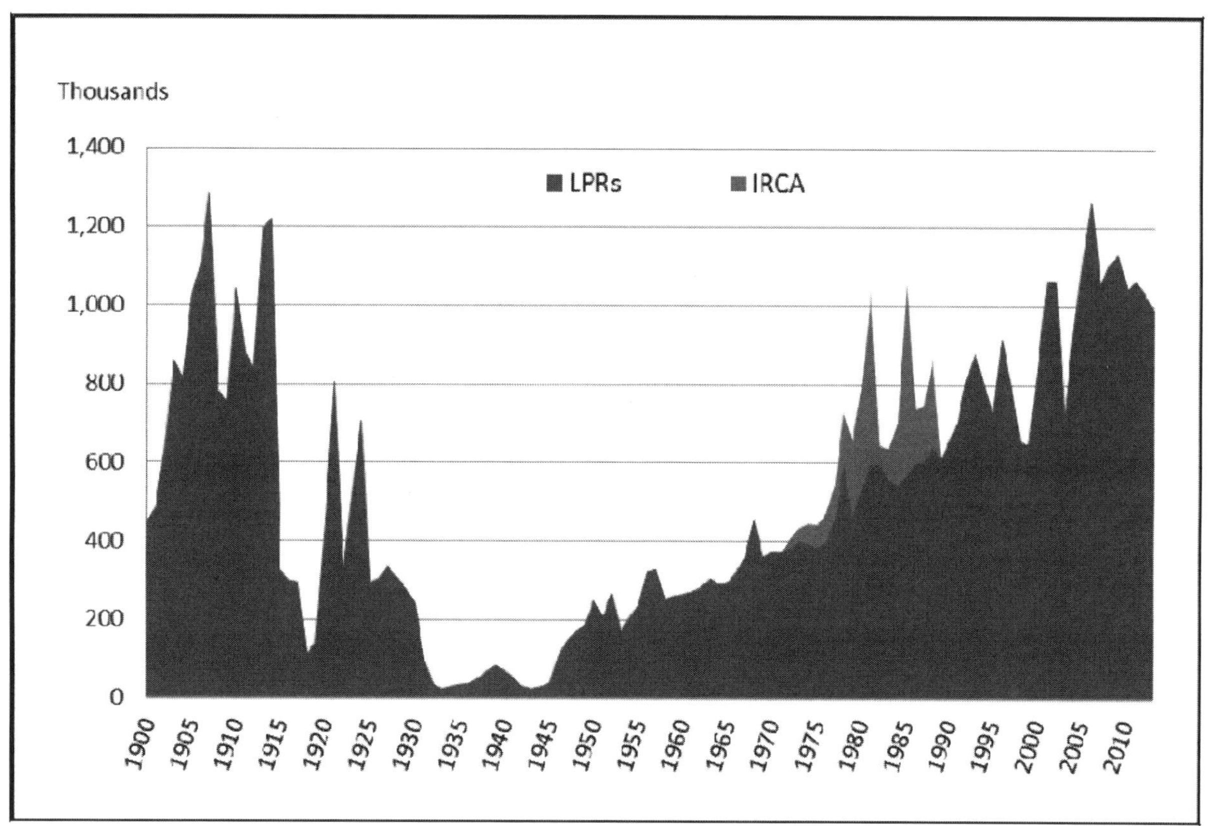

Figure 23-1: Annual Immigration Admissions 1900-2010 [1, p. 2]

The growth in immigration after 1980 is partly attributable to the total number of LPRs entering through the preference system as well as immediate relatives of U.S. citizens. The Immigration Reform and Control Act of 1986 enabled 2.1 million unauthorized aliens residing in the United States as of 1982 to become LPRs. In addition, the number of refugees admitted increased from 718,000 in the period 1966-1980 to 1.6 million during the period 1981-1995, after the enactment of the Refugee Act of 1980. The Refugee Act established permanent provisions for refugees and asylees to become LPRs. [1, p. 2]

Congress has significantly amended the INA several times since 1952, most notably by the Immigration Amendments of 1965, the Refugee Act of 1980, the Immigration Reform and Control Act (IRCA) of 1986, the Immigration Act of 1990, and the Illegal Immigration Reform and Immigrant Responsibility Act (IIRIRA) of 1996.

The Immigration Act of 1990 was the last significant revision of legal permanent immigration. It set a statutory worldwide level of 675,000 LPRs annually, but certain categories of LPRs, most notably immediate relatives of U.S. citizens and refugees, are permitted to exceed the limits. The INA further holds countries to an annual numerical limit of 7% of the worldwide level of U.S. immigrant admissions, known as per-country limits or country caps. Immigration to the United States today has reached levels comparable to the early years of the 20th century. In FY2013, 990,553 aliens became LPRs through admissions (459,751) or status adjustments (530,802). [1, pp. 2-3]

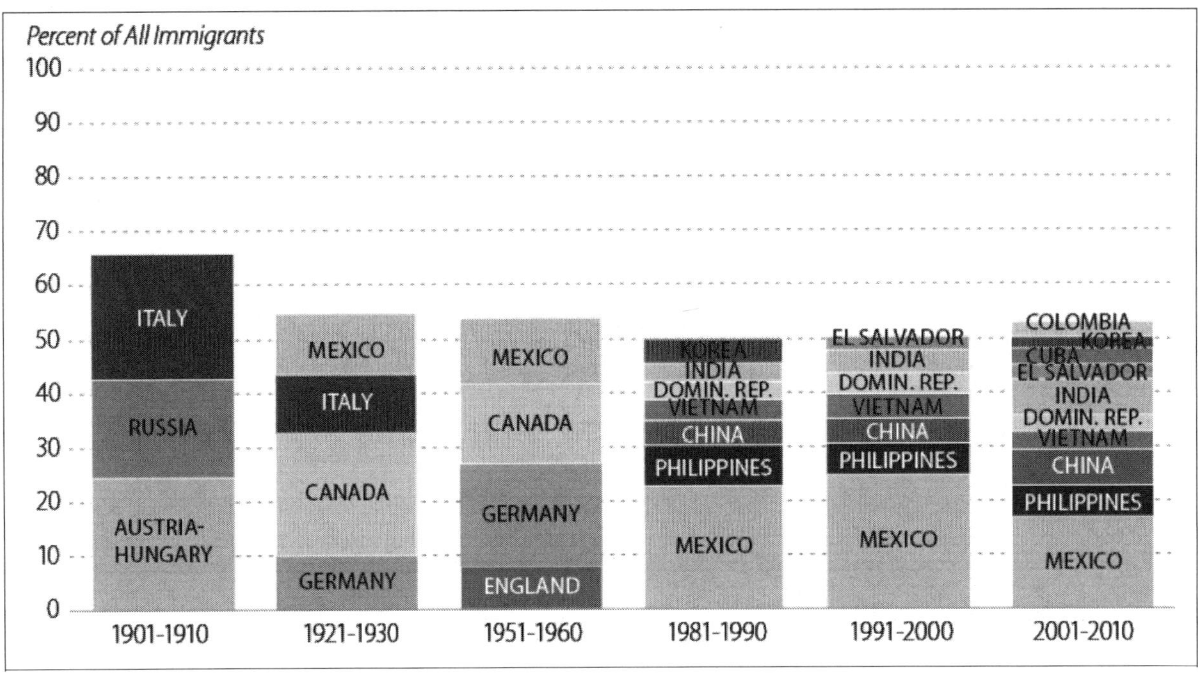

Figure 23-2: Immigrant Countries of Origin 1900-2010 [1, p. 3]

Where We Come From

In any given period of U.S. history, a handful of countries have dominated the flow of immigrants, but the dominant countries have varied over time. Mexico has been a top sending country for most of the 20th century—largely after 1970—and into the 21st century.

In any given period of U.S. history, a handful of countries have dominated the flow of immigrants, but the dominant countries have varied over time. Figure 2 presents trends in the top immigrant-sending countries (together comprising at least 50% of the immigrants admitted) for selected decades. The Immigration Act of May 19, 1921, imposed the first numerical limits on LPR admissions to the United States, and it set the level of admission of aliens from specific countries to 3% of the foreign-born persons of that nationality who lived in the United States in 1910. A few years later, the Immigration Act of May 26, 1924, established the national origins system, which set quotas based on the number of foreign-born persons of that nationality in the country in 1890 and 1920. Both laws exempted Western Hemisphere countries from the limits. The Immigration Amendments of 1965 replaced the national origins quota system with per-country ceilings. [1, p. 3]

Figure 2 illustrates that immigration over the last few decades of the 20th century was not as dominated by three or four countries as it was earlier in the century. Although Europe was home to the countries sending the most immigrants during the early 20th century (e.g., Germany, Italy, Austria-Hungary, and the United Kingdom), Mexico has been a top sending country for most of the 20th century—largely after 1970—and into the 21st century. Other top sending countries from FY2001 through FY2010 were the Dominican Republic, El Salvador, Colombia, and Cuba (Western Hemisphere); and the Philippines, India, China, South Korea, and Vietnam (Asia). [1, p. 3]

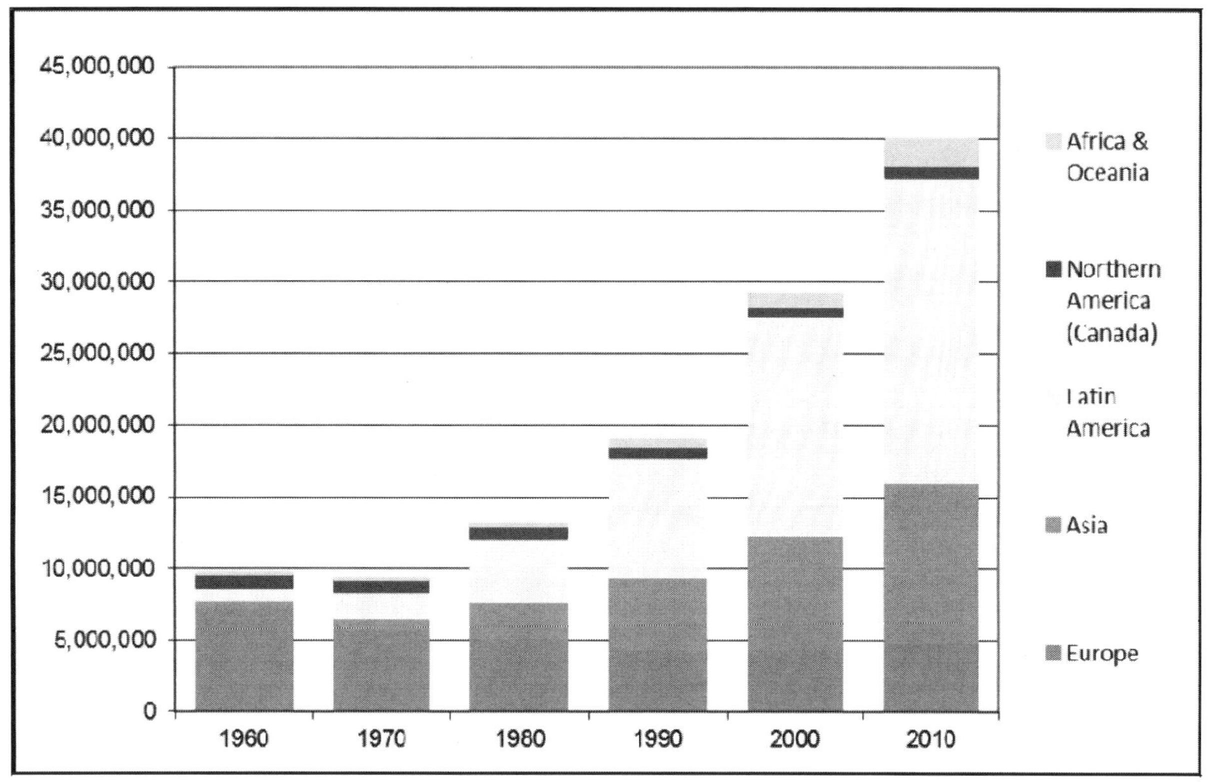

Figure 23-3: Foreign-Born Residents by Region of Origin 1960-2010 [1, p. 4]

These data suggest that the per-country ceilings established in 1965 had some effect. As Figure 2 illustrates, immigrants from only three or four countries made up more than half of all LPRs prior to 1960. By the last two decades of the 20th century, immigrants from seven to eight countries comprised about half of all LPRs, and this pattern has continued into the 21st century. [1, p. 4]

The number of foreign -born residents in the United States is at the highest level in U.S. history. In the past 50 years, the number of foreign-born residents of the United States has gone from just under 10 million in 1960 to 40 million in 2010, a 313% increase.

The number of foreign-born residents in the United States is at the highest level in U.S. history. In the past 50 years, the number of foreign-born residents of the United States has gone from just under 10 million in 1960 to 40 million in 2010, a 313% increase, as Figure 3 illustrates. As part of this increase, the source regions of foreign-born residents have shifted from Europe (74% in 1960) to Latin America and Asia (81% in 2010). Foreign-born residents made up 12.9% of the U.S. population in 2010. [1, p. 4]

More recently, between 2000 and 2010, the foreign born contributed 32% of the total U.S. population increase. Foreign-born residents comprised most of the increase in the prime 25-54 working age population over this decade. Almost one-third of current foreign-born residents arrived in the United States since 2000. [1, p. 5]

The Department of Homeland Security (DHS) Office of Immigration Statistics (OIS) estimated that 13.3 million foreign-born residents were LPRs as of January 1, 2012. OIS has also estimated that 1.9 million foreign-residents were legally present on long-term temporary visas and about 11.4 million were aliens residing in the United States without legal authorization. [1, p. 5]

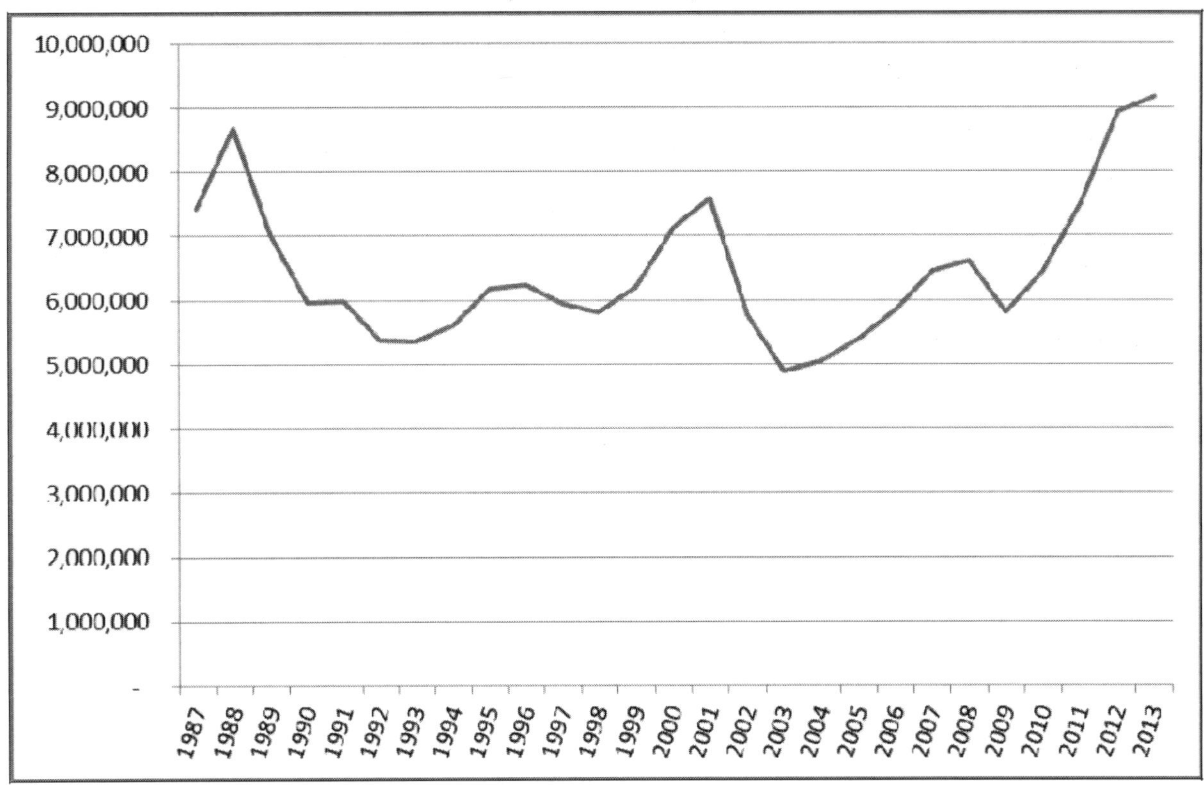

Figure 23-4: Nonimmigrant Visas Issued by U.S. Department of State 1987-2013 [1, p. 9]

As of 2012, the DHS Office of Immigration Statistics (OIS) estimates that about 11.4 million aliens are residing in the United States without legal authorization.

Just Visiting

The INA provides for the temporary admission of various categories of foreign nationals, known as nonimmigrants. Nonimmigrants are admitted for a temporary period of time and a specific purpose, including as tourists, students, and temporary workers. There are 24 major nonimmigrant visa categories, and over 70 specific types of nonimmigrant visas are issued currently. Most of these nonimmigrant visa categories are defined in §101(a)(15) of the INA. These visa categories are commonly referred to by the letter and numeral that denotes their subsection in §101(a)(15); for example, B-2 tourists, E-2 treaty investors, F-1 foreign students, H-1B temporary professional workers, and J-1 cultural exchange participants. Many nonimmigrant visas are valid for multiple entries as well as multiple years. [1, p. 9]

The U.S. Department of State (DOS) consular officer who issues the visa must be satisfied that the foreign national is entitled to a nonimmigrant status. Notably, INA §214(b) generally presumes that all aliens seeking admission to the United States are coming to live permanently; as a result, most aliens seeking to qualify for a nonimmigrant visa must demonstrate that they are not coming to reside permanently. Nonimmigrant visas issued abroad had dipped to 5.0 million in FY2004 after peaking at 7.6 million in FY2001, as Figure 4 shows. Nonimmigrant visa issuances reached 9.2 million in FY2013. Expansion of the visa waiver program (VWP), which allows nationals from 36 countries to enter the United States as temporary visitors for business or pleasure without obtaining a visa from a U.S. consulate abroad, has affected these trends. [1, p. 9]

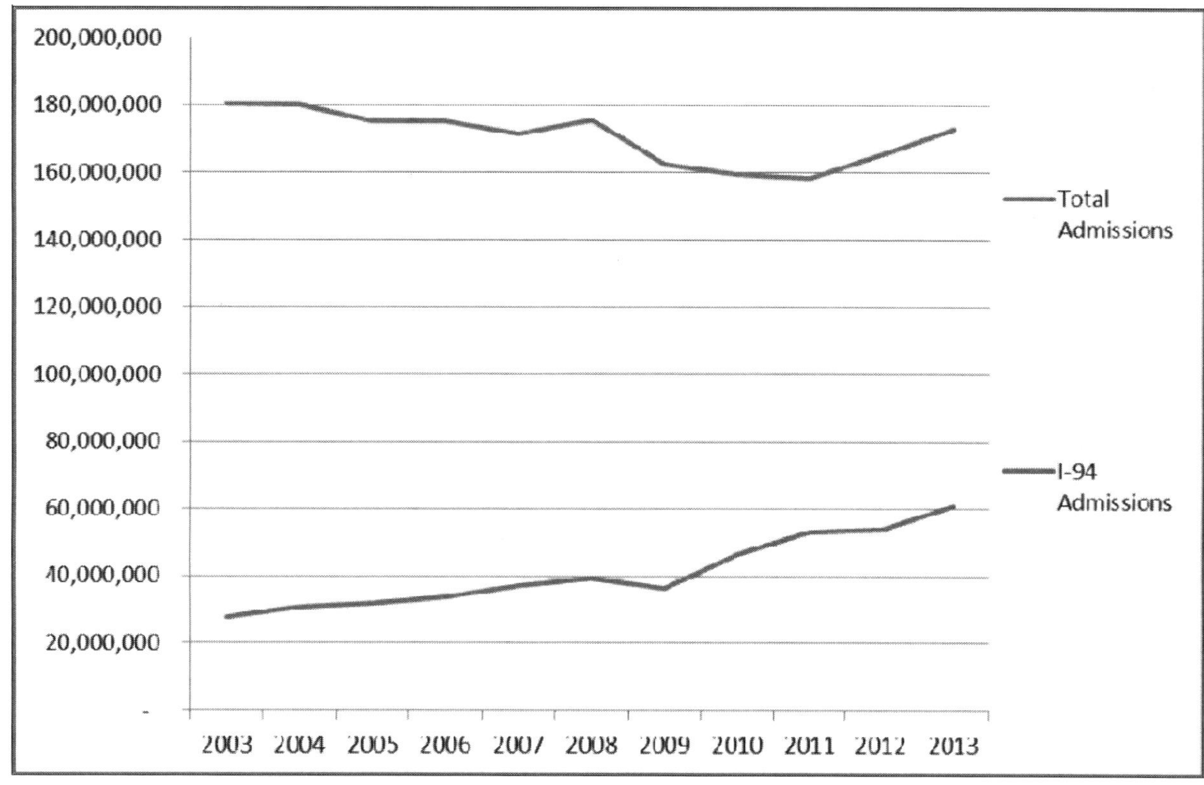

Figure 23-5: Nonimmigrant Admissions at U.S. Ports of Entry 2003-2013 [1, p. 11]

INA allows foreigners not seeking to immigrate to visit the country temporarily for a specific purpose, such as tourists, students, and temporary workers. There are 24 major nonimmigrant visa categories, and over 70 specific types of nonimmigrant visas are issued currently.

In addition to DOS consular officers interviewing aliens applying for visas, DHS Customs and Border Protection (CBP) inspects foreign nationals when they seek to enter the United States. CBP policy typically requires about one-quarter of nonimmigrants entering the United States to fill out the arrival records, which are colloquially called I-94 admissions because I-94 is the immigration form number. For example, Mexican nationals with border crossing cards and Canadian nationals traveling for business or tourist purposes are specifically excluded from the I-94 admission totals. I-94 data presented in Figure 5 recorded admissions rather than persons. [1, p. 11]

As can be seen in Figure 5, I-94 admissions have generally inched upwards from FY2003 to FY2013, largely due to CBP's expanded use of I-94 forms at land ports in FY2005. The total nonimmigrant admissions recorded by CBP has declined somewhat over this same period. In FY2013, the 18.3 million visitors entering under the VWP constituted about 40% of all temporary visitors. [1, p. 11]

Visitors dominated the 61.0 million I-94 admissions in FY2013. Almost four-fifths of all I -94 admissions were tourists in FY2013 and another 10% were business visitors. The other substantial categories were students and exchange visitors (4%) and temporary workers and families (5%). [1, p. 12]

Not Welcome

The INA requires the inspection of all aliens who seek entry into the United States; possession of a visa or another form of travel document does not guarantee admission into the United States. As a result, all persons seeking admission to the United States must demonstrate to a CBP inspector that they are a foreign national with a valid visa and/or passport or that they are a U.S. citizen. CBP officers can permit an alien to voluntarily withdraw their application for admission and return to their home country. CBP officers can also summarily exclude an alien arriving through the Visa Waiver Program and those arriving without proper documentation, unless the alien expresses the intention to apply for asylum or has a fear of persecution or torture. Immigration judges with the U.S. Department of Justice's Executive Office for Immigration Review (EOIR) decide all other inadmissibility cases resulting from inspections. [1, p. 14]

Possession of a visa or another form of travel document does not guarantee admission into the United States. All persons seeking admission to the United States must demonstrate to a CBP inspector that they are a foreign national with a valid visa and/or passport or that they are a U.S. citizen.

As Figure 6 shows, the number of inadmissible aliens at ports of entry has not fluctuated greatly over the nine-year period for which data are available. Reports published by the DHS Office of Immigration Statistics indicate that CBP recorded 204,108 foreign nationals arriving at a port of entry who were inadmissible in FY2013. [1, p. 15]

According to the DHS Office of Immigration Statistics, Mexican nationals accounted for 28% of inadmissible aliens, followed by persons from Canada (14%), the Philippines (11%), and Cuba (9%). These four countries accounted for almost two-thirds of all aliens whom CBP deemed inadmissible in FY2013. [1, p. 15]

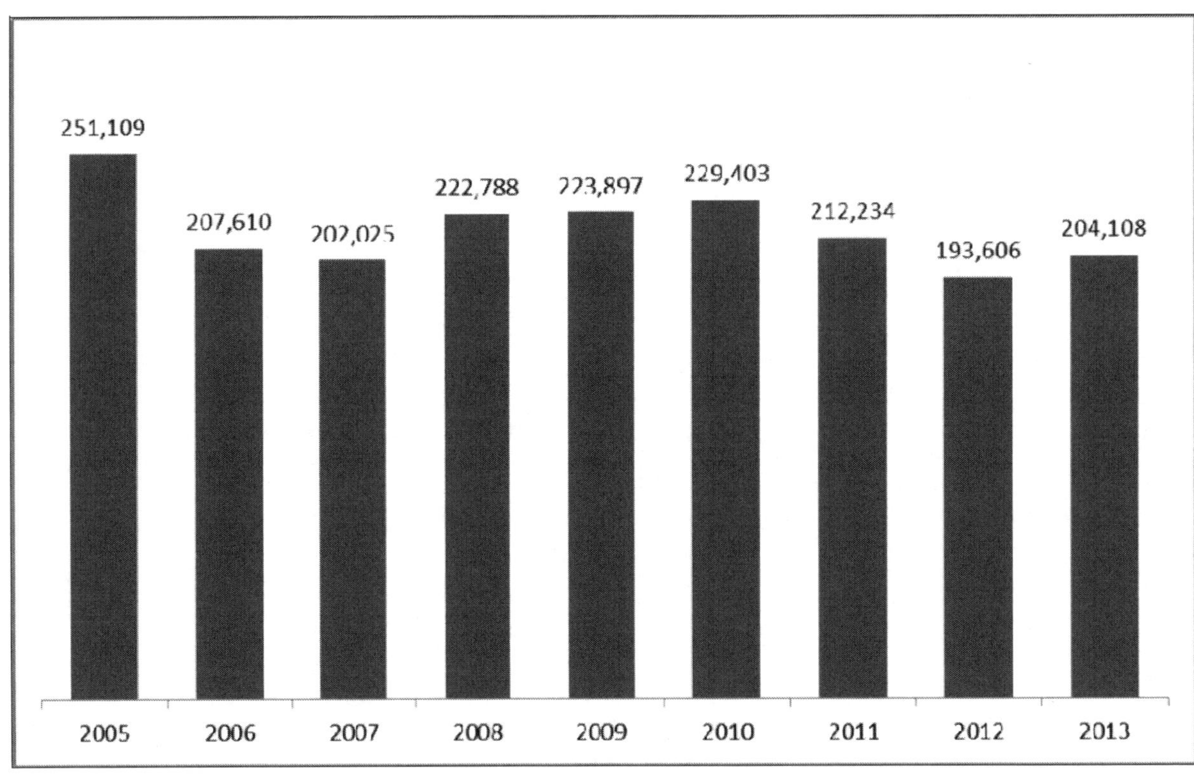

Figure 23-6: Inadmissible Aliens at Ports of Entry 2005-2013 [1, p. 15]

Illegal Workers

All employers are currently required to participate in a paper-based employment eligibility verification system in which they examine documents presented by every new hire to verify the person's identity and work eligibility. The INA states that an employer is in compliance "if the document reasonably appears on its face to be genuine." The new hire must submit a document that establishes both identity and authorization to work (e.g., U.S. passport or LPR card) or submit two documents, one establishing identity (e.g., driver's license) and the other establishing authorization to work (e.g., Social Security card). Employers must retain these employment eligibility verification (I-9) forms. [1, p. 17]

All employers are currently required to participate in a paper-based employment eligibility verification system in which they examine documents presented by every new hire to verify the person's identity and work eligibility. The INA states that an employer is in compliance "if the document reasonably appears on its face to be genuine."

Employers may opt to participate in an electronic employment eligibility verification program, E-Verify, which checks the new hire's employment authorization through Social Security Administration and, if necessary, DHS databases. E-Verify evolved from the Basic Pilot program, one of the three employment verification pilots authorized by the Illegal Immigration Reform and Immigrant Responsibility Act of 1996 to be implemented and the only one still in operation. It began in November 1997 in the five states with the largest unauthorized alien populations at the time. In December 2004, in accordance with P.L. 108-156, the program became available nationwide. The number of employers enrolled in E-Verify grew from 5,900 in FY2005 to 483,000 by the end of FY2013. These data indicate that approximately 8% of U.S. employers were participating in E-Verify by the close of FY2013. [1, pp. 16-17]

Under INA §274A, it is unlawful for an employer to knowingly hire, recruit or refer for a fee, or continue to employ an alien who is not authorized to be so employed. Employers who engage in unlawful employment may be subject to civil and/or criminal penalties. If DHS's Immigration and Customs Enforcement (ICE) believes that an employer has committed a civil violation, the employer may receive a "Final Order" for civil money penalties, a settlement, or a dismissal. In April 2009, ICE issued new guidance on immigration-related worksite enforcement. The 2009 guidance emphasized targeting criminal aliens and employers who cultivate illegal workplaces. [1, p. 18]

Native Americans

The Federal government recognizes tribal nations as "domestic dependent nations" with inherent authority to govern themselves within the borders of the United States. Whereas the Fourteenth Amendment to the Constitution accords citizenship to any person born in the U.S., it was generally interpreted to restrict the citizenship rights of most Native people. In 1924, the Indian Citizenship Act was signed by President Coolidge granting full U.S. citizenship to America's indigenous peoples. The law was enacted partially in recognition of the thousands of Native people who served in the armed forces during World War I.

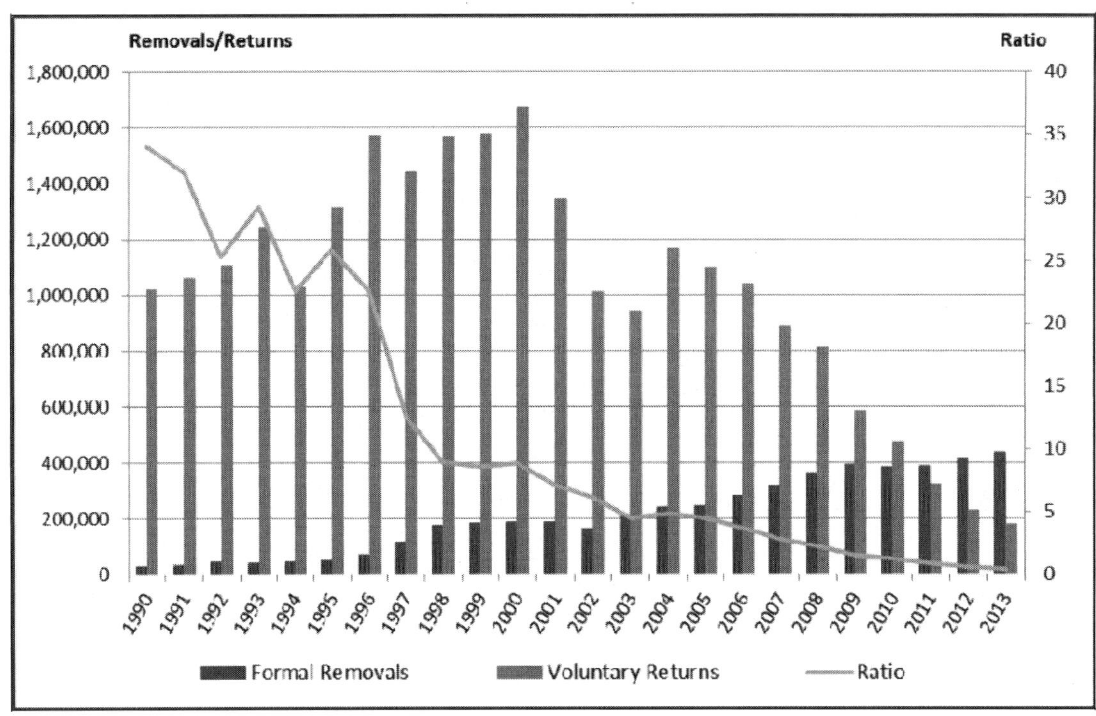

Figure 23-7: Alien Formal Removals and Voluntary Returns 1990-2013 [1, p. 20]

Under INA §274A, it is unlawful for an employer to knowingly hire, recruit or refer for a fee, or continue to employ an alien who is not authorized to be so employed. Employers who engage in unlawful employment may be subject to civil and/or criminal penalties.

According to data provided by ICE, 637 employers were subject to civil penalties in FY2013, up from zero in FY2006. A total of $15.8 million in administrative fines were imposed in FY2013—a figure that exceeds the level of total fines imposed from FY1999 through FY2009. [1, p. 18]

Employers convicted of having engaged in a pattern or practice of knowingly hiring or continuing to employ unauthorized aliens may face criminal fines and/or imprisonment. It is also a criminal offense for a person to knowingly produce, use, or facilitate the production or use of fraudulent immigration documents. Criminal fines peaked at $36.6 million in FY2010. [1, p. 18]

The specific grounds for which foreign nationals are removed from the United States are found in INA §237. These grounds are comparable to the inadmissibility grounds. They include foreign nationals who are inadmissible at time of entry or violate their immigration status; commit certain criminal offenses (e.g., crimes of moral turpitude, aggravated felonies, alien smuggling, high speed flight); fail to register (if required under law) or commit document fraud; are security risks (such as aliens who violate any law relating to espionage, engage in criminal activity that endangers public safety, partake in terrorist activities, or genocide); become a public charge within five years of entry; or vote unlawfully. Generally, an immigration judge determines whether an alien is removable. [1, p. 20]

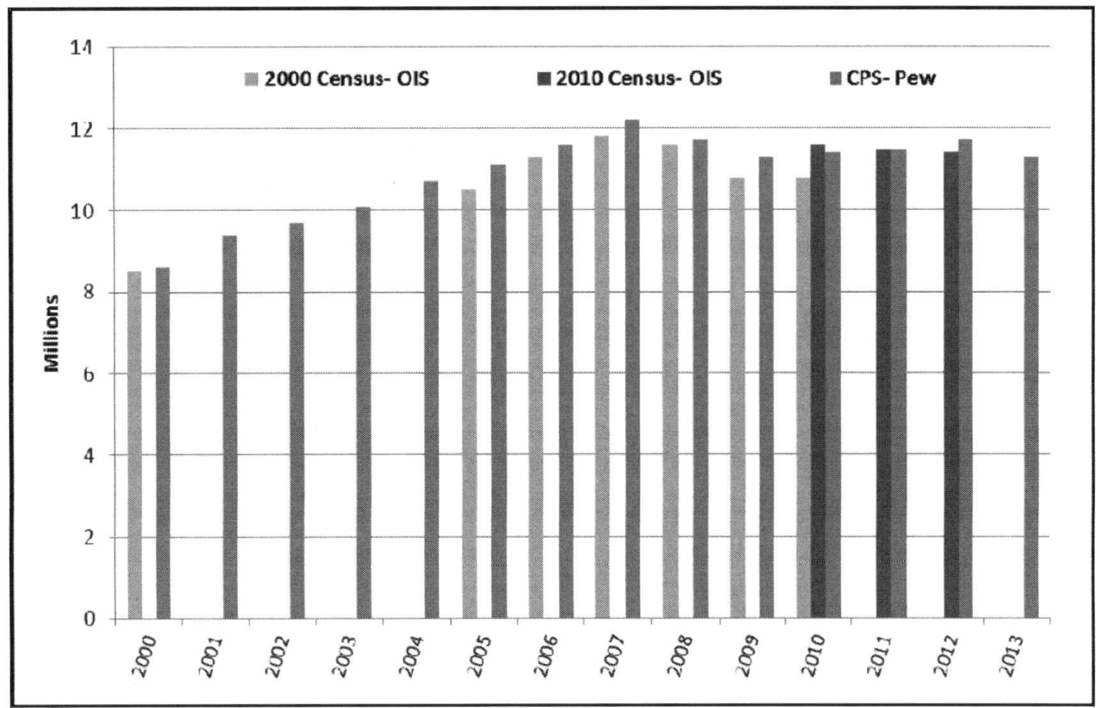

Figure 23-8: Estimated Number of Unauthorized Resident Aliens [1, p. 23]

Formal removals grew from 30,039 in FY1990 to 438,421 in FY2013. Since FY2001, formal removals have increased by over 100%. The trends for direct returns at the border and voluntary departures (i.e., permitting aliens to leave the United States on their own recognizance and at their own expense) within the interior are depicted in Figure 7. As can be seen, the ratio of voluntary departures to formal removals has gone from 34:1 in FY1990 to under 1:2 by FY2013. [1, p. 20]

The three main components of the unauthorized resident alien population are (1) aliens who enter the country surreptitiously without inspection, (2) aliens who overstay their nonimmigrant visas, and (3) aliens who are admitted on the basis of fraudulent documents. In all three instances, the aliens are in violation of the INA and subject to removal.

Illegal Immigrants

The three main components of the unauthorized resident alien population are (1) aliens who enter the country surreptitiously without inspection, (2) aliens who overstay their nonimmigrant visas, and (3) aliens who are admitted on the basis of fraudulent documents. In all three instances, the aliens are in violation of the INA and subject to removal. [1, p. 23]

Estimates derived from the Current Population Survey (CPS) based on the 2010 census indicate that the unauthorized resident alien population rose from 8.6 million in 2000 to 11.3 million in 2013, as Figure 8 shows. The demographers at the Pew Research Center, which produced many of the unauthorized population estimates, concluded that the size of the unauthorized resident alien population has declined from an estimated 12.2 million unauthorized immigrants living in the United States in March 2007. [1, p. 24]

Demographers at the Department of Homeland Security's Office of Immigration Statistics published their estimates of the unauthorized resident alien population and yielded results consistent with Pew Research estimates. OIS demographers drew their estimates from the decennial censuses of 2000 and 2010, adjusted with the American Community Survey (ACS). Although their ACS estimates tend to be lower than the Pew estimates using the Current Population Survey, the trends are comparable. [1, p. 24]

The most recent OIS report estimated that 42% of the 11.4 million unauthorized residents in 2012 had entered from 2000 to 2010. Although increased border security, a record number of alien removals, and high unemployment, among other factors, have depressed the levels of illegal migration in recent years, the estimated number of unauthorized aliens residing in the United States has remained above 10 million for a decade. [1, p. 24]

The most recent OIS report estimated that 42% of the 11.4 million unauthorized residents in 2012 had entered from 2000 to 2010.

Conclusion

Immigration is a legitimate security concern. On November 13, 2015, seven men armed with explosives and automatic weapons mounted coordinated attacks in Paris, killing 130 and injuring 368 innocent victims. According to the French prime minister, several of the gunmen had exploited Europe's immigration crisis to enter the continent undetected. But just as much as it is a security concern, immigration is also a political and economic concern. Debate rages over whether immigrants are a boost or a bust to the economy; the question remains unresolved. Immigrants can also change traditional voting patterns, causing grave concern to those in office. Given these considerations, it is uncertain which will weigh most in determining the future direction of U.S. immigration policy.

Challenge Your Understanding

The following questions are designed to challenge your understanding of the material presented in this chapter. Some questions may require additional research outside this book in order to provide a complete answer.

1. What is a migrant?
2. How does a migrant become a legal permanent resident?
3. How is immigration screening similar to border screening?
4. How is immigration screening different from border screening?
5. Why, as a nation of immigrants, are we concerned about controlling migration?
6. What is the reigning legislation forming the foundation for U.S. immigration policy?
7. List and describe three ways people may illegally remain in this country.
8. What are the restrictions and penalties for hiring an illegal immigrant?
9. Why doesn't DHS have a precise count of illegal immigrants?
10. Describe the circumstances attendant to your U.S. residency status.

Part IV: Mission Components

In this section we will explore DHS components and try and describe "who's who and what do they do". The task is complicated because the Department remains an organization in continual evolution. As seen in Chapter 11, some of the restructuring was self-initiated under authorities granted in the 2002 Homeland Security Act, and some of it was externally directed by Congress, such as the 2006 Post-Katrina Emergency Reform Act and 2007 Implementing the Recommendations of the 9/11 Commission Act. All were done to better orient the Department towards its assigned missions, or expand it to accommodate new missions. One indication of how much the Department has changed is that the number of employees has expanded over 30% from 180,000 in 2003 to 240,000 in 2015. We understand that the information presented in this section is perishable. Accordingly, we do not attempt to address all components within the Department, but focus on those most directly related to its primary missions. In order to maintain a manageable scope, we further restrict our review to higher level components consisting of agencies (e.g., USCG, FEMA, etc.), directorates (e.g., NPPD, CBP, etc.), and offices (DNDO, I&A, etc.). In order to facilitate understanding, each chapter is organized to 1) provide background on the component's origin, 2) identify its specific mission, 3) outline its internal structure, and 4) describe what it is doing.

Chapter 24

National Protection & Programs Directorate

Learning Outcomes

Careful study of this chapter will help a student do the following:

- Explain the mission of the organization.
- Describe some key components of the organization.
- Discuss some of the work of the organization.

"Proactive and coordinated efforts are necessary to strengthen and maintain secure, functioning, and resilient critical infrastructure – including assets, networks, and systems – that are vital to public confidence and the Nation's safety, prosperity, and well-being. "

- 2013 Presidential Policy Directive No. 21

Introduction

If indeed critical infrastructure offers an avenue for domestic catastrophic destruction, then the National Protection and Programs Directorate (NPPD) may be considered one of the most important directorates within the Department of Homeland Security (DHS).

The National Protection and Programs Directorate (NPPD) leads national efforts to strengthen the security and resilience of the Nation's critical infrastructure against terrorist attacks, cyber events, natural disasters, other large-scale incidents, and during national security special events.

Background

The National Protection and Programs Directorate traces its lineage to the original Information Analysis & Infrastructure Protection (IA&IP) Directorate. The IA&IP was headed by an Undersecretary supported by two Assistant Secretaries, one for Information Analysis and the other for Infrastructure Protection. The Assistant Secretary for Infrastructure Protection was assigned responsibility for actively protecting the nation's critical infrastructure and developing an overall National Infrastructure Protection Plan (NIPP). [1, pp. 8-9] Responding to Congressional mandates imposed by the 2006 Post-Katrina Emergency Management Reform Act, and using his own authorities under the 2002 Homeland Security Act, in 2007 Secretary Chertoff formed NPPD, headed by an Undersecretary, to consolidate both physical and cyber protection of the nation's critical infrastructure. [2, p. 17]

Mission

The National Protection and Programs Directorate leads national efforts to strengthen the security and resilience of the Nation's critical infrastructure against terrorist attacks, cyber events, natural disasters, other large-scale incidents, and during national security special events. To accomplish its mission, NPPD collaborates with the owners and operators of infrastructure to maintain near real-time situational awareness of both physical and cyber events and share information that may disrupt critical infrastructure. Through partnerships with Federal, State, local, tribal, territorial, international, and private-sector entities, NPPD identifies and enables mitigation and risk reduction to infrastructure and builds capacity to secure the Nation. [3, p. 77]

NPPD works with infrastructure owners and operators, along with others in the private sector; Federal, State, local, territorial, and tribal officials; and international partners to ensure timely information, analysis, and assessments in order to maintain and provide situational awareness, increase resilience, and understand and mitigate risk through its field force and headquarters components. Through established partnerships, NPPD leads the national unity of effort for infrastructure security and resilience and builds capacity of partners across the nation through activities like bombing prevention, technical assistance, training, analysis, and assessments. NPPD also directly protects Federal infrastructure against both physical and cyber threats and responds to incidents which threaten infrastructure at the local level. [3, p. 77]

NPPD leads the national effort for infrastructure security and resilience and builds capacity of partners across the nation.

The goal of the National Protection and Programs Directorate is to advance the Department of Homeland Security's risk-reduction mission. Reducing risk requires an integrated approach that encompasses both physical and virtual threats and their associated human elements.

Organization

The NPPD is organized into five offices:

1. Office of Infrastructure Protection
2. Office of Cybersecurity and Communications
3. Office of Biometric Identity Management
4. Office of Cyber & Infrastructure Analysis
5. Federal Protective Service

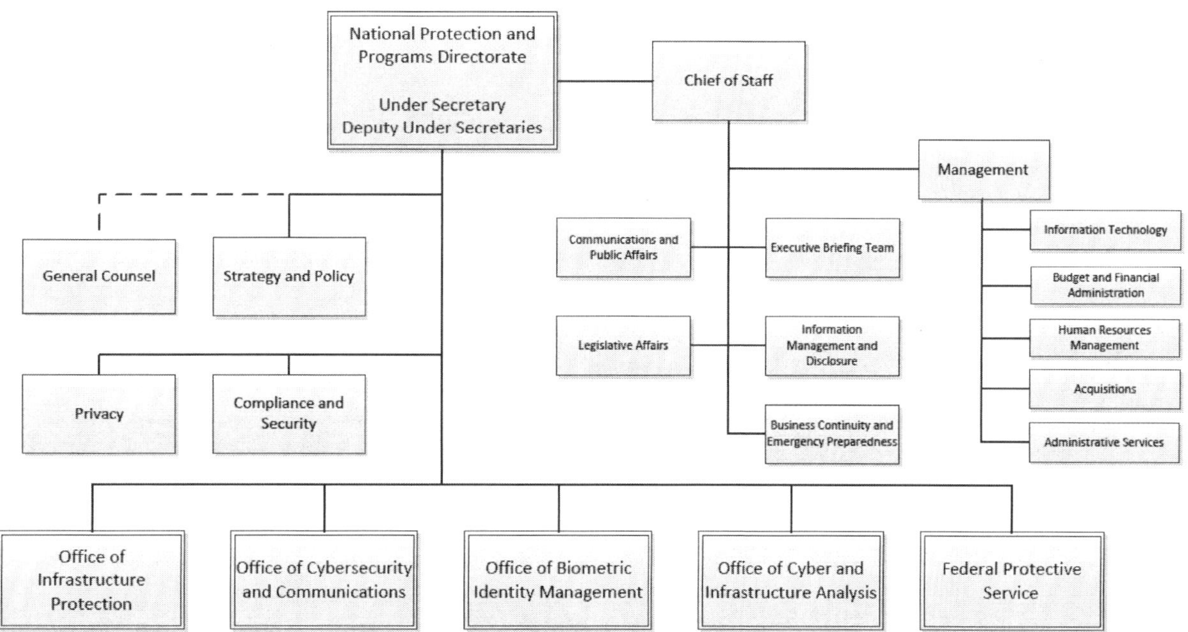

Figure 24-1: NPPD Organization Chart [4]

Office of Infrastructure Protection

The Office of Infrastructure Protection (IP) leads and coordinates national programs and policies on critical infrastructure security and resilience and has established strong partnerships across government and the private sector. The office conducts and facilitates vulnerability and consequence assessments to help critical infrastructure owners and operators and State, local, tribal, and territorial partners understand and address risks to critical infrastructure. IP provides information on emerging threats and hazards so that appropriate actions can be taken. The office also offers tools and training to partners to help them manage the risks to their assets, systems, and networks. [5]

The Office of Infrastructure Protection (IP) leads and coordinates national programs and policies on critical infrastructure security and resilience .

IP's protection efforts are focused on 16 critical infrastructure sectors whose assets, systems, and networks, whether physical or virtual, are considered so vital to the United States that their incapacitation or destruction would have a debilitating effect on security, national economic security, national public health or safety, or any combination thereof. The 16 sectors identified in Presidential Policy Directive 21 (PPD-21) include:

Table 24-1: Critical Infrastructure Sectors

1. Chemical Facilities	9. Financial Services
2. Commercial Facilities	10. Food & Agriculture
3. Communications Assets	11. Government Facilities
4. Critical Manufacturing Facilities	12. Healthcare and Public Health
5. Dams	13. Information Technology
6. Defense Industrial Base	14. Nuclear Reactors, Materials, and Waste
7. Emergency Services	15. Transportation
8. Energy	16. Water and Wastewater Systems

IP's protection efforts are guided by the National Infrastructure Protection Plan. First introduced in 2006, the NIPP was revised in 2009 and again in 2013. The current NIPP advocates protecting critical infrastructure through public/private partnerships predicated on a Risk Management Framework (RMF). The RMF is a 5-step processing for assessing risk and prioritizing countermeasures to reduce the vulnerability of the nation's critical infrastructure. [6]

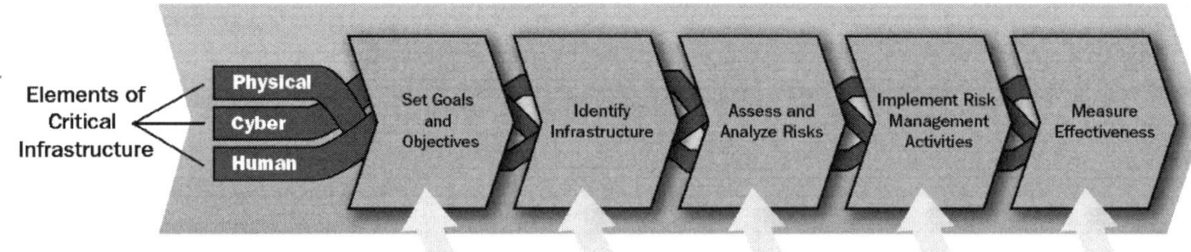

Figure 24-1: NIPP Risk Management Framework [6, p. 15]

The 2013 NIPP represents an evolution from concepts introduced in the initial versions. It is streamlined and adaptable to the current risk, policy, and strategic environments. It provides the foundation for an integrated and collaborative approach to achieve the vision of: "[a] Nation in which physical and cyber critical infrastructure remain secure and resilient, with vulnerabilities reduced, consequences minimized, threats identified and disrupted, and response and recovery hastened." The 2013 NIPP was developed through a collaborative process involving stakeholders from all 16 critical infrastructure sectors, all 50 states, and from all levels of government and industry. [6]

IP actively monitors the health of the nation's critical infrastructure through the National Infrastructure Coordinating Center (NICC). The NICC is an element of the Department's National Operations Center (NOC) which maintains active watch over all homeland security threats. When an incident or event impacting critical infrastructure occurs that requires coordination between DHS and the owners and operators of critical infrastructure, the NICC is the national coordination hub to support the security and resilience of physical critical infrastructure assets. The NICC collaborates with Federal departments, State and Local governments, and private sector partners to monitor potential, developing, and current regional and national operations of the Nation's critical infrastructure sectors. [7, p. 1]

IP actively monitors the health of the nation's critical infrastructure through the National Infrastructure Coordinating Center (NICC). Similarly, the National Cybersecurity and Communications Integration Center (NCCIC) stands watch for national cyber threats.

Similarly, the National Cybersecurity and Communications Integration Center (NCCIC) stands watch for national cyber threats. It issues alerts and coordinates response through law enforcement agencies, the Intelligence Community (IC), international computer emergency readiness teams, domestic Information Sharing And Analysis Centers (ISACs), and critical infrastructure partners. [7, p. 2]

Both the NICC and NCCIC maintain active relationships with Federal partners, law enforcement, and emergency management communities. Other government agencies also work with the NICC and NCCIC and share interest in critical infrastructure-related information. For example, the NICC works closely with the State Department's Overseas Security Advisory Council, which provides information regarding threats to physical infrastructure overseas to American organizations and can ensure this information is available to the domestic critical infrastructure community. At the same time, the NCCIC works on a daily basis with other Federal cyber centers to exchange critical information and coordinate analytical and response processes. Both centers provide reports to the National Operations Center to facilitate shared situational awareness across the Federal community. [7, pp. 4-5]

Important components of the NCCIC include the United States Computer Emergency Readiness Team (US-CERT) and Industrial Control Systems Cyber Emergency Response Team (ICS-CERT). They maintain web-based, collaborative tools to share sensitive cybersecurity prevention, protection, mitigation, response, and recovery information with validated partners. They provide access to a secure portals which provides information regarding cyber indicators, incidents, advisories, and malware digests for critical infrastructure systems. [7, p. 3]

- The Cobalt Compartment is an information hub for enterprise systems security.
- The Control System Compartment provides material on industrial control systems, limited to control system asset owners and operators.
- A National Cyber Awareness System provides timely alerts, bulletins, tips, and technical documents to those who sign up.
- Cybersecurity incident reporting provides critical infrastructure partners with a secure means to report cybersecurity incidents.

The Infrastructure Information Collection Division (IICD) within the NPPD's Office of Infrastructure Protection (IP) leads the Department's efforts to gather and manage vital information regarding the nation's critical infrastructure.

The Infrastructure Information Collection Division (IICD) within the NPPD's Office of Infrastructure Protection (IP) leads the Department's efforts to gather and manage vital information regarding the nation's critical infrastructure. The Web-based infrastructure surveys and assessments, available through the Infrastructure Protection (IP) Gateway, allow users to capture valuable data on a facility's physical and operational security and its resilience to attacks and natural hazards. The collected data is analyzed to determine the facility's relative security and resilience in comparison to the national average for similar facilities. This information is used to develop dashboards that equip the facility's owners and operators with the knowledge to detect and prevent physical, cyber, and natural threats, and better respond to, recover from, and remain resilient against all hazards. [8]

To enhance information-sharing efforts among the public and private sectors, the Protected Critical Infrastructure Information (PCII) program provides congressionally mandated protections from public disclosure to qualifying critical infrastructure information. The success of the nation's collaborative critical infrastructure protection program relies on participation from critical infrastructure owners and operators. The PCII program supports this effort by providing owners and operators with the assurance that their sensitive information can be protected. [8]

To support the efforts of critical infrastructure planners and other IP mission partners, IICD has integrated data visualization and mapping capabilities within the IP Gateway. The secure, web-based, geospatial mapping tool integrates commercial and government-owned data and imagery from multiple sources, to support complex data analysis or provide comprehensive situational and strategic awareness. [8]

The OneView program is also available as an alternative visualization capability for Geospatial Information Infrastructure (GII). OneView provides a rich interface for viewing maps of critical infrastructure, natural hazards data, and other user defined data sources, as well as enhanced imagery, geocoding, and routing features. [8]

IICD manages infrastructure information partnerships with homeland security geospatial stakeholders in state and local governments, as well as the private sector. These partnerships include activities such as working to define better geospatial information requirements and to improve data sharing, creating geospatial data sets for partner use, assigning staff to work in the field and serve as focal points for state and local data needs, and managing workshops to address future geospatial information issues in homeland security and emergency response. [8]

The Office of Cybersecurity and Communications (CS&C) is responsible for enhancing the security, resilience, and reliability of the Nation's cyber and communications infrastructure.

Office of Cybersecurity and Communications

The Office of Cybersecurity and Communications (CS&C) is responsible for enhancing the security, resilience, and reliability of the Nation's cyber and communications infrastructure. CS&C works to prevent or minimize disruptions to critical information infrastructure in order to protect the public, the economy, and government services. CS&C leads efforts to protect the federal ".gov" domain of civilian government networks and to collaborate with the private sector—the ".com" domain—to increase the security of critical networks. [9]

Within CS&C is the Office of Emergency Communications (OEC). Established in 2007 in response to communications challenges faced during the attacks on September 11, 2001 and Hurricane Katrina, the OEC supports and promotes communications used by emergency responders and government officials to keep America safe, secure, and resilient. The office leads the Nation's operable and interoperable public safety and national security and emergency preparedness (NS/EP) communications efforts. OEC provides training, coordination, tools, and guidance to help its federal, state, local, tribal, territorial and industry partners develop their emergency communications capabilities. OEC's programs and services coordinate emergency communications planning, preparation and evaluation, to ensure safer, better-prepared communities nationwide.

CS&C coordinates national security and emergency preparedness through the Stakeholder Engagement and Cyber Infrastructure Resilience (SECIR) office. CS&C relies on SECIR to streamline coordination and engagement with external partners, while leveraging capabilities and significant subject matter expertise in order to meet stakeholder requirements.

The Federal Network Resilience (FNR) office within CS&C is responsible for developing metrics to drive cybersecurity risk management for Federal departments and agencies. FNR also gathers cybersecurity requirements and develops operational policies for the Federal government. It collaborates with, and provides outreach to, the Office of Management and Budget (OMB), the Federal Chief Information Officer (CIO) Council, and individual agency Chief Information (CIOs) and Chief Information Security Officers (CISOs) of various Federal agencies. FNR is a clearing house for cyber best practices and cyber lessons learned in support of Federal departments and agencies.

The CS&C Network Security Deployment (NSD) office works collaboratively with public, private, and international entities to secure cyberspace and America's cyber assets. NSD serves as the cybersecurity engineering and acquisition "Center of Excellence" within CS&C. In support of that role, NSD provides development, acquisition, deployment, operational, and customer support to satisfy the Department's mission requirements under the Comprehensive National Cybersecurity Initiative (CNCI). [9]

The Office of Biometric Identity Management (OBIM) is responsible for collecting, maintaining, and sharing biometric data with the law enforcement and intelligence communities and strategic foreign partners. As part of this mission, it maintains the Automated Biometric Identification System (IDENT)—DHS's central repository for biometric data.

Finally, CS&C operates the Enterprise Performance Management Office (EPMO), which ensures that the Assistant Secretary's strategic goals and priorities are reflected across all CS&C programs. EPMO measures the effectiveness of initiatives, programs, and projects that support those goals and priorities, and facilitates cross-functional mission coordination and implementation between CS&C components within DHS, and among the interagency. [9]

Office of Biometric Identity Management (OBIM)

The Office of Biometric Identity Management (OBIM) is responsible for collecting, maintaining, and sharing biometric data with the law enforcement and intelligence communities and strategic foreign partners. As part of this mission, it maintains the Automated Biometric Identification System (IDENT)—DHS's central repository for biometric data. [10, p. 11] OBIM was created in March, 2013, replacing the United States Visitor and Immigration Status Indicator Technology (US-VISIT) Program, the system used by the DHS for keeping track of all visitors to the country and checking all of their identity through various biometric technologies. [11]

Formerly US-VISIT, the OBIM uses biometrics to help make travel simple, easy and convenient for legitimate visitors, but virtually impossible for those who wish to do harm or violate U.S. laws. Biometrics collected by OBIM and linked to specific biographic information enable a person's identity to be established, then verified, by the U.S. government. With each encounter, from applying for a visa to seeking immigration benefits to entering the United States, OBIM:

Checks a person's biometrics against a watch list of known or suspected terrorists, criminals and immigration violators

Checks against the entire database of all of the fingerprints the Department of Homeland Security has collected since OBIM began to determine if a person is using an alias and attempting to use fraudulent identification.

Checks a person's biometrics against those associated with the identification document presented to ensure that the document belongs to the person presenting it and not someone else. [12]

OBIM provides the results of these checks to decision makers when and where they need it. These services help prevent identity fraud and deprive criminals and immigration violators of the ability to cross U.S. borders. Based on biometrics alone, OBIM has helped stop thousands of people who were ineligible to enter the United States. Biometrics are unique physical characteristics, such as fingerprints, that can be used for automated recognition. Biometrics form the foundation of OBIM's identification services because they are reliable, convenient and virtually impossible to forge. [12]

The Office of Cyber & Infrastructure Analysis (OCIA) performs integrated analysis of critical infrastructure, and identifies critical infrastructure where cyber incidents could have catastrophic impacts. To assist with these responsibilities, the OCIA manages the National Infrastructure Simulation and Analysis Center (NISAC) on Kirtland Air Force Base in Albuquerque, NM.

Privacy is an integral part of the OBIM and it is essential to the program mission. OBIM takes privacy into account from conception through planning and development, and during the execution of every aspect of the OBIM program. Personal information collected by OBIM is to be used only for the purposes for which it was collected, unless specifically authorized or mandated by law. OBIM has carefully monitored systems and security practices in place to protect the privacy of those whose data are collected and to ensure the integrity of that data. OBIM has dedicated privacy personnel to further ensure that the information collected is protected from misuse by anyone inside or outside OBIM. [12]

Office of Cyber & Infrastructure Analysis

Formerly the Infrastructure Analysis and Strategy Division (IASD) within the Office of Infrastructure Protection (IP), OCIA was established as an office of the NPPD in 2014. OCIA has an important role in DHS's efforts to implement Presidential Policy Directive 21 (PPD-21), which calls for integrated analysis of critical infrastructure, and Executive Order 13636, identifying critical infrastructure where cyber incidents could have catastrophic impacts to public health and safety, the economy, and national security.

OCIA builds on the recent accomplishments of the Department's Homeland Infrastructure Threat and Risk Analysis Center (HITRAC) and manages the National Infrastructure Simulation and Analysis Center (NISAC) to advance understanding of emerging risks crossing the cyber-physical domain. OCIA represents an integration and enhancement of DHS's analytic capabilities, supporting stakeholders and interagency partners.

Federal Protective Service

The Federal Protective Service (FPS), within the National Protection and Programs Directorate is responsible for the protection and security of federal property, personnel, and federally owned and leased buildings. In general, FPS operations focus on security and law enforcement activities that reduce vulnerability to criminal and terrorist threats. FPS protection and security operations include all-hazards based risk assessments; emplacement of criminal and terrorist countermeasures, such as vehicle barriers and closed-circuit cameras; law enforcement response; assistance to federal agencies through Facility Security Committees; and emergency and safety education programs. FPS also assists other federal agencies, such as the U.S. Secret Service (USSS) at National Special Security Events (NSSE), with additional security. FPS is the lead "Government Facilities Sector Agency" for the National Infrastructure Protection Plan (NIPP). There are more than 1,300 Law Enforcement Officers, Security Specialists, Special Agents and Mission Support Staff protecting federal facilities and tenants (4) along with approximately 13,000 contract security guards. [10, p. 10]

The Federal Protective Service (FPS), within NPPD is responsible for the protection and security of federal property, personnel, and federally owned and leased buildings.

The Federal Protective Service provides integrated security and law enforcement services to more than 9,500 federal facilities nationwide. These services include: conducting facility security assessments; responding to crimes and other incidents to protect life and property; and detecting, investigating, and mitigating threats. [13] Protective services of the FPS also include:

- Designing countermeasures for tenant agencies
- Maintaining uniformed law enforcement presence
- Maintaining armed contract security guards
- Performing background suitability checks for contract employees
- Offering special operations including K - 9 explosive detection
- Monitoring security alarms via centralized communication centers
- Sharing intelligence among local/state/federal
- Protecting special events
- Training federal tenants in crime prevention and occupant emergency planning

> In the spring of 2013, the Federal Protective Service (FPS) implemented a new directive entitled the Prohibited Items Program (FPS Directive 15.9.3.1. (Rev. 1). The Prohibited Items Program sets forth FPS' policy for applying security force countermeasures to mitigate prohibited item entry at Federal properties. The intent of the policy is to provide risk-based recommendations to Facility Security Committees regarding security screening, visitor processing, and the development of prohibited items lists and accommodation policies as well as establishing FPS policies and procedures for addressing prohibited items. The Facility Security Committee is responsible for determining the security countermeasures and prohibited item list for a particular Federal facility. FPS is responsible for implementing the security countermeasures and enforcing the prohibited items list developed by the Facility Security Committee.

Within the Federal Protective Service, the Office for Bombing Prevention (OBP) leads the DHS's efforts to implement the National Policy for Countering Improvised Explosive Devices (IED) and enhance the nation's ability to prevent, protect against, respond to, and mitigate the use of explosives against critical infrastructure; the private sector; and federal, state, local, tribal, and territorial entities. OBP was born of terrorism events, such as Lockerbie, Oklahoma City, 9/11, Madrid, and London through its mission to protect life and critical infrastructure by building capabilities within the general public and across the public and private sectors to prevent, protect against, respond to, and mitigate bombing incidents. [14]

The FPS also has other specialized capabilities. FPS Explosive Detection Canine (EDC) teams conduct searches for a variety of explosive materials near building exteriors, parking lots, office areas, vehicles, packages, and people in and around Federal facilities. They also provide a strong visible and psychological deterrent against criminal and terrorist threats. The teams are available to assist federal, state, and local law enforcement partners. EDC teams play a critical role in FPS' comprehensive preventive security measures by supporting strategic explosive detection activities. They also provide immediate and specialized response to bomb threats and unattended packages or other such dangerous items. Most often, these detection activities allow the EDC teams to detect or quickly rule out the presence of dangerous materials and allow the business of the government to continue with minimal or no interruption. FPS has also initiated a Personnel Screening Detection (PSD) program. PSD canines are specially trained to detect explosives carried by people or in moving containers, such as luggage or backpacks. [13]

Within the Federal Protective Service, the Office for Bombing Prevention (OBP) leads the DHS's efforts to implement the National Policy for Countering Improvised Explosive Devices (IED).

FPS mobile command vehicles (MCV) are deployed to enhance or reestablish communication and coordination during emergency incidents and special security events nationwide. These assets leverage satellite and internet access, as well as interoperable radios and video capabilities to enhance communication between FPS assets and other federal and local response and support assets. The MCVs can rapidly deploy to any location in the continental United States where the communications infrastructure is inadequate or has been disrupted, or where enhanced interoperability among law enforcement agencies is needed.

Conclusion

While, arguably, NPPD may have the most important job in DHS, without doubt it also has one of the most challenging jobs in DHS. Critical infrastructure protection remains a work in progress. Although DHS has succeeded in engaging owners and operators in a dialog about critical infrastructure protection, it has made little progress in actually reducing vulnerabilities as the Department was tasked to do by the 2002 Homeland Security Act. In part, the predicament is the result of an absence of workable solutions. Critical infrastructure protection is a job easier said than done. This assessment is evidenced by 1) the Department's inability to compile a definitive list of critical infrastructure, 2) develop a transparent and

Challenge Your Understanding

The following questions are designed to challenge your understanding of the material presented in this chapter. Some questions may require additional research outside this book in order to provide a complete answer.

1. What is the mission of the National Protection and Programs Directorate?
2. Which NPPD component has primary responsibility for critical infrastructure protection?
3. Which NPPD component monitors the nation's infrastructure?
4. Which NPPD component stands watch for national cyber threats?
5. Which NPPD component collects and manages information about critical infrastructure?
6. Which NPPD component is responsible for protecting the ".gov" Internet domain?
7. Which NPPD component collects and manages law enforcement biometric data?
8. Which NPPD component performs integrated analysis of critical infrastructure?
9. Which NPPD component performs modeling and simulation of critical infrastructure?
10. Which NPPD component works to counter improvised explosive devices?

Chapter 25

Science & Technology Directorate

Learning Outcomes

Careful study of this chapter will help a student do the following:

- Explain the mission of the organization.
- Describe some key components of the organization.
- Discuss some of the work of the organization.

"Just as science and technology have helped us defeat past enemies overseas, so too will they help us defeat the efforts of terrorists to attack our homeland and disrupt our way of life."

- 2002 National Strategy for Homeland Security

Introduction

As the 1995 Tokyo Subway Attacks raised the prospect of domestic WMD attack by non-state actors, the United States found that its traditional methods of deterring WMD attack by nation states were no longer effective. New means had to be discovered to prevent and protect against this new threat. Accordingly, the Department of Homeland Security was given the means and the mandate to harness the nation's research and development capacity to deliver innovative technologies that would render the country less vulnerable to WMD attack.

The Department of Homeland Security Science and Technology Directorate (DHS S&T) was established by the 200 Homeland Security Act to develop countermeasures to chemical, biological, radiological, and nuclear threats.

Background

The Department of Homeland Security Science and Technology Directorate (S&T) was established by the Homeland Security Act of 2002 (P.L. 107-296). DHS S&T is headed by an Under Secretary for Science and Technology. The Homeland Security Act gave the Under Secretary a wide-ranging list of responsibilities and authorities, chief among them the objective of developing countermeasures to chemical, biological, radiological, and nuclear threats.

Mission

In general, DHS S&T conducts basic and applied research, development, testing, and evaluation to:

- Deliver new capabilities and knowledge products;
- Enhance processes and efficiencies;
- Provide acquisition support; and
- Help understand homeland security risks and opportunities. [1, pp. 1 - 2]

DHS S&T's current approach emphasizes research and development (R&D) deliverables with high impact, the ability to rapidly transition products to use in the field, and a high return on investment. [1, p. 2]

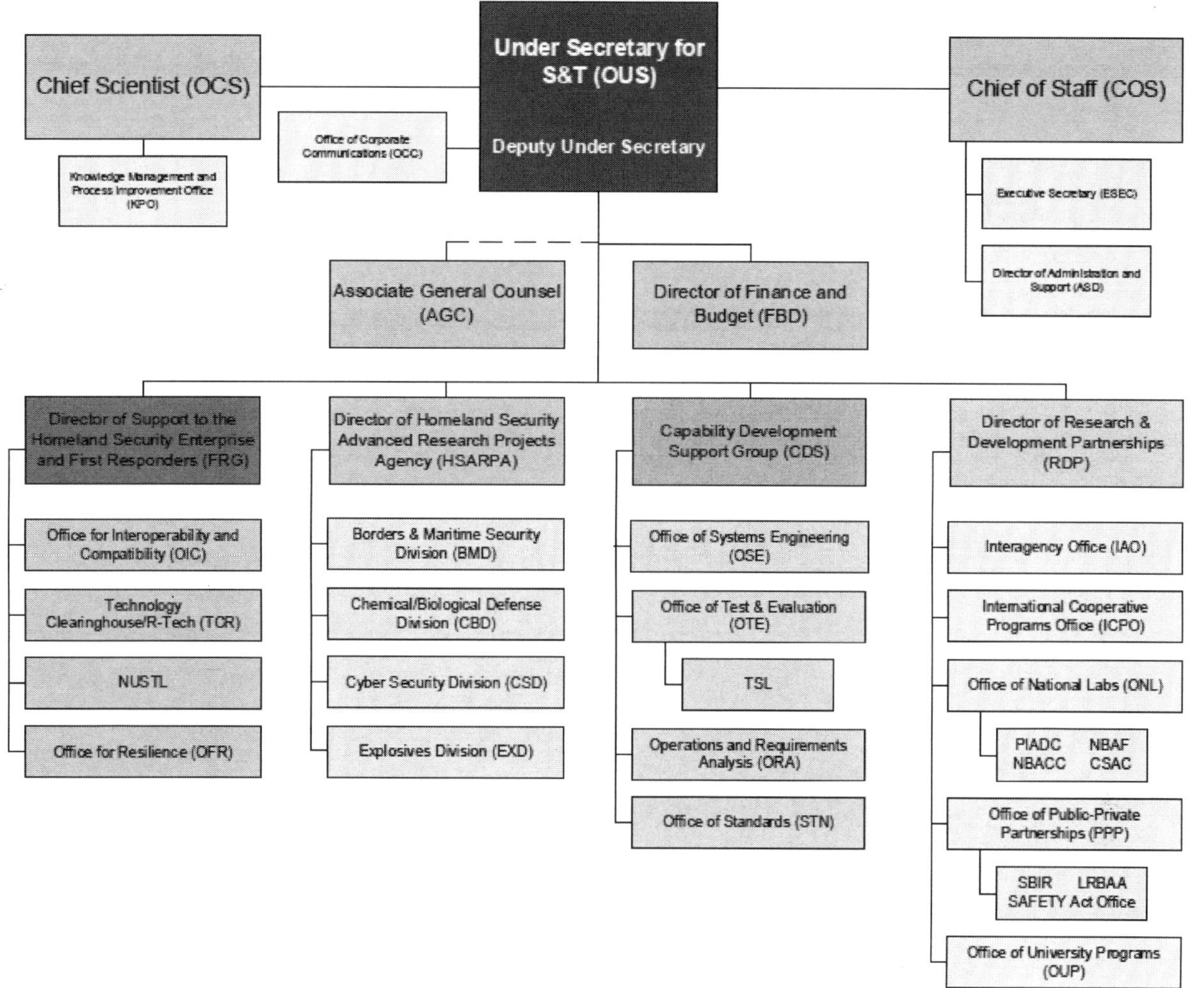

Figure 25-1: DHS S&T Organization [3]

Organization

The statutory language creating DHS did not define the structure of the S&T Directorate; the Under Secretary has discretion to reorganize as needed. Each Under Secretary has had a different vision for the organization and activities of the S&T Directorate and has organized or reorganized the S&T Directorate accordingly. The current structure, since 2010, organizes the S&T Directorate into four groups, each headed by a Director. The groups are:

1. Support to the Homeland Security Enterprise and First Responders Group (FRG), which is responsible for technology interoperability and compatibility, transfers technologies to first responders, and oversees the National Urban Security Technology Laboratory (formerly the Environmental Measurements Laboratory);
2. Homeland Security Advanced Research Projects Agency (HSARPA), which contains six technical divisions that manage R&D in different topical areas and the Special Projects Office that oversees the directorate's classified R&D; [1, p. 3]

3. The Capability Development Support (CDS) Group works closely with the DHS components to ensure programs and systems reduce or mitigate the challenges in the safest, most efficient and most cost-effective manner. CDS responds to DHS component needs for standards, test and evaluation, operations and requirements analysis and systems engineering. [2]

4. Research and Development Partnerships (RDP) Division, which serves as the primary external interface for the S&T Directorate, coordinates work with the DHS University Centers of Excellence, oversees several DHS laboratories, and manages the relationship between the S&T Directorate and the Department of Energy national laboratories. [1, p. 3]

DHS is currently organized into four groups: 1) First Responders Group, 2) HSARPA, 3) Capability Development Support Group, and 4) Research and Development Partnerships Division.

In addition to these groups, the 2010 reorganization created a Chief Scientist position reporting to the Under Secretary.

First Responders Group

FRG works in close partnership with first responders at all levels to identify, validate, and facilitate the fulfillment of needs through the use of existing and emerging technologies, knowledge products and standards. Prioritized areas of FRG focus and initiatives include:

1. Making First Responders Safer
2. Helping First Responders Share Data and Critical Information
3. Helping First Responders Communicate Through Interoperability
4. Engaging, Communicating and Partnering with First Responders [4]

FRG is comprised of four divisions:

1. National Urban Security Technology Laboratory (NUSTL): NUSTL tests, evaluates and analyzes homeland security capabilities while serving as a technical authority to first responder, state and local entities in protecting our cities. NUSTL leads and provides independent federal oversight for test programs, pilots, demonstrations and other forms of evaluations of homeland security capabilities both in the field and in the laboratory.

2. Office for Interoperability and Compatibility (OIC): OIC provides local, tribal, state and federal stakeholders with the tools, technologies, methodologies and guidance to enable improved communications interoperability at all levels of government. OIC manages a comprehensive research, development, testing, evaluation and standards program to enhance emergency interoperable communications and improve alerts and warnings.

3. First Responder Technologies (R-Tech): R-Tech rapidly disseminates technology information on products and services to local, tribal, state and federal agencies and private sector entities in order to encourage technological innovation and facilitate the mission of DHS. R-Tech provides information, resources and technology solutions that address mission capability gaps identified by the emergency response community.

4. System Assessment and Validation for Emergency Responders (SAVER): DHS established the SAVER program to assist first responders in making procurement decisions. The SAVER program conducts objective assessments and validations of commercial equipment and systems and provides those results along with other relevant equipment information to the response community. [4]

Given its name association, many believed that, like DARPA, HSARPA would fund high-risk, high-reward R&D. Attempts to make HSARPA more like DARPA were unsuccessful because HSARPA doesn't have the organizational capacity of DARPA. Today, HSARPA is more focused on transitioning technology to the field.

HSARPA

When Congress established DHS, it created within the S&T Directorate the Homeland Security Advanced Research Projects Agency, which was to administer a newly established Acceleration Fund for Research and Development of Homeland Security Technologies. The scope of HSARPA has evolved since Congress created it. Initially, it was unclear how the S&T Directorate would implement HSARPA. Given the similarity of its name to the Defense Advanced Research Projects Agency (DARPA), some policy makers and experts in the scientific community believed that, like DARPA, it would fund high-risk, high-reward R&D. Instead, the S&T Directorate initially used HSARPA to conduct essentially all of its extramural activities, most of which were conventional R&D with only moderate risk. To be fair, the strategy was intentionally devised to accumulate rapid success. An attempt to make HSARPA more like DARPA was unsuccessful because HSARPA doesn't have the organizational capacity of DARPA. Today, HSARPA is more focused on transitioning technology to the field. A consequence of this change has been a reduction in the number of projects and programs, from 250 in 2010 to 75 in 2012. While the number of projects rose to 100 in 2014, the challenge for S&T is maintaining a number of programs and projects sufficient to cover the range of homeland security threats while also providing each program and project with sufficient resources to achieve meaningful progress or success. [1, p. 17]

Capability Development Support

CDS provides an innovative, systems-based approach to help operators define their needs and develop technologies and solutions that can be quickly deployed to frontline operators. CDS' analytic and systems engineering approach assesses the operational environment and fiscal limitations to ensure the best solutions are chosen. CDS' expertise includes systems engineering, operations analysis, test and evaluations, standards and acquisition. CDS focuses on accuracy and analysis to make smart investment decisions that deliver enhanced capabilities to the Homeland Security Enterprise. CDS does this in a variety of ways:

- Office of Test and Evaluation. Through delegation by the Secretary of Homeland Security under the Homeland Security Act of 2002, CDS acts as the principal advisor on operational test and evaluation and oversees test and evaluation for DHS major acquisitions, ensuring homeland security technologies are reliable, interoperable and effective. CDS provides test and evaluation (T&E) oversight for 135 major DHS acquisition programs totaling about $150 billion. The Office of Test and Evaluation includes the Transportation Security Laboratory (TSL) specializing in evaluating screening and contraband detection technologies.
- Standards. CDS develops and oversees DHS standards that ensure reliable, interoperable and effective technologies and processes. This includes coordination and representation on a number of standard-setting bodies and organizations.
- Operations and Requirements Analysis. Established in 2012, CDS' Operations and Requirements Analysis uses technical and analytic expertise to identify and prioritize cross-DHS capability gaps and find solutions for DHS component operations. The goal is to save money and time while meeting DHS critical missions and to support S&T with transitioning technologies to operational use. The office also supports the DHS Joint Requirements Council (JRC), a DHS component-led body designed to identify and prioritize cross-department capability gaps and recommend investments to address those gaps. CDS supports the JRC by providing capabilities and requirements analysis enabling DHS leadership to address the gaps, overlaps and duplications at the enterprise-level rather than at the individual component level.
- Systems Engineering. CDS's systems engineering promotes a rigorous systems engineering process that transforms customer needs and requirements into operational capabilities.

RDP was created in November 2010 to develop, foster and leverage innovative partnerships and serve as a primary resource in establishing and managing world class Centers of Excellence and federal laboratories.

As the Component Acquisition Executive, CDS represents S&T on a number of acquisition and policy steering committees and provides advice on acquisition issues. [2]

Research and Development Partnerships

RDP was created in November 2010 to develop, foster and leverage innovative partnerships and serve as a primary resource in establishing and managing world class Centers of Excellence and federal laboratories. RDP manages the Homeland Security Science and Technology Advisory Committee, International Cooperative Programs Office, the Office of National Laboratories, Public-Private Partnership Offices, and Office of University Programs. [5]

- The Homeland Security Science and Technology Advisory Committee (HSSTAC) serves as a source of independent expert advice to the Under Secretary for Science and Technology. [6] The HSSTAC provides independent, consensus scientific and technical advice and recommendations to the Under Secretary for Science and Technology. Its activities focus on the S&T mission to strengthen America's security and resiliency by providing knowledge products and innovative technology solutions for the Homeland Security Enterprise. The committee addresses science and technology needs and trends, management processes and organizational constructs, and other matters of special interest to the Under Secretary for S&T and will ensure the identification of new technologies in those areas that strengthen homeland security. It supports the priority needs of HSARPA and First Responders Group. [7]

- The International Cooperative Programs Office (ICPO) develops partnerships with foreign governments and international organizations to enhance scientific and technical knowledge for the Homeland Security Enterprise. These partnerships provide the HSE with access to innovative research and development knowledge, funding and other unique capabilities and resources. ICPO was established in accordance with Title 6 U.S. Code Section 195c ("Promoting antiterrorism through international cooperation program"). [8]

RDP oversees research projects at five DHS laboratories, thirteen DOE laboratories, and manages sixteen academic Centers of Excellence.

- The Office of National Laboratories (ONL) oversees a coordinated network of the five DHS laboratories listed in Table 1. DHS also coordinates homeland security research at the 13 Department of Energy (DOE) national laboratories listed in Table 2. [9]

Table 25-1: DHS Laboratories [9]

1.	Chemical Security Analysis Center, Aberdeen Proving Ground, MD
2.	National Bio and Agro-Defense Facility, Manhattan, KS
3.	National Biodefense Analysis and Countermeasures Center, Fort Detrick, MD
4.	National Urban Security Technology, Manhattan, NY
5.	Plum Island Animal Disease Center, Orient Point, NY

Table 25-2: DOE Laboratories [10]

1.	Ames Lab, Ames, IA
2.	Argonne National Lab, Argonne, IL
3.	Brookhaven National Lab, Upton, NY
4.	Idaho National Lab, Idaho Falls, ID
5.	Los Alamos National Lab, Los Alamos, NM
6.	National Energy Technology Lab, Albany, OR
7.	National Renewable Energy Lab, Golden, CO
8.	Oak Ridge National Lab, Oak Ridge, TN
9.	Pacific Northwest National Lab, Richland, WA
10.	Princeton Plasma Physics Lab, Plainsboro, NJ
11.	Sandia National Labs, Albuquerque, NM
12.	Savannah River National Lab, Aiken, SC
13.	Thomas Jefferson National Accelerator Facility, Newport News, VA

Table 25-3: DHS Centers of Excellence [16]

1.	**Arctic Domain Awareness Center of Excellence (ADAC)**, led by the University of Alaska Anchorage, develops and transitions technology solutions, innovative products, and educational programs to improve situational awareness and crisis response capabilities related to emerging maritime challenges posed by the dynamic Arctic environment.
2.	**Center for Advancing Microbial Risk Assessment (CAMRA)**, co-led by Michigan State University and Drexel University and established jointly with the U.S. Environmental Protection Agency, fills critical gaps in risk assessments for mitigating microbial hazards.
3.	**Center for Borders, Trade, and Immigration Research (CBTIR)**, led by the University of Houston, develops technology-based tools, techniques, and educational programs for border management, immigration, trade facilitation, and targeting and enforcement of transnational borders.
4.	**Center for Maritime, Island and Remote and Extreme Environment Security (MIREES)**, co-led by the University of Hawaii and Stevens Institute of Technology, focuses on developing robust research and education programs addressing maritime domain awareness to safeguard populations and properties in geographical areas that present significant security challenges.
5.	**Center for Visualization and Data Analytics (CVADA), co-led by Purdue University (visualization sciences – VACCINE)** and Rutgers University (data sciences – CCICADA), creates the scientific basis and enduring technologies needed to analyze large quantities of information to detect security threats to the nation.
6.	**Center of Excellence for Awareness and Localization of Explosives-Related Threats (ALERT)**, led by Northeastern University, develops new means and methods to protect the nation from explosives-related threats.
7.	**Center of Excellence for Zoonotic and Animal Disease Defense (ZADD)**, co-led by Texas A&M University and Kansas State University, protects the nation's agriculture and public health sectors against high-consequence foreign animal, emerging and zoonotic disease threats.
8.	**Coastal Hazards Center of Excellence (CHC)**, co-led by the University of North Carolina at Chapel Hill and Jackson State University, performs research and develops education programs to enhance the nation's ability to safeguard populations, properties and economies from catastrophic natural disasters.
9.	**Coastal Resilience Center of Excellence (CRC)**, led by the University of North Carolina at Chapel Hill, conducts research and education to enhance the Nation's ability to safeguard people, infrastructure, and economies from catastrophic coastal natural disasters such as floods and hurricanes.
10.	**Critical Infrastructure Resilience Institute (CIRI)**, led by the University of Illinois at Urbana-Champaign, conducts research and education to enhance the resilience of the Nation's critical infrastructure and its owners and operators.
11.	**Food Protection and Defense Institute (FPDI)**, led by the University of Minnesota, defends the safety and security of the food system by conducting research to protect vulnerabilities in the food supply chain. FPDI was formerly named the National Center for Food Protection and Defense (NCFPD).
12.	**Maritime Security Center of Excellence (MSC)**, led by Stevens Institute of Technology, enhances Maritime Domain Awareness and develops strategies to support Marine Transportation System resilience and educational programs for current and aspiring homeland security practitioners.
13.	**National Center for Border Security and Immigration (NCBSI)**, co-led by the University of Arizona and the University of Texas at El Paso, develops novel technologies, tools and advanced methods to balance immigration and commerce with effective border security.
14.	**National Center for the Study of Preparedness and Catastrophic Event Response (PACER)**, led by Johns Hopkins University, optimizes the nation's medical and public health preparedness, mitigation and recovery strategies in the event of a high-consequence natural or man-made disaster.
15.	**National Consortium for the Study of Terrorism and Responses to Terrorism (START)**, led by the University of Maryland, provides policy makers and practitioners with empirically grounded findings on the human elements of the terrorist threat and informs decisions on how to disrupt terrorists and terrorist groups.
16.	**National Transportation Security Center of Excellence (NTSCOE)** was established in accordance with H.R.1, Implementing the Recommendations of the 9/11 Commission Act of 2007, in August 2007. NTSCOE is a seven-institution consortium focused on developing new technologies, tools and advanced methods to defend, protect and increase the resilience of the nation's multi-modal transportation infrastructure.

- RDP manages a number of incentive programs and program offices designed to promote innovation within the private sector. RDP manages the InnoPrize Program which elicits ideas directly from citizens. [11] The Small Business Innovation Research (SBIR) program provides grants to foster small business research. [12] The Office of SAFETY Act Implementation oversees provisions of the 2002 Homeland Security Act that protects manufacturers or sellers of effective anti-terrorism technologies from undue litigation. [13] The Technology Transfer Program Office expedites technology transition from DHS laboratories to commercial markets. [14] And the Long-Range Broad Agency Announcement (LBRAA) program manages a standing, open invitation to the scientific and technical communities to fund pioneering research and development in support of the nation's security. [15]
- The Office of University Programs manages the Centers of Excellence Program, Minority Serving Institutions Program, and Workforce Development Initiatives. The Center of Excellence Program awards three-year grants to colleges and universities conducting research on priority topics of interest as listed in Table 3. [16] The Minority Serving Institutions Program is designed to build a diverse homeland security science and engineering workforce through the Centers of Excellence. And Workforce Development Initiatives educate and train homeland security science and engineering students and professionals for the current and future workforce. [17]

Funding for the S&T Directorate fell in FY2012 to its lowest level since Congress began appropriating funding for DHS. The reductions reflected several competing priorities within the S&T Directorate. One is establishing the appropriate balance between long-term R&D investments and near-term operational needs.

Program Priorities

Funding for the S&T Directorate fell in FY2012 to its lowest level since Congress began appropriating funding for DHS. The reductions reflected several competing priorities within the S&T Directorate. One is establishing the appropriate balance between long-term R&D investments and near-term operational needs. [1, p. 5]

In contrast to other R&D organizations in DHS, the S&T Directorate has a broad scope. The S&T Directorate bases its priority-setting on DHS mission areas as articulated in the Quadrennial Homeland Security Review (QHSR), the Administration's National Security Strategy, and first responder requirements. The directorate derives its priorities and requirements from assessing near- and long-term threats, national needs, and operational vulnerabilities. In addition, the S&T Directorate attempts to identify technical areas suitable for development. [1, p. 7]

Identifying specific priorities, based on these general principles, and then planning and executing integrated R&D activities to accomplish those priorities remain formidable tasks. Among the approaches the S&T Directorate has taken toward meeting this challenge are strategic planning, a portfolio review process, and partnerships with DHS operational components to identify high priority activities. [1, p. 7]

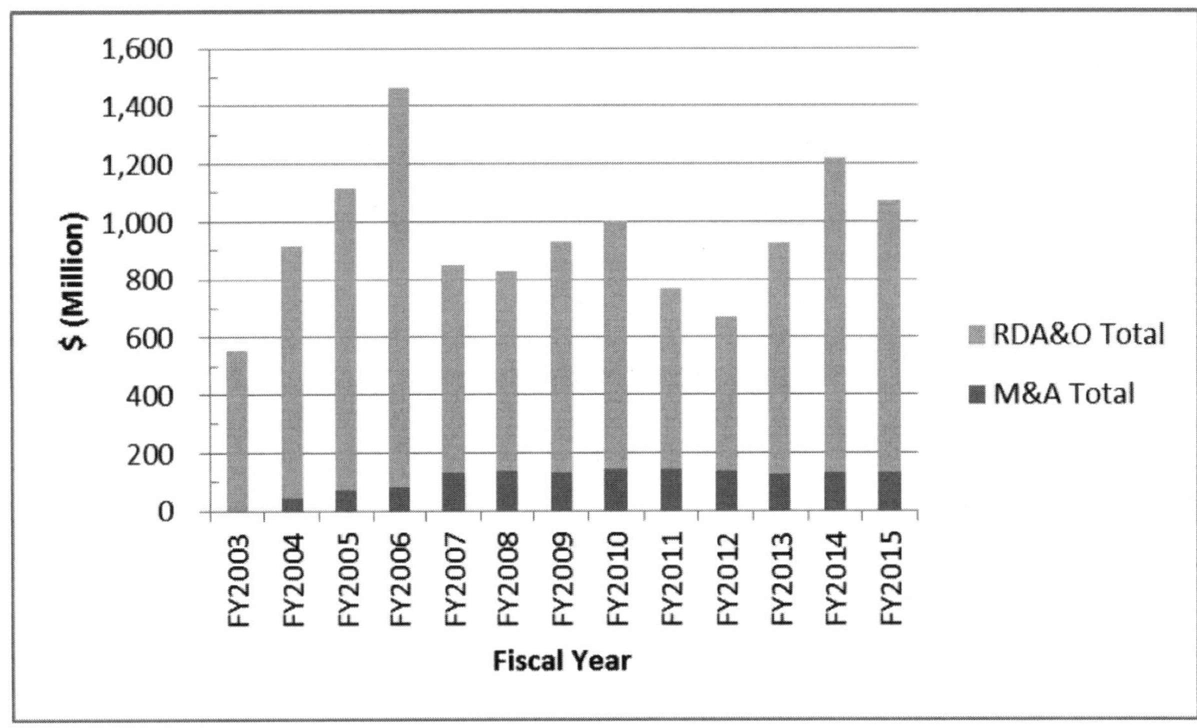

Figure 25-2: DHS S&T Annual Funding [1, p. 5]

A significant change in the S&T Directorate's R&D strategy was the creation in 2011 of what DHS calls Apex projects. Apex projects aim to solve urgent problems identified by the head of a DHS operational component.

A significant change in the S&T Directorate's R&D strategy was the creation in 2011 of what DHS calls Apex projects. Apex projects aim to solve urgent problems identified by the head of a DHS operational component. As a consequence, the S&T Directorate designates Apex projects as high-priority investments. S&T had two Apex projects in FY2013, and has capacity for a total of three or four simultaneous Apex projects. One Apex project with the U.S. Secret Service was successfully completed. The other Apex-like project with Customs and Border Protection (CBP) was terminated by mutual agreement. [1, pp. 12-13]

R&D Projects

S&T projects fall under six primary commodity areas that directly support DHS component missions and fulfill S&T's statutory responsibility to support federal, state, and local first responders:

1. First Responders. These programs expand first responder capabilities and improve their effectiveness, efficiency, and safety.
2. Borders and Maritime Security. These programs enhance security at the nation's borders and upon its waterways without impeding the flow of commerce.
3. Chemical and Biological Defense. These programs develop new and improved means for detecting, protecting against, responding to, and recovering from chemical and biological incidents.
4. Cybersecurity. These programs contribute to a safe, secure, and resilient cyber environment.

5. Explosives. These programs help protect people and infrastructure from the devastating effects of explosives.

6. Resilience. These programs improve the nation's preparedness for natural and man-made catastrophes. [18, p. 6]

DHS S&T currently manages over 100 R&D projects. The following sections summarize some of those highlighted in the 2014 S&T Portfolio Review.

First Responder Projects

- Multi-Band Radio. Handheld radio that can communicate across several frequencies and thus enable seamless communications among agencies operating on different channels.
- Land Mobile Radio Bridging System. Recognizing that budget limitations will delay the integration of a nationwide public safety broadband network in some communities, this project is developing solutions to maintain interoperability between older land mobile radio systems and broadband systems.
- Wireless Emergency Alerts. Sends geographically targeted notices to mobile devices notifying citizens of imminent threats and significant events based on their location.
- Finding Individuals for Disaster and Emergency Response (FINDER). Uses microwave radar to detect a human heartbeat buried beneath 30 feet of crushed materials, or 20 feet of solid concrete, or from a distance of 100 feet in open space.
- Virtual USA. Provides First Responders with latest status of power outages, road closures, traffic incidents, hospitals, shelters, and weather conditions, graphically depicted on an active map display.
- Improved Firefighting Structure Gloves. Firefighter gloves made from new materials affording enhanced dexterity, water repellency, and fire resistance.
- Wildland Firefighter Advanced Personal Protection System. Enhanced gear to improve heat protection, reduce heat stress, and provide better form, fit, and function for wildland firefighters.
- Enhanced Dynamic Geo-Social Environment (EDGE). Multiplayer video game providing realistic firefighter training in lieu of more expensive full-scale exercises.
- Radiological Emergency Management System (REMS). A fixed-site network of gamma radiation sensors designed for response and recovery after a radiological or nuclear incident.
- System Assessment and Validation for Emergency Responders (SAVER). The SAVER program conducts objective assessments of First Responder equipment and validates that technologies meet responder requirements. [18, pp. 16-21]

S&T had two Apex projects in FY2013, and has capacity for a total of three or four simultaneous Apex projects.

Borders and Maritime Security Projects

- Reusable Electronic Conveyance Security Devices (RECONS). Technology to detect unauthorized intrusion into cargo containers and provide real-time tracking of cargo through the supply chain.
- Mobile Surveillance System Upgrade (MSS-U). Improved automated target detection and tracking to reduce false alarms up to 97 percent in winds greater than 15 mph, thereby allowing operation in inclement weather.
- Pollen Forensics. Rapid and cost-effective means for identifying pollen samples to help determine a cargo's country of origin to better enforce trade compliance.
- Coastal Surveillance System (CSS). Advanced detection, identification, and tracking capabilities along the maritime borders for rapid, coordinated response to maritime anomalies and threats. [18, pp. 27-28]

Chemical and Biological Defense Projects

- Biological Terrorism Risk Assessment (BTRA). Develop improved means for assessing biological threats and recommending mitigation strategies.
- Chemical Terrorism Risk Assessment (CTRA). Provide comprehensive analysis of homeland security risks associated with a broad range of chemical threat agents.
- Integrated Terrorism Risk Assessment (ITRA). A management tool to help maintain the quality and availability of essential drugs in the Strategic National Stockpile (SNS).
- Detect-to-Protect (D2P) Program. Develop advanced bio-sensors capable of rapidly identifying harmful biological organisms and determining their rate of spread.
- Foot-and-Mouth Disease (FMD) Vaccine Project. Develop improved FMD vaccine that doesn't carry the risk of current vaccines made from live FMD virus. [18, pp. 29-31]

Cybersecurity Projects

- Defense Technology Experimental Research (DETER). A testbed for evaluating emerging and advanced cybersecurity technologies.
- Rapid Prototyping. The Cyber Forensics Working Group works with law enforcement to rapidly prototype forensic analysis tools useful for cyber crime investigations.
- Transition to Practice (TTP). Assists with rapidly deploying cybersecurity technologies developed in Federal research laboratories. [18, pp. 32-33]

Explosive Countermeasures

- Homemade Explosive Emulators. Simulated explosive devices to assist with safely training canine detection teams.
- Next Generation Passenger Checkpoint (NexGen). Development of phase-based imaging and X-ray diffraction technologies for improved detection of Homemade Explosive Devices (HMEs) and liquid-based explosives in passenger carry-on items. [18, pp. 34-35]

Resilience Projects

- Actionable Indicators and Countermeasures Project. Program to more efficiently and accurately evaluate threats posed by violent extremists by developing an integrated database based on analysis of terrorist disengagement, re-engagement, and recidivism.
- Resilient Tunnel Project (RTP). An inflatable balloon capable of plugging a tunnel and making a seal to prevent flooding.
- Inherently Fault Current Limiting, High Temperature Superconducting (IFCL-HTS) Cable. A new cable that allows electric distribution networks to interconnect and share power while eliminating the risk of cascading faults. [18, pp. 35-36]

HSARPA Apex Programs

- Border Enforcement Analytics Program (BEAP). Mines multiple, disparate data sets to generate investigative leads related to export enforcement and counter proliferation.
- Air Entry and Exit Re-Engineering (AEER). Program to develop next-generation airport screening technology. [18, p. 26]

Conclusion

Both congressional and executive branch policy makers assert that science and technology play significant roles in improving homeland security. Congress established the Directorate of Science and Technology within the Department of Homeland Security to ensure that DHS has access to science and technology advice and research and development capabilities. DHS supports both short- and long-term R&D activities. However, successful R&D activities may not result in a deployable product for many years. The S&T Directorate and other DHS offices have not developed technological advances at the rate some Members of Congress expected. Since the establishment of DHS, the appropriations committees have often expressed displeasure at the rate of technology transfer, the direction of R&D efforts, and the ability of the S&T Directorate to align its resources and mission. In a time of increasing fiscal constraint, some Members have questioned whether S&T Directorate R&D activities should receive priority over other non-R&D activities. [1, p. 1]

Challenge Your Understanding

The following questions are designed to challenge your understanding of the material presented in this chapter. Some questions may require additional research outside this book in order to provide a complete answer.

1. What is the mission of the Science and Technology Directorate?
2. Which S&T component is developing technologies for first responders?
3. Which S&T component is focused on transitioning technology to the field?
4. Which S&T center of excellence is researching critical infrastructure resilience?
5. Which S&T center of excellence is researching plant and animal diseases?
6. Which R&D project is developing gear to reduce heat stress on wildland firefighters?
7. Which R&D project is developing devices to detect unauthorized intrusion of shipping containers?
8. Which R&D project is developing a foot -and-mouth vaccine?
9. Which R&D project is developing a next generation passenger checkpoint?
10. Which R&D project is developing a balloon to prevent tunnels from flooding?

Chapter 26

Domestic Nuclear Detection Office

Learning Outcomes

Careful study of this chapter will help a student do the following:

- Explain the mission of the organization.
- Describe some key components of the organization.
- Discuss some of the work of the organization.

"The Office shall be responsible for coordinating Federal efforts to detect and protect against the unauthorized importation, possession, storage, transportation, development, or use of a nuclear explosive device, fissile material, or radiological material in the United States, and to protect against attack using such devices or materials against the people, territory, or interests of the United States."

- 2006 SAFE Port Act

Introduction

In 2005, the Domestic Nuclear Detection Office (DNDO) was established within the Department of Homeland Security to centralize coordination of the federal response to an unconventional nuclear threat. The office was codified in 2006 through the passage of the SAFE Port Act (P.L. 109-347) and given specific statutory responsibilities to protect the United States against radiological and nuclear attack, including the responsibility to develop a "global nuclear detection architecture." Determining the range of existing federal efforts protecting against nuclear attack, coordinating the outcomes of these efforts, identifying overlaps and gaps between them, and integrating the results into a single architecture are likely to be evolving, ongoing tasks. [1, p. ii]

DNDO is the primary entity in the U.S. government for implementing domestic nuclear detection efforts for a managed and coordinated response to radiological and nuclear threats, as well as integration of federal nuclear forensics programs.

Mission

The Domestic Nuclear Detection Office is a jointly staffed office within the Department of Homeland Security. DNDO is the primary entity in the U.S. government for implementing domestic nuclear detection efforts for a managed and coordinated response to radiological and nuclear threats, as well as integration of federal nuclear forensics programs. Additionally, DNDO is charged with coordinating the development of the global nuclear detection and reporting architecture, with partners from federal, state, local, and international governments and the private sector. [2]

Organization

The Director of the Domestic Nuclear Detection Office is appointed by the President, but reports to the Secretary of Homeland Security. The DNDO is comprised of seven directorates:

1. Architecture and Plans Directorate - Determines gaps and vulnerabilities in the existing global nuclear detection architecture, then formulates recommendations and plans to develop an enhanced architecture.
2. Product Acquisition & Deployment Directorate - Carries out the engineering development, production, developmental logistics, procurement and deployment of current and next-generation nuclear detection systems.

3. Transformational & Applied Research Directorate - Conducts, supports, coordinates, and encourages an aggressive, long-term research and development program to address significant architectural and technical challenges unresolved by research and development efforts on the near horizon.

4. Operations Support Directorate - Develops the information sharing and analytical tools necessary to create a fully integrated operating environment. Residing in the Operations Support Directorate is the Joint Analysis Center, which is an interagency coordination and reporting mechanism and central monitoring point for the Global Nuclear Detection Architecture.

5. Systems Engineering & Evaluation Directorate - Ensures that DNDO proposes sound technical solutions and thoroughly understands systems performance and potential vulnerabilities prior to deploying those technologies.

6. Red Team & Net Assessments - Independently assesses the operational performance of planned and deployed capabilities, including technologies, procedures, and protocols.

7. National Technical Nuclear Forensics Center - Provides national-level stewardship, centralized planning and integration for an enduring national technical nuclear forensics capability. [2]

The Director of the Domestic Nuclear Detection Office is appointed by the President, but reports to the Secretary of Homeland Security.

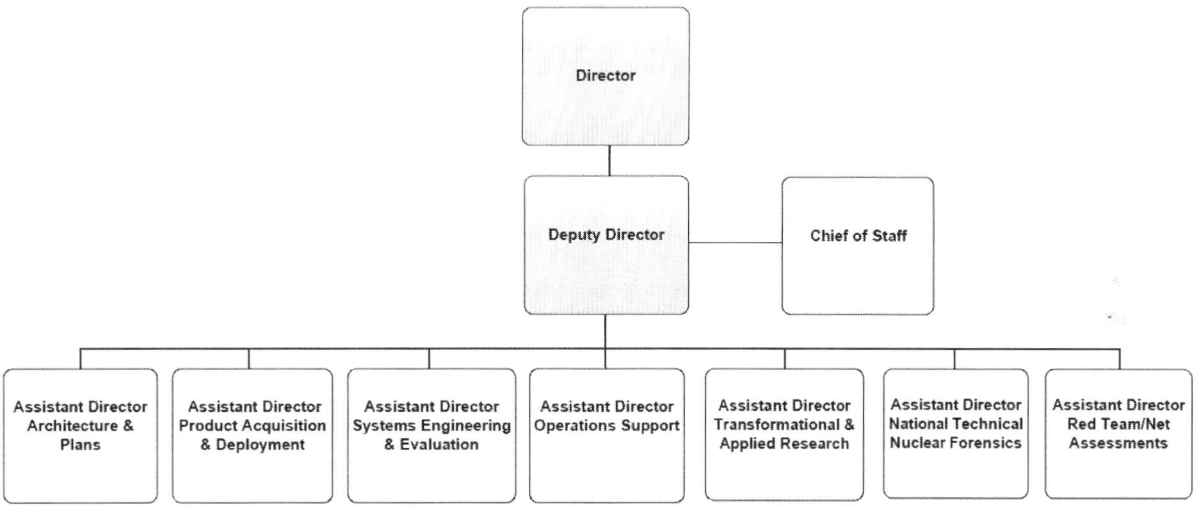

Figure 26-1: DNDO Organization [3]

Detection of Nuclear Weapons and Materials

Detection of nuclear weapons and special nuclear material (SNM), plutonium, and certain types of uranium, is crucial to thwarting nuclear proliferation and terrorism and to securing weapons and materials worldwide. [4, p. ii] A key research objective is to reduce the number of "false positives" and "false negatives" inherent in current detection devices. False positives indicating the presence of nuclear materials when they are not there impede the flow of commerce and undermine confidence in the devices themselves. Conversely, false negatives indicate the absence of nuclear materials when they are present, ultimately failing in their task of thwarting the movement of illicit agents. [4, p. 19] It is because of these shortcomings that research and development (R&D) into improved technologies is an active and ongoing concern.

Nuclear weapons contain special nuclear material (SNM), plutonium, and certain types of uranium, which produce suspect signatures that can be detected. SNM emits radiation, notably gamma rays (high-energy photons) and neutrons. SNM is dense, so it produces a bright image on a radiograph (a picture like a medical x-ray) when x-rays or gamma rays are beamed through a container in which it is hidden.

Nuclear weapons contain SNM, which produces suspect signatures that can be detected. It emits radiation, notably gamma rays (high-energy photons) and neutrons. SNM is dense, so it produces a bright image on a radiograph (a picture like a medical x-ray) when x-rays or gamma rays are beamed through a container in which it is hidden. Using lead or other shielding to attenuate gamma rays would make that image larger. Nuclear weapons produce detectable signatures, such as radiation or a noticeable image on a radiograph. Other detection techniques are also available. [4, p. ii]

Eight technologies illustrate the detection portfolio:

1. A new scintillator material to improve detector performance and lower cost. This project was terminated in January 2010.
2. GADRAS, an application using multiple algorithms to determine the materials in a container by analyzing gamma-ray spectra. If materials are the "eyes and ears" of detectors, algorithms are the "brains."
3. A project to simulate large numbers of experiments to improve detection system performance.
4. Two Cargo Advanced Automated Radiography Systems (CAARS) to detect high-density material based on the principle that it becomes less transparent to photons of higher energy, unlike other material.
5. A third CAARS to detect material with a high atomic number (Z, number of protons in an atom's nucleus) based on the principle that Z affects how material scatters photons. This project was terminated in March 2009.
6. A system to generate a 3-D image of the contents of a container based on the principle that Z and density strongly affect the degree to which muons (a subatomic particle) scatter.

7. Nuclear resonance fluorescence imaging to identify materials based on the spectrum of gamma rays a nucleus emits when struck by photons of a specific energy.
8. The Photonuclear Inspection and Threat Assessment System to detect SNM up to 1 km away, unlike other systems that operate at very close range. It would beam high energy photons at distant targets to stimulate fission in SNM, producing characteristic signatures that may be detected.

These technologies are selected not because they are necessarily the "best" in their categories, but rather to show a variety of approaches, in differing stages of maturity, performed by different types of organizations, relying on different physical principles, and covering building blocks (materials, algorithms, models) as well as systems, so as to convey many points on the spectrum of detection technology development. [4, p. ii]

The 2006 SAFE Port Act that created DNDO requires it to establish an "enhanced global nuclear detection architecture." The global nuclear detection architecture is a multi-layered system of detection technologies, programs, and guidelines designed to enhance the nation's ability to detect and prevent a radiological or nuclear attack.

From these examples it becomes apparent that it is difficult to predict the schedule or capabilities of new detection technologies. It is easier and less costly to accelerate a program in R&D than in production. [4, p. ii] Making the tough choices which technologies to back and how best to implement them is a problem for the global nuclear detection architecture.

Global Nuclear Detection Architecture

The U.S. government has implemented a series of programs to protect the nation against terrorist nuclear attack. Some of these programs predate 9/11, while others were established since then. Most programs are within the Nuclear Regulatory Commission; the Departments of Defense, Energy, and State; and agencies that became part of DHS upon its creation, and they are focused on detecting the illicit acquisition and shipment of nuclear and radiological materials and protecting and securing nuclear weapons. [1, p. ii]

The 2006 SAFE Port Act that created DNDO requires it to establish an "enhanced global nuclear detection architecture." [1, p. 3] The global nuclear detection architecture is a multi-layered system of detection technologies, programs, and guidelines designed to enhance the nation's ability to detect and prevent a radiological or nuclear attack. Among its components are existing programs in nuclear detection operated by other federal agencies and new programs put into place by DNDO. The global nuclear detection architecture as developed by DNDO in coordination with other federal agencies implementing nuclear detection efforts and this coordination is essential to the success of the architecture. [1, p. ii]

The current global nuclear detection architecture includes programs at DHS, the Department of Defense (DoD), the Department of Energy (DOE), the Department of State (DOS), and other agencies. According to DHS, before the formation of DNDO these programs were "a disparate patchwork of systems, distributed and implemented in recent years across multiple departments, jurisdictions and locations without any degree of coordination." The DNDO has organized these programs into a global nuclear detection architecture framework, a combined system of systems, which relies heavily on its technological component. The deployment of radiation detectors at points of entry, commercial ports, and other border crossings is key to its effectiveness. [1, p. 4]

The global nuclear detection architecture encompasses more than just sensors. Other elements include site security of known nuclear or radiological material, use of sensor data to inform decision makers, effective reaction to a detection event, and interdiction following detection.

Although much focus has been given to technologies to detect nuclear or radiological material that have been developed or procured by DNDO, the global nuclear detection architecture encompasses more than just these sensors. Other elements include site security of known nuclear or radiological material, use of sensor data to inform decision makers, effective reaction to a detection event, and interdiction following detection. According to the Government Accountability Office, "combating nuclear smuggling requires an integrated approach that includes equipment, proper training of border security personnel in the use of radiation detection equipment, and intelligence gathering on potential nuclear smuggling operations." Other experts have concluded that the deployment of radiation detectors needs to be highly integrated with other federal efforts, prioritized on identified threats, configured for flexibility and efficiency, and organized as a global approach including international institutions. [1, p. 4]

A layered, defense-in-depth approach to a global nuclear detection architecture was recommended by the Defense Science Board when considering how to protect DOD assets against unconventional nuclear threats. Successful application of a layered defense provides multiple opportunities to detect and interdict threats. According to DNDO, "It is recognized that no single layer of protection can ever be one hundred percent successful," and a layered defense strategy acknowledges this difficulty. If one sublayer fails to detect a threat, the next may succeed. [1, p. 6]

This increase in the likelihood of detection occurs in two different ways. In one case, a threat may avoid the detector in an outer layer, but then encounter a detector in an inner layer. In this case, having more detection opportunities makes it more likely that a detector is encountered. An example of this approach could be the use of detection technology at U.S. borders coupled with random truck screening at weigh stations on interstate highways. [1, p. 6]

Layer	Sublayer	Example
Exterior	Foreign Origin	Foreign sites with nuclear material that could be misused.
Exterior	Foreign Transit	Illicit trafficking of nuclear material within the exterior layer
Exterior, Border	Foreign Departure	Foreign seaport with cargo containers destined for the U.S.
Exterior, Border	Transit to U.S.	Ships transporting cargo from overseas to U.S.
Border	U.S. Border	Official U.S. ports of entry and between official land and sea ports of entry
Interior	U.S. Origin	Hospital with nuclear medicine equipment or industrial site
Interior	U.S. Regional	Areas surrounding origins of nuclear material in the U.S.
Interior	Target Vicinity	Areas surrounding potential targets of nuclear attack
Interior	Target	Potential locations of nuclear attack within the U.S.

Figure 26-2: Layers of the Nuclear Detection Architecture [1, p. 5]

Accordingly, the DNDO has attempted to align existing federal programs so that their capabilities can be compared and integrated into an organizing framework that can help identify gaps and duplication. This framework consists of three partially overlapping layers with nine sub-layers as shown in Figure 2. [1, p. 4]

The layers are distinguished geographically: interior, border, and exterior. The overlap between the exterior and border layers may make analysis of priorities between and within the layers more difficult. The sublayers correspond mainly to conceptual steps in the transportation of a threat object to a target. [1, p. 5]

The global nuclear detection architecture has a broad, international scope, so implementing it is difficult. Multiple agency initiatives and programs must be relied on to achieve the architecture's goals, and its effectiveness is dependent on many factors outside of DNDO's direct authority and control. [1, p. 5]

A significant advantage to establishing a global nuclear detection architecture is that it provides a framework for analysis of the overall effectiveness of federal nuclear detection efforts. Thus the performance of programs in each layer of the architecture can be measured and judged within the context of the overall structure rather than in isolation. In this way, effectiveness and efficiency can be maximized for the architecture overall rather than for each program individually. [1, p. 7]

Gaps and vulnerabilities in the global nuclear detection architecture, depending on their nature, may be addressed now or in the future. In some cases, no solutions to these gaps and vulnerabilities are currently available, and a solution will need to be identified through research and development.

By categorizing existing programs in this architecture, DNDO can analyze federal nuclear detection capabilities, identifying gaps and vulnerabilities through which a potential adversary might be able to avoid detection. These gaps may be filled by redirecting existing efforts, increasing existing efforts, deploying available technology, and implementing research and development programs that develop solutions to such gaps. [1, p. 5]

Priority Setting

Gaps and vulnerabilities in the global nuclear detection architecture, depending on their nature, may be addressed now or in the future. In some cases, no solutions to these gaps and vulnerabilities are currently available, and a solution will need to be identified through research and development. The DNDO has stated that "there are still key, long-term challenges and vulnerabilities in our detection architecture that require long-range, higher risk research programs that will need to be evaluated in terms of risk reduction, direct and indirect costs, operational feasibility, and other relevant decision factors." In other cases, the available near-term solution is an incremental improvement over existing approaches. In these cases, policymakers must decide whether to invest in a near-term, potentially incomplete solution; accept the presence of a gap or vulnerability and invest in a long-term program to develop a more complete solution; or do both. Choosing between these options requires an understanding of the risk posed by the existing vulnerabilities, the benefits available through the near- and long-term options, and their relative costs. [1, p. 10]

Decision makers are faced with difficult choices when setting priorities for implementing the global nuclear detection architecture. In the case of existing programs, incremental increases in the performance of a system may be challenged on the basis of their perceived costs and benefits. In the case of new programs, questions may arise about whether the effort expended on a new program would have provided more benefits if applied elsewhere. Finally, given that improvement of the global nuclear detection architecture is a multi-year project, one must determine which portion of the architecture to focus on at any given time. [1, p. 10]

A likely benefit of casting federal efforts at nuclear detection into the framework of a global architecture is the ability to prioritize, in a quantitative or qualitative fashion, across programs. Even without a rigorous method to discriminate finely between the results of different investments, the global nuclear detection architecture may be able to provide a rank ordering of vulnerabilities and gaps, and thus a rank ordering of investment priorities. Thus, it may provide an interagency tool to analyze current technology options and R&D investments relative to the federal government's detection needs. [1, p. 10]

As well as developing the global nuclear detection architecture, DNDO is also responsible for coordinating the activities of other federal agencies whose programs make up the global nuclear detection architecture.

Interagency Coordination

As well as developing the global nuclear detection architecture, DNDO is also responsible for coordinating the activities of other federal agencies whose programs make up the global nuclear detection architecture. For the architecture to be successful, substantial interagency coordination must occur on the operational and policy levels. [1, p. 11]

Congress recognized the need for DNDO to have access to specific talent resident in other agencies. The SAFE Port Act authorizes the DHS Secretary to "request that the Secretary of Defense, the Secretary of Energy, the Secretary of State, the Attorney General, the Nuclear Regulatory Commission, and the directors of other Federal agencies, including elements of the Intelligence Community, provide for the reimbursable detail of personnel with relevant expertise to [DNDO]." Under this authority and that of the Intergovernmental Personnel Act (IPA), DNDO has established a significant interagency workforce, including personnel from DOD, DOE, the Federal Bureau of Investigation, the Department of State, and the Nuclear Regulatory Commission, as well as intra-agency personnel from the Science and Technology Directorate, U.S. Customs and Border Protection, the Transportation Security Administration, and the U.S. Coast Guard. [1, pp. 11-12]

The DNDO uses the detailees and IPAs as part of its coordinating function. By using these experts as conduits back to their agencies, DNDO is able to draw on the expertise and address the needs and concerns of these agencies. The DNDO also has established a more senior policy coordinating body, the Interagency Coordination Council, to address higher level policy issues and further coordinate activities between agencies, but the extent to which this body is able to implement and develop new policy for the participating agencies is not known. The Interagency Coordination Council was reportedly used to develop the deployment strategy for the global nuclear detection architecture and studies of maritime and aviation threats. [1, p. 12]

Beyond the interagency activities organized within DNDO, coordination of DNDO activities with other portions of the federal government occurs within the White House through the Domestic Nuclear Defense Policy Coordinating Committee.

The DNDO also has implemented an Advisory Council consisting of officials from other DHS components. The DNDO uses the Advisory Council to solicit the opinions of and resolve intra-agency issues within DHS. [1, p. 12]

Beyond the interagency activities organized within DNDO, coordination of DNDO activities with other portions of the federal government occurs within the White House through the Domestic Nuclear Defense Policy Coordinating Committee. This joint policy coordination body was created jointly by the Homeland Security Council and the National Security Council and provides a high-level forum for the generation of guidance and coordination among federal agencies with responsibilities for nuclear defense, detection, and interdiction. Other interagency planning activities, such as coordination of long-term research and development, occur through subcommittees of the National Science and Technology Council. [1, pp. 12-13]

Conclusion

The DNDO aims to improve "the probability of detection by integrating and deploying current technologies, continually improving these technologies through both near-term enhancements and transformational research and development, and expanding detection capabilities at the Federal, State and local levels." In expanding and improving the global nuclear detection architecture, DNDO and other participating agencies are faced with a temporal choice. Vulnerabilities and gaps identified through the global nuclear detection architecture could be reduced by applying immediately available technologies that provide a partial solution or by investing in research and development to develop technologies that will provide a more complete solution in the long-term. [1, p. 16] Determining the optimal process for creating a robust global nuclear detection architecture, understanding the capabilities of near- and long-term technology and their potential effect on the global nuclear detection architecture, and assessing the adequacy of the metrics used to measure the risk reduction benefits present significant challenges. The success of DNDO's activities will require ongoing evaluation and oversight into the future. [1, p. 17]

Challenge Your Understanding

The following questions are designed to challenge your understanding of the material presented in this chapter. Some questions may require additional research outside this book in order to provide a complete answer.

1. What is the mission of the Domestic Nuclear Detection Office?
2. Which DNDO component looks for gaps and vulnerabilities in the global nuclear detection architecture?
3. Which DNDO component conducts and supports long -term research and development?
4. Which DNDO component analyzes proposed solutions to make certain they are technically sound?
5. What is "special nuclear material" and how can it be detected?
6. Why are sensors by themselves insufficient for monitoring and detecting special nuclear material?
7. What is the Global Nuclear Detection Architecture and why was it created?
8. Why is the Global Nuclear Detection Architecture organized into a layered defense?
9. Why is the Global Nuclear Detection Architecture incomplete?
10. Who owns and operates the Global Nuclear Detection Architecture?

Chapter 27

Intelligence & Analysis

Learning Outcomes

Careful study of this chapter will help a student do the following:

- Explain the mission of the organization.
- Describe some key components of the organization.
- Discuss some of the work of the organization.

"Earlier in this report we detailed various missed opportunities to thwart the 9/11 plot. Information was not shared, sometimes inadvertently or because of legal misunderstandings. Analysis was not pooled. Effective operations were not launched. Often the handoffs of information were lost across the divide separating the foreign and domestic agencies of the government."

- 2004 9/11 Commission Report

Introduction

Congress made information sharing a top priority of the Department's intelligence component in the Homeland Security Act of 2002 and underscored its importance through the Intelligence Reform and Terrorism Prevention Act of 2004. Since the 2SR reorganization, Congress imposed additional requirements for intelligence analysis; information sharing; department-wide intelligence integration; and support to state, local, tribal governments, and the private sector through the Implementing Recommendations of the 9/11 Commission Act of 2007. [1, p. ii]

The mission of the Office of Intelligence and Analysis is to equip the Homeland Security Enterprise with the intelligence and information it needs to keep the homeland safe, secure, and resilient.

Background

At the outset, the mission of the Department of Homeland Security (DHS) was to "prevent terrorist attacks within the United States, reduce the vulnerability of the United States to terrorism, and minimize the damage, and assist in the recovery from terrorist attacks that do occur in the United States. Since its inception in 2003, DHS has had an intelligence component to support this mission and has been a member of the U.S. Intelligence Community (IC). [1, p. ii]

Following the Second Stage Review (2SR) reorganization in July 2005, former Secretary of Homeland Security, Michael Chertoff established a strengthened Office of Intelligence and Analysis (I&A) and made the Assistant Secretary for Information Analysis (now Under Secretary for Intelligence and Analysis) the Chief Intelligence Officer for the Department. He also tasked I&A with ensuring that intelligence is coordinated, fused, and analyzed within the Department to provide a common operational picture; provide a primary connection between DHS and the IC as a whole; and to act as a primary source of information for state, local and private sector partners. [1, p. ii]

After the 2SR reorganization, Congress imposed additional requirements for intelligence analysis; information sharing; department-wide intelligence integration; and support to state, local, tribal governments, and the private sector through the Implementing Recommendations of the 9/11 Commission Act of 2007. [2]

As part of the department-wide intelligence integration initiative, I&A today serves as the central coordinator for the DHS Intelligence Enterprise (DHS IE). The DHS IE consists of those elements within DHS that have an intelligence mission. These include I&A, the Office of Cyber & Infrastructure Analysis (OCIA), and the Intelligence Division of the Office of Operations Coordination and Planning (all located at the DHS headquarters), and the intelligence elements of six DHS operational components: U.S. Customs and Border Protection (CBP), U.S. Immigration and Customs Enforcement (ICE). U.S. Citizenship and Immigration Services (USCIS), the Transportation Security Administration (TSA), U.S. Coast Guard (USCG), and U.S. Secret Service (USSS). [1, p. ii]

Mission

The mission of the Office of Intelligence and Analysis is to equip the Homeland Security Enterprise with the intelligence and information it needs to keep the homeland safe, secure, and resilient. [3]

Under Secretary for Intelligence and Analysis directly manages four major offices:

1. *State & Local Program Office*
2. *Enterprise & Mission Support*
3. *Analysis Office*
4. *Plans, Policy, & Performance Management*

Organization

I&A is led by an Under Secretary, a position subject to Senate confirmation. The Under Secretary also serves as the department's Chief Intelligence Officer (CINT). [1, p. 8] The Under Secretary for Intelligence and Analysis directly manages four major offices:

1. State & Local Program Office (SLPO). The SLPO serves in the central coordination role for DHS interaction with State and Local Fusion Centers (SLFCs). [4, p. 3]
2. Enterprise & Mission Support (EMS). EMS is responsible for homeland security intelligence integration activities; policies governing enterprise-wide production and standardization of reports; the I&A Strategic Plan; training, and the implementation of a comprehensive information systems architecture. [2, p. 13]
3. Analysis. The Analysis Office is responsible for the analytic mission of I&A. The office has been focused on five "analytic thrusts" aligned with the principal threats to the Homeland: 1) border security, including narcotics trafficking, alien and human smuggling, and money laundering; 2) radicalization and extremism; particular groups entering the United States that could be exploited by terrorists or criminals; 3) critical infrastructure and key resources; and 4) weapons of mass destruction (WMD) and 5) health threats. [2, pp. 8-9]
4. Plans, Policy, & Performance Management (PPPM). PPPM is responsible for developing an effective department-wide operations planning and coordination capability to support DHS integration. In short, the key function of PPPM is the application of intelligence research and analysis to conditions on the ground that must be considered for effective planning and operations and the development of a Common Intelligence Picture (CIP)[1][2, pp. 18-19]

[1]DHS is mute on the current internal organization of I&A. The specific responsibilities of EMS, Analysis, and PPPM are inferred from functions ascribed to previous I&A components as cited.

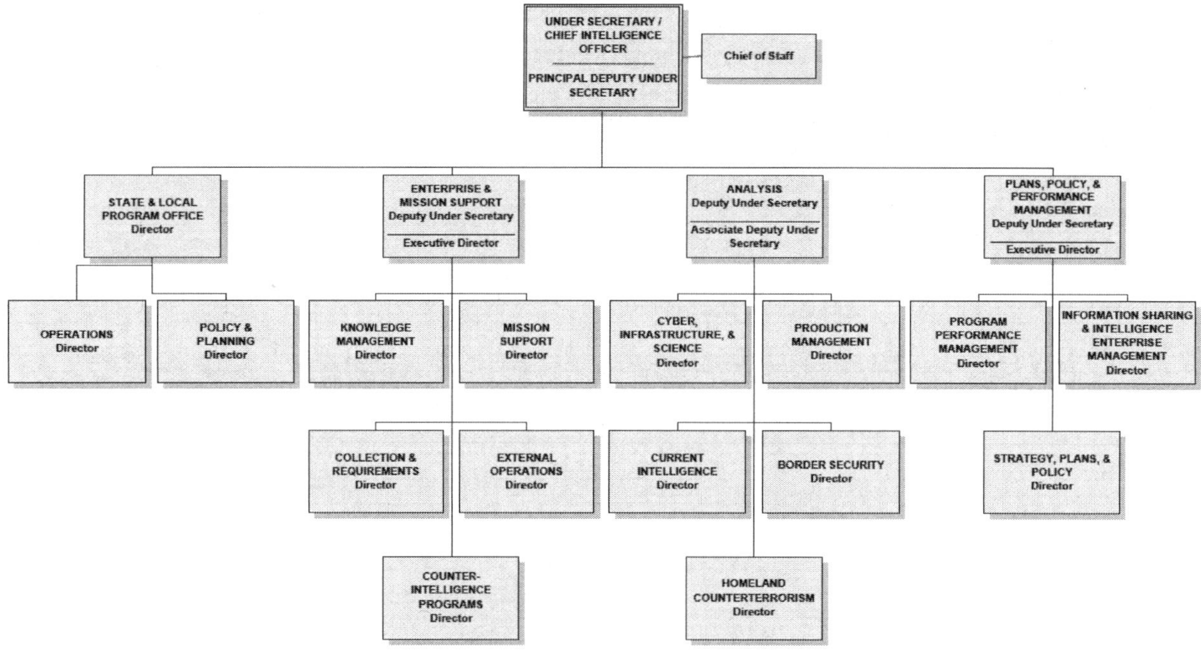

Figure 27-1: DHS Office of Intelligence & Analysis Organization Chart [5]

Homeland Security Intelligence

Prior to 9/11, it was possible to make a distinction between "domestic intelligence"—primarily law enforcement information collected within the United States—and "foreign intelligence"— primarily military, political, and economic intelligence collected outside the country. Today, threats to the homeland posed by terrorist groups are now national security threats. Intelligence collected outside the United States is often very relevant to the threat environment inside the United States and vice versa. [6, p. ii]

Prior to 9/11, it was possible to make a distinction between "domestic intelligence"—primarily law enforcement information collected within the United States—and "foreign intelligence"—primarily military, political, and economic intelligence collected outside the country.

Although the activities involved in homeland security intelligence (HSINT) itself are not new, the relative importance of state, local, and private sector stakeholders; the awareness of how law enforcement information might protect national security; and the importance attached to homeland security intelligence have all increased substantially since the events of 9/11. [6, p. ii]

There are numerous intelligence collection disciplines through which the U.S. Intelligence Community collects intelligence to support informed national security decision-making at the national level and the allocation of tactical military and law enforcement resources at the local level. The collection disciplines are generally referred to as those which fall within national technical means or non-technical means. Technical means include signals intelligence (SIGINT), measurement and signatures intelligence (MASINT), and imagery intelligence (IMINT). Nontechnical means include human intelligence (HUMINT) and open source intelligence (OSINT). Each of these collection disciplines is source-specific—that is, a technical platform or human source, generally managed by an agency or mission manager, collects intelligence that is used for national intelligence purposes. [6, p. ii]

HSINT, however, is generally not source specific, as it includes both national technical and nontechnical means of collection. For example, HSINT includes human intelligence collected by federal border security personnel or state and local law enforcement officials, as well as SIGINT collected by the National Security Agency (NSA). Reasonable individuals can differ, therefore, with respect to the question of whether HSINT is another collection discipline, or whether homeland security is simply another purpose for which the current set of collection disciplines is being harnessed. Homeland security information, as defined by the 2002 Homeland Security Act, pertains directly to (1) terrorist intentions and capabilities to attack people and infrastructure within the United States, and (2) U.S. abilities to deter, prevent, and respond to potential terrorist attacks. [6, p. ii]

I&A Intelligence Processing

To accomplish its mission, I&A participates in all aspects of the intelligence cycle" – the process by which information is acquired, converted into finished intelligence, and made available to policymakers. Generally the cycle comprises five steps: planning and direction, collection, processing, analysis, and production and dissemination." It is an iterative process in which collection requirements based on national security threats are developed, and intelligence is collected, analyzed, and disseminated to a broad range of consumers. [1, p. 5]

Although the activities involved in homeland security intelligence (HSINT) itself are not new, the relative importance of state, local, and private sector stakeholders are new.

Intelligence planning and direction is guided by a Program of Analysis (POA) that is framed as Key Intelligence Questions (KIQs). I&A KIQs are organized by time frame:

- Immediate and Ongoing Threat KIQs focus on short term or operational issues such as imminent terrorist threats to the homeland. Production that addresses these threats provides the Administration and DHS leadership with the intelligence analysis to better inform near-term operational decision to increase the nation's security.
- Strategic Context KIQs focus on providing context, trend, or pattern analysis. Production that addresses these KIQs helps customers understand recent threats in a broader, global, or historical perspective and they shape strategies to combat the threats or address gaps in homeland security. These would include, for example, how the evolving cartel-related violence in Mexico compares to past cartel wars or how threats to our national infrastructure are changing.
- Opportunity KIQs focus on emerging issues or topics for which reporting streams are new or fragmentary; for example, these KIQs may describe the kinds of polices or activities that have been effective in combating newly emerging threats. [7]

Key Intelligence Questions subsequently inform Homeland Security Standing Information Needs (HSEC SINs). These form the foundation for information collection activities within the Department and provide other Intelligence Community and Homeland Security Enterprise members the ability to focus their collection, analytic, and reporting assets in support of the homeland security mission. The HSEC SINs are updated and published annually to ensure the information needs of the Homeland Security Enterprise are continuously collected, identified, and documented. [7]

DHS does not generally engage in traditional intelligence collection activities. For the most part, I&A is the recipient of intelligence data received from components of the DHS Intelligence Enterprise and the broader Intelligence Community.

DHS does not generally engage in traditional intelligence collection activities. For the most part, I&A is the recipient of intelligence data received from components of the DHS Intelligence Enterprise and the broader Intelligence Community.

DHS Intelligence Enterprise

I&A is the recipient of intelligence data collected by DHS components with an intelligence mission integral to performing their primary function.

The Office of Cyber and Infrastructure Analysis (OCIA) within the DHS National Protection and Programs Directorate (NPPD), formerly the Homeland Infrastructure Threat and Risk Analysis Center (HITRAC), is responsible for protecting the nation's critical infrastructure from both physical and cyber threats. OCIA conducts integrated analysis of critical infrastructure to identify threats that could have catastrophic impacts to public health and safety, the economy, and national security. Accordingly, OCIA 1) Provides analytic support to DHS leadership, operational components, and field personnel during steady-state and crises on emerging threats and incidents impacting the nation's critical infrastructure; 2) Assesses and informs national infrastructure risk management strategies on the likelihood and consequence of emerging and future risks; and 3) Develops and enhances capabilities to support crisis action by identifying and prioritizing infrastructure through the use of analytic tools and modeling capabilities. [8]

The Office of Operations Coordination manages the DHS National Operations Center (NOC), a 24-hour center responsible for monitoring and responding to homeland security threats against the nation. The NOC provides real-time situational awareness and monitoring of the homeland, coordinates incidents and response activities, and, in conjunction with the Office of Intelligence and Analysis, issues advisories and bulletins concerning threats to homeland security, as well as specific protective measures. The NOC coordinates information sharing to help deter, detect, and prevent terrorist acts and to manage domestic incidents. Information on domestic incident management is shared with Emergency Operations Centers at all levels through the Homeland Security Information Network (HSIN). [9]

U.S. Customs and Border Protection. CBP is the agency responsible for securing the nation's borders at and between ports of entry (POE). CBP accomplishes its various missions by inspecting persons and goods to determine if they are authorized to enter the United States. CBP officers and Border Patrol agents intercept illegal narcotics, firearms, counterfeit merchandise, and other types of contraband. They also interdict unauthorized aliens and enforce more than 400 laws and regulations at the border. CBP intelligence operations are designed to support the full range of CBP missions, particularly its primary mission of preventing the entry of terrorists and the instruments of terrorism. CBP gathers and analyzes large amounts of data concerning persons and cargo inbound to the U.S. as well as information derived from the apprehensions of illegal aliens, drug seizures, and other border enforcement activities. All of this data is a unique source of operational intelligence that is potentially very useful to I&A and other Federal agencies with national security missions. CBP coordinates its intelligence activities through its Office of Intelligence and Operations Coordination (OIOC). [1, pp. 20-22]

Immigration and Customs Enforcement (ICE). ICE is the largest investigative organization within DHS. ICE's mission is to enforce trade and immigration laws through the investigation of activities, persons and events that may pose a threat to the safety or security of the United States and its people. ICE also investigates illegal trafficking in weapons (including weapons of mass destruction), the smuggling of narcotics and other contraband, human smuggling and trafficking, money laundering and other financial crimes, fraudulent trade practices, identity and benefit fraud, child pornography, child sex tourism, and health and public safety dangers. ICE's intelligence activities are coordinated and managed within its Office of Intelligence. The office is responsible for collecting, analyzing, and disseminating strategic and tactical intelligence for use by the operational elements of ICE and DHS. [1, pp. 28-29]

U.S. Citizenship and Immigration Services (USCIS). USCIS oversees lawful immigration to the United States. USCIS is not a law enforcement agency nor a member of the IC and the vast majority of its funding is derived from fees collected from immigration benefit applicants and petitioners. Thus its activities are limited to adjudication of immigration benefits, which includes conducting background checks on the individuals and organizations who submit applications and petitions, as well as the intended beneficiaries. As part of that process, USCIS collects biometrics, in the form of digital photographs and fingerprints. On average each day, USCIS processes 30,000 applications for immigration benefits, issues 7,300 Permanent Resident Cards (Green Cards), adjudicates 400 refugee applications, and naturalizes 3,400 new civilian citizens and 30 new citizens who are member of the U.S. Armed Forces. USCIS also has the authority to detect and combat immigration fraud. In 2004, USCIS established the Office of Fraud Detection and National Security (FDNS). Within FDNS, there is an Intelligence Branch that manages the analysis, reporting, production, and dissemination of immigration-based intelligence products. Those products are designed to focus on the identification of fraud trends or vulnerabilities that are being exploited in the immigration benefits processes while also enhancing national security efforts. Intelligence Research Specialists within the branch conduct research and analysis to identify previously unknown links, associations, emerging trends, correlations, anomalies, and indications and warnings with national security or public security threat implications. [1, pp. 34-36]

I&A combines the unique information collected by DHS components as part of their operational activities with foreign intelligence from the IC; law enforcement information from Federal, state, local, and tribal sources; private sector data about critical infrastructure and key resources; and information from domestic open sources to develop homeland security intelligence.

Transportation Security Administration (TSA). The TSA is most commonly known for its aviation security role, particularly the security screening of airline passengers and their baggage. However, TSA is also responsible for security in all modes of transportation – aviation, maritime, mass transit, highway and motor carrier, freight rail, and pipeline. The size of the transportation sector in the United States makes it impossible for the Federal government to provide security for all modes. The exception is the commercial aviation sector. But, TSA does provide threat and other intelligence information to support security programs for each sector. In addition, TSA collaborates with industry and government operators and other stakeholders to develop strategies, policies, and programs to reduce security risks and vulnerabilities within each mode. Finally, it seeks to enhance capabilities to detect, deter, and prevent terrorist attacks and respond to and recover from attacks and security incidents, should they occur. The Assistant Secretary for TSA is responsible "to receive, assess, and distribute intelligence information related to transportation security and to assess threats specifically related to transportation. The TSA intelligence function is centered in its Office of Intelligence (TSA-OI) and led by an Assistant Administrator for Intelligence. [1, pp. 36-37]

The U.S. Coast Guard (USCG). The USCG is a military, multi-mission, maritime service that is the "principal Federal agency responsible for safety, security, and stewardship within the maritime domain. These missions are performed in any maritime region where those interests may be at risk, including international waters and America's coasts, ports, and inland waterways. Given a range of complex and ambiguous threats, the Coast Guard places a premium on knowledge and shared understanding of the maritime domain. This knowledge and shared understanding is termed "maritime domain awareness" and is defined as "the effective understanding of anything associated with the global maritime domain that could impact the security, safety, economy, or environment of the United States." The achievement of maritime domain awareness is, therefore, the principal objective of the USCG intelligence program. It is a collaborative effort—especially between the USCG and U.S. Navy—and also with DHS components, such as CBP and ICE, other Federal agencies, and the broader maritime community. Coast Guard intelligence collection begins at the port level and encompasses the entire maritime domain and features maritime surveillance activities by patrol aircraft, unmanned aerial vehicles, shore-based radar, and shipboard sensors including radar and passive electronic surveillance systems. The Coast Guard Intelligence Coordination Center (ICC) is the national-level coordinator for collection, analysis, production, and dissemination of Coast Guard intelligence. It is the focal point of interaction with the intelligence components of other government entities such as the Department of Defense and Federal law enforcement agencies at the national level. The ICC is co-located with the U.S. Navy's Office of Naval Intelligence at the National Maritime Intelligence Center in Suitland, Maryland. [1, pp. 43-46]

U.S. Secret Service (USSS). The USSS is best known for its responsibility to protect the President and Vice President of the United States and visiting foreign heads of state and government. Additionally, the USSS is responsible for maintaining the integrity of the nation's financial infrastructure and payment systems. The USSSS Protective intelligence and Assessment Division (PID) is responsible for evaluating, disseminating, and maintaining information concerning subjects (individuals and groups) and activities that pose a known, potential, or perceived threat to persons, property, and events protected by the USSS; investigating those subjects and activities; and conducting protective intelligence 'advances' preceding protectee travel. The PID includes the National Threat Assessment Center (NTAC) which uses historical information, investigative records, interviews, and other primary source material to produce long-term behavioral research studies that leverage USSS expertise in the protection of persons for homeland security or public safety purposes. [1, pp. 48-50]

I&A produces numerous products for its customers.

I&A Intelligence Products

I&A combines the unique information collected by DHS components as part of their operational activities (e.g., at airports, seaports, and the border) with foreign intelligence from the IC; law enforcement information from Federal, state, local, and tribal sources; private sector data about critical infrastructure and key resources; and information from domestic open sources to develop homeland security intelligence. This encompasses a broad range of homeland security threats. It includes border security information to counter human smuggling and trafficking, cargo data to prevent the introduction of dangerous items, information to protect critical infrastructure against all hazards, information about infectious diseases, and demographic data and other research about 'violent radicalization. [1, p. 5]

I&A produces numerous products for its customers. In 2008, there was a realignment and standardization of the I&A finished intelligence product line which now include:

- Homeland Security Threat Assessment (HSTA). This is an annual threat assessment that represents the analytical judgments of DHS and assesses the major threats to the homeland for which the nation must prepare and respond. This includes the actions, capabilities, and intentions of domestic and foreign terrorists and extremists and the possible occurrence of systemic threats. It focuses on domestic extremists, international terrorists operating in the homeland or directing attacks against it, and systemic threats such as pandemics and transnational criminal organizations. The HSTA is produced in classified and "Unclassified/For Official Use Only" versions.

- Intelligence Warning. Contains urgent intelligence.
- Intelligence Note. Contains timely information or analysis on a current topic.
- Homeland Security Assessment. Consists of in-depth analysis on a topic.
- Homeland Security Monitors. These are produced monthly in collaboration with the components and may be classified or unclassified. Examples include:
    - Border Security Monitor
    - Cyber Security Monitor
    - Cuba-Gram
- Reference Aids. These are less analytical and more descriptive. For example, they might describe what an anthrax lab looks like or the latest on improvised explosive devices (IED) and fuses. They contain photos and diagrams and inform law enforcement and first responders what to look for and what actions to take if they are encountered.
- Joint Homeland Security Assessment/FBI Intelligence Bulletin. These are joint reports done in conjunction with the FBI. [1, pp. 9-10]

I&A makes the products of its analysis available to state and local officials through classified and unclassified intelligence networks.

I&A also produces Homeland Intelligence Reports (HIR) which contain information that has yet to be fully evaluated. These are similar to the Intelligence Information Report (IIR) produced by other IC agencies. An HIR could contain information related to border encounters, information shared by a state or local fusion center, or other information of homeland security interest. There are also Homeland Security Intelligence Reports (HSIR) that are produced by the DHS component agencies. HSIR's, however, do contain some analysis. [1, p. 10]

I&A makes the products of its analysis available to state and local officials through classified and unclassified intelligence networks: The Homeland Security Information Network is a secured, web-based platform that facilitates Sensitive But Unclassified information sharing and collaboration between federal, state, local, tribal, private sector, and international partners. It is managed by the DHS Directorate of Operations Coordination and Planning. The HSIN platform was created to interface with existing information sharing networks to support the diverse communities of interest engaged in preventing, protecting from, responding to, and recovering from all threats, hazards and incidents under the jurisdiction of DHS. It provides real-time, interactive connectivity between states and major urban areas and the National Operations Center. [1, p. 10]

The Homeland Secure Data Network (HSDN) provides access to collateral Secret-level terrorism related information. This includes NCTC Online, a classified repository that serves as the counterterrorism community's library of terrorism information. I&A has deployed HSDN terminals to 33 state and local fusion centers and intends to install terminals in all of the fusion centers as soon as security requirements are met. [1, p. 11]

State and Local Fusion Center Program

In an effort to strengthen intelligence and information sharing and analysis capabilities following the 9/11 attacks, states and major urban areas established intelligence fusion centers. Congress has defined fusion centers as a "collaborative effort of two or more Federal, state, local, or tribal government agencies that combines resources, expertise, or information with the goal of maximizing the ability of such agencies to detect, prevent, investigate, apprehend, and respond to criminal or terrorist activity." At the end of 2009, there were 72 DHS/FBI designated state and Urban Area Security Initiative (UASI) fusion centers. [1, p. 11]

In an effort to strengthen intelligence and information sharing and analysis capabilities following the 9/11 attacks, states and major urban areas established intelligence fusion centers.

I&A intelligence officers assigned to fusion centers are responsible for providing intelligence support, including briefings to state and local officials; reviewing and analyzing suspicious activity reports and writing Homeland Intelligence Reports based on state and local information; supporting the development of state and local intelligence products; posting material on the HSDN and the Homeland Security State and Local Intelligence Community of Interest (HS-SLIC) portal; and reaching back to I&A for intelligence products and IT resources. [1, p. 12]

Fusion centers contribute to the Information Sharing Environment (ISE) through their role in receiving threat information from the federal government; analyzing that information in the context of their local environment; disseminating that information to local agencies; and gathering tips, leads, and suspicious activity reporting (SAR) from local agencies and the public. Fusion centers receive information from a variety of sources, including SAR from stakeholders within their jurisdictions, as well as federal information and intelligence. They analyze the information and develop relevant products to disseminate to their customers. These products assist homeland security partners at all levels of government to identify and address immediate and emerging threats. [10]

Beyond serving as a focal point for information sharing, fusion centers add significant value to their customers by providing a state and local context to help enhance the national threat picture. Fusion centers provide the federal government with critical state and local information and subject matter expertise that it did not receive in the past – enabling the effective communication of locally generated threat-related information to the federal government. Integrating and connecting these state and local resources creates a national capacity to gather, process, analyze, and share information in support of efforts to protect the country. [10]

National Terrorism Advisory System

In 2011, the Department of Homeland Security (DHS) replaced the color-coded alerts of the Homeland Security Advisory System (HSAS) with the National Terrorism Advisory System (NTAS).

In 2011, the Department of Homeland Security (DHS) replaced the color-coded alerts of the Homeland Security Advisory System (HSAS) with the National Terrorism Advisory System (NTAS), designed to more effectively communicate information about terrorist threats by providing timely, detailed information to the American public. [11]

When it was launched, NTAS featured an advisory system that consisted of two types of "Alerts": Elevated and Imminent. An "Elevated Alert" is intended to warn of a credible terrorist threat against the United States and its territories that is general in both timing and potential location such that it is reasonable to recommend implementation of protective measures to thwart or mitigate against an attack. An "Imminent Alert" is intended to warn of a credible, specific, and impending terrorist threat or on-going attack.

Because neither the circumstances nor threat streams rose to the required level, DHS never issued an Alert after introducing NTAS. Accordingly, in December 2015 DHS introduced the NTAS "Bulletin" to provide greater awareness of the general threat, short of any specific indicators or warnings. NTAS Bulletins are designed to provide information describing broader or more general trends and current developments regarding threats of terrorism. They will share important terrorism-related information with the American public and various partners and stakeholders, including in those situations where additional precautions may be warranted, but where the circumstances do not warrant the issuance of an "elevated" or "imminent" Alert. An NTAS Bulletin will summarize the issue and why it is important for public awareness, outline U.S. Government counterterrorism efforts, and offer recommendations to the public on how it can contribute to the overall counterterrorism effort. [12]

With the introduction of the Bulletin, NTAS will now consist of two types of advisories: Bulletins and Alerts. As under the existing system, if there is sufficient information regarding a credible, specific terrorist threat against the United States, such that it is reasonable to recommend implementation of protective measures to thwart or mitigate against an attack, DHS will share an NTAS Alert – either Elevated or Imminent

– with the American public. The Alert may include specific information, if available, about the nature of the threat, including the geographic region, mode of transportation, or critical infrastructure potentially affected by the threat, as well as steps that individuals and communities can take to protect themselves and help prevent, mitigate, or respond to the threat. [12]

NTAS advisories – whether they be Alerts or Bulletins – encourage individuals to follow the guidance provided by state and local officials and to report suspicious activity. Where possible and applicable, NTAS advisories include steps that individuals and communities can take to protect themselves from the threat as well as help detect or prevent an attack before it happens. Individuals are encouraged review the information contained in the Alert or Bulletin, and based upon the circumstances, take the recommended precautionary or preparedness measures for themselves and their families. [11]

Conclusion

In 2014, the Government Accountability Office (GAO) was asked to review I&A's analysis efforts. I&A customers had mixed views on the extent to which its analytic products and services are useful. GAO's interviews with representatives of I&A's five customer groups indicated that two groups—DHS leadership and state, local, tribal, and territorial partners—found products to be useful, while three groups—DHS components, the Intelligence Community, and the private sector—generally did not. Representatives of four of the five groups said that they found other types of services, such as briefings, to be useful. Results from surveys that are attached to I&A products indicate that most customers were very satisfied with the products' usefulness, but the results are not generalizable because they reflect only the views of customers who chose to respond. [13, p. ii] The difficult task of balancing liberty and security while trying to prevent another 9/11 means that I&A's job will necessarily continue to evolve. Whether or not they will be successful remains to be seen. In the meantime, though, they have filled an essential role that was previously absent and could have made a significant difference before 9/11.

Challenge Your Understanding

The following questions are designed to challenge your understanding of the material presented in this chapter. Some questions may require additional research outside this book in order to provide a complete answer.

1. What is the mission of the Intelligence and Analysis Office?
2. Which I&A component is responsible for the analytic mission?
3. How is foreign intelligence different from domestic intelligence?
4. How is homeland security intelligence different from both foreign and domestic intelligence?
5. Which DHS component provides I&A with threat data to critical infrastructure?
6. Which DHS component provide I&A with threat data to transportation systems?
7. Which I&A product provides an annual assessment of major threats to the United States?
8. Which I&A product contains urgent intelligence?
9. What are fusion centers and why were they created after 9/11?
10. How is the National Terrorism Advisory System different than the previous Homeland Security Advisory System?

Chapter 28

FEMA

Learning Outcomes

Careful study of this chapter will help a student do the following:

- Explain the mission of the organization.
- Describe some key components of the organization.
- Discuss some of the work of the organization.

"Under the President's proposal, the Department of Homeland Security, building on the strong foundation already laid by the Federal Emergency Management Agency (FEMA), will lead our national efforts to create and employ a system that will improve our response to all disasters, both manmade and natural."

- 2002 National Strategy for Homeland Security

Introduction

The Federal Emergency Management Agency (FEMA) coordinates the federal government's role in preparing for, preventing, mitigating the effects of, responding to, and recovering from all domestic disasters, whether natural or man-made, including acts of terror. [1] FEMA has a major role in on-ground support of disaster response and recovery efforts by providing state, local, and tribal governments with experts in specialized fields and funding for relief and rebuilding efforts. FEMA also provides funds for first responders to train throughout the United States and its territories as part of the agency's preparedness agenda.

The Federal Emergency Management Agency (FEMA) coordinates the federal government's role in preparing for, preventing, mitigating the effects of, responding to, and recovering from all domestic disasters, whether natural or man-made.

Background

FEMA can trace its beginnings to the Congressional Act of 1803. This act, generally considered the first piece of disaster legislation, provided assistance to a New Hampshire town following an extensive fire. In the century that followed, ad hoc legislation was passed more than 100 times in response to hurricanes, earthquakes, floods and other natural disasters. [1]

By the 1930s, when the federal approach to disaster-related events became popular, the Reconstruction Finance Corporation was given authority to make disaster loans for repair and reconstruction of certain public facilities following an earthquake, and later, other types of disasters. [1]

- In 1934, the Bureau of Public Roads was given authority to provide funding for highways and bridges damaged by natural disasters.
- The Flood Control Act of 1965, which gave the U.S. Army Corps of Engineers greater authority to implement flood control projects, was also passed.
- The 1960s and early 1970s brought massive disasters requiring major federal response and recovery operations by the Federal Disaster Assistance Administration, established within the Department of Housing and Urban Development (HUD).
- In 1968, the National Flood Insurance Act created the Federal Insurance Administration and made flood insurance available for the first time to homeowners.

- The Flood Disaster Protection Act of 1973 made the purchase of flood insurance mandatory for the protection of property located in Special Flood Hazard Areas.
- In the year following, President Nixon passed into law the Disaster Relief Act of 1974, firmly establishing the process of Presidential disaster declarations.

This piecemeal approach to disaster assistance was problematic. Accordingly, it prompted legislation to require greater cooperation between federal agencies and authorized the President to coordinate these activities. These events served to focus attention on the issue of natural disasters and brought about increased legislation. However, emergency and disaster activities were still fragmented. When hazards associated with nuclear power plants and the transportation of hazardous substances were added to natural disasters, more than 100 federal agencies were involved in some aspect of disasters, hazards and emergencies. Many parallel programs and policies existed at the state and local level, simplifying the complexity of federal disaster relief efforts. The National Governor's Association sought to decrease the many agencies with which state and local governments were forced to work. They asked President Carter to centralize federal emergency functions. On April 1, 1979, President Jimmy Carter signed Executive Order 12127 that created the Federal Emergency Management Agency (FEMA) charged with leading America to prepare for, prevent, respond to and recover from disasters with a vision of "A Nation Prepared". [1]

The Robert T. Stafford Disaster Relief and Emergency Assistance Act (Public Law 100-707) was signed into law November 23, 1988 amending the Disaster Relief Act of 1974 (Public Law 93-288). The Stafford Act as it came to be known created the system in place today by which a presidential disaster declaration of an emergency triggers financial and physical assistance through FEMA.

President Carter's 1979 executive order merged many of the separate disaster-related responsibilities into the Federal Emergency Management Agency (FEMA) by absorbing the following agencies:

- The Federal Insurance Administration
- The National Fire Prevention and Control Administration
- The National Weather Service Community Preparedness Program
- The Federal Preparedness Agency of the General Services Administration
- The Federal Disaster Assistance Administration activities from HUD
- Civil defense responsibilities were also transferred to the new agency from the Defense Department's Defense Civil Preparedness Agency

The Robert T. Stafford Disaster Relief and Emergency Assistance Act (Public Law 100-707) was signed into law November 23, 1988 amending the Disaster Relief Act of 1974 (Public Law 93-288). The Stafford Act as it came to be known created the system in place today by which a presidential disaster declaration of an emergency triggers financial and physical assistance through FEMA. The Stafford Act gives FEMA the responsibility for coordinating government-wide relief efforts which are designed to bring an orderly and systemic means of federal natural disaster assistance for state and local governments in carrying out their responsibilities to aid citizens. Congress' intention was to encourage states and localities to develop comprehensive disaster preparedness plans, prepare for better intergovernmental coordination in the face of a disaster, encourage the use of insurance coverage, and provide federal assistance programs for losses due to a disaster. The Stafford Act constitutes the statutory authority for most federal disaster response activities especially as they pertain to FEMA and FEMA programs. [1]

As a result of 9/11, the Homeland Security Act of 2002 made FEMA a part of the new Department of Homeland Security to bring a coordinated approach to national security from emergencies and disasters – both natural and manmade.

The new agency was faced with many unusual challenges in its first few years that emphasized how complex emergency management can be. Early disasters and emergencies included the contamination of Love Canal, the Cuban refugee crisis, and the accident at the Three Mile Island nuclear power plant. Later, the Loma Prieta Earthquake in 1989 and Hurricane Andrew in 1992 focused major national attention on FEMA. In 1993, President Clinton nominated James L. Witt as the new FEMA director making him the first agency director with experience as a state emergency manager. He initiated sweeping reforms that streamlined disaster relief and recovery operations, insisted on a new emphasis regarding preparedness and mitigation, and focused agency employees on customer service. The end of the Cold War also allowed Witt to redirect more of FEMA's limited resources from civil defense into disaster relief, recovery and mitigation programs.

As a result of the Homeland Security Act of 2002, in March, 2003, FEMA officially joined 22 other federal agencies, programs, and offices in becoming the Department of Homeland Security bringing a coordinated approach to national security from emergencies and disasters – both natural and manmade. As part of DHS, FEMA's Office of National Preparedness was given responsibility for helping to ensure that the nation's first responders were trained and equipped to deal with weapons of mass destruction. Within months, the terrorist attacks of Sept.11th focused the agency on issues of national preparedness and homeland security, and tested the agency in unprecedented ways. Billions of dollars of new funding were directed to FEMA to help communities face the threat of terrorism. Just a few years past its 20th anniversary, FEMA was actively directing its "all-hazards" approach to disasters toward homeland security issues. [1]

On August 29, 2005, Hurricane Katrina struck the Gulf coasts of Louisiana, Alabama, and Mississippi resulting in severe and widespread damage to the region. The response of the federal government, especially FEMA, in the aftermath of the storm was widely criticized. Some of the criticism focused on the organizational arrangements involving

FEMA and its parent organization, DHS. On October 4, 2006, President George W. Bush signed into law the Post-Katrina Emergency Reform Act. The act significantly reorganized FEMA, provided it substantial new authority to remedy gaps that became apparent in the response to Hurricane Katrina, the most devastating natural disaster in U.S. history, and included a more robust preparedness mission for FEMA.

Natural disasters continued to plague the U.S. and the nation's next major storm that impacted the operational objectives of FEMA was Hurricane Sandy, also known as "Superstorm Sandy" hitting the New England coast on October 29, 2012. [2, pp. 3-4] Sandy was massive in size and drove a catastrophic storm surge and subsequent flooding into the New Jersey, New York, and Connecticut coastal areas. [2, p. 8] Hurricane Sandy caused extensive human suffering and damage to public and private property. In response to this catastrophic event, Congress considered legislation to provide supplemental appropriations to federal disaster assistance programs to include revising the Stafford Act. [3, p. i] On January 29, 2013, President Barack Obama signed into law the Sandy Recovery Improvement Act (SRIA) of 2013 and the accompanying Disaster Relief Appropriations Act, 2013. In many ways, the passage of SRIA represents the most significant legislative change to FEMA's substantive authorities since the enactment of the Stafford Act. The law authorizes several significant changes to the way FEMA may deliver federal disaster assistance to survivors. [4]

As a result of Hurricane Katrina, the 2006 Post-Katrina Emergency Reform Act restored many of the previous functions and elevated FEMA as a separate agency within the Department of Homeland Security.

Mission

FEMA's mission is to support American citizens and first responders to work together as a nation to build, sustain and improve its capability to prepare for, protect against, respond to, recover from and mitigate all hazards. [1] To serve disaster victims and communities more quickly and effectively, FEMA builds on experience, applies lessons learned and best practices from field operations, gathers feedback from many sources, and constantly strives to improve upon its operational core competencies of service to disaster victims, integrated preparedness, operational planning and preparedness, incident management, disaster logistics, hazard mitigation, emergency and public disaster communications, and continuity programs. [5, pp. 2-3]

- Mission Support (MS) is organized around the following six functional offices [1]:
- Office of the Chief Administrative Officer
- Office of the Chief Component Human Capital Officer
- Office of the Chief Information Officer
- Office of the Chief Procurement Officer
- Office of the Chief Security Officer

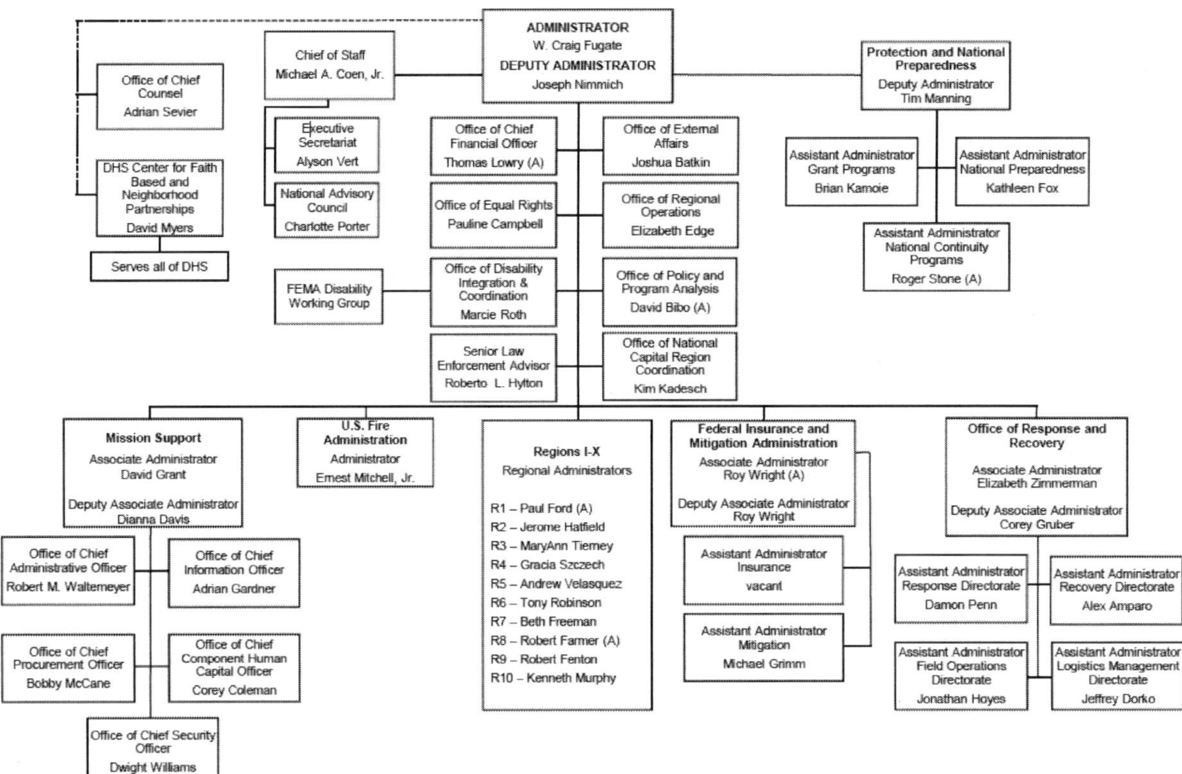

Figure 28-1: FEMA Leadership Organization Chart [6]

Organization

FEMA staff work together with tribal, state and local emergency management personnel to prepare communities before a disaster, and to respond effectively when needed. FEMA's efforts at the national and regional levels are led by individuals with a broad range of hands-on emergency management, fire, rescue, emergency medical services, law enforcement, military and private sector experience. FEMA employees are committed to their mission of protecting lives and communities. [5, p. 4]

In addition to its headquarters in Washington, D.C., FEMA has 10 permanent regional offices (Figure 28-2), three permanent area offices, and various temporary disaster-related sites that carry out the agency's operations throughout the United States and its territories. These offices work more closely with other federal agencies, strategic partners and tribal, state and local officials in their regions, further supporting the agency's mission and core competencies. FEMA has additional facilities across the country. [5, p. 6]

Figure 28-2: FEMA Regions [7]

FEMA is organized into ten regions, with headquarters in Washington, DC.

FEMA Headquarters
500 C St., SW
Washington DC 20472

FEMA Region I
99 High St., 6th Floor
Boston, MA 02110

FEMA Region II
26 Federal Plaza, Suite 1337
New York, NY 10278-0002

FEMA Region III
615 Chestnut St.
One Independence Mall, 6th Floor
Philadelphia, PA 19106-4404

FEMA Region IV
3003 Charublee-Tucker Rd.
Atlanta, GA 30341

FEMA Region V
536 South Clark St., 6th Floor
Chicago, IL 60605

FEMA Region VI
Federal Regional Center
800 North Loop 288
Denton, TX 76209

FEMA Region VII
9221 Ward Parkway, Suite 300
Kansas City, MO 64114-3372

FEMA Region VIII
Federal Center, Bldg. 710
P.O. Box 25267
Denver, CO 80225

FEMA Region IX
1111 Broadway
Suite 1200
Oakland, CA 94607-4052

FEMA Region X
130 228th St., SW
Bothell, WA 98021-8627

Offices and Directorates

The FEMA National Advisory Council (NAC) was established by the enactment of the Post-Katrina Emergency Management Reform Act of 2006 to ensure effective and ongoing coordination of Federal preparedness, protection, response, recovery, and mitigation for natural disasters, acts of terrorism, and other manmade disasters. The NAC advises the FEMA Administrator on all aspects of emergency management. The NAC incorporates state, local, and tribal governments; nonprofit, and private sector input in the development and revision of the National Preparedness Goal, the National Preparedness System, the National Incident Management System, and other related plans and strategies. [1]

The FEMA National Advisory Council (NAC) advises the FEMA Administrator on all aspects of emergency management. The NAC was established to ensure effective and ongoing coordination of Federal preparedness, protection, response, recovery, and mitigation for natural disasters, acts of terrorism, and other manmade disasters.

In 2010, FEMA established the Office of Disability Integration and Coordination (ODIC) to lead FEMA's commitment to achieve whole community emergency management, inclusive of individuals with disabilities. Each of the ten FEMA regions is staffed with a Regional Disability Integration Specialist, a third of whom are interpreters as qualified sign language providers and certified deaf interpreters, who provide guidance, training, and tools for facilitating disability-inclusive emergency preparedness, response, recovery and mitigation. Regional Disability Integration Specialists work closely with the states to ensure that their disaster planning is inclusive of people with disabilities and others with access and functional needs. Simultaneously, they work with local nonprofit disability groups to reach the disability community encouraging them to participate in federal, state, local, and community emergency planning meetings. [1]

The Office of External Affairs (OAE) was created in 2007, bringing together several independent offices and adding two new divisions to enhance a coordinated communications program for the agency. The Office's purpose is to maintain visibility regarding public and internal communications; coordinate routine and special communications; ensure accurate, useful, timely, synchronized, targeted communication; and provide continuous messaging to meet the needs of the situation. The Office also serves as an advisor to FEMA program and support offices on decision making, development, and maintenance of policies and programs to ensure that activities are responsive to stakeholder, media, congressional and other audiences. [1]

As part of the Office of External Affairs, the Congressional Affairs Division is FEMA's primary liaison with the United States Congress. The mission is to proactively engage and communicate with Members of Congress and their staffs to build strong working relationships that will advance the agency's legislative and emergency management priorities. [1] This mission is accomplished by:

- Informing Congress of agency efforts to support citizens and first responders in preparing for, protecting against, responding to, recovering from, and mitigating all hazards;

- Responding to various Congressional inquiries related to emergency management and disaster response/recovery issues;
- Providing Members of Congress and their staffs with regular updates on key developments in Presidentially-declared disasters; and
- Advising the FEMA Administrator, and other senior agency officials, on legislative matters pertaining to emergency management.

The Office of Policy and Program Analysis (OPPA) fosters strategic coherence; ensures availability of critical resources; leads Agency policy, strategy, and innovation; provides objective analysis; and drives strategy, budget, execution, performance integration and accountability. The OPPA ensures FEMA's strategic direction, informs sound decisions with independent analysis, and facilitates cross-agency interactions. The Strategic Planning and Analysis Division, the Defense Production Act Program, and the International Affairs Division all fall under the OPPA . [1]

The Office of Response and Recovery (ORR) provides coordination of all Federal emergency management response operations, response planning and integration of Federal, state, tribal and local disaster programs. This coordination ensures efficient and effective delivery of immediate emergency assistance to individuals and communities impacted and overwhelmed by these disasters.

The Office of Response and Recovery (ORR) provides the core, coordinated Federal operational response capability needed to save and sustain lives, minimize suffering, and protect property in a timely and effective manner in communities that become overwhelmed by natural disasters, acts of terrorism, or other emergencies. Response program activities encompass the coordination of all Federal emergency management response operations, response planning and integration of Federal, state, tribal and local disaster programs. This coordination ensures efficient and effective delivery of immediate emergency assistance to individuals and communities impacted and overwhelmed by these disasters, emergencies, or acts of terrorism. [1]

The Disaster Emergency Communications Division of the ORR establishes, maintains, and coordinates effective disaster emergency communications services and information systems critical to FEMA's role in coordinating the Federal government's response, continuity efforts, and restoration of essential services before, during, and after an incident or planned event. The DEC Division promotes and provides operable and interoperable communications and information systems capabilities across all levels of government to ensure mission–critical information and situational awareness for emergency management decision makers and support elements. [1] This is accomplished through:

- Supporting effective tactical operable and interoperable voice, video, and information systems for federal emergency response teams.
- Identifying and documenting mission-critical disaster emergency communication and information systems capabilities, requirements, solutions, and mitigation strategies.
- Developing effective command and control communications frameworks.

- Supporting the coordination and delivery of secure communications solutions.
- Promoting communications interoperability with Federal, State, tribal, and local emergency response providers.

The Recovery Directorate through its Disaster Survivor Assistance Program, National Emergency Family Registry and Locator System, and Transitional Shelter Assistance programs supports communities in rebuilding so individuals, civic institutions, businesses, and governmental organizations can function on their own, return to normal life, and protect against future hazards. [1]

Protection and National Preparedness (PNP) is responsible for the coordination of preparedness and protection related activities throughout FEMA, including grants, planning, training, exercises, individual and community preparedness, assessments, lessons learned, continuity of government and national capital region coordination.

In addition to the Response and Recovery Directorates, the ORR houses the Logistics Management Directorate and the Office of Federal Disaster Coordination. [1]

- FEMA's Logistics Management Directorate provides an efficient, transparent, and flexible logistics capability to procure and deliver goods and services to support disaster survivors and communities responding to and recovering from disasters. The primary mission of the Logistics Management Directorate is to deliver the right resources to the right place at the right time in support of state, local, tribal governments and territories.
- The mission of the Office of Federal Disaster Coordination is to access, train, equip, and manage FEMA's Federal Coordinating Officers (FCO) and Federal Disaster Recovery Coordinators (FDRC) to ensure their availability for rapid deployment in response to any disaster; deliver training to develop and sustain FCO and FDRC professional competencies, and coordinate both FCO and FDRC assignments to meet the on-scene needs of FEMA and its emergency management partners.

Protection and National Preparedness (PNP) is responsible for the coordination of preparedness and protection related activities throughout FEMA, including grants, planning, training, exercises, individual and community preparedness, assessments, lessons learned, continuity of government and national capital region coordination. [1] The PNP consists of:

- The Grant Programs Directorate (GPD), formally created on April 1, 2007 in accordance with the Post-Katrina Emergency Management Reform Act, is to strategically and effectively administer and manage FEMA grants to ensure critical and measurable results for customers and stakeholders. The mission is to manage federal assistance to measurably improve capability and reduce the risks the Nation faces in times of man-made and natural disasters. The focus of GPD is to provide exceptional customer service to all grantees, as well as internal and external partners; establish and promote consistent outreach and communication with state, local and tribal stakeholders; ensure transparency in the grant process; and enhance the Nation's level of preparedness and the public's ability to prevent, protect and mitigate against, and respond to and recover from all hazards.

- FEMA's National Continuity Programs (NCP) is the Federal Executive Branch Lead Agent for continuity of national essential functions. The goal of the NCP is to minimize the disruption of essential operations in order to guarantee an Enduring Constitutional Government in response to a full-threat spectrum of emergencies. The scope of this mandate includes development and promulgation of continuity directives and guidance, education, and training, as well as coordination between the Federal, State, local, territorial, tribal, and private sectors. NCP also coordinates and participates in Federal, State, and local continuity exercises. FEMA serves as the lead agent for coordinating continuity operations and activities of Federal agencies and collaborating with State, territorial, tribal, and local government jurisdictions. Viable continuity capabilities ensure FEMA is ready to respond to a continuity event. NCP also manages the Integrated Public Alert and Warning System (IPAWS), the Nation's next generation alert and warning capability developed by NCP in partnership with multiple Federal Departments and Agencies. IPAWS meets the requirements of Executive Order 13407, signed by the President in 2006, which called for the development and implementation of an "effective, reliable, integrated, flexible, and comprehensive system to alert and warn the American people... and to ensure under all conditions the President can communicate with the American people."

FEMA's National Continuity Programs (NCP) is the Federal Executive Branch Lead Agent for continuity of national essential functions. NCP also manages the Integrated Public Alert and Warning System (IPAWS), the Nation's next generation alert and warning capability.

- The National Preparedness Directorate (NPD) provides the doctrine, programs, and resources to prepare the Nation to prevent, protect, mitigate, respond to and recover from disasters while minimizing the loss of lives, infrastructure, and property. NPD carries out these responsibilities through the following NPD divisions:
    - National Integration Center (NIC)
    - Individual and Community Preparedness Division (ICPD)
    - National Training & Education (NTE), which includes:
        - Center for Domestic Preparedness (CDP)
        - Emergency Management Institute (EMI)
        - National Training and Education Division (NTED)
    - National Exercises Division (NED)
    - Technological Hazards Division (THD)
    - National Preparedness Assessment Division (NPAD)

National Preparedness

National preparedness is a shared responsibility—everyone has a role to play to ensure that the nation's greatest risks can be addressed effectively and efficiently. The National Preparedness Goal defines what it means for the whole community to be prepared for all types of disasters and emergencies. [8]

The National Preparedness Goal sets the vision for preparedness nationwide and identifies the core capabilities necessary to achieve that vision across the five mission areas: Prevention, Protection, Mitigation, Response and Recovery. The goal itself is succinct and remains unchanged:

The National Preparedness Goal sets the vision for preparedness nationwide and identifies the core capabilities necessary to achieve that vision across the five mission areas: Prevention, Protection, Mitigation, Response and Recovery.

> *"A secure and resilient nation with the capabilities required across the whole community to prevent, protect against, mitigate, respond to, and recover from the threats and hazards that pose the greatest risk."*
>
> - 2015 National Preparedness Goal

These risks include events such as natural disasters, disease pandemics, chemical spills and other man-made hazards, terrorist attacks and cyber attacks. The National Preparedness Goal also outlines 32 activities or core capabilities that address the greatest risks to the nation. [8]

Each of these core capabilities is tied to a capability target. These targets recognize that everyone needs the flexibility to determine how they apply their resources, based on the threats that are most relevant to them and their communities. A Midwestern city, for example, may determine it is at high risk for a catastrophic tornado. As a result, the city could set a target to have a certain number of shelters in place. The same applies across all potential risks, understanding that each risk is different; therefore, each target is different. [8]

The National Preparedness Goal is the cornerstone of implementing the National Preparedness System. Several National Preparedness System components contribute to building, sustaining, and delivering the core capabilities described in the National Preparedness Goal [9, p. 21]. These include:

- A National Planning System, which supports the integration of planning across all levels of government and the whole community to provide an agile, flexible, and accessible delivery of the core capabilities.

- A series of National Frameworks and Federal Interagency Operational Plans. The National Frameworks address the roles and responsibilities across the whole community to deliver the core capabilities. The Federal Interagency Operational Plans address the critical tasks, responsibilities, and resourcing, personnel, and sourcing requirements for the core capabilities.
- A National Preparedness Report, which provides a summary of the progress being made toward building, sustaining, and delivering the core capabilities described in the Goal. The annual National Preparedness Report provides an opportunity to measure the advancement the whole community has made in preparedness and to identify where challenges remain.
- A Campaign to Build and Sustain Preparedness, which provides an integrating structure for new and existing community-based, nonprofit, and private sector preparedness programs, research and development activities to include post-event evaluation of the use of science and technology tools, and preparedness assistance.

Preparedness is the shared responsibility of the entire nation. The whole community contributes, beginning with individuals and communities, the private and nonprofit sectors, faith-based organizations, and all governments (local, regional/metropolitan, state, tribal, territorial, insular area, and Federal).

Whole Community

Preparedness is the shared responsibility of the entire nation. The whole community contributes, beginning with individuals and communities, the private and nonprofit sectors, faith-based organizations, and all governments (local, regional/metropolitan, state, tribal, territorial, insular area, and Federal). [9, p. 1]

A government-centric approach to emergency management is not enough to meet the challenges posed by a catastrophic incident. Whole Community is an approach to emergency management that reinforces the fact that FEMA is only one part of the nation's emergency management team; that all of the resources of the collective team must be leveraged in preparing for, protecting against, responding to, recovering from and mitigating against all hazards; and that collectively the needs of the entire community in each of these areas must be met. This larger collective emergency management team includes not only FEMA and its partners at the federal level, but also local, tribal, state and territorial partners; non-governmental organizations like faith-based and non-profit groups and private sector industry; and individuals, families and communities, who continue to be the nation's most important assets as first responders during a disaster. Both the composition of the community and the individual needs of community members, regardless of age, economics, or accessibility requirements, must be accounted for when planning and implementing disaster strategies. [10]

When the community is engaged in an authentic dialogue, it becomes empowered to identify its needs and the existing resources that may be used to address them. Only together can the whole community determine the best ways to organize and strengthen community assets, capacities, and interests. This allows the nation to expand its reach and deliver services more efficiently and cost effectively to build, sustain, and improve the capability to prepare for, protect against, respond to, recover from, and mitigate all hazards. [10]

Reservist Program

Community Emergency Response Teams (CERT) train and organize volunteers that provide assistance to their communities before, during, and after disasters.

FEMA Reservists are a type of Incident Management responder, hired under The Stafford Act as temporary, intermittent employees. They are a significant FEMA Incident Management work component, staffing Joint Field Offices and other activities. These employees, when listed as available, can deploy to perform disaster field activities directly related to specific disasters, emergencies, projects, or activities of a non-continuous nature. FEMA is committed to deploy each Reservist at least annually. However, as deployment opportunities are dictated by disaster activity and certain limitations apply regarding their use, Reservists are not guaranteed to deploy. Rather than serve as an alternative to permanent full-time staff, Reservists are a necessary augmentation of permanent full-time staffing. [11]

Community Emergency Response Teams (CERT)

The Community Emergency Response Teams (CERT) train and organize teams of volunteers that provide assistance to their communities before, during, and after disasters. CERT volunteers help others following disasters when professional responders are not immediately available to help, and supplement and support the efforts of professional responders upon their arrival. Volunteers also support emergency response agencies by organizing and participating in local preparedness projects and initiatives. The CERT program educates participants about how to prepare for hazards that may impact their communities and trains them in basic disaster response skills, such as fire safety search and rescue, team organization, and disaster medical operations. [12]

Urban Search and Rescue

Urban search and rescue (US&R) involves the location, rescue (extrication), and initial medical stabilization of individuals trapped in confined spaces. Structural collapse is most often the cause for people being trapped, but individuals may also be trapped in transportation accidents, mines, and collapsed trenches. Urban search and rescue is considered a "multi-hazard" discipline, as it may be needed for a variety of emergencies or disasters, including earthquakes, hurricanes, typhoons, storms, tornadoes, floods, dam failures, technological accidents, terrorist activities, and hazardous materials releases. The events may be slow in developing, as in the case of hurricanes, or sudden, as in the case of earthquakes. [13]

Voluntary Agency and Donations Coordination

FEMA Voluntary Agency Liaisons promote the interest of voluntary, faith-based, and community-based stakeholders by advocating for them and empowering their activities and integration across the disaster life-cycle and in every subject area in which they engage. FEMA Voluntary Agency Liaisons (VALs) and Donations Specialists build relationships among Federal, State, and tribal governments and voluntary, faith-based, and community-based organizations by reporting to and from FEMA and other government agencies on programs of voluntary organizations active during disasters, providing information and guidance to organizations, and helping strengthen National and State Voluntary Organizations Active in Disaster (VOADs). [14]

FEMA Voluntary Agency Liaisons (VALs) and Donations Specialists build relationships among Federal, State, and tribal governments and voluntary, faith-based, and community -based organizations by reporting to and from FEMA and other government agencies on programs of Voluntary Organizations Active in Disaster (VOADs).

Disaster Recovery Centers

A Disaster Recovery Center is a readily accessible facility or mobile office where survivors may go for information about FEMA's programs or other disaster assistance programs, and to ask questions related to their case. [15] Some of the services may include:

- Guidance regarding disaster recovery
- Clarification of any written correspondence received
- Housing Assistance and Rental Resource information
- Answers to questions, resolution to problems and referrals to agencies that may provide further assistance
- Status of applications being processed by FEMA
- Small Business Administration (SBA) program information
- Crisis Counseling Program
- Disaster Legal Services
- Disaster Unemployment
- Funeral Assistance - Individuals and Households Program

Ready.gov

Launched in February 2003, Ready is a national public service advertising (PSA) campaign designed to educate and empower Americans to prepare for and respond to emergencies including natural and man-made disasters. The goal of the campaign is to get the public involved and ultimately to increase the level of basic preparedness across the nation.

Ready and its Spanish language version Listo ask individuals to do three key things: 1) build an emergency supply kit, 2) make a family emergency plan and 3) be informed about the different types of emergencies that could occur and their appropriate responses.

FEMA has also worked with a variety of public and private sector organizations to develop tailored preparedness information for specific Americans. The Department worked with American Kennel Club, American Society for the Prevention of Cruelty to Animals, American Veterinary Medical Association and The Humane Society of the United States to create materials that highlight the key steps pet owners should take to prepare themselves and their animals. FEMA also worked with American Association of Retired Persons, the American Red Cross, the National Organization on Disability, and the National Fire Protection Association to create emergency information for seniors and Americans with disabilities and special needs.

In 2008, The Ready Campaign added a section on their web site for military families. The entire Department highlights emergency preparedness through National Preparedness Month (NPM), a nationwide effort held each September to encourage Americans to take simple steps to prepare for emergencies in their homes, businesses and schools. [16]

Conclusion

The Congressional Act of 1803 was the earliest effort to provide disaster relief on a federal level after a fire devastated a New Hampshire town. From that point forward, assorted legislation provided disaster support. In 1979, the Federal Emergency Management Agency (FEMA) was established by an executive order, which merged many of the separate disaster-related responsibilities into a single agency. Since then, FEMA has dedicated itself to the mission of helping communities nationwide prepare for, respond to and recover from natural and manmade disasters – a mission strengthened when the agency became part of the Department of Homeland Security (DHS) in 2003. [5, p. 2]

To serve disaster victims and communities more quickly and effectively, FEMA builds on experience, applies lessons learned and best practices from field operations, gathers feedback from many sources, and constantly strives to improve upon its operational core competencies of service to disaster victims, integrated preparedness, operational planning and preparedness, incident management, disaster logistics, hazard mitigation, emergency communications, public disaster communications, and continuity programs. [5, pp. 2-3]

Challenge Your Understanding

The following questions are designed to challenge your understanding of the material presented in this chapter. Some questions may require additional research outside this book in order to provide a complete answer.

1. What is the mission of the Federal Emergency Management Agency?
2. Under what authority does FEMA coordinate Federal assistance to States?
3. Why was FEMA made part of DHS?
4. How did FEMA's position within DHS change after Hurricane Katrina?
5. The U.S. Virgin Islands and Puerto Rico are part of which FEMA region?
6. Which FEMA component provides the core operational response capability?
7. Which FEMA component helps communities rebuild following a disaster?
8. Which FEMA component awards grants to improve emergency preparedness?
9. What is the purpose of the National Preparedness Goal?
10. What FEMA program helps organize and train volunteers to assist with emergency management?

Chapter 29

U.S. Coast Guard

Learning Outcomes

Careful study of this chapter will help a student do the following:

- Explain the mission of the organization.
- Describe some key components of the organization.
- Discuss some of the work of the organization.

"Semper Paratus. Stand a taut watch."

- 2014 Doctrine for the U.S. Coast Guard

Introduction

The United States Coast Guard (USCG) is one of the most unique organizations within the Department of Homeland Security. Implemented in 1790 as the "Revenue Marine" and renamed the U.S. Revenue Cutter Service in 1894, it is the oldest defense organization in the U.S. and served as the nation's sole armed maritime presence until the Naval Act of 1794 declared it a standing naval force. [1, pp. 1-2] It was not until 1915 upon merging with the U.S. Life Saving Service, that the U.S. Revenue Cutter Service officially became the U.S. Coast Guard. Subsequently, the Coast Guard incorporated the Lighthouse Service, the Steamboat Inspection Service, and the Bureau of Navigation and Lifesaving Service all having similar missions. The Coast Guard moved across several federal departments from the Department of the Treasury, where it first resided, to the newly formed Department of Transportation in 1967 before finally coming to rest within the Department of Homeland Security in 2002. Initially, the Coast Guard protected the U.S. maritime ports to promote and safeguard legal trade, as a law enforcement arm to collect taxes, and to perform maritime rescue services. [2] Much of these mission areas have not changed and it is this broad mission area that makes the Coast Guard unique even today.

The U.S. Coast Guard is one of the nation's seven uniformed services of the United States and the only military organization within the Department of Homeland Security.

Military Mission

The U.S. Coast Guard is one of the nation's seven uniformed services of the United States and the only military organization within the Department of Homeland Security. Its mission is unique among the U.S. military services due to its defense and federal regulatory authority. While it currently operates under the Department of Homeland Security, it can easily be transferred to the Department of the Navy at any time under a presidential order, particularly during times of war as it had been during both World Wars I and II. [3] The Coast Guard has a different legal authority under the U.S. Code than that of the other U.S. military branches. Title 14 establishes the Coast Guard as a branch of the U.S., but it also serves simultaneously under Title 10, which outlines the role of the armed forces allowing the Coast Guard to conduct military operations under the Department of Defense, and Title 6 which governs domestic security allowing the Coast Guard to enforce laws within the 3.4 million square mile exclusive economic zone. [4] One of the most unique features of the Coast Guard is its exclusion from the Posse Comitatus Act of 1878 that prevents other military services from conducting law enforcement activities. As such, the Coast Guard has the legal authority to board any vessel within U.S. jurisdiction, or to make inquiries, examinations, inspections, searches, seizures, and arrests upon the high seas or waterways in which the U.S. has jurisdiction. [5, p. 11] The Coast Guard also has the unique capability of applying its military mission toward guarding against the importation of illegal drugs and other illicit goods, disrupting transnational terrorist and criminal organizations, enforcing legal immigration laws, while also providing humanitarian support in rescue and disaster operations. [5, p. 12]

Homeland Security Mission

Following the terrorist attacks of September 11, 2001, Congress passed the Homeland Security and the Maritime Transportation Security Acts of 2002, and transferred the Coast Guard to the newly created Department of Homeland Security (DHS). By law, the U.S. Coast Guard is the lead federal agency for maritime homeland security with eleven specific missions:

- ports, waterways, and coastal security,
- drug interdiction,
- aids to navigation,
- search and rescue,
- living marine resources,
- marine safety,
- defense readiness,
- migrant interdiction,
- marine environmental protection,
- ice operations, and
- other law enforcement.

The Coast Guard is exempt from the Posse Comitatus Act of 1878 that prevents other military services from conducting law enforcement activities. As such, the Coast Guard has the legal authority to board any vessel within U.S. jurisdiction, or to make inquiries, examinations, inspections, searches, seizures, and arrests upon the high seas.

The Coast Guard's inclusion into DHS affected their priorities, but it did not alter the fundamental goals or the importance of their work. As criminals and terrorists try to exploit or blend in with legitimate maritime activity, maritime governance becomes a critical component of DHS strategy to protect the homeland. As a first responder and an integral part of the DHS–led comprehensive emergency management system, the Coast Guard fulfilled an expanded role in response operations during Hurricanes Katrina and Rita in 2005, the 2010 Haiti earthquake, the Deepwater Horizon oil spill, and other natural and man-made disasters. The Coast Guard continues to build and leverage relationships with federal, state, local, and tribal governments, the private sector, and international partners. [5, p. 7]

The Coast Guard's distinct blend of authorities, capabilities, competencies, and partnerships provide the President, Secretary of Homeland Security, Secretary of Defense, and other national leaders with the capabilities to lead or support a range of operations to ensure safety, security, and stewardship in the maritime domain.

Maritime Safety

The U.S. government has a fundamental interest in safeguarding the lives of its people. In the maritime realm, the Coast Guard serves this interest. They improves safety at sea through complementary programs such as accident prevention, search and rescue, and accident investigation, while working with other federal agencies, state, local, and tribal governments, marine industries, and individual mariners. [5, p. 7] The Coast Guard also provides prevention activities to include the development of standards and regulations, various plan reviews, compliance inspections, and a number of safety programs designed to protect mariners. In addition, they develop and enforce vessel construction standards and domestic shipping and navigation regulations. [5, p. 7] They are America's voice in the International Maritime Organization (IMO), which develops measures to improve shipping safety and security, prevent pollution, train mariners, and standardize certifications. To ensure compliance, they review and approve plans for ship construction, repair, and alteration. They inspect vessels, mobile offshore drilling units, and marine facilities for safety. [5, p. 7] With regard to international standards, the Port State Control program is aimed at ensuring vessel compliance, a key element since the majority of the passenger and cargo ships operating in U.S. waters are foreign flagged. The commercial fishing vessel safety programs are designed to safeguard commercial fishermen, many of whom earn their living performing some of the most dangerous work in the world. [5, p. 8]

The Coast Guard's distinct blend of authorities, capabilities, competencies, and partnerships provide the President, Secretary of Homeland Security, Secretary of Defense, and other national leaders with the capabilities to lead or support a range of operations to ensure safety, security, and stewardship in the maritime domain.

The Coast Guard operates the International Ice Patrol to safeguard ships transiting the North Atlantic shipping lanes and document U.S. flag vessels and license commercial mariners. America has approximately 22 million recreational boats and as the National Recreational Boating Safety Coordinator, the Coast Guard works to minimize loss of life, personal injury, property damage, and environmental harm associated with recreational boating. The boating safety program involves public education efforts, regulation of boat design and construction, approval of boating safety equipment, and vessel safety checks for compliance with federal requirements. [5, p. 8]

The maritime domain is large and complex, and the sea is powerful and unforgiving. Despite the Coast Guard's best efforts, mariners sometimes find themselves in harm's way. When they do, the Coast Guard has a long heritage of providing immediate response to save lives and property in peril. As the lead agency for maritime search and rescue (SAR) in U.S. waters, they coordinate the SAR efforts of Coast Guard units with those of other federal, state, and local responders. They also coordinate with the world's merchant fleet to rescue mariners in distress around the globe through the Automated Mutual Assistance Vessel Rescue (AMVER) system. [5, p. 9]

The Coast Guard's activities in support of maritime safety are often inseparable from those they perform to protect the marine environment or secure the U.S. Marine Transportation System (MTS). For example, a routine inspection for safety compliance may uncover a serious risk to the environment. In addition, Coast Guard vessel traffic services not only reduce the risk of vessel collisions, but also provide maritime domain awareness. Such efforts may quickly divert to a SAR activity while managing a buoy tender working to aid navigation, for instance. [5, p. 10] The integration of all Coast Guard missions has saved many lives, helped secure citizens, and contributed to the nation's economic and environmental well-being.

The Coast Guard maintains safety at sea through complementary programs such as accident prevention, search and rescue, and accident investigation, while working with other federal agencies, state, local, and tribal governments, marine industries, and individual mariners.

Maritime Security

Maritime law enforcement and border control are among the oldest of the Coast Guard's numerous responsibilities. In the early days of the Revenue Marine, cutters patrolled outside the approaches to U.S. coasts and seaports, boarding ships at sea to more effectively frustrate smuggling and enforce the customs laws of the fledgling Republic. Over two centuries later, that early maritime security challenge has evolved into a global obligation. The core capability to interdict ships at sea provides the foundation for today's broader and more complex maritime security operations. Because their specialized capabilities are complementary, the Coast Guard is able to leverage its military nature to project force abroad, sustain their traditional missions, or respond to emergent national incidents that often do not involve the use of other military forces. [5, p. 11]

As the Nation's primary maritime law enforcement service, the Coast Guard enforces, or assists in enforcing, federal laws, treaties, and other international agreements on waters subject to U.S. jurisdiction and on the high seas. They are the designated lead agency for maritime interdiction under the National Drug Control Strategy and the co-lead agency for air interdiction operations with U.S. Customs and Border Protection. As such, the Coast Guard defends the approaches to America's maritime borders against a torrent of illegal drugs and other illicit goods. For more than three decades, their cutters and aircraft have forward deployed off Central and South America and in the drug transit zones. They have disrupted trans-national terrorist and criminal organizations by intercepting thousands of tons of contraband that otherwise would have found its way to America's streets, apprehended thousands of suspected narco-terrorists and smugglers, and supported successful prosecutions in the United States and in many other countries. [5, p. 12]

The Coast Guard enforces, or assists in enforcing, federal laws, treaties, and other international agreements on waters subject to U.S. jurisdiction and on the high seas. They are the designated lead agency for maritime interdiction under the National Drug Control Strategy and the co-lead agency for air interdiction operations with U.S. Customs and Border Protection.

The Coast Guard's undocumented migrant interdiction operations are law enforcement missions with an important humanitarian dimension. Migrants often take great risks and endure significant hardships in their attempts to flee their countries and enter the United States. In many cases, migrant vessels interdicted at sea are overloaded and unseaworthy, lack basic safety equipment, and are operated by inexperienced mariners. Many of these undocumented migrant cases actually begin as SAR incidents. [5, p. 12]

From a national security standpoint, the Coast Guard has served in all American wars, primarily along with the U.S. Navy as a naval augmentation force providing specialized capabilities as required for the defense of the nation. This began with the Quasi-War with France in 1798, and continued through the Civil War, both World Wars, the Korean Conflict, Vietnam, and Operations Desert Shield, Desert Storm, Iraqi Freedom and Enduring Freedom. [5, p. 13]

Today, as a critical component of the U.S. National Fleet, the Coast Guard maintains a high state of readiness to operate as a specialized service alongside the Navy and Marine Corps and to provide direct support to combatant commanders. Coast Guard competencies and resources are included in the National Military Strategy and other national-level defense and security strategies with special emphasis on the following Coast Guard national defense capabilities:

- Maritime interception and interdiction;
- Military environmental response;
- Port operations, security, and defense;
- Theater security cooperation;
- Coastal sea control;

• Rotary wing air intercept;

• Combating terrorism; and

• Maritime Operational Threat Response support

These support the unified combatant commanders and require that the Coast Guard to execute essential military operations in peacetime, crisis, and war. [5, p. 13]

The Coast Guard's domestic law enforcement and port security expertise are uniquely valuable today as combatant commanders work to build foreign nation capacity for security and governance. The Coast Guard has been requested to conduct at-sea interception and anti-piracy operations, foreign liaison, and other supporting warfare tasks in all key theaters. In addition, the Coast Guard can reduce international tension by promoting global economic security through enhanced international capacity to preserve sustainable fish stocks and other living marine resources. [5, p. 14]

The 2002 Maritime Transportation Security Act designated Coast Guard Captains of the Port responsibility for coordinating all maritime security planning and operations in U.S. ports and waterways. These activities encompass all efforts to prevent or respond to threats and hazards.

The Coast Guard has been responsible for the security of the ports and waterways of the United States during times of war since the enactment of the 1917 Espionage Act. After World War II, the Magnuson Act of 1950 assigned the Coast Guard an ongoing responsibility to safeguard U.S. ports, harbors, vessels, and waterfront facilities from accidents, sabotage, or other subversive actions. Building on this foundation, the Coast Guard provides expeditionary port security and harbor defense as a key component of national defense operations. [5, p. 14]

The national security environment has changed since the end of the Cold War and especially after the terrorist attacks against the United States on September 11, 2001. Port, waterways, and coastal security took on increased importance as a result. Denying terrorists the use of the U.S. maritime domain and the U.S. MTS to mount attacks on American territory, population, or critical infrastructure has become a critical objective. [5, p. 15]

Coast Guard authorities were further strengthened with the passage of the Maritime Transportation Security Act of 2002. This designated Coast Guard Captains of the Port as the Federal Maritime Security Coordinators (FMSC). Thus they became the lead agency for coordinating all maritime security planning and operations in U.S. ports and waterways. These activities encompass all efforts to prevent or respond to threats and hazards. [5, p. 15]

Maritime security is a continuing theme running throughout the Coast Guard's history of service to America. It requires a breadth of experience and skills—seamanship, diplomacy, legal expertise, and combat readiness. In conjunction with the other areas of traditional Coast Guard expertise-peacetime military engagement and humanitarian assistance-these skills have been honed for more than two centuries. No other federal agency offers this combination of law enforcement and military capabilities, together with the legal authorities to carry them out. [5, p. 15]

Maritime Stewardship

The Coast Guard's efforts, however, go beyond the safety and security missions. They respond to oil spills, provide relief supplies to victims of war or man-made and natural disasters, ensure safe marine transportation, conduct peacetime engagement visits to foreign countries, or work with international organizations to improve the safety of commercial shipping. These activities add a distinctive humanitarian dimension to their character, and help define who they are. [5, p. 11]

The Coast Guard serves as the primary federal agency for at-sea fisheries enforcement. In coordination with other federal and state agencies, they enforce marine resource management and protection regimes to preserve healthy and sustainable stocks of fish and other living marine resources.

The U.S. waters are vital to the nation's well-being and economy. The marine environment of the United States is one of the most valuable natural resources on Earth, containing one-fifth of the world's fisheries resources. It is also a region of extraordinary recreation, energy and mineral resources, and transportation activities. Finally, it is an inseparable part of the national heritage and the daily fabric of life in its coastal communities. [5, p. 16]

The Coast Guard's role in protecting natural resources dates back to the 1820s when Congress tasked the Revenue Marine with the protection of federal stocks of live oak trees in Florida. These trees were deemed critical to the security of the young nation because they provided the best wood for shipbuilding. As the exploitation of the U.S.'s valuable marine resources—whales, fur bearing animals, and fish—increased, the Coast Guard was given the duty to protect these living resources as well.

The Coast Guard serves as the primary federal agency for at-sea fisheries enforcement. In coordination with other federal and state agencies, they enforce marine resource management and protection regimes to preserve healthy and sustainable stocks of fish and other living marine resources. Their actions also help to safeguard a multi-billion dollar industry, preserving thousands of jobs. [5, p. 16] In 1976, the Magnuson-Stevens Fishery Conservation and Management Act created an Exclusive Economic Zone (EEZ), extending the U.S. sovereign rights out to 200 nautical miles for fisheries and other natural resources. The Coast Guard patrols these areas to uphold U.S. sovereignty and protect precious resources. Today, international fisheries agreements have extended U.S. jurisdiction to waters beyond the EEZ.

The Coast Guard stewardship role has expanded to include enforcing laws intended to protect the environment for the common good. As a result, they safeguard sensitive marine habitats, mammals, and endangered species. They enforce laws protecting U.S. waters from the discharge of oil, hazardous substances, and non-indigenous invasive species.

To do all of this, the Coast Guard conducts a wide range of activities. These include education and prevention; law enforcement; emergency response and containment; and disaster recovery. They also provide critical command and control support for forces responding to environmental disasters in the maritime domain. Under the National Oil and Hazardous Substances Pollution Contingency Plan, Coast Guard Captains of the Port (COTPs) are the pre-designated Federal On-Scene Coordinators (FOSC) for oil and hazardous substance incidents in all coastal and some inland areas. The FOSC is the President's designated on-scene representative and, as such, is responsible for coordinating effective response operations among a diverse group of government and commercial entities in sometimes emotionally charged and often dangerous emergency situations. [5, p. 17]

The Coast Guard is responsible for providing a safe, efficient, and navigable waterway system to support domestic commerce, international trade, and military sealift. They provide short-range aids to navigation; navigation schemes and standards; support for mapping and charting; tide, current, and pilotage information; vessel traffic services; domestic icebreaking to facilitate commerce; and technical assistance and advice.

While the health of U.S. waters and marine resources is vital to the economy, its waterways are also an economic highway essential to the nation's access to several billion tons of foreign and domestic freight annually. Waterborne trade generates millions of jobs and contributes hundreds of billions of dollars to the U.S. gross domestic product each year. The U.S. MTS and its inter-modal links support economic prosperity, military strength, and national security. This complex system includes international and domestic passenger services, commercial and recreational fisheries, and recreational boating. [5, p. 17]

The Coast Guard carries out numerous port and waterways management tasks as well. They are responsible for providing a safe, efficient, and navigable waterway system to support domestic commerce, international trade, and military sealift requirements for national defense. They provide short-range aids to navigation; navigation schemes and standards; support for mapping and charting; tide, current, and pilotage information; vessel traffic services; domestic icebreaking to facilitate commerce; and technical assistance and advice. Finally, with increasing human activity and international interest in the Arctic, the Coast Guard is at the forefront in protecting the U.S. northern frontier. They train and equip their personnel to operate in the extreme Polar environment and ensure they are ready to respond to crises in both Polar Regions. With improved Arctic awareness, modernized maritime governance, and broadened partnerships, their service is postured to protect national interests and promote international cooperation. The Coast Guard's ability to ensure maritime safety, security, and stewardship makes them truly a unique instrument of national strategy. They not only safeguard U.S. coasts and the maritime community, they safeguard the nation's economic prosperity. [5, p. 19]

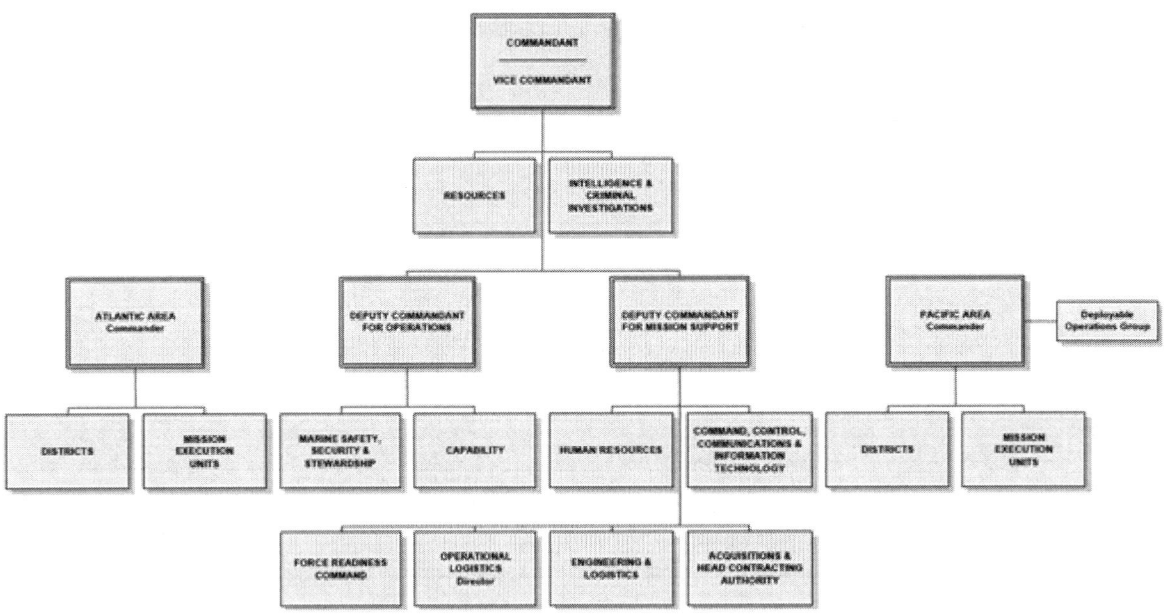

Figure 29-1: United States Coast Guard Organization Chart [6]

Workforce

Mission success is made possible by the combined activities of Coast Guard operational and support personnel. The Coast Guard's missions are accomplished by its forces which have evolved as they have grown and today reflect the uniqueness of its Service. Coast Guardsmen (men and women of the Active, Reserve, Civilian, and Auxiliary) are their most valuable resource. This teamwork is key to ensuring Coast Guard readiness, agility, and operational excellence. They also rely on the help of its many federal, state, local, tribal, and private sector partners. The Coast Guard's full-time workforce is made up of approximately 42,000 active duty military personnel and over 6,800 civilian employees. They are augmented when necessary by small numbers of civilians working under contract. [5, p. 20]

The Coast Guard's full-time workforce is made up of approximately 42,000 active duty military personnel and over 6,800 civilian employees.

The Coast Guard Reserve offers the opportunity to serve in the military part-time while maintaining a separate civilian career. The Reserve provides the Coast Guard highly trained and well qualified personnel for active duty in times of war and national emergency, and for augmentation of Coast Guard forces during natural or man-made disasters or accidents. The Coast Guard Reserve, numbering nearly 8,000 members, provides the Coast Guard surge capacity and flexibility to respond to all threats and all hazards. [5, p. 21]

In addition, the over 32,000 men and women of the uniformed all volunteer U.S. Coast Guard Auxiliary spend thousands of hours each year, often on their personal vessels and aircraft, helping to carry out Coast Guard missions. On some waterways, Auxiliarists are the principal Coast Guard personnel serving the public. They are probably best known for their boating safety classes and courtesy vessel safety checks. However, since 1997 they have supported all Coast Guard missions except those

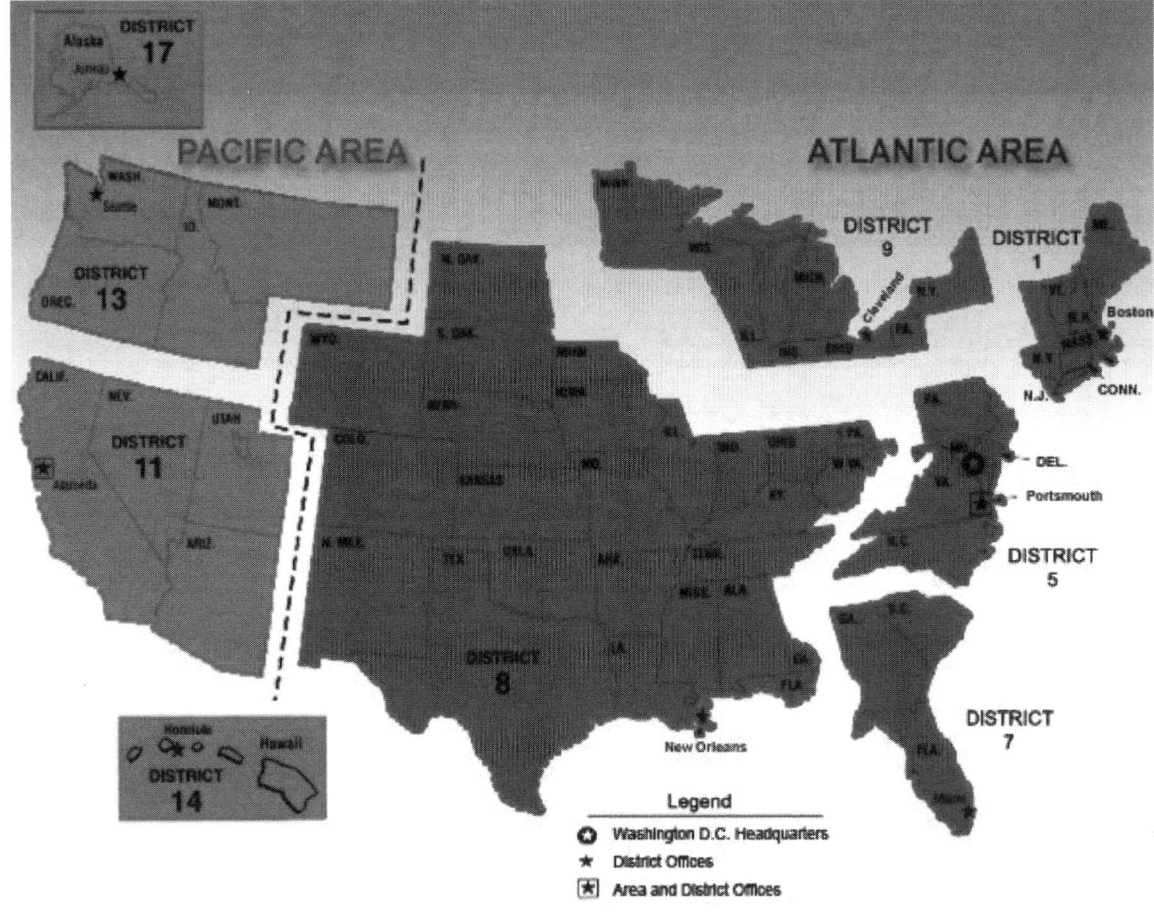

Figure 29-2: United States Coast Guard Districts [7]

involving military operations, law enforcement, and intelligence. The Coast Guard Auxiliary is the only all-volunteer component within the Department of Homeland Security. All together, the Coast Guard manages to carry out its missions with a combined force of approximately 88,800 active, reserve, auxiliarist, and civilian personnel. Figure 1 the organizational structure of the Coast Guard. By comparison, the next smallest U.S. Armed Force is the U.S. Marine Corps with more than 180,000 active duty members alone. [5, p. 21]

Coast Guard forces operate within nine geographic regions encompassing the continental United States, Alaska, and Hawaii.

Service Area

The Coast Guard grew as the nation grew providing its services across several districts based upon the location of each station's home port. Today, the Coast Guard is organized across nine districts as depicted in Figure 2.

America's enduring maritime interests—its reliance on the seas for commerce, sustenance, and defense—has changed little since colonial days. The U.S. Coast Guard exists to uphold and protect these interests. The United States is a maritime nation, with extensive interests in its waters and far beyond. Having 95,000 miles of shoreline and nearly 4.5 million square miles (3.4 million square nautical miles) of Exclusive Economic Zone (EEZ), the United States will always remain tied to the sea. The seas link the nation with world trade and commerce. Utilizing the seas allows the Coast Guard to project military power beyond U.S. shores, protect important U.S. interests, and assist allies and friends. Alternatively, the seas also serve as highways for criminal and terrorist threats that honor no national borders. The Coast Guard protects the nation's territorial integrity; its natural and economic resources; critical infrastructure; and the U.S. Marine Transportation System—from all threats, internal and external, natural and man-made. The MTS is comprised of 25,000 miles of inland, intracoastal, and coastal waterways encompassing nearly 200 locks, 361 commercial sea and river ports, and 1,000 harbor channels; along America's coasts; in international waters; and in any other maritime region where they may be at risk. [5, p. 5]

Coast Guard forces are operationally organized into 1) Shore-Based Forces, 2) Maritime Patrol and Interdiction Forces, and 3) Deployable Specialized Forces.

Operational Force Structure

Coast Guard forces are organized into a maritime trident of forces. Shore-Based Forces are comprised of Sector Commands and specific subordinate units that operate in ports, waterways, and coastal regions of the U.S. and its territories. [5, p. 22] Sector commands include a command and control element and staff (with organic mission support and intelligence functions), and prevention and response elements. Prevention elements conduct marine inspections, waterways management, and marine investigations activities (e.g., aids-to-navigation, issuing safety and security zones, inspecting regulated vessels and facilities, investigating marine casualties). Response elements conduct incident management and enforcement activities. (e.g., SAR, pollution investigation, security patrols, vessel boardings). Shore-based forces execute the broad legal authorities and roles of the Sector Commander, which include:

- Captain of the Port (COTP), with authority over maritime commerce and waterways;
- Federal Maritime Security Coordinator (FMSC), with authority over maritime security;
- Officer in Charge of Marine Inspection (OCMI), with authority over vessel standards compliance;
- Search and Rescue Mission Coordinator (SMC), with authority over rescue operations; and
- Federal On-Scene Coordinator (FOSC), with authority over oil and hazardous material spill response and preparedness.

Subordinate shore-based units include boat stations, aids to navigation teams, marine safety units, vessel traffic services, river, construction, and buoy tenders, and harbor and icebreaking tugs. Although Coast Guard air stations are shore-based commands, all fixed-wing and rotary-wing aircraft that deploy from air stations are categorized as maritime patrol forces because of the capabilities and employment. [5, p. 22]

Maritime Patrol and Interdiction Forces

Maritime patrol forces are comprised of Coast Guard cutters and aircraft and their crews. These assets deploy primarily in coastal and offshore areas to conduct prevention and response operations through patrol, presence, and at-sea operations (e.g., interdiction, boarding, enforcement, search and rescue). Cutters provide armed, persistent presence and command and control capabilities throughout the maritime domain. In addition to conducting Coast Guard operations, cutters project U.S. presence and protect U.S. sovereignty. These forces provide unique capabilities to the Department of Defense (DoD) for joint operations, including warfighting under combatant commander operational control. Cutters also include the polar icebreakers, the nation's only capability for providing access to Polar Regions when restricted by ice. Maritime patrol forces also conduct intelligence, surveillance, and reconnaissance (ISR) activities in support of Coast Guard and national requirements. Maritime patrol forces can also operate in inland areas when required, such as performing mobile command and control, prevention and response operations following a disaster or disruption to normal Sector operations, or when Sectors require augmenting forces. [5, p. 23]

Coast Guard Deployable Specialized Forces engage in a broad range of activities including traditional law enforcement, short notice maritime response to threats delivered from the sea, high-end pollution and hazardous materials response, and military diving operations.

Deployable Specialized Forces

Deployable specialized forces (DSF) are teams of readily available and globally deployable personnel and assets with specialized capabilities, organized into unit types by specialty function and capabilities. [5, p. 24] DSF conduct operations across a broad range of Coast Guard missions where their unique capabilities are required.

The DSF engage in a broad range of activities including traditional law enforcement, short notice maritime response to threats delivered from the sea, high-end pollution and hazardous materials response, and military diving operations. The DSF, which include some reserve units, may be combined with other forces, both within and outside of the Coast Guard, to form integrated, multi-agency force packages. [5, p. 25] These forces include:

- Port Security Units
- Maritime Safety and Security Teams
- Maritime Security Response Teams
- Law Enforcement Detachments
- National Strike Force
- Military Divers

Conclusion

The Coast Guard's ability to fulfill its three broad roles— maritime safety, maritime security, and maritime stewardship— makes them truly a unique instrument of national policy and well-being. More than simply "guarding the coast," the Coast Guard helps safeguard the global maritime commons. To meet the challenges of the dynamic maritime environment, the Coast Guard executes a layered, security-in-depth concept of operations, built upon a multi-dimensional framework of authorities, capabilities, competencies, and partnerships to apply its core operational concept of Prevention—Response. Through this approach, the Coast Guard seeks to prevent dangerous or illicit maritime activities, and if undesirable or unlawful events do occur—whether deliberate or accidental—to rapidly and effectively respond in order to protect the United States, minimize the impact, and recover.

Challenge Your Understanding

The following questions are designed to challenge your understanding of the material presented in this chapter. Some questions may require additional research outside this book in order to provide a complete answer.

1. What is the military mission of the United States Coast Guard
2. What is the homeland security mission of the United States Coast Guard
3. Which USCG role involves inspecting vessels, offshore drilling units, and marine facilities?
4. Which USCG role involves enforcing the nation's laws and controlling its borders?
5. Which USCG role involves protecting the nation's fisheries and maintaining its navigable waterways?
6. How big is the USCG in comparison to the NYPD?
7. Which USCG district might be called upon to rescue fishermen casting for king crab?
8. Which USCG district might be called upon to board and inspect the Michipicoten?
9. What is the Captain of the Port's responsibility with respect to oil spills?
10. What can USCG Deployable Specialized Forces do?

Chapter 30

Transportation & Security Administration

Learning Outcomes

Careful study of this chapter will help a student do the following:

- Explain the mission of the organization.
- Describe some key components of the organization.
- Discuss some of the work of the organization.

"On November 19, 2001, the President signed into law the Aviation and Transportation Security Act of 2001. The act established a series of challenging but important milestones toward achieving a secure air travel system. More broadly, however, the act fundamentally changed the way transportation security will be performed and managed in the United States."

• 2002 National Strategy for Homeland Security

Introduction

The Transportation Security Administration was created in response to the 9/11 attacks as part of the Aviation and Transportation Security Act (ATSA, Public Law 107-71) passed by the U.S. Congress and signed into law by President George W. Bush on November 19, 2001 which among other things established the new Transportation Security Administration (TSA).

The Transportation Security Administration (TSA) was created in the wake of 9/11 to strengthen the security of the nation's transportation systems while ensuring the freedom of movement for people and commerce. Within a year, TSA assumed responsibility for security at the nation's airports and deployed a federal workforce to meet Congressional deadlines for screening all commercial airline passengers and baggage. In March 2003, TSA transferred from the Department of Transportation to the Department of Homeland Security. [1]

The TSA employs a risk-based strategy to secure U.S. transportation systems, working closely with stakeholders in aviation, rail, transit, highway, and pipeline sectors, as well as the partners in the law enforcement and intelligence community. The agency continuously sets the standard for excellence in transportation security through its people, processes, technologies and use of intelligence to drive operations.

The TSA employs over 50,000 full-time employees charged with protecting U.S. transportation systems and the traveling public who serve on the front lines at more than 450 U.S. airports as well as across all modes of transportation in the U.S. 100 percent of all checked and carry-on baggage is screened for explosives and the TSA continually assesses intelligence to develop countermeasures in order to enhance its multiple layers of security at airports and onboard aircraft. TSA also secures and safeguards mass transit and railroad operations through a variety of programs. By performing baseline and collaborative risk assessments in the mass transit and passenger railroad domains, TSA is able to engage state and local partners to identify ways to reduce vulnerabilities, assess risk, and improve security efforts. [2] Ultimately, the TSA looks for bombs at checkpoints in airports, inspects rail cars, patrols subways with its law enforcement partners, and works to make all modes of transportation safe.

Background

The Transportation Security Administration was created in response to the 9/11 attacks as part of the Aviation and Transportation Security Act (ATSA, Public Law 107-71) passed by the U.S. Congress and signed into law by President George W. Bush on November 19, 2001 which among other things established the new Transportation Security Administration within the Department of Transportation. Under the Homeland Security Act of 2002, Public Law 107-296, TSA transferred to DHS in March, 2003. [3] The organization was charged with developing policies to protect U.S. transportation to include airport security, aircraft hijacking, and other forms of transportation including highways, railroads, buses, mass transit systems, pipelines and ports.

Mission

TSA's mission is to protect the nation's transportation systems to ensure freedom of movement for people and commerce.

The TSA's mission is to protect the nation's transportation systems to ensure freedom of movement for people and commerce. The TSA, an agency in the Department of Homeland Security, is responsible for protecting the nation's transportation networks from attack. Specifically, it safeguards airports and airplanes, mass-transit systems, highways, seaports, railroads and buses. Ultimately, the TSA's vision is to provide the most effective transportation security while serving as a high performing counter-terrorism organization. [4]

Organization

As a federal operation, the TSA is a component of the Department of Homeland Security promoting confidence by deploying personnel to detect, deter, and defeat hostile acts targeting all modes of transportation in the U.S. With state, local and regional partners, the TSA oversees security for highways, railroads, buses, mass transit systems, pipelines, ports, and over 450 U.S. airports. [1]

The TSA's leadership and organization is comprised of the Administrator and Deputy Administrator, along with various administrative, law enforcement, and security operations personnel.

Given that the bulk of the TSA's efforts are in aviation security, the TSA employs Transportation Security Officers, colloquially known as screeners, as well as Federal Air Marshals, Transportation Security Specialists and Transportation Security Inspectors, and oversees the training and testing of explosives detection canine teams with very specific job responsibilities:

- The Transportation Security Officer (TSO), also known as a screener, performs security screening of persons and property and controls entry and exit points within an airport. They also practice surveillance of several areas before and beyond the checkpoints with specialized programs. [5, p. 6]
- Behavioral Detection Officers are personnel who, as part of the Screening of Passengers by Observation Techniques (SPOT) program, are trained to serve as an additional layer of security in airports by providing a non-intrusive means of identifying individuals who may pose a risk of terrorism or criminal activity. In behavior-based screening, trained personnel attempt to identify anomalous behaviors by observing passengers and comparing what they see to an established behavioral baseline of other passengers developed in the same general location and within the same timeframe. [5, p. 17]
- The Federal Air Marshal (FAM) is a federal law enforcement officer who, while blending in with passengers, are tasked with detecting, deterring, and defeating terrorist or other criminal hostile acts targeting U.S. air carriers, airports, passengers, crew, and when necessary, other transportation modes within the U.S.'s general transportation systems. [6]
- Transportation Security Inspectors (TSIs) have the authority to enforce security regulations and to help stakeholders improve their security in the surface modes, which include the mass transit, freight rail, highway, and pipeline sectors. [7, p. 2]
- The TSA's National Explosives Detection Canine Team Program prepares dogs and handlers to serve as mobile teams that can quickly locate and identify dangerous materials that may present a threat to transportation systems. [8, p. 15]

TSA employs Transportation Security Officers (TSOs), Federal Air Marshals (FAMs), Transportation Security Specialists (TSSs) and Transportation Security Inspectors (TSIs), and oversees the training and testing of explosives detection canine teams.

After the 2004 Madrid train bombings, which killed 191 people and wounded 1,800 more, TSA developed the Visible Intermodal Prevention and Response (VIPR) program to augment the security of any mode of transportation at any location within the United States. These teams are comprised of people from each of the above areas, where applicable, that are deployed at the request of local, state and federal law enforcement to support their efforts and enhance the security presence during specific alert periods or major high-profile events. [5, p. 17]

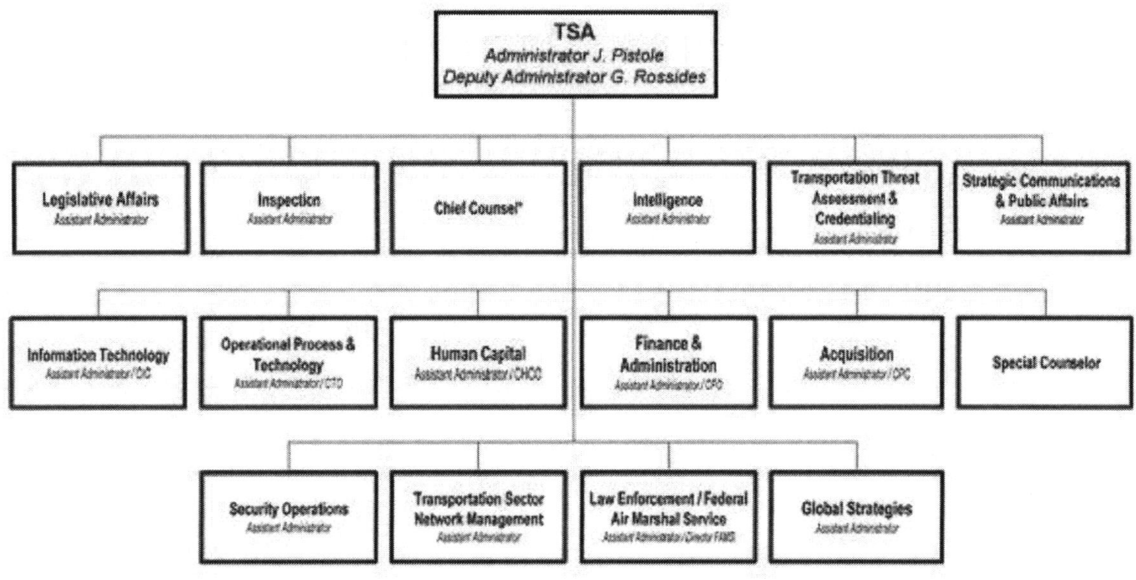

Figure 30-1: TSA Organization Chart 2010 [9]

Operations

The U.S. transportation systems accommodate: approximately 660 million domestic and international aviation passengers per year; 751 million passengers traveling on buses each year; more than 10 billion passenger trips on mass transit per year; 24 million students daily on school buses traveling more than 4 million miles annually; nearly 800,000 shipments of hazardous materials transported every day (95 percent by truck); more than 140,000 miles of railroad track; 3.9 million miles of roads; 604,000 bridges each spanning over 20 feet; 366 highway tunnels each over 300 feet in length; and nearly 2.6 million miles of pipeline. [10, p. 57]

The focus of the TSA is to identify, prioritize, and mitigate risks, ultimately minimizing the impact of potential incidents. Information sharing among agencies and stakeholders – including intelligence information – is a cornerstone of the risk management model.

The focus of the TSA is to identify, prioritize, and mitigate risks, ultimately minimizing the impact of potential incidents. Information sharing among agencies and stakeholders – including intelligence information – is a cornerstone of the risk management model.

The TSA recognizes the unique attributes of each transportation mode and works to ensure passenger and cargo security and to preserve public confidence in the security of the U.S. transportation system overall. The TSA's specific responsibilities include:

- Ensuring a thorough and efficient screening of all aviation passengers and baggage;
- Promoting confidence by deploying Federal Air Marshals to detect, deter, and defeat hostile acts targeting air carriers;

- Managing security risks of the surface transportation systems by establishing clear lines of communication and collaborative working relationships with federal, local, and private stakeholders, providing support and programmatic direction, conducting on-site inspections, and developing security programs; and
- Developing and implementing more efficient, reliable, integrated, and cost effective terrorist-related screening programs. [10, pp. 57-58]

Service to the Public

The TSA's responsibilities, which span all modes of transportation, ensure the provision of proactive security measures and a quick and efficient response to any threat, including terrorist incidents and natural disasters. Public confidence in the security of the nation's transportation systems ensures the continued success and growth of the industry. TSA engages the public in the security of the transportation system by encouraging them to report suspicious behavior. TSA also strives to provide excellent customer service to all travelers. TSA provides information to all travelers through its TSA Contact Center, Customer Service Managers in airports nationwide, the TSA website and blog, and Twitter and other social media outlets. Additionally, TSA Cares is a dedicated toll free number established to assist passengers or their loved ones with disabilities, medical conditions, or other special circumstances to prepare for the screening process.

TSA uses a layered approach for airport security, beginning with passenger checkpoints, and including intelligence gathering and analysis, checking passenger manifests against watch lists, random canine team searches at airports, federal air marshals, federal flight deck officers and more security measures both visible and not visible to the public.

Aviation Security

The TSA employs several programs and initiatives to achieve its goal of security in all modes of transportation. Using the layered security approach to ensure the security of the traveling public and the nation's transportation system, the TSA not only uses passenger checkpoints at airports, but includes intelligence gathering and analysis, checking passenger manifests against watch lists, random canine team searches at airports, federal air marshals, federal flight deck officers and more security measures both visible and not visible to the public.

As an additional layer of security, the TSA Secure Flight program conducts passenger watch list matching for 100 percent of covered U.S. aircraft operator and foreign air carrier flight. The program is designed to identify any passengers who may pose a threat to aviation or national security and designate them for enhanced screening or, as appropriate, prohibit them from boarding an aircraft. This program identifies individuals who may pose a threat to aviation or national security and designates them for enhanced screening or, as appropriate, prohibits them from boarding an aircraft. Although the TSA does not conduct passenger screening abroad, it requires airports that serve as the last point of departure to the U.S. to meet stringent security standards. The TSA assesses the security programs of all U.S. and foreign air carriers that serve last points of departure. [11]

Security Screening

TSA has evolved from a one-size-fits-all security screening approach to a risk-based, intelligence-driven strategy designed to improve both security and the passenger experience. This approach permits the TSA to provide expedited screening for trusted travelers and to focus on high-risk and unknown passengers at security checkpoints. TSA officers may use risk-based security measures to identify, mitigate and resolve potential threats at the airport security checkpoint. These officers may ask questions about passengers' travel to include identity, travel itinerary and property. The TSA may use a variety of screening processes, including random screening, regardless of whether an alarm is triggered. In addition, the TSA uses random and unpredictable security measures throughout the airport and no individual is guaranteed expedited screening.

TSA has evolved from a one-size-fits-all security screening approach to a risk-based, intelligence-driven strategy designed to improve both security and the passenger experience.

TSA Pre® is an expedited security screening program connecting travelers departing from the United States with smarter security and a better air travel experience. Passengers considered low-risk who qualify for the program can receive expedited screening either as a member of the program or another specific trusted traveler group.

TSA SPOT

A 2012 article in the New York Times criticized the Transportation Security Administration's behavior detection program as one of racial profiling. The article stated that over 30 federal officers from Boston Logan International Airport reportedly expressed concerns that the program targets Middle Easterners, blacks, Hispanics, and other minorities as a race-based program rather than a behavioral-based program. The TSA responded by stating that the agency "in no way encourages or tolerates profiling and bans singling out passengers based on nationality, race, ethnicity or religion." Yet, officers indicated that minorities are frequently targeted in response to the pressure from management to attain a certain threshold of referrals to law enforcement agencies and to demonstrate that the program is producing results. The TSA indicated that the behavioral detection program is designed to assess passengers "for unusual activity, but also to speak individually with each passenger and gauge their reactions while asking about their trip or for other information. The assessors look for inconsistencies in the answers and other signs of unusual behavior, like avoiding eye contact, sweating or fidgeting...a passenger considered to be acting suspiciously can be pulled from the line and subjected to more intensive questioning". [5]

TSA began deploying the SPOT program in fiscal year 2007—and has since spent about $900 million—to identify persons who may pose a risk to aviation security through the observation of behavioral indicators. In May 2010, GAO concluded, among other things, that TSA deployed SPOT without validating its scientific basis and SPOT lacked performance measures. The GAO recommended that Congress should consider the absence of scientifically validated evidence for using behavioral indicators to identify threats to aviation security when assessing the potential benefits and cost in making future funding decisions for aviation security. GAO included this matter because DHS did not concur with GAO's recommendation that TSA limit future funding for these activities until it can provide such evidence, in part because DHS disagreed with GAO's analysis of indicators. [6]

Screening Technology

TSA uses millimeter wave advanced imaging technology and walk-through metal detectors to screen passengers. Millimeter wave advanced imaging technology safely screens passengers without physical contact for metallic and non-metallic threats, including weapons and explosives, which may be concealed under clothing. Passengers have the option to request a pat-down as an alternative. The advanced imaging technology is considered safe and meets national health and safety standards. This technology uses non-ionizing radio-frequency energy in the millimeter spectrum with no known adverse health effects. It does not use X-ray technology. The TSA has strict privacy standards when using advanced imaging technology to protect passengers' privacy. Advanced imaging technology uses automated target recognition software that eliminates passenger-specific images and instead auto-detects potential threats by indicating their location on a generic outline of a person. [12]

TSA uses millimeter wave advanced imaging technology and walk-through metal detectors to screen passengers. Millimeter wave advanced imaging technology safely screens passengers without physical contact for metallic and non-metallic threats, including weapons and explosives, which may be concealed under clothing.

Pat-down Screening

If a passenger cannot or chooses not to be screened by advanced imaging technology or a walk-through metal detector, they will undergo a pat-down procedure instead. Passengers may also undergo a pat-down procedure if they alarm the screening equipment and/or at random. [12]

DHS Traveler Redress Inquiry Program (TRIP)

The Department of Homeland Security Traveler Redress Inquiry Program (DHS TRIP) is a single point of contact for individuals who have inquiries or seek resolution regarding difficulties they experienced during their travel screening at transportation hubs—like airports and train stations—or crossing U.S. borders. This includes:

- watch list issues;
- screening problems at ports of entry; or
- situations where travelers believe they have been unfairly or incorrectly delayed, denied boarding or identified for additional screening at U.S. transportation hubs.

DHS TRIP is part of an effort by the departments of State and Homeland Security to welcome legitimate travelers while still securing the nation from those who want to do harm. People who have been denied or delayed airline boarding; have been denied or delayed entry into or exit from the U.S. at a port of entry or border crossing; or have been repeatedly referred to additional (secondary) screening can file an inquiry to seek redress. [13]

Aviation Training Programs

The TSA provides flight crew training programs to prepare them for potential threat conditions that may occur onboard an aircraft. These programs include the Federal Flight Deck Officer Program which authorizes flight crew members to use firearms to defend against an act of criminal violence and air piracy while attempting to gain control of an aircraft; the Crew Member Self Defense Training Program which provides 4-hours of training to prepare active crew members of all domestic scheduled carriers for potential physical altercations both on and off the aircraft; and the Federal Air Marshal Service provides training of armed security officers required on approved flights associated with restoration of general aviation and charter flight operations at Washington Reagan National Airport (DCA). The training is designed to better prepare the qualified active, retired and former law enforcement officer to react within the unique general aircraft environment in the event of an in-flight crisis on approved flights into DCA. [14]

TSA uses a multi-layered approach to air cargo security, including enhanced screening requirements for known and established shippers, explosive detection canine teams, and covert tests and no-notice inspections of cargo operations in order to promote the efficient and secure movement of goods.

Alien Flight Student Program

The TSA conducts Security Threat Assessments (STA) on individuals who are not U.S. citizens or nationals and other individuals designated by TSA seeking flight instruction or recurrent training from Federal Aviation Administration (FAA)-certified flight training providers to ensure that aliens and other individuals designated by TSA seeking such training do not pose a threat to aviation or national security. [15, p. 1]

Cargo Screening

Securing the global supply chain, while ensuring its smooth functioning, is essential to national security and economic prosperity. This vital system provides the goods that feed the nation's domestic critical infrastructures and supports the American way of life. The Department of Homeland Security uses a multi-layered approach to air cargo security, including enhanced screening requirements for known and established shippers, explosive detection canine teams, and covert tests and no-notice inspections of cargo operations in order to promote the efficient and secure movement of goods. [16]

Other nations worldwide also rely upon the goods transported by the global supply chain system – in that sense it is a global asset that all stakeholders must collaboratively work to strengthen. The international community has also made significant progress in protecting the global supply chain through Program Global Shield, which was launched in 2011 in collaboration with the World Customs Organization, the United Nations Office on Drugs and Crime, and Interpol. [16]

In conjunction with the U.S. Customs and Border Protection Container Security Initiative (CSI), the TSA is responsible for ensuring the security of cargo placed aboard airplanes and particularly focuses on passenger-carrying planes. As required by the 9/11 Act, 100 percent of all cargo transported on passenger aircraft departing U.S. airports is now screened commensurate with screening of passenger checked baggage and international inbound air cargo is more secure than it has ever been, with 100 percent of identified high risk cargo being screened. [16]

Mass Transit and Rail Security

The Transportation Security Administration is responsible for security in all modes of transportation, including mass transit and passenger rail systems.

The Transportation Security Administration is responsible for security in all modes of transportation, including mass transit and passenger rail systems. The U.S. passenger rail network is critical to the American way of life, transporting more than 12 million commuters each day. Passenger rail systems face a dynamic landscape of potential natural disasters, accidents, and terrorist attacks. Since 1995, there have been more than 250 terrorist attacks worldwide against rail targets, resulting in nearly 900 deaths and more than 6,000 injuries. The Transportation Security Administration, the Federal Transit Administration, the Federal Railroad Administration, and the Federal Emergency Management Agency share responsibilities, programs, and resource investments to mass transit and passenger rail emergencies. [17, p. 1]

- The Baseline Assessment and Security Enhancement (BASE) program is a voluntary program implemented by Transportation Security Inspectors in the Office of Security Operations. Inspectors review documents, question passenger rail personnel, and observe security measures within the transit system. The BASE program seeks to identify program gaps or weaknesses and develop best practices applicable to all passenger rail systems. [17, p. 3]
- The Public Transportation Emergency Preparedness Workshops (Connecting Communities) integrate mass transit and passenger rail security, operations, and emergency management officials with law enforcement and emergency response partners in their operating areas. The goal of the workshops is to unite passenger rail stakeholders from a variety of organizations, including first responders, to foster dialogue, improve planning efforts, review past experiences, analyze best practices, and identify assets and resources to enhance overall interoperability and response during passenger rail incidents. [17, p. 3]

- The Training Matrix and Recommended Courses List is coordinated by the Office of Transportation Sector Network Management to support mass transit and passenger rail agencies' security and emergency management training. The list includes recommended instruction in security awareness, behavior recognition, immediate-emergency response, the National Incident Management System, and Operations Control Center Readiness. The TSGP provides funds to owners and operators of mass transit and passenger rail systems to protect the critical surface transportation infrastructure and the traveling public from acts of terrorism, major disasters, and other emergencies. [17, p. 4]
- The Intermodal Security Training and Exercise Program (I-STEP) is designed to improve the intermodal transportation industry's ability to prepare for and respond to transportation security incidents by increasing awareness, improving processes, creating partnerships, and delivering training exercises to mass transit and passenger rail stakeholders. Through the I-STEP, TSA employs multi-phased workshops, table top exercises, and working groups to integrate mass transit and passenger rail agencies with regional law enforcement and emergency response partners to expand and enhance coordinated deterrent and incident management capabilities. [17, p. 4]

Conclusion

Established in 2001, the Transportation Security Administration (TSA) employs a layered, risk-based approach to secure U.S. transportation systems, working closely with stakeholders in aviation, rail, transit, highway, and pipeline sectors, as well as the partners in the law enforcement and intelligence community. The agency continuously sets the standard for excellence in transportation security through its people, processes, technologies and use of intelligence to drive operations. The TSA is committed to evolving its systems to enhance the safety of the traveling public as well as individual passenger experiences whenever possible. The agency's risk-based, intelligence-driven approach to aviation security is evolving from what may have seemed like a one-size-fits-all approach and is establishing TSA as a high performing counterterrorism agency. The TSA is now focusing resources on those the agency knows the least about, and using intelligence in better ways to inform the screening process. This risk-mitigation strategy makes both good business and security sense. [1]

Challenge Your Understanding

The following questions are designed to challenge your understanding of the material presented in this chapter. Some questions may require additional research outside this book in order to provide a complete answer.

1. What is the mission of the Transportation Security Administration?
2. Which TSA personnel, commonly known as "screeners", perform security checks at airports?
3. Which TSA personnel have law enforcement authority, yet travel incognito and try to avoid recognition?
4. List and describe the different layers of security found at an airport.
5. List and describe two benefits and two risks of the TSA Pre® program.
6. What is the primary advantage of using advanced imaging technology at airports compared to magnetometers?
7. What can you do if you are unfairly or incorrectly delayed or denied boarding at an airport?
8. What methods does TSA generally employ to screen air cargo?
9. Which TSA program performs voluntary security assessments for passenger rail owners/operators?
10. Which TSA program conducts workshops uniting passenger rail stakeholders from different organizations?

Chapter 27

U.S. Customs & Border Protection

Learning Outcomes

Careful study of this chapter will help a student do the following:

- Explain the mission of the organization.
- Describe some key components of the organization.
- Discuss some of the work of the organization.

"The border and immigration system of the United States must remain a visible manifestation of our belief in freedom, democracy, global economic growth, and the rule of law, yet serve equally well as a vital element of counterterrorism."

- 2004 9/11 Commission Report

Introduction

The U.S. Customs and Border Protection (CBP), within the Department of Homeland Security (DHS), is responsible for facilitating international trade while keeping terrorists and weapons of mass destruction from entering the United States.

CBP is the primary agency charged with monitoring, regulating, and facilitating the flow of goods through U.S. ports of entry (POEs), and protecting the nation's borders.

Background

CBP traces its origins to the Directorate of Border and Transportation Security (BTS) originally stipulated in the 2002 Homeland Security Act. In late January 2003, as components of DHS were being transferred to the department's operational control, President George W. Bush modified his original reorganization plan for DHS to reconfigure the functions of certain border security agencies into two new components — the Bureau of Customs and Border Protection and the Bureau of Immigration and Customs Enforcement — within the Border and Transportation Security Directorate. As part of his Second Stage Review (2SR), Secretary Chertoff dismantled BTS to form a new Office of Operations Coordination (OOC). As a consequence, CBP became an independent bureau reporting directly to the Secretary of Homeland Security. [1]

Mission

CBP is the primary agency charged with monitoring, regulating, and facilitating the flow of goods through U.S. ports of entry (POEs), and protecting the nation's borders. CBP's policies are designed to (1) ensure the smooth flow of imported cargo through U.S. POEs; (2) enforce trade and customs laws designed to protect U.S. consumers and business and to collect customs revenue; and (3) prevent weapons of mass destruction, illegal drugs, and other contraband from entering the United States—a complex and difficult mission. [2, p. ii]

International trade is a critical component of the U.S. economy, with U.S. goods trade amounting to about $4 trillion in 2014, with merchandise imports of $2.4 trillion and exports of $1.6 trillion. The efficient flow of legally traded goods in and out of the United States is thus a vital element of the country's economic security. While U.S. trade in imports depends on the smooth flow of legal cargo through U.S. ports of entry, the goal of trade facilitation often competes with two additional goals: enforcement of U.S. trade laws and import security. How to strike the appropriate balance among these three goals is a fundamental question at the heart of U.S. import policies. [2, p. 1]

Striking the appropriate balance among competing import policy goals is made more difficult due to the volume and complexity of trade inflows. U.S. Customs and Border Protection, the agency charged with managing the import process at the border, admitted about 30.4 million import entries per year through over 300 U.S. POEs, in fiscal year (FY) 2013. The largest volume of imports comes through land (truck and rail) and maritime flows, which together account for over 25 million shipping containers per year. Air cargo consists mainly of lower volume, higher value goods. [2, p. 1]

International trade is a critical component of the U.S. economy, with U.S. goods trade amounting to about $4 trillion in 2014, with merchandise imports of $2.4 trillion and exports of $1.6 trillion. The efficient flow of legally traded goods in and out of the United States is thus a vital element of the country's economic security.

CBP's current import strategy emphasizes a risk management approach that segments importers into higher and lower risk pools and focuses trade enforcement and import security procedures on higher-risk imports, while expediting lower-risk flows. CBP's "multi-layered" risk management approach means that security screening and enforcement occur at multiple points in the import process, beginning before goods are loaded in foreign ports (pre-entry) and continuing long after the time goods have been admitted into the United States (post-entry). [2, p. ii]

Border enforcement is a core element of the Department of Homeland Security's effort to control unauthorized migration and importation of contraband, with the U.S. Border Patrol (USBP) within the U.S. Customs and Border Protection as the lead agency along most of the border. Border enforcement has been an ongoing subject of congressional interest since the 1970s, when illegal immigration to the United States first registered as a serious national problem and received additional attention after the terrorist attacks of 2001. [3, p. ii]

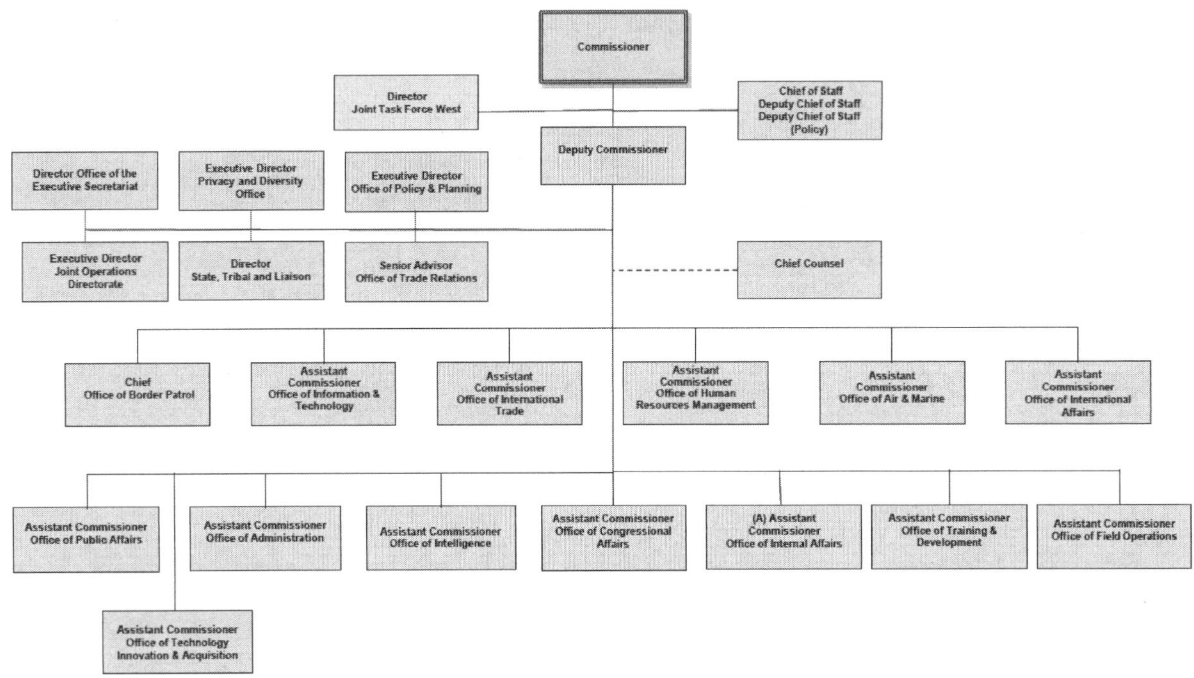

Figure 31-1: CBP Organization Chart [6]

Organization

CBP is headed by a Commissioner who reports to the Secretary of Homeland Security. Working for the Commissioner are 14 assistant commissioners who oversee CBP law enforcement, regulatory, intelligence, technology, and other support efforts. The office of the commissioner also oversees executive offices that provide an array of expertise from policy and planning to trade relations and privacy and civil rights. [4]

Office of Administration. The Office of Administration is headed by an Assistant Commissioner, who is the Chief Financial Officer (CFO) and the Chief Administrative Officer (CAO) for the U.S. Customs and Border Protection. This office is responsible for administering the broad range of financial management activities delineated under the CFO Act of 1990, including accounting, budgeting, procurement, logistics, financial systems, policy, planning, and audit oversight. An annual Accountability Report is prepared and submitted to the Department of Homeland Security Pursuant to the CFO Act, the Government Performance and Results Act of 1993 (GPRA), and the Government Management Reform Act of 1994 (GMRA), this report includes the annual audited financial statements and auditors' opinion. The report also includes: financial analysis; a description of the effectiveness of management controls; program performance results related to agency mission, goals, and objectives; and an assessment of data validity and reliability in support of performance measures. [5]

Air and Marine Operations. The mission of Air and Marine Operations is to protect the American people and Nation's critical infrastructure through the coordinated use of integrated air and marine forces to detect, interdict and prevent acts of terrorism and the unlawful movement of people, illegal drugs and other contraband toward or across the borders of the United States. [5]

United States Border Patrol. The United States Border Patrol, headed by the Chief, U.S. Border Patrol, is the headquarters of the primary federal law enforcement organization responsible for preventing terrorists and terrorist weapons from entering the United States between official U.S. Customs and Border Protection ports of entry. Their traditional mission is to enforce immigration laws and to detect, interdict and apprehend those who attempt to illegally enter or smuggle people or contraband across U.S. borders between official ports of entry. The Border Patrol has a workforce of over 21,000 agents assigned to patrol the more than 6,000 miles of America's land borders. The Border Patrol has an operating budget of $1.4 billion, which provides for operations coordinated by 20 sector offices. [5]

The U.S. Border Patrol, headed by the Chief, U.S. Border Patrol, is the headquarters of the primary federal law enforcement organization responsible for preventing terrorists and terrorist weapons from entering the United States between official U.S. Customs and Border Protection ports of entry.

Office of Congressional Affairs. The Office of Congressional Affairs, headed by an Assistant Commissioner, is responsible for advising CBP managers on legislative and congressional matters; and for assisting members of Congress and their staffs in understanding current and proposed CBP programs. [5]

Office of Field Operations (OFO). The Office of Field Operations is the largest component in CBP and is responsible for border security—including antiterrorism, immigration, anti-smuggling, trade compliance, and agriculture protection—while simultaneously facilitating the lawful trade and travel at U.S. ports of entry. OFO is headed by an Assistant Commissioner who is responsible for overseeing the operations of 20 major field offices, 328 ports of entry, and 70 locations in over 40 countries internationally, with a staff of more than 28,000 employees, and an operating budget of $3.2 billion. [5]

Office of Human Resources Management. The Office of Human Resources Management is responsible for providing human resources support within CBP. It promotes and enables mission accomplishment through human capital planning and utilization; strategic leadership to CBP employees; efficient processes and practices which meet customer's operational needs; a safe work environment; advocacy for fair treatment; effective delivery of services (including filling positions, providing employee services and benefits, processing personnel actions and facilitating workforce effectiveness). [5]

Office of Information and Technology (OIT). The Office of Information and Technology, headed by an Assistant Commissioner, is responsible for implementation and support of information technology, research and development functions, and automation and technological strategies for meeting mission-related needs. Specifically, the Office is responsible for automated information systems, management of the research and development functions and all forensic and laboratory support of the agency. OIT personnel manage all computer and related resources including all operational aspects of the Computer Security Program; establish requirements for computer interfaces between U.S. Customs and Border Protection and various trade groups and government agencies; and manage matters related to automated import processing and systems development. OIT personnel are responsible for managing all aspects of tactical communications, including the 24x7 operations of the National Law Enforcement Communications Center. [5]

The Office of Intelligence is a coordinating facilitator that integrates U.S. Customs and Border Protection's diverse intelligence capabilities into a single cohesive intelligence enterprise.

Office of Intelligence (OI). The Office of Intelligence is a coordinating facilitator that integrates U.S. Customs and Border Protection's diverse intelligence capabilities into a single cohesive intelligence enterprise. OI supports CBP's mission through a multi-layered approach that includes an intelligence field support capability, a strategic analysis capability focusing on terrorist, geo-political and economic threats, a daily CBP executive leadership briefing capability and intelligence, surveillance and reconnaissance capabilities as such pertain to the National Border Geospatial Intelligence Strategy, the Law Enforcement Technical Collections (LETC) initiative and the Confidential Human Source (CHS) initiative. [5]

Office of Internal Affairs (IA). Office of Internal Affairs, headed by an Assistant Commissioner, has oversight authority for all aspects of CBP operations, personnel and facilities. IA is responsible for ensuring compliance with all CBP-wide programs and policies relating to corruption, misconduct, or mismanagement and for executing the internal security, integrity, and management inspections program. Through the national headquarters in Washington, D.C., and strategically located regional field offices, IA investigates criminal and serious administrative misconduct by CBP employees. IA also screens potential CBP employees for suitability; educates employees concerning ethical standards and integrity responsibilities; evaluates physical security threats to CBP employees, facilities, and sensitive information; and inspects CBP operations and processes for managerial effectiveness and improvements. [5]

Office of International Affairs (INA). The Office of International Affairs is responsible for coordinating and supporting foreign initiatives, programs and activities within CBP. INA strives to extend U.S. borders by implementing programs and initiatives that promote anti-terrorism, global border security, non-proliferation, export controls, immigration and capacity building. INA focuses on international cooperation and strengthening multi- and bi-lateral relationships to achieve international agreements and joint efforts that both facilitate and secure legitimate trade. INA promotes expansion of the World Customs Organization (WCO) Framework of Standards for supply chain security and facilitation by providing targeted countries with training and advisory support through programs such as, Capacity Building and Export Control and Border Security (EXBS). INA provides in-country advisory support for broad-based customs reform and modernization and ensures CBP is represented at overseas posts and influencing policy throughout the world. [5]

Office of International Trade (OT). The Office of International Trade consolidates the trade policy, program development, and compliance measurement functions of CBP into one office. The Office provides uniformity and clarity for the development of CBP's national strategy to facilitate legitimate trade and manages the design and implementation of results-driven strategic initiatives of trade compliance and enforcement. It directs national enforcement responses through effective targeting of goods crossing the border as well as strict, swift punitive actions against companies participating in predatory trade practices. Through coordination with international partners and other U.S. government agencies it directs the enforcement of intellectual property rights, the identification of risks to detect and prevent the importation of contaminated agricultural or food products and the enforcement of free trade agreement eligibility. By promoting trade facilitation through partnership programs, the Office of Trade will streamline the flow of legitimate shipments and foster corporate self-governance as a means of achieving compliance with trade laws and regulations. A risk-based audit program is used to respond to allegations of commercial fraud and to conduct corporate reviews of internal controls to ensure importers comply with trade laws and regulations. Finally, the Office of Trade provides the legal tools to promote facilitation and compliance with customs, trade and border security requirements through the issuance of all CBP regulations, legally binding rulings and decisions, informed compliance publications and structured programs for external CBP training and outreach on international trade laws and CBP regulations. [5]

The Office of International Affairs promotes expansion of the World Customs Organization (WCO) Framework of Standards for supply chain security.

Office of Public Affairs (OPA). The Office of Public Affairs, headed by an Assistant Commissioner, communicates CBP's mission and operations. OPA continually informs the agency's chief stakeholders, the American public, through media outreach and public awareness campaigns conducted via media events, news, video and photography as well as the public website CBP.gov, informational brochures, and a national customer service call center to address public questions and complaints. OPA also provides continual information to the CBP workforce through an intranet site and frequent leadership messages. A regular news magazine, Frontline, is developed for CBP personnel and stakeholders throughout the nation and abroad. OPA acts as a conduit for information to and guidance from the Department of Homeland Security. [5]

Office of Technology Innovation and Acquisition (OTIA). The Office of Technology Innovation and Acquisition is responsible for two major functions essential to the future effectiveness of CBP. First, it ensures all of CBP's technology efforts are properly and innovatively focused on the mission and are well integrated across CBP. Secondly, it strengthens CBP's expertise and effectiveness in acquisition and program management of contractor-delivered products and services. The office provides the necessary training to its acquisition workforce, administers policy and acquisition oversight for all program management offices (including those established to manage Level 1, 2 and 3 acquisition programs) across CBP, and develops standard requirements coordination processes for CBP. OTIA is also exploring innovation and its critical role in inspiring and catalyzing a culture of innovation across all of CBP. [5]

Office of Training and Development (OTD). The Office of Training and Development is responsible for centralized leadership and direction of all Customs and Border Protection training programs. OTD ensures that all training efforts support the CBP mission and strategic goals, meet the needs of a diverse and dispersed workforce, and contribute to measurable outcomes and results. OTD establishes standards and policies for designing, developing, delivering, and evaluating training. The Office directly executes career development programs, basic and advanced training to all occupations (e.g., anti-terrorism training to CBP Officers, Border Patrol Agents, and other occupations), and management and executive development programs. OTD develops and implements the annual training plan for the agency. OTD defines and implements evaluation measures, data collection processes, and inspection methods for ongoing assessment of all CBP training programs. OTD is responsible for the continuous improvement and expansion of CBP learning capabilities. To accomplish its organizational mission and strategic plan, OTD has eight divisions – Training Production and Standards Division, Use of Force Policy Division, Leadership and Organization Development Division, Advanced Training Center, Operations Division, U.S. Border Patrol Academy, CBP Field Operations Academy, and the CBP Canine Program Headquarters. [5]

Office of Chief Counsel. The Chief Counsel is the chief legal officer of CBP and reports to the General Counsel of the Department of Homeland Security through the Assistant General Counsel, Borders and Transportation Security. The Chief Counsel serves as the Ethics Officer for the organization and is the principal legal advisor to the CBP commissioner and its officers. The Office of the Chief Counsel provides legal advice to, and legal representation of, CBP officers in matters relating to the activities and functions of CBP. The office is also responsible for reviewing proposed actions to ensure compliance with legal requirements, preparing formal legal opinions, preparing or reviewing responses in all court actions, civil or criminal, involving CBP, and developing, implementing, and evaluating nationwide programs, policies, and procedures within its functional areas. The office has both a headquarters and a field structure. The headquarters office is located in Washington, D.C. and its activities are divided broadly into three functional areas: Ethics, Labor and Employment, Enforcement, and Trade and Finance, under the supervision of Associate Chief Counsels. The field structure consists of Associate and Assistant Chief Counsels located in major cities across the U.S. who advise CBP field managers in their geographic areas. [7]

Office of Non-Government Organization Liaison. The Non-Government Office (NGO) Liaison is the agency's principal liaison to non-governmental organizations to include faith-based and advocacy groups. Responsibilities of the NGO Liaison include facilitating dialogue on behalf of CBP to the NGO community in close collaboration with DHS components, and other federal agencies as appropriate. Formalizing this position is a critical step toward building and enhancing the agency's relationship with this important community. [7]

Office of Policy and Planning. The Office of Policy and Planning is responsible for assisting CBP leadership in defining and advancing U.S. Customs and Border Protection mission priorities through the effective development, review and implementation of key policy and planning initiatives. In partnership and coordination and with other CBP offices, the Department of Homeland Security and other governmental agencies, the office develops policy, provides oversight of the CBP policy function and ensures a common framework and alignment to CBP strategic intent. This team acts as the commissioner's executive agent for CBP policy and aligns CBP policy across offices. Additionally, in collaboration with other CBP offices, the office promotes an integrated approach toward strategic planning for CBP by formalizing the use of the planning, programming, budgeting, and accountability process to align out-year planning with budget priorities. [7]

Office of State, Local and Tribal Liaison. The CBP State, Local and Tribal Liaison is responsible for advising the commissioner, deputy commissioner and program offices on the impact of CBP policies and initiatives with regard to state, local and tribal stakeholders. To accomplish this mission, the liaison office strives to maintain open communication and build effective relationships with state, local and tribal governments. The office assists these stakeholders through regular, transparent and proactive communication by maintaining partnerships through active outreach. [7]

Office of Trade Relations. The Office of Trade Relations is responsible for managing CBP's outreach and communications with the international trade community. The office ensures that the trade community and the public understand that trade is an integral part of CBP's mission: making America safer, stronger, more prosperous, and economically competitive. The office's mission is to continually improve relations between CBP and the trade community by enhancing collaboration, cooperation, and inform decision making at all levels including operational, legislative, and political. The office also is responsible for organizing and presenting formal CBP outreach efforts to the trade community, including CBP's annual Trade Symposium, monthly trade day meetings, trade roundtable meetings, and webinars. The office manages the Advisory Committee on Commercial Operations of U.S. Customs and Border Protection (COAC), a congressionally mandated trade advisory group. Finally, the office is the designated regulatory fairness representative for the agency with responsibility for promoting compliance with the Small Business Regulatory Enforcement Fairness Act. [7]

Privacy and Diversity Office. The Privacy and Diversity Office is responsible for developing and implementing the policies, procedures and internal controls necessary to: Create a culture of privacy by ensuring and safeguarding all personally identifiable information (PII) pursuant to the Privacy Act; process Freedom of Information Act (FOIA) requests; ensure that CBP respects and protects the civil rights and civil liberties of the trade and traveling public; comply with Limited English Proficiency (LEP) requirements; receive and process equal employment opportunity (EEO) complaints filed by applicants and current CBP employees; advance CBP's Diversity and Inclusion initiatives; and to ensure compliance with the Prison Rape Elimination Act (PREA). [7]

CBP's trade strategy emphasizes risk management, which means that CBP collects advance information about shippers, importers, and cargo to evaluate cargo for potential import security and trade enforcement risks,

The Import Process

Under the Homeland Security Act of 2002 (P.L. 107-296) as amended in 2003, CBP is the lead agency charged with enforcing the trade laws under the Mod Act and the security measures under the Maritime Transportation Security Act (MTSA), the SAFE Port Act, and the other post-9/11 laws. CBP's trade strategy emphasizes risk management, which means that CBP collects advance information about shippers, importers, and cargo to evaluate cargo for potential import security and trade enforcement risks, and focuses enforcement efforts primarily on cargo and shippers identified as relatively high risk. Conversely, those deemed lower-risk imports (including, e.g., shipments of "trusted traders") are less likely to be targeted for CBP enforcement and may be eligible for expedited processing— thus advancing CBP's trade facilitation goal and freeing up resources for targeting higher-risk imports. [2, p. 16]

CBP's trade strategy also emphasizes layered enforcement, meaning that risk assessment and risk-based enforcement happen at a number of different points in the import process, beginning well before cargo arrives at a U.S. port of entry, and continuing long after cargo has been formally admitted to the United States. CBP attempts to target high-risk flows as early as possible in the import process, but its ability to conduct enforcement activities at different stages of the import process is designed to create multiple opportunities to interdict illegal imports. [2, p. 16]

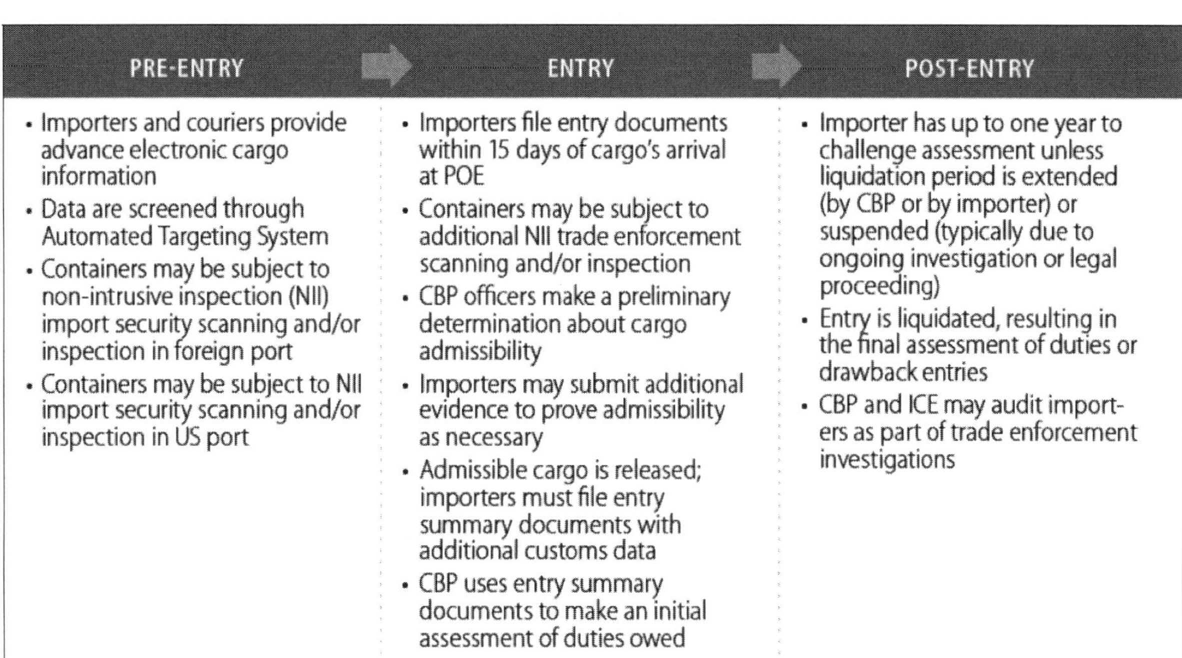

Figure 31-2: The U.S. Import Process [2, p. 17]

The import process includes three main stages, as illustrated in Figure 2. First, prior to entry at a U.S. POE, importers and carriers file paperwork and provide advance electronic cargo information, and all imports are subject to risk-based screening. Based on the results of this screening, certain goods are subject to import security scanning and inspection in foreign ports and/or upon arrival at a U.S. port. Second, importers file "entry documents" when cargo reaches a U.S. port, and cargo may be subject to additional scanning and inspection for import security and trade enforcement purposes. Admissible cargo is released from the port, and importers file an additional set of "entry summary" documents, which CBP uses to calculate customs duties and to make an initial assessment of taxes, fees, and duties owed. Third, following cargo entry, importers may challenge the assessment for up to a year, or longer under certain circumstances, until the final assessment of taxes and fees, a process known as liquidation. Trade enforcement activities may continue through audits and other post-entry investigations. [2, pp. 16-17]

The import process begins well before cargo arrives at a U.S. port of entry (POE). During the pre-entry stage of the process, importers of record submit electronic cargo manifests and other shipment data to CBP. This information may be submitted through CBP's Automated Customs System (ACS) or its Automated Customs Environment (ACE). CBP uses these advanced filing data to pre-clear cargo for admission, facilitate inflows, and target certain cargo for import security and trade enforcement. Cargo may be subject to import security scanning and inspections in foreign ports prior to being loaded on U.S.-bound ships and/or upon arrival at a U.S. port of entry (POE). [2, p. 17]

Import Security and Trade Enforcement Terminology and Procedures

Cargo being imported to the United States may be subject to multiple and varied types of import security and trade enforcement reviews, including the following:

- Screening: A risk assessment based on an analysis of data elements (e.g., cargo manifest, country of origin, shipper and consignee information) provided by an importer or carrier.
- Scanning: An analysis of container contents based on non-intrusive inspection (NII) technologies, including x-ray and gamma ray imaging systems and other technologies. NII scanning produces a high -resolution image of container contents that is reviewed by law enforcement officers to detect hidden cargo and other anomalies that suggest container contents do not match reported manifest data. If an officer detects an abnormality, containers may be "cracked open" for a physical examination. Scanning may also refer to radiation detection.
- Radiation detection: An analysis of container contents based on radiation portal monitors, handheld radiation detection monitors, and/or other radiation detection technology to detect nuclear material that may be part of a nuclear weapon or dirty bomb.
- Examination: A physical examination of container contents (requires that the container be opened and, in some cases, unpacked).
- Primary inspection: A review of entry documents to determine whether cargo may be admissible to the United States.
- Secondary inspection: A review of container contents to confirm that cargo is admissible to the United States. Secondary inspections may include NII scanning and/or a physical examination of container contents.
- Liquidation: The final assessment of import-related taxes and fees; typically occurs a year or more after cargo enters the United States. [2, p. 16]

One of CBP's primary tools for risk management is the use of trusted trader programs, including the Customs-Trade Partnership Against Terrorism (C-TPAT).

One of CBP's primary tools for risk management is the use of trusted trader programs, including the Customs-Trade Partnership Against Terrorism (C-TPAT), which was established in November 2001, after the 9/11 attacks, and subsequently authorized as part of the SAFE Port Act of 2006. Trusted trader programs are voluntary public-private partnership programs that permit certain import-related businesses to register with CBP, follow instructions prescribed by the agency to secure their supply chains, and thereby become recognized as low-risk actors and become eligible for expedited processing and other benefits. [2, p. 18]

The SAFE Port Act of 2006 also authorizes a pair of programs to conduct radiation detection and NII scanning in foreign ports: the Secure Freight Initiative and the Container Security Initiative.

- The Secure Freight Initiative (SFI) is a pilot program to test CBP's ability, working with international partners, to conduct radiation detection and NII scanning of 100% of cargo containers being loaded on U.S.-bound ships in certain ports. The SFI employs an integrated scanning system consisting of radiation portal monitors (provided by the Department of Energy) and NII imaging systems (provided by CBP) in a single location. CBP officers review the scanning data to determine which containers should be subject to secondary inspections. Secondary inspections, when called for, are conducted by host-state law enforcement agencies.

- The Container Security Initiative (CSI) is a partnership program among CBP, Immigration and Customs Enforcement, and law enforcement agencies in CSI countries. Under the program, CBP officers and other federal agents at the National Targeting Center–Cargo (NTC-C) in Herndon, VA, review advanced sea cargo data and identify high-risk containers. High-risk containers are targeted for radiation detection and NII scanning within CSI ports. Host state law enforcement agents typically conduct physical scans in the foreign ports, and CBP personnel located in the port or in the United States evaluate the scan results. When an abnormality is detected, host state law enforcement agents conduct a physical inspection before the container is loaded on a U.S.- bound ship. CBP officers and ICE agents participate in such inspections either remotely or as partners within foreign ports. [2, pp. 21-23]

The Container Security Initiative (CSI) is a partnership program among CBP, Immigration and Customs Enforcement, and law enforcement agencies in CSI countries.

Imported goods are not legally entered until after the shipment has arrived within the port of entry, entry of the merchandise has been authorized by CBP, and all estimated duties have been paid. The importer of record (i.e., the owner, purchaser, or a licensed customs broker) has the option to enter the goods for consumption, enter them into a bonded warehouse at the port of entry, or to transport the cargo in-bond to another port of entry for processing. [2, p. 23]

If goods are being entered for consumption (e.g., going directly into U.S. commerce) importers are typically required to file entry documents within 15 calendar days of a shipment arriving at a U.S. port of entry. These documents may include an entry manifest or other form of merchandise release, evidence of the right to make entry, commercial invoices, packing lists, and other documents necessary to determine admissibility. Since most cargo is released electronically, however, packing lists and invoices are rarely requested. [2, p. 23]

Importers also must provide evidence that a bond has been posted with CBP to cover estimated duties, taxes, and charges that may accrue. If the goods are to be released from CBP custody, an entry summary must be filed and estimated duties deposited at the port within 10 days of the entry of the merchandise. [2, p. 23]

Based on screening of the cargo and a review of the entry documents, CBP officers at the port make a preliminary determination about cargo admissibility and either release or challenge the shipment. For cargo that is challenged, importers may be required to provide additional documents or take other steps to prove admissibility. [2, p. 23]

Cargo that is found to be admissible and cleared through security and trade enforcement inspections is formally released into U.S. commerce. In these cases, importers must file additional entry summary documentation within 10 days to provide detailed information about the shipment (including customs classification, weight, and duty rates) that CBP will use to determine that all import requirements have been satisfied. Importers must pay storage and transportation costs during the cargo release period, and must pay initial customs duties and fees assessed prior to taking possession of imported goods. [2, pp. 27-28]

In addition to a workforce of over 20,000 agents, the USBP deploys vehicles, aircraft, watercraft, and many different technologies to defend the border.

CBP responsibilities do not end when a product has entered the United States. Importers have up to 180 days from the date of entry to challenge CBP's assessment of duties owed, after which CBP makes a final determination of the rate and amount of duty owed, a process known as liquidation, and importers pay additional duties or receive refunds to reconcile any differences between estimated and final duties owed. CBP trade specialists and other federal agencies involved in trade enforcement may conduct additional enforcement activities in the period after cargo enters the United States, including audits of importers' records to ensure compliance with U.S. trade laws. [2, pp. 30-31]

As a general rule, CBP requires that all records regarding imports of merchandise be kept for a period of five years after the date of entry. These documents must be made available to CBP officials if they request an audit to determine if any additional duties, fees, and taxes are owed, or to insure that the importer is in compliance with laws administered by CBP. [2, pp. 31-32]

Border Patrol

In the decade following 9/11 the USBP saw its budget and manpower more than triple. This expansion was the direct result of congressional concerns about illegal immigration and the agency's adoption of "Prevention Through Deterrence" as its chief operational strategy in 1994. The strategy called for placing USBP resources and manpower directly at the areas of greatest illegal immigration in order to detect, deter, and apprehend aliens attempting to cross the border between official points of entry. Post 9/11, the USBP refocused its strategy on preventing the entry of terrorists and weapons of mass destruction, as laid out in its recently released National Strategy. In addition to a workforce of over 20,000 agents, the USBP deploys vehicles, aircraft, watercraft, and many different technologies to defend the border. [8, p. ii]

In the course of discharging its duties, the USBP patrols 8,000 miles of American international borders with Mexico and Canada and the coastal waters around Florida and Puerto Rico. However, there are significant geographic, political, and immigration-related differences between the northern border with Canada and the Southwest border with Mexico. Accordingly, the USBP deploys a different mix of personnel and resources along the two borders. Due to the fact that approximately 98.7% of unauthorized migrant apprehensions by the USBP occur along the Southwest border, the USBP deploys over 85% of its agents there to deter illegal immigration. The northern border is more than two times longer than the Southwest border, and features far lower numbers of aliens attempting to enter illegally, but may be more vulnerable to terrorist infiltration. As a consequence of this, the USBP has focused its northern border efforts on deploying technology and cooperating closely with Canadian authorities through the creation of International Border Enforcement Teams. [8, p. ii]

USBP patrols 8,000 miles of American international borders with Mexico and Canada and the coastal waters around Florida and Puerto Rico.

Across a variety of indicators, the United States has substantially expanded border enforcement resources over the last three decades. Particularly since 2001, such increases include border security appropriations, personnel, fencing and infrastructure, and surveillance technology. In addition to increased resources, the USBP has implemented several strategies over the past several decades in an attempt to thwart illegal migration. [3, p. ii]

Since 2005, CBP has attempted to discourage repeat illegal migrant entries and disrupt migrant smuggling networks by imposing tougher penalties against certain unauthorized aliens, a set of policies eventually described as "enforcement with consequences." Most people apprehended at the Southwest border are now subject to "high consequence" enforcement outcomes. [3, p. ii]

The Border Patrol collects data on several different border enforcement outcomes such as border apprehensions, recidivism, and estimated "got aways" and "turn backs". Yet none of these existing data are designed to measure illegal border flows or the degree to which the border is secured. But a range of evidence suggests a substantial drop in illegal inflows in 2007-2011, followed by a slight rise in 2012 and a more dramatic rise in 2013. Enforcement, along with the economic downturn in the United States, likely contributed to the drop in unauthorized migration, though the precise share of the decline attributable to enforcement is unknown. [3, p. ii]

Conclusion

How effectively CBP has performed its import policy mission is a matter of some debate. Some participants in CBP's "trusted trader" programs argue that the concessions (e.g., expedited processing; fewer container inspections) CBP provides at the border do not adequately justify the effort and expense to certify their supply chains. Questions have also been raised about CBP's management of trade facilitation, especially the means through which the Automated Commercial System trade data management system is being phased out in favor of the newer Automated Commercial Environment. Some critics also assert that CBP has not adequately fulfilled its trade enforcement role, especially its duties for preventing illegal transshipments, protecting U.S. intellectual property rights, and collecting duties. Still others criticize CBP's performance of its security functions, especially because it does not yet physically scan 100% of maritime cargo as mandated by the SAFE Port Act of 2006, as amended. [2, p. ii]

The results from increased border security are also mixed. To the extent that border enforcement successfully deters illegal entries, such enforcement may reduce border-area violence and migrant deaths, protect fragile border ecosystems, and improve the quality of life in border communities. But to the extent that aliens are not deterred, the concentration of enforcement resources on the border may increase border area violence and migrant deaths, encourage unauthorized migrants to find new ways to enter illegally and to remain in the United States for longer periods of time, damage border ecosystems, harm border-area businesses and the quality of life in border communities, and strain U.S. relations with Mexico and Canada. [3, p. ii]

Challenge Your Understanding

The following questions are designed to challenge your understanding of the material presented in this chapter. Some questions may require additional research outside this book in order to provide a complete answer.

1. What is the mission of U.S. Customs and Border Protection?
2. What is the essential difficulty of screening every traveler and cargo container transiting a port of entry?
3. What is the essential difficulty of preventing smuggling between ports of entry?
4. What illicit good provides an indicator how well CBP is thwarting smugglers?
5. Which CBP component enforces immigration law and apprehends smugglers between ports of entry?
6. Which CBP component enforces immigration law and apprehends smugglers at ports of entry?
7. List and describe the three stages of the import process.
8. How is CBP's risk management strategy applied to the import process?
9. How do trusted trader programs support CBP's risk management strategy?
10. What three conditions must be met before a cargo can be cleared through a port of entry?

Chapter 32

U.S. Secret Service

Learning Outcomes

Careful study of this chapter will help a student do the following:

- Explain the mission of the organization.
- Describe some key components of the organization.
- Discuss some of the work of the organization.

"Your main objective is to restore public confidence in the money of the country."

- Treasury Secretary Hugh McCulloch, July 5, 1865

Introduction

Most are familiar with the protection mission provided by the U.S. Secret Service to the President, Vice President, visiting dignitaries and their families. The Secret Service has been providing this protection for over 100 years. Fewer are familiar, though, with the Service's investigation mission, protecting the nation's currency and financial institutions. The Secret Service has been providing this protection for the past 150 years. The missions and history of the U.S. Secret Service are the subject of this chapter.

The U.S. Secret Service has two missions—criminal investigations and protection. Criminal investigation activities encompass financial crimes, identity theft, counterfeiting, computer fraud, and computer-based attacks on the nation's financial, banking, and telecommunications infrastructure.

Background

The U.S. Secret Service traces its origins to the American Civil War. By 1865, an estimated half of all U.S. currency in circulation was counterfeit. As a result of this currency crisis, the Secretary of Treasury established a Secret Service Division (SSD) to investigate counterfeiting under authority given to it by Congress in the 1863 National Currency Act. At the request of President Grover Cleveland, Secret Service agents provided security to him and his family at their vacation home in the summer of 1894. President William McKinley also received SSD protection during the Spanish-American War and limited protection following the end of the war. Three SSD agents were present when President McKinley was assassinated in Buffalo, NY, but reportedly they were not fully in charge of the protection mission. Accordingly, Congress assigned SSD with protecting the President following the assassination of President McKinley in 1901. The USSS pretty much maintained its investigative and protection roles within the Treasury Department for the next 100 years until 9/11. [1, pp. 5-8] In 2002, as part of his proposal, President Bush recommended adding the U.S. Secret Service to the new Department of Homeland Security. [2, p. 3] In March 2003, the USSS was transferred to DHS under authority of the 2002 Homeland Security Act.

Mission

The U.S. Secret Service has two missions—criminal investigations and protection. Criminal investigation activities encompass financial crimes, identity theft, counterfeiting, computer fraud, and computer-based attacks on the nation's financial, banking, and telecommunications infrastructure. The protection mission is the more publicly visible of the two, covering the President, Vice President, their families, former Presidents, and major candidates for those offices, along with the White House and the Vice President's residence (through the Service's Uniformed Division). Protective duties of the Service also extend to foreign missions (such as embassies, consulates, and foreign dignitary residences) in the District of Columbia and to designated individuals, such as the Homeland Security Secretary and visiting foreign dignitaries. Separate from these specific mandated assignments, USSS is also responsible for security at designated National Special Security Events (NSSEs) which include presidential inaugurations, national political conventions, major international conferences, and the Super Bowl. [1]

The USSS employs approximately 3,500 special agents, 1,350 Uniformed Division officers, and more than 1,800 other technical, professional, and administrative support personnel. They work at the headquarters in Washington, D.C. and in 142 field offices and units within the United States and its territories and 22 offices in 18 foreign countries.

Organization

The USSS employs approximately 3,500 special agents, 1,350 Uniformed Division officers, and more than 1,800 other technical, professional, and administrative support personnel. They work at the headquarters in Washington, D.C. and in 142 field offices and units within the United States and its territories and 22 offices in 18 foreign countries. The USSS is organized into seven offices: Investigations, Protective Operations, Protective Research, Professional Responsibility, Government and Public Affairs, Human Resources and Training, and Administration. The two principal operational offices are Investigations and Protective Operations. [3, p. 49]

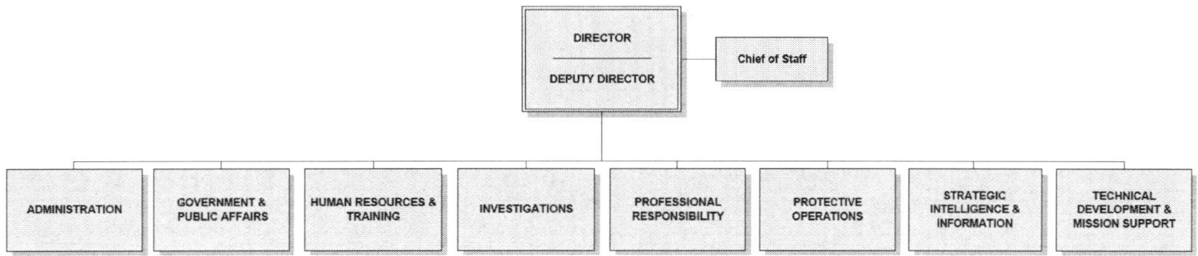

Figure 32-1: U.S. Secret Service Organization Chart [4]

The USSS also operates the National Threat Assessment Center (NTAC). The NTAC was established in 1998 as an effort to dedicate resources to better understand, and find ways to prevent targeted violence; to share this knowledge with others; and to continue to provide leadership in the field of threat assessment. The premise for NTAC was developed in the wake of an original assassination research study, the Exceptional Case Study Project (ECSP), conducted in collaboration with the Department of Justice. The ECSP was a study of individuals who had assassinated, attacked, or approached with lethal means, public officials or public figures from 1949-1996 in the United States. One major product from this study was a guidebook on protective intelligence and threat assessment investigations. NTAC uses historical information, investigative records, interviews, and other primary source material to produce long-term behavioral research studies that leverage USSS expertise in the protection of persons for homeland security or public safety purposes. Through the Presidential Threat Protection Act of 2000, Congress formally authorized NTAC to provide assistance to Federal, state, and local law enforcement, and others with protective responsibilities, on training in the area of threat assessment; consultation on complex threat assessment cases or plans; and research on threat assessment and the prevention of targeted violence. [3, p. 50]

The USSS also operates the National Threat Assessment Center (NTAC). NTAC uses historical information, investigative records, interviews, and other primary source material to produce long-term behavioral research studies that leverage USSS expertise in the protection of persons for homeland security or public safety purposes.

Investigative Mission

The original mission of the Service was to investigate the counterfeiting of United States currency. This mission has been expanded throughout the agency's history through presidential, departmental, and congressional action. At times, early in the agency's history, Secret Service agents conducted investigations that were not related to financial system crimes. [1, p. 2] In 1889, the Service was directed to investigate espionage activities during the Spanish- American War, and again during World War I. These missions were phased out at the end of each war. Additionally, in the early 1900s, the Service was directed to investigate land fraud in the western United States; another area outside its purview. [1, p. 6]

In the first half of the 20th Century, Congress continued to authorize the Treasury Secretary to "direct and use" the Secrete Service to "detect, arrest, and deliver into custody of the United States marshal having jurisdiction any person or persons violating" counterfeit laws. In 1948, the Service was also authorized to investigate crimes against the Federal Deposit Insurance Corporation, federal land banks, joint-stock land banks, and national farm loan associations. As throughout USSS's history, Congress continued to amend the Service's investigation mission from 1950 to 1984. Among the provisions, the USSS was authorized to confiscate and purchase counterfeit currency. [1, p. 6]

Due to the increased use of computers and electronic devices in financial crime, Congress, in 1984, authorized the USSS to investigate violations related to credit card and computer fraud. In the 1990s, Congress continued to amend laws affecting the investigation, prosecution, and punishment of crimes against United States financial systems. One such amendment authorized USSS investigation of crimes against financial systems by authorizing the Service to conduct civil or criminal investigations of federally insured financial institutions. Another law was the Violent Crime Control and Law Enforcement Act of 1994 (P.L. 103-322), which made international manufacturing, trafficking, and possession of counterfeit United States currency a crime as if it were committed in the United States. Congress also enacted laws related to telemarketing fraud (P.L. 105-184) and identity theft (P.L. 105-318), both of which are used in committing financial fraud and crime. [1, p. 7]

The original mission of the Service was to investigate the counterfeiting of United States currency. The 2001 USA PATRIOT Act expanded the Secret Service's responsibilities for protecting the U.S. financial system and investigating electronic device crimes. It also authorized the Service to establish nationwide electronic crime task forces to assist in detecting and suppressing computer-based crimes.

Following the terrorist attacks of September 11, 2001, Congress enacted the USA PATRIOT Act. Among numerous provisions addressing the protection of the United States financial systems and electronic device crimes, the act authorized the Service to establish nationwide electronic crime task forces to assist law enforcement, private sector, and academic entities in detecting and suppressing computer-based crimes. [1, p. 7]

Today, USSS conducts criminal investigations into counterfeiting and financial crimes. Within the investigative mission area is the USSS's forensic services division. USSS forensic services personnel conduct analyses of evidence, some of which includes documents, fingerprints, false identification documents, and credit cards, to assist in USSS investigations. USSS's investigative support is also responsible for developing and implementing a criminal and investigative intelligence program. One of the components of this program is the Criminal Research Specialist Program, which provides intelligence analysis related to infrastructure protection, conducts forensic financial analysis, and provides research and analytical support to USSS criminal investigations. Additionally, in 1994, Congress mandated that USSS provide forensic and technical assistance to the National Center for Missing and Exploited Children. [1, p. 2]

Protection Mission

Following the assassination of President McKinley, in 1901, congressional leadership asked that the Secret Service Division protect the President. Five years later Congress, for the first time, appropriated funds for the protection of the President with the passage of the Sundry Civil Expenses Act for 1907 (enacted in 1906). [1, pp. 7-8]

In 1908, SSD's protection mission was expanded to include the President-elect. In that same year, President Theodore Roosevelt transferred a number of SSD agents to the Department of Justice, which served as the foundation for the Federal Bureau of Investigation. Annual congressional authorization of the mandate to protect the President and President-elect began in 1913. [1, p. 8]

During World War I threats against the President began to arrive at the White House, which resulted in a 1917 law making it a crime to threaten the President. Additionally, later that same year, Congress authorized SSD to protect the President's immediate family. [1, p. 8]

USSS protection includes not only the presence of agents in close proximity to the protectee, but also advance security surveys of locations to be visited, coordination with state and local enforcement entities, and intelligence analysis of present and future threats.

In addition to the expansion of the protection of the President and the President's family, the White House Police Force was created in 1922 to secure and patrol the Executive Mansion and grounds in Washington, DC. Initially, the White House Police Force was not supervised or administered by SSD; but rather by the President or his appointed representative. In 1930, however, Congress mandated that the White House Police Force be supervised by the SSD. [1, p. 8] In 1970 the White House Police Force was renamed the Executive Protection Service (EPS). The EPS is responsible for protection of

- The Executive Mansion and grounds in the District of Columbia;
- Any building with presidential offices;
- The President and immediate family;
- Foreign diplomatic missions located in the metropolitan DC area; and
- Foreign diplomatic missions located in the United States, its territories, and its possessions—as directed by the President. [1, p. 9]

For the first time, Congress, in 1943, appropriated funding for both the investigation and protection missions. The appropriation was specifically for "suppressing" counterfeiting and "other" crimes; protecting the President, the President-elect, and their immediate families; and providing funding for the White House Police Force. Similarly, in 1951, Congress permanently authorized the "U.S. Secret Service" to protect the President, his immediate family, the President-elect, and the Vice President—if the Vice President so desired. In 1954, Congress used the title "U.S. Secret Service" in an appropriation act for the first time. [1, p. 8]

Over the ensuing decades, the list of Secret Service protectees continued to evolve and grow. Today, the following individuals are authorized USSS protection:

- President, Vice President, President - and Vice President-elect;
- The immediate families of those listed above;
- Former Presidents and their spouses;
- Former Presidents' children under age 16;
- Visiting heads of foreign states or governments;
- Distinguished foreign visitors and official United States representatives on special missions abroad;
- Major presidential and vice presidential candidates, within 120 days of the general presidential elections, their spouses; and
- Former Vice Presidents, their spouses, and their children under the age of 16. [5]

On December 19, 2000, President Clinton signed P.L. 106 -544, the Presidential Threat Protection Act of 2000, authorizing the USSS—when directed by the President—to plan, coordinate, and implement security operations at National Special Security Events (NSSEs).

The form of protection has also evolved. Originally, USSS protection entailed agents being, what could be described as "bodyguards." Now protection includes not only the presence of agents in close proximity to the protectee, but also advance security surveys of locations to be visited, coordination with state and local enforcement entities, and intelligence analysis of present and future threats. The USSS protection mission uses human resources and physical barriers, technology, and a review of critical infrastructures and their vulnerabilities to increase security to meet evolving threats. [1, pp. 3-4]

On December 19, 2000, President Clinton signed P.L. 106-544, the Presidential Threat Protection Act of 2000, authorizing the USSS—when directed by the President—to plan, coordinate, and implement security operations at special events of national significance. The special events were designated National Special Security Events (NSSEs). Some events categorized as NSSEs include presidential inaugurations, major international summits held in the United States, major sporting events, and political party nominating conventions. [1, p. 11]

Reform

On March 26, 2015, Representative Bob Goodlatte (R-VA) introduced House Resolution 1656 titled "The Secret Service Improvement Act of 2015". The bill was motivated by a series of security breaches and scandals that had undermined confidence in the agency over the preceding years. In April 2012, during a Presidential trip to Columbia, several USSS agents reportedly hired prostitutes and took them back to their hotel rooms. Several of the agents were subsequently fired. In September 2014, a person carrying a knife gained unauthorized entrance into the White House after climbing the perimeter fence. In January 2015, an unmanned aerial drone flew over the White House fence and landed within the grounds. In March 2015, it became public knowledge that senior -ranking Secret Service officials, including an agent on President Obama's personal detail, crashed a government car into a barrier at the White House after drinking. H.R. 1656 provides resources and creates new performance and accountability measures in an attempt to better enable the U.S. Secret Service (USSS) to carry out its mission. [5]

- Improved Security and Safety—the bill clarifies that it is a federal crime to knowingly cause, with the intent to impede or disrupt the orderly conduct of Government business or official functions, any object to enter restricted buildings or grounds, including the White House and the Vice President's residence. The bill requires the USSS to evaluate ways technology at the White House can be used to improve safety and counter threats posed by unmanned aerial systems or explosive devices. The bill also requires the USSS to evaluate the use of additional weaponry, including non-lethal weapons. The bill amends current law to permit the USSS to investigate threats against former Vice Presidents. [5]
- Enhanced Evidence Evaluation and Reporting Requirements—the bill requires the USSS to evaluate how it retains evidence and to report its findings to Congress. [5]
- Enhanced Training Requirements–the bill requires the Director of the USSS to increase the number of hours spent training, and directs the agency to provide joint training between Uniformed Division officers and Special Agents. The bill also authorizes the Director to construct facilities at the Rowley Training Center necessary to improve the training of USSS officers. [5]
- Increased Uniformed and Plain Clothing Agents—the bill authorizes the hiring of no fewer than 200 additional Uniformed Division officers and 80 additional Special Agents. [5]
- Senate Confirmation of the USSS Director — the bill requires the Director of the USSS to be confirmed by the Senate. [5]

On July 27, 2015, H.R. 1656 was passed by the House of Representatives and forwarded to the Senate. Upon receiving the bill, it was read twice in the Senate and referred to the Committee on Homeland Security and Governmental Affairs. [6]

Conclusion

Both the U.S. Secret Service Investigation and Protection missions have distinctive characteristics and histories, and each has been affected by informal decisions and congressional action. [1, p. 5] Since 9/11, though, there have been consistent and continuing questions regarding the Secret Service's two missions and whether they are compatible. The recent lapses in security and scandals have convinced some that the Protection mission is not receiving the attention it should. Some are even questioning whether the Department of Homeland Security is the appropriate home for the Secret Service. [1, p. ii] Whether or not the Secret Service will retain both its Investigation and Protection missions, and whether or not the Secret Service will remain in the Department of Homeland Security will be determined, as it has for the past 150 years, by Congress.

Challenge Your Understanding

The following questions are designed to challenge your understanding of the material presented in this chapter. Some questions may require additional research outside this book in order to provide a complete answer.

1. Why was the U.S. Secret Service originally formed?
2. What are the two missions of the U.S. Secret Service?
3. Which USSS component uses historical information, investigative records, and interviews to produce long-term behavioral research studies to prevent targeted violence?
4. Which USSS component provides investigative support by analyzing fingerprints, forged documents, and stolen credit cards?
5. Which USSS program provides intelligence analysis related to infrastructure protection?
6. List and describe three measures the USSS employs to protect assigned individuals.
7. Which of the following individuals are not USSS protectees?
    a. Former President's children under age 16.
    b. Current National Security Advisor and statutory members of the National Security Council.
    c. Distinguished foreign visitors and official U.S. representatives on special missions abroad.
8. Which of the following are not National Special Security Events?
    a. Super Bowl
    b. Air Force Academy Graduation
    c. Democratic National Convention
9. List and describe two different presidential assassination attempts in the last 50 years.
10. Did the attempted assassins harbor terrorist motives?

Chapter 33

U.S. Immigration & Customs Enforcement

Learning Outcomes

Careful study of this chapter will help a student do the following:

- Explain the mission of the organization.
- Describe some key components of the organization.
- Discuss some of the work of the organization.

"Our investigation showed that two systemic weaknesses came together in our border system's inability to contribute to an effective defense against the 9/11 attacks: a lack of well-developed counterterrorism measures as a part of border security, and an immigration system not able to deliver on its basic commitments, much less support counterterrorism."

- 2004 9/11 Commission Report

Introduction

The U.S. Immigration and Customs Enforcement (ICE) agency was created in 2003 through a merger of the investigative and interior enforcement elements of the former U.S. Customs Service and the Immigration and Naturalization Service. ICE now has more than 20,000 employees in more than 400 offices in the United States and 48 foreign countries. [1] ICE is the largest investigative agency in the Department of Homeland Security (DHS), and one of three agencies charged with administering the nation's immigration system, together with Customs and Border Protection (CBP), and the U.S. Customs and Immigration Service (USCIS). [2]

ICE is the largest investigative agency in the Department of Homeland Security (DHS), and one of three agencies charged with administering the nation's immigration system, together with Customs and Border Protection (CBP), and the U.S. Customs and Immigration Service (USCIS).

Mission

U.S. Immigration and Customs Enforcement enforces federal laws governing border control, customs, trade and immigration to promote homeland security and public safety. [1] This mission is executed through the enforcement of more than 400 federal statutes and focuses on smart immigration enforcement, preventing terrorism and combating the illegal movement of people and goods. [3]

Organization

U.S. Immigration and Customs Enforcement is organized into three directorates: 1) Homeland Security Investigations (HSI); 2) Enforcement and Removal Operations (ERO); and 3) Management and Administration (M&A). [1]

1. Homeland Security Investigations. The HSI directorate is responsible for investigating a wide range of domestic and international activities arising from the illegal movement of people and goods into, within and out of the United States. [1]
2. Enforcement and Removal Operations. ERO enforces the nation's immigration laws in a fair and effective manner. It identifies and apprehends removable aliens, detains these individuals when necessary and removes illegal aliens from the United States. This unit prioritizes the apprehension, arrest and removal of convicted criminals, those who pose a threat to national security, fugitives and recent border entrants. Individuals seeking asylum also work with ERO. [1]
3. Management and Administration. M&A provides professional management and mission support to advance the ICE mission. [1]

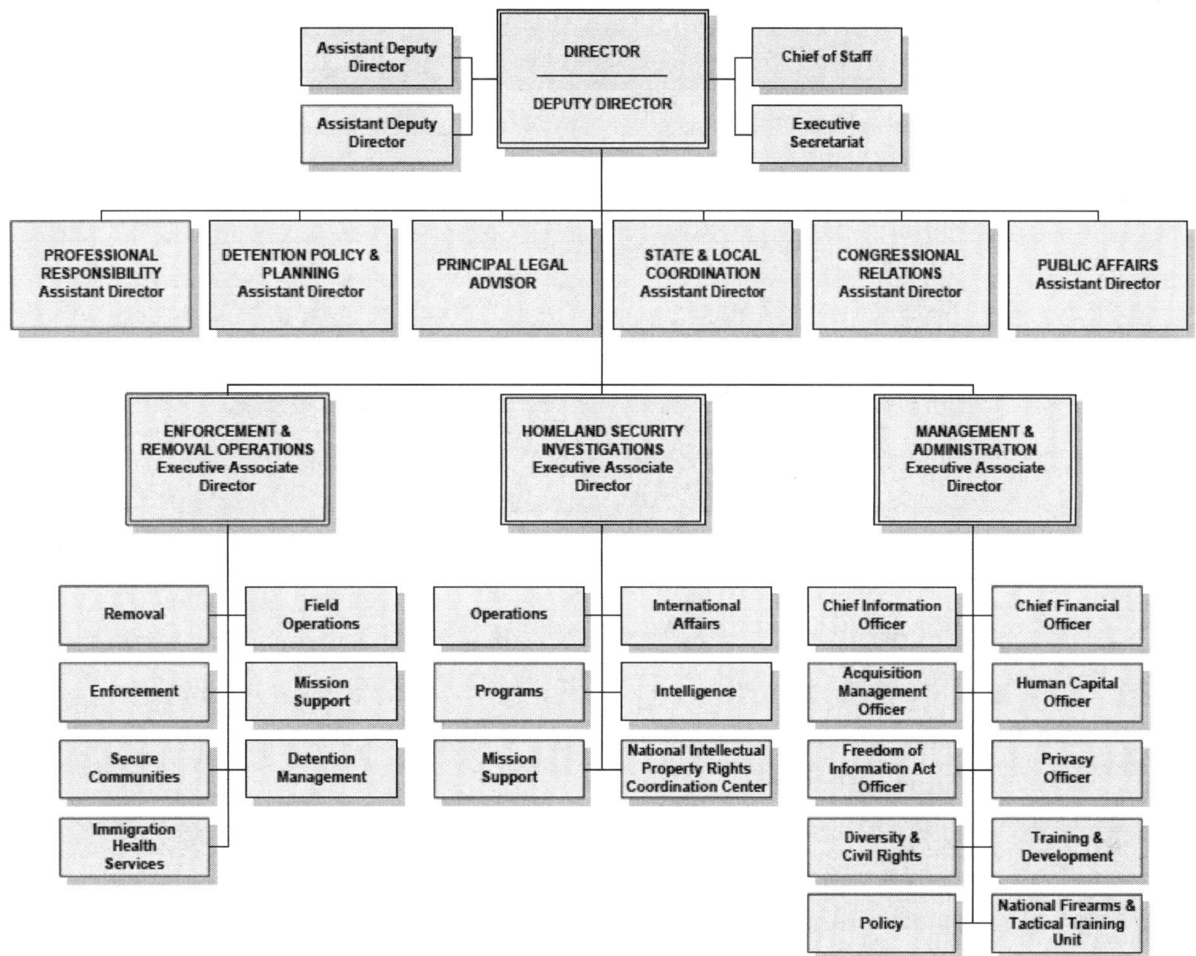

Figure 33-1: ICE Organization Chart [4]

Investigating Illegal Movement of People and Goods

ICE special agents, officers and attorneys enforce provisions of approximately 400 federal statutes. This large and diverse body of laws is reflected in the wide array of offices, programs and projects that make up ICE. People are smuggled and trafficked, while children are sexually exploited at home and abroad. Illegal trade, in a very general sense, predominately involve guns, money and drugs, but ICE's responsibilities extend much further into all kinds of illegal and counterfeit merchandise coming into the country. For instance, ICE's responsibilities include the repatriation of cultural treasures out of the country to original owners abroad, and combatting the trade of child pornography and much more. [3]

Human trafficking is one of the most heinous crimes that ICE investigates. In its worst manifestation, human trafficking is akin to modern-day slavery. Victims pay to be illegally transported into the United States only to find themselves in the thrall of traffickers. They are forced into prostitution, involuntary labor and other forms of servitude to repay debts – often incurred during entry into the United States. In certain cases, the victims are mere children. They find themselves surrounded by an unfamiliar culture and language without identification documents, fearing for their lives and the lives of their families. [5] ICE has embarked on an ambitious strategy to dismantle organized human smuggling networks:

- First, ICE pursues intelligence-driven investigations to target large-scale smuggling organizations regardless of where they operate. Particular emphasis is placed on smuggling rings that pose a national security risk, jeopardize lives or engage in violence, abuse, hostage-taking or extortion.
- Second, ICE coordinates with partners at U.S. Customs and Border Protection to ensure aggressive investigation and prosecution of smuggling cases along the border.
- Third, ICE targets all links in the smuggling chain, beyond the immediate smugglers. For example, ICE seeks to target the overseas recruiters and organizers, the fraudulent document vendors, and the transportation and employment networks that benefit from alien smuggling within the United States.
- Finally, ICE pursues legislation to increase penalties against organized smugglers and provide additional criminal offenses to better address spotters who assist criminals with smuggling aliens and contraband. [6]

Human trafficking is one of the most heinous crimes that ICE investigates. In its worst manifestation, human trafficking is akin to modern-day slavery.

In recent decades, U.S. law enforcement has encountered an increasing number of major financial crimes, frequently resulting from the needs for drug trafficking organizations to launder large sums of criminal proceeds through legitimate financial institutions and investment vehicles.

- Cornerstone is ICE's initiative to detect and close down weaknesses within U.S. financial, trade and transportation sectors that can be exploited by criminal networks. Law enforcement entities share criminal typologies and methods with businesses and industries that manage the very systems that terrorists and criminal organizations seek to exploit. This sharing of information allows the financial and trade community to take precautions in order to protect themselves from exploitation.
- The El Dorado Task Force consists of more than 260 members from more than 55 law enforcement agencies in New York and New Jersey – including federal agents, state and local police investigators, intelligence analysts and federal prosecutors. The El Dorado Task Force is headquartered at the New York Special Agent in Charge Office and at other locations in the New York/New Jersey Metropolitan area. The El Dorado Task Force targets financial crime at all levels. Task force agents educate the private financial sector to identify and eliminate vulnerabilities and promote anti-money laundering legislation through training and other outreach programs. Prosecutors use a full range of criminal and civil laws to prosecute targets and forfeit the proceeds of their illicit activity. The El Dorado Task Force uses a systems-based approach to investigating financial crimes by targeting vulnerabilities such as the Black Market Peso Exchange and commodity-based money laundering.

- Many developing nations are plagued by corrupt foreign officials who plunder state coffers for personal gain and then attempt to place those funds in the U.S. financial system. ICE leads investigations against corrupt foreign public officials who have used U.S. financial institutions and other investment vehicles to facilitate criminal acts involving the laundering of proceeds emanating from foreign public corruption, bribery or embezzlement.

- Trade-based money laundering is an alternative remittance system that allows illegal organizations the opportunity to earn, move and store proceeds disguised as legitimate trade. Value can be moved through this process by false-invoicing, over-invoicing and under-invoicing commodities that are imported or exported around the world. Criminal organizations frequently exploit global trade systems to move value around the world by employing complex and sometimes confusing documentation associated with legitimate trade transactions. ICE established the Trade Transparency Unit initiative to target trade-based money laundering worldwide. [7]

- The Homeland Security Investigations' National Bulk Cash Smuggling Center identifies, investigates and disrupts bulk cash smuggling activities around the world. The center is located at the ICE Law Enforcement Support Center in Williston, Vt. [8]

HSI and its law enforcement partners target the illegal movement of U.S. origin firearms, ammunition, and explosive weapons with the ultimate goal of preventing the procurement of these items by drug cartels, terrorists, human rights violators, foreign adversaries, and other transnational criminal organizations and individuals that utilize these weapons to facilitate criminal activity and commit acts of violence. HSI's investigative strategy includes the identification and prosecution of criminal networks and individuals responsible for the acquisition and movement of firearms and other dangerous weapons from the United States, as well as the seizure and forfeiture of money and valuable property derived from or used to facilitate this criminal activity. [9]

HSI and its law enforcement partners target the illegal movement of U.S. origin firearms, ammunition, and explosive weapons with the ultimate goal of preventing the procurement of these items by drug cartels, terrorists, human rights violators, foreign adversaries, and other transnational criminal organizations .

In 2005, in response to the significant increase in violence along the Southwest Border in Mexico, the U.S Immigration and Customs Enforcement, Homeland Security Investigations, in partnership with U.S. Customs and Border Protection, as well as other federal, state, local, and international law enforcement officials created the Border Enforcement Security Task Force (BEST) in Laredo, Texas. ICE partners with more than 100 fellow law enforcement agencies in BEST teams across 16 states. Each team focuses on disrupting criminal smuggling and trafficking operations and on denying criminal organizations the opportunity to transport their illicit funds. Since its creation in 2005, BEST has initiated more than 9,000 cases. [10]

Federal importation laws give HSI the authority to take a leading role in investigating crimes involving the illicit importation and distribution of cultural property and art. Customs laws allow HSI to seize cultural property and art that are brought into the United States illegally, especially when objects have been reported lost or stolen. Specially trained investigators assigned to domestic and international offices partner with federal, state and local agencies; private institutions; and foreign governments to conduct investigations. These entities share HSI's mission to protect these objects and preserve cultural heritage. Since 2007, HSI special agents have participated in a training program to learn the latest techniques and trends for conducting criminal investigations of cultural property. As part of this program, the Smithsonian Institution's Museum Conservation Institute provides HSI special agents with on-site training on how to handle, store, photograph and authenticate cultural property and works of art. [11]

One of HSI's top priorities is to combat criminal activity conducted on or facilitated by the Internet. HSI's Cyber Crimes Center (C3) delivers computer-based technical services to support domestic and international investigations into cross-border crime.

The Homeland Security Investigations' Forensic Laboratory (HSI-FL) provides a broad range of forensic, intelligence and investigative support to ICE, DHS and many other U.S. and foreign law enforcement agencies. The Latent Print (LP) Section provides finger and palm print services and support across all investigative disciplines. These services include, but are not limited to, processing evidence for latent prints (e.g., drug packaging and paraphernalia, firearms, computers, currency, compact discs), latent print comparison, inked print comparison, searching automated fingerprint identification system databases, and providing crime scene assistance. The Questioned Document (QD) Section specializes in determining the authenticity of documents and identifying the presence of alterations within those documents. Specialized equipment may be used during the examination process that will not affect or damage the original document. [12]

One of HSI's top priorities is to combat criminal activity conducted on or facilitated by the Internet. HSI's Cyber Crimes Center (C3) delivers computer-based technical services to support domestic and international investigations into cross-border crime. C3 is made up of the Cyber Crimes Unit, the Child Exploitation Investigations Unit and the Computer Forensics Unit. C3 offers cyber-crime support and training to federal, state, local and international law enforcement agencies. C3 also operates a fully equipped computer forensics laboratory, which specializes in digital evidence recovery, and offers training in computer investigative and forensic skills. [13]

As part of ICE's Cyber Crimes Center, the Child Exploitation Investigations Unit (CEIU) uses cutting edge investigative techniques to bring justice to consumers, producers and distributors of child pornography, as well as to predators engaging in child sex tourism. Collaborating with law enforcement partners around the country and the world, Operation Predator brings together an array of resources to target these child predators. As part of the effort:

- HSI participates on all 61 Internet Crimes Against Children (ICAC) Task Forces across the United States, which are led by state and local law enforcement agencies.
- HSI established a National Victim Identification Program at its Cyber Crimes Center, combining the latest technology with traditional investigative techniques to rescue child victims of sexual exploitation.
- HSI is the U.S. representative to the Interpol working group that locates new child sexual abuse material on the Internet and refers cases to the country that the abuse is believed to be occurring in for further investigation. Also, HSI special agents stationed internationally work with foreign governments, Interpol and others to enhance coordination and cooperation on crimes that cross borders.
- HSI works in partnership with the National Center for Missing & Exploited Children and other federal agencies to help solve cases and rescue sexually exploited children.
- HSI is a founding member and current chair of the Virtual Global Taskforce, joining law enforcement agencies, non-governmental organizations and private sector partners around the world to fight child exploitation information and images that travel over the Internet. [14]

As part of ICE's Cyber Crimes Center, the Child Exploitation Investigations Unit (CEIU) uses cutting edge investigative techniques to bring justice to consumers, producers and distributors of child pornography, as well as to predators engaging in child sex tourism.

Preventing Terrorism

Most ICE offices and programs have a role in preventing terrorism. Several are on the front lines of this effort, either identifying dangerous persons before they enter the U.S. or finding them as they violate immigration or customs laws. ICE also works to prevent the illegal export of U.S. technology that could be used or repurposed to do harm. [3]

The National Security Unit (NSU) serves as a comprehensive unit to provide for the complete integration of national security investigations and counterterrorism efforts within the National Security Investigations Division. NSU has programmatic oversight of HSI's participation on the FBI's Joint Terrorism Task Forces (JTTF), serves in a leadership position on the National Joint Terrorism Task Force, and works directly with the National Security Council and senior leadership throughout the interagency to develop, facilitate, and implement unified interagency policy in support of the counterterrorism mission. [15]

The Counterterrorism Section (CTS) within NSU provides programmatic oversight and investigative support to HSI's Special Agents assigned to every JTTF nationwide. CTS ensures that HSI Special Agents assigned to the JTTF program are engaged in every investigation where our unique immigration or trade-based authorities may be used to disrupt terrorist networks and prevent attacks against the homeland. [15]

The National Security Threat Section (NSTS) within NSU is co-located with the U.S. Customs and Border Protection, National Targeting Center – Passenger. NSTS provides ongoing reviews of individuals who are possibly of national security concern as well as any threats to national security and U.S. interests overseas, and notifies HSI Special Agents both domestically and abroad when this information is received. [15]

The Counterterrorism and Criminal Exploitation Unit (CCEU) is part of ICE's Homeland Security Investigations' National Security Investigations Division. The unit prevents terrorists and other criminals from exploiting the nation's immigration system through fraud. It investigates non-immigrant visa holders who violate their immigration status and places a high priority on scrutinizing the activities of known or suspected terrorists and terrorist associations. It also combats criminal exploitation of the student visa system. [16]

Homeland Security Investigations' Counter-Proliferation Investigations (CPI) Program prevents sensitive U.S. technologies and weapons from reaching terrorists, criminal organizations and foreign adversaries.

The Student and Exchange Visitor Program (SEVP) is also part of the National Security Investigations Division and acts as a bridge for government organizations that have an interest in information on nonimmigrants whose primary reason for coming to the United States is to be students. SEVP manages schools and nonimmigrant students in the F and M visa classifications and their dependents. The Department of State (DoS) manages Exchange Visitor Programs, nonimmigrant exchange visitors in the J visa classification and their dependents. Both SEVP and DoS use the Student and Exchange Visitor Information System (SEVIS) to track and monitor schools; exchange visitor programs; and F, M and J nonimmigrants while they visit the United States and participate in the U.S. education system. [17]

Homeland Security Investigations' Counter-Proliferation Investigations (CPI) Program, also within the National Security Investigations Division, prevents sensitive U.S. technologies and weapons from reaching terrorists, criminal organizations and foreign adversaries. The CPI program combats the trafficking and illegal export of the following commodities and services:

- Weapons of mass destruction and associated delivery systems
- Conventional military weaponry, equipment and technology
- Controlled dual - use commodities and technology
- Firearms and ammunition
- Financial and business transactions with sanctioned / embargoed countries and terrorist organizations. [18]

The CPI Export Enforcement Coordination Center (EECC) serves as the primary forum within the federal government for executive departments and agencies to coordinate and enhance their export control enforcement efforts. [19]

Project Shield America is an industry and academic outreach program, the intent of which is to obtain the assistance and cooperation of those companies involved in the manufacture and export of U.S. origin strategic goods, technologies, and munitions items as well as academic researchers who study and research these and other strategic fields. The focus of Project Shield America is to prevent the proliferation of export-controlled technology and components, the acquisition of nuclear, chemical and biological weapons, and the unlawful exportation of weapon systems and classified or controlled technical data. [20]

The CPI Export Enforcement Coordination Center (EECC) serves as the primary forum within the federal government for executive departments and agencies to coordinate and enhance their export control enforcement efforts.

The Visa Security Program (VSP) deploys HSI special agents with immigration law enforcement expertise to diplomatic posts worldwide to conduct visa security activities, such as:

- Examining visa applications for fraud,
- Initiating investigations,
- Coordinating with law enforcement partners, and
- Providing law enforcement training and advice to Department of State consulates. [21]

The Illicit Pathways Attack Strategy (IPAS) is aimed against Transnational Organized Crime (TOC). IPAS elements include:

- Extended operating borders.
- Prioritized networks and pathways.
- Maintaining robust interagency engagement.
- Coordinating with foreign partners in specific regions.
- Supporting efforts to combat crime through laws and policy. [22]

Immigration Enforcement

Immigration enforcement is the largest single area of responsibility for ICE. While certain responsibilities and close cooperation with U.S. Customs and Border Protection (CBP), U.S. Citizenship and Immigration Services (USCIS), and others require significant ICE assets near the border, the majority of immigration enforcement work for ICE takes place in the country's interior. ICE special agents strive to help businesses secure a lawful workforce and enforce immigration laws against those who encourage and rely on unauthorized workers, sometimes taking advantage of their situation to offer low pay and inadequate conditions. Multiple programs help ICE focus and improve on stated priorities to find and remove illegal aliens who are criminals, fugitives or recent arrivals. Immigration enforcement entails cracking down on those who produce fraudulent documents to enable unlawful activity. Additionally, several robust efforts seek to continue improving the safe and humane detention and removal of persons subject to those actions. [3]

ICE's role in the immigration enforcement system is focused on two primary missions: (1) the identification and apprehension of criminal aliens and other removable individuals located in the United States; and (2) the detention and removal of those individuals apprehended in the interior of the U.S.

ICE's role in the immigration enforcement system is focused on two primary missions: (1) the identification and apprehension of criminal aliens and other removable individuals located in the United States; and (2) the detention and removal of those individuals apprehended in the interior of the U.S., as well as those apprehended by CBP officers and agents patrolling our nation's borders. In executing these responsibilities, ICE has prioritized its limited resources on the identification and removal of criminal aliens and those apprehended at the border while attempting to unlawfully enter the United States. [23]

Undocumented workers secure jobs through fraudulent means such as presenting false documents, completing fraudulent benefit applications and stealing someone's identity. To combat unlawful employment and reduce vulnerabilities that help illegal aliens gain such employment, ICE announced the Mutual Agreement between Government and Employers (IMAGE) program in July 2006. Employers enrolling in the IMAGE program obtain access to E-Verify, an Internet-based system that compares information from an employee's Form I-9, Employment Eligibility Verification, to data from U.S Department of Homeland Security and Social Security Administration records. Through this cross-check, E-Verify can confirm employment eligibility status. [24]

ICE works with the private sector to educate employers about their responsibilities to hire only authorized workers and how to accurately verify employment eligibility. However, ICE will also investigate employers to verify that they comply with U.S. law and are not themselves exploiting unauthorized workers. Worksite enforcement investigations often involve egregious violations of criminal statutes by employers and widespread abuses. Such cases often involve additional violations such as alien smuggling, alien harboring, document fraud, money laundering, fraud or worker exploitation. ICE also investigates employers who employ force, threats or coercion (for example, threatening to have employees deported) in order to keep the unauthorized alien workers from reporting substandard wage or working conditions. An effective worksite enforcement strategy must address both employers who knowingly hire illegal workers, as well as the workers themselves. In worksite cases, ICE investigators adhere to high investigative standards, including the following:

- ICE will look for evidence of the mistreatment of workers, along with evidence of trafficking, smuggling, harboring, visa fraud, identification document fraud, money laundering and other such criminal conduct.
- ICE will obtain indictments, criminal arrests or search warrants, or a commitment from a U.S. Attorney's Office to prosecute the targeted employer before arresting employees for civil immigration violations at a worksite. [25]

Apprehended aliens may be placed in secure custody or released on their own recognizance until their case can be heard in immigration court. ERO keeps track of both "detained" and "non-detained" aliens until their case is decided.

Apprehended aliens may be placed in secure custody or released on their own recognizance until their case can be heard in immigration court. ERO keeps track of both "detained" and "non-detained" aliens until their case is decided. The exception is children. Unaccompanied alien minors are turned over to the Department of Health and Human Services Office of Refugee Resettlement until their cases can be heard. [26]

The removal of criminal aliens from the US is a national priority. The National Fugitive Operations Program (NFOP) helps complete this task by identifying, locating and arresting removable criminal aliens. A fugitive alien is a person who has failed to leave the United States after he or she receives a final order of removal, deportation or exclusion, or who has failed to report to ICE after receiving notice to do so. The NFOP's "Absconder Apprehension Initiative" uses data available from National Crime Information Center databases to help find fugitive aliens who have also committed crimes. As part of the Alien Absconder Initiative, ERO developed and coordinated the "ICE ERO Most Wanted" program. This program publicizes the names, faces and other identifying features of the 10 most wanted fugitive criminals by ERO. In FY2012, NFOP efforts resulted in more than 37,000 arrests. [27]

Fugitive criminal aliens are also pursued under the Criminal Alien Program (CAP). CAP provides ICE-wide direction and support in the biometric and biographic identification, arrest, and removal of priority aliens who are incarcerated within federal, state, and local prisons and jails, as well as at-large criminal aliens that have circumvented identification. It is incumbent upon ICE to ensure that all efforts are made to investigate, arrest, and remove individuals from the United States that ICE deems priorities by processing the alien expeditiously and securing a final order of removal for an incarcerated alien before the alien is released to ICE custody. The identification and processing of incarcerated criminal aliens, before release from jails and prisons, decreases or eliminates the time spent in ICE custody and reduces the overall cost to the Federal Government. Additionally, integral to the effective execution of this program is the aggressive prosecution of criminal offenders identified by ERO officers during the course of their duties. ERO, in conjunction with the Offices of the United States Attorneys, actively pursues criminal prosecutions upon the discovery of offenses of the nation's criminal code and immigration laws. This further enhances public safety and provides a significant deterrent to recidivism. [28]

ICE also investigates fraud perpetrated by immigrants seeking to become naturalized citizens. ICE places a high priority on investigating document and benefit fraud. These types of fraud pose a severe threat to national security and public safety because they create a vulnerability that may enable terrorists, other criminals and illegal aliens to gain entry to and remain in the United States. Document and benefit fraud are elements of many immigration-related crimes, such as human smuggling and human trafficking, critical infrastructure protection, worksite enforcement, visa compliance enforcement and national security investigations.

ICE also investigates fraud perpetrated by immigrants seeking to become naturalized citizens. ICE places a high priority on investigating document and benefit fraud.

- Document fraud, also known as identity fraud, is the manufacturing, counterfeiting, alteration, sale, and/or use of identity documents and other fraudulent documents to circumvent immigration laws or for other criminal activity. Identity fraud in some cases also involves identity theft, a crime in which an imposter takes on the identity of a real person (living or deceased).
- Benefit fraud is the willful misrepresentation of a material fact on a petition or application to gain an immigration benefit. Benefit fraud can be an extremely lucrative form of white-collar crime, often involving sophisticated schemes and multiple co-conspirators. These schemes can take years to investigate and prosecute. [29]

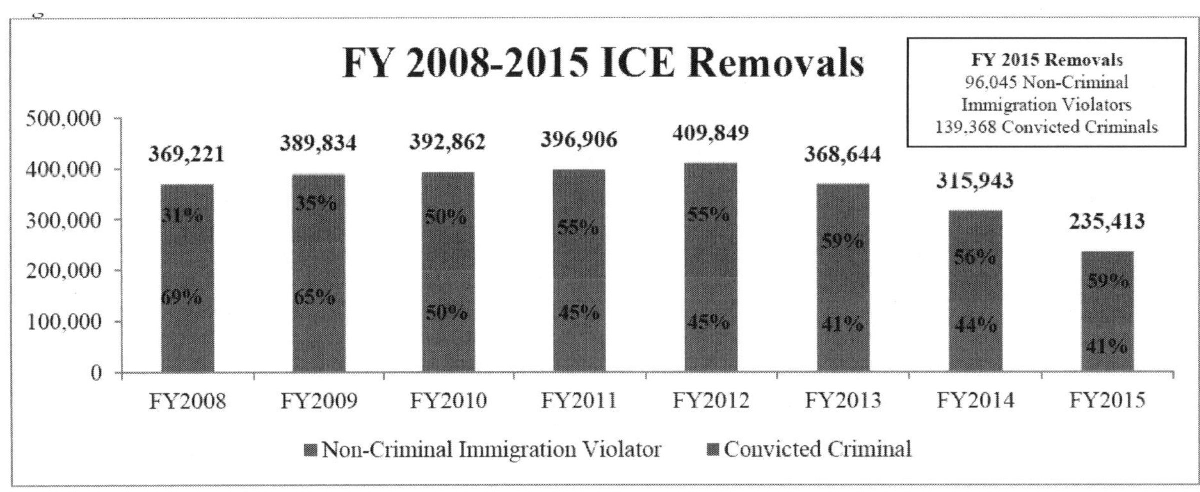

Figure 33-2: ICE Removal Statistics [30]

In 2015, ICE deported 96,045 non-criminal aliens, and 139,368 criminal violators. The decreasing trend in deportations seen in Figure 33-2 is attributed to changing immigration enforcement directives and priorities. [30]

The Identity and Benefit Fraud Unit is charged with investigating and disrupting document and benefit fraud schemes. It coordinates its investigative efforts with other U.S. Department of Homeland Security components, such as U.S. Customs and Border Protection and U.S. Citizenship and Immigration Services, as well as other federal agencies such as the U. S. Department of State and U.S. Department of Labor. The unit also develops and advances policy initiatives and proposes legislative changes to address vulnerabilities in the immigration process to deter fraud and reduce the incentives for committing document and benefit fraud. [29]

Performance Analysis

Congress has a long-standing interest in seeing that immigration enforcement agencies identify and deport criminal aliens. Despite the interest in criminal aliens, inconsistencies in data quality, data collection, and definitions make it impossible to precisely enumerate the criminal alien population, all noncitizens ever convicted of a crime.

Congress has a long-standing interest in seeing that immigration enforcement agencies identify and deport criminal aliens. The expeditious removal of such aliens has been a statutory priority since 1986, and the Department of Homeland Security and its predecessor agency have operated programs targeting criminal aliens since 1988. These programs have grown substantially since FY2005, and deportations of criminal aliens—along with other unauthorized immigrants— have grown proportionally. [31, p. ii]

Despite the interest in criminal aliens, inconsistencies in data quality, data collection, and definitions make it impossible to precisely enumerate the criminal alien population, all noncitizens ever convicted of a crime. The Congressional Research Service (CRS) estimates the number of noncitizens incarcerated in federal and state prisons and local jails—a subset of all criminal aliens—at 183,830 in 2011 (the most recent year for which complete data are available), with state prisons and local jails each accounting for somewhat more incarcerations than federal prisons. The overall proportion of noncitizens in prisons and jails corresponds closely to the proportion of noncitizens in the total U.S. population. [31, p. ii]

While consensus exists on the overarching goal of identifying and removing serious criminal aliens, these programs have generated controversy, in part because many of the aliens identified by ICE have never been convicted of a crime, or have been convicted only of minor criminal offenses. Thus, the programs focus attention on questions about when—if ever—DHS should exercise "prosecutorial discretion" by not asserting its full enforcement authority in certain cases. ICE and DHS officials have testified that resource constraints mean that the department can deport only about 400,000 aliens per year—far fewer than the total number of potentially removable aliens identified. Officials have released a series of memoranda describing criteria to prioritize certain aliens for removal, and to consider exercising discretion in other cases. [31, p. ii]

Another area of concern is ICE's performance in worksite enforcement. ICE's worksite enforcement program is focused primarily on critical infrastructure facilities and cases involving employers who commit "egregious" violations of criminal statutes and engage in worker exploitation. Various measures are available to examine the performance of ICE's worksite enforcement program. They include Final Orders for civil monetary penalties, administrative fines, administrative arrests, criminal arrests, criminal indictments, criminal convictions, and criminal fines and forfeitures. In addition to examining annual changes and trends in the various performance measure data, these data can be considered in relation to the estimated size of the unauthorized workforce or the potential number of employers employing these workers. When considered in this context, ICE's worksite enforcement program can seem quite limited. [32, p. ii]

Conclusion

ICE promotes homeland security and public safety through the strategic and wide-ranging criminal and civil enforcement of hundreds of federal laws governing border control, customs, trade, and immigration. ICE primarily consists of two operational programs: Enforcement and Removal Operations and Homeland Security Investigations. Guided by ICE's prioritized enforcement principles, ERO identifies and apprehends convicted criminals and other individuals deemed removable, detains or places these individuals in alternatives to detention programs, and removes individuals determined to be illegally present (or otherwise subject to removal) from the United States. HSI is responsible for a wide range of domestic and international criminal investigations arising from the illegal movement of people and merchandise into, within, and out of the United States, often in coordination with other Federal agencies. [33]

Challenge Your Understanding

The following questions are designed to challenge your understanding of the material presented in this chapter. Some questions may require additional research outside this book in order to provide a complete answer.

1. What is the mission of the U.S. Immigration and Customs Enforcement agency?
2. How is the ICE mission similar to CBP?
3. How is the ICE mission different from CBP?
4. How is financial crime related to ICE's mission?
5. Which ICE component investigates and disrupts bulk cash smuggling around the world?
6. How is cyber crime related to ICE's mission?
7. Which ICE component investigates and targets purveyors of child pornography?
8. How is counterproliferation related to ICE's mission?
9. Which ICE program aims to prevent the export of sensitive U.S. technology, weapons, and ammunition?
10. What happens to illegal aliens apprehended by ICE?

Chapter 34

U.S. Citizenship & Immigration Services

Learning Outcomes

Careful study of this chapter will help a student do the following:

- Explain the mission of the organization.
- Describe some key components of the organization.
- Discuss some of the work of the organization.

"The Administration will complete reform of the Immigration and Naturalization Service (INS), separating the agency's enforcement and service functions within, as the President has proposed, the new Department of Homeland Security."

- 2002 National Strategy for Homeland Security

Introduction

U.S. Citizenship and Immigration Services (USCIS) adjudicates immigration and naturalization petitions, considers refugee and asylum claims and related humanitarian and international concerns, and provides a range of immigration-related services, such as issuing employment authorizations and processing nonimmigrant change-of-status petitions. Processing immigrant petitions remains USCIS's leading function. In FY2014, it handled roughly 6 million petitions for immigration-related services and benefits. [1, p. ii] USCIS currently funds over 95% of its budget by charging user fees to petitioners for its services. [1, p. 1]

U.S. Citizenship and Immigration Services is the federal agency that oversees lawful immigration to the United States.

Background

USCIS was established with the Homeland Security Act of 2002 and assumed responsibility for the immigration service functions of the federal government on March 1, 2003. [1, p. 2] USCIS replaced the former Immigration and Naturalization Service (INS), whose authorities and responsibilities were split among USCIS, Immigration and Customs Enforcement (ICE), and Customs and Border Protection (CBP). [2]

Mission

U.S. Citizenship and Immigration Services is the federal agency that oversees lawful immigration to the United States. [3]

Services

- Citizenship. Individuals who wish to become U.S. citizens through naturalization submit their applications to USCIS. USIS determines eligibility, processes the applications and, if approved, schedules the applicant for a ceremony to take the Oath of Allegiance. USCIS also determines eligibility and provide documentation of U.S. citizenship for people who acquired or derived U.S. citizenship through their parents.
- Immigration of Family Members. USCIS manages the process that allows current permanent residents and U.S. citizens to bring close relatives to live and work in the United States.

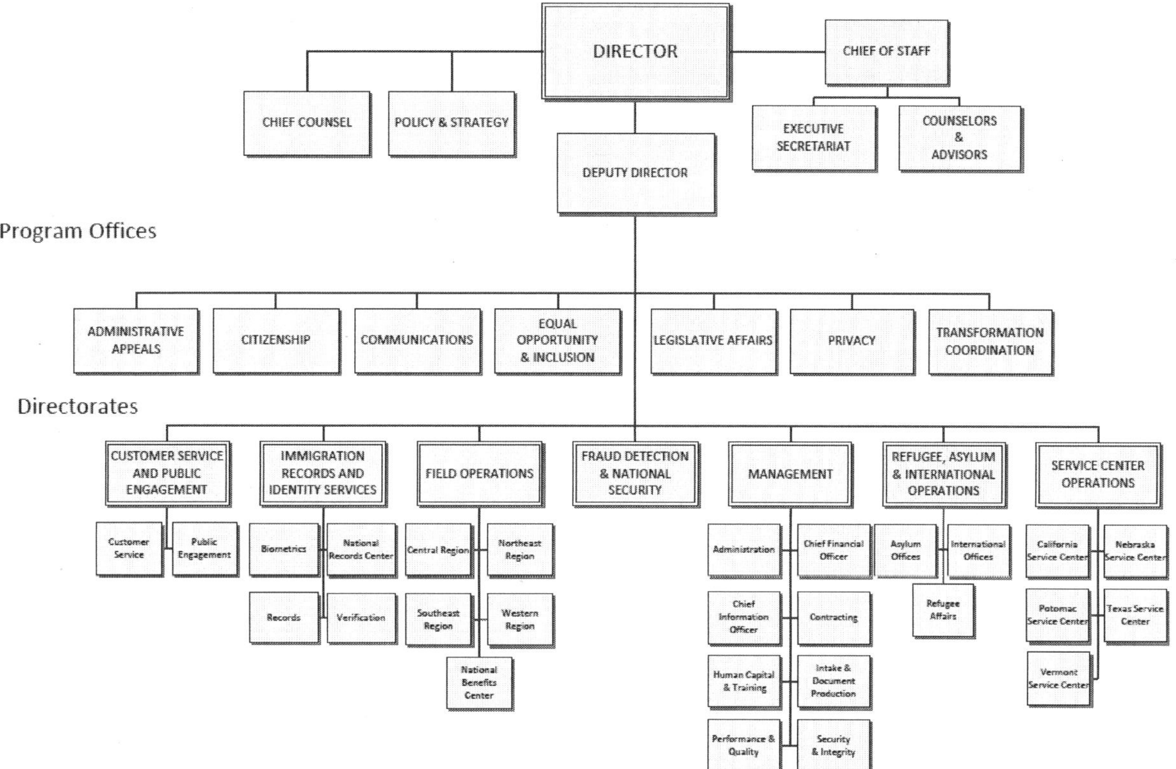

Figure 34-1: USCIS Organization Chart [4]

- Work Authorization. USCIS manages the process that allows individuals from other countries to work in the United States. Some of the opportunities are temporary, and some provide a path to a green card (permanent residence).
- Work Verification. USCIS manages the E - Verify system that allows participating employers to electronically verify the employment eligibility of their newly hired employees.
- Humanitarian Programs. USCIS administers humanitarian programs that provide protection to individuals inside and outside the United States who are displaced by war, famine and civil and political unrest, and those who are forced to flee their countries to escape the risk of death and torture at the hands of persecutors.
- Adoption. USCIS manages the first step in the process for U.S. citizens to adopt children from other countries. Approximately 20,000 adoptions take place each year.
- Civic Integration. USCIS promotes instruction and training on citizenship rights and responsibilities and provides immigrants with the information and tools necessary to successfully integrate into American civic culture.
- Genealogy. Eligible historical records are placed online and otherwise made publicly available to assist in genealogical research. [3]

Organization

USCIS has over 200 offices around the world and employs roughly 19,000 employees and contractors within its directorates and program offices. Processing petitions and applications, which is most of the agency's workload, occurs in four major USCIS Service Centers and 83 Field Offices in the United States, Puerto Rico, and Guam. [1, p. 2]

USCIS Directorates

Processing petitions and applications, which is most of the agency's workload, occurs in four major USCIS Service Centers and 83 Field Offices in the United States, Puerto Rico, and Guam.

The Customer Service and Public Engagement Directorate provides clear, accurate, and timely response to customer concerns and questions, and engage the public through transparent dialogue that promotes participation and feedback.

- The Customer Service Division (CSD) is dedicated to proactively providing information and guidance to USCIS applicants, petitioners and advocates regarding immigration benefits.
- The Public Engagement Division (PED) develops and maintains collaborative relationships with community-based and faith-based organizations, and advances outreach and communication to state, local, territorial, and tribal partners. [5]

The Field Operations Directorate ensures the integrity of the immigration system and lends assistance to applicants, petitioners, and beneficiaries through field offices and the National Benefits Center.

- 83 field offices and field support offices deliver immigration benefit services directly to applicants and petitioners in communities across the United States and its territories.
- The National Benefits Center (NBC) performs centralized front-end processing of applications and petitions that require field office interviews (primarily, family-based I-485s and N-400s). In addition, the NBC adjudicates some form types to completion including I-765s, I-131s, immigration benefits associated with the LIFE Act, legalization-related applications and international adoption cases.
- A headquarters office, four regional offices and 26 district offices provide oversight, direction and support to the field offices, field support offices and the NBC. [6]

The Fraud Detection and National Security Directorate (FDNS) determines whether individuals or organizations filing for immigration benefits pose a threat to national security, public safety, or the integrity of the nation's legal immigration system. FDNS officers resolve background check information and other concerns that surface during the processing of immigration benefit applications and petitions. Resolution often requires communication with law enforcement or intelligence agencies to make sure that the information is relevant to the applicant or petitioner at hand and, if so, whether the information would have an impact on eligibility for the benefit. FDNS officers are located in every USCIS Center, District, Field, and Asylum Office. FDNS officers are also located in other government agencies. [7]

The Refugee, Asylum, and International Operations Directorate (RAIO) provides immigration, protection, and humanitarian services for people who are fleeing oppression, persecution, or torture; facing urgent humanitarian situations; and military members and overseas residents who need replacement documents to return to the U.S.

The Fraud Detection and National Security Directorate (FDNS) determines whether individuals or organizations filing for immigration benefits pose a threat to national security, public safety, or the integrity of the nation's legal immigration system.

- The Refugee Affairs Division provides resettlement benefits to people who are outside their countries and cannot or are unwilling to return to their homes because they fear serious harm.
- The Asylum Division manages the U.S. affirmative asylum process, which allows individuals who are already in the U.S. (or at a port of entry), to remain here because they have been persecuted or fear persecution. The individual must not be in removal proceedings to apply under affirmative asylum procedures.
- The International Operations Division, with offices around the world, is the face of USCIS abroad. These offices reunite families, enable adoptive children to come to join permanent families in the U.S., consider parole requests from individuals outside the U.S. for urgent humanitarian reasons or significant public benefit, and provide information services and travel documents to people around the world. [8]

The Service Center Operations Directorate (SCOPS) provides services to people seeking immigration benefits while ensuring the integrity of the immigration system. SOPS provides decisions to individuals who want to receive immigration benefits, and supports components at headquarters and service centers. Work performed by the service centers is organized by these distinct product lines:

- Business services process Immigrant (Permanent) and Nonimmigrant (Temporary) classifications for individuals of extraordinary ability; outstanding researchers and professors; executives and managers; advanced degree professionals; athletes, entertainers; skilled and unskilled workers; individuals working in specialty occupations; religious workers; agricultural workers and temporary and seasonal workers, among others.
- Family services process petitions for immediate family members and fiancés.

- Humanitarian services process benefit requests filed by refugees and asylees and their accompanying family members, individuals seeking consideration of deferred action for childhood arrivals (DACA), and individuals seeking temporary protected status (TPS); relief for victims of abuse, crimes, and severe forms of trafficking; waivers of inadmissibility; and posthumous naturalization based on death in active military service, among other humanitarian benefits.
- Students services process requests for practical training in a field of study and waivers for medical doctors to enable them to work in medically underserved areas. [9]

The Office of Citizenship engages and supports partners to welcome immigrants, promote English language learning, and education on the rights and responsibilities of citizenship.

USCIS Offices

The Administrative Appeals Office (AAO) conducts administrative review of immigrant appeals to ensure consistency and accuracy in the interpretation of immigration law and policy. AAO generally issues "non-precedent" decisions, which apply existing law and policy to the facts of a given case. After review by the Attorney General, AAO may also issue "precedent" decisions to provide clear and uniform guidance to adjudicators and the public on the proper interpretation of law and policy. AAO exercises appellate jurisdiction over approximately 50 different immigration case types. [10]

The Office of Intake and Document Production designs, prints, and distributes USCIS forms; manages the paper (USCIS Lockbox facilities) intake system; troubleshoots intake issues, adjudicates fee waivers and resolves problems with applications; and produces and delivers secure benefit documents and cards, such as Permanent Resident Cards. [11]

The Office of Citizenship engages and supports partners to welcome immigrants, promote English language learning, and education on the rights and responsibilities of citizenship. The office supports national and community-based organizations that prepare immigrants for citizenship by providing grants, educational materials, and technical assistance; and conducts training workshops for educators and organizations preparing immigrants for citizenship. [12]

The Office of Communications (OCOMM) oversees and coordinates official USCIS communications to both internal and external audiences. OCOMM manages communications and messaging to external audiences; and informs the public regarding USCIS immigration services and benefits. [13]

The Office of Legislative Affairs (OLA) maintains relationships with Congress by ensuring prompt replies to constituent concerns; reaching out on issues of interest; and providing ongoing educational activities for Congressmen and staff. [14]

The Office of Privacy maintains privacy protections for individuals and promotes transparency of USCIS operations. [15]

The Office of Transformation Coordination manages and oversees the development of the USCIS Electronic Immigration System (USCIS ELIS) to move the agency from a paper -based application and adjudication process to an electronic one. [16]

USCIS Functions

Three major activities dominate USCIS functions: adjudication of immigration petitions, adjudication of naturalization petitions, and consideration of refugee and asylum claims and related humanitarian and international concerns. USCIS also provides a range of immigration-related services, such as employment authorizations and change-of-status petitions. [1, p. 2]

Three major activities dominate USCIS functions:

1. *Adjudication of immigration petitions;*
2. *Adjudication of naturalization petitions; and*
3. *Consideration of refugee and asylum claims and related humanitarian and international concerns.*

Immigration Adjudication. USCIS processes roughly 6 million petitions each year, including about 1 million for permanent status and 5 million for temporary nonimmigrant status. USCIS adjudicators determine the eligibility of immediate relatives and other family members of U.S. citizens and lawful permanent residents (LPRs); employees that U.S. businesses have demonstrated that they need (and their immediate family members); and other foreign nationals who meet specified criteria. They also must determine whether a foreign national in the United States on a temporary visa (i.e., a nonimmigrant) is eligible to change to another nonimmigrant status or adjust to LPR status. [1, p. 3]

Work Authorization. USCIS adjudicates work authorizations for aliens who meet certain conditions. [1, p. 3]

Employment Verification. USCIS is responsible for the Electronic Employment Eligibility Verification (E-Verify) program used by employers to ensure that their employees possess lawful status to work in the United States. Since FY2007, congressional appropriations have supported the E-Verify program. [1, p. 3]

International Services. The USCIS Office of International Affairs adjudicates refugee applications and conducts background and record checks related to some immigrant petitions abroad. The largest component of this program is the asylum officer corps, a small but occasionally high-profile part of USCIS's workload, whose members interview and screen asylum applicants. [1, p. 3]

Fraud Detection and National Security. USCIS must confirm that all applicants are eligible for the particular immigration status they are seeking, or alternatively, determine they should be rejected because they fail to meet other legal requirements. USCIS established the Office of Fraud Detection and National Security at the agency's inception in 2003 to work with the appropriate law enforcement entities to handle foreign nationals whose applications and petitions trigger national security and criminal database notifications and to identify systemic fraud in the application process. Many such duties formerly performed by the Immigration and Naturalization Service enforcement arm are now the responsibility of DHS's Immigration and Customs Enforcement (ICE). [1, pp. 3-4]

USCIS is responsible for naturalization, a process that grants U.S. citizenship to Legal Permanent Residents (LPRs) who fulfill the related requirements established by Congress in the Immigration and Nationality Act of 1952.

Civic Integration. USCIS promotes instruction and training on citizenship rights and responsibilities and provides immigrants with the information and tools necessary to successfully integrate into American civic culture. This includes maintaining a Citizenship Resource Center website and managing the Immigrant Integration Grants Program, which assists public or private nonprofit organizations that provide citizenship instruction and naturalization application services to Lawful Permanent Residents. [1, p. 4]

Naturalization. USCIS is responsible for naturalization, a process that grants U.S. citizenship to LPRs who fulfill the related requirements established by Congress in the Immigration and Nationality Act of 1952 (INA). Adjudicators must determine whether aliens have continuously resided in the United States for a specified period; possess good moral character, are able to read, write, speak, and understand English; and possess a basic knowledge of U.S. civics and history. [1, p. 4]

USCIS Operations

USCIS funds the processing and adjudication of immigrant, nonimmigrant, refugee, asylum, and citizenship benefits through its user fees deposited into the Immigration Examination Fee Account (IEFA). This account is not subject to annual congressional approval. The INA states that user fees be set at a level that ensures recovery of the full costs of providing adjudication and naturalization services, including similar services to those people who are not charged, such as asylum applicants. User fees can also be set at levels to cover "costs associated with the administration of the fees collected." [1, p. 6]

In 1998, Congress passed the American Competitiveness and Workforce Improvement Act (ACWIA), which, among other provisions, temporarily increased the number of temporary skilled H-1B workers admitted to the United States. To provide training for American workers and thus reduce employer reliance on immigrant workers, the act established the H-1B Nonimmigrant Petitioner Fee Account to fund training and education programs administered by the Department of Labor and the National Science Foundation, thereby establishing an affirmative role for U.S. employers to assist with education and training efforts for U.S. workers. The statutorily set H-1B Nonimmigrant Petitioner Fee is currently $1,500 ($750 if the employer has 25 or fewer full-time equivalent employees). USCIS receives 5% of the fees paid into the account by all employers participating in the H-1B program. In FY2014, the USCIS share of funding in this account was $13 million, representing 0.07% of the USCIS budget. [1, p. 7]

USCIS customers who seek immigration services and benefits often face challenges as they navigate the complexity of U.S. immigration laws and regulations. Obtaining answers to questions and resolving issues may require visits to USCIS offices that can be time-consuming and inconvenient. According to the DHS Inspector General's office, USCIS was relying on paper-based processes to manage the filing and adjudication of immigration benefits as recently as 2011.

On December 8, 2004, Congress passed the H-1B Visa Reform Act of 2004, which established the Fraud Prevention and Detection Account. This account receives funds for fraud detection and prevention activities from a "Fraud Fee" (currently $500) that must be submitted with a petition seeking an initial grant of H-1B, H-2B, or L visa classification to foreign nationals or by an employer seeking to change an alien's employer within those classifications. USCIS receives 33% of the Fraud Detection and Prevention Account fees. As with the H-1B Nonimmigrant Petitioner Fee, the Fraud Prevention and Detection Fee is set by statute, and DHS has no authority to adjust it. In FY2014, the USCIS share of funding in this account was $41 million, representing 1.36% of the USCIS budget. [1, pp. 7-8]

USCIS customers who seek immigration services and benefits often face challenges as they navigate the complexity of U.S. immigration laws and regulations. Obtaining answers to questions and resolving issues may require visits to USCIS offices that can be time-consuming and inconvenient. For many services, USCIS customers must apply for most benefits by mail. USCIS employees then review submitted paper files and ship documents between offices to complete their adjudication. [1, p. 12]

According to the DHS Inspector General's office, USCIS was relying on paper-based processes to manage the filing and adjudication of immigration benefits as recently as 2011. [1, p. 12] This mode of operation generates complaints of lost files. Many observers comment that it is entirely outmoded to meet the growing workload and challenges facing the agency. [1, p. 4]

As part of a comprehensive set of initiatives to modernize the agency, USCIS embarked on an agency-wide investment referred to as "transformation" that began transitioning the agency from a fragmented, paper-based operational environment to a centralized and consolidated environment facilitating electronic processing of the adjudication function. In 2012, USCIS formally launched the first two phases of its electronic immigration application system, known as ELIS. Under ELIS, eligible individuals can establish an account and apply online to extend or change their nonimmigrant status for certain visa types. ELIS enables USCIS officers to review and adjudicate filings online. It also includes tools to combat fraud and identify national security concerns. Nevertheless, ELIS still possesses limited features and must expand substantially before USCIS can move to an entirely electronic platform. [1, p. 13]

Capacity

As part of a comprehensive set of initiatives to modernize the agency, USCIS embarked on an agency-wide investment referred to as "transformation" that began transitioning the agency from a fragmented, paper-based operational environment to a centralized and consolidated environment facilitating electronic processing.

USCIS regularly faces concerns from immigration observers about the agency's ability to manage adjudication workloads, particularly during surges in application volume that result from changes in immigration policy or other major events. Such an event occurred in November 2014 when President Obama announced the Immigration Accountability Executive Action deferring removals on certain classes of unauthorized aliens. The executive order encompassed nearly 5 million unauthorized aliens, sparking a surge in new applications. The move was unprecedented, but not unusual, as USCIS processed roughly 2.7 million additional applications between 1987 and 1989 following passage of the Immigration Reform and Control Act of 1986 (IRCA, P.L. 99-603), which, by most accounts, was successfully administrated. However, the Government Accountability Office noted that when the 3 million individuals legalized under IRCA in 1986 became eligible for naturalization in 1995, the application backlog increased markedly. Processing backlogs may affect processing times for other petitions as resources within the agency are reconfigured to address urgent needs. This latter concern has been raised by some who argue the agency is diverting resources used to process petitions of those immigrating to the United States legally in order to process petitions that benefit the unauthorized alien population. [1, p. 14]

Critics also describe a processing system that continues to rely primarily on paper applications and postal mail and argue that other agency services will suffer from the diversion of USCIS resources to attend to the pressing caseload caused by the 2014 executive action. After it was announced in November 2014, the agency made plans to hire over 1,000 full and part-time personnel to handle the workload. Costs for the new hires were to be covered by other petition fees. [1, pp. 14-15]

Conclusion

For several years, some Members of Congress have favored "comprehensive immigration reform" (CIR), a label that commonly refers to omnibus legislation that includes increased border security and immigration enforcement, expanded employment eligibility verification, revision of nonimmigrant visas and legal permanent immigration, and legalization for some unauthorized aliens residing in the country. Other Members of Congress prefer incremental revisions to the Immigration and Nationality Act that would address some but not all of these elements, and with sequential reforms that would tackle border security and interior enforcement provisions prior to revising legal immigration or enacting legalization pathways. [17, p. ii] In 2013, the Senate passed S. 744 calling for comprehensive immigration reform. After the bill was blocked by the House, President Obama undertook executive action that inflamed both legislative branches. Unfortunately, while everybody agrees immigration reform is needed, nobody agrees how to accomplish it.

Challenge Your Understanding

The following questions are designed to challenge your understanding of the material presented in this chapter. Some questions may require additional research outside this book in order to provide a complete answer.

1. What is the mission of the U.S. Citizenship and Immigration Services?
2. Which USCIS component has 83 field offices to process applications for citizenship and other benefits?
3. Which USCIS component determines if people applying for citizenship pose a threat to national security?
4. Which USCIS component assists people seeking asylum from persecution or have urgent humanitarian needs?
5. What is the difference between a U.S. immigrant, nonimmigrant, refugee, asylee, and naturalized citizen?
6. Which of the following is not a naturalization requirement under the 1952 Immigration and Nationalization Act?
    a. Understanding of the English language.
    b. A knowledge and understanding of U.S. government.
    c. A profession or trade capable of providing a living wage.
7. List and describe the three major activities that dominate USCIS functions.
8. How are USCIS operations funded?
9. What countermeasure did Congress enact in 1998 when it lifted the quota on temporary workers in the U.S.?
10. Should the U.S. increase or decrease immigration quotas? Explain your answer.

Part V: Mission Partners

This section examines selected partners in the Homeland Security Enterprise. It is beyond the scope of this book to address all partners identified in Chapter 13. For the sake of brevity, we have tried to address those who play a larger role within the context of DHS missions. Congress is integral to DHS funding and oversight; The National Security Council is the central coordinating body for all Federal interagency planning and execution; DHS is a member of the Intelligence Community, both as a recipient and contributor; DoD is a supporting agency for all Emergency Support Functions, and an essential partner for large-scale incident response; the National Guard under command of their State Governors are exempt from Posse Comitatus restrictions on law enforcement, and typically the first military units on-scene following disaster; While the FBI remains the Lead Federal Agency for counterterrorism, they work closely with DHS to develop leads and issue alerts; Through its Fusion Center program, DHS maintains a communications pathway for sharing intelligence data between the Federal government and State and Local law enforcement; and, of course, DHS continues to help First Responders become better prepared through the National Preparedness System. Though some of the material here was seen in earlier chapters, in this section we try to give the partners more comprehensive treatment with respect to their roles and responsibilities in working with DHS to safeguard the U.S. from domestic catastrophic destruction.

Chapter 35

Congress

Learning Outcomes

Careful study of this chapter will help a student do the following:

- Describe the relationship between Congress and DHS.
- Explain the purpose of congressional oversight.
- Discuss different means for conducting oversight.
- Evaluate current oversight of DHS.

"If men were angels, no government would be necessary. If angels were to govern men, neither external nor internal controls on government would be necessary. In framing a government which is to be administered by men over men, the great difficulty lies in this: you must first enable the government to control the governed; and in the next place, oblige it to control itself."

- James Madison, Federalist No. 51, 1788

Introduction

Congress created the Department of Homeland Security. Congress funds the Department. Congress also maintains oversight of its activities. This chapter examines the oversight role of Congress and how it has been applied to the Department of Homeland Security.

Congress created the Department of Homeland Security. Congress funds the Department. Congress also maintains oversight of its activities.

Background

Power in American national government is decentralized, divided, dispersed, and limited. This distribution of power derives in part from the Constitution, through limitations imposed on the government, the system of checks and balances among the three branches, and independent bases of support and authority for each branch. [1, p. 1]

Congress, the President, and the Supreme Court have separate and distinct political bases under the Constitution, to foster each branch's independence and integrity. The ultimate purpose behind this separation, James Madison argued in the Federalist Papers, is to prevent a "faction" — that is, a group "adverse to the rights of other citizens, or to the permanent and aggregate interest of the community" — from gaining control over the entire government. [1, p. 2]

Under the Constitution, the three branches have both enumerated and implied powers that reinforce their institutional independence and political power. Accompanying these, however, is shared responsibility for public policy and a system of checks and balances. These "auxiliary precautions," as Madison called them in the Federalist Papers, are designed so that the "several constituent parts may, by their mutual relations, be the means of keeping each other in their proper places ... [and] may be a check on the other." [1, p. 5]

The key function of lawmaking is shared, with the President able to veto legislation passed by both chambers of Congress; to override his veto requires a two-thirds vote in each house. Further, the Supreme Court, through its implied power of judicial review, can declare a statute or a part of it unconstitutional, as it did initially, two centuries ago, in Marbury v. Madison. [1, p. 5]

Control of national security policy is also divided. While the President is commander in chief of the armed forces, Congress has authority to declare war, raise and support armies, and make rules governing the land, air, and naval forces. While the President holds the sword, as commander in chief, Congress holds the purse strings, through the appropriations process. The Supreme Court too can affect the military capacity of the United States, as the Court did when it overturned the President's seizure of the steel mills during the Korean War. [1, p. 5]

Control of national security policy is also divided. While the President is commander in chief of the armed forces, Congress has authority to declare war, raise and support armies, and make rules governing the land, air, and naval forces. While the President holds the sword, as commander in chief, Congress holds the purse strings.

Although "executive power is vested in a President" by the Constitution (Article II, Section 1), he shares official responsibility for enforcing, implementing, and administering public law and policy with other officers and offices. Individual agencies and subordinate officers in the executive branch and elsewhere have been delegated duties and authority directly by statute. [1, p. 6]

The Constitution does not establish specific departments or agencies; these are created and sustained by legislation. As a result, a wide range and variety of organizations administer public policy. These include not only the cabinet departments — which now number 15, with the new Department of Homeland Security — but also other executive branch agencies, such as the Environmental Protection Agency and the Central Intelligence Agency. [1, p. 6]

The constitutional system — through its founding premise of limited government and an intricate system of separated institutions, checks and balances, and shared responsibilities — strives to meet two core values of democracy. One is to ensure majority rule, through, for instance, the popular election of officials who make public policy; the other is to protect individual rights and civil liberties, through specific constitutional safeguards and indirectly through restraints on and competition among the three branches. [1, p. 6]

Congressional Oversight

Oversight is an implicit constitutional obligation of Congress. According to Historian Arthur Schlesinger, Jr., the framers believed it was not necessary to make specific reference to "oversight" in the Constitution. "[I]t was not considered necessary to make an explicit grant of such authority," wrote Schlesinger. "The power to make laws implied the power to see whether they were faithfully executed." The Constitution also granted Congress an array of formal powers—the purse strings, lawmaking, impeachment, among others—to hold the president and the administration accountable for their actions or inactions. In short, oversight plays a key role in our system of checks and balances. [2, p. 5]

A fundamental objective of congressional oversight is to hold executive officials accountable for the implementation of delegated authority.

There is a large number of overlapping purposes associated with oversight. This array can be divided into three basic types: programmatic, political, and institutional. Programmatic purposes include such objectives as making sure agencies and programs are working in a cost-effective and efficient manner; ensuring executive compliance with legislative intent; evaluating program performance; improving the economy of governmental performance; investigating waste, fraud, and abuse in governmental programs; reviewing the agency rulemaking process; acquiring information useful in future policymaking; or determining whether agencies or programs are fulfilling their statutory mission. [2, p. 5]

There are also political purposes associated with oversight, such as generating favorable publicity for lawmakers, winning the electoral support of constituents and outside groups, or rebutting criticisms of favorite programs or agencies. After all, oversight occurs in an ever-present political context in which Congress's relationship with administrative entities can range from cooperation to conflict. There are, moreover, inherent constitutional and political tensions between Congress and the President even during periods of unified government (one party in charge of the House, Senate, and White House). Partisan and inter-branch conflicts are not uncommon in the conduct of the legislative review function. [2, pp. 5-6]

In addition, there are institutional oversight purposes that merit special mention, because they serve to protect congressional prerogatives and strengthen the American public's ability to evaluate and reevaluate executive activities and actions. Three institutional purposes include checking the power of the executive branch; investigating how a law is being administered; and informing Congress and the public. [2, p. 6]

A fundamental objective of congressional oversight is to hold executive officials accountable for the implementation of delegated authority. This objective is especially important given the huge expansion of executive influence in the modern era. If the Founding Fathers returned to observe their handiwork, they would likely be surprised by such developments as the creation of a "presidential branch" of government (the Office of Management and Budget, the National Security Council, and the like) and the establishment of so many federal departments and agencies. From three departments in 1789 (State, Treasury, and War, renamed Defense in 1947), a dozen more have been added to the cabinet. [2, p. ii]

Clearly, given the role and scope of the federal establishment, the importance of Congress's review function looms large in checking and monitoring the delegated authority that it grants to federal departments and agencies. [2, p. ii]

A traditional method of congressional oversight is hearings and investigations into executive branch operations.

Oversight Mechanisms

In carrying out its oversight responsibilities, Congress may choose from a variety of techniques to hold agencies accountable, so that if one technique proves to be ineffective, committees and Members can employ others singly or in combination. Most of these techniques are utilized by the committees of Congress: standing, subcommittee, select, or special. [2, p. 9]

A traditional method of congressional oversight is hearings and investigations into executive branch operations. Legislators need to know how effectively federal programs are working and how well agency officials are responding to legislative or committee directives. And they want to know the scope and intensity of public support for government programs to assess the need for statutory changes. Although the terms "hearings" and "investigations" overlap ("investigative hearings," for example) and they may look alike in their formal setting and operation, a shorthand distinction is that hearings focus generally on the efficiency and effectiveness of federal agencies and programs. Investigations, too, may address programmatic efficiency and effectiveness, but their primary focus—triggered by widespread public interest and debate—is often on allegations of wrongdoing, lack of agency preparedness or competence, fraud and abuse, conflicts of interest, and the like. Famous examples include investigations so well-known that a few words are often enough to trigger the attentive public's recollection, such as the 1972 Watergate break-in, the 1987 Iran-Contra affair, or the Hurricane Katrina debacle of 2005. [2, p. 9]

Congress can pass authorizing legislation that establishes, continues (a reauthorization), or abolishes (a de-authorization) a federal agency or program. It can enact "statutes authorizing the activities of the departments, prescribing their internal organization and regulating their procedures and work methods." Once an agency or program is created, the reauthorization process, which typically occurs on an annual or multiyear cycle, can be an important oversight tool. Significant issues are often raised during the authorization or reauthorization process. Lawmakers may ask such questions as: Can the agency be made smaller? If this program or agency did not exist, would it be created today? Should functions that overlap several agencies be merged or consolidated? What fundamental changes need to be made in how the department operates? [2, p. 10]

Congress probably exercises its most effective oversight of agencies and programs through the appropriations process.

Congress probably exercises its most effective oversight of agencies and programs through the appropriations process. As James Madison wrote in The Federalist Papers No. 58: "The power of the purse may, in fact, be regarded as the most complete and effectual weapon with which any constitution can arm the immediate representatives of the people, for obtaining a redress of every grievance, and for carrying into effect every just and salutary measure." By cutting off or reducing funds, Congress can effectively abolish agencies or curtail federal programs. For example, in its various committee reports to accompany FY2010 appropriations measures, the House Appropriations Committee includes "a three-part list of terminations, program reductions and White House initiatives that have been denied." By increasing funds, appropriators can build up neglected program areas. In either case, the appropriating panels in each chamber have formidable power to shape ongoing federal agencies and programs. A noted, congressional budget expert remarked that the appropriating process as an oversight method is comparable to a Janus (after the mythical Roman god)-like weapon: "The stick of spending reductions in case agencies cannot satisfactorily defend their budget requests and past performance, and the carrot of more money if agencies produce convincing success stories or the promise of future results." [2, p. 11]

Congress has created statutory offices of inspectors general (IGs) in nearly 70 major federal entities and departments. The IGs, for example, are located in all fifteen cabinet departments, the Central Intelligence Agency (CIA), and the independent regulatory commissions. Granted substantial independence by the Inspectors General Act of 1978, as amended in 1988 and again in 2008, these officials are authorized to conduct investigations and audits of their agencies to improve efficiency, end waste and fraud, discourage mismanagement, and strengthen the effectiveness and economy of agency operations. Appointed in various ways—in most cases either by the President subject to Senate confirmation or by agency heads—IGs report their findings and recommendations to (1) the Attorney General in cases of suspected violations of federal criminal law, (2) semiannually to the agency head, who must transmit the IG report to Congress within thirty days with no changes to the report but with his or her suggestions; and (3) in the case of "particularly serious or flagrant problems," immediately to the agency head who must send the report to Congress within seven days unaltered but with his or her recommendations. Inspectors generals, said a Senator, are "the government's first line of defense against fraud." [2, p. 11]

The Government Accountability Office (GAO), formerly titled the General Accounting Office until the name change in 2004, was established by the Budget and Accounting Office of 1921. With about 3,100 employees, GAO functions as Congress's investigative arm, conducting financial and program audits and evaluations of executive activities, operations, and programs. For example, in one study, GAO reported "that 19 of 24 Federal agencies ... could not fully explain how they had spent taxpayer money appropriated by Congress." The head of GAO is the Comptroller General (CG), who is nominated by the President (following a recommendation process involving the bipartisan leaders of the House and Senate) and subject to the advice and consent of the Senate for a non-renewable 15-year term. The GAO conducts field investigations of administrative activities and programs, prescribes accounting standards for the executive branch, prepares policy analyses, adjudicates bid protests, makes recommendations for legislative action, evaluates programs, and provides legal opinions on government actions and activities. The office submits hundreds of reports to Congress annually, describing ways to root out waste and mismanagement in executive branch programs and to promote program performance. One of its traditional reports to Congress is on government programs and activities that are "high risk," that is, they require significant improvements in their operations and performance. [2, p. 12]

The Government Accountability Office (GAO), formerly titled the General Accounting Office until the name change in 2004, was established by the Budget and Accounting Office of 1921. With about 3,100 employees, GAO functions as Congress's investigative arm, conducting financial and program audits and evaluations of executive activities, operations, and programs.

Numerous laws require executive agencies to submit reports periodically, and as required by specific events or certain conditions, to Congress and its committees. Generally the report requirement encourages self-evaluation by the executive branch and promotes agency accountability to Congress. Reporting requirements involve weighing Congress's need for information and analysis to conduct evaluations of agencies and programs against the imposition of burdensome or unnecessary obligations on executive entities. (Recall, too, that IGs regularly report to Congress.) [2, p. 12]

Each lawmaker's office handles thousands of requests each year from constituents seeking help in dealing with executive agencies. The requests range from inquiries about lost Social Security checks or delayed pension payments to disaster relief assistance and complicated tax appeals to the Internal Revenue Service. "Constituents perceive casework in nonpolitical terms," wrote two scholars. "They expect their representatives to provide [this service]." Casework, an ombudsman-like function, has the positive effect of bringing quirks in the administrative machinery to Members' attention. Solutions to an individual constituent's problems can suggest legislative remedies on a broader scale. On occasion, constituents' casework requests may be used in oversight hearings by Members to highlight and lend support to a problem or shortcoming in the operations of a program or agency. [2, p. 13]

Congressional Oversight of Homeland Security

For all the reasons cited, congressional oversight is an important and necessary function of the legislative branch to ensure the will of the people are maintained by the executive branch of U.S. government. Congress, however, must maintain a balance to ensure its oversight functions don't become overly burdensome and impede the functions of the executive agencies invested with the authority to perform their designated role. It was with this in mind that the 9/11 Commission originally recommended that "Congress should create a single, principal point of oversight and review for homeland security. Congressional leaders are best able to judge what committee should have jurisdiction over this department and its duties. But we believe that Congress does have the obligation to choose one in the House and one in the Senate, and that this committee should be a permanent standing committee with a nonpartisan staff." [3, p. 421] Unfortunately, this view did not prevail, and ten years later it was seen as the most important unfulfilled recommendation of the 9/11 Commission. [4, p. 37]

Ninety-two committees and subcommittees of Congress now exercise some jurisdiction over the Department of Homeland Security. Every former Secretary of Homeland Security as well as current high-level DHS officials report—as they have for a decade—that this fragmented oversight is a significant impediment to the department's successful development.

According to a retrospective analysis on the tenth anniversary of the 9/11 Commission Report (July 2014), the Annenberg Public Policy Center found:

> "Ninety-two committees and subcommittees of Congress now exercise some jurisdiction over the Department of Homeland Security. Every former Secretary of Homeland Security as well as current high-level DHS officials report—as they have for a decade—that this fragmented oversight is a significant impediment to the department's successful development. This Balkanized system of oversight detracts from the department's mission and has made Americans less safe. It is long past time for Congress to oversee the department as a cohesive organization rather than a collection of disparate parts. Only a committee with responsibility for all DHS components will be able to provide the department with useful strategic guidance. Reducing jurisdictional overlap." [4, p. 37]

The 9/11 Commission saw agility as an essential capability required to counter a nimble enemy. In its 2004 report, the 9/11 Commission observed that Congress, as a whole, adjusted slowly to the rise of transnational terrorism as a threat to national security. In the years before September 11, terrorism seldom registered as important, and Congress did not reorganize itself after the end of the Cold War to address new threats. Committee jurisdiction over terrorism was splintered in both the House and

Senate. The 9/11 Commission assessed Congress's treatment of terrorism before 9/11 as episodic and inadequate; its overall attention level was low. It regarded Congress's oversight of intelligence and terrorism as "dysfunctional." [4, p. 20]

An oppressive bureaucracy impedes agility, which is why the 9/11 Commission recommended streamlining congressional oversight. They foresaw, though, it would not be easy. According to the 2004 9/11 Commission Report, few things were more difficult to change in Washington than congressional committee jurisdiction and prerogatives. To a member, these assignments are almost as important as the map of their own congressional district. [3, p. 419] Unfortunately, we were right. While the executive branch has undergone historic change and institutional reform, Congress has proved deeply resistant to needed change. It has made some minor adjustments, but not the necessary structural changes in oversight and appropriations for homeland security and intelligence. [4, p. 20]

As the Department of Homeland Security was assembled from various components of 22 existing Federal agencies, instead of consolidating oversight, Congress chose to leave oversight with their original committees.

As the Department of Homeland Security was assembled from various components of 22 existing Federal agencies, instead of consolidating oversight, Congress chose to leave oversight with their original committees. [5] More than 90 committees and subcommittees have some jurisdiction over DHS, nearly three times the number that oversee the Defense Department. And that doesn't count nearly 30 other congressional bodies such as task forces and commissions. [6] The cost is significant. DHS must divert crucial resources to answer the varied committees' requests. Between 2009 and 2010, for example, DHS conducted over 3,900 briefings and testified before Congress more than 285 times. The cost of such oversight to the Department is estimated in the tens of millions of dollars, with thousands of lost work hours that DHS could have spent executing its mission. [5]

There is wide consensus among former DHS officials, former congressional leaders, and homeland security experts that simplifying congressional oversight of DHS is necessary if the department is to do its part to ensure the prosperity, safety and security of the United States. [7] In its tenth anniversary review of the 9/11 Commission Report, the Annenberg Public Policy Center reiterated the original recommendation:

> "Congress should oversee and legislate for DHS through one primary authorizing committee. The Department of Homeland Security should receive the same streamlined oversight as the Department of Defense. At the very minimum, the next Congress should sharply reduce the number of committees and subcommittees with some jurisdiction over the department." [4, p. 38]

Conclusion

The Founding Fathers established Congress to express the will of the people in governing themselves. As the nation grew and faced new challenges, the executive branch expanded to deal with new threats and complexities faced by the nation as a whole. Accordingly, Congress expanded its oversight to ensure executive agencies acted according to the will of the people it represented. Unfortunately, Congress was too slow to change to the evolving terrorist threat manifested by 9/11. Despite the lessons learned and recommendations made by the 9/11 Commission, Congress remains resistant to change. The result is that the Department of Homeland Security has been burdened with excessive oversight that detracts from its primary mission, and Congress is no more agile than it was before 9/11 to counter the threat of a nimble enemy.

Challenge Your Understanding

The following questions are designed to challenge your understanding of the material presented in this chapter. Some questions may require additional research outside this book in order to provide a complete answer.

1. What is the relationship between Congress and DHS?
2. List and describe two elements of national security delegated to Congress by the Constitution.
3. What is the basic purpose of congressional oversight?
4. Which oversight method is often triggered by public concern over agency competency and preparedness?
5. Which oversight method is employed to make a determination on program continuation?
6. Which oversight method is employed to make a determination on program funding?
7. Which congressional agency conducts financial and program audits of executive agencies?
8. How many congressional committees and subcommittees exercise oversight of DHS?
9. What is the cost of so much congressional oversight?
10. As a member of Congress, why would you not want to relinquish your oversight authority?

Chapter 36

National Security Council

Learning Outcomes

Careful study of this chapter will help a student do the following:

- Explain the purpose and organization of the National Security Council.
- Identify key components of the NSC system.
- Analyze the NSC system.

"Yet a subtler and more serious danger is that as the NSC staff is consumed by these day-to-day tasks, it has less capacity to find the time and detachment needed to advise a president on larger policy issues."

- 2004 9/11 Commission Report

Introduction

The National Security Council (NSC) was established by statute in 1947 to create an interdepartmental body to advise the President with respect to the integration of domestic, foreign, and military policies relating to the national security so as to enable the military services and the other departments and agencies of the Government to cooperate more effectively in matters involving the national security. Currently, statutory members of the Council are the President, Vice President, the Secretary of State, the Secretary of Defense, and, since 2007, the Secretary of Energy; but, at the President's request, other senior officials participate in NSC deliberations. The Chairman of the Joint Chiefs of Staff and the Director of National Intelligence are statutory advisers. [1, p. ii]

Throughout most of the history of the United States, until the twentieth century, policy coordination centered on the President, who was virtually the sole means of such coordination.

Background

Throughout most of the history of the United States, until the twentieth century, policy coordination centered on the President, who was virtually the sole means of such coordination. The Constitution designates the President as Commander-in-Chief of the armed forces (Article II, Section 2) and grants him broad powers in the areas of foreign affairs (Article II, Section 2), powers that have expanded considerably in the twentieth century through usage. Given limited U.S. foreign involvements for the first hundred or so years under the Constitution, the small size of the armed forces, the relative geographic isolation of the Nation, and the absence of any proximate threat, the President, or his executive agents in the Cabinet, provided a sufficient coordinative base. [1, p. 2]

However, the advent of World War I, which represented a modern, complex military effort involving broad domestic and international coordination, forced new demands on the system that the President alone could not meet. In 1916, the Council of National Defense was established by statute (Army Appropriation Act of 1916). It reflected proposals that went back to 1911 and consisted of the Secretaries of War, Navy, Interior, Agriculture, Commerce and Labor. The statute also allowed the President to appoint an advisory commission of outside specialists to aid the Council. The Council of National Defense was intended as an economic mobilization coordinating group, as reflected by its membership—which excluded the Secretary of State. His inclusion would have given the Council a much wider coordinative scope. Furthermore, the authorizing statute itself limited the role of the Council basically to economic mobilization issues. The Council of National Defense was disbanded in 1921, but it set a precedent for coordinative efforts that would be needed in World War II. [1, p. 2]

The President remained the sole national security coordinator until 1938, when the prewar crisis began to build in intensity, presenting numerous and wide-ranging threats to the inadequately armed United States. The State Department, in reaction to reports of Axis activities in Latin America, proposed that interdepartmental conferences be held with War and Navy Department representatives. In April 1938, Secretary of State Cordell Hull, in a letter to President Franklin Roosevelt, formally proposed the creation of a standing committee made up of the second ranking officers of the three departments, for purposes of liaison and coordination. The President approved this idea, and the Standing Liaison Committee, or Liaison Committee as it was also called, was established, the members being the Under Secretary of State, the Chief of Staff of the Army, and the Chief of Naval Operations. The Standing Liaison Committee was the first significant effort toward interdepartmental liaison and coordination, although its work in the area was limited and uneven. The Liaison Committee largely concentrated its efforts on Latin American problems, and it met irregularly. Although it did foster some worthwhile studies during the crisis following the fall of France, it was soon superseded by other coordinative modes. It was more a forum for exchanging information than a new coordinative and directing body. [1, pp. 2 -3]

The President remained the sole national security coordinator until 1938, when the prewar crisis began to build in intensity. An informal coordinating mechanism evolved during weekly meetings established by Secretary of War Henry L. Stimson. with his Navy counterpart, Frank Knox, and Cordell Hull. These meetings grew into a significant coordinative body by 1945, with the formal creation of the State, War, Navy Coordinating Committee (SWNCC).

An informal coordinating mechanism, which complemented the Standing Liaison Committee, evolved during weekly meetings established by Secretary of War Henry L. Stimson, who took office in June 1940. Stimson arranged for weekly luncheons with his Navy counterpart, Frank Knox, and Cordell Hull. These meetings grew into a significant coordinative body by 1945, with the formal creation of the State, War, Navy Coordinating Committee (SWNCC). SWNCC had its own secretariat and a number of regional and topical subcommittees; its members were assistant secretaries in each pertinent department. The role of SWNCC members was to aid their superiors "on politico-military matters and [in] coordinating the views of the three departments on matters in which all have a common interest, particularly those involving foreign policy and relations with foreign nations...." SWNCC was a significant improvement in civilian-military liaison, and meshed well with the military Joint Chiefs of Staff (JCS). [1, pp. 3-4]

The creation of SWNCC, virtually at the end of the war, and its continued existence after the surrender of Germany and Japan reflected the growing awareness within the Federal Government that better means of coordination were necessary. The World War II system had largely reflected the preferred working methods of President Roosevelt, who relied on informal consultations with various advisers in addition to the JCS structure. However, the complex demands of global war and the post-war world rendered this system inadequate, and it was generally recognized that a return to the simple and limited prewar system would not be possible if the United States was to take on the responsibilities thrust upon it by the war and its aftermath. [1, p. 4]

National Security Council

The National Security Council (NSC) was created by the National Security Act of 1947. The function of the Council was to advise the President with respect to the integration of domestic, foreign, and military policies relating to the national security so as to enable the military services and the other departments and agencies of the Government to cooperate more effectively in matters involving the national security.

The NSC was created by the National Security Act, which was signed by the President on July 26, 1947. The NSC appears in Section 101 of Title I, Coordination for National Security, and its purpose is stated as follows:

(a) ... The function of the Council shall be to advise the President with respect to the integration of domestic, foreign, and military policies relating to the national security so as to enable the military services and the other departments and agencies of the Government to cooperate more effectively in matters involving the national security.

(b) In addition to performing such other functions as the President may direct, for the purpose of more effectively coordinating the policies and functions of the departments and agencies of the Government relating to the national security, it shall, subject to the direction of the President, be the duty of the Council

> (1) to assess and appraise the objectives, commitments, and risks of the United States in relation to our actual and potential military power, in the interest of national security, for the purpose of making recommendations to the President in connection there with; and
>
> (2) to consider policies on matters of common interest to the departments and agencies of the Government concerned with the national security, and to make recommendations to the President in connection therewith. . . .

(d) The Council shall, from time to time, make such recommendations, and such other reports to the President as it deems appropriate or as the President may require. [1, p. 6]

The following officers were designated as members of the NSC: the President; the Secretaries of State, Defense, Army, Navy, and Air Force; and the Chairman of the National Security Resources Board. The President could also designate the following officers as members "from time to time:" secretaries of other executive departments and the Chairmen of the Munitions Board and the Research and Development Board. Any further expansion required Senate approval. The NSC was provided with a staff headed by a civilian executive secretary, appointed by the President. [1, p. 6]

The National Security Act also established the Central Intelligence Agency under the NSC, but the Director of Central Intelligence (DCI) was not designated as an NSC member. The act also created a National Military Establishment (NME), with three executive departments (Army, Navy, and Air Force) under a Secretary of Defense. [1, p. 6] In 1949 the NME was re-designated the Department of Defense (DOD).

The creation of the NSC was a definite improvement over past coordinative methods and organization, bringing together as it did the top diplomatic, military, and resource personnel with the President. The addition of the CIA, subordinate to the NSC, also provided the necessary intelligence and analyses for the Council so that it could keep pace with events and trends. The changeable nature of its organization and its designation as an advisory body to the President also meant that the NSC was a malleable organization, to be used as each President saw fit. Thus, its use, internal substructure, and ultimate effect would be directly dependent on the style and wishes of the President. [1, p. 7]

The National Security Council is the principal forum for consideration of national security policy issues requiring Presidential determination. It is chaired by the President and is called into session at the President's discretion. Today, its statutory members are the President, Vice President, and the Secretaries of State, Defense and Energy. The Chairman of the Joint Chiefs of Staff is the statutory military advisor to the Council, and the Director of National Intelligence is the intelligence advisor.

NSC Organization

The National Security Council is the principal forum for consideration of national security policy issues requiring Presidential determination. It is chaired by the President and is called into session at the President's discretion. Today, its statutory members are the President, Vice President, and the Secretaries of State, Defense and Energy. The Chairman of the Joint Chiefs of Staff is the statutory military advisor to the Council, and the Director of National Intelligence is the intelligence advisor. [2, p. 12]

The National Security Advisor is the President's personal advisor responsible for the daily management of national security affairs, and advises the President on the entirety of national security matters and coordinates the development of interagency policies. The President alone decides national security policy, but the National Security Advisor is responsible for ensuring that the President has all the necessary information, that a full range of policy options have been identified, that the prospects and risks of each option have been evaluated, that legal and funding considerations have been addressed, that potential difficulties in implementation have been identified, and that all NSC principals have been included in the policy development and recommendation process. [2, p. 13]

The professionals who work directly for the President under the National Security Advisor's direction constitute the National Security Staff. the NSS is charged with running a proactive and rigorous interagency policy process, consisting of Interagency Policy Committees (IPCs), chaired by a Senior Director and consisting primarily of interagency Assistant Secretaries; Deputies Committees (DCs), chaired by either the Deputy National Security Advisor or the Assistant to the President for Homeland

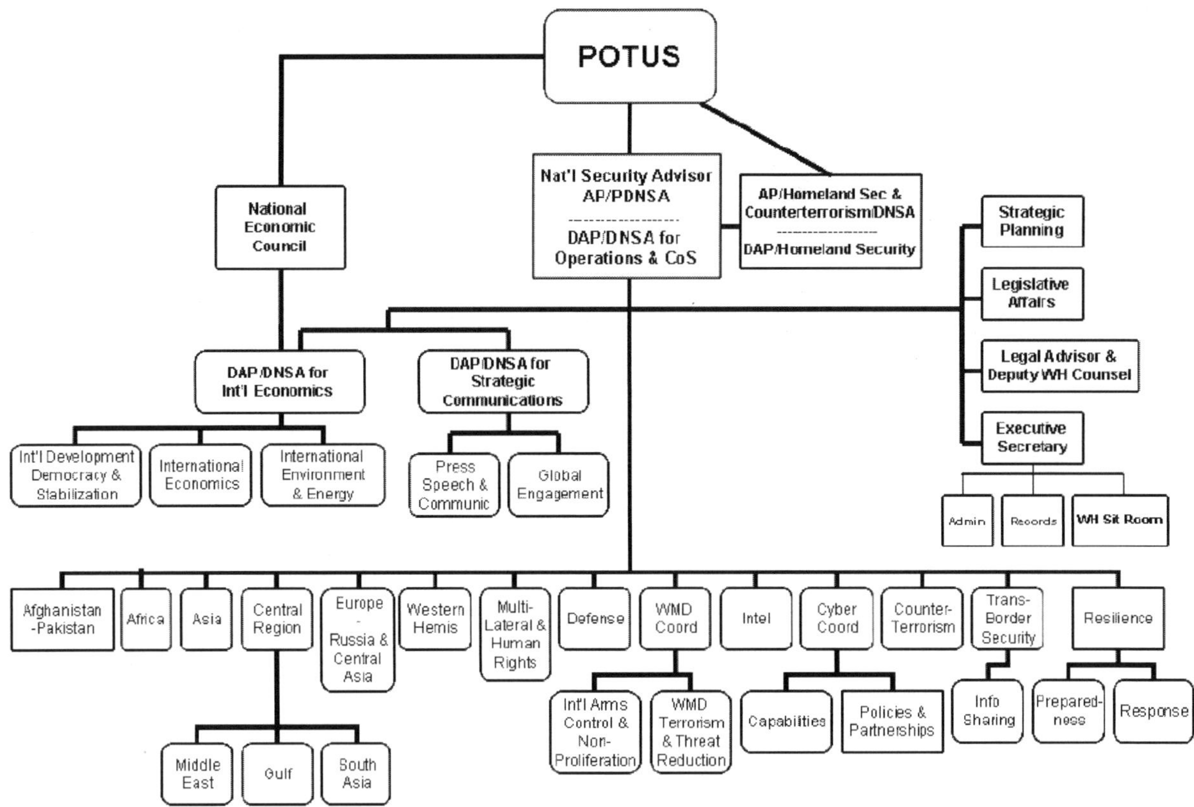

Figure 36-1: National Security Council Organization [2, p. 69]

The National Security Advisor is the President's personal advisor responsible for the daily management of national security affairs, and advises the President on the entirety of national security matters and coordinates the development of interagency policies.

Security and Counterterrorism and consisting primarily of interagency Deputy Secretaries; and Principals Committees (PCs), chaired by either the National Security Advisor or, at times, the Assistant to the President for Homeland Security and Counterterrorism and consisting primarily of interagency Secretaries. The IPCs, DC, and PCs can all make decisions, but must do so by consensus of its interagency members. The chair, including the NSA, cannot make decisions or "break ties." [2, p. 14]

NSS staff members handling substantive issues include political appointees (frequently experts from think tanks and academia), senior professionals on detail from Executive Branch departments, and military officers. The expertise of career Foreign Service Officers in foreign affairs, for example, often means that the senior positions of the NSS regional directorates are assigned to State Department personnel. This staff conducts the day-to-day management of national security affairs for the White House and currently numbers approximately 320, with around 175 policy positions and the remainder support positions (including the White House Situation Room staffed by approximately 35 watch officers and 35 technical/communications staffers). However, the NSC and its staff also are able to rely on a network of former NSC members, staffers, and other trusted policy experts, if needed, when reviewing policy issues. [2, p. 14]

The most senior interagency group is the Principals Committee (NSC/PC). The PC for all practical purposes is the membership of the NSC without the President and Vice President. The PC is called into session and chaired by the National Security Advisor. In addition to the National Security Advisor, the other principal members of the PC are the Secretaries of State, Defense, Treasury, Homeland Security, and Energy, the National Security Advisor, the Attorney General, the Director of the Office of Management and Budget, the Representative of the United States of America to the United Nations, the Chief of Staff to the President, the Director of National Intelligence, and Chairman of the Joint Chiefs of Staff. [2, p. 15]

Other key Executive Branch officials may be invited to attend Principals Committee meetings when issues related to their areas of responsibility are discussed. Regularly invited attendees include the White House Chief of Staff, Counsel to the President, and the Assistant to the Vice President for National Security Affairs. Topic area invitees may include the Secretary of Commerce, the United States Trade Representative, and the Assistant to the President for Economic Policy when international economic issues are on the Agenda. Topic area invitees for homeland security or counterterrorism related issues usually include the Assistant to the President for Homeland Security and Counterterrorism (who also serves as the PC chair on homeland security topics). Topic area invitees for science and technology related issues might include the Director of the Office of Science and Technology Policy. Similar to NSC meetings, the heads of other executive departments and agencies, along with additional senior officials, may be invited to PC meetings as appropriate. [2, p. 15]

The most senior interagency group is the Principals Committee (NSC/PC). The PC for all practical purposes is the membership of the NSC without the President and Vice President. The PC is called into session and chaired by the National Security Advisor.

Subordinate to the Principals Committee is the Deputies Committee (NSC/DC). As the senior sub-Cabinet interagency forum, the DC is responsible for directing the work of interagency working groups and ensuring that issues brought before the PC or the NSC have been properly analyzed and prepared for high-level deliberation. Historically, the DC is where the bulk of the government's policy decisions are made in preparation for the PC's review and the President's decision. Issues decided above the DC level either are the most sensitive national security decisions, are very contentious within the interagency, or both. In some circumstances (e.g., crisis situations) a significant portion of interagency policy development and coordination may be done at the DC level rather than at lower levels. [2, pp. 15-16]

The DC is composed of the deputy or relevant undersecretaries to the cabinet secretaries. The DC is chaired by the Assistant to the President and Deputy National Security Advisor (AP/DNSA) or the Assistant to the President for Homeland Security and Counterterrorism. The regular members of the DC include the Deputy Secretary of

State (who in practice sometimes may be represented by the Under Secretary of State for Political Affairs), Under Secretary of the Treasury (who sometimes may be represented by the Under Secretary of the Treasury for International Affairs), Deputy Secretary of Defense (who sometimes may be represented by the Under Secretary of Defense for Policy), Deputy Attorney General, Deputy Secretary of Energy, Deputy Director of the Office of Management and Budget, Deputy to the United States Representative to the United Nations, Deputy Director of National Intelligence (or sometimes the Director of the National Counterterrorism Center if counterterrorism issues are being considered), Vice Chairman of the Joint Chiefs of Staff, and Assistant to the Vice President for National Security Affairs. [2, p. 16]

Subordinate to the Principals Committee is the Deputies Committee (NSC/DC). As the senior sub-Cabinet interagency forum, the DC is responsible for directing the work of interagency working groups and ensuring that issues brought before the PC or the NSC have been properly analyzed and prepared for high-level deliberation. Historically, the DC is where the bulk of the government's policy decisions are made in preparation for the PC's review and the President's decision.

Like the PC, other senior executive branch officials may participate in DC meetings when appropriate for the substantive issues on the agenda. The Assistant to the President for Homeland Security and Counterterrorism and Deputy National Security Advisor chairs DC meetings when homeland security or counterterrorism related issues are on the agenda, and attends meetings on other topics as appropriate. Likewise, the Deputy Assistant to the President and Deputy National Security Advisor for International Economics will attend DC meetings when international economic issues are on the agenda and may be directed to chair the meeting at the discretion of the AP/DNSA. [2, pp. 16-17]

Subordinate to the DC are a variety of interagency working groups called Interagency Policy Committees (NSC/IPCs). These interagency committees are composed of substantive experts and senior officials from the departments and agencies represented on the DC. Although bounded by how much control is exerted over policy issues by the PC and DC groups, IPC-type committees historically are the main forum for interagency coordination. These groups conduct the day-to-day interagency analysis, generation of courses of action, policy development, coordination, resource determination, and policy implementation planning. Sometimes events may affect this traditional role, as when crisis situations or other high level national security developments warrant considerable attention by the PC or NSC. [2, p. 17]

Contingent upon the scope of their responsibilities, some IPCs may meet regularly (weekly or even several times daily in a crisis situation) while others meet only when developments or planning require policy synchronization. They are responsible for managing the development and implementation of national security policies when they involve more than one government agency. IPCs provide policy analysis for consideration by the more senior committees of the NSC system (e.g., the DC and PC) and ensure timely responses to decisions made by the President. The role of each IPC in policy development and implementation has tended to vary from administration to administration according to the amount of authority and responsibility delegated to them by the DC and PC. In the Obama administration, IPCs are expected whenever possible to find consensus before elevating issues to DCs. They are organized around either regional or functional issues. [2, p. 17]

Regional IPCs normally are headed by Assistant Secretaries of State while functional IPCs are headed by senior department officials or NSS Senior Directors. [2, p. 17]

Subordinate to the DC are a variety of interagency working groups called Interagency Policy Committees (NSC/IPCs). These interagency committees are composed of substantive experts and senior officials from the departments and agencies represented on the DC.

9/11

In February 2001, President George W. Bush issued National Security Presidential Directive-1, Organization of the National Security Council System." NSPD-1 indicated that the NSC system was to advise and assist the President and "coordinate executive departments and agencies in the effective development and implementation" of national security policies. [1, p. 22] However, the advent of the terrorist attacks of September 11, 2001 resulted in numerous changes to the original intentions for the Bush administration in the conduct of national security affairs. [2, p. 10]

One of the major findings of both the 9/11 Commission, and the congressional Joint Inquiry into Intelligence Community Activities before and after the Terrorist Attacks of September 11, 2001 (JIICATAS911) was that there were significant signals of a looming terrorist attack in different parts of the intelligence community, but information and analysis sharing and synthesis was inadequate. One result of these findings was the creation of the Homeland Security Council (HSC) and the Department of Homeland Security (DHS). These institutions brought new organizational responsibilities and perspectives to the consideration of national security affairs. The increased concern with domestic as well as foreign terrorist threats raised a range of new policy issues including debates over what constitutes "national" versus "homeland" security, separate and overlapping staff responsibilities (as reflected in the number of officials who were members both of the NSC and HSC), and the involvement of state and local governments as considerations in national policy making. National security policy development and coordination was heavily influenced by the Global War on Terrorism, Operation Enduring Freedom, Operation Iraqi Freedom, and by the significant concentration of operational imperatives and resources in the Department of Defense and U.S. Central Command. [2, pp. 10-11]

Executive Office of the President

The National Security Advisor is a senior aide in the Executive Office of the President (EOP). Since 1939, federal agencies immediately assisting the President have been located in the EOP. Within these entities are many, if not most, of the President's closest advisers and assistants on matters of policy, politics, administration, and management. Some of these EOP components have been creations of the President; others have been established by Congress. While some have endured, others have been brief experiments; some have been transferred to other quarters of the executive branch, others have been abolished with no successor. In large measure, the tenure and durability of an Executive Office agency is dependent upon its usefulness to the President — as a managerial or coordinative auxiliary, a national symbol, or a haven of political patronage, among other considerations. [3, pp. CRS-1]

The Executive Office of the President represents an institutional response to needs felt by every occupant of the Oval Office, beginning with George Washington, who, of course, served before there even was a White House. Primarily, these were, and remain, needs for advice and assistance. Undoubtedly, there have always been many who are ready and more than willing to offer the President their advice. However, what has probably always been desired by Presidents in this regard were a few loyal and intelligent individuals who would offer counsel when asked and would keep such consultations confidential. Loyalty, competence, and ability to keep confidences were also qualities to be sought in individuals providing immediate assistance — with correspondence and records maintenance, appointments and scheduling, bookkeeping, and, in time, many more sophisticated tasks. [3, pp. CRS-1]

Following 9/11, President Bush created a Homeland Security Council to focus on homeland security issues. Shortly after taking office in 2009, President Obama re-integrated the HSC into the NSC to ensure more effective coordination. the former Homeland Security Advisor became the Assistant to the President for Homeland Security and Counterterrorism.

Another significant change was instituted by the 2004 Intelligence Reform and Terrorism Prevention Act (P.L. 108-458) creating a new Director of National Intelligence (DNI). The Office of the Director of National Intelligence (ODNI) was given enhanced authorities over the entire Intelligence Community, providing centralized oversight of the U.S. National Intelligence Program. Accordingly, the Director of National Intelligence replaced the Director of Central Intelligence on the NSC to become the new principal intelligence advisor to the President. [1, p. 23]

President Obama, shortly after taking office in 2009, promulgated Presidential Policy Directive-1 (PPD-1), "Organization of the National Security Council System," which established the procedures for assisting the President in carrying out his responsibilities in the area of national security. As part of this policy, he merged the Homeland Security Council Staff and the National Security Council Staff into a single National Security Staff (NSS). While the National Security Advisor remained in charge of the new NSS, the former position of Homeland Security Advisor was re-designated the Assistant to the President for Homeland Security and Counterterrorism. Today, this assistant serves as the chair for Principal Committees responsible for homeland security topics. [2, p. 14]

NSC Reform

The increasing difficulties in separating national security issues from law enforcement and international economic concerns has led some observers to urge that the lines separating various international staffs at the White House be erased and that a more comprehensive policymaking entity be created. It is argued that such reforms could most effectively be accomplished without legislation. President Obama's move to combine the National Security Council and the Homeland Security Council was considered only a first step. Such initiatives, though, raise complex questions, including the role of congressional oversight. Whereas Congress has traditionally deferred to White House leadership in national security matters, to a far greater extent than in international economic affairs, there might be serious questions about taking formal steps to place resolution of a wide range of international policies, including economic and law enforcement issues, in the hands of officials who receive little congressional oversight. [1, p. 31]

The Project for National Security Reform (PNSR) was established with congressional support to study the adequacy of the organization of the government for dealing with national security issues. Its membership was initially comprised of former officials with extensive national security experience, including former National Security Adviser Brent Scowcroft. A November 2008 report, Forging a New Shield, addressed the functions of the NSC along with other parts of the "national security system." PNSR argued that the current organizational structure is ill coordinated and is placing the nation at risk in an international environment that requires agile and coordinated efforts by all instruments of power. To replace the National Security Council and the Homeland Security Council, PNSR recommended the creation of a President's Security Council and a Senate-confirmed Director of National Security who would have broader responsibilities than the existing National Security Adviser. The Director would "direct the implementation of national security missions identified by the present as inherently interagency." The office of the new Director of National Security would be comprised of some 500 people. A number of members of the PNSR effort joined the Obama Administration, including National Security Adviser James Jones and DNI Dennis Blair although both subsequently departed. Some of the principal PNSR initiatives would require legislative changes, but, as yet, a broad consensus has not emerged that would result in substantial realignments of organizational authorities in the executive branch or committee jurisdictions in the legislative branch. [1, p. 31]

Conclusion

While the Secretary of Homeland Security reports directly to the President, the programs and activities of the Department of Homeland Security must be closely coordinated with those of other departments and agencies within the Executive Branch of Federal government. This coordination is conducted within the auspices of the National Security Council. Allegations that the NSC failed to anticipate 9/11 fuel concerns that it is inadequate to the task of preventing future such attacks. Reform, however, is not easy, and as seen with the split and then merger of the National Security Council and Homeland Security Council, highly dependent upon the temperament and style of the incumbent President.

Challenge Your Understanding

The following questions are designed to challenge your understanding of the material presented in this chapter. Some questions may require additional research outside this book in order to provide a complete answer.

1. For most of U.S. history, who was the single individual who coordinated national security?
2. Why was the National Security Council formed after World War II?
3. Who are the statutory members of the National Security Council?
4. Who is the chief military advisor to the President?
5. Who is the chief intelligence advisor to the President?
6. What is the function of the National Security Advisor?
7. What is the function of the National Security Staff?
8. What is the designation of the NSC senior policy group?
9. What is the designation of the NSC policy groups that are the main forum for interagency coordination?
10. List and describe at least two potential pitfalls of the NSC system.

Chapter 37

Intelligence Community

Learning Outcomes

Careful study of this chapter will help a student do the following:

- Define the term "intelligence".
- Discuss the purpose and performance of the CIA prior to 2004.
- Compare the authorities of the ODNI and CIA.
- Identify different members of the Intelligence Community.
- Identify different intelligence disciplines.
- Describe the intelligence cycle.
- Explain the necessary predicate for conducting surveillance of U.S. citizens.

"Since the Pearl Harbor attack of 1941, the intelligence community has devoted generations of effort to understanding the problem of forestalling a surprise attack."

- 2004 9/11 Commission Report

Introduction

The U.S. Intelligence Community (IC) is a coalition of 17 agencies and organizations, within the Executive Branch that work both independently and collaboratively to gather and analyze the intelligence necessary to conduct foreign relations and national security activities. [1]

The United States has carried out intelligence activities since the days of George Washington, but only since World War II have they been coordinated on a government-wide basis.

Background

Intelligence is secret, state activity to understand or influence foreign entities. [2] The United States has carried out intelligence activities since the days of George Washington, but only since World War II have they been coordinated on a government -wide basis. President Franklin D. Roosevelt appointed New York lawyer and war hero, William J. Donovan, to become first the Coordinator of Information, and then, after the U.S. entered World War II, head of the Office of Strategic Services (OSS) in 1942. The OSS had a mandate to collect and analyze strategic information. After World War II, however, the OSS was abolished along with many other war agencies and its functions were transferred to the State and War Departments. [3]

At about the time the OSS was being disbanded, a study commissioned by Navy Secretary James Forrestal and chaired by private businessman Ferdinand Eberstadt was published. While the report dealt principally with the issue of military unification, it also recommended coordination of the intelligence function through the establishment of a National Security Council (NSC) and a Central Intelligence Agency (CIA). The NSC would coordinate the civilian and military national security policy for the President. The CIA, under the auspices of the NSC, would serve "to coordinate national security intelligence." [4]

On July 27, 1947, President Truman signed into law the National Security Act of 1947, creating a postwar national security framework. A National Security Council was created to coordinate national security policy. The Act created the position of Secretary of Defense and unified the separate military departments (the Army, the Navy, and the newly-created Air Force) under this position. The Act also established the Joint Chiefs of Staff to serve as the principal military advisers to the President and the Secretary of Defense. Finally, a Central Intelligence Agency was established with the Director of Central Intelligence as its head. [4]

As the head of the CIA, the Director of Central Intelligence (DCI) served as the principal adviser to the President for intelligence matters related to national security. According to the 1947 National Security Act, such national intelligence was to be timely, objective, independent of political considerations, and based upon all sources available to the Intelligence Community. To coordinate the efforts of the Intelligence Community, the DCI was given authority over a National Intelligence Council (NIC), comprised of senior analysts from the Intelligence Community and substantive experts from the public and private sector. The focus of the National Intelligence Council was to produce National Intelligence Estimates (NIEs) for the Government. To enforce cooperation among the Intelligence Community, the National Security Act of 1947 made the DCI the "Head of the Intelligence Community" responsible for 1) developing and presenting the annual budget for National Foreign Intelligence Programs; 2) establishing requirements and priorities for the collection of intelligence by elements of the IC; and 3) approving collection priorities for national collection assets. [5]

The establishment of the CIA was borne out of a collective failure to anticipate Japan's attack on the U.S. Pacific Fleet at Pearl Harbor that led to America's entry into World War II. Now engaged in a Cold War to contain further expansion of the Soviet Union, a primary objective of the CIA was to prevent an "Atomic Pearl Harbor" that could lead to World War III.

The establishment of the CIA was borne out of a collective failure to anticipate Japan's attack on the U.S. Pacific Fleet at Pearl Harbor that led to America's entry into World War II. Now engaged in a Cold War to contain further expansion of the Soviet Union, a primary objective of the CIA was to prevent an "Atomic Pearl Harbor" that could lead to World War III. A number of significant "intelligence failures" over the ensuring decades led some to question whether the CIA had the requisite authority to effectively coordinate the efforts of the Intelligence Community.

- In April 1961, a CIA-planned effort by Cuban exiles to overthrow Fidel Castro's regime and replace it with a non-communist, U.S.-friendly government went horribly awry when an aerial attack on Cuba's air force flopped and the 1,400-strong "Assault Brigade 2506" came under heavy fire from the Cuban military after landing off the country's southern coast. The botched invasion poisoned U.S.-Cuban relations.
- On Jan. 31, 1968, during the Tet holiday in Vietnam, North Vietnam's communist forces stunned the United States by launching a massive, coordinated assault against South Vietnam. While the communist military gains proved fleeting, the Tet Offensive was arguably the most decisive battle of Vietnam. Americans grew disillusioned with the war, prompting U.S. policymakers to shift gears and focus on reducing America's footprint in Vietnam.
- While the CIA accurately analyzed the Six-Day War between Israel and neighboring Arab states in 1967, it was caught flat-footed only six years later when Egyptian and Syrian forces launched coordinated attacks on Israeli forces in the Sinai Desert and the Golan Heights during the Jewish holiday of Yom Kippur. The conflict, which ended with a ceasefire in October 1973, tested U.S.-Soviet relations and pushed the Arab-Israeli conflict to the top of Washington's foreign-policy agenda.

- In August 1978, six months before the U.S-backed Shah Mohammed Reza Pahlavi fled Iran, the CIA infamously concluded that "Iran is not in a revolutionary or even a pre-revolutionary situation." Subsequently, the Ayatollah Ruhollah Khomeini rose to power in the Islamic Revolution of 1979, opening up a rift between Iran and the United States that persists to this day.
- The Soviet Union's military incursion into Afghanistan, which began in December 1979 and devolved into a bloody, nine-year occupation, took the Carter administration by surprise. The U.S. intelligence community had assumed that the specter of a costly quagmire would deter the Soviets from invading Afghanistan. Former CIA official Douglas MacEachin recalls that in the days after the invasion, a dark joke began circulating around the agency that "the analysts got it right, and it was the Soviets who got it wrong."
- Conventional wisdom holds that the U.S. intelligence community failed to predict the Soviet Union's demise in 1991, presaged as it was by President Mikhail Gorbachev's reforms, the deteriorating Soviet economy, the collapse of communism in east-central Europe, and the moves toward independence by several Soviet republics. As the BBC recently noted, "the Soviet example illustrates the problem that intelligence gatherers are great counters: they can look at missiles, estimate the output of weapons factories, and so on. But the underlying political and social dynamics in a society are much harder to read." [6]

Given a number of high-profile intelligence failures over the years, many outside observers argued that the DCI position was unworkable. They contended that DCIs, frustrated by the challenges involved in managing the entire intelligence community, focused narrowly on the CIA, and that the result was an ill-coordinated intelligence effort that poorly served the nation.

Many outside observers, Members of Congress, and various commissions over the years argued that the DCI position was unworkable. They contended that DCIs, frustrated by the challenges involved in managing the entire intelligence community, focused narrowly on the CIA, and that the result was an ill-coordinated intelligence effort that poorly served the nation. Some also asserted that DCIs lacked adequate legal authorities to establish priorities and to ensure compliance by intelligence agencies beyond the CIA. In particular, it was suggested that major intelligence agencies in the Department of Defense (DOD)—the National Security Agency (NSA), the National Reconnaissance Office (NRO), and the National Geospatial-Intelligence Agency (NGA)—had been more responsive to the needs of the military services than to the requirements of national policymakers. And, finally, some observers, while conceding that DCI authorities under the National Security Act were limited, nevertheless contended that DCIs failed to fully assert their authorities, particularly when their priorities conflicted with those of the Secretary of Defense, viewed by many as the dominant voice in the intelligence community because of the Secretary's control over an estimated 85% of the intelligence budget. [7, p. 1]

Ultimately, it was the failure to anticipate 9/11 that prompted Congress to enact reform. In its report on the terrorist attacks of Sept. 11, 2001, the 9/11 Commission noted that the Intelligence Community, assailed by "an overwhelming number of priorities, flat budgets, an outmoded structure, and bureaucratic rivalries," had failed to pin down the big-picture threat posed by "transnational terrorism" throughout the 1990s and up to 9/11. [6] In response, Congress approved significantly larger intelligence budgets and, in December 2004, passed the most extensive reorganization of the intelligence community since the National Security Act of 1947. The Intelligence Reform and Terrorism Prevention Act of 2004 (P.L. 108-458) created a new Director of National Intelligence to head the Intelligence Community, and serve as the principal intelligence adviser to the President, and oversees and directs the acquisition of major collections systems. [8, p. 1]

Office of the Director of National Intelligence

The 2004 Intelligence Reform Act was designed to address the findings of the 9/11 Commission that there had been inadequate coordination of the national intelligence effort and that the Intelligence Community, as then organized, could not serve as an agile information gathering network in the struggle against international terrorists. [8, p. 1] The resulting Office of the Director of National Intelligence (ODNI) was consequently commissioned to improve information sharing, promote a strategic, unified direction, and ensure integration across the U.S. Intelligence Community. The ODNI stood up on April 21, 2005. [9, p. 15]

The 2004 Intelligence Reform Act assigned to the Director of National Intelligence (DNI) two of the three principal responsibilities formerly performed by the Director of Central Intelligence. The DNI would provide intelligence to the President, other senior officials, and Congress, and the DNI would head the Intelligence Community. The 2004 Intelligence Reform Act further strengthened the DNIs authority by providing enhanced budget authorities that were unavailable to the DCI.

The 2004 Intelligence Reform Act assigned to the Director of National Intelligence (DNI) two of the three principal responsibilities formerly performed by the Director of Central Intelligence. The DNI would provide intelligence to the President, other senior officials, and Congress, and the DNI would head the Intelligence Community. But, unlike the DCI, the DNI would not oversee the CIA. Rather, the act renamed the DCI the DCIA, and subordinated their position to the DNI. [8, p. 2]

The 2004 Intelligence Reform Act further strengthened the DNIs authority by providing enhanced budget authorities that were unavailable to the DCI.

- First, it provides that at the DNI's exclusive direction, the Director of the Office of Management and Budget (OMB) shall "apportion," or direct, the flow of congressionally appropriated funds from the Treasury Department to each of the Cabinet level agencies containing intelligence community elements. This change is designed to strengthen the DNI's control over intelligence community spending. If, for example, an agency fails to comply with certain of the DNI's spending priorities, the DNI can withhold that agency's funding. DCIs had no such authority.

- Second, the DNI is authorized to "allot" or "allocate" appropriations directly at the sub-Cabinet agency and department level, providing the DNI additional control over spending. If a departmental comptroller refuses to act in accordance with a DNI spending directive, the law requires that the DNI notify Congress of such refusal. The DCI had no such authority or reporting obligation.
- Third, the DNI is authorized to "develop and determine" the National Intelligence Program (NIP; former "NFIP") budget. By contrast, DCIs were authorized to "facilitate the development" of the intelligence community's annual budget.
- Fourth, the DNI is authorized to "ensure the effective execution of the budget," and to monitor its implementation and execution. Except in the case of the CIA, DCIs had no such authority.
- Fifth, the DNI is authorized to provide budget guidance to those elements of the Intelligence Community not falling within the NIP. Again, DCIs had no such authority. [8, p. 6]

To assist with accomplishing its mission, the 2004 Intelligence Reform Act gave ODNI statutory authority over the National Counterterrorism Center (NCTC), National Counterproliferation Center (NCPC), the National Counterintelligence Executive (NCIX), and the National Intelligence Council.

The 2004 Intelligence Reform Act also authorized the DNI to "manage and direct the tasking of, collection, analysis, production, and dissemination of national intelligence ... by approving requirements and resolving conflicts." Although DCIs were authorized to exercise certain collection authorities, statutory authorities did not explicitly address analysis, production, and dissemination authorities. [8, p. 8]

To assist with accomplishing its mission, the 2004 Intelligence Reform Act gave ODNI statutory authority over the National Counterterrorism Center (NCTC), National Counterproliferation Center (NCPC), the National Counterintelligence Executive (NCIX), and the National Intelligence Council. [9, p. 15]

The National Counterterrorism Center has primary responsibility within the U.S. Government for counterterrorism intelligence analysis and counterterrorism strategic operational planning. NCTC's components are the Directorate of Intelligence, Directorate of Strategic Operational Planning, Directorate of Operations Support, Directorate of Terrorist Identities, and the Office of National Intelligence Management. Their functions are:

- Directorate of Intelligence leads the production and integration of counterterrorism analysis for the U.S. Government.
- Directorate of Strategic Operational Planning directs the U.S. Government's planning efforts to focus all elements of national power against the terrorist threat.
- Directorate of Operations Support provides the common intelligence picture for the counterterrorism community with 24 hours a day/7 days a week situational awareness; terrorism threat reporting; management and incident information tracking; and support for worldwide, national, and international special events.

- Directorate of Terrorist Identities maintains a consolidated repository of information on international terrorist identities and ensures Federal agencies can access the information they need through the Terrorist Identities Datamart Environment (TIDE).
- Office of National Intelligence Management provides strategic management of all national intelligence related to the IC's counterterrorism mission to set analytic and collection priorities; advance analytic tradecraft and training; and lead strategic planning, evaluation, and budgeting. [9, p. 16]

The National Counterproliferation Center is the bridge from the IC to the policy community for activities within the U.S. Government associated with countering the proliferation of weapons of mass destruction (WMD). NCPC conducts strategic counterproliferation planning for the IC to support policy efforts to prevent, halt, or mitigate the proliferation of WMDs, their delivery systems, and related materials and technologies. This includes both states of concern and, in partnership with the National Counterterrorism Center, non-state actors. NCPC achieves this by drawing on the expertise of counterproliferation professionals in the IC, the U.S. Government, industry, and academia. These relationships foster an atmosphere of collaboration and intelligence sharing in order to protect the U.S.'s interests at home and abroad. [9, pp. 16-17]

The National Counterproliferation Center is the bridge from the IC to the policy community for activities within the U.S. Government associated with countering the proliferation of weapons of mass destruction (WMD).

The National Counterintelligence Executive (NCIX) serves as the head of national counterintelligence and security for the U.S. Government. Per the Counterintelligence Enhancement Act of 2002, the NCIX is charged with promulgating an annual strategy for all counterintelligence elements of the U.S. Government. The Office of the NCIX is charged with integrating the activities of all counterintelligence programs to make them coherent and efficient. They also coordinate counterintelligence policy and budgets to the same end. It is also responsible for evaluating the performance of the counterintelligence community against the strategy. NCIX's Special Security Division is responsible for security policy and uniformity across the U.S. Government. [9, p. 17]

The National Intelligence Council (NIC), a Congressionally-mandated council, is a component of the ODNI that conducts mid- and long-term strategic analysis through the use of all-source intelligence. Since its formation in 1979, the NIC has been a source of deep substantive expertise on intelligence matters and a facilitator of integrated, IC coordinated strategic analysis on issues of key concern to senior U.S. policymakers. Some of the NIC's core functions are to:

- Produce National Intelligence Estimates — the IC's most authoritative written assessments on national security issues, as well as a broad range of other Community coordinated products.

- Foster outreach to nongovernmental experts in academia and the private sector to broaden the IC's perspective.

Articulate substantive intelligence priorities to guide intelligence collection and analysis. [9, p. 17]

The core mission of the ODNI is to lead the IC in Intelligence Integration, forging a community that delivers the most insightful intelligence possible. Intelligence Integration is the key to ensuring that the highest quality of intelligence is delivered with the right inputs, at the right time, in defense of the Homeland. [9, p. 15]

The core mission of the ODNI is to lead the IC in Intelligence Integration, forging a community that delivers the most insightful intelligence possible.

The Intelligence Community

The Director of National Intelligence is responsible for coordinating the combined efforts of the Intelligence Community. The IC is defined in 50 U.S.C. 401a(4) as consisting of the following:

1. The Office of the Director of National Intelligence (ODNI)
2. Central Intelligence Agency (CIA)
3. Bureau of Intelligence and Research, Department of State (INR)
4. Defense Intelligence Agency (DIA)
5. National Security Agency (NSA)
6. National Reconnaissance Office (NRO)
7. National Geospatial -Intelligence Agency (NGA)
8. The National Security Branch, Federal Bureau of Investigation (FBI)
9. Army Intelligence
10. Navy Intelligence
11. Air Force Intelligence
12. Marine Corps Intelligence
13. Coast Guard Intelligence
14. The Office of Intelligence and Analysis, Department of the Treasury
15. The Office of Intelligence, Department of Energy
16. The Office of National Security Intelligence, Drug Enforcement Administration (DEA)
17. The Office of Intelligence and Analysis, Department of Homeland Security [8, p. 2]

Except for the CIA, intelligence offices or agencies are components of Cabinet departments with other roles and missions. The intelligence offices/agencies, however, participate in intelligence community activities while supporting the other efforts of their departments. [8, p. 2]

The CIA remains the keystone of the analytic efforts of the intelligence community. It has all-source analytical capabilities that cover the whole world outside U.S. borders. It produces a range of studies that address virtually any topic of interest to national security policymakers. The CIA also collects intelligence with human sources and, on occasion, undertakes covert actions at the direction of the President. (A covert action is an activity or activities of the U.S. government to influence political, economic, or military conditions abroad, where it is intended that the U.S. role will not be apparent or acknowledged publicly.) [8, p. 2]

The CIA remains the keystone of the analytic efforts of the intelligence community. It has all-source analytical capabilities that cover the whole world outside U.S. borders. It produces a range of studies that address virtually any topic of interest to national security policymakers. The CIA also collects intelligence with human sources and, on occasion, undertakes covert actions at the direction of the President.

Three major national-level intelligence agencies in the Department of Defense—the National Security Agency, the National Reconnaissance Office, and the National Geospatial-Intelligence Agency—absorb the larger part of the national intelligence budget. NSA is responsible for signals intelligence and has collection sites throughout the world. The NRO develops and operates reconnaissance satellites. The NGA prepares the geospatial data—ranging from maps and charts to sophisticated computerized databases—necessary for humanitarian operations and for targeting in an era in which military operations are dependent upon precision-guided weapons. In addition to these three agencies, the Defense Intelligence Agency (DIA) is responsible for defense attachés and for providing DOD with a variety of analytical products. It serves as the premier all-source analytic unit within DOD. Although the Intelligence Reform Act provides extensive budgetary and management authorities over these agencies to the DNI, it does not revoke the responsibilities of the Secretary of Defense for these agencies. [8, pp. 2-3]

The State Department's Bureau of Intelligence and Research (INR) is one of the smaller components of the intelligence community but is widely recognized for the high quality of its analysis. INR is strictly an analytical agency; diplomatic reporting from embassies, though highly useful to intelligence analysts, is not considered an intelligence function (nor is it budgeted as one). [8, p. 3]

The key intelligence functions of the FBI relate to counterterrorism and counterintelligence. The former mission has grown enormously in importance since September 2001, many new analysts have been hired, and the FBI has been reorganized in an attempt to ensure that intelligence functions are not subordinated to traditional law enforcement efforts. Most importantly, law enforcement information, including counterterrorism and counterintelligence information, is now expected to be

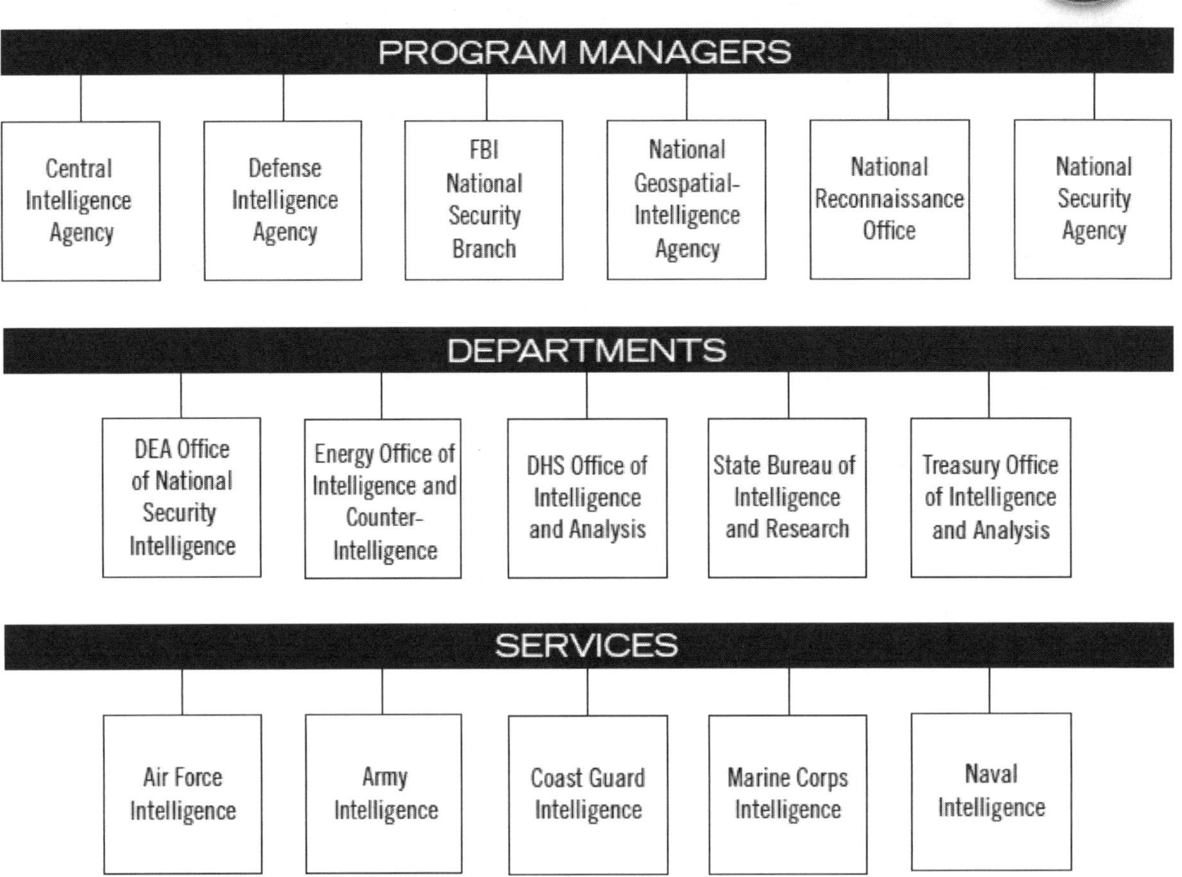

Figure 37-1: The U.S. Intelligence Community [9]

forwarded to other intelligence agencies for use in all-source products. The intelligence organizations of the four military services concentrate largely on concerns related to their specific missions. Their analytical products, along with those of DIA, supplement the work of CIA analysts and provide greater depth on key military and technical issues. [8, p. 3]

The intelligence organizations of the four military services concentrate largely on concerns related to their specific missions. Their analytical products, along with those of DIA, supplement the work of CIA analysts and provide greater depth on key military and technical issues. [8, p. 3]

The Homeland Security Act (P.L. 107-296) provided the Department of Homeland Security (DHS) responsibilities for fusing law enforcement and intelligence information relating to terrorist threats to the homeland. The Office of Intelligence and Analysis in DHS participates in the inter-agency counterterrorism efforts and, along with the FBI, has focused on ensuring that state and local law enforcement officials receive information on terrorist threats from national level intelligence agencies. [8, p. 3]

The Coast Guard, as part of DHS, deals with information relating to maritime security and homeland defense. The Energy Department analyzes foreign nuclear weapons programs as well as nuclear nonproliferation and energy-security issues. It also has a robust counterintelligence effort. The Treasury Department collects and processes information that may affect U.S. fiscal and monetary policies. Treasury also covers the terrorist financing issue. [8, p. 3]

The Intelligence Cycle

The Intelligence Cycle is the process of developing raw information into finished intelligence for use by policymakers, military commanders, and other consumers in decision making. This six-step cyclical process is highly dynamic, continuous, and never-ending. The sixth step, evaluation (which includes soliciting feedback from users) is conducted for each of the other five steps individually and for the Intelligence Cycle as a whole. [9, p. 10]

The Intelligence Cycle is the process of developing raw information into finished intelligence for use by policymakers, military commanders, and other consumers in decision making. This six-step cyclical process is highly dynamic, continuous, and never-ending.

Step 1: Planning and Direction. The planning and direction step sets the stage for the Intelligence Cycle. It is the springboard from which all Intelligence Cycle activities are launched. Oftentimes, the direction part of the step precedes the planning part. Generally, in such cases, the consumer has a requirement for a specific product. That product may be a full report, a graphic image, or raw information that is collected, processed, and disseminated, but skips the analysis and production step. Given the customer's requirement, the intelligence organization tasked with generating the product will then plan its Intelligence Cycle activities. [9, p. 11]

Step 2: Collection. Data collection is performed to gather raw data related to the five basic intelligence sources: 1) GEOINT, 2) HUMINT, 3) MASINT, 4) OSINT, and 5) SIGINT. The sources of the raw data may include, but are not limited to, news reports, aerial imagery, satellite imagery, and government and public documents. [9, p. 11]

Step 3: Processing and Exploitation. The processing and exploitation step (see the Glossary of Terms for a definition of "exploitation") involves the use of highly trained and specialized personnel and technologically sophisticated equipment to turn the raw data into usable and understandable information. Data translation, data decryption, and interpretation of filmed images and other imagery are only a few of the processes used for converting data stored on film, magnetic, or other media into information ready for analysis and production. [9, p. 11]

Step 4: Analysis and Production. The analysis and production step also requires highly trained and specialized personnel (in this case, analysts) to give meaning to the processed information and to prioritize it against known requirements. Synthesizing the processed information into a finished, actionable intelligence product enables the information to be useful to the customer. Note that, in some cases, the Intelligence Cycle may skip this step (for example, when the consumer needs only specific reported information or products such as raw imagery). This was the case during the Cuban Missile Crisis (October 1962) when President Kennedy needed only the actual number of pieces of Soviet equipment in Cuba and facts concerning reports on observed Soviet activity with no analysis of that information. [9, p. 12]

There are six basic intelligence sources, or collection disciplines:

1. GEOINT

2. HUMINT

3. MASINT

4. OSINT

5. SIGINT

6. IMINT

Step 5: Dissemination. The consumer that requested the information receives the finished product, usually via electronic transmission. Dissemination of the information typically is accomplished through such means as websites, email, Web 2.0 collaboration tools, and hardcopy distribution. The final, finished product is referred to as "finished intelligence." After the product is disseminated, further gaps in the intelligence may be identified, and the Intelligence Cycle begins all over again. [9, p. 12]

Step 6: Evaluation. Constant evaluation and feedback from consumers are extremely important to enabling those involved in the Intelligence Cycle to adjust and refine their activities and analysis to better meet consumers' changing and evolving information needs. [9, p. 12]

Intelligence Sources

There are six basic intelligence sources, or collection disciplines:

1. Geospatial Intelligence (GEOINT) is the exploitation and analysis of imagery, imagery intelligence (IMINT) (see the Glossary of Terms), and geospatial information to describe, assess, and visually depict physical features and geographically referenced activities on the earth. [9, p. 54]
2. Human Intelligence (HUMINT) is the collection of information—either orally or via documentation— that is provided directly by a human source. It is the only type of intelligence for which collectors speak directly to the sources of information, control the topic of discussion, and direct the source's activities. Human sources can obtain access to information that is not obtainable any other way. [9, pp. 53-54] The Director of the CIA serves as the National HUMINT Manager, but has delegated the day-to-day responsibilities of this position to the Director of the National Clandestine Service (D/NCS). [10]
3. Measurement and Signatures Intelligence (MASINT) is intelligence produced through quantitative and qualitative analysis of the physical attributes of targets and events to characterize and identify those targets and events. [9, p. 53]

Examples of this might be the distinctive radar signatures of specific aircraft systems or the chemical composition of air and water samples. The Directorate for MASINT and Technical Collection (DT), a component of the Defense Intelligence Agency, is the focus for all national and Department of Defense MASINT matters. [10]

4. Open-Source Intelligence (OSINT) is intelligence produced from publicly available information that is collected, exploited, and disseminated in a timely manner to an appropriate audience for the purpose of addressing a specific intelligence requirement. [9, p. 54]

5. Signals Intelligence (SIGINT) is intelligence gathered from data transmissions, including Communications Intelligence (COMINT), Electronic Intelligence (ELINT), and Foreign Instrumentation Signals Intelligence (FISINT). SIGINT includes both raw data and the analysis of that data to produce intelligence. [9, p. 54] The National Security Agency is responsible for collecting, processing, and reporting SIGINT. The National SIGINT Committee within NSA advises the Director, NSA, and the DNI on SIGINT policy issues and manages the SIGINT requirements system. [10]

6. Imagery Intelligence (IMINT) includes representations of objects reproduced electronically or by optical means on film, electronic display devices, or other media. Imagery can be derived from visual photography, radar sensors, and electro -optics. The National Geospatial-Intelligence Agency is the manager for all imagery intelligence activities, both classified and unclassified, within the government, including requirements, collection, processing, exploitation, dissemination, archiving, and retrieval. [10]

Counterintelligence (CI) is the business of identifying and dealing with foreign intelligence threats to the United States and its interests.

Counterintelligence

Counterintelligence (CI) is the business of identifying and dealing with foreign intelligence threats to the United States and its interests. Its core concern is the intelligence services of foreign states and similar organizations of non-state actors, such as transnational terrorist groups. Counterintelligence has both a defensive mission - protecting the nation's secrets and assets against foreign intelligence penetration - and an offensive mission - finding out what foreign intelligence organizations are planning to better defeat their aims. [10]

As defined in Executive Order 12333 (and amended on 30 July 2008), "counterintelligence means information gathered and activities conducted to identify, deceive, exploit, disrupt, or protect against espionage, other intelligence activities, sabotage, or assassinations conducted for or on behalf of foreign powers, organizations, or persons, or their agents, or international terrorist organizations or activities." [10]

The Office of the National Counterintelligence Executive (ONCIX), under the leadership of the National Counterintelligence Executive (NCIX), was created to serve as the head of national counterintelligence for the USG and provide strategic direction to the counterintelligence community. [10]

ONCIX, through established programs, coordinates counterintelligence outreach efforts and the dissemination of warnings to the private sector on intelligence threats to the U.S. Visit the ONCIX website at www.ncix.gov for an in-depth look into the counterintelligence vision and mission for preserving our national security. [10]

In practice, U.S. law affords Fourth Amendment protection to all within the United States, citizen or not, and to all U.S. citizens everywhere, in the U.S. or not. Accordingly, "probable cause" must be demonstrated in order to obtain a warrant before conducting surveillance on somebody in the U.S., or a U.S. citizen abroad.

Domestic Surveillance

The Fourth Amendment to the U.S. Constitution guarantees "The right of people to be secure in their persons, house, papers, and effects, against unreasonable searches and seizures, shall not be violated, and no Warrants shall issue, but upon probable cause, supported by Oath or affirmation, and particularly describing the place to be searched, and the persons or things to be seized." In practice, U.S. law affords Fourth Amendment protection to all within the United States, citizen or not, and to all U.S. citizens everywhere, in the U.S. or not. Accordingly, "probable cause" must be demonstrated in order to obtain a warrant before conducting surveillance on somebody in the U.S., or a U.S. citizen abroad. For matters of national security, domestic surveillance warrants may be sought under provisions of the 1978 Foreign Intelligence Surveillance Act (FISA). [11]

In 2013, Edward Snowden, a former contractor employee working as a computer system administrator at an NSA facility in Hawaii, was charged with leaking top secret documents related to certain NSA programs to the Guardian and Washington Post newspapers. [12, p. 7]

The first program collected in bulk the phone records—including the number that was dialed from, the number that was dialed to, and the date and duration of the call—of customers of Verizon and possibly other U.S. telephone service providers. It did not collect the content of the calls or the identity of callers. The data was collected pursuant to Section 215 of the USA PATRIOT ACT, which amended the Foreign Intelligence Surveillance Act of 1978. Section 215 allowed the FBI, in this case on behalf of the NSA, to apply to the Foreign Intelligence Surveillance Court (FISC) for an order compelling a person to produce "any tangible thing," such as records held by a telecommunications provider, if the tangible things sought are "relevant to an authorized investigation." Some commentators expressed skepticism regarding how such a broad amount of data could be said to be "relevant to an authorized investigation," as required by the statute. In response to these concerns, the Obama Administration subsequently declassified portions of the FISC order authorizing the program and issued a "whitepaper" describing the Administration's legal reasoning. [13, p. ii]

The second program, called PRISM, targeted the electronic communications, including content, of foreign targets overseas whose communications flow through American networks. These data were collected pursuant to Section 702 of FISA, which was added by the FISA Amendments Act of 2008. This program acquired information from Internet service providers, as well as through what NSA termed "upstream" collection that appeared to acquire Internet traffic while it was in transit from one location to another. Although the program targeted the communications of foreigners who were abroad, the Administration acknowledged that technical limitations in the "upstream" collection resulted in the collection of some communications that were unrelated to the target or that could take place between persons in the United States. Notwithstanding these technical limitations, the FISC held that this program was consistent with the requirements of both Section 702 and the Fourth Amendment provided that there were sufficient safeguards in place to identify and limit the retention, use, or dissemination of such unrelated or wholly domestic communications. [13, p. ii]

Following a contentious debate, the USA FREEDOM Act was finally passed and signed into law on June 2, 2015. Among its provisions, the USA FREEDOM Act restricted the use of FISA Section 215, effectively ending the NSA bulk collection programs.

The revelations prompted several lawsuits challenging the NSA programs. Congress also conducted hearings over their legitimacy. Following a contentious debate, the USA FREEDOM Act was finally passed and signed into law on June 2, 2015. Among its provisions, the USA FREEDOM Act restricted the use of FISA Section 215, effectively ending the NSA bulk collection programs. [14]

Conclusion

Since the 9/11 terrorist attacks, Congress has focused considerable attention on how intelligence is collected, analyzed, and disseminated in order to protect the homeland against terrorist threats. Prior to 9/11, it was possible to make a distinction between "domestic intelligence"—primarily law enforcement information collected within the United States—and "foreign intelligence"— primarily military, political, and economic intelligence collected outside the country. Today, threats to the homeland posed by terrorist groups are now national security threats. Intelligence collected outside the United States is often very relevant to the threat environment inside the United States and vice versa. [15, p. ii]

Challenge Your Understanding

The following questions are designed to challenge your understanding of the material presented in this chapter. Some questions may require additional research outside this book in order to provide a complete answer.

1. What is national intelligence?
2. Why was the CIA formed after World War II?
3. List and describe two high -profile intelligence failures over the last 30 years.
4. How did the 2004 Intelligence Reform Act enhance the authorities of the DNI compared to the DCI?
5. What is the purpose and function of the National Counterterrorism Center?
6. List and describe three different members of the Intelligence Community.
7. List and describe the six steps of the Intelligence cycle.
8. List and describe three different intelligence disciplines.
9. What is the necessary predicate to conduct surveillance of U.S. citizens?
10. Do you think Edward Snowden's actions were of benefit or harm to the nation? Explain your answer.

Chapter 38

Department of Defense

Learning Outcomes

Careful study of this chapter will help a student do the following:

- Explain the difference between active and reserve military forces.
- Describe the unique capabilities of the National Guard.
- Discuss the homeland defense mission.
- Discuss defense support of civil authorities.
- Explain the purpose and authority of a dual - status commander.
- Identify unique roles and responsibilities of USNORTHCOM.

"Demonstrate to the world there is 'No Better Friend, No Worse Enemy' than a U.S. Marine."

- 2003, Major General James Mattis, USMC

Introduction

We previously described the Department of Defense's role in counterterrorism and countering weapons of mass destruction. In this chapter we will examine DoD's missions in Homeland Defense and Defense Support of Civil Authorities.

U.S. military forces are drawn from active and reserve components of the Army, Air Force, Navy, Marine Corps, and Coast Guard.

Background

In order to understand the Department of Defense's (DoD's) role in Homeland Defense (HD) and Defense Support of Civil Authority (DSCA), it is necessary to examine DoD's combatant organization and legal authorization with respect to protecting United States territory.

Table 38-1: Organization of U.S. Military Forces

Departments	Army	Air Force	Navy		
Services	Army	Air Force	Navy	Marines	Coast Guard
Components	Active	Active	Active	Active	Active
	Reserve	Reserve	Reserve	Reserve	Reserve
	National Guard	National Guard			
Combat Units	Division	Air Force	Fleet	Expeditionary Force	Task Force
	Brigade	Wing	Strike Group	Expeditionary Brigade	
	Battalion	Squadron	Wing	Expeditionary Unit	
	Company		Squadron	Specialized Task Force	
	Platoon				

DoD is a very large and complex organization. Three service departments organize, train, and equip four services: Army, Navy, Marines, and Air Force. The United States Marine Corps (USMC) is part of the Navy Department. The United States Coast Guard (USCG) is also an arm of the United States Navy (USN); the USCG, however, is organized, trained, and equipped by the Department of Homeland Security. Each service has both an active and reserve component: United States Army Reserve (USAR), United States Navy Reserve (UNSR), United States Marine Corps Reserve (USMCR), and United States Air Force Reserve (USAFR). Active forces serve and are paid full-time; reserve forces serve and are paid part-time. The Reserve Component (RC) provides cost-effective military capability and a ready means to rapidly expand the Active Component (AC) during times of crisis. Both active and reserve components serve under Title 10 U.S. law at the direction of the President of the United States. In addition to having both an active and reserve component, the United States Army and United States Air Force also have National Guard components. Both the Army National Guard (ARNG) and Air National Guard (ANG) serve at the direction of their respective State Governors, either in State Active Duty (SAD) or Title 32 status. Under Title 32, the Feds pay, while under SAD, the State pays. The Feds also pay when the National

Table 38-2: National Guard Direction, Payment, & Authorities

	President Commander	Governor Commander
Feds Pay	T10	T32
States Pay		SAD

Guard is called up to serve the President under Title 10 status. The National Guard units are descended from the original State militias, but today serve to 1) maintain State civil order, 2) provide State disaster support, and 3) perform assigned Federal military missions. When serving in either SAD or Title 32 status, NG forces are exempt from Posse Comitatus. This 1878 law, as interpreted, precludes the use of Federal military forces to enforce domestic law. As Congress has chosen to continue upholding this law, it means that the National Guard can perform in domestic roles prohibited to Federal active duty forces. On the other hand, the United States Coast Guard is specifically authorized to enforce U.S. laws under Title 14 of United States Code. This allows the USCG to also perform unique roles prohibited to Federal active duty forces. Posse Comitatus and other laws affect how and when Federal military forces can be used for HD and DSCA compared to the USCG and National Guard. [1]

U.S. military forces are operationally assigned to four-star Combatant Commanders with Areas of Responsibility (AORs) assigned by the Unified Command Plan (UCP).

The DoD is also a matrix organization. Though Army, Navy, Marine, and Air Force units are organized, trained, and equipped by their separate service departments, they fight together as a team under the direction of a single combatant commander. Army, Navy, Marine, and Air Force units may be assigned to one of nine Combatant Commands (COCOMs) specified in the Unified Command Plan (UCP). The UCP was created in 1946 based on the command relationships formed in the European and Pacific theaters during World War II. Today, the concept of theater command has evolved into six Geographic Combatant Commands (GCCs) plus three Functional Combatant Commands (FCCs) listed in Table 3. Each COCOM is commanded by a four-star general or admiral appointed by the President. Each combatant commander has direction over military forces assigned to their Area of Responsibility (AOR). For the six geographic commands, the AOR encompasses a specific region of the world as delineated in Figure 1. For the three functional commands, the AOR is the entire world. The operational chain of command for authorizing and directing military action begins with the President and runs directly to the four-star combatant commander

Table 38-3: U.S. Combatant Commands

	Command	Designation	Type	Headquarters
1.	U.S. Africa Command	USAFRICOM	GCC	Kelley Barracks, Stuttgart, Germany
2.	U.S. Central Command	USCENTCOM	GCC	MacDill Air Force Base, FL
3.	U.S. European Command	USEUCOM	GCC	Patch Barracks, Stuttgart, Germany
4.	U.S. Northern Command	USNORTHCOM	GCC	Peterson Air Force Base, CO
5.	U.S. Pacific Command	USPACOM	GCC	Camp H. M. Smith, HI
6.	U.S. Southern Command	USSOUTHCOM	GCC	Miami, FL
7.	U.S. Special Operations Command	USSOCOM	FCC	MacDill Air Force Base, FL
8.	U.S. Cyber Command[1]	USCYBERCOM	FCC	Fort Meade, MD
9.	U.S. Strategic Command	USSTRATCOM	FCC	Offutt Air Force Base, NE
10.	U.S. Transportation Command	USTRANSCOM	FCC	Scott Air Force Base, IL

[1]USCYBERCOM is a subunified command of USTRATCOM

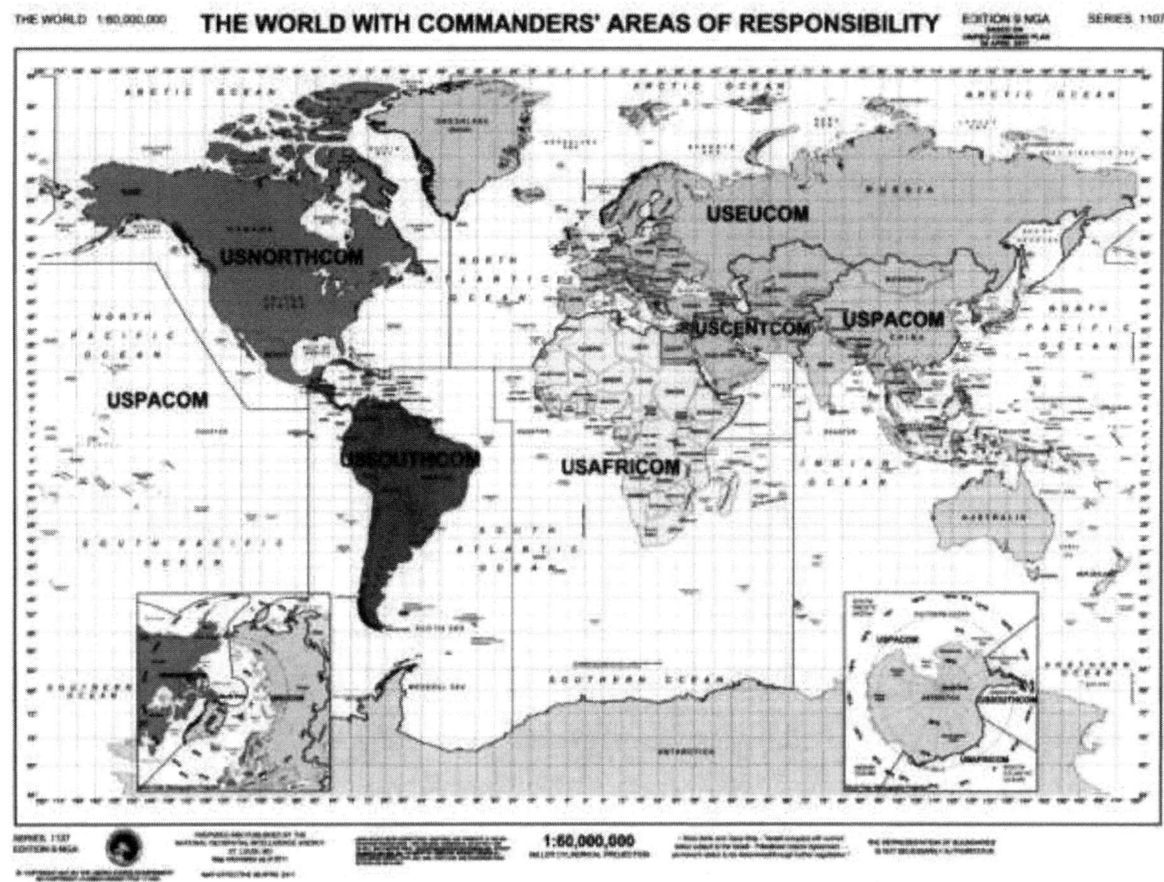

Figure38- 1: Geographic Combatant Commands' Areas of Responsibility

The Homeland Defense Mission is assigned to the Commanders of U.S. Pacific Command and U.S. Northern Command whose AORs include all U.S. territory.

who directs assigned forces to achieve assigned objectives according to their assigned missions. Because their AOR encompasses U.S. territorial possessions, United States Northern Command (USNORTHCOM) and United States Pacific Command (USPACOM) are responsible for Homeland Defense and Defense Support of Civil Authorities. [1]

Homeland Defense

The U.S. homeland is the physical region that includes the continental United States, Alaska, Hawaii, U.S. territories, and surrounding territorial waters and airspace. [2, p. vii]

> *Homeland Defense is the protection of U.S. sovereignty, territory, domestic population, and critical infrastructure against external threats and aggression, or other threats as directed by the President. [2, pp. I-1]*

Put more succinctly, HD is about defending U.S. territory from direct attack by State and Non-State actors. [3, p. 9]

According to the 2013 Strategy for Homeland Defense and Defense Support of Civil Authorities, homeland defense relies on an active, layered global defense. [3, p. 9] This defense strategy integrates U.S. capabilities in the forward regions of the world, in the geographic approaches to U.S. territory, and within the U.S. homeland. [2, pp. I-9]

- The forward regions essentially encompass all foreign territories around the world. In the forward regions, the objective is to detect, deter, prevent, or when necessary, defeat threats to the U.S. Actions may include combat operations, military engagement activities, peace operations, or preemptive measures such as direct action missions, cyberspace operations, or global strike. [2, p. ix]
- The approaches extend from U.S. territorial boundaries to the forward regions. The primary objective of actions within the approaches is to locate threats as far from the homeland as possible and defeat them at a safe distance. [2, p. ix]
- The homeland encompasses all U.S. territory and territorial possessions. The DoD strategy to prevent terrorist attacks on the homeland is predicated on supporting State, Local, and Federal law enforcement. [3, p. 11]

In most forward regions around the world, prevention is the predominate strategy. Prevention is facilitated regionally through military exchanges and collaborative ventures between the Geographic Combatant Commands and their foreign military counterparts. Prevention is facilitated globally by United States Strategic Command (USSTRATCOM) who maintains the alert posture and readiness status of U.S. nuclear forces. Direct actions continue in United States Central Command's (USCENTCOM's) AOR where U.S. forces remain actively engaged in combat missions in Afghanistan and other parts of the region to prevent terrorist organizations from gaining safe havens as they had before 9/11.

Homeland Defense is about defending U.S. territory from direct attack by state and non-state actors.

In the approaches, USPACOM and USNORTHCOM are responsible for countering air and maritime threats at a safe distance from U.S. territory. Both commands work closely with the Federal Aviation Administration (FAA) to identify potential air threats and scramble interceptors as necessary. Air defense within the USNORTHOM AOR is conducted in partnership with Canada through the North American Aerospace Defense Command (NORAD). [3, pp. 9-10] NORAD, though, is designed to counter military threats, and was unprepared to intercept civilian airliners on 9/11. To safeguard U.S. airspace from the expanded threat posed by suicide hijackings, USNORTHCOM performs additional air surveillance and patrols under the aegis of Operation NOBLE EAGLE. [4] In the maritime domain, USPACOM and USNORTHCOM work closely with the Department of Homeland Security to coordinate intercepts of suspected hostile agents by vessels belonging to the U.S. Navy and U.S. Coast Guard. Additionally, USNORTHCOM works with Canada Command to coordinate intercepts by vessels belonging to the Royal Canadian Navy. Coordination is accomplished through a formal process called the Maritime Operational Threat Response (MOTR) plan, facilitated by the Global MOTR Coordination Center (GMCC). [5] Homeland Defense in the approaches depends upon 1) persistent air and maritime domain awareness, 2) capable and responsive air defense forces, and 3) capable and responsive maritime forces. [3, p. 9]

Working by themselves or together with other Combatant Commands, USPCACOM and USNORTHCOM can project military force into the forward regions and approaches to deter and defeat potential adversaries.

In the homeland, the DoD strategy is to prevent terrorist attacks by supporting law enforcement. As mentioned previously, federal military forces are expressly prohibited from conducting law enforcement under Posse Comitatus. Because it is not subject to the constraints imposed by Posse Comitatus, the National Guard can be used to conduct law enforcement and has been used extensively to augment the U.S. Border Patrol. Even though Posse Comitatus prevents federal military forces from directly conducting law enforcement, it has been generally interpreted as not preventing them from acting in a support capacity. Thus, when National Guard forces were deployed in support of U.S. Border Patrol, they were accompanied by active Army personnel who filled administrative positions to help field more border agents. Similarly, federal military forces may lend equipment and personnel to operate in a supporting capacity when requested by local law enforcement. [6, p. x] Because of its extensive experience countering Improvised Explosive Devices (IEDs) in Afghanistan and Iraq, the DoD is specifically prepared to lend counter-IED support when requested by law enforcement. Additionally, the DoD shares foreign intelligence with the Federal Bureau of Investigation specifically, and the National Counterterrorism Center (NCTC) in general. [3, pp. 12-13] While both the Army and Marines maintain Quick Reaction Forces (QRFs), the chances they would be deployed to confront armed terrorist attacks in the United States are very small since State and Federal law enforcement have significant tactical capability within their own jurisdictions. However, both USPACOM and USNORTHCOM maintain organizational structures and contingency plans to defend U.S. territory in the highly unlikely event of invasion.

Defense Support of Civil Authorities

Recall that Federal support in response to a serious incident is provided under authority of the Robert T. Stafford Act following procedures laid out in the National Response Framework (NRF). Also recall that incident response is a bottom-up process whereby assistance is requested from the next higher authority only when all local resources are exhausted. Assistance is provided in Emergency Support Functions (ESFs) that are integrated into the local Incident Command System (ICS) applying organizational concepts described in the National Incident Management System (NIMS). The entire process is facilitated between the State Coordinating Officer (SCO) representing the State Governor and the Federal Coordinating Officer (FCO) representing the Federal Emergency Management Agency (FEMA). Under provisions of the Robert T. Stafford Act, the State may be reimbursed upwards to 75% of any incurred costs for Federal assistance, meaning the State still has to pay a 25% balance which can still be significant, and why the SCO is cautious when requesting Federal assistance. [7]

Emergency Support Functions are maintained by a Federal ESF Coordinator designated by the Secretary of Homeland Security. The Coordinator oversees the preparedness activities for a particular ESF by working with its Primary and Support agencies. ESF Primary Agencies (PAs) have significant authorities, roles, resources, and capabilities for a particular ESF. ESF Support Agencies (SAs) have specific capabilities or resources that support the Primary Agency in executing its ESF mission. According to the 2013 National Response Framework, there are fifteen ESFs, even though ESF #14 (Long Term Community Recovery) has been superseded by the National Disaster Recovery Framework. Of the fifteen ESFs, the Department of Defense is both the ESF Coordinator and PA for ESF #3, Public Works and Engineering. [7, pp. 31-36] Additionally, according to the ESF Annex, DoD is also the Primary Agency for ESF #9, Search and Rescue, and the Supporting Agency for all other ESFs. This means the DoD can potentially be called in for any incident in which Federal assistance is requested. [8]

Inside U.S. territorial boundaries, USPACOM and USNORTHCOM work within the strictures of Posse Comitatus to support law enforcement, and stand ready to provide Defense Support of Civil Authorities (DSCA) following disaster, either natural or manmade.

DoD assistance can be highly specialized and very expensive. That is why a Defense Coordinating Officer (DCO) supported by a Defense Coordinating Element (DCE) is assigned to each of the ten FEMA Regions to help the SCO and FCO make informed decisions when requesting DoD support. Emergency Preparedness Liaison Officers (EPLOs) are also assigned within each FEMA Region to advise State and Local authorities with requesting DoD support. When DoD support does indeed become necessary, the Federal Coordinating Officer will submit a Request For Assistance (RFA) to the Secretary of Defense (SecDef). If SecDef agrees to fulfill the request, the RFA will be made into a Mission Assignment (MA) and forwarded to the appropriate Geographic Combatant Commander, either at USPACOM or USNORTHCOM. [6]

Before a Mission Assignment ever arrives at USPACOM or USNORTHCOM, they will start forming their command organization and build a Joint Task Force (JTF). The JTF commander will be a National Guard officer specially trained and given temporary authority as a Dual-Status Commander (DSC) to command both National Guard and active duty Federal forces. Theoretically, the DSC works simultaneously for both the Governor and President. To assist the DSC with this complex task, they may be supported by an active duty Army Deputy Commander (CD). Together, the DSC and CD will organize and direct assigned forces comprising the Joint Task Force. The JTF will perform tasks compatible with the original Mission Assignment, and complimentary to the Incident Action Plan (IAP) formulated by the civilian Incident Commander (IC). While DoD forces remain under military command at all times, their actions are similarly governed at all times by civilian authorities. [6, pp. C-1 - C-9]

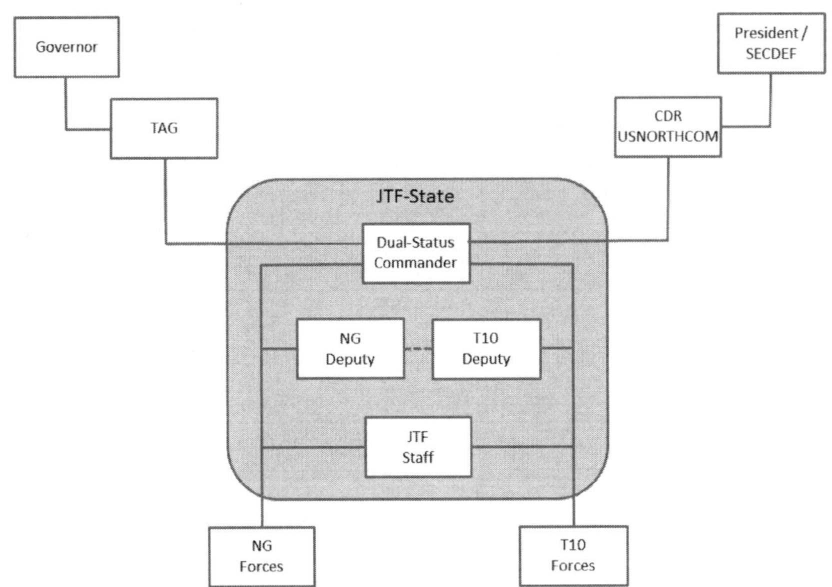

Figure 38-2: Dual-Status Commander Chain of Command

Unless otherwise provided, Title 10 active duty military forces will work at the discretion of the State Governor in support of the designated Incident Commander at the direction of a National Guard appointed Dual-Status Commander.

Sometimes there just isn't enough time to wait for a formal request for Defense Support of Civil Authorities. In accordance with Department of Defense Document (DODD) 3025.18, commanders have Immediate Response Authority (IRA) to render local assistance at their own discretion. However, such assistance must be 1) requested by civil authorities, and must be necessary to 2) save lives, 3) prevent human suffering, or 4) mitigate great property damage, under 5) imminently serious conditions within the United States. [6, pp. I-7]

United States Northern Command

USNORTHCOM was established after 9/11 in 2002. Before 9/11, there was no single unified command directly responsible for the United States. USNORTHCOM is headquartered at Peterson Air Force Base, Colorado. USNORTHCOM's AOR includes the continental United States, Alaska, Canada, Mexico, and surrounding waters out to approximately 500 nautical miles, including the Gulf of Mexico and the Straits of Florida. USNORTHCOM's mission is to "anticipate and conduct Homeland Defense and Civil Support operations within the assigned area of responsibility to defend, protect, and secure the United States and its interests." The USNORTHCOM Commander also commands NORAD. [9, pp. CRS-1]

USNORTHCOM has no permanently assigned forces. Forces are assigned to USNORTHCOM by SecDef when necessary to perform assigned missions. Assigned units are released back to their corresponding service departments when the missions are done. While USNORTHCOM has no assigned forces, it does have assigned subordinate commands and Joint Tasks Forces ready to direct forces when assigned. [9, pp. CRS-2]

Army North (ARNORTH). Based at Fort Sam Houston, Texas, 5th Army assumed responsibility for its USNORTHCOM mission in October 2005. Commanded by an active duty three-star general, this organization shed its traditional role of training reservists to focus on supporting civil authorities. It assigns Defense Coordinating Officers to all ten FEMA regional offices to streamline DSCA coordination. [9, pp. CRS-2]

Air Force North (AFNORTH). First Air Force is headquartered at Tyndall Air Force Base, Florida, and in February 2006, it was designated as USNORTHCOM's air component or AFNORTH. The organization is commanded by an Air National Guard two-star general who also serves as commander of the Continental NORAD Region encompassing the airspace over the continental United States (not including Alaska or Hawaii). [9, pp. CRS -2]

Marine Forces North (MARFORNORTH). In the fall of 2004, DOD designated Marine Forces Reserve Command in New Orleans, Louisiana, as a USNORTHCOM component. The reserve three-star Marine commander is responsible for force-protection of Marine installations and coordinating Marine forces assigned to USNORTHCOM. Additionally, to assist USNORTHCOM DSCA planning, the command has 32 Emergency Preparedness Liaison Officers (EPLOs) assigned to the 10 FEMA regions. [9, pp. CRS-3]

Joint Task Force Civil Support (JTF-CS). assists lead federal agencies managing the consequences of a chemical, biological, radiological, nuclear, or high-yield explosive incident in the United States or its territories and possessions.

Joint Task Force North (JTF-N). Established in September 2004, JTF-N aids law enforcement agencies protecting U.S. borders. The Fort Bliss, Texas-based unit inherited 15 years of interagency experience from its predecessor JTF-6. Whereas JTF-6 assisted with counter-drug operations on the southern border, JTF-N now has a broader Homeland Defense focus as it integrates military capabilities with Federal, State and Local law enforcement. In addition to exercises and planning, JTF-N operations include reconnaissance, surveillance, detection, and infrastructure construction missions that often leverage military units training for overseas deployment. [9, pp. CRS-3]

Joint Task Force Alaska (JTF-AK). JTF-AK is headquartered at Joint Base Elmendorf-Richardson, Alaska, and is tasked to coordinate land defense and Defense Support of Civil Authorities in Alaska. [9, pp. CRS-4]

Joint Task Force Civil Support (JTF-CS). Headquartered at Fort Eustis, outside Newport News Virginia, this JTF assists lead federal agencies managing the consequences of a chemical, biological, radiological, nuclear, or high-yield explosive incident in the United States or its territories and possessions. It was established in 1999 under U.S. Joint Forces Command, and its coordination with agencies like FEMA is more mature. The JTF is also works with state National Guard civil support teams. [9, pp. CRS-4]

Joint Force Headquarters National Capital Region (JFHQ-NCR). Activated in June 2003, this JTF is located at Fort Lesley J. McNair in Washington, D.C. It facilitates planning, training, and exercising among four local service components. Additionally, it coordinates with Coast Guard District 5, the DHS Office of National Capitol Region, and other Federal, State, and Local agencies to ensure unity of effort in the event of manmade or natural catastrophes. [9, pp. CRS-4]

In order to maintain readiness for its DSCA mission, USNORTHCOM must be prepared to work with many other agencies at the State, Local, and Federal levels of government. As such, USNORTHCOM participates in the Joint Interagency Coordination Group (JIACG) and maintains strong relationships with the Department of Homeland Security and the National Guard. Additionally, USNORTHCOM is an active participant in National Level Exercises (NLE) and integral component of the National Exercise Plan. [9, pp. CRS-4]

In order to perform its HD mission, USNORTHCOM must work closely with both Canada and Mexico. In addition to the NORAD agreement, USNORTHCOM and Canada Command are the acting agencies for a Civil Assistance Plan (CAP) that allows the military from one nation to support the armed forces of the other nation during a civil emergency. Cooperation with Mexico is less robust, but still evolving. For the most part, USNORTHCOM works with Mexico in counter-drug support through JTF-N. [9, pp. CRS-6 - CRS-7]

Conclusion

In addition to its counterterrorism and counter-WMD missions, the Department of Defense is also responsible for Homeland Defense and Defense Support of Civil Authorities. HD operations are limited to supporting law enforcement within U.S. territory. In the approaches, HD operations are hampered by the ability to differentiate friend from foe in both the maritime and air domains. In the forward regions, HD is mostly facilitated by diplomatic engagement, backed up by a credible nuclear deterrent and unprecedented capability to project conventional force anywhere in the world. Unfortunately, all this is not enough to prevent disaster back home, either natural or manmade. Accordingly, DoD is also prepared to assist civil authorities as requested following disaster. While military forces remain under military command at all time, their actions remain at all times under the direction of the Incident Commander.

Challenge Your Understanding

The following questions are designed to challenge your understanding of the material presented in this chapter. Some questions may require additional research outside this book in order to provide a complete answer.

1. What is the primary advantage of maintaining a Reserve Component?
2. How is the National Guard uniquely positioned compared to the Active Component?
3. What is the purpose and advantage of a Combatant Command?
4. What is homeland defense?
5. Which two Combatant Commands are responsible for homeland defense?
6. List and describe the three different layers of homeland defense.
7. What is DoD's strategy for preventing terrorist attack on the homeland?
8. What is Defense Support of Civil Authorities?
9. How are Title 10 forces coordinated together with National Guard responding to a disaster?
10. Which Combatant Command coordinates DSCA within the continental United States and Alaska?

Chapter 39

National Guard

Learning Outcomes

Careful study of this chapter will help a student do the following:

- Describe the different missions of the National Guard.
- Discuss how the National Guard uniquely contributes to homeland security and homeland defense.
- Explain the different command and control arrangements for National Guard under State and Federal authorities.

"The National Guard has served America as both a wartime force and the first military responders in times of domestic crisis. Hundreds of times each year, the nation's governors call upon their Guard troops to respond to fires, floods, hurricanes and other natural disasters."

- LTG Russell Honore, Commander, JTF-Katrina

Introduction

Historically, the National Guard has served as a critical resource in emergencies and can be an effective force multiplier to civil authorities in responding to acts of terrorism at the state, local, and federal levels.

Historically, the National Guard has served as a critical resource in emergencies and can be an effective force multiplier to civil authorities in responding to acts of terrorism at the state, local, and federal levels. In the wake of the September 11, 2001, terrorist attacks, the National Guard has expanded its traditional role in homeland defense and homeland security and readily supports Local, Territorial, State, and Federal response agencies with needed equipment, facilities, and personnel. National Guard activities such as conducting vulnerability assessments; planning, training, and exercising with civilian emergency responders; and securing strategic facilities, such as airports, pharmaceutical labs, nuclear power plants, communications towers, and border crossings, have been a cornerstone in protecting our citizens from domestic acts of terrorism. Unless and until activated for Federal service, the National Guard is under the control of the Governor as Commander-in-Chief. [1, pp. 3-4]

The National Guard

The National Guard is descended from the colonial militias which existed prior to the adoption of the Constitution. With the adoption of the Constitution, the Federal government acquired authority to organize, arm, and discipline the militia, and to call the militia into Federal service in order to execute the laws of the Union, to suppress insurrection, and to repel invasion. Additionally, Federal laws passed in the early 20th century designated part of the militia — now called the National Guard — as a Federal reserve of the Army, thereby enhancing Federal authority over the Guard in certain respects. As a result of this history, the National Guard is neither a purely State nor a purely Federal organization. Rather, it is both a State and Federal organization. [2, pp. 6-7]

The National Guard of the United States is made up of 54 separate National Guard organizations: one for each state, and one each for Puerto Rico, Guam, the U.S. Virgin Islands, and the District of Columbia. While the District of Columbia National Guard is an exclusively Federal organization and operates under Federal control at all times, the other 53 National Guards operate as State or Territorial organizations most of the time. In this capacity, each of these 53 organizations is identified by its state or territorial name (e.g. ,the California National Guard or the Puerto Rico National Guard), and is controlled by its respective Governor. [2, p. 7]

The National Guard is comprised of both an Army National Guard (ARNG) and Air National Guard (ANG). Both elements consist mainly of part-time personnel, supplemented by a small cadre of full-time staff. The Army National Guard is authorized approximately 358,000 soldiers. The Air National Guard is authorized approximately 105,000 airmen. Each state's National Guard forces have a dual role in both Federal and State missions. [3, pp. 4-5]

Federal Mission

According to Title 10 Section 10102 of United States Code, the purpose of the National Guard is to "provide trained units and qualified persons available for active duty in the armed forces in time of war or national emergency, and at such other times as the national security may require." The National Guard together with the Federal Reserve make up the Reserve Component (RC) of the United States military. Together with the Active Component (AC), the three components comprise the Total Force of the United States military. The basic advantage of maintaining a Reserve Component is that it is much cheaper than the Active Component. The Army National Guard comprises 32% of the Total Force, yet incurs less than 13% of the total cost. Likewise, the Air National Guard comprises 20% of the Total Force, yet incurs less than 7% of the total cost. [3, p. 5] This cost differential has played an important role shaping the mix of AC and RC forces over time.

The National Guard together with the Federal Reserve make up the Reserve Component (RC) of the United States military. Together with the Active Component (AC), the three components comprise the Total Force of the United States military. The basic advantage of maintaining a Reserve Component is that it is much cheaper than the Active Component.

From the founding of the nation to the Cold War era, the bulk of force structure was maintained in the Reserve Component, especially the militia/National Guard, except in times of major conflicts. When major conflicts arose—such as the Civil War, World War I, and World War II—the comparatively small active component was expanded through the activation of militia and federal reserves, recruitment of additional volunteers for the AC, and the use of conscription. At the end of the conflict, active force levels were dramatically reduced. For example, in 1939, there were fewer than 350,000 active duty personnel in all branches of the U.S. armed forces. During World War II, this number grew enormously, reaching over 12 million service members on duty by 1945. With the end of World War II, the United States radically reduced the size of its active armed forces to about 1.5 million in 1947-1950. [4, p. 3]

This approach changed with the onset of the Cold War. With the advent of the Korean War in 1950, the United States doubled the size of its active forces by 1951 to approximately 3.2 million. This increase included a major reserve mobilization, with over 850,000 members of the National Guard and Reserves called to active duty. However, with the end of the war in 1953, the size of the active component did not decrease nearly as much as it would have in earlier eras. For the next decade, it remained roughly between 2.5 million and 3 million for all services, while the size of the reserve component hovered around 1 million. In response to the Vietnam War, the size of the active component was increased again to about 3.5 million (1968), but there was no major reserve mobilization. Thus, since the Korean War and continuing to the present, the United States has maintained most of its force structure in the AC. [4, p. 3]

This shift to an AC-centric force structure model in the aftermath of World War II began to ebb somewhat starting in the 1970s. The downsizing that followed the Vietnam War, the end of the comparatively inexpensive manpower provided by conscription, budgetary pressures, and dissatisfaction with the negative consequences of not using reserve forces more extensively during Vietnam led to a renewed focus on using RC forces to supplement the AC. The Total Force Policy, established in 1973 by Secretary of Defense James Schlesinger on the basis of the 1970 Total Force Concept developed by Secretary of Defense Melvin Laird, sought to integrate "the Active, Guard and Reserve forces into a homogenous whole" and emphasized that, instead of draftees, "Guard and Reserve forces will be used as the initial and primary augmentation of active forces." [4, pp. 3-4]

For most of U.S. history, its military forces were comprised of a small core of full-time military supplemented during war with part-time militia. This model was reversed following WWII, when the ability to attack across continents shrunk from weeks to hours.

General Creighton Abrams, the Chief of Staff of the Army from 1972-74, implemented this policy for the Army by instituting changes which deeply integrated reserve forces into the active force structure. This deeper integration helped General Abrams rebuild the Army to 16 divisions while staying within budgetary limits; it also effectively ensured that the Army could not be sent to war again without the Guard and Reserve, as had occurred in Vietnam. The most notable manifestation of this increased active-reserve integration was the roundout brigade program, which involved restructuring of certain AC divisions to include an RC brigade. Normally, an AC division would have three AC brigades assigned to it. At Abrams' direction, some AC divisions were assigned two AC brigades, along with a "roundout" National Guard brigade; other AC divisions kept three AC brigades but had some of their AC battalions replaced with "roundout" RC battalions. Congress passed a new law in 1976 to make it easier for the President to activate RC personnel and units. [4, pp. 4-5] The President can call up RC personnel under provisions in Title 10 United States Code listed in Figure 1.

Statute	Provisions
10 U.S.C. 12301(a) "Full Mobilization"	Declared by Congress: In time of war or national emergency No limit on numbers of soldiers called to active duty For duration of war plus 6 months
10 U.S.C. 12302 "Partial Mobilization"	Declared by the President: In time of national emergency No more than 1,000,000 reservists can be on active duty No more than 24 consecutive months
10 U.S.C. 12304 "Presidential Reserve Call-up"	Determined by the President: To augment the active duty force for operational missions No more than 200,000 reservists can be on active duty No more than 270 days

Figure 39-1: Reserve Component Mobilization Authorities [4, p. 5]

Other initiatives to improve active-reserve integration in the 1970s and 1980s included more modernized equipment for the RC, greater overseas training opportunities, and rotations at the newly established National Training Center. [4, pp. 4-5]

The first major test of this greater active-reserve integration came during the 1990-91 Persian Gulf War, which saw the activation of over 238,000 RC personnel, including about 60,000 members of the Army National Guard and some 88,000 members of the Army Reserve. In many respects, RC performance in this conflict strengthened support for the Total Force Policy among defense policymakers. However, there were areas of RC readiness identified as needing improvement. This was most apparent with respect to the roundout brigades. Three ARNG roundout brigades were mobilized, somewhat belatedly, and deployed to the National Training Center for post-mobilization training. Amid claims of serious readiness deficiencies, however, they were not certified as combat ready until the war was over. [4, p. 5]

In the 1970s, General Creighton Abrams conceived the "Total Force" concept, and began to more actively integrate the Reserve Component into active duty military missions. With minor exceptions, the concept passed its first major test in the 1990-91 Persian Gulf War. Since then, the Reserve Component, including the National Guard, have played an increasingly larger role in U.S. military engagements, including both Iraq and Afghanistan.

The Persian Gulf War experience led Congress to address identified readiness shortcomings through passage of the Army National Guard Combat Readiness Reform Act of 1992 (also known as "Title XI," in reference to its location within the 1993 National Defense Authorization Act). The reforms focused primarily, though not exclusively, on ARNG combat units. Title XI contained 19 provisions which sought to improve the readiness of Army Guard units and their compatibility with AC units by: increasing experience and leadership levels in the ARNG by recruiting more prior-service personnel, Service Academy graduates, and ROTC graduates; revising the training focus for combat units; providing for a more robust medical and dental evaluation process; ensuring the compatibility of personnel, supply, maintenance and finance systems across the AC, ARNG, and USAR; reforming the Army's readiness system for USAR and ARNG units; directing the Secretary of the Army to conduct inspections to ensure that ARNG units met deployability standards; and mandating that the Army provide greater funding to deploying ARNG and USAR units. [4, p. 6]

Although the Department of Defense effectively ended the roundout brigade program in 1993, the disintegration of the Soviet Union gave further impetus to the ongoing integration of the AC and RC. With the demise of the United States' main military competitor, the requirement for large numbers of ground forces at a high state of readiness was considered less critical for national security. Subsequently, AC force structure was substantially reduced in the 1990s. [4, p. 6]

The post-Cold War drawdown was followed by the increased employment of RC forces in Iraq (low-intensity conflict with Iraq, 1998-2003), Bosnia (1995-2004), Kosovo (1999-present), and Haiti (1994-1996). As the use of RC units increased and they gained experience through repetitive deployments, the distinction between components faded somewhat, and RC units began to be more seriously considered as suitable substitutes for AC units—provided they received necessary personnel, equipment, training and preparation time prior to being deployed. This perspective was further reinforced by the large-scale and continuing mobilizations of RC forces for the wars in Iraq and Afghanistan, which led many public officials and policy analysts to conclude that the performance of the RC in these conflicts largely validated the Total Force Policy. Some Army officials argued, however, that AC and RC units were not interchangeable, with one senior Army officer indicating that this was the reason RC BCTs were used for less complex missions in Iraq and Afghanistan than their AC counterparts. RC advocates countered that they had no control over the missions they were assigned in Iraq and Afghanistan, that they were effective in all the missions they were given, and that they could have successfully completed combined arms maneuver missions if they had been given the opportunity. [4, p. 7]

The National Guard is located in all 54 states and territories. It is typically a major state emergency responder and a vital part of the state's ability to protect its people and property from disaster and to recover after disaster has struck.

In addition to the large scale mobilization of RC units during the wars in Iraq and Afghanistan, Congress authorized significant expansions of the active Army and Marine Corps. This led to an increase in the ratio of AC to RC forces in those Services. However, with the end of the war in Iraq and the ongoing reduction of forces in Afghanistan, a multi-year drawdown of AC forces is underway in these Services. This drawdown has rolled back the war-time increases in AC strength and will likely end at a level lower than existed prior to the war. As such, the proportion of AC to RC forces will also likely decline in those Services. [4, p. 7]

State Mission

The National Guard is located in all 54 states and territories. It is typically a major state emergency responder and a vital part of the state's ability to protect its people and property from disaster and to recover after disaster has struck. [5, p. 55]

Normally, the National Guard operates under the control of State and Territorial governors. In response to disasters and civil disorders, governors can order National Guard personnel to perform full-time duty, commonly referred to as "state active duty." In this state capacity, National Guard personnel operate under the control of their Governor, are paid according to state law, can perform typical disaster relief tasks and are not subject to the restrictions of the Posse Comitatus Act. [2, p. 7]

> *"Whoever, except in cases and under circumstances expressly authorized by the Constitution or Act of Congress, willfully uses any part of the Army or Air Force as a posse comitatus or otherwise to execute the laws shall be fined under this title or imprisoned not more than two years, or both."*
>
> - Title 18, United States Code, Section 1385

The Posse Comitatus Act prohibits the use of Title 10 Army and Air Force personnel as enforcement officials to execute State or Federal law or to perform direct law enforcement functions. The Navy and Marine Corps are included in this prohibition as a result of Department of Defense (DOD) policy articulated in DODD 3025.21, Defense Support of Civilian Law Enforcement Agencies. [3, pp. III-1]

When activated under Title 10 status, the National Guard also becomes subject to Posse Comitatus and cannot perform law enforcement. However, there are exceptions provided by the Constitution and Congress. The Insurrection Act (10 U.S.C. §§ 331-335) allows the President to call the National Guard into Federal service to suppress insurrection against a State government (10 U.S.C. § 331), enforce Federal laws and suppress rebellion against the authority of the United States (10 U.S.C. §332), and prevent interference with State and Federal laws, if that interference deprives a class of people of rights, privileges, immunities, or protections named in the Constitution (10 U.S.C. § 333). Similar authority is contained in 10 U.S.C. § 12406, which permits the President to call members and units of the National Guard into Federal service to repel invasion, suppress rebellion, or execute the laws of the United States. [2, p. 9]

Normally, the National Guard operates under the control of State and Territorial governors. In response to disasters and civil disorders, governors can order National Guard personnel to perform full-time duty, commonly referred to as "state active duty."

Another way in which National Guard personnel can be activated and remain under the control of their Governor is under the authority of 32 U.S.C. 502(f). This provision of Federal law provides that "a member of the National Guard may...without his consent, but with the pay and allowances provided by law...be ordered to perform training or other duty in addition to [inactive duty for training or annual training]." The advantage of using this authority is that the National Guard personnel called will receive Federal pay and benefits and are entitled to certain legal protections as though they were in Federal service, but they remain under the control of their Governor and are therefore not subject to the restrictions of the Posse Comitatus Act. This is the provision of law which was used to provide federal pay and benefits to the National Guard personnel who provided security at many of the nation's airports in the aftermath of the terrorist attacks of September 11, 2001. [2, p. 7]

As the chief executives of their states, governors are vested with a primary responsibility to protect the life and property of their citizens, and are the senior civilian officials in charge of most emergency preparedness and disaster response efforts in our nation. As the commanders in chief of their respective state National Guard units, governors have a major interest in how their state National Guard units and personnel are trained, equipped, and utilized. And as commanders in chief, they are responsible for their Guard before and after its use, whether the units are deployed on a state mission, a federal mission, or a combination of both. [5, p. 55]

National Guard forces are commanded by The Adjutant General (TAG) of each State. In 49 states, Puerto Rico, Guam, and the United States Virgin Islands, the Adjutant General is appointed by the Governor. The exceptions are Vermont, where the Adjutant General is appointed by the legislature; and the District of Columbia, where a commanding general is appointed by the President of the United States. [7]

The Adjutant General commands their respective Army National Guard and Air National Guard forces from a Joint Force Headquarters (JFHQ).

The Adjutant General commands their respective Army National Guard and Air National Guard forces from a Joint Force Headquarters (JFHQ). JFHQ-State evolved from predecessor ARNG and ANG headquarters in each state that were established in the 1980s. In 2003, at the direction of the Chief of the National Guard Bureau, the predecessor headquarters were combined into the 54 Joint Force Headquarters-State. This arrangement was formally recognized by DOD in 2011 with the issuance of DOD Instruction 5105.83. The state Joint Force headquarters each consist of a Joint staff element, Army staff element, and Air staff element. These headquarters are responsible for coordinating the planning, training, and execution of National Guard homeland defense, civil support, and other domestic emergency missions within the United States. They also manage the National Guard's readiness and prepare National Guard units for federal mobilization. [3, pp. 8, 54]

JFHQ-State is supported by the National Guard Bureau (NGB). The NGB is the National Guard representative to DOD. The NGB works with the Army and Air Force staffs to provide for the organization, maintenance, and operation of National Guard units. While the NGB is not an operational command, it does provide an important communication between DOD and the states during national emergencies. The National Guard Bureau is headed by the Chief of the National Guard Bureau (CNGB). In 2011, the CNGB was elevated to a 4-star position and made a member of the Joint Chiefs of Staff. The NGB, in turn, is supported by the Army National Guard Directorate and the Air National Guard Readiness Center. [3, p. 51]

- The Army National Guard Directorate assists the Chief of the National Guard Bureau with carrying out the functions as they relate to the Army National Guard. Most of these functions involve providing for equipment, maintenance, and training of Army National Guard forces. [3, p. 51]
- The Air National Guard Readiness Center, likewise, assists the Chief of the National Guard with carrying out their functions as they relate to the Air National Guard. Similarly, these functions involve providing for equipment, maintenance and training of Air National Guard forces. However, they also include rotating alert sites for air defense interceptors; managing airlift and aeromedical evacuations; and arranging weather flights and search and rescue missions. [3, p. 51]

When disaster strikes, State governors may mobilize their National Guard to support incident response under the direction of Local Incident Commanders within their State. If additional National Guard forces are required for the task, State governors may call upon their neighbors to lend assistance under provisions of the Emergency Management Assistance Compact (EMAC). [6, p. 17] EMAC was established by Congress and signed into law in 1996 (Public Law 104-321). All 54 States and Territories are covered under its authorities. EMAC provides the means for States to assist each other on a cost-reimbursable basis with potential Federal assistance. The advantage of EMAC is that it resolves liability issues in advance, allowing States to expeditiously lend assistance to one another. [9] EMAC resulted in the largest deployment of military forces within the U.S. since the Civil War after it was activated in response to Hurricane Katrina.

In the wake of Hurricane Katrina, the National Guard performed a range of missions, including search and rescue, security, evacuations, and distribution of food and water.

Hurricane Katrina in 2005 was the costliest natural disaster ($108 billion) and one of the five deadliest (1,245 fatalities) hurricanes in U.S. history. Katrina caused severe destruction along the Gulf coast from central Florida to Texas, much of it due to storm surge and levee failure. It was New Orleans, however, that sustained the most damage when Katrina came ashore as a Category 3 hurricane and passed directly over the city on August 29. The rain swollen canals quickly overtopped the levees and flooded 80% of the city. [10] Within four hours of landfall, Army National Guard helicopters were airborne and actively performing rescue missions, with other National Guard personnel joining the effort on the ground. [6, p. 38]

Guardsmen performed a range of missions, including search and rescue, security, evacuations, and distribution of food and water. In Mississippi, National Guard forces prepared Camp Shelby as a staging point for incoming forces and also engaged in law enforcement support, debris removal, shelter support and other vital operations. Guardsmen from Texas and Pennsylvania supplied satellite phone communications to the response. When a group of Pennsylvania Guardsmen arrived to fix a Louisiana woman's roof, she told the group: "That's a long way to come to help us. We're really grateful ... you boys are going to heaven, I tell you." By August 29, sixty-five National Guard helicopters were positioned throughout the Gulf Coast. By September 2, nearly 22,000 National Guard soldiers and airmen had deployed to the region — including 6,500 in New Orleans alone—breaking the National Guard's previous record for the largest response to a domestic emergency. Eventually, over 50,000 National Guard members from fifty-four States, Territories, and the District of Columbia deployed to the Gulf Coast. Active duty military and National Guard personnel provided critical emergency response and security support to the Gulf Coast during the height of the crisis. State active duty and Title 32 National Guard forces that deployed to Louisiana and Mississippi operated under the command of their respective Governors. The robust National Guard response played a crucial role in the effort to bring stability to the areas ravaged by Hurricane Katrina. [8, pp. 42-43] But all did not go well.

A fragmented deployment system and lack of an integrated command structure for both active duty and National Guard forces exacerbated communications and coordination issues during the initial response. Deployments for Title 32 National Guard forces were coordinated State-to-State through EMAC agreements and also by the National Guard Bureau. Title 10 active duty force deployments were coordinated through U.S. Northern Command (USNORTHCOM). Once forces arrived in the Joint Operations Area, they fell under separate command structures, rather than one single command. The separate commands divided the area of operations geographically and supported response efforts separately. [6, p. 43]

Unfortunately, the National Guard's response to Hurricane Katrina was not well coordinated with Title 10 forces working under Task Force Katrina, nor with FEMA. The Dual-Status Commander concept was subsequently developed to improve coordination between the National Guard, Title 10 forces, and FEMA in future large-scale disasters.

For the first two days of Katrina response operations, USNORTHCOM did not have situational awareness of what forces the National Guard had on the ground. Joint Task Force Katrina (JTF-Katrina) simply could not operate at full efficiency when it lacked visibility of over half the military forces in the disaster area. Neither the Louisiana National Guard nor JTF-Katrina had a good sense for where each other's forces were located or what they were doing. For example, the JTF-Katrina Engineering Directorate had not been able to coordinate with National Guard forces in the New Orleans area. As a result, some units were not immediately assigned missions matched to on-the-ground requirements. Further, FEMA requested assistance from DOD without knowing what State National Guard forces had already deployed to fill the same needs. [6, p. 55]

Also, the Commanding General of JTF-Katrina and the Adjutant Generals of Louisiana and Mississippi had only a coordinating relationship, with no formal command relationship established. This resulted in confusion over roles and responsibilities between National Guard and Federal forces and highlighted the need for a more unified command structure. [6, p. 55]

In the years following the divided military response to Katrina, State governors and DOD officials realized the urgent need for policy changes and the requirement for an improved coordination mechanism between State and Federal Government, and National Guard and Federal military forces. Unable to legislate an agreeable command arrangement, in 2010 the Council of Governors and Secretary of Defense (SecDef) signed a Joint Action Plan agreeing to employ Dual-Status Command (DSC) when Federal forces are deployed to a State. In 2012, the National Defense Authorization Act (NDAA) made DSC the law as the "usual and customary command and control arrangement". [12, pp. 14-17]

The Government Accountability Office defines a Dual-Status Commander as a "Military officer who serves as an intermediate link between the separate chains of command for state and federal forces—has authority over both National Guard forces under state control and active duty forces under federal control during a civil support incident or special event." More simply stated, a DSC is "responsible for performing two separate and distinct but related jobs with two separate and distinct teams for two separate and distinct bosses, all at the same time." [11, p. 7] The DSC concept was first put to the test during Hurricane Sandy in 2012.

Hurricane Sandy was the largest and most damaging Atlantic hurricane on record and the second most costly in U.S. history, eclipsed only by Hurricane Katrina. At the peak of the October-November 2012 military response to Hurricane Sandy in New York, more than 4,000 National Guard personnel, along with Active and Reserve Soldiers, Sailors, Airmen, and Marines were engaged in supporting civil authorities as part of Joint Task Force Sandy (JTF-Sandy). [11, p. 1]

For the most part, the Dual-Status Commander concept proved itself well after Hurricane Sandy came ashore in New Jersey and flooded much of New York City in October 2012.

In October 2012, Hurricane Sandy came ashore along one of the most densely populated regions in the country. Even though Sandy was downgraded to tropical storm status prior to landfall, it was a massive storm that affected east coast cities from Washington, DC, to New York City. As was the case with Katrina, the storm's magnitude overwhelmed State and Local responders. Requests for military support were widespread, resulting in an over-convergence of military forces inside the region within days of the storm's arrival. Again, like Katrina, National Guard forces in both State Active Duty and Title 32 status operated alongside Title 10 Federal forces in support of civil authorities responding to the storm's damage. Unlike Katrina, however, this response effort was a historical first for the U.S. military. For the first time, National Guard and Federal military forces executed unplanned civil support operations under the tactical command of Dual-Status Commanders. [12, p. 2]

As the storm approached the coast on October 28, 2012, President Barack Obama signed Stafford Act emergency declarations for Connecticut; Washington, DC; Maryland; Massachusetts; New Jersey; and New York. Over the next 24 hours, Hurricane Sandy weakened from a category 1 hurricane to a tropical storm. The storm made landfall slightly north of Atlantic City near Brigantine, NJ, at approximately 11:30 p.m. on October 29, 2012. That same day, President Obama signed additional disaster declarations for Delaware, Rhode Island, and Pennsylvania; and declared major disaster areas in New Jersey and New York following massive storm surges along each coast. [12, p. 28]

With the new disaster declarations approved, the Secretary of Defense, through the Chairman of the Joint Chiefs of Staff, issued a standing execution order directing USNORTHCOM to provide Defense Support of Civil Authorities (DSCA) to the affected states. Owing to the Joint Action Plan, State governors had the option to request a Dual-Status Commander for the pending DSCA response. Ultimately, six states received authorization to employ a DSC: New York, New Jersey, Maryland, New Hampshire, Massachusetts, and Rhode Island. Of the six states receiving DSC authorizations, only two—New York and New Jersey—actually activated a DSC to lead the military response efforts. [12, pp. 28-29]

Brigadier General Bud Grant from the New Jersey Army National Guard and Brigadier General Michael Swezey from the New York Army National Guard were each given Title 10 and Title 32 orders authorizing them to command both State National Guard and Federal military forces. [12, p. 29] On the one hand they reported to their State Governor who remained Commander-in-Chief over their State National Guard. On the other hand they reported to the President of the United States who remained Commander-in-Chief over Federal military forces assigned through USNORTHCOM. These two National Guard officers became the coordinating point for Defense Support of Civil Authorities within their respective states.

The National Guard also supports the Homeland Defense mission. First Air Force is commanded by an Air National Guard two-star general responsible for protecting the airspace over the Continental United States and Alaska.

Hurricane Sandy caused a great deal of damage in the New York metropolitan area. However, Sandy was only a Category 1 storm when it made landfall and quickly dissipated after coming ashore. While the storm surge was one of the most significant in New York's history, the storm could have been worse. [12, p. 53]

Hurricane Sandy demonstrated that Dual-Status Command could provide effective coordination of National Guard and Title 10 forces through the successful integration of liaison officers (LNOs), and a strategic forward-leaning approach to the operation, including pre-positioning Title 10 assets. However, while the DSC concept proved sound, the execution during Sandy was flawed. Lessons learned from this incident can help refine the concept further and help improve coordination in future such disasters [12, pp. 54, 113]

Homeland Missions

In addition to providing for Federal military capability and State disaster response, the National Guard has specific roles assigned for Homeland Defense and Homeland Security.

Homeland Defense (HD) is defined in the 2002 National Strategy for Homeland Security as "the protection of U.S. sovereignty, territory, domestic population, and critical defense infrastructure against external threats or aggression, or other threats as directed by the President." Protecting the sovereignty of U.S. airspace is a key HD mission assigned to the National Guard. [13, pp. B-1]

First Air Force at Tyndall Air Force Base, Florida, is the designated air component to USNORTHCOM, called AFNORTH. AFNORTH is commanded by an Air National Guard two-star general responsible for protecting the airspace over the Continental United States and Alaska. AFNORTH maintains joint surveillance of U.S. airspace together with the Federal Aviation Administration (FAA). U.S. airspace is protected by Air National Guard squadrons flying the F-22 Raptor, F-15 Eagle, and F-16 Falcon. In the event of unknown or suspicious radar tracks, fighters can be vectored from patrol or launched from alert to investigate. Since 9/11, the Commander of UNORTHCOM has been authorized to shoot down suspicious or hostile aircraft. That authority is delegated to the AFNORTH Commander. Homeland Defense missions are designated Operation NOBLE EAGE to distinguish them from NORAD missions flown by the same units. National Guard aircraft maintain continuous and constant watch over U.S airspace. [14, pp. 2-3]

Since the 1980s, DOD, including the National Guard, as authorized by Congress, has conducted a wide variety of counterdrug support missions along the borders of the United States.

Border security remains a core mission of homeland security. The U.S. Border Patrol within the Customs and Border Protection (CBP) Directorate of the Department of Homeland Security (DHS) has primary responsibility for detecting and preventing illegal entry across nearly 7,000 miles of border with Mexico and Canada, and over 2,000 miles of coastline. It is DOD's role to support DHS in this responsibility. Since the 1980s, DOD, including the National Guard, as authorized by Congress, has conducted a wide variety of counterdrug support missions along the borders of the United States. Since 9/11, DOD's support role in counterdrug and counterterrorism has increased its profile in border security. [15, p. 1]

In 2006, in response to requests for support enforcing federal immigration laws from the governors of Arizona, California, New Mexico, and Texas, President George W. Bush announced the deployment of up to 6,000 National Guard troops along the southern border to support the Border Patrol. During 2006–2008, more than 30,000 individuals participated in the mission "Operation Jump Start." The troops provided engineering, aviation, and entry identification teams, as well as technical, logistical, and administrative support. The Guard units, serving pursuant to Title 32 of the U.S. Code, remained under the control of the respective governors, but were fully funded by the Federal government and were not involved in direct law-enforcement activities. Throughout Operation Jump Start, the federal government continued to recruit and train thousands of additional Border Patrol agents, thereby reducing the number of National Guard troops required to support the southern border. Operation Jump Start officially concluded on July 15, 2008. [15, p. 1]

In response to increasing drug traffic and murders along the U.S.-Mexico border, in 2010 President Obama sent 1,200 National Guard troops to support Border Patrol along the southern border. A year later the number of troops was drawn down and the remaining 300 relegated mostly to conducting aerial surveillance. [15, p. 1]

Because of their unique legal status, the National Guard remains a ready manpower reserve to draw on for border security during times of crisis or emergency.

And while the National Guard actively protect against enemy intrusion on sovereign U.S. territory, they are also prepared to respond in the event a WMD attack employing chemical, biological, radiological, or nuclear (CBRN) agents.

Congress in 1998 approved the development of Federally funded, State controlled, National Guard WMD Civil Support Teams (CSTs). The CSTs' principal mission is to assist civil authorities in the United States in responding to catastrophic terrorism, including the use of chemical, biological, radiological, nuclear, or high-yield explosive weapons and agents.

Congress in 1998 approved the development of Federally funded, State controlled, National Guard WMD Civil Support Teams (CSTs). The CSTs' principal mission is to assist civil authorities in the United States in responding to incidents involving WMD or catastrophic terrorism, including the use of chemical, biological, radiological, nuclear, or high-yield explosive weapons and agents. The CSTs are to identify these agents and substances, assess current or projected consequences, advise civil authorities on response measures, and assist with requests for additional support. Like traditional National Guard units, the CSTs are under the control of the governors of their respective states and territories, unless they are activated for Federal service, at which time they would fall under the control of the Department of Defense. However, unlike traditional National Guard units, these highly specialized teams are each composed of 22 members who are on full-time duty. The teams include both Army and Air National Guard personnel who are divided into six sections, including command, operations, administration/logistics, medical science, communications, and survey. The teams possess highly technical mobile laboratory and communications equipment to accomplish their mission. [16, p. 1] There are 58 full-time teams: one in every U.S. state, Washington, D.C., Puerto Rico, Germany, Guam and the US Virgin Islands, and an additional team each in California, Florida and New York. [17]

In the event of large-scale employment of WMD anywhere in the nation, the National Guard is ready to deploy Homeland Response Forces (HRFs) to the scene of the incident. A HRF is comprised of around 570 National Guard personnel trained in CBRN response. There are 10 designated HRFs, one for each FEMA region. Eight are hosted in WA, CA, UT, TX, MO, GA, OH, and PA. In Region I, HRF units are stationed in VT, MA, and CT. Region II elements are shared between NY and NJ. The Adjutant General may activate a HRF in response to an incident within their State, or to support the Governor of another State under the provisions of EMAC. Once activated, HRFs can assemble within 6-12 hours, and deploy in less than 24 hours. Once on-scene, HRFs are capable of conducting command and control; casualty assistance; search and extraction; decontamination; medical triage and stabilization, fatality search and recovery; and otherwise save lives and mitigate human suffering. HRFs provide a rapid response capability when Local jurisdictions are overwhelmed and Federal assistance is still on its way. [18]

International Diplomacy

In addition to its many roles protecting the nation, the National Guard also serves as an international ambassador under the State Partnership Program (SPP). SPP is a Department of Defense security cooperation program designed to build defense relationships with foreign military partners, develop allied and friendly military capabilities, and foster international relations through peaceful engagement. [19, p. 1]

The SPP evolved from an effort begun in 1992 to use professional contacts between the U.S. military and the militaries of the newly independent nations of the former Soviet Union to help reform the defense establishments of those nations. The program has expanded greatly since then. Today, it is a significant component of DOD's security cooperation efforts, linking state and territorial National Guards in 63 partnerships with 70 partners nations. Nearly every state National Guard participates in the SPP, as do the National Guard of Guam, Puerto Rico, the U.S. Virgin Islands, and the District of Columbia. [19, p. 1]

In addition to its many roles protecting the nation, the National Guard also serves as an international ambassador under the State Partnership Program (SPP).

The SPP conducts a variety of activities in support of partner nations. The focus of SPP activities varies depending on the needs of the partner nation, the capabilities of the state National Guard, the goals of the respective U.S. ambassador and the combatant commander, and statutory authorities and restrictions. According to National Guard Bureau, the typical SPP event is a week-long subject matter expert exchange, with three to five National Guard subject matter experts participating. Examples of different types of exchanges are listed here.

- Subject Matter Expert Exchanges. During these events, National Guard personnel with expertise in a certain area share their knowledge with partner nation personnel.
- Familiarizations. These are demonstrations of certain capabilities that the Army or Air National Guard has, or discussions of policy issues related to those capabilities.
- Senior Leader Visits. These are visits between senior leaders of the state National Guard, such as the adjutant general, and senior leaders of the partner nation's armed forces.
- Operational Mentor and Liaison Teams. Operational Mentor and Liaison Teams (OMLTs) provide mentoring and training for the Afghan National Army (ANA) and serve as liaisons between the ANA and the International Security Assistance Force (ISAF) in Afghanistan. They are composed of 13-30 personnel from one or more countries. National Guard personnel have embedded with their partner nation's OMLTs and accompanied them throughout their deployments to Afghanistan (they have also conducted similar embedded operations with partner nation forces in Iraq and Kosovo). [19, pp. 4-6]

One unique aspect of the SPP is the ability to forge relationships between particular individuals over a long period of time. For active component personnel, a duty assignment that includes regular contact with the military of a foreign nation would typically last for about two to three years. At the end of the tour of duty, the U.S. service member would normally be reassigned as part of his or her career progression. In contrast, National Guard personnel participating in the SPP may well participate in engagements with partner nation military personnel repeatedly throughout their career. This is due to both the duration of the state National Guard and foreign nation partnership—some of which have been in existence for nearly two decades—and the frequency with which National Guard personnel serve their entire reserve careers within one state National Guard. Thus, for example, individuals who joined the Michigan National Guard in 1993 and continued to serve to the present would have had the opportunity to participate in SPP activities with Latvia numerous times over the past 18 years. In that time, both the Guard personnel and the foreign military personnel with whom they engaged will have been promoted to higher ranks, potentially providing for strong relationships between the now fairly senior National Guard and foreign military personnel. The ability to develop such long-term relationships is rare for active component personnel because of career assignment policies. An additional benefit of an enduring relationship is that it provides National Guard personnel with the opportunity to develop cultural knowledge, and potentially even language skills, based on their recurring contacts with the partner nation. [19, pp. 6-7]

One unique aspect of the SPP is the ability to forge relationships between particular individuals over a long period of time. For active component personnel, a duty assignment typically last for about two to three years. In contrast, National Guard personnel participating in the SPP may well participate in engagements with partner nation military personnel repeatedly throughout their career.

Another aspect of the SPP that distinguishes it from similar engagements by active component forces stems from the National Guard's dual status as both a state and a federal organization. In its federal status, the National Guard is a reserve component of the Army and the Air Force and is trained, organized, and equipped to conduct a wide spectrum of military activities. However, the National Guard is also the organized militia of each state and in that capacity it routinely operates under the control of its state governor, typically to respond to disasters and civil disorders. National Guard personnel in a "Title 32 status" have also conducted counterdrug, border security, and airport security missions. The practical expertise the National Guard has acquired in these areas may be complemented by the skills that National Guard personnel develop in their civilian occupations. For example, a National Guard soldier may serve as an infantryman in his Guard unit, but may be a state trooper, paramedic, or emergency dispatcher in his civilian job. [19, p. 7]

The expertise that National Guard units have acquired in conducting these types of operations are often in demand among foreign militaries, which frequently play a major role in their nation's disaster response plans, and which may play significant roles in their nation's border security, civil disorder, or counterdrug operations. Although active component forces have significant expertise in these areas—as evidenced, for example, by the role played by active component personnel in responding to the earthquake in Haiti and the floods in Pakistan in 2010—it is typically not exercised with the frequency of National Guard forces and, in certain cases, is intentionally limited by law. [19, p. 7]

A final area in which the SPP differs from active component security cooperation activities lies in the role of individual states in the relationship. Active component security cooperation activities are purely Federal in nature; there is no connection with any U.S. state. SPP activities have both a Federal and a State connection, and this latter relationship can be important from several perspectives. For the State and the foreign nation, the SPP provides a link between senior State and foreign nation officials. The Adjutant General is typically a senior official in his or her State government, normally heading up the state department of military affairs, and sometimes leading the state department of emergency management or homeland security. This can provide a conduit for the State and the foreign nation to develop relationships beyond that with the state National Guard—for example, enhancing economic ties or conducting educational exchanges. From the Federal perspective, a strong relationship between a state and a foreign nation could potentially contribute to a stronger relationship between the United States and the foreign nation. [19, p. 8]

Conclusion

Among homeland security partners, the National Guard may be considered the most versatile. They provide an effective combat force that comprises a significant yet cost-effective proportion of the nation's total military might. Because of their unique status, they stand ready to maintain civil order and respond to Local disasters within each State. Moreover, they are available to assist their neighbors in the most expeditious manner under the worst conceivable circumstances. And finally, they are agents of diplomacy, helping reduce global tensions and improve U.S. relations internationally.

Challenge Your Understanding

The following questions are designed to challenge your understanding of the material presented in this chapter. Some questions may require additional research outside this book in order to provide a complete answer.

1. What are the two types of National Guard forces?
2. What is the Federal mission of the National Guard?
3. Under what circumstances may the President call up the National Guard?
4. What is the State mission of the National Guard?
5. How is the Washington DC National Guard different from all other State National Guard?
6. How was the National Guard deployed for Hurricane Katrina?
7. What was the motivation behind the dual -status commander concept?
8. List and describe two roles the National Guard perform in homeland defense.
9. What capability can the National Guard bring in response to a WMD incident?
10. How does the National Guard uniquely contribute to international diplomacy?

Chapter 40

Federal Bureau of Investigation

Learning Outcomes

Careful study of this chapter will help a student do the following:

- Describe the primary homeland security mission of the FBI.
- Identify legal and procedural changes that expanded FBI investigative authorities after 9/11.
- Explain why it is difficult to identify dangerous radicals.
- Discuss how external factors influence FBI tactics and techniques.
- Explore the boundaries between freedom and security.

"A tension between order and liberty is inevitable in any society."

-1976 Church Commission

Introduction

The Federal Bureau of Investigation (FBI, the Bureau) is the lead federal law enforcement agency charged with counterterrorism investigations. Since 9/11, the FBI has implemented a series of reforms intended to transform itself from a largely reactive law enforcement agency focused on investigations of criminal activity into a more proactive, agile, flexible, and intelligence-driven agency that can prevent acts of terrorism. [1, p. ii]

The FBI is the lead agency for investigating the federal crime of terrorism, which is defined under law as "an offense that is calculated to influence or affect the conduct of government by intimidation or coercion, or to retaliate against government conduct." This includes terrorist acts committed within and outside U.S. national boundaries.

Post-9/11 Transformation

The FBI is the lead agency for investigating the federal crime of terrorism, which is defined under law as "an offense that is calculated to influence or affect the conduct of government by intimidation or coercion, or to retaliate against government conduct." This includes terrorist acts committed within and outside U.S. national boundaries. [1, p. 1]

The 9/11 terrorist attacks have been called a major security, law enforcement, and intelligence failure. Prior to 9/11, the FBI was largely a reactive law enforcement agency—pursuing suspects after they had allegedly committed crimes. Since 9/11, the Bureau has arguably taken a much more proactive posture, particularly regarding counterterrorism. It now views its role as both "predicting and preventing" the threats facing the nation, drawing upon enhanced resources. [1, p. 1]

The FBI's post-9/11 transformation is particularly evident in four areas: 1) The USA PATRIOT Act provided the FBI additional authorities and enhanced investigative tools; 2) The FBI and DOJ altered the way the Bureau investigated terrorism with the 2008 revision of The Attorney General's Guidelines for Domestic FBI Operations; 3) The FBI expanded operationally via a proliferation of Joint Terrorism Task Forces (JTTFs) across the United States; and 4) In so doing, it also increased its cooperation with state, local, and federal agencies. [1, p. 3]

USA PATRIOT Act

Shortly after the 9/11, Congress provided the FBI new investigative tools and expanded its authority to monitor and search suspects in terrorism-related investigations. Many of these tools and authorities were contained in the USA PATRIOT Act (P.L. 107-56) signed by President George W. Bush on October 26, 2001. The act amended several existing statutes, such as the Foreign Intelligence Surveillance Act (FISA) of 1978 (P.L. 95-511), the Electronic Communications Privacy Act of 1986 (P.L. 99-508), and the various National Security Letter (NSL) statutes. These changes enhanced the FBI's investigative abilities by:

- Dismantling "the Wall" that inhibited the sharing of information between intelligence and criminal investigators;
- Facilitating roving wiretaps;
- Expanding the use of devices that record the sources of incoming and outgoing communications;
- Accommodating "Sneak and Peek" search warrants;
- Increasing access to business records; and
- Expanding use of National Security Letters. [1, p. 3]

Shortly after the 9/11, Congress provided the FBI new investigative tools and expanded its authority to monitor and search suspects in terrorism-related investigations. Many of these tools and authorities were contained in the USA PATRIOT Act .

FISA regulates intelligence collection directed at foreign powers and agents of foreign powers in the United States to include those engaged in international terrorism. FISA required the government to certify that "the purpose" of surveillance was to gather foreign intelligence information. Prior to the USA PATRIOT Act, the Department of Justice (DOJ) turned the "primary purpose" standard into written policy that had the effect of limiting the coordination between intelligence and criminal investigators. This came to be known as "the Wall" between intelligence and law enforcement and the "unfortunate consequences" of this barrier to information sharing were noted in the 9/11 Commission Report. Section 218 of the USA PATRIOT Act amended FISA to replace the phrase "the purpose" with the phrase "a significant purpose." As one legal scholar described it, by moving the FISA requirement from the purpose to a significant purpose, the USA PATRIOT Act "knocked out the foundation for 'the Wall.'" This removed impediments to the exchange of information about terrorism or other national security threats between intelligence and law enforcement personnel. [1, p. 4]

Federal law enforcement officers have the authority, subject to court approval, to conduct wiretaps and electronic surveillance on persons suspected of committing federal crimes. A "roving" wiretap allows law enforcement officers to "follow" a subject and lawfully intercept that person's communications with a single court order even if the target attempts to evade surveillance by changing telephones or other communications devices. According to an Assistant U.S. Attorney, "Prior to roving wiretaps, law enforcement agents and federal prosecutors had to invest substantial time and resources in obtaining a separate wiretap order for each additional telephone used by a subject during an investigation ... [Q]uite often this resulted in a loss of valuable evidence through missed wiretap conversations relating to the criminal activity being monitored." Before the USA PATRIOT Act, the concept behind roving wiretaps did not apply to FISA. The USA PATRIOT Act amended the electronic surveillance portion of FISA to allow government agents to continue surveillance when "the target of the surveillance switches from a facility (e.g., a telephone) associated with one service provider (e.g., a telephone company) to a different facility associated with a different provider. [1, p. 5]

A trap and trace device shows all incoming phone numbers to a particular telephone. A pen register shows all outgoing phone numbers a particular telephone has called. Prior to 2001, FISA allowed law enforcement officers to collect incoming and outgoing numbers on a telephone line. The USA PATRIOT Act expanded the law to permit the capture of comparable information related to other forms of communication including the Internet, electronic mail, web surfing, and all other forms of electronic communications.

A trap and trace device shows all incoming phone numbers to a particular telephone. A pen register shows all outgoing phone numbers a particular telephone has called. Prior to 2001, FISA allowed law enforcement officers to collect incoming and outgoing numbers on a telephone line. The USA PATRIOT Act expanded the law to permit the capture of comparable information related to other forms of communication including the Internet, electronic mail, web surfing, and all other forms of electronic communications. [1, pp. 5-6]

In general, police officers serving a warrant must "knock and announce"—that is, give the subject notice that they are the police and are serving a warrant. They may enter and search even if the subject is not present at the premises to be searched, but they must leave a copy of the warrant and an inventory of what was seized, giving notice that the premises was searched. The USA PATRIOT Act amended Title 1833 to allow federal law enforcement officers to request from the courts a delayed-notice (so-called "sneak and peek") search warrant allowing officers to enter and search a premises without immediately notifying the owner when such notice may have an adverse result (e.g., tipping off a suspect or co-conspirators). This authority has been used rarely in terrorism cases. [1, p. 6]

The USA PATRIOT Act amended FISA to authorize the FBI to seek an order from the FISA Court for the production of any tangible things (including books, records, papers, documents, and other items) in a terrorism or counterintelligence investigation provided that such investigation of a United States person is not conducted solely upon the basis of activities protected by the First Amendment. [1, p. 6]

National Security Letters (NSL) are regularly used in FBI counterterrorism investigations and are roughly comparable to administrative subpoenas. They have been described as "form letters signed by an FBI agent" used to request and collect non-content consumer records and related information from "telephone companies, Internet service providers, consumer credit reporting agencies, banks, and other financial institutions." According to the FBI, "NSLs are indispensable investigative tools that serve as building blocks in many counterterrorism and counterintelligence investigations." The USA PATRIOT Act expanded the circumstances under which an NSL could be applied. For one thing, the USA PATRIOT Act allowed the FBI to issue NSLs for full consumer credit reports. Additionally, it widened the number of FBI officials who could issue NSLs. [1, p. 7]

Revised Attorney General Guidelines

The FBI and DOJ also emphasized their forward-leaning approach with the September 29, 2008, revision of the Attorney General's Guidelines for Domestic FBI Operations, which they claim "make the FBI's operations in the United States more effective by providing simpler, clearer, and more uniform standards and procedures." Referred to as the "Mukasey Guidelines" after Michael B. Mukasey, who was Attorney General at the time of their release, this is the latest in a series of guidelines stretching back to 1976 that govern the FBI's investigative activities. The Mukasey Guidelines went into effect on December 1, 2008. [1, p. 11]

The Mukasey Guidelines consolidated a number of previous standalone directives into a single modified volume called the Domestic Investigations and Operations Guide (DIOG). One of the most significant changes brought about by this consolidation was the expanded use of "assessments." Assessments allow the FBI to look into a broader range of potential criminal activities, subject to First Amendment protections, that might otherwise escape detection.

The Mukasey Guidelines consolidated a number of previous standalone directives into a single modified volume called the Domestic Investigations and Operations Guide (DIOG). One of the most significant changes brought about by this consolidation was the expanded use of "assessments." Previously, investigations could only be initiated if the FBI had some level of factual predication. Preliminary investigations required an "allegation or information indicative of possible criminal activity or threats to national security." A full investigation required an "articulable factual basis of possible criminal or national threat activity." The revised guidelines allowed for an "assessment" without any factual predication. Assessments allow the FBI to look into a broader range of potential criminal activities, subject to First Amendment protections, that might otherwise escape detection. [1, pp. 11-12]

The Bureau has incorporated assessments into its investigative processes. According to numbers made publicly available in March 2011, the FBI initiated 11,667 assessments to check leads on individuals, activities, groups, or organizations between December 2008 and March 2009. These, in turn, led to 427 preliminary or full investigations. Officials noted that about one-third of the assessments resulted from vague tips. Reportedly, between March 2009 and March 2011, the Bureau opened 82,325 assessments. About half of the assessments from this time frame focused on determining whether specific groups or individuals were spies or terrorists. This pool of 42,888 assessments produced just under 2,000 full or preliminary investigations. [1, p. 12]

Enhancing State and Local Cooperation

JTTFs are locally based, multi-agency teams of investigators, analysts, linguists, SWAT experts, and other specialists who investigate terrorism and terrorism-related crimes. Seventy-one of the more than 100 JTTFs operated by DOJ and the FBI were created since 9/11. Over 4,400 federal, state, and local law enforcement officers and agents—more than four times the pre-9/11 total— work in them. These officers and agents come from more than 600 state and local agencies and 50 federal agencies. [1, p. 12]

The FBI considers the JTTFs "the nation's front line on terrorism." They "investigate acts of terrorism that affect the U.S., its interests, property and citizens, including those employed by the U.S. and military personnel overseas." As this suggests, their operations are highly tactical and focus on investigations, developing human sources (informants), and gathering intelligence to thwart terrorist plots. [1, pp. 13-14]

JTTFs are locally based, multi-agency teams of investigators, analysts, linguists, SWAT experts, and other specialists who investigate terrorism and terrorism-related crimes. Seventy-one of the more than 100 JTTFs operated by DOJ and the FBI were created since 9/11.

JTTFs also offer an important conduit for the sharing of intelligence developed from FBI -led counterterrorism investigations with outside agencies and state and local law enforcement. To help facilitate this, especially as the threat of homegrown jihadists has emerged, the number of top-secret security clearances issued to local police working on JTTFs has increased from 125 to 878 between 2007 and 2009. [1, p. 14]

There is also a National JTTF, which was established in July 2002 to serve as a coordinating mechanism with the FBI's partners. Some 40 agencies are now represented in the National JTTF, which has become a focal point for information sharing and the management of large-scale projects that involve multiple partners. [1, p. 14]

Intelligence Reform

The FBI's post-9/11 transformation has placed greater emphasis on intelligence and analysis in order to prevent future such attacks. One of the most visible manifestations of this transformation was creation of a Directorate of Intelligence (DI) at FBI headquarters. The DI was also made party to a new National Security Branch which integrated the FBI's Counterterrorism and Counterintelligence Divisions with the Weapons of Mass Destruction Directorate, and Terrorist Screen Center. Perhaps more fundamentally, the FBI established Field Intelligence Groups (FIGs) at each of its 56 field offices. FIGs improve the Bureau's intelligence capacity by combining its intelligence and investigative capabilities. Comprised of agents, analysts, linguists, and surveillance specialists, a FIG's principal mission is to identify intelligence gaps, obtain and analyze raw intelligence from FBI investigations and sources, and generate intelligence products and disseminate them to the intelligence and law enforcement communities in order to help guide investigations, programs, and policy. Arguably, the mission of the FIGs is nothing less than to "drive," or inform the direction of, the FBI's counterterrorism effort by identifying, assessing, and attacking emerging threats "before they flourish." [1, pp. 14-15]

The transformation has not been easy. Historically, investigative agents have garnered more resources and promotions than intelligence agents at the Bureau. Despite efforts to instill institutional changes across the Bureau, critics in both the FBI and Congress contend that it is "still a work in progress". [1, p. 16]

Tactics and Techniques

Stopping terrorists before they strike is no easy task. The new proactive posture entails new challenges for the Bureau—especially in determining when individuals move from radical activity involving First Amendment-protected behavior to violent extremism. Because not all terrorist suspects follow a single radicalization roadmap on their way to executing plots, U.S. law enforcement faces the task of discerning exactly when radicalized individuals become real threats. [1, p. 19]

Stopping terrorists before they strike is no easy task. The new proactive posture entails new challenges for the Bureau—especially in determining when individuals move from radical activity involving First Amendment-protected behavior to violent extremism. Because not all terrorist suspects follow a single radicalization roadmap on their way to executing plots, U.S. law enforcement faces the task of discerning exactly when radicalized individuals become real threats.

As suggested, timing is everything. To preemptively stop terrorists, law enforcement requires accurate and timely intelligence. The FBI generates terrorism cases from a number of sources. Information about terrorist threats or suspicious incidents is brought to the attention of the FBI by the public; other government agencies (particularly those in the intelligence community); state and local law enforcement; ongoing FBI investigations (including sources, surveillance, financial analysis, and tactical analysis); and FBI Legal Attachés stationed abroad. Most FBI investigations develop from information or leads generated by pre-existing FBI investigations, or casework and liaison with other federal agencies or international counterparts. A handful of leads stem from information generated by local or state law enforcement and filtered up to the FBI via intelligence fusion centers. [1, p. 19]

To counter violent plots, U.S. law enforcement has employed two tactics that have been described by one scholar as the "Al Capone" approach and the use of "agent provocateurs." The Capone approach involves apprehending individuals linked to terrorist plots on lesser, nonterrorism- related offenses such as immigration violations. In agent provocateur cases—often called sting operations—government undercover operatives befriend suspects and offer to facilitate their activities. As the "Al Capone" moniker suggests, historically these tactics have been employed against many types of targets such as mafia bosses, white-collar criminals, and corrupt public servants. While these techniques combined with the cultivation of informants as well as surveillance (especially in and around mosques) may be effective in stymieing rapidly developing terrorist plots, their use has fostered concern within U.S. Muslim communities. [1, p. 19]

Lying to an FBI Special Agent is a charge reminiscent of the Capone approach. An example from 2010 stands out. On July 21, 2010, Paul Rockwood, Jr., a U.S. citizen and Muslim convert, pled guilty to making false statements to the FBI. Rockwood's wife, Nadia Rockwood, also pled guilty to making false statements related to her husband's case. By early 2010, while living in King Salmon, AK, Paul Rockwood had developed a list of 15 people he planned to kill, believing that they had desecrated Islam. He had also researched explosives and shared with others ideas about mail bombs or using firearms to kill his targets. It appears that prosecutors did not pursue a case based on more substantive terrorism charges and opted to neutralize a threat—someone apparently preparing to kill people—by using a false statement charge. [1, p. 20]

Agent provocateur cases—sting operations—rely on expert determination by law enforcement that a specific individual or group is likely to move beyond radicalized talk and engage in violence or terrorist plotting.

Lesser charges against a suspect in a terrorism case may also act as a placeholder until evidence to support a more serious charge is gathered. The utility of this preventative technique coupled with actual terrorism charges was exhibited by the FBI in its case against Najibullah Zazi. He arrived in New York on September 10, 2009, with explosive material and plans to detonate bombs in New York's subway system. Zazi feared authorities had caught up with him and returned to Denver on September 12. Between September 10 and 19, the FBI monitored his activities and bolstered its case with searches of a vehicle and locations linked to him in New York and Denver. Zazi also agreed to interviews with the FBI in Denver. Then, on September 19 FBI special agents arrested Zazi in Aurora, CO, for knowingly and willfully lying to the FBI. Presumably this was done because he might flee. Four days later, a grand jury returned a more substantive one-count indictment against him on weapons of mass destruction charges. [1, pp. 20-21]

Agent provocateur cases—sting operations—rely on expert determination by law enforcement that a specific individual or group is likely to move beyond radicalized talk and engage in violence or terrorist plotting. The ultimate goal is to catch a suspect committing an overt criminal act such as pulling the proverbial trigger but on a dud weapon. By engaging in such strategy, investigators hope to obtain ironclad evidence against suspects. [1, p. 21]

One FBI investigation exemplifies this approach. On November 26, 2010, Mohamed Osman Mohamud was arrested after he attempted to set off what he believed was a vehicle bomb at an annual Christmas tree lighting ceremony in Portland, OR. Mohamud thought he had plotted with terrorists to detonate the bomb. In actuality, the device was a dud assembled by his coconspirators, who were FBI undercover operatives. Mohamud offered the target for the strike, provided components for assembly of the device, gave instructions for the operation, and mailed passport photographs for his getaway plan to FBI undercover operatives. What specifically caused the FBI to begin its sting operation against Mohamud is unclear from publicly available sources. At some point, someone from the local Muslim community alerted the FBI to Mohamud, a 19-year-old Somali-born naturalized U.S. citizen. Media reports have suggested that a family member, perhaps Mohamud's father, relayed concerns about the young man to officials. [1, p. 21]

In a number of FBI terrorism sting operations, defense attorneys have alleged that the FBI had entrapped defendants. Ten defendants charged with terrorism-related crimes formally argued the entrapment defense in six trials between 9/11 and early December 2011. However, since 9/11 this defense has been unsuccessful in federal courts. In at least some investigations, FBI undercover employees test suspects to ascertain the depth of their intent to do harm. For example, the FBI evaluated Mohamud's resolve on a number of occasions. Two stand out. Mohamud's first meeting with an undercover FBI operative entailed a discussion in which the would-be violent jihadist was told that he could help "the cause" in "a number of ways ... ranging from simply praying five times a day to becoming a martyr." The young man responded, saying that he wanted to become "operational" and needed help in staging an attack. When Mohamud suggested the Christmas tree lighting ceremony as his intended target in a following meeting, an FBI undercover employee noted that children attend such events. Mohamud responded by saying that he wanted a large crowd "that will ... be attacked in their own element with their families celebrating the holidays." [1, pp. 21-22]

In a number of FBI terrorism sting operations, defense attorneys have alleged that the FBI had entrapped defendants. Ten defendants charged with terrorism-related crimes formally argued the entrapment defense in six trials between 9/11 and early December 2011. However, since 9/11 this defense has been unsuccessful in federal courts.

Balancing Civil Liberties

As discussed, the FBI's DIOG articulates a need to proactively gather intelligence in counterterrorism investigations and establishes the assessment as a technique to do so. Balancing civil liberties against the need for preventative policing to combat terrorism is a key policy challenge. [1, p. 22]

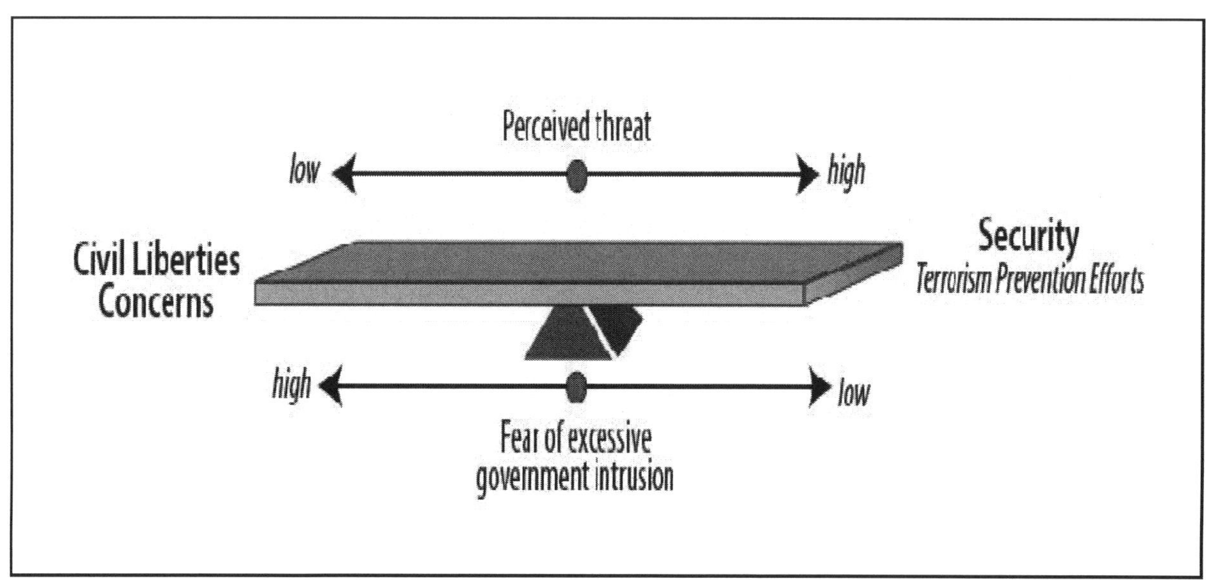

Figure 40-1: Balancing Civil Liberties

Figure 1 suggests how competing elements influence the balance between civil liberties and security—largely defined today in terms of terrorism prevention efforts. As a historical example, the FBI had developed intrusive domestic intelligence collection measures and counter-radical operations stretching from the late 1930s through the 1960s. Of course, the focus of the FBI's efforts in this period was not counterterrorism. These decades featured domestic security concerns during World War II and fears of espionage and communist infiltration of American institutions during the Cold War. The FBI worked to prevent this activity. For much of this period, a national consensus suggested that serious threats were posed by foreign agents, revolutionaries, or outside agitators operating in the United States. Within this context, the FBI had broad authority for investigation of and intelligence collection regarding domestic subversive activity from Presidents Harry S. Truman and Dwight D. Eisenhower and Attorney General Robert F. Kennedy. The Bureau developed a number of programs to combat what it saw as internal threats. [1, p. 23]

Balancing civil liberties and security is not easy. The FBI's tactics and techniques remain subject to scrutiny based on an immeasurable perception of the national threat.

During this period, the FBI engaged in what can be described as preventive, covert, intelligence-based efforts to target and contain people, groups, or movements suspected by the Bureau to be '"rabble rousers,' 'agitators,' 'key activists,' or 'key black extremists.'" A hallmark was the FBI's Counterintelligence Program (COINTELPRO), which lasted from 1956 to 1971. Subjects investigated by the FBI under its domestic intelligence programs did not have to be suspected of criminal activity. Instead of bringing criminal cases to court, the Bureau acted outside of legal processes and relied on illegal means to curb constitutionally protected activity it deemed threatening to national security. [1, pp. 23-24]

By the 1970s, as Cold War fears ebbed, the balance between civil liberties and prevention tipped in the other direction—favoring concerns over civil liberties. This is highlighted by the development of the original set of Attorney General guidelines. Issued in 1976 and known as the Domestic Security Investigation Guidelines, these responded to FBI abuses embodied in programs such as COINTELPRO. These first guidelines were intended to prevent the FBI's monitoring of groups that had unpopular or controversial public views and greatly circumscribed the Bureau's domestic intelligence gathering capabilities and investigations related to national security-related issues. [1, p. 24]

Since the 1976 guidelines, and especially after 9/11, the balance has shifted in favor of security and terrorism prevention efforts. As suggested, the Mukasey Guidelines and FBI DIOG offer more investigative flexibility to proactively counter terrorist actors. Critics have stated that subsequent guidelines have excessively loosened the constraints on FBI intelligence collection and investigation. In essence, these critics suggest that concerns over terrorism and security have outweighed fears of systemic abuse by investigators. [1, pp. 24-25]

The balance remains tenuous and the task uneasy. The FBI's tactics and techniques are subject to scrutiny based on an immeasurable perception of the national threat. While the Mukasey Guidelines and FBI DIOG address these competing forces, their implementation understandably raise concerns among civil liberties groups.

Conclusion

Confronted with the intelligence failures that failed to prevent 9/11, the FBI has taken measures to transform itself into a more proactive, intelligence-focused agency. Four major changes have helped facilitate this transformation: 1) The USA PATRIOT Act removed the "wall" between law enforcement and intelligence investigations; 2) The Mukasey Guidelines have streamlined internal procedures and made it easier to initiate terrorist "assessments"; 3) A proliferation of Joint Terrorism Task Forces have expanded the FBI's intelligence collection abilities, as well as 4) increased cooperation with State and Local agencies. The FBI's more proactive approach has been further accommodated by organizational changes designed institutionalize the increased emphasis on intelligence and analysis. Still, the FBI faces a fundamental challenge of discerning real threats from protected First Amendment rights of expression. To help distinguish the difference, the FBI has adopted tactics that were instrumental in capturing a number of terrorists before they could strike. The tactics are not without their critics, particularly with regard to protecting civil liberties. Balancing security needs against civil liberties is a justifiable concern given past indiscretions, and one that will continue to challenge the FBI as it seeks to prevent future catastrophic attacks.

Challenge Your Understanding

The following questions are designed to challenge your understanding of the material presented in this chapter. Some questions may require additional research outside this book in order to provide a complete answer.

1. What is the primary homeland security mission of the FBI?
2. How did the USA PATRIOT Act expand FBI authorities to conduct terrorism investigations?
3. How did the Mukasey Guidelines expand FBI authorities to conduct terrorism investigations?
4. What is the purpose of a Joint Terrorism Task Force?
5. Why is it difficult to identify dangerous radicals?
6. Explain why an FBI sting operation might be considered entrapment.
7. How do external factors influence FBI tactics and techniques?
8. Do you think the FBI COINTELPRO was justified by the communist threat? Explain.
9. As an innocent citizen, would you feel comfortable with the FBI collecting your phone contacts?
10. As an innocent citizen, would you feel comfortable with the FBI browsing your Facebook® page?

Chapter 41

State & Local Law Enforcement

Learning Outcomes

Careful study of this chapter will help a student do the following:

- Explain why State and Local law enforcement are bound up into homeland security.
- Describe the purpose and function of State and Local fusion centers.
- Discuss the potential risks associated with fusion centers.
- Evaluate the cost benefit proposition of fusion centers.

"In a free country we punish men for the crimes they commit but never for the opinions they have."

- President Truman, 1950

Introduction

Improving intelligence gathering and information sharing at all levels of government has been a major concern and priority since the terrorist attacks of September 11, 2001. To promote greater information sharing and collaboration among Federal, State, and Local intelligence and law enforcement entities, State and Local authorities established fusion centers throughout the country. These centers are a collaborative effort of two or more agencies that provide resources, expertise, and information to the center with the goal of maximizing its ability to detect, prevent, investigate, and respond to criminal and terrorist activity. [1, p. 1]

Improving intelligence gathering and information sharing at all levels of government has been a major concern and priority since the terrorist attacks of September 11, 2001. To promote greater information sharing and collaboration among Federal, State, and Local intelligence and law enforcement entities, State and Local authorities established fusion centers throughout the country.

Background

The Homeland Security Act of 2002 established the Department of Homeland Security (DHS) and charged it with coordinating activities and improving information sharing efforts among Federal, State, Local, and Tribal government agencies and the private sector. Furthermore, the 9/11 Commission concluded that a lack of information sharing contributed to the inability to prevent the attacks. Moreover, in its 2004 final report, the 9/11 Commission promoted the value of State and Local agencies in the information sharing process and recommended that DHS have the responsibility of coordinating these efforts. [1, p. 2]

Although the Commission did not refer to fusion centers in its recommendations, advocates of the centers, including DHS, interpreted the panel's recommendations to improve information-sharing as a call for Federal support for fusion centers. [2, p. 11]

The Commission's report spurred Congress and the White House to action, passing bills and issuing executive orders which reorganized U.S. government agencies' roles and responsibilities in fighting terrorism. Those moves boosted the importance of federal-state-local information-sharing efforts. They also all but shifted responsibility for facilitating information sharing, integrating intelligence, and analyzing threat information at the federal level from DHS to a new federal interagency body, the National Counterterrorism Center (NCTC), part of the Office of the Director of National Intelligence. [2, p. 11]

The 2004 Intelligence Reform Act gave the NCTC responsibility for integrating and analyzing terrorist threat intelligence from all sources, as well as the job of assessing the terrorist threat to the United States. That law, and Executive Order 13356, also created a new office, the Program Manager for the Information Sharing Environment (PM-ISE), to help Local, State and Federal agencies better share terrorism-related information. [2, p. 12]

As other federal agencies and offices took the lead in compiling and analyzing counterterrorism information at the federal level, DHS's intelligence operations began to focus on a responsibility that received less attention in subsequent reform laws and executive orders: information sharing with State, Local and Tribal partners. [2, p. 12]

At that time, DHS was working with 18 state and local intelligence and fusion centers to share threat-related information, and officials were working on how to best develop a coordinated effort to build their capabilities. [2, p. 12]

In 2006, DHS's then intelligence chief, Charles E. Allen, submitted a detailed fusion center plan to his superior, then DHS Secretary Michael Chertoff, which highlighted fusion centers' potential to aid federal counterterrorism efforts. [2, p. 12]

In 2004, DHS was working with 18 state and local intelligence and fusion centers to share threat-related information, and officials were working on how to best develop a coordinated effort to build their capabilities. In 2006, DHS's then intelligence chief, Charles E. Allen, submitted a detailed fusion center plan to his superior, then DHS Secretary Michael Chertoff, which highlighted fusion centers' potential to aid federal counterterrorism efforts.

DHS Secretary Chertoff approved the plan in June 2006. [2, p. 13] Secretary Chertoff signed the DHS Support Implementation Plan for State and Local Fusion Centers and designated the Office of Intelligence and Analysis (I&A) as its executive agent for managing the department's role in the nationwide fusion center Initiative. The implementation plan identified state and local governments among DHS' primary partners. It also explained DHS' role in supporting and developing state and local partnerships and highlighted domestic information gathering and analysis as DHS' "unique contribution to the national-level mission" to protect the Nation. [1, p. 5] By the end of that year, at least 37 fusion centers had begun operations in states including Connecticut, Delaware, Indiana, Maine, and North Carolina. [2, p. 13]

The following year, both Congress and the White House took steps to bolster DHS's involvement with fusion centers. Congress passed the "Implementing Recommendations of the 9/11 Commission Act of 2007," which explicated DHS's role in sharing information with state and local agencies, even as it called the Department's outreach to those state and local officials "haphazard and often accompanied by less than timely results." In the law, legislators directed DHS to provide support and coordinate federal involvement with fusion centers. [2, p. 13]

In the law, Congress established a DHS State, Local, and Regional Fusion Center Initiative. The law directed DHS to provide to fusion centers "operational and intelligence advice;" conduct exercises with them; provide management assistance; and "review information . . . including homeland security information, terrorism information, and weapons of mass destruction information that is gathered by State, local, and regional fusion centers; and to incorporate such information, as appropriate, into the Department's own such information." [2, p. 13]

To underscore the point, Congress urged DHS to "increase its involvement with State and Local fusion centers] and appropriately incorporate their non-Federal information into the Department's intelligence products." [2, p. 14]

From the 2007 Implementing Recommendations of the 9/11 Commission Act, Congress established the DHS State, Local, and Regional Fusion Center Initiative. The law directed DHS to support fusion centers with training, personnel, and materiel.

The law also directed DHS to detail intelligence personnel to the centers if the centers met certain criteria, several of which required a center to demonstrate a focus on and commitment to a counterterrorism mission. Among the criteria the law suggested were "whether the fusion center . . . focuses on a broad counterterror approach," whether the center has sufficient personnel "to support a broad counterterrorism mission," and whether the center is appropriately funded by non-federal sources "to support its counterterrorism mission." [2, p. 14]

Also in 2007, the Bush Administration focused on improving how officials at all levels of government shared terrorism-related information. That October, President Bush released his "National Strategy for Information Sharing: Successes and Challenges in Improving Terrorism- Related Information Sharing," in which he called for fusion centers to be "the focus . . . within the State and local environment for the receipt and sharing of terrorism information, homeland security information, and law enforcement information related to terrorism." [2, p. 14]

President Bush's 2007 report also directed the Federal government to develop for the first time a set of minimum operational standards for fusion centers, which would allow officials to determine whether a fusion center had "achieved a baseline level of capability." [2, p. 14]

In response, in September 2008, the Departments of Justice and Homeland Security published "Baseline Capabilities for State and Major Urban Area Fusion Centers." The document outlined the basic "structures, processes and tools" fusion centers needed to have in place in order to functionally participate in sharing counterterrorism intelligence information with the federal government. The capabilities included having a governance structure, a staffing plan, and a privacy policy; installing sufficient physical security; developing a funding strategy; having a plan to provide training to intelligence analysts; and having processes and protocols in place to share relevant information with federal agencies. [2, p. 14]

Since then, hundreds of millions of dollars have been poured into State and Local fusion centers to develop their capabilities, and make them an effective partner in the nation's counterterrorism strategy.

Fusion Centers

State and major urban area fusion centers serve as focal points within the state and local environment for the receipt, analysis, gathering, and sharing of threat-related information between the federal government and State, Local, Tribal, Territorial (SLTT) and private sector partners. Fusion centers are state-created entities largely financed and staffed by the States

State and major urban area fusion centers serve as focal points within the state and local environment for the receipt, analysis, gathering, and sharing of threat-related information between the federal government and State, Local, Tribal, Territorial (SLTT) and private sector partners. [3]

Fusion centers are state-created entities largely financed and staffed by the States, and there is no one "model" for how a center should be structured. State and local law enforcement and criminal intelligence seem to be at the core of many of the centers. Although many of the centers initially had purely counterterrorism goals, for numerous reasons, they have increasingly gravitated toward an all-crimes and even broader all-hazards approach. [4, p. II]

The Federal role in supporting fusion centers consists largely of providing financial assistance, the majority of which has flowed through the Homeland Security Grant Program; sponsoring security clearances; providing human resources; producing some fusion center guidance and training; and providing congressional authorization and appropriation of national foreign intelligence program resources, as well as oversight hearings. [4, p. II]

There are currently 78 fusion centers located around the country. DHS classifies them as either a "primary" or "recognized" facility. There are 53 primary fusion centers. A primary fusion center serves as the focal point within the State and Local environment for the receipt, analysis, gathering, and sharing of threat-related information. Primary fusion centers also receive the highest priority for the allocation of available Federal resources, including the deployment of DHS personnel and connectivity with Federal data systems. Any fusion center not designated as "primary" is otherwise referred to as "recognized". There are 25 recognized fusion centers across the country. [4]

A fusion center is defined as a "collaborative effort of two or more agencies that provide resources, expertise, and information to the center with the goal of maximizing their ability to detect, prevent, investigate, and respond to criminal and terrorist activity." Among the primary focuses of fusion centers are the intelligence and fusion processes, through which information is collected, integrated, evaluated, analyzed, and disseminated. [5, p. 3]

The value proposition for fusion centers is that by integrating various streams of information and intelligence, including that flowing from the federal government, state, local, and tribal governments, as well as the private sector, a more accurate picture of risks to people, economic infrastructure, and communities can be developed and translated into protective action. The ultimate goal of fusion is to prevent manmade (terrorist) attacks and to respond to natural disasters and manmade threats quickly and efficiently should they occur. [6, p. ii]

The value proposition for fusion centers is that by integrating various streams of information and intelligence, including that flowing from the federal government, state, local, and tribal governments, as well as the private sector, a more accurate picture of risks to people, economic infrastructure, and communities can be developed and translated into protective action.

It has been argued that State, Local, Tribal law enforcement, first responders, and other public and private sector entities are uniquely positioned to collect information to identify emerging threats and assist in the development of a more comprehensive threat assessment. Many would agree that the 800,000 plus law enforcement officers across the country know their communities most intimately and, therefore, are best placed to function as the "eyes and ears" of an extended national security community. They have the experience to recognize what constitutes anomalous behavior in their areas of responsibility and can either stop it at the point of discovery (a more traditional law enforcement approach) or follow the anomaly or criminal behavior, either unilaterally or jointly with the Federal Bureau of Investigation (FBI), to extract the maximum intelligence value from the activity (a more intelligence-based approach) [4, p. 7]

The fusion process turns information into actionable intelligence. The fusion process supports the implementation of risk-based, information-driven prevention, response, and consequence management programs. At the same time, it supports efforts to address immediate or emerging threat-related circumstances and events. [5, p. 3]

Data fusion involves the exchange of information from different sources—including law enforcement, public safety, and the private sector—and, with analysis, turning this information into actionable intelligence. Fusion also allows for continuous reevaluation of existing data in context with new data in order to provide constant updates. [5, p. 3]

The public safety and private sector components are integral in the fusion process because they provide fusion centers with crime-related information, including risk and threat assessments, and subject-matter experts who can aid in threat identification. [5, p. 3]

However, the potential fusion center use of private sector data, the adoption of a more proactive approach, and the collection of intelligence by fusion center staff and partners has led to questions about possible civil liberties abuses. Arguments against fusion centers often center around the idea that such centers are essentially pre-emptive law enforcement — that intelligence gathered in the absence of a criminal predicate is unlawfully gathered intelligence. The argument is that the further law enforcement, public safety and private sector representatives get away from a criminal predicate, the greater the chances that civil liberties may be violated. [4, p. 11]

However, the potential fusion center use of private sector data, the adoption of a more proactive approach, and the collection of intelligence by fusion center staff and partners has led to questions about possible civil liberties abuses.

Because of the need to protect civil liberties, it is not the intent of fusion centers to combine federal databases containing personally identifiable information with State, Local, and Tribal databases into one system or warehouse. Rather, when a threat, criminal predicate, or public safety need is identified, fusion centers will allow information from all sources to be readily gathered, analyzed, and exchanged, but only in connection with a specific case and only within the confines of criminal predicate. [5, p. 3]

The ultimate goal is to provide a mechanism through which government, law enforcement, public safety, and the private sector can come together with a common purpose and improve the ability to safeguard the homeland and prevent criminal activity. [5, p. 3]

DHS Program Management

As the executive agent for managing DHS' fusion center program, Intelligence & Analysis is responsible for coordinating among its federal, state, local, tribal, and private sector partners to ensure the program's success. Each I&A division has a specific mission that in some way relates to the program. I&A is headed by an Under Secretary, who also serves as the department's Chief Intelligence Officer. The State and Local Program Office, which coordinates the fusion center program, is directed by a program manager. The State and Local Program Office contains three divisions:

- State and Local Fusion Center Program Management Office;
- Information Sharing Fellows Program; and
- Law Enforcement Liaison Team. [1, p. 6]

The Program Management Office directs the day-to-day operations of DHS' fusion center program, including the management and coordination of deployed officers and Homeland Secure Data Network (HSDN) access. Through the Information Sharing Fellows Program, state or local representatives are detailed temporarily to I&A to familiarize state and local entities with DHS missions, capabilities, roles, and programs, and to promote information sharing among federal, state, and local entities. Law Enforcement Liaison Team representatives liaise with state and local law enforcement entities to advise them about DHS' role in the nationwide Fusion Center Initiative, promote state and local use of DHS systems and databases such as the Homeland Security Information Network (HSIN), and improve information sharing. [1, p. 6]

The DHS State & Local Fusion Center (SLFC) program seeks to enhance lawful sharing of information through 1) efficient and effective communication; 2) collaborative analysis, assessment, and planning; 3) better understanding of both side's capabilities; 4) quicker coordination through increased transparency; and 5) improved management through implementation of Global Fusion Center Guidelines.

Program Objectives

The State & Local Fusion Center (SLFC) program aims to enhance the lawful sharing of information consistent with DHS' statutory mission as defined by the Homeland Security Act of 2002. Success is dependent upon five essential elements: Communication, Collaboration, Understanding, Coordination, and Management Support. [7, p. 9]

Communication. DHS must ensure that communication with SLFCs is efficient and effective. The Department has created the Single Point of Service (SPS) for DHS information and intelligence support to State and local fusion centers to ensure that all inquiries are responded to expeditiously by the appropriate elements within DHS. The SPS will not preclude the SLFCs from interacting with DHS components directly. The SPS is responsible for identifying the appropriate DHS resources to address requests, providing transparency across DHS entities, and tracking requests through to completion. DHS will continue to enhance its relationships with the SLFCs, by providing mechanisms to improve visibility to the appropriate stakeholders of DHS activities, such as analysts' conferences and regular DHS representative visits to the fusion centers. The Department will continue to develop other communications tools, including the Homeland Secure Data Network, the Homeland Security Information Network and the HSIN-Intelligence portal — to improve communications with fusion centers. DHS will develop Standing Operating Procedures (SOPs) to determine the specific organizations within DHS associated with specific types of SLFC interactions. These SOPs will address coordination of interactions across the Department in greater detail. [7, p. 9]

Collaboration. To enhance the partnership with SLFCs and deepen connections between DHS and SLFC analysts, DHS will expand existing collaborative analysis, assessment, and planning capabilities. DHS will continue to develop mechanisms to more effectively identify opportunities to collaborate to include the Fire Service, Public Health, and Emergency Management. DHS and SLFCs will expand the development of joint products and explore tools to improve the collaborative environment. The

Department will also continue to support and develop collaborative bodies like the Homeland Security State and Local Intelligence Community of Interest (HS-SLIC). Operational components, in concert with the SLPO and other components, will conduct strategic planning, including resource projections, necessary to support field interactions with SLFCs. [7, p. 9]

Understanding. As partnerships expand and are strengthened, DHS and the SLFCs will enhance their understanding of each other's capabilities and needs. DHS will enhance support to SLFCs on three critical dimensions of information support: 1) Response to the SLFCs' requests for information; 2) SLFC Priority Information Needs (PINS) that align with I&A analytic production to SLFC needs; and 3) Training and technical assistance tailored to the needs of the SLFC analytic cadre. The Department will expand its active engagement of SLFCs to understand their needs. SLFCs will better understand how information can be combined at the Federal level, and what types of DHS support are available and appropriate to meet their needs. Further, DHS will continue to work with the fusion centers to maintain an open dialogue about needs and capabilities and will educate the fusion centers on DHS headquarters and component capabilities. DHS will also provide SLFCs feedback on information received, and identify the types of information most useful for integration into DHS products. [7, p. 10]

Coordination. DHS will continue to develop processes and tools to increase the transparency of activities and information exchanged with the fusion centers. All DHS components will be able to quickly view the recent and planned activities, such as conferences or site visits. The SPS will continue to facilitate coordination among the DHS components and ensure requests are responded to in a timely manner. The DHS Homeland Security Intelligence Council's Integrated Intelligence Board (HIIB), a body composed of the heads of intelligence functions from all DHS components and chaired by the Chief Intelligence Officer, will ensure mechanisms are in place to coordinate across DHS on analytic collaboration with SLFCs. Similar mechanisms will be implemented to provide visibility into products distributed to or available to the fusion centers, as well as training opportunities or assistance to increase awareness of what information and resources fusion centers have access to. [7, p. 10]

Management Support. In an effort to establish a baseline level of capability in all fusion centers through the implementation of the Global Fusion Center Guidelines and the Office of the Director of National Intelligence – Information Sharing Environment Implementation Plan, DHS will continue to provide an integrated suite of support programs. DHS may revise the Homeland Security Grant Program Guidance as needed to enable the full implementation of the fusion process. In addition, the joint DHS/ Department of Justice Fusion Process Technical Assistance Program will continue to support the establishment of baseline capabilities through the following activities:

- Fusion Process Technical Assistance Services;
- Fusion Center Exchange Program;
- Fusion Center Fellowship Program;
- Online Fusion Process Resource Center; and
- Other Specialized Fusion Process Support Services. [7, p. 11]

Program Risks

There are several potential risks associated with fusion center development. Risks focus on factors that could ultimately diminish political and popular support for fusion centers, and ultimately result in their demise or marginalized contribution to the national homeland security mission. [4, p. 9]

There are several potential risks associated with fusion center development. Risks focus on factors that could ultimately diminish political and popular support for fusion centers, and ultimately result in their demise or marginalized contribution to the national homeland security mission.

Violations of Civil Liberties.

One of the risks to the fusion center concept is that individuals who do not necessarily have the appropriate law enforcement or broader intelligence training will engage in intelligence collection that is not supported by law. The concern is to what extent, if at all, First Amendment protected activities may be jeopardized by fusion center activities. [4, p. 11]

For purposes of criminal intelligence systems, most fusion centers operate under Federal regulations, in addition to any applicable State policies, laws or regulations. At the Federal level, the authorities which guide the FBI in collection of intelligence are the Attorney General's Guidelines for FBI National Security Investigations and Foreign Intelligence Collection. At the state and local levels, if there is any analogue to the Attorney General's guidelines for multijurisdictional criminal intelligence systems, it is 28 Code of Federal Regulations (CFR) (Judicial Administration), Chapter 1 (Department of Justice), Part 23 (criminal intelligence systems operating policies). Many centers cite 28 CFR, Part 23 as the guiding legal mechanism for their criminal intelligence operations. By its terms, 28 CFR, Part 23, applies to "all criminal intelligence systems operating through support under the Omnibus Crime Control and Safe Streets Act of 1968, as amended." From the perspective of intelligence collection, the 28 CFR, Part 23 standard is reasonable suspicion. One of the operating principles of 28 CFR, Part 23 is that:

"A project shall collect and maintain criminal intelligence information concerning an individual only if there is reasonable suspicion that the individual is involved in criminal conduct or activity and the information is relevant to that criminal conduct or activity." [4, p. 13]

Reasonable Suspicion or Criminal Predicate is established when information exists which established sufficient facts to give a trained law enforcement or criminal investigative agency officer, investigator, or employee a basis to believe that there is a reasonable possibility that an individuals or organization is involved in a definable criminal activity or enterprise. [4, p. 14]

The question of how to balance civil liberties with security remains an open issue the country often weighs. The balancing is, arguably, a moving target driven by the country's collective sense of security and safety. The nation cannot necessarily have absolute security, nor absolute liberty; a pendulum swings between relative amounts of each of these "public goods." The question, to which there is no definitive answer, raised here is how aggressive should fusion centers be in proactively collecting and analyzing intelligence that may go beyond that which may be entered into criminal intelligence systems that fall under federal law? Which entity at the Federal level is auditing the activities of fusion centers to ensure civil liberties are not violated? Given that these centers are creations of State and Local governments, should an entity of the federal government be the ultimate arbiter of civil liberties protection? [4, p. 14]

One of the risks to the fusion center concept is that individuals who do not necessarily have the appropriate law enforcement or broader intelligence training will engage in intelligence collection that is not supported by law.

Time

Some homeland security observers suggest that the rush to establish and enhance state fusion centers is a post-9/11 reaction and that over time some of the centers may dissolve. It could be argued that in the absence of another terrorist attack or catastrophic natural disaster, over the course of the next 5 to 10 years, state and regional fusion centers may be eliminated and/or replaced by regional fusion organizations. The state fusion regional representation organizations may be an entity to facilitate future center consolidation efforts. Issues that may lead to state and regional fusion center consolidation into regional organizations include:

- Perceived lack of need by state leaders;
- State and federal financial constraints;
- Duplication of effort without showing tangible products and services within a given center; and
- Reduction of risks to a given geographic location. [4, p. 14]

Alternatively, if there are additional terrorist attacks or natural disasters in the near future and fusion centers can demonstrate their tangible value by serving as proactive, analytic and/or operational information/intelligence hubs, it is plausible that substantial additional federal, state, and local funds may flow to these centers. [4, p. 14]

Funding

Another potentially time-related risk is the threat diminished or eliminated federal and/or state funding poses to fusion center development. If the United States is not the target of a successful terrorist attack, homeland security funding, arguably, may decrease. If overall federal funding levels for homeland security decrease, it is possible that there will be some level of decrease in Homeland Security Grant Program (HSGP) funding. Such a decrease might force states to re-prioritize funds for those programs deemed the most critical to their jurisdiction. Specific federal programs that fund and/or support fusion centers (i.e. DHS and FBI detailee programs) could potentially also suffer under funding cuts. It is unclear how fusion centers would fare in such a situation. It is likely that the fate of fusion centers would differ drastically from state to state, depending on a range of factors, to include, their level of maturity, buy-in from other agency partners, their resource needs, and noted successes, balanced with other critical issues and programs within the jurisdiction. [4, p. 15]

A 2012 Senate investigation found that DHS's support of fusion centers yielded little, if any, benefit to federal counterterrorism intelligence efforts.

One fusion center official stated that if federal funding went away, his fusion center would continue to operate, albeit with less staff and possibly with a more limited scope. It could be argued in some states that fusion centers would not be able to continue long after federal dollars and support ceases to exist. Others might disagree, believing it is quite possible that many fusion centers would survive despite dwindling federal support. It is even possible that many fusion centers would survive even after drastic decline in state and local funding because states and localities would be in a difficult position to officially dismantle these centers. [4, p. 15]

Performance Analysis

Sharing terrorism-related information between State, Local and Federal officials is crucial to protecting the United States from another terrorist attack. Achieving this objective was the motivation for Congress and the White House to invest hundreds of millions of taxpayer dollars in support of dozens of State and Local fusion centers across the United States. However, a 2012 Senate investigation found that DHS's support of fusion centers yielded little, if any, benefit to federal counterterrorism intelligence efforts. [2, p. 1]

After reviewing 13 months' worth of reporting originating from fusion centers from 2009 to 2010, the Subcommittee investigation found that DHS-assigned detailees forwarded "intelligence" of uneven quality – often times shoddy, rarely timely, sometimes endangering citizens' civil liberties and Privacy Act protections, occasionally taken from already-published public sources, and more often than not unrelated to terrorism. [2, p. 27]

According to a former DHS Senior Reports Officer, "A lot of [the reporting] was predominantly useless information." "You had a lot of data clogging the system with no value." Overall, the former official estimated 85 percent of reports coming out of the Reporting Branch were "not beneficial" to any entity, from Federal intelligence agencies to State and Local fusion centers. [2, p. 27]

Regarding the centers themselves, the Subcommittee investigation learned that a 2010 assessment of State and Local fusion centers conducted at the request of DHS found widespread deficiencies in the centers' basic counterterrorism information-sharing capabilities. The findings of the 2010 assessment and another done in 2011 contradicted public statements by DHS officials who described fusion centers as "one of the centerpieces of our counterterrorism strategy," and "a major force multiplier in the counterterrorism enterprise." [2, p. 2]

Despite reviewing 13 months' worth of reporting originating from fusion centers from April 1, 2009 to April 30, 2010, the Subcommittee investigation could identify no reporting which uncovered a terrorist threat, nor could it identify a contribution such fusion center reporting made to disrupt an active terrorist plot.

Despite reviewing 13 months' worth of reporting originating from fusion centers from April 1, 2009 to April 30, 2010, the Subcommittee investigation could identify no reporting which uncovered a terrorist threat, nor could it identify a contribution such fusion center reporting made to disrupt an active terrorist plot. [2, p. 2]

Conversely, obtaining information from DHS is also problematic. Many state and local fusion center officials praised I&A's efforts on the nationwide Fusion Center Initiative. However, fusion center officials remain concerned that I&A has not developed an action plan to ensure that it understands and can meet the centers' evolving and unique needs. Such needs include:

- Receiving adequate and timely information from DHS;
- Assistance in navigating DHS' complex organization, and
- Obtaining initial and ongoing training for state and local analysts. [1, p. 8]

Fusion centers have experienced difficulty receiving adequate and timely information from DHS. Many fusion center officials said that they received irrelevant or outdated information in the past. In addition, center officials could not determine whether the information was adequately processed through all relevant systems or coordinated with other intelligence or law enforcement entities. However, according to I&A officials, I&A is striving to meet the needs of fusion centers. In an April 2008 speech, the Under Secretary for I&A recognized that state and local authorities have been analyzing and acting on information for years and the federal government must aggressively support these endeavors. As a result, I&A plans to increase its support to state and local partners in three main areas: standing information needs, Requests for Information, and use of open source information. [1, p. 8]

Many fusion center officials reported frustrations when navigating DHS' complex organization, and are confused by the department's structure. As a result, state and local officials rely on their assigned I&A officer for fast, efficient, and adequate responses to their information needs. In response, I&A officials said that I&A continues to identify ways to improve the Request for Information process. For example, one I&A representative said that when there is an administrative request, such as a Request for Information about security clearances, the representative refers the request to I&A's State and Local Program Office, who could be immediately and appropriately tasked. In another example, should a request involve an analytical product, the representative refers the request to one of I&A's analytical branches for resolution. To discourage the practice of several fusion center officials contacting multiple DHS components directly for information, another I&A representative suggested creating a single email address to receive requests from fusion center officials and provide one "DHS answer." DHS is taking steps to facilitate efficient and coordinated communications between it and the fusion centers by enhancing I&A's Request for Information process and by requesting that each state that has multiple fusion centers designate one of its centers as the primary point of contact with DHS. [1, p. 12]

Conversely, obtaining information from DHS is also problematic. Fusion centers have experienced difficulty receiving adequate and timely information from DHS. Many fusion center officials reported frustrations when navigating DHS' complex organization, and are confused by the department's structure.

Fusion center officials reported benefits from DHS communications, training, and outreach efforts, as these efforts enhance state and local officials' understanding of the federal intelligence community and their role within the community. However, fusion center officials expressed a need to obtain more structured and formalized analytical training to improve their ability to generate products for the intelligence community, and to facilitate coordination and communication between DHS and the fusion centers. Fusion center officials also reported that budget constraints limit their ability to send personnel to out-of-state training. One fusion center director said funds are not routinely available to send personnel to off-site training or conferences, and it can be difficult convincing state governments to fund such travel. A number of fusion center officials suggested that DHS conduct training outside of the Washington, DC, metropolitan area and explore the feasibility of online training modules to provide low - or no-cost training to state and local field personnel. [1, p. 13]

Conclusion

Fusing foreign intelligence with a wide spectrum of domestic information is the stated primary purpose of most fusion centers. Locally gathered information collected from a broad array of law enforcement, public health and safety, as well as private sector sources, is fused with intelligence collected and produced by the Federal Intelligence Community to better understand threat and assist in directing national security resources. The same benefit also works in reverse. For example, when a bombing occurs overseas, it can be very helpful for modus operandi and other tactical information surrounding that bombing to be communicated to states and localities in a timely fashion so they may align their protective resources accordingly. The fusion centers, through their connectivity with the federal Intelligence Community via either systems and/or federal personnel collocated at the centers, can serve as the single focal point for timely dissemination of that information. [4, pp. 5-6] While the system remains unproven and continues to mature, the lessons from 9/11 attest to the criticality of the function and the need to continue fostering development of the nation's fusion centers.

Challenge Your Understanding

The following questions are designed to challenge your understanding of the material presented in this chapter. Some questions may require additional research outside this book in order to provide a complete answer.

1. How are State and Local law enforcement bound up into homeland security?
2. What is the value proposition of fusion centers?
3. How are fusion centers similar to JTTFs?
4. How are fusion centers different from JTTFs?
5. What risks do fusion centers pose to civil liberties?
6. What support does DHS lend to fusion centers?
7. What is the State and Local view of DHS support to fusion centers?
8. How is DHS working to make fusion centers more effective?
9. How have fusion centers contributed to counterterrorism?
10. As a taxpayer, do you think fusion centers provide an adequate return on investment? Explain.

Chapter 42

First Responders

Learning Outcomes

Careful study of this chapter will help a student do the following:

- Explain why first responders are the "first line of defense" against domestic catastrophic destruction.
- Discuss what was different about 9/11 that necessitated improved emergency preparedness.
- Describe the relationship between the NPG, NPS, HSGP, and THIRA.
- Assess the state of national emergency preparedness today.

"Every day, first responders put their own lives on the line to ensure our safety. The least we can do is make sure they have the tools to protect and serve their communities."

- Senator Joe Lieberman

Introduction

America's first line of defense in the aftermath of any terrorist attack is its first responder community—police officers, firefighters, emergency medical providers, public works personnel, and emergency management officials. Nearly three million state and local first responders regularly put their lives on the line to save the lives of others and make our country safer. These individuals include specially trained hazardous materials teams, collapse search and rescue units, bomb squads, and tactical units. [1, p. 41]

America's first line of defense in the aftermath of any terrorist attack is its first responder community—police officers, firefighters, emergency medical providers, public works personnel, and emergency management officials.

Background

On September 11, the nation suffered the largest loss of life—2,973—on its soil as a result of hostile attack in its history. The Fire Department of New York (FDNY) suffered 343 fatalities— the largest loss of life of any emergency response agency in history. The Port Authority Police Department (PAPD) suffered 37 fatalities—the largest loss of life of any police force in history. The New York Police Department (NYPD) suffered 23 fatalities—the second largest loss of life of any police force in history, exceeded only by the number of PAPD officers lost the same day. [2, p. 311]

The emergency response to the attacks on 9/11 was necessarily improvised. In New York, the FDNY, NYPD, the Port Authority, World Trade Center (WTC) employees, and the building occupants themselves did their best to cope with the effects of an unimaginable catastrophe—unfolding furiously over a mere 102 minutes—for which they were unprepared in terms of both training and mindset. [2, p. 315]

The National Institute of Standards and Technology has estimated that between 16,400 and 18,800 civilians were in the WTC complex as of 8:46 am on September 11. At most 2,152 individuals died at the WTC complex who were not (1) fire or police first responders, (2) security or fire safety personnel of the WTC or individual companies, (3) volunteer civilians who ran to the WTC after the planes' impact to help others, or (4) on the two planes that crashed into the Twin Towers. Out of this total number of fatalities, the workplace location of 2,052 individuals, or 95.35 percent can be accounted. Of this number, 1,942 or 94.64 percent either worked or were supposed to attend a meeting at or above the respective impact zones of the Twin Towers; only 110, or 5.36 percent of those who died, worked below the impact zone. While a given person's office location at the WTC did not definitively indicate where that individual died that morning or whether he or she could have evacuated, the data strongly suggests that the evacuation was a success for civilians below the impact zone. [2, p. 316]

First responders played a significant role in the success of the evacuation. Some specific rescues are quantifiable, such as an FDNY company's rescue of civilians trapped on the 22d floor of the North Tower, or the success of FDNY, PAPD, and NYPD personnel in carrying non-ambulatory civilians out of both the North and South Towers. In other instances, intangibles combined to reduce what could have been a much higher death total. It is impossible to measure how many more civilians who descended to the ground floors would have died but for the NYPD and PAPD personnel directing them—via safe exit routes that avoided jumpers and debris—to leave the complex urgently but calmly. It is impossible to measure how many more civilians would have died but for the determination of many members of the FDNY, PAPD, and NYPD to continue assisting civilians after the South Tower collapsed. It is impossible to measure the calming influence that ascending firefighters had on descending civilians or whether but for the firefighters' presence the poor behavior of a very few civilians could have caused a dangerous and panicked mob flight. But the positive impact of the first responders on the evacuation came at a tremendous cost of first responder lives lost. [2, pp. 316-317]

The lesson of 9/11 for civilians and first responders can be stated simply: in the new age of terror, they—we—are the primary targets. The losses America suffered that day demonstrated both the gravity of the terrorist threat and the commensurate need to prepare ourselves to meet it. [2, p. 323]

The first responders of today live in a world transformed by the attacks on 9/11. Because no one believes that every conceivable form of attack can be prevented, civilians and first responders will again find themselves on the front lines. We must plan for that eventuality. A rededication to preparedness is perhaps the best way to honor the memories of those we lost that day. [2, p. 323]

The first responders of today live in a world transformed by the attacks on 9/11. Because no one believes that every conceivable form of attack can be prevented, civilians and first responders will again find themselves on the front lines. We must plan for that eventuality. A rededication to preparedness is perhaps the best way to honor the memories of those we lost that day.

National Preparedness Goal

Americans responded with great skill and courage on 9/11. However, in 2001 there were too many seams and gaps in the nation's response plans and capabilities. At the time, at least five different plans—the Federal Response Plan, the National Contingency Plan, the Interagency Domestic Terrorism Concept of Operations Plan, the Federal Radiological Emergency Response Plan, and a nascent bioterrorism response plan—governed the Federal government's response. Those plans and the government's overarching policy for counterterrorism were based on a distinction between "crisis management" and "consequence management." In addition, different organizations at different levels of the government put in place different incident management systems and communications equipment. All too often, those systems and equipment do not function together well enough. [1, p. 42]

Within months of enactment of the Homeland Security Act, President Bush issued Homeland Security Presidential Directive 5 (HSPD-5) directing the Secretary of Homeland Security to develop and administer a National Incident Management System (NIMS) and a National Response Plan (NRP).

Furthermore, many areas of the country had little or no capability to respond to a terrorist attack using weapons of mass destruction. Even the best prepared States and localities did not possess adequate resources to respond to the full range of terrorist threats we face. Many did not have mutual aid agreements to facilitate cooperation with their neighbors in time of emergency. Federal support for domestic preparedness efforts was relatively small and disorganized, with eight different departments and agencies providing money in a tangled web of grant programs. [1, p. 42]

The Homeland Security Act of 2002 established the Emergency Preparedness and Response (EPR) Directorate within the Department of Homeland Security (DHS) to consolidate and coordinate emergency management for the nation. [3, p. 1]

Within months of enactment of the Homeland Security Act, President Bush issued Homeland Security Presidential Directive 5 (HSPD-5) directing the Secretary of Homeland Security to develop and administer a National Incident Management System (NIMS) and a National Response Plan (NRP). These two documents were to be used to "enhance the ability of the United States to manage domestic incidents by establishing a single, comprehensive national incident management system." [4, p. 1]

The NIMS was meant to fix the absence of standardized procedures, operating systems, and terminology that complicated response efforts at the World Trade Center on 9/11. Released in March 2004, NIMS introduced the Incident Command System (ICS) and described a system for integrating response agencies from across jurisdictions into a unified whole, and coordinating their actions towards a single purpose. The NIMS established standard operational components and procedures to ensure that first responders could communicate and cooperate to achieve the most efficient and effective response to a disaster. [4, p. 19]

The NRP consolidated various Federal plans into a single document. Released in January 2005, the NRP introduced Emergency Support Functions for providing Federal support, and procedures for requesting Federal support under the terms of the 1988 Robert T. Stafford Act. [4, pp. 22-23]

Both NIMS and the NRP provided a foundation allowing first responders from across the nation to work together according to standard principals of organization and operation. Still, work needed to be done to enhance their capabilities, particularly with respect to a potential WMD attack. Accordingly, President Bush issued HSPD-8 directing development of a National Preparedness Goal (NPG). Released in December 2005, the NPG established an objective for guiding the nation's emergency preparedness efforts, and target capabilities for attaining it. [4, p. 3]

Both NIMS and the NRP provided a foundation allowing first responders from across the nation to work together according to standard principals of organization and operation. Still, work needed to be done to enhance their capabilities, particularly with respect to a potential WMD attack.

The 2005 National Preparedness Goal established an objective "To engage Federal, State, local, and tribal entities, their private and nongovernmental partners, and the general public to achieve and sustain risk-based target levels of capability to prevent, protect against, respond to, and recover from major events in order to minimize the impact on lives, property, and the economy." [5, p. 1]

The 2005 National Preparedness Goal established 36 target capabilities deemed essential to reduce losses and successfully respond to disaster. The Target Capabilities List (TCL) was drawn from a much larger Universal Task List (UTL). The UTL identified operations and tasks that would be necessary to successfully respond to the 15 National Planning Scenarios. The National Planning Scenarios identified potential worst case disasters, both natural and manmade, encompassing all forms of WMD. [4, pp. 7-14]

What was absent from this scheme was a system for driving incremental but continuous improvement. Emergency preparedness is a cycle. It begins with planning to establish goals. It proceeds with organization, equipping, and training to attain those goals. Then a series of exercises and evaluations are necessary to assess progress towards those goals. Then the cycle must begin anew to set new goals and attain them. [6, pp. I-4] In September 2007, DHS belatedly introduced a National Preparedness System as part of its National Preparedness Guidelines [7, p. 22], only to be trumped a month later by the Homeland Security Management System advocated in the 2007 National Strategy for Homeland Security prepared by the White House Homeland Security Council. [7, p. 42] Neither survived to maturity as events, both natural and manmade, would change the direction of homeland security.

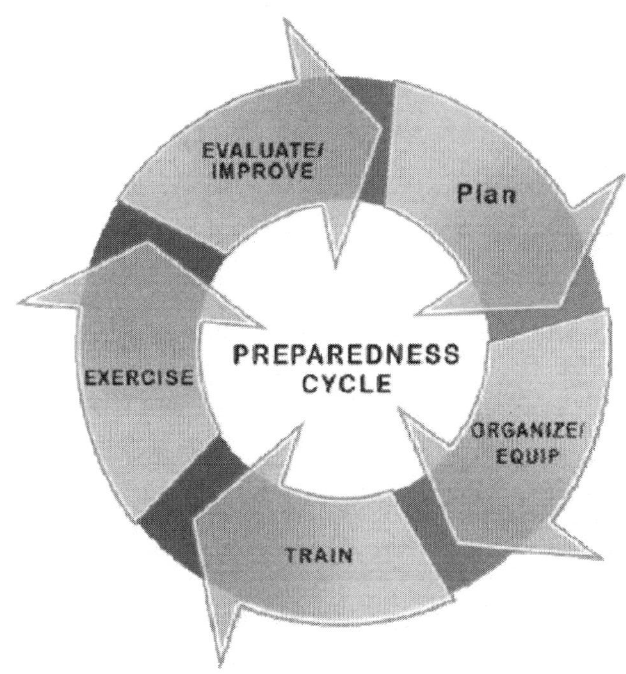

Figure 42-1: Emergency Preparedness Cycle [6, pp. I-4]

Accordingly, President Bush issued HSPD-8 directing development of a National Preparedness Goal (NPG). Released in December 2005, the NPG established an objective for guiding the nation's emergency preparedness efforts, and target capabilities for attaining it.

Reports issued by committees of the 109th Congress, the White House, federal offices of Inspector General, and the Government Accountability Office (GAO), among others, concluded that the losses caused by Hurricane Katrina were due, in part, to deficiencies such as questionable leadership decisions and capabilities, organizational failures, overwhelmed preparation and communication systems, and inadequate statutory authorities. As a result, the Post-Katrina Emergency Management Reform Act of 2006 revised federal emergency management policies vested in the President; reorganized the Federal Emergency Management Agency (FEMA); and enhanced and clarified the mission, functions, and authorities of the agency, as well as those of its parent, the Department of Homeland Security (DHS). [9, p. ii]

Effective March 31, 2007, the Post-Katrina Reform Act restored to FEMA all its former authorities, taken away by the 2002 Homeland Security Act, subsumed the former DHS EPR Directorate within its organization, and made the FEMA Administrator a direct-report to the Secretary of Homeland Security. The Post-Katrina Act reorganized DHS with a reconfigured FEMA with consolidated emergency management functions, and elevated status within DHS. [9, p. 5]

As a result of the Post-Katrina Reform Act, FEMA gained control over the majority of grants and training provided by DHS. These included the State Homeland Security Grant Program (HSGP), the Law Enforcement Terrorism Prevention Program, and the Urban Area Security Initiative (UASI); all essential to enhancing first responder preparedness. [9, p. 27]

Also as part of the Post-Katrina Reform Act, the FEMA Administrator was given responsibility for the National Preparedness Goal and National Preparedness System. The act further amended the Stafford Act to require that all emergency preparedness grants awarded by FEMA to the States be based upon plans consistent with the NPG, NIMS, and NRP. [9, p. 28]

The National Response Plan was released in January when Hurricane Katrina struck at the end of August 2005. Few people knew about the plan, let alone its contents. Still, it took a beating in the post-disaster recriminations, and was subsequently replaced by the National Response Framework (NRF) in 2008; same plan, different wrapper, slimmer package. By the same token, the National Incident Management System was also revised in 2008.

In March 2011, President Obama issued Presidential Policy Directive No. 8 (PPD-8) overriding the previous HSPD-8 and calling for a new National Preparedness Goal: "A secure and resilient Nation with the capabilities required across the whole community to prevent, protect against, mitigate, respond to, and recover from the threats and hazards that pose the greatest risk." [10, p. 1]

In March 2011, President Obama issued PPD-8 overriding HSPD-8 and enunciating a new National Preparedness Goal. To see to its implementation, FEMA released a new National Preparedness System in November 2011. HSGP funding is now tied to attainment of NPG Core Capabilities, as determined by State assessments using the FEMA Threat and Hazard Identification and Risk Assessment (THIRA) system.

The new NPG placed emphasis on resilience, the ability to rapidly recover from disaster. Additionally, PPD-8 replaced Target Capabilities with Core Capabilities, and called for a family of frameworks to compliment the National Response Framework. The new frameworks were to propose preparedness measures across the spectrum of integrated emergency management: Prevention, Protection, Mitigation, Response, and Recovery. [11]

In November 2011, FEMA released a new National Preparedness System to support implementation of its new National Preparedness Goal. In accordance with the 2006 Post-Katrina Reform Act, the new NPS was not only capabilities-based, it was much more process focused. In order to compete for funds from the Homeland Security Grants Program, States would have to complete a Threat and Hazard Identification and Risk Assessment (THIRA) demonstrating progress towards the NPG Core Capabilities. In 2015 the Core Capabilities were revised, but otherwise remain the measure for assessing a State's progress towards the National Preparedness Goal. [12, pp. 1-2]

Conclusion

Before 9/11, Federal support to first responders was minimal and fragmented. On 9/11 the nation's finest in the FDNY, PAPD, and NYPD paid the price for this vulnerability. In the wake of 9/11, the Department of Homeland Security was given the mission of consolidating Federal support and preparing first responders for future catastrophes, including those employing WMD. Both the National Incident Management System and National Response Plan were unprecedented for fostering first responder integration across the nation. And while the National Preparedness Goal and National Preparedness System matured more slowly, today they underpin a systematic and continuous improvement process to ensure that first responders are prepared to meet all hazard challenges of the future.

Challenge Your Understanding

The following questions are designed to challenge your understanding of the material presented in this chapter. Some questions may require additional research outside this book in order to provide a complete answer.

1. Why are first responders recognized as the "first line of defense" against domestic catastrophic destruction?
2. What was different about 9/11 that necessitated improved emergency preparedness?
3. What is the National Preparedness Goal?
4. What is the relationship between the NPG and core capabilities?
5. What is the relationship between the NPG and the National Preparedness System?
6. List and describe the five steps of the preparedness cycle.
7. What is the purpose of the Homeland Security Grant Program?
8. How do first responders apply for HSGP funding?
9. How is HSGP funding related to the preparedness cycle?
10. Overall, do you think DHS has improved national emergency preparedness? Explain.

Appendix A: DHS Budgets

The Department of Homeland was established by the Homeland Security Act, signed into law by President Bush on November 25, 2002. Former Pennsylvania Governor Tom Ridge was appointed the first Secretary of Homeland Security. Between November 2002 and January 2003, Secretary Ridge consolidated 180,000 personnel from twenty-two Federal agencies to form the new Department of Homeland Security. On January 23, 2003, President Bush issued Executive Order 13284 activating the new Department.

As with all Federal agencies, the Department of Homeland Security is funded by Congress and must compete for limited taxpayer dollars together with other Federal agencies. The Federal budget process is managed according to the Congressional Budget Act of 1974. The process starts in February when the President submits a detailed budget request for the coming fiscal year which begins October 1st. The budget request is developed through an interactive process between Federal agencies and the President's Office of Management and Budget (OMB) that begins the previous spring or earlier.

Table A-1: DHS and US Budgets

FY	DHS Budget (billions)	US Budget (billions)	Portion
2003	$37.7	$2,159.899	1.7455%
2004	$36.2	$2,292.841	1.5788%
2005	$40.2	$2,471.957	1.6262%
2006	$41.1	$2,655.050	1.5480%
2007	$42.7	$2,728.686	1.5649%
2008	$46.4	$2,982.544	1.5557%
2009	$50.5	$3,517.677	1.4356%
2010	$55.1	$3,457,079	0.0016%
2011	$56.3	$3,603,056	0.0016%
2012	$57.0	$3,536,951	0.0016%
2013	$59.0	$3,454,647	0.0017%
2014	$60.0	$3,506,114	0.0017%
2015	$60.9	$3,688,292	0.0017%
2016	$64.9	$3,951,307	0.0016%
Totals	$708.00	$25,216,254.65	0.0028%

This appendix provides a summary of DHS budgets from FY03 to FY16. The numbers were drawn from the corresponding DHS Budget in Brief[1], submitted annually to OMB for the President's Budget. These budgets represent what was requested from Congress and not what was actually spent, but otherwise provide a reasonable approximation[2]. The specific request for each fiscal year is cited together with any accompanying justification. Also, where available, table summaries were included indicating how DHS planned to allocate its budget.

FY03, Oct 02 - Sep 03
Thomas Ridge, Secretary
Title: Securing the Homeland, Strengthening the Nation

"The President's Budget for 2003- the Federal government's first post-September 11 budget- reflects his absolute commitment to achieving a more secure homeland. The FY 2003 Budget directs $37.7 billion to homeland security, up from $19.5 billion in 2002[3]. This mass infusion of Federal resources reflects the priority the President has attached to the homeland security agenda."

	2002 Enacted Base	FY 2002 Supp.	FY 2003 Proposed
Supporting First Responders	291	651	3,500
Defending Against Biological Terrorism	1,408	3,730	5,898
Securing America's Borders	8,752	1,194	10,615
Using 21st Century Technology to Defend the Homeland	155	75	722
Aviation Security	1,543	1,035	4,800
Other Non-Department of Defense (DOD) Homeland Security	3,186	2,384	5,352
DOD Homeland Security (Outside Initiatives)	4,201	689	6,815
Total	19,535	9,758	37,702

Figure A-1: FY03 DHS Budget Allocation

1Copies of these budgets may be found at www.dhs.gov/dhs-budget.
2Listed US Budget data excerpted from www.whitehouse.gov/omb/budget/Historicals
3Refers to funds requested for homeland security missions in 2002, before DHS was formed.

FY04, Oct 03 - Sep 04

Thomas Ridge, Secretary

Title: Department of Homeland Security Budget in Brief

"The President's 2004 Budget provides the necessary resources for the Department to succeed. The budget includes a total of $36.2 billion, 7.4 percent more than the 2003 level and over 64 percent more than the FY 2002 level for these activities. The President's 2004 budget supports a new Department whose primary mission is to protect the American people and the homeland. In addition, it unifies principal border and transportation security agencies; further coordinates a cohesive network of disaster response capabilities; creates a central point for analysis and dissemination of intelligence and other information pertaining to terrorist threats to protect America's critical infrastructure; and unites research and development efforts to detect and counter potential terrorist attacks and recognize the multi-missions of so many of our agencies. "

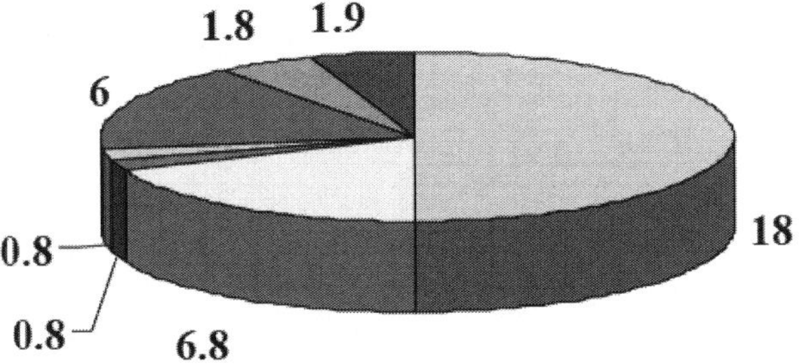

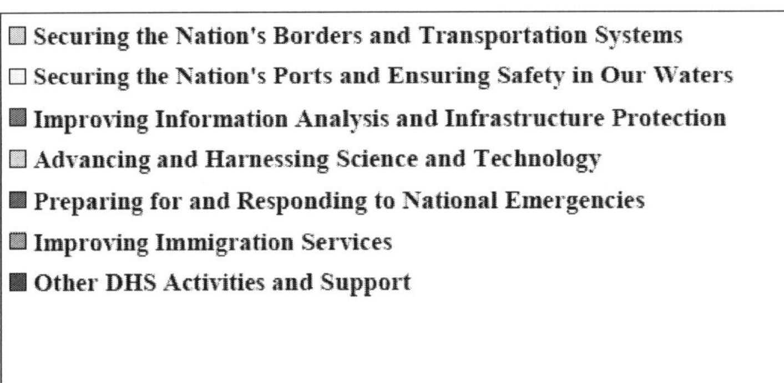

Figure A-2: FY04 DHS Budget Allocation

FY05, Oct 04 - Sep 05

Thomas Ridge, Secretary

Title: Department of Homeland Security Budget in Brief

"The Fiscal Year 2005 budget for the Department of Homeland Security builds upon the significant investments to date that improve our safeguards against terrorism, while also sustaining the many important departmental activities not directly related to our fight against terrorism. The President's budget clearly demonstrates the continuing priority placed on Homeland Security in requesting total new resources for FY 2005 of $40.2 billion. This is an increase of 10% above the comparable FY 2004 resource level. This includes all sources of funding, such as discretionary and mandatory appropriations, offsetting collections from user fees, and trust funds."

ORGANIZATION	*FY 2003*	*FY 2004* [2]	*FY 2005*	*(+/-) Change FY 2004 to FY 2005*
SECURITY, ENFORCEMENT, & INVESTIGATIONS	21,566	22,606	24,691	2,085
BTS Under Secretary	0	8	10	2
US VISIT	380	328	340	12
Bureau of Customs & Border Protection	5,887	5,942	6,199	257
Bureau of Immigration & Customs Enforcement	3,262	3,654	4,011	357
Transportation Security Administration	4,648	4,405	5,297	892
United States Coast Guard	6,196	6,935	7,471	536
United States Secret Service	1,193	1,334	1,363	29
PREPAREDNESS & RECOVERY	5,175	5,493	7,372	1,879
EP&R Federal Emergency Management Agency (Less Biodefense) [1]	*5,175*	*4,608*	*4,844*	*236*
Biodefense	*0*	*885*	*2,528*	*1,643*
RESEARCH, DEVELOPMENT, TRAINING, ASSESSMENTS & SERVICES	2,330	3,591	3,810	219
Bureau of Citizenship & Immigration Services	1,422	1,653	1,711	58
Federal Law Enforcement Training Center	170	191	196	5
Information Analysis & Infrastructure Protection Directorate	185	834	864	30
Science & Technology Directorate	553	913	1,039	126
DEPARTMENTAL MANAGEMENT AND OPERATIONS	2,111	4,851	4,294	-557
Departmental Management	2,040	4,771	4,212	-559
Departmental Operations	*22*	*211*	*405*	*194*
Technology Investments	*47*	*184*	*226*	*42*
Counter-Terrorism Fund	*10*	*10*	*20*	*10*
Office for Domestic Preparedness	*1,961*	*4,366*	*3,561*	*-805*
Inspector General	71	80	82	2
TOTAL	31,182	36,541	40,167	3,626

Figure A-3: FY05 DHS Budget Allocation

FY06, Oct 05 - Sep 06

Michael Chertoff, Secretary

Title: Department of Homeland Security Budget in Brief

"The President's FY 2006 budget request includes a total of $41.1 billion for the Department of Homeland Security. This is an increase in total budgetary authority of 7 percent over the enacted FY 2005 funding, excluding Project BioShield, and clearly demonstrates the Administration's continued commitment to making further improvements in the nation's homeland security. Among the operating entities with significant budgetary increases are Immigration and Customs Enforcement (a 13.5 percent increase) and the U.S. Coast Guard (an increase of more than 9 percent, adjusting for transferred programs). The budget also streamlines screening programs, increasing resources for these activities under a new screening office by 68 percent."

	FY 2004 Enacted 1	FY 2005 Enacted 2	FY 2006 President's Budget	FY 2006 +/- FY05 Enacted
	$000	$000	$000	$000
BTS Under Secretary	$8,058	$9,617	$10,617	$1,000
US-VISIT	328,053	340,000	-	(340,000)
Screening Coordination and Operations Office (SCO)	-	-	846,913	846,913
U.S. Customs & Border Protection	5,997,287	6,416,398	6,725,010	308,612
U.S. Immigration & Customs Enforcement	3,669,615	3,845,178	4,364,270	519,092
Transportation Security Administration	4,578,043	5,405,375	5,561,792	156,417
Federal Law Enforcement Training Center	191,643	222,357	223,998	1,641
U.S. Coast Guard	6,994,222	7,558,560	8,146,912	588,352
U.S. Secret Service	1,334,128	1,375,758	1,403,782	28,024
FEMA (EP&R Directorate) [4]	4,671,782	5,038,256	5,365,288	327,032
U.S. Citizenship & Immigration Services	1,549,733	1,775,000	1,854,000	79,000
IAIP Directorate	834,348	893,708	873,245	(20,463)
S&T Directorate	912,751	1,115,450	1,368,446	252,996
SLGCP	4,192,120	3,984,846	3,564,756	(420,090)
Departmental Operations	394,435	524,457	664,672	140,215
Counter-Terrorism Fund	9,941	8,000	10,000	2,000
Inspector General	80,318	82,317	83,017	700
TOTAL:	$35,746,477	$38,595,277	$41,066,718	$2,471,441
Less Rescission of Prior Year Carryover Funds: [3]	(142,385)	(84,760)	-	84,760
ADJUSTED TOTAL BUDGET AUTHORITY: [4]	$35,604,092	$38,510,517	$41,066,718	$2,556,201
BIOSHIELD: [4]	884,749	2,507,776	n/a	(2,507,776)

Figure A-4: FY06 DHS Budget Allocation

FY07, Oct 06 - Sep 07

Michael Chertoff, Secretary

Title: Department of Homeland Security Budget in Brief

"The implementation of 2SR instituted a fundamental reform of policies and procedures critical to achieving the mission of the Department. As a result, the FY 2007 budget proposal for the Department of Homeland Security is driven by a mission and risk-based approach to allocating the Department's resources, requesting $42.7 billion in funding, an increase of 6 percent over FY 2006. The Department's FY 2007 gross discretionary budget is $35.4 billion, an increase of 6 percent. Gross Discretionary funding includes appropriated budget authority and discretionary fee collections such as funding for the Federal Protective Service; aviation security passenger and carrier fees; and premium collections. It does not include funding such as Coast Guard's retirement pay accounts and fees paid for immigration benefits. The Department's FY 2007 net discretionary budget is $30.9 billion."

	FY 2005 Revised Enacted [1]	FY 2006 Revised Enacted [2]	FY 2007 President's Budget	FY 2007 +/- FY 2006 Enacted	FY 2007 +/- FY 2006 Enacted
	$000	$000	$000	$000	%
Departmental Operations	$ 527,257	$ 559,230	$ 674,791	$ 115,561	21%
Counter-Terrorism Fund	8,000	1,980	-	(1,980)	-100%
Office of Screening Coordination and Operations	-	3,960	3,960	-	-
Office of the Inspector General	82,317	82,187	96,185	13,998	17%
US--VISIT	340,000	336,600	399,494	62,894	19%
U.S. Customs & Border Protection	6,344,398	7,109,875	7,846,681	736,806	10%
U.S. Immigration & Customs Enforcement	3,127,078	3,866,443	4,696,932	830,489	21%
Transportation Security Administration	6,068,275	6,167,014	6,299,462	132,448	2%
Preparedness Directorate	-	678,395	669,980	(8,415)	-1%
Preparedness: Office of Grants & Training	-	3,352,437	2,750,009	(602,428)	-18%
Analysis and Operations	-	252,940	298,663	45,723	18%
Federal Emergency Management Agency	5,038,256	4,834,744	5,326,882	492,138	10%
U.S. Citizenship & Immigration Services	1,775,000	1,887,850	1,985,990	98,140	5%
U.S. Secret Service	1,385,758	1,399,889	1,465,103	65,214	5%
U.S. Coast Guard	7,558,560	8,193,797	8,422,075	228,278	3%
Federal Law Enforcement Training Center	222,357	279,534	244,556	(34,978)	-13%
S&T Directorate	1,115,450	1,487,075	1,002,271	(484,804)	-33%
Domestic Nuclear Detection Office	-	-	535,788	535,788	-
Legacy DHS Organizations					
BTS Under Secretary	9,617	-	-	-	-
IAIP Directorate	887,108	-	-	-	-
SLGCP	3,984,846	-	-	-	-
TOTAL:	$ 38,474,277	$ 40,493,950	$ 42,718,822	$ 2,224,872	5%
Less Rescission of Prior Year Carryover Funds: [3]	(104,760)	(148,603)	(16,000)	132,603	-89%
ADJUSTED TOTAL BUDGET AUTHORITY:	$ 38,369,517	$ 40,345,347	$ 42,702,822	$ 2,357,475	6%
BIOSHIELD: [4]	$ 2,507,776	-	-	-	-
SUPPLEMENTAL: [5/6]	$ 67,329,867	$ (23,076,917)	-	-	-

Figure A-5: FY07 DHS Budget Allocation

FY08, Oct 07 - Sep 08

Michael Chertoff, Secretary

Title: Department of Homeland Security Budget in Brief

"As the Department reflects on the fifth anniversary of the tragic events that occurred on September 11, 2001, we remain committed to our duty of securing our homeland, directing our resources toward the greatest risks, and being flexible to changing threats. The FY 2008 budget request for the Department of Homeland Security represents an eight percent increase over FY 2007, with a total request of $46.4 billion in funding. The Department's FY 2008 gross discretionary budget is $37.7 billion, an increase of eight percent. Gross Discretionary funding does not include funding such as Coast Guard's retirement pay accounts and fees paid for immigration benefits. The Department's FY 2008 net discretionary budget is $34.3 billion, which does not include fee collections such as funding for the Federal Protective Service (ICE), aviation security passenger and carrier fees (TSA), credentialing fees (such as TWIC - TSA), and premium collections (National Flood Insurance Fund, FEMA). It should also be noted that the FY 2008 President's Budget request reflects the Notice of Implementation of the Post–Katrina Emergency Reform Act of 2006 (P.L. 109-295) and of Additional Changes Pursuant to Section 872 of the Homeland Security Act of 2002, provided to Congress on January 18, 2007. The Department continues to be disciplined in its use of resources, and has structured its budget request to target the Secretary's five highest priorities."

	FY 2006 Revised Enacted [1]	FY 2007 Revised Enacted [2]	FY 2008 President's Budget [3]	FY 2008 +/- FY 2007 Enacted	FY 2008 +/- FY 2007 Enacted
	$000	$000	$000	$000	%
Departmental Operations [4/5]	$ 559,230	$ 626,123	$ 683,189	$ 57,066	9%
Analysis and Operations	252,940	299,663	314,681	15,018	5%
Office of the Inspector General	82,187	98,685	99,111	426	0%
U.S. Customs & Border Protection	7,113,495	7,743,581	10,174,114	2,430,533	31%
U.S. Immigration & Customs Enforcement	3,866,443	4,696,641	5,014,500	317,859	7%
Transportation Security Administration	6,167,014	6,329,291	6,401,178	71,887	1%
U.S. Coast Guard	8,268,797	8,553,352	8,775,088	221,736	3%
U.S. Secret Service	1,399,889	1,479,158	1,608,996	129,838	9%
National Protection and Programs Directorate [5]	-	-	1,046,567	1,046,567	-
Office of Health Affairs [5]	-	-	117,933	117,933	-
Counter-Terrorism Fund	1,980	-	-	-	-
Federal Emergency Management Agency [5]	4,834,744	5,223,503	5,824,204	600,701	11%
FEMA: Office of Grant Programs [5]	-	-	2,196,000	2,196,000	-
FEMA: Office of Grant Programs with PSIC Grants [9]			*[3,196,000]*	*[3,196,000]*	-
U.S. Citizenship & Immigration Services	1,887,850	1,985,990	2,568,872	582,882	29%
Federal Law Enforcement Training Center	279,534	253,279	263,056	9,777	4%
S&T Directorate	1,487,075	973,109	799,100	(174,009)	-18%
Domestic Nuclear Detection Office	-	480,968	561,900	80,932	17%
Legacy DHS Organizations					
Preparedness Directorate [5]	678,395	618,577	-	(618,577)	-100%
Preparedness: Office of Grants & Training [5]	3,352,437	3,393,000	-	(3,393,000)	-100%
US-VISIT [5]	336,600	362,494	-	(362,494)	-100%
TOTAL:	$ 40,568,610	$ 43,117,414	$ 46,448,489	$ 3,331,075	8%
Less Rescission of Prior Year Carryover Funds: [6]	(148,603)	(313,005)	(48,787)	264,218	-84%
ADJUSTED TOTAL BUDGET AUTHORITY:	$ 40,420,007	$ 42,804,409	$ 46,399,702	$ 3,595,293	8%

Figure A-6: FY08 DHS Budget Allocation

FY09, Oct 08 - Sep 09

Michael Chertoff, Secretary

Title: Department of Homeland Security Budget in Brief

"The Department remains dedicated to fulfilling our duty to protect our country. Six years after September 11, 2001 we are moving beyond operating as an agency in transition to an agency diligently working to protect our borders and critical infrastructure, prevent dangerous people and goods from entering our country, and recover from natural disasters effectively. The total FY 2009 budget request for the Department of Homeland Security is $50.5 billion in funding; a 7 percent increase over the FY 2008 enacted level excluding emergency funding. The Department's FY 2009 gross discretionary budget request is $40.7 billion, an increase of 8 percent over the FY 2008 enacted level excluding emergency funding. Gross Discretionary funding does not include funding such as Coast Guard's retirement pay accounts and fees paid for immigration benefits. The Department's FY 2009 net discretionary budget request is $37.6 billion, which does not include fee collections such as funding for the Federal Protective Service (ICE), aviation security passenger and carrier fees (TSA), credentialing fees (such as TWIC - TSA), and premium collections (National Flood Insurance Fund, FEMA). In pursuit of our five priorities established in 2007, the Department continues to efficiently align resources to lead a unified national effort in securing America."

	FY 2007 Revised Enacted [1]	FY 2008 Enacted [2]	FY 2009 President's Budget [3]	FY 2009 +/- FY 2008 Enacted	FY 2009 +/- FY 2008 Enacted
	$000	$000	$000	$000	%
Departmental Operations [3]	$ 603,525	$ 571,791	$ 752,593	$ 180,802	32%
Analysis and Operations	299,663	306,000	333,521	27,521	9%
Office of the Inspector General	98,685	108,711	101,023	(7,688)	-7%
U.S. Customs & Border Protection	7,746,259	9,306,725	10,941,231	1,634,506	18%
U.S. Immigration & Customs Enforcement	4,696,641	5,054,317	5,676,085	621,768	12%
Transportation Security Administration	6,329,291	6,819,859	7,101,828	281,969	4%
U.S. Coast Guard	8,554,067	8,741,053	9,346,022	604,969	7%
U.S. Secret Service	1,485,617	1,595,496	1,639,346	43,850	3%
National Protection and Programs Directorate	942,436	902,076	1,286,100	384,024	43%
Office of Health Affairs	9,917	116,500	161,339	44,839	38%
Federal Emergency Management Agency	4,571,716	5,522,178	6,566,794	1,044,616	19%
FEMA: Grants [4]	4,048,500	4,117,800	2,200,000	(1,917,800)	-47%
U.S. Citizenship & Immigration Services	2,216,240	2,539,845	2,689,726	149,881	6%
Federal Law Enforcement Training Center	253,279	267,666	274,126	6,460	2%
S&T Directorate	968,131	830,335	868,837	38,502	5%
Domestic Nuclear Detection Office	480,968	484,750	563,800	79,050	16%
TOTAL:	$ 43,304,935	$ 47,285,102	$ 50,502,371	$ 3,217,269	7%
Less Rescission of Prior Year Carryover Funds: [5]	(313,005)	(262,249)	-	262,249	-100%
ADJUSTED TOTAL BUDGET AUTHORITY:	$ 42,991,930	$ 47,022,853	$ 50,502,371	$ 3,479,518	7%
EMERGENCY FUNDING/SUPPLEMENTAL: [6]	$ 7,290,193	$ 5,630,000	$ -	$ (5,630,000)	$ -

Figure A-7: FY09 DHS Budget Allocation

FY10, Oct 09 - Sep 10

Janet Napolitano, Secretary

Title: Department of Homeland Security Budget in Brief

"The total FY 2010 budget request for the Department of Homeland Security is $55.1 billion in funding; a 4.9 percent increase over the FY 2009 enacted level excluding supplemental funding. The Department's FY 2010 gross discretionary budget request1 is $45.7 billion, an increase of 5.9 percent over the FY 2009 enacted level excluding emergency funding. The Department's FY 2010 net discretionary budget request is $42.7 billion."

	FY 2008 Revised Enacted [1]	FY 2009 Enacted [2]	FY 2010 President's Budget [3]	FY 2010 +/- FY 2009 Enacted	FY 2010 +/- FY 2009 Enacted
	$000	$000	$000	$000	%
Departmental Operations [4]	$ 573,983	$ 644,553	$ 904,673	$ 260,120	40%
Analysis and Operations	304,500	327,373	357,345	29,972	9%
Office of the Inspector General	108,711	98,513	127,874	29,361	30%
U.S. Customs & Border Protection	9,285,001	11,274,783	11,436,917	162,134	1%
U.S. Immigration & Customs Enforcement	5,054,317	5,928,210	5,762,800	(165,410)	-3%
Transportation Security Administration	6,809,359	6,990,778	7,793,576	802,798	11%
U.S. Coast Guard	8,631,053	9,623,779	9,955,663	331,884	3%
U.S. Secret Service	1,629,496	1,637,954	1,709,584	71,630	4%
National Protection and Programs Directorate	896,476	1,158,263	1,958,937	800,674	69%
Office of Health Affairs	118,375	157,191	138,000	(19,191)	-12%
Federal Emergency Management Agency	5,515,178	5,985,805	6,612,287	626,482	10%
FEMA: Grant Programs	4,117,800	4,245,700	3,867,000	(378,700)	-9%
U.S. Citizenship & Immigration Services	2,822,012	2,690,926	2,867,232	176,306	7%
Federal Law Enforcement Training Center	273,302	332,986	288,812	(44,174)	-13%
S&T Directorate	830,335	932,587	968,391	35,804	4%
Domestic Nuclear Detection Office	484,750	514,191	366,136	(148,055)	-29%
TOTAL:	$ 47,454,648	$ 52,543,592	$ 55,115,227	$ 2,571,635	4.89%
Less Rescission of Prior Year Carryover Funds: [5]	(124,985)	(61,373)	-	61,373	-100%
ADJUSTED TOTAL BUDGET AUTHORITY:	$ 47,329,664	$ 52,482,219	$ 55,115,227	$ 2,633,008	5%
SUPPLEMENTAL: [6]	$ 15,129,607	$ 2,967,000	$ -	$ (2,967,000)	$ -

Figure A-8: FY10 DHS Budget Allocation

FY11, Oct 10 - Sep 11

Janet Napolitano, Secretary

Title: Department of Homeland Security Budget in Brief

"The total FY 2011 budget request for the Department of Homeland Security is $56.3 billion in total funding; a 2 percent increase over the FY 2010 enacted level. The Department's FY 2011 gross discretionary budget request1 is $47.1 billion, an increase of 2 percent over the FY 2010 enacted level. The Department's FY 2011 net discretionary budget request is $43.6 billion2, an increase of 3 percent over the FY 2010 enacted level. For purposes of comparison the Overseas Contingency Operation funding and transfer from the National Science Foundation are not included in the FY 2010 enacted level."

	FY 2009 Revised Enacted [1] $000	FY 2010 Revised Enacted [2] $000	FY 2011 President's Budget $000	FY 2011 +/- FY 2010 Enacted $000	FY 2011 +/- FY 2010 Enacted %
Departmental Operations [3]	$ 659,109	$ 802,931	$ 1,270,821	$ 467,890	58%
Analysis and Operations	327,373	335,030	347,930	12,900	4%
Office of the Inspector General	114,513	113,874	129,806	15,932	14%
U.S. Customs & Border Protection	11,250,652	11,449,283	11,180,018	(269,265)	-2%
U.S. Immigration & Customs Enforcement	5,968,015	5,741,752	5,835,187	93,435	2%
Transportation Security Administration	6,992,778	7,656,066	8,164,780	508,714	7%
U.S. Coast Guard	9,624,179	10,122,963	10,078,317	(44,646)	0%
U.S. Secret Service	1,640,444	1,702,644	1,811,617	108,973	6%
National Protection and Programs Directorate	1,188,263	2,432,755	2,361,715	(71,040)	-3%
Office of Health Affairs	157,621	139,250	212,734	73,484	53%
Federal Emergency Management Agency	5,971,159	6,194,268	6,527,406	333,138	5%
FEMA: Grant Programs	4,220,858	4,165,200	4,000,590	(164,610)	-4%
U.S. Citizenship & Immigration Services	2,876,348	2,859,997	2,812,357	(47,640)	-2%
Federal Law Enforcement Training Center	332,986	282,812	278,375	(4,437)	-2%
S&T Directorate	932,587	1,006,471	1,018,264	11,793	1%
Domestic Nuclear Detection Office	514,191	383,037	305,820	(77,217)	-20%
TOTAL:	$ 52,771,076	$ 55,388,333	$ 56,335,737	$ 947,404	1.71%
Less Rescission of Prior Year Carryover Funds: [4]	(61,373)	(40,474)	-	40,474	-100%
ADJUSTED TOTAL BUDGET AUTHORITY:	$ 52,709,703	$ 55,347,859	$ 56,335,737	$ 987,878	2%
SUPPLEMENTAL: [5]	$ 3,354,503	$ 295,503	$ -	$ (295,503)	$ -
Less Rescission of Prior Year Carryover Funds: [5]	$ (100,000)	$ -	$ -	$ -	

Figure A-9: FY11 DHS Budget Allocation

FY12, Oct 11 - Sep 12

Janet Napolitano, Secretary

Title: Department of Homeland Security Budget in Brief

"The demands on the Department of Homeland Security (DHS) have never been greater and the threats we face pose new challenges that require an innovative and focused response. Today's threat picture features an adversary who evolves and adapts quickly and who is determined to strike us here at home – from the aviation system and the global supply chain to surface transportation systems, critical infrastructure, and cyber networks. The Department's Fiscal Year (FY) 2012 Budget allows us to continue to meet these evolving threats and challenges by prioritizing our essential operational requirements – while reflecting an unprecedented commitment to fiscal discipline that maximizes the effectiveness of every security dollar we receive. The FY 2012 budget request for DHS is $57.0 billion in total funding, $47.4 billion in gross discretionary funding, and $43.2 billion in net discretionary funding."

	FY 2010 Revised Enacted [1]	FY 2011 Continuing Resolution [2]	FY 2012 President's Budget	FY 2012 +/- FY 2011	FY 2012 +/- FY 2011
	$000	$000	$000	$000	%
Departmental Operations [3]	$ 809,531	$ 800,931	$ 947,231	$ 146,300	18%
Analysis and Operations (A&O)	333,030	335,030	355,368	20,338	6%
Office of the Inspector General (OIG)	113,874	129,874	144,318	14,444	11%
U.S. Customs & Border Protection (CBP)	11,540,501	11,544,660	11,845,678	301,018	3%
U.S. Immigration & Customs Enforcement (ICE)	5,741,752	5,748,339	5,822,576	74,237	1%
Transportation Security Administration (TSA)	7,656,066	7,649,666	8,115,259	465,593	6%
U.S. Coast Guard (USCG)	10,789,076	10,151,543	10,338,545	187,002	2%
U.S. Secret Service (USSS)	1,710,344	1,722,644	1,943,531	220,887	13%
National Protection and Programs Directorate (NPPD)	2,429,455	2,432,756	2,555,449	122,693	5%
Office of Health Affairs (OHA)	136,850	139,250	160,949	21,699	16%
Federal Emergency Management Agency (FEMA)	6,200,618	6,181,718	6,218,433	36,715	1%
FEMA: Grant Programs	4,165,200	4,165,200	3,844,663	(320,537)	-8%
U.S. Citizenship & Immigration Services (USCIS)	2,870,997	3,054,829	2,906,866	(147,963)	-5%
Federal Law Enforcement Training Center (FLETC)	282,812	282,812	276,413	(6,399)	-2%
Science &Technology Directorate (S&T)	1,006,471	1,006,471	1,176,432	169,961	17%
Domestic Nuclear Detection Office (DNDO)	383,037	383,037	331,738	(51,299)	-13%
TOTAL BUDGET AUTHORITY:	$ 56,169,614	$ 55,728,760	$ 56,983,449	$ 1,254,689	2.25%
Mandatory, Fee, and Trust Funds	(10,179,438)	$ (9,697,347)	$ (9,578,910)	$ 118,437	-1.22%
Discretionary Offsetting Fees	(3,533,561)	(3,442,780)	(4,180,357)	(737,577)	21%
NET DISC. BUDGET AUTHORITY:	$ 42,456,615	$ 42,588,633	$ 43,224,182	$ 635,549	-
Less Rescission of Prior-Year Carryover - Regular Appropriations: [4]	(151,582)	(40,474)	(41,942)	-	0%
ADJUSTED NET DISC. BUDGET AUTHORITY:	$ 42,305,033	$ 42,548,159	$ 43,182,240	$ 634,081	1%
SUPPLEMENTAL: [5]	$ 5,865,603	-	-	-	-

Figure A-10: FY12 DHS Budget Allocation

FY13, Oct 12 - Sep 13

Janet Napolitano, Secretary

Title: Department of Homeland Security Budget in Brief

"The FY 2013 Budget for DHS is $59.0 billion in total budget authority, $48.7 billion in gross discretionary funding, and $39.5 billion in net discretionary funding. Net discretionary budget authority is 0.5 percent below the FY 2012 enacted level. An additional $5.5 billion for the Disaster Relief Fund (DRF) is provided separately, pursuant to the Budget Control Act of 2011 (BCA). Ten years after the September 11th attacks, America is stronger and more secure today, thanks to the strong support of the President; Congress; the work of the men and women of the Department of Homeland Security (DHS) and local, State and Federal partners across the homeland security enterprise. While we have made significant progress, threats from terrorism – including, but not limited to al-Qaeda and al-Qaeda related groups – persist and continually evolve, and the demands on DHS continue to grow."

	FY 2011 Enacted [1]	FY 2012 Enacted [2]	FY 2013 President's Budget	FY 2013 +/- FY 2012	FY 2013 +/- FY 2012
	$000	$000	$000	$000	%
Departmental Operations [3]	$ 839,292	$ 802,885	$ 812,978	$ 10,093	1%
Analysis and Operations (A&O)	334,360	338,068	321,982	(16,086)	-5%
Office of the Inspector General (OIG)	129,614	141,000	143,664	2,664	2%
U.S. Customs & Border Protection (CBP)	11,245,410	11,737,569	11,979,454	241,885	2%
U.S. Immigration & Customs Enforcement (ICE)	5,805,420	5,862,453	5,644,061	(218,392)	-4%
Transportation Security Administration (TSA)	7,687,552	7,841,019	7,644,585	(196,434)	-3%
U.S. Coast Guard (USCG)	10,193,685	10,348,886	9,966,651	(382,235)	-4%
U.S. Secret Service (USSS)	1,755,299	1,911,617	1,850,863	(60,754)	-3%
National Protection and Programs Directorate (NPPD)	2,331,197	2,531,339	2,518,778	(12,561)	0%
Office of Health Affairs (OHA)	139,455	167,449	166,458	(991)	-1%
Federal Emergency Management Agency (FEMA)	7,073,862	11,549,247	10,659,504	(889,743)	-8%
FEMA: Grant Programs	3,372,741	2,374,681	2,900,212	525,531	0%
U.S. Citizenship & Immigration Services (USCIS)	2,983,422	3,078,465	3,005,383	(73,082)	-2%
Federal Law Enforcement Training Center (FLETC)	270,832	271,413	258,324	(13,089)	-5%
Science &Technology Directorate (S&T)	827,578	668,000	831,472	163,472	24%
Domestic Nuclear Detection Office (DNDO)	341,744	290,000	327,977	37,977	13%
TOTAL BUDGET AUTHORITY:	$ 55,331,462	$ 59,914,091	$ 59,032,346	$ (881,745)	-1.47%
Mandatory, Fee, and Trust Funds	(9,682,503)	$ (10,118,541)	$ (10,333,516)	$ (214,975)	2.12%
Discretionary Offsetting Fees	(3,442,780)	(3,547,405)	(3,756,720)	(209,315)	6%
NET DISC. BUDGET AUTHORITY:	$ 42,206,179	$ 46,248,145	$ 44,942,110	$ (1,306,035)	-
Less Rescission of Prior-Year Carryover - Regular Appropriations: [4]	(524,185)	(200,736)	-	-	0%
ADJUSTED NET DISC. BUDGET AUTHORITY:	$ 41,681,994	$ 46,047,409	$ 44,942,110	$ (1,105,299)	-2%
Supplemental: [5]	-	-	-	-	-

Figure A-11: FY13 DHS Budget Allocation

FY14, Oct 13 - Sep 14

Janet Napolitano, Secretary

Title: Department of Homeland Security Budget in Brief

"The FY 2014 Budget for DHS is $60.0 billion in total budget authority, $48.5 billion in gross discretionary funding, and $39.0 billion in net discretionary funding. An additional $5.6 billion for the Disaster Relief Fund (DRF) is provided separately, pursuant to the Budget Control Act of 2011 (BCA). This year marks the 10th anniversary of the creation of the Department of Homeland Security (DHS), the largest reorganization of the U.S. Government since the formation of the Department of Defense (DOD). After 10 years of effort, DHS has transformed 22 agencies from across the Federal Government into a single integrated Department, building a strengthened homeland security enterprise and a more secure America better equipped to confront the range of threats we face."

	FY 2012 Revised Enacted [1]	FY 2013 Annualized CR [2]	FY 2014 Pres. Budget [3]	FY 2014 +/- FY 2012	FY 14 +/- FY 12
	$000	$000	$000	$000	%
Departmental Operations [4]	$ 804,136	$ 802,768	$ 810,773	$ 6,637	1%
Analysis and Operations (A&O)	338,068	339,957	309,228	(28,840)	-8%
Office of the Inspector General (OIG)	141,000	141,863	143,309	2,309	2%
U.S. Customs & Border Protection (CBP)	11,781,438	11,863,849	12,900,103	1,118,665	9%
U.S. Immigration & Customs Enforcement (ICE)	5,982,977	5,878,209	5,341,722	(641,255)	-11%
Transportation Security Administration (TSA)	7,855,938	7,910,532	7,398,295	(457,643)	-6%
U.S. Coast Guard (USCG)	10,422,410	10,497,057	9,793,981	(628,429)	-6%
U.S. Secret Service (USSS)	1,914,445	1,920,706	1,801,389	(113,056)	-6%
National Protection and Programs Directorate (NPPD)	2,525,688	2,804,087	2,568,543	42,855	2%
Office of Health Affairs (OHA)	165,049	168,356	131,797	(33,252)	-20%
Federal Emergency Management Agency (FEMA)	11,638,525	11,867,560	11,327,685	(310,840)	-3%
FEMA: Grant Programs	2,285,403	2,308,826	2,123,200	(162,203)	-7%
U.S. Citizenship & Immigration Services (USCIS)	3,078,465	3,077,782	3,219,466	141,001	5%
Federal Law Enforcement Training Center (FLETC)	271,413	272,703	271,429	16	0%
Science &Technology Directorate (S&T)	673,000	671,807	1,527,096	854,096	127%
Domestic Nuclear Detection Office (DNDO)	290,000	290,695	291,320	1,320	0%
TOTAL BUDGET AUTHORITY:	$ 60,167,956	$ 60,816,756	$ 59,959,337	$ (208,619)	-0.34%
Less: Mandatory, Fee, and Trust Funds	10,271,646	$ 10,616,486	$ 11,501,970	$ 1,230,324	11.59%
Less: Discretionary Offsetting Fees	3,515,166	3,639,720	3,785,021	269,855	7%
NET DISC. BUDGET AUTHORITY:	$ 46,381,144	$ 46,560,550	$ 44,672,346	$ (1,708,798)	-
Less Rescission of Prior-Year Carryover - Regular Appropriations: [5]	(196,468)	(131,412)	-	-	-
ADJUSTED NET DISC. BUDGET AUTHORITY:	$ 46,184,675	$ 46,429,138	$ 44,672,346	$ (1,512,329)	-3%
Supplemental: [6]	-	$ 12,071,908	-	-	-

Figure A-12: FY14 DHS Budget Allocation

FY15, Oct 14 - Sep 15

Jeh Johnson, Secretary

Title: Department of Homeland Security Budget in Brief

"The FY 2015 Budget for DHS is $60.9 billion in total budget authority, $49.0 billion in gross discretionary funding, $38.2 billion in net discretionary funding, and $4.4 billion in discretionary fees. As part of total DHS funding, $6.4 billion for the Disaster Relief Fund (DRF) is provided separately from discretionary amounts, pursuant to the Budget Control Act of 2011 (BCA). The Budget focuses resources on key capabilities in each of the Department's mission areas. The basic missions of the Department of Homeland Security are preventing terrorism and enhancing security; securing and managing our borders; enforcing and administering our immigration laws; safeguarding and securing cyberspace; and, preparing for and responding to disasters. In addition, the Department's request also includes proposals for funding a portion of the Federal Emergency Management Agency's (FEMA) and National Protection and Programs Directorate's (NPPD) activities through the President's Opportunity, Growth, and Security Initiative."

	FY 2013 Revised Enacted[1]	FY 2014 Enacted[2]	FY 2015 Pres. Budget[3]	FY 2015 +/- FY 2014	FY 2015 +/- FY 2014
	$000	$000	$000	$000	%
Departmental Operations[4]	$ 708,695	$ 728,269	$ 748,024	$ 19,755	2.7%
Analysis and Operations (A&O)	301,853	300,490	302,268	1,778	0.6%
Office of the Inspector General (OIG)	137,910	139,437	145,457	6,020	4.3%
U.S. Customs & Border Protection (CBP)	11,736,990	12,445,616	12,764,835	319,219	2.6%
U.S. Immigration & Customs Enforcement (ICE)	5,627,660	5,614,361	5,359,065	(255,296)	-4.5%
Transportation Security Administration (TSA)	7,193,757	7,364,510	7,305,098	(59,412)	-0.8%
U.S. Coast Guard (USCG)	9,972,425	10,214,999	9,796,995	(418,004)	-4.1%
U.S. Secret Service (USSS)	1,808,313	1,840,272	1,895,905	55,633	3.0%
National Protection and Programs Directorate (NPPD)	2,638,634	2,813,213	2,857,666	44,453	1.6%
Office of Health Affairs (OHA)	126,324	126,763	125,767	(996)	-0.8%
Federal Emergency Management Agency (FEMA)	11,865,196	11,553,899	12,496,517	942,618	8.2%
FEMA: Grant Programs	2,373,540	2,530,000	2,225,469	(304,531)	-12.0%
U.S. Citizenship & Immigration Services (USCIS)	3,378,348	3,219,142	3,259,885	40,743	1.3%
Federal Law Enforcement Training Center (FLETC)	243,111	258,730	259,595	865	0.3%
Science &Technology Directorate (S&T)	794,227	1,220,212	1,071,818	(148,394)	-12.2%
Domestic Nuclear Detection Office (DNDO)	302,981	285,255	304,423	19,168	6.7%
TOTAL BUDGET AUTHORITY:	$ 59,209,964	$ 60,655,168	$ 60,918,787	$ 263,619	0.4%
Less: Mandatory, Fee, and Trust Funds:	(11,308,307)	(11,526,210)	(11,890,496)	(364,286)	3.2%
GROSS DISC. BUDGET AUTHORITY:	47,901,657	49,128,958	49,028,291	(100,667)	-0.2%
Less: Discretionary Offsetting Fees:	(3,553,282)	(3,733,428)	(4,414,798)	(681,370)	18.3%
NET DISC. BUDGET AUTHORITY:	$ 44,348,375	$ 45,395,530	$ 44,613,493	$ (782,037)	-1.7%
Less: FEMA Disaster Relief - Major Disasters Cap Adjustment:	$ (6,075,554)	$ (5,626,386)	$ (6,437,793)	$ (811,407)	14.4%
Less: Rescission of Prior-Year Carryover - Regular Appropriations:[5]	(151,463)	(543,968)	-	543,968	-100.0%
ADJUSTED NET DISC. BUDGET AUTHORITY:	$ 38,121,358	$ 39,225,176	$ 38,175,700	$ (1,049,476)	-2.7%
Supplemental:[6]	$ 11,483,313	-	-	-	-

Figure A-13: FY15 DHS Budget Allocation

FY16, Oct 15 - Sep 16

Jeh Johnson, Secretary

Title: Department of Homeland Security Budget in Brief

"The FY 2016 Budget for DHS is $64.9 billion in total budget authority, $51.9 billion in gross discretionary funding, $41.2 billion in net discretionary funding, and $4.0 billion in discretionary fees. As part of total DHS funding, $6.7 billion for the Disaster Relief Fund (DRF) is provided separately from discretionary amounts, pursuant to the Budget Control Act of 2011. The Budget focuses resources on key capabilities in each of the Department's mission areas: prevent terrorism and enhance security, secure and manage our borders, enforce and administer our immigration laws, safeguard and secure cyberspace, and strengthen national preparedness and resilience."

	FY 2014 Revised Enacted	FY 2015 Pres. Budget	FY 2016 Pres. Budget	FY 2016 +/- FY 2015	FY 2016 +/- FY 2015
	$000	$000	$000	$000	%
Departmental Management and Operations (DMO)	$ 728,269	$ 748,024	$ 960,627	$ 212,603	28.4%
Analysis and Operations (A&O)	300,490	302,268	269,090	(33,178)	-11.0%
Office of the Inspector General (OIG)	139,437	145,457	166,284	20,827	14.3%
U.S. Customs & Border Protection (CBP)	12,463,893	12,764,835	13,565,294	800,459	6.3%
U.S. Immigration & Customs Enforcement (ICE)	5,948,161	5,359,065	6,281,637	922,572	17.2%
Transportation Security Administration (TSA)	7,420,517	7,305,098	7,346,924	41,826	0.6%
U.S. Coast Guard (USCG)	10,098,753	9,810,468	9,963,914	153,446	1.6%
U.S. Secret Service (USSS)	1,845,272	1,895,905	2,204,122	308,217	16.3%
National Protection and Programs Directorate (NPPD)	2,810,413	2,857,666	3,102,862	245,196	8.6%
Office of Health Affairs (OHA)	126,763	125,767	124,069	(1,698)	-1.4%
Federal Emergency Management Agency (FEMA)	10,869,247	12,179,177	13,235,589	1,056,412	8.7%
FEMA: Grant Programs	2,530,000	2,225,469	2,231,424	5,955	0.3%
U.S. Citizenship & Immigration Services (USCIS)	3,368,805	3,770,026	4,003,638	233,612	6.2%
Federal Law Enforcement Training Center (FLETC)	258,730	259,595	266,694	7,099	2.7%
Science & Technology Directorate (S&T)	1,220,212	1,071,818	778,988	(292,830)	-27.3%
Domestic Nuclear Detection Office (DNDO)	288,055	304,423	357,327	52,904	17.4%
TOTAL BUDGET AUTHORITY:	$ 60,417,017	$ 61,125,061	$ 64,858,484	$ 3,733,423	6.1%
Less: Mandatory, Fee, and Trust Funds:	(10,826,987)	(11,987,538)	(12,909,477)	(921,939)	7.7%
GROSS DISC. BUDGET AUTHORITY:	49,590,030	49,137,523	51,949,007	2,811,484	5.7%
Less: Discretionary Offsetting Fees:	(3,526,605)	(4,505,990)	(4,042,340)	463,650	-10.3%
NET DISC. BUDGET AUTHORITY:	$ 46,063,425	$ 44,631,533	$ 47,906,667	$ 3,275,134	7.3%
Less: FEMA Disaster Relief - Major Disasters Cap Adjustment:	$ (5,626,386)	$ (6,437,793)	$ (6,712,953)	$ (275,160)	4.3%
Less: Rescission of Prior-Year Carryover - Regular Appropriations:	(543,968)			-	
ADJUSTED NET DISC. BUDGET AUTHORITY:	$ 39,893,071	$ 38,193,740	$ 41,193,714	$ 2,999,974	7.9%

Figure A-14: FY16 DHS Budget Allocation

Appendix B: Glossary

2SR Second Stage Review

AAO Administrative Appeals Office

AAR Association of American Railroads

AASHTO American Association of State and Highway Transportation Officials

ABSTP Arizona Border Surveillance Technology Plan

AC Active Component

ACARS Aircraft Communications Addressing and Reporting System

ACE Automated Customs Environment

ACFD Arlington County Fire Department

ACPD Arlington County Police Department

ACS American Community Survey

ACS Automated Customs System

ACWIA American Competitiveness and Workforce Improvement Act

ADAC Arctic Domain Awareness Center of Excellence

ADS-B Automatic Dependent Surveillance - Broadcast

AEER Air Entry and Exit Re - Engineering

AFDX Avionics Full Duplex Switched Ethernet

AFNORTH Air Force North

AIT Advanced Imaging Technology

ALERT Center of Excellence for Awareness and Localization of Explosives-Related Threats

AMOC Air and Marine Operations Center

AMOSS Air and Marine Operations Surveillance System

AMRA Aviation Model Risk Assessment

AMVER Automated Mutual Assistance Vessel Rescue

ANA Afghan National Army

ANG Air National Guard

AOR Area of Responsibility

AP/DNSA Assistant to the President and Deputy National Security Advisor

APHIS Animal and Plant Health Inspection Service

APIS Advance Passenger Information System

APSS Agent Portable Surveillance System

APTA American Public Transportation Association

ARNG Army National Guard

ARNORTH Army North

ASME American Society of Mechanical Engineers

ATC Air Traffic Control

ATON Aids to Navigation

ATR Automated Targeting Recognition

ATS Air Transportation System

ATSA Aviation and Transportation Security Act

ATS-C Advance Targeting System - Cargo

AVC Arms Control Verification and Compliance

AWWA American Water Works Association

BASE Baseline Assessment and Security Enhancement

BDO Behavior Detection Officer

BEAP Border Enforcement Analytics Program

BEST Border Enforcement Security Task Force

BTRA Biological Terrorism Risk Assessment

BTS Border and Transportation Security

BUR Bottom - Up Review

C3 Cyber Crimes Center

CAARS Cargo Advanced Automatic Radiography

CAMRA Center for Advancing Microbial Risk Assessment

CAO Chief Administrative Officer

CAP Criminal Alien Program

CAP Civil Assistance Plan

CAPPS Computer Assisted Passenger Prescreening System

CAPTA Costing Asset Protection Guide

CARMA Cyber Assessment Risk Management Approach

CBP Customs and Border Protection

CBRN Chemical, Biological, Radiological, and Nuclear

CBTIR Center for Borders, Trade, and Immigration Research

CCEU Counterterrorism and Criminal Exploitation Unit

CCTG CBRN Counterterrorism Group

CD Army Deputy Commander

CDP Center for Domestic Preparedness

CDS Capability Development Support

CEIU Child Exploitation Investigations Unit

CEM Comprehensive Emergency Management

CERT Community Emergency Response Teams

CFO Chief Financial Officer

CFR Code of Federal Regulations

CG Comptroller General

CHC Coastal Hazards Center of Excellence

CHEMTREC Chemical Transportation Emergency Center

CI Counterintelligence

CIA Catastrophic Incident Annex

CIA Central Intelligence Agency

CIKR Critical Infrastructure and Key Resources

CINT Chief of Intelligence

CIO Chief Information Officer

CIP Common Intelligence Picture

CIR Comprehensive Immigration Reform

CIRG Critical Incident Response Group

CIRI Critical Infrastructure Resilience Institute

CISO Chief Information Security Officer

CM Consequence Management

CMF Cyber Mission Force

CMT Combat Mission Team

CNCI Comprehensive National Cybersecurity Initiative

CNGB Chief of the National Guard Bureau

COAC Committee on Commercial Operations of U.S. Customs and Border Protection

COCOM Combatant Command

COINTELPRO Counterintelligence Program

COM Chief of Mission

COMINT Communications Intelligence

COTP Captain of the Port

COTS Commercial - Off-The-Shelf

CP Counterproliferation

CPB Coastal Patrol Boat

CPI Counter - Proliferation Investigations

CPRC Counterproliferation Program Review Committee

CPS Current Population Survey

CPT Cyber Protection Team

CRC Coastal Resilience Center of Excellence

CRS Congressional Research Service

CS&C Office of Cybersecurity and Communications

CSD Customer Service Division

CSG Counterterrorism Security Group

CSI Container Security Initiative

CSS Coastal Surveillance System

CSSP Control Systems Security Program

CST Civil Support Team

C-TPAT Customs - Trade Partnership Against Terrorism

CTRA Chemical Terrorism Risk Assessment

CTS Counterterrorism Section

CVADA Center for Visualization and Data Analytics

CWMD Combat Weapons of Mass Destruction

CXPST Cross - Plane Session Termination

D/NCS Director of the National Clandestine Service

D2P Detect - to-Protect

DACA Deferred Action for Childhood Arrivals

DARPA Defense Advanced Research Projects Agency

DC Deputies Committee

DCE Defense Coordinating Element

DCI Director of Central Intelligence

DCO Defense Coordinating Officer

DDoS Distributed Denial of Service

DEA Drug Enforcement Administration

DEST Domestic Emergency Support Team

DETER Defense Technology Experimental Research

DHHS Department of Health and Human Services

DHS Department of Homeland Security

DHS IE DHS Intelligence Enterprise

DI Directorate of Intelligence

DIA Defense Intelligence Agency

DIOG Domestic Investigations and Operations Guide

DNDO Domestic Nuclear Detection Office

DNI Director of National Intelligence

DNS Domain Name Service

DOC Department of Commerce

DoD Department of Defense

DoDD Department of Defense Directive

DoE Department of Energy

DOI Department of the Interior

DoJ Department of Justice

DoS Department of State

DOT Department of Transportation

DPS Defense Protective Service

DSC Dual - Status Commander

DSCA Defense Support of Civil Authorities

DSF Deployable Specialized Force

DSL Digital Service Link

DST Direct Support Team

DT Directorate for MASINT and Technical Collection

DTRA Defense Threat Reduction Agency

ECC Emergency Communications Center

ECIP Enhanced Critical Infrastructure Protection

ECSP Exceptional Case Study Project

EDC Explosive Detection Canine

EDGE Enhanced Dynamic Geo - Social Environment

EECC Export Enforcement Coordination Center

EEO Equal Employment Opportunity

EEZ Economic Exclusion Zone

EEZ Exclusive Economic Zone

EFB Electronic Flight Bag

ELINT Electronic Intelligence

ELIS Electronic Immigration System

EM Emergency Manager

EMAC Emergency Management Assistance Compact

EMI Emergency Management Institute

EMP Electromagnetic Pulse

EMS Emergency Medical Service

EMS Emergency Medical Services

EMS Enterprise & Mission Support

EO Executive Order

EOC Emergency Operations Center

EOIR Executive Office for Immigration Review

EOP Executive Office of the President

EPA Environmental Protection Agency

EPLO Emergency Preparedness Liaison Officer

EPMO Enterprise Performance Management Office

EPR Emergency Preparedness and Response

EPS Executive Protection Service

ERO Enforcement and Removal Operations

ESF Emergency Support Function

ESU Emergency Service Units

E-Verify Electronic Employment Eligibility Verification

EXBS Export Control and Border Security

FAA Federal Aviation Administration

FAM Federal Air Marshal

FBI Federal Bureau of Investigation

FCC Functional Combatant Command

FCO Federal Coordinating Officer

FDNS Office of Fraud Detection and National Security

FDNS Fraud Detection and National Security Directorate

FDNY Fired Department New York

FDRC Federal Disaster Recovery Coordinator

FEMA Federal Emergency Management Agency

FHWA Federal Highway Administration

FIG Field Intelligence Group

FINDER Finding Individuals for Disaster and Emergency Response

FISA Foreign Intelligence Surveillance Act

FISC Foreign Intelligence Surveillance Court

FISINT Foreign Instrumentation Signals Intelligence

FLETC Federal Law Enforcement Training Center

FMCSA Federal Motor Carrier Safety Administration

FMD Foot - and-Mouth Disease

FMSC Federal Maritime Security Coordinator

FNR Federal Network Resilience

FOIA Freedom of Information Act

FOSC Federal On - Scene Coordinator

FPDI Food Protection and Defense Institute

FPS Federal Protective Service

FRA Federal Railroad Administration

FRC Fast Response Cutter

FRG First Responders Group

FTA Federal Transit Administration

FY Fiscal Year

G8 Group of Eight

GAO Government Accountability Office

GCC Geographic Combatant Command

GDP Grant Programs Directorate

GEOINT Geospatial Intelligence

GII Geospatial Information Infrastructure

GMCC Global MOTR Coordination Center

GMRA Government Management Reform Act

GPC General - Purpose Controller

GPRA Government Performance and Results Act

GPS Global Positioning System

HAZMAT Hazardous Material

HD Homeland Defense

HEU Highly Enriched Uranium

HIIB Homeland Security Council's Integrated Intelligence Board

HIR Homeland Intelligence Report

HIS Homeland Security Investigations

HITRAC Homeland Infrastructure Threat and Risk Analysis Center

HM-232 Hazardous Materials Transportation Security Requirements

HMC Highway Infrastructure and Motor Carrier

HME Homemade Explosive Device

HRF Homeland Response Force

HSARPA Homeland Security Advanced Research Projects Agency

HSAS Homeland Security Advisory System

HSC Homeland Security Council

HSDN Homeland Secure Data Network

HSEC SIN Homeland Security Standing Information Needs

HSEEP Homeland Security Exercise and Evaluation Program

HSIC Homeland Security Intelligence Council

HSI-FL Homeland Security Investigations' Forensic Laboratory

HSIN Homeland Security Information Network

HSINT Homeland Security Intelligence

HSPD Homeland Security Presidential Directive

HS-SLIC Homeland Security State and Local Intelligence Community of Interest

HSSTAC Homeland Security Science and Technology Advisory Committee

HSTA Homeland Security Threat Assessment

HTUA High Threat Urban Area

HUD Housing and Urban Development

HUMINT Human Intelligence

HUMS Health and Usage Monitoring System

I&A Information and Analysis

I&A Intelligence and Analysis

IA Office of Internal Affairs

IA&IP Information Analysis & Infrastructure Protection

IANA Internet Assigned Numbers Authority

IAP Incident Action Plan

IASD Infrastructure Analysis and Strategy Division

IBSGP Intercity Bus Security Grant Program

IC Intelligence Community

IC Incident Commander

ICAC Internet Crimes Against Children

ICAD Integrated Computer Assisted Detection

ICANN Internet Corporation for Assigned Names and Numbers

ICC Intelligence Coordination Center

ICE Immigration and Customs Enforcement

ICP Incident Command Post

ICPD Individual and Community Preparedness Division

ICPO International Cooperative Programs Office

ICS Incident Command System

ICS Industrial Control System

ICS-CERT Industrial Control System Cyber Emergency Response Team

ICSJWG Industrial Control System Joint Working Group

ICW Intercostal Waterway

IDENT Automated Biometric Identification System

IED Improvised Explosive Device

IEFA Immigration Examination Fee Account

IFCL-HTS Inherently Fault Current Limiting, High Temperature Superconducting Cable

IFE Inflight Entertainment System

IG Inspector General

IICD Infrastructure Information Collection Division

IICS infrastructure Information Collection System

IIR Intelligence Information Report

IIRIRA Immigration Reform and Immigrant Responsibility Act

IMAGE Mutual Agreement Between Government and Employers

IMAT Incident Management Assistance Team

IMF International Monetary Fund

IMINT Imagery Intelligence

IMO International Maritime Organization

INA Immigration and Nationality Act

INA Office of International Affairs

INA Immigration Nationality Act

IND Improvised Nuclear Device

INR Bureau of Intelligence and Research, Department of State

INS Immigration and Naturalization Service

IP Infrastructure Protection

IPA Intergovernmental Personnel Act

IPAS Illicit Pathways Attack Strategy

IPAWS Integrated Public Alert and Warning System

IPC Interagency Policy Committee

IRA Immediate Response Authority

IRCA Immigration Reform and Control Act

IS Islamic State

ISAC Information Sharing and Analysis Center

ISAF International Security Assistance Force

ISE Information Sharing Environment

ISI Inter-Services Intelligence

ISN Bureau of International Security and Nonproliferation

ISP Internet Service Provider

ISR Intelligence, Surveillance, and Reconnaissance

IST Incident Support Team

ISTEP Intermodal Security Training and Exercise Program

IT Information Technology

ITRA Integrated Terrorism Risk Assessment

ITSRA IT Sector Baseline Risk Assessment

IT-SSP IT Sector Specific Plan

IXP Internet Exchange Point

JCS Joint Chiefs of Staff

JFHQ Joint Force Headquarters

JFHQ-NCR Joint Force Headquarters National Capital Region

JFO Joint Field Office

JIACG Joint Interagency Coordination Group

JIC Joint Information Center

JIICATAS911 Joint Inquiry into Intelligence Community Activities Before and After the Terrorist Attacks of September 11, 2001

JOC Joint Operations Centers

JOC Joint Operations Center

JRC Joint Requirements Council

JTAC Joint Terminal Attack Controller

JTF Joint Task Force

JTF-AK Joint Task Force Alaska

JTF-CS Joint Task Force Civil Support

JTF-N Joint Task Force North

JTTF Joint Terrorism Task Force

KIQ Key Intelligence Questions

KSM Khalid Sheikh Mohammed

LA Lead Agency

LAX Lost Angeles International Airport

LBRAA Long - Range Broad Agency Announcement

LEDET Law Enforcement Detachment

LEP Limited English Proficiency

LETC Law Enforcement Technical Collections

LNO Liaison Officer

LP Latent Print

LPR Legal Permanent Resident

LPR Lawful Permanent Resident

LRS Long Range Surveillance

M&A Management and Administration

MA Mission Assignment

MAA Mutual Aid Agreement

MAK Maktab al - Khidamat

MANPADS Man -Portable Air Defense System

MARFORNORTH Marine Forces North

MASINT Measurement and Signatures Intelligence

MCV Mobile Command Vehicle

MDW Military District of Washington

MIREES Center for Maritime, Island and Remote and Extreme Environment Security

MOTR Maritime Operational Threat Response

MRR Medium Range Response

MS Mission Support

MSC Maritime Security Center of Excellence

MSD Marine Safety Detachment

MSRT Maritime Security Response Team

MSST Maritime Safety and Security Team

MSS-U Mobile Surveillance System Upgrade

MSU Marine Safety Unit

MTB Mobile Training Branch

MTS Maritime Transportation System

MTSA Maritime Transportation Safety Act

MVSS Mobile Vehicle Surveillance System

MWAA Metropolitan Washington Airports Authority

NAC Nebraska Avenue Complex

NAC National Advisory Council

NADB National Asset Database

NAS National Airspace System

NBC National Benefits Center

NBPS National Border Patrol Strategy

NCBSI National Center for Border Security and Immigration

NCCIC National Cybersecurity and Communications Integration Center

NCIPP National Critical Infrastructure Prioritization Program

NCIRP National Cyber Incident Response Plan

NCIX National Counterintelligence Executive

NCP National Continuity Programs

NCPC National Counterproliferation Center

NCRAL National Cyber Risk Alert Level

NCRS National Capital Response Squad

NCSC National Cyber Security Center

NCSD National Cyber Security Division

NCTC National Counterterrorism Center

NDAA National Defense Authorization Act

NDMS National Disaster Medical System

NED National Exercise Division

NEP National Exercise Program

NERT Nuclear Emergency Response Team

NexGen Next Generation Passenger Checkpoint

NFIP National Foreign Intelligence Program

NFOP National Fugitive Operations Program

NG National Guard

NGA National Geospatial - Intelligence Agency

NGB National Guard Bureau

NGO Non - Governmental Organization

NHSA National Homeland Security Agency

NHSD National Homeland Security Department

NIC National Integration Center

NIC National Intelligence Council

NICC National Incident Coordinating Center

NIE National Intelligence Estimate

NII Non - Intrusive Inspection

NIMS National Incident Management System

NIP National Intelligence Program

NIPP National Infrastructure Protection Plan

NISAC National Infrastructure Simulation and Analysis Center

NIST National Institute of Standards and Technology

NLE National Level Exercise

nm Nautical Mile

NMCC National Military Command Center

NME National Military Establishment

NMF National Mission Force

NMSZ New Madrid Seismic Zone

NNSA National Nuclear Security Administration

NOC National Operations Center

NORAD North American Aerospace Defense Command

NP Nonproliferation

NPAD National Preparedness Assessment Division

NPD National Preparedness Directorate

NPG National Preparedness Goal

NPM National Preparedness Month

NPPD National Protection and Program Directorate

NPRM Notice of Proposed Rule Making

NPS National Preparedness System

NPT Nonproliferation Treaty

NRCC National Response Coordination Center

NRF National Response Framework

NRO National Reconnaissance Office

NRP National Response Plan

NS/EP National Security and Emergency Preparedness

NSA National Security Agency

NSC National Security Cutter

NSC National Security Council

NSD Network Security Deployment

NSF National Strike Force

NSL National Security Letter

NSP National Strategic Plan

NSS National Security Staff

NSSE National Special Security Event

NST National Support Team

NSTA National School Transportation Association

NSTS National Security Threat Section

NSU National Security Unit

NTAC National Threat Assessment Center

NTAS National Terrorism Advisory System

NTC-C National Targeting Center - Cargo

NTE National Training & Education

NTED National Training and Education Division

NTSCOE National Transportation Security Center of Excellence

NUSTL National Urban Security Technology Laboratory

NYPD New York Police Department

OAE Office of External Affairs

OBIM Office of Biometric Identity Management

OCC National Operations Control Center

OCIA Office of Cyber and Infrastructure Analysis

OCMI Officer in Charge of Marine Inspection

OCOMM Office of Communications

ODIC Office of Disability Integration and Coordination

ODNI Office of the Director of National Intelligence

ODP Office of Domestic Preparedness

OEM Office of Emergency Management

OEP Office of Emergency Preparedness

OFO Office of Field Operations

OHS Office of Homeland Security

OI Office of Intelligence

OIC Office for Interoperability and Compatibility

OIOC Office of Intelligence and Operations Coordination

OIS Office of Immigration Statistics

OIT Office of Information Technology

OLA Office of Legislative Affairs

OMB Office of Management and Budget

OMLT Operational Mentor and Liaison Team

ONCIX Office of the National Counterintelligence Executive

ONDCP Office of National Drug Control Policy

ONL Office of National Laboratories

OOC Office of Operations Coordination

OPA Office of Public Affairs

OPC Offshore Patrol Cutter

OPPA Office of Policy and Program Analysis

ORR Office of Response and Recovery

OSC On - Scene Commander

OSI Open System Interconnection

OSINT Open Source Intelligence

OSS Office of Strategic Services

OT Office of International Trade

OTD Office of Training and Development

OTIA Office of Technology Innovation and Acquisition

P.L. Public Law

PA Primary Agency

PACER National Center for the Study of Preparedness and Catastrophic Event Response

PAPD Port Authority Police Department

PC Principals Committee

PCC Policy Coordination Committee

PCII Protected Critical Infrastructure Information

PDD Presidential Decision Directive

PED Public Engagement Division

PFO Principal Federal Official

PHMSA Pipeline Hazardous Materials Safety Administration

PID Protective Intelligence and Assessment Division

PINS Priority Information Needs

PLC Programmable Logic Controller

PLE Principal Level Exercise

PM Bureau of Political-military Affairs

PM-ISE Program Manager for the Information Sharing Environment

PMTL Protected Measures Target List

PN Partner Nation

PNP Protection and National Preparedness

PNSR Project for National Security Reform

POA Program of Analysis

POE Port of Entry

POTUS President of the United States

PPD Presidential Policy Directive

PPPM Plans, Policy, & Performance Management

PREA Prison Rape Elimination Act

PSA Protective Security Advisor

PSA Public Service Advertising

PSD Personnel Screening Detection

PSU Port Security Unit

PT-ISAC Public Transportation Information Sharing and Analysis Center

PTN Public Telecommunications Network

PWCS Ports, Waterways, and Coastal Security

QD Questioned Document

QHSR Quadrennial Homeland Security Review

QRF Quick Reaction Force

R&D Research and Development

RAIO Refugee, Asylum, and International Operations Directorate

RAMCAP Risk Analysis and Management for Critical Asset Protection

RAM-W Risk Assessment Methodology - Water

RAN Railroad Alert Network

RC Reserve Component

RDD Radiological Dispersal Device

RDL Regional Dive Locker

RDP Research and Development Partnerships

RDT&E Research, Development, Test, and Evaluation

RECONS Reusable Electronic Conveyance Security Devices

REMS Radiological Emergency Management System

RFA Request for Assistance

RMA Risk Mitigation Activity

RMF Risk Management Framework

RRAP Regional Resiliency Assessment Program

RRCC Regional Response Coordination Center

RSC Rail Security Coordinator

RSCN Rail Security Coordinator Network

RSSM Rail Security - Sensitive Materials

R-Tech First Responder Technologies

RTP Resilient Tunnel Project

RVS Remote Video Surveillance

RVSS Remote Video Surveillance System

S&T Science and Technology Directorate

SA Support Agency

SAC Special Agent - in-Charge

SAD Special Activities Division

SAD State Active Duty

SAI Security Action Item

SAR Search and Rescue

SAR Suspicious Activity Report

SAV Site Assistance Visit

SAVER System Assessment and Validation for Emergency Responders

SBA Small Business Administration

SBI Secure Border Initiative

SBIR Small Business Innovation Research

SCADA Supervisory Control and Data Acquisition

SCC Sector Coordinating Council

SCO State Coordinating Officer

SCOPS Service Center Operations Directorate

SecDef Secretary of Defense

SECIR Stakeholder Engagement and Cyber Infrastructure Resilience

SEOC State Emergency Operations Center

SEVIS Student and Exchange Visitor Information System

SEVP Student and Exchange Visitor Program

SFI Secure Freight Initiative

SGLCP State and Local Government Coordination and Preparedness

SHSGP State Homeland Security Grant Program

SHSS State Homeland Security Strategy

SIGINT Signals Intelligence

SIOC Strategic Information Operations Center

SLFC State and Local Fusion Center

SLPO State & Local Program Office

SLTT State, Local, Tribal, Territorial

SMC Search and Rescue Mission Coordinator

SMES Security and Environmental Management System

SNM Special Nuclear Material

SOF Special Operations Forces

SOP Standing Operating Procedure

SPOT Screening Passengers by Observational Techniques

SPP State Partnership Program

SPS Single Point of Service

SRIA Sandy Recovery Improvement Act

SRR Short Range Response

SSA Supervisory Special Agent

SSA Sector - Specific Agency

SSD Secret Service Division

SSP Sector Security Plan

STA Security Threat Assessments

START National Consortium for the Study of Terrorism and Response to Terrorism

ST-ISAC Surface Transportation ISAC

SWNCC State, War, Navy Coordinating Committee

T&E Test and Evaluation

TACLET Tactical Law Enforcement Team

TAG The Adjutant General

TCL Target Capabilities List

TCP Transmission Control Protocol

THD Technological Hazards Division

THIRA Threat and Hazard Identification and Risk Assessment

TIC Toxic Industrial Chemical

TIDE Terrorist Identities Datamart Environment

TIH Toxic Inhalation Hazard

TLD Top - Level Domain

TMC Thrust Management Computer

TOC Transnational Organized Crime

TPS Temporary Protected Status

TREAS Department of Treasury

TRIP Traveler Redress Inquiry Program

TRT Technical Rescue Team

TSA Transportation Security Administration

TSA-FRSD TSA Freight Rail Security Division

TSA-OI TSA Office of Intelligence

TSDP Terrorist Screening Database

TSI Transportation Security Inspector

TSL Transportation Security Laboratory

TSO Transportation Security Officer

TSSRA Transportation Systems Sector Security Risk Assessment

TSWG Transportation Sector Working Group

TTP Transition to Practice

TWIC Transportation Worker Identification Credential

UAE United Arab Emirates

UAS Unmanned Aerial System

UASI Urban Area Security Initiative

UCP Unified Command Plan

UDP User Datagram Protocol

US&R Urban Search and Rescue

USA Unites States Army

USAF United States Air Force

USAFR Unites States Air Force Reserve

USAR United States Army Reserve

USBP U.S. Border Patrol

USC United States Code

USCENTCOM United States Central Command

US-CERT U.S. Computer Emergency Readiness Team

USCG United States Coast Guard

USCIS U.S. Citizenship and Immigration Services

USDA U.S. Department of Agriculture

USFA United States Fire Administration

USG U.S. Government

USMC United States Marine Corps

USMCR United States Marine Corps Reserve

USN United States Navy

USNORTHCOM United States Northern Command

USNR United States Navy Reserve

USPACOM United States Pacific Command

USSS United States Secret Service

USSTRATCOM United States Strategic Command

UTL Universal Task List

VAL Voluntary Agency Liaison

VBIED Vehicle - borne Improvised Explosive Device

VIPR Visible Intermodal Prevention and Response

VOAD Volunteer Organizations Active in Disaster

VSAT Vulnerability Self - Assessment Tool

VSP Visa Security Program

VTS Vessel Traffic Services

VWP Visitor Waiver Program

WBI Whole Body Imaging

WCO World Customs Organization

WFO Washington Field Office

WLAN Wireless Local Area Network

WMD Weapons of Mass Destruction

WTC World Trade Center

ZADD Center of Excellence for Zoonotic and Animal Disease Defense

Appendix C: Index

C

D

E

H

I

J

K

O

P

T

Appendix D: Works Cited

Part I: Hard Lessons

Chapter 1: Turning Point

[1] Natural Resources Defense Council, "Archive of Nuclear Data," [Online]. Available: http://www.nrdc.org/nuclear/nudb/datainx.asp. [Accessed 4 August 2015].

[2] A. F. Woolf, "Nonproliferation and Threat Reduction Assistance: U.S. Programs in the Former Soviet Union," Congressional Research Service, Washington, DC, 2012.

[3] G. Bunn and J. B. Rhinelander, "Looking Back: The Nuclear Nonproliferation Treaty Then and Now," 8 July 2008. [Online]. Available: https://www.armscontrol.org/act/2008_07-08/lookingback. [Accessed 5 August 2015].

[4] Wikipedia Contributors, "Tokyo Subway Sarin Attack," Wikipedia, The Free Encyclopedia, 31 July 2015. [Online]. Available: https://en.wikipedia.org/w/index.php?title=Tokyo_subway_sarin_attack&oldid=673899076. [Accessed 3 August 2015].

[5] Wikipedia Contributors, "Sarin," Wikipedia, The Free Encyclopedia, 18 July 2015. [Online]. Available: https://en.wikipedia.org/w/index.php?title=Sarin&oldid=672034061. [Accessed 3 August 2015].

[6] Advisory Panel to Assess Domestic Response Capabilities for Terrorism Involving Weapons of Mass Destruction, "First Annual Report to The President and The Congress: Assessing the Threat," RAND Corporation, Washington, DC, 1999.

[7] United States Army Training and Doctrine Command, "Handbook No. 1.04: Terrorism and WMD," US Army TRADOC, Fort Leavenworth, KS, 2007.

[8] Homeland Security Council, "Planning Scenarios: Executive Summaries," The White House, Washington, DC, 2005.

[9] J. D. Brake, "Terrorism and the Military's Role in Domestic Crisis Management: Background and Issues for Congress," Congressional Research Service, Washington, DC, 2001.

[10] US General Accounting Office, "Combating Terrorism: Selected Challenges and Related Recommendations," GAO, Washington, DC, 2001.

[11] National Commission on Terrorism, "Report of the National Commission on Terrorism," US Congress, Washington, DC, 2000.

[12] Advisory Panel to Assess Domestic Response Capabilities for Terrorism Involving Weapons of Mass Destruction, "II. Toward A National Strategy for Combating Terrorism," RAND Corp., Washington, DC, 2000.

[13] U.S. Commission on National Security/21st Century, "Road Map for National Security: Imperative for Change," US Congress, Washington, DC, 2001.

Chapter 2: Lost Opportunities

[1] Wikipedia Contributors, "George W. Bush," Wikipedia, The Free Encyclopedia, 7 August 2015. [Online]. Available: https://en.wikipedia.org/w/index.php?title=George_W._Bush&oldid=674938412. [Accessed 8 August 2015].

[2] National Commission on Terrorist Attacks Upon the United States, "The 9/11 Commission Report," Government Printing Office, Washington, DC, 2004.

[3] Wikipedia Contributors, "Osama bin Laden," Wikipedia, The Free Encyclopedia, 5 August 2015. [Online]. Available: https://en.wikipedia.org/w/index.php?title=Osama_bin_Laden&oldid=674671389. [Accessed 8 August 2015].

[4] Wikipedia Contributors, "Soviet-Afghan War," Wikipedia, The Free Encyclopedia, 8 August 2015. [Online]. Available: https://en.wikipedia.org/w/index.php?title=Soviet%E2%80%93Afghan_War&oldid=675096642. [Accessed 8 August 2015].

[5] Wikipedia Contributors, "Taliban," Wikipedia, The Free Encyclopedia, 9 August 2015. [Online]. Available: https://en.wikipedia.org/w/index.php?title=Taliban&oldid=675255918. [Accessed 9 August 2015].

[6] Rocky Mountain Public Broadcasting Service, "Bin Laden's Fatwa," PBS NEWSHOUR, 23 August 1996. [Online]. Available: http://www.pbs.org/newshour/updates/military-july-dec96-fatwa_1996/. [Accessed 9 August 2015].

[7] Wikipedia Contributors, "Cruise Missile Strikes on Afghanistan and Sudan (August 1998)," Wikipedia, The Free Encyclopedia, 27 July 2015. [Online]. Available: https://en.wikipedia.org/w/index.php?title=Cruise_missile_strikes_on_Afghanistan_and_Sudan_(August_1998)&oldid=673297053. [Accessed 10 August 2015].

[8] Wikipedia Contributors, "2000 Millennium Attack Plots," Wikipedia, The Free Encyclopedia, 22 March 2015. [Online]. Available: https://en.wikipedia.org/w/index.php?title=2000_millennium_attack_plots&oldid=653048633. [Accessed 10 August 2015].

[9] National Commission on Terrorist Attacks Upon the United States, "Staff Statement No. 16: Outline of the 9/11 Plot," Washington, DC, 2004.

[10] Federal Bureau of Investigation Office of the Inspector General, "A Review of the FBI's Handling of Intelligence Information Related to the September 11 Attacks," FBI OIG, Washington, DC, 2006.

[11] Wikipedia Contributors, "Zacarias Moussaoui," Wikipedia, The Free Encyclopedia, 10 August 2015. [Online]. Available: https://en.wikipedia.org/w/index.php?title=Zacarias_Moussaoui&oldid=675361416. [Accessed 11 August 2015].

Chapter 3: We Have Some Planes

[1] National Commission on Terrorist Attacks Upon the United States, "The 9/11 Commission Report," US Government Printing Office, Washington, DC, 2004.

Chapter 4: And They Saved Many

[1] National Commission On Terrorist Attacks Upon the United States, "Staff Statement No. 13: Emergency Preparedness and Response," Washington, DC, 2004.

Chapter 5: Not By Chance

[1] National Commission on Terrorist Attacks Upon The United States, "Staff Statement No. 14: Crisis Management," Washington, DC, 2004.

[2] Wikipedia Contributors, "The Pentagon," Wikipedia, The Free Encyclopedia, 10 August 2015. [Online]. Available: https://en.wikipedia.org/w/index.php?title=The_Pentagon&oldid=675363116. [Accessed 14 August 2015].

[3] Titan Systems Corporation, "Arlington County After Action Report on the Response to the September 11 Terrorist Attack on the Pentagon," Titan Systems Corporation, 2002.

Chapter 6: Surpassing Disproportion

[1] D. K. Nanto, "9/11 Terrorism: Global Economic Costs," Congressional Research Service, Washington, DC, 2004.

[2] National Commission on Terrorist Attacks Upon the United States, "The 9/11 Commission Report: Executive Summary," Government Printing Office, Washington, DC, 2004.

[3] National Commission on Terrorist Attacks Upon the United States, "The 9/11 Commission Report," Government Printing Office, Washington, DC, 2004.

[4] J. D. Moteff, "Critical Infrastructures: Background, Policy, and Implementation," Congressional Research Service, Washington, DC, 2011.

[5] President's Commission on Critical Infrastructure Protection, "Critical Foundations: Protecting America's Infrastructures," Washington, DC, 1997.

[6] Wikipedia Contributors, "List of Disasters in the United States by Death Toll," Wikipedia, The Free Encyclopedia, 13 August 2015. [Online]. Available: https://en.wikipedia.org/w/index.php?title=List_of_disasters_in_the_United_States_by_death_toll&oldid=675890190. [Accessed 25 August 2015].

[7] Wikipedia Contributors, "Virginia Tech Shooting," Wikipedia, The Free Encyclopedia, 22 August 2015. [Online]. Available: https://en.wikipedia.org/w/index.php?title=Virginia_Tech_shooting&oldid=677363010. [Accessed 24 August 2015].

[8] Wikipedia Contributors, "2008 Mumbai Attacks," Wikipedia, The Free Encyclopedia, 24 August 2015. [Online]. Available: https://en.wikipedia.org/w/index.php?title=2008_Mumbai_attacks&oldid=677554005. [Accessed 24 August 2015].

[9] Police Executive Research Forum, "Critical Issues in Policing: The Police Response to Active Shooter Incidents," Police Executive Research Forum, Washington, DC, 2014.

[10] US Department of Homeland Security, "Ammonium Nitrate Security Program," [Online]. Available: http://www.dhs.gov/ammonium-nitrate-security-program. [Accessed 24 August 2015].

[11] Wikipedia Contributors, "1993 World Trade Center Bombing," Wikipedia, The Free Encyclopedia, 11 August 2015. [Online]. Available: https://en.wikipedia.org/w/index.php?title=1993_World_Trade_Center_bombing&oldid=675580375. [Accessed 25 August 2015].

[12] Wikipedia Contributors, "Atomic Bombings of Hiroshima and Nagasaki," Wikipedia, The Free Encyclopedia, 23 August 2015. [Online]. Available: https://en.wikipedia.org/w/index.php?title=Atomic_bombings_of_Hiroshima_and_Nagasaki&oldid=677529173. [Accessed 24 August 2015].

[13] Advisory Panel to Assess Domestic Response Capabilities for Terrorism Involving Weapons of Mass Destruction, "I. Assessing the Threat," RAND Corporation, Washington, DC, 1999.

[14] Wikipedia Contributors, "Chernobyl Disaster," Wikipedia, The Free Encyclopedia, 20 August 2015. [Online]. Available: https://en.wikipedia.org/w/index.php?title=Chernobyl_disaster&oldid=676938404. [Accessed 24 August 2015].

[15] Wikipedia Contributors, "Bhopal Disaster," Wikipedia, The Free Encyclopedia, 23 August 2015. [Online]. Available: https://en.wikipedia.org/w/index.php?title=Bhopal_disaster&oldid=677446793. [Accessed 24 August 2015].

[16] The White House, "The National Strategy to Secure Cyberspace," The White House, Washington, DC, 2003.

[17] Wikipedia Contributors, "1995 Chicago Heat Wave," Wikipedia, The Free Encyclopedia, 19 July 2015. [Online]. Available: https://en.wikipedia.org/w/index.php?title=1995_Chicago_heat_wave&oldid=672140319. [Accessed 29 August 2015].

[18] Wikipedia Contributors, "2003 European Heat Wave," Wikipedia, The Free Encyclopedia, 7 August 2015. [Online]. Available: https://en.wikipedia.org/w/index.php?title=2003_European_heat_wave&oldid=675050801. [Accessed 29 August 2015].

[19] The White House, "The National Strategy for the Physical Protection of Critical Infrastructure and Key Assets," The White House, Washington, DC, 2003.

[20] Wikipedia Contributors, "1986 United States Bombing of Libya," Wikipedia, The Free Encyclopedia, 27 August 2015. [Online]. Available: https://en.wikipedia.org/w/index.php?title=1986_United_States_bombing_of_Libya&oldid=678063523. [Accessed 29 August 2015].

[21] Wikipedia Contributors, "Osama bin Laden," Wikipedia, The Free Encyclopedia, 29 August 2015. [Online]. Available: https://en.wikipedia.org/w/index.php?title=Osama_bin_Laden&oldid=678395152. [Accessed 30 August 2015].

[22] Wikipedia Contributors, "FBI Most Wanted Terrorists," Wikipedia, The Free Encyclopedia, 30 August 2015. [Online]. Available: https://en.wikipedia.org/w/index.php?title=FBI_Most_Wanted_Terrorists&oldid=678604719. [Accessed 30 August 2015].

Chapter 7: Failure of Imagination

[1] National Commission on Terrorist Attacks Upon the United States, "The 9/11 Commission Report," US Government Printing Office, Washington, DC, 2004.

[2] National Commission on Terrorist Attacks Upon the United States, "Entry of the 9/11 Hijackers into the United Stats: Staff Statement No. 1," Washington, DC, 2004.

Chapter 8: Failure of Initiative

[1] Select Bipartisan Committee to Investigate the Preparation for the Response to Hurricane Katrina, "A Failure of Initiative," Government Printing Office, Washington, DC, 2006.

[2] Wikipedia Contributors, "Hurricane Katrina," Wikipedia, The Free Encyclopedia, 1 September 2015. [Online]. Available: https://en.wikipedia.org/w/index.php?title=Hurricane_Katrina&oldid=678919666. [Accessed 2 September 2015].

[3] History.Com, "Hurricane Katrina," The History Channel, [Online]. Available: http://www.history.com/topics/hurricane-katrina. [Accessed 2 September 2015].

[4] Wikipedia Contributors, "Effects of Hurricane Katrina in New Orleans," Wikipedia, The Free Encyclopedia, 25 August 2015. [Online]. Available: https://en.wikipedia.org/w/index.php?title=Effects_of_Hurricane_Katrina_in_New_Orleans&oldid=677704593. [Accessed 2 September 2015].

[5] Senate Committee on Homeland Security and Governmental Affairs, "Hurricane Katrina: A Nation Still Unprepared," Washington, DC, 2006.

[6] nola.com, "The Katrina Files," [Online]. Available: http://www.nola.com/katrina/timeline/. [Accessed 1 September 2015].

Part II: HS, DHS, & HS Enterprise

Chapter 9: Homeland Security

[1] Advisory Panel to Assess Domestic Response Capabilities for Terrorism Involving Weapons of Mass Destruction, "First Annual Report to The President and The Congress: Assessing the Threat," RAND Corporation, Washington, DC, 1999.

[2] U.S. Commission on National Security/21st Century, "Road Map for National Security: Imperative for Change," Washington, DC, 2001.

[3] Wikipedia Contributors, "U.S. Commission on National Security/21st Century," Wikipedia, The Free Encyclopedia, 6 August 2015. [Online]. Available: https://en.wikipedia.org/w/index.php?title=U.S._Commission_on_National_Security/21st_Century&oldid=674857266. [Accessed 8 September 2015].

[4] U.S. Commission on National Security/21st Century, "Seeking a National Strategy: A Concert for Preserving Security and Promoting Freedom," Washington, DC, 2000.

[5] The White House, "EO 13228: Establishing the Office of Homeland Security and the Homeland Security Council," The White House, Washington, DC, 2001.

[6] Homeland Security Council, "National Strategy for Homeland Security," Washington, DC, 2007.

[7] The White House, "National Security Strategy," Washington, DC, 2010.

[8] The White House, "National Security Strategy," The White House, Washington, DC, 2015.

[9] Department of Homeland Security, "Quadrennial Homeland Security Review Report: A Strategic Framework for a Secure Homeland," Washington, DC, 2010.

[10] Department of Homeland Security, "The 2014 Quadrennial Homeland Security Review," Department of Homeland Security, Washington, DC, 2014.

[11] US Commission on National Security/21st Century; the Hart-Rudman Commission, "New World Coming: American Security in the 21st Century," Washington, DC, 1999.

[12] National Commission on Terrorism, "Report of the National Commission on Terrorism," US Congress, Washington, DC, 2000.

[13] National Commission on Terrorist Attacks Upon the United States, "The 9/11 Commission Report," Government Printing Office, Washington, DC, 2004.

[14] The Telegraph, "Bush Gives Taliban Ultimatum," [Online]. Available: http://www.telegraph.co.uk/news/1341196/Bush-gives-Taliban-ultimatum.html. [Accessed 10 September 2015].

[15] The Guardian, "Taliban Defy Bush Ultimatum," [Online]. Available: http://www.theguardian.com/world/2001/sep/21/september11.usa15. [Accessed 10 September 2015].

[16] Wikipedia Contributors, "Taliban," Wikipedia, The Free Encyclopedia, 7 September 2015. [Online]. Available: https://en.wikipedia.org/w/index.php?title=Taliban&oldid=679837499. [Accessed 10 September 2015].

[17] Wikipedia Contributors, "War in Afghanistan (2001 - Present)," Wikipedia, The Free Encyclopedia, 4 September 2015. [Online]. Available: https://en.wikipedia.org/w/index.php?title=War_in_Afghanistan_(2001%E2%80%93present)&oldid=679372417. [Accessed 10 September 2015].

[18] Wikipedia Contributors, "Osama bin Laden," Wikipedia, The Free Encyclopedia, 7 September 2015. [Online]. Available: https://en.wikipedia.org/w/index.php?title=Osama_bin_Laden&oldid=679848439. [Accessed 10 September 2015].

[19] Wikipedia Contributors, "Zacarias Moussaoui," Wikipedia, The Free Encyclopedia, 7 September 2015. [Online]. Available: https://en.wikipedia.org/w/index.php?title=Zacarias_Moussaoui&oldid=679829362. [Accessed 10 September 2015].

[20] Wikipedia Contributors, "Khalid Sheikh Mohammed," Wikipedia, The Free Encyclopedia, 2 September 2015. [Online]. Available: https://en.wikipedia.org/w/index.php?title=Khalid_Sheikh_Mohammed&oldid=679021147. [Accessed 10 September 2015].

Chapter 10: DHS Formation

[1] National Commission on Terrorist Attacks Upon the United States, "The 9/11 Commission Report," Government Printing Office, Washington, DC, 2004.

[2] The White House, "Executive Order 13228 Establishing the Office of Homeland Security and the Homeland Security Council," Washington, DC, 2001.

[3] Scardaville, Michael, "Principles for Creating an Effective Dept. of Homeland Security," 12 June 2002. [Online]. Available: http://www.heritage.org/research/reports/2002/06/principles-for-creating-an-effective-dept-of-homeland-security. [Accessed 13 September 2015].

[4] White House Press Office, "President to Propose Department of Homeland Security," The White House, Washington, DC, 2002.

[5] CONGRESS.GOV, "H.R. 5005 - Homeland Security Act of 2002," [Online]. Available: https://www.congress.gov/bill/107th-congress/house-bill/5005. [Accessed 13 September 2015].

[6] Wikipedia Contributors, "United States Department of Homeland Security," Wikipedia, The Free Encyclopedia, 21 August 2015. [Online]. Available: https://en.wikipedia.org/w/index.php?title=United_States_Department_of_Homeland_Security&oldid=677188948. [Accessed 23 October 2004].

[7] Arms Control Center, "DHS Countdown: Play-by-Play Archive," [Online]. Available: http://www.armscontrolcenter.org/terrorism/playbyplay/archive.html. [Accessed 4 December 2004].

[8] U.S. Department of Homeland Security, "Performance and Accountability Report: Fiscal Year 2003," Department of Homeland Security, Washington, DC, 2004.

[9] The White House, "Reorganization Plan for the Department of Homeland Security," Government Printing Office, Washington, DC, 2002.

[10] U.S. Department of Homeland Security, "History: Who Became Part of the Department?," [Online]. Available: http://www.dhs.gov/dhspubli/display?theme=59&content=4081&print=true. [Accessed 7 April 2005].

[11] The White House, "The Department of Homeland Security," The White House, Washington, DC, 2002.

[12] United States Congress, "Public Law 107-296: Homeland Security Act," Washington, DC, 2002.

[13] J. Frittelli, "Transportation Security: Issues for the 109th Congress," Congressional Research Service, Washington, DC, 2005.

[14] H. C. Relyea, "Organizing for Homeland Security: The Homeland Security Council Reconsidered," Congressional Research Service, Washington, DC, 2008.

[15] J. Moteff, "Critical Infrastructures: Background, Policy, and Implementation," Congressional Research Service, Washington, DC, 2011.

Chapter 11: DHS Evolution

[1] Drucker Institute, "Peter Drucker's Life and Legacy," Drucker Institute, [Online]. Available: http://www.druckerinstitute.com/peter-druckers-life-and-legacy/. [Accessed 28 September 2015].

[2] The White House, "Executive Order 13228 Establishing the Office of Homeland Security and the Homeland Security Council," Washington, DC, 2001.

[3] Office of Homeland Security, "National Strategy for Homeland Security," The White House, Washington, DC, 2002.

[4] U.S. Department of Homeland Security, "Performance and Accountability Report: Fiscal Year 2003," Department of Homeland Security, Washington, DC, 2004.

[5] H. C. Relyea and H. B. Hogue, "Department of Homeland Security Reorganization: The 2SR Initiative," Congressional Research Service, Washington, DC, 2005.

[6] The White House, "The Department of Homeland Security," The White House, Washington, DC, 2002.

[7] General Services Administration, "U.S. Department of Homeland Security Nebraska Avenue Complex Master Plan: Draft Environmental Impact Statement," General Services Administration, Washington, DC, 2014.

[8] J. Markon, "Planned Homeland Security Headquarters, Long Delayed and Over Budget, Now in Doubt," 20 May 2014. [Online]. Available: http://www.washingtonpost.com/politics/planned-homeland-security-headquarters-long-delayed-and-over-budget-now-in-doubt/2014/05/20/d0df2580-dc42-11e3-8009-71de85b9c527_story.html. [Accessed 15 September 2015].

[9] U.S. Department of Homeland Security, "Brief Documentary History of the Department of Homeland Security," Department of Homeland Security History Office, Washington, DC, 2009.

[10] United States Congress, "Public Law 107-296: Homeland Security Act," Washington, DC, 2002.

[11] Wikipedia Contributors, "Tom Ridge," Wikipedia, The Free Encyclopedia, 8 September 2015. [Online]. Available: https://en.wikipedia.org/w/index.php?title=Tom_Ridge&oldid=679980534. [Accessed 15 September 2015].

[12] Wikipedia Contributors, "Michael Chertoff," Wikipedia, The Free Encyclopedia, 9 September 2015. [Online]. Available: https://en.wikipedia.org/w/index.php?title=Michael_Chertoff&oldid=680150200. [Accessed 15 September 2015].

[13] U.S. Department of Homeland Security, "Performance and Accountability Report: Fiscal Year 2006," Department of Homeland Security, Washington, DC, 2006.

[14] K. Bea, "Federal Emergency Management Policy Changes After Hurricane Katrina: A Summary of Statutory Provisions," Congressional Research Service, Washington, DC, 2007.

[15] Homeland Security Council, "National Strategy for Homeland Security," Washington, DC, 2007.

[16] B. W. Blanchard, "Guide to Emergency Management and Related Terms, Definitions, Concepts, Acronyms, Organizations, Programs, Guidance & Legislation," Emergency Management Institute, Emmetsburg, MD, 2008.

[17] Wikipedia Contributors, "9/11 Commission," Wikipedia, The Free Encyclopedia, 11 September 2015. [Online]. Available: https://en.wikipedia.org/w/index.php?title=9/11_Commission&oldid=680468979. [Accessed 27 September 2015].

[18] Govtrack.us, "H.R. 1 (110th): Implementing Recommendations of the 9/11 Commission Act of 2007," Govtrack.us, [Online]. Available: https://www.govtrack.us/congress/bills/110/hr1. [Accessed 27 September 2015].

[19] Public Law 110-53, "Implementing Recommendations of the 9/11 Commission Act of 2007," US Government Printing Office, Washington, DC, 2007.

[20] U.S. Department of Homeland Security, "Organization Chart," Department of Homeland Security, Washington, DC, 2008.

[21] Wikipedia Contributors, "Janet Napolitano," Wikipedia, The Free Encyclopedia, 13 August 2015. [Online]. Available: https://en.wikipedia.org/w/index.php?title=Janet_Napolitano&oldid=675914533. [Accessed 27 September 2015].

[22] U.S. Department of Homeland Security, "Bottom-Up Review Report," Department of Homeland Security, Washington, DC, 2010.

[23] U.S. Department of Homeland Security, "Quadrennial Homeland Security Review Report: A Strategic Framework for a Secure Homeland," Department of Homeland Security, Washington, DC, 2010.

[24] National Initiative for Cybersecurity Careers and Studies, "Explore Terms: A Glossary of Common Cybersecurity Terminology," [Online]. Available: https://niccs.us-cert.gov/glossary#letter_c. [Accessed 2 October 2015].

[25] President's Commission on Critical Infrastructure Protection, "Critical Foundations: Protecting America's Infrastructures," Washington, DC, 1997.

[26] The White House, "The National Strategy to Secure Cyberspace," The White House, Washington, DC, 2003.

[27] List 25, "25 Biggest Cyber Attacks in History," [Online]. Available: http://list25.com/25-biggest-cyber-attacks-in-history/. [Accessed 2 October 2015].

[28] Wikipedia Contributors, "United States Secretary of Homeland Security," Wikipedia, The Free Encyclopedia, 2 September 2015. [Online]. Available: https://en.wikipedia.org/w/index.php?title=United_States_Secretary_of_Homeland_Security&oldid=679043607. [Accessed 2 October 2015].

[29] U.S. Department of Homeland Security, "The 2014 Quadrennial Homeland Security Review," Department of Homeland Security, Washington, DC, 2014.

[30] U.S. Department of Homeland Security, "Organizational Chart," Department of Homeland Security, 13 July 2015. [Online]. Available: http://www.dhs.gov/organizational-chart. [Accessed 2 October 2015].

[31] Google, [Online]. Available: https://www.google.com/?gws_rd=ssl#q=definition+strategy. [Accessed 2 October 2015].

[32] S. S. Hsu, "Obama Combines Security Councils, Adds Offices for Computer and Pandemic Threats," 27 May 2009. [Online]. Available: http://www.washingtonpost.com/wp-dyn/content/article/2009/05/26/AR2009052603148.html. [Accessed 11 November 2011].

[33] United States Congress, "Public Law 99-433, "Goldwater-Nichols Act"," Washington, DC, 1986.

[34] The White House, "National Security Strategy," The White House, Washington, DC, 2010.

[35] The White House, "National Security Strategy," The White House, Washington, DC, 2015.

Chapter 12: DHS Progress

[1] U.S. Government Accountability Office, "Department of Homeland Security: Progress Report on Implementation of Mission and Management Functions," Government Accountability Office, Washington, DC, 2007.

[2] U.S. Government Accountability Office, "Department of Homeland Security: Progress Made and Work Remaining in Implementing Homeland Security Missions 10 Years after 9/11," Government Accountability Office, Washington, DC, 2011.

[3] U.S. Government Accountability Office, "Department of Homeland Security: Progress Made, but More Work Remains in Strengthening Management Functions," Government Accountability Office, Washington, DC, 2015.

Chapter 13: HS Enterprise

[1] U.S. Department of Homeland Security, "Quadrennial Homeland Security Review Report: A Strategic Framework for a Secure Homeland," Department of Homeland Security, Washington, DC, 2010.

Part III: Mission Areas

Chapter 14: Critical Infrastructure Protection

[1] J. D. Moteff, "Critical Infrastructures: Background, Policy, and Implementation," Congressional Research Service, Washington, DC, 2014.

[2] U.S. Department of Homeland Security, "Interim National Preparedness Goal," Washington, DC, 2005.

[3] U.S. Department of Homeland Security, "NIPP 2013: Partnering for Critical Infrastructure Security and Resilience," Department of Homeland Security, Washington, DC, 2013.

[4] U.S. Department of Homeland Security, "Progress in Developing the National Asset Database," Department of Homeland Security Office of Inspector General, Washington, DC, 2006.

[5] Public Law 110-53, "Implementing Recommendations of the 9/11 Commission Act of 2007," US Government Printing Office, Washington, DC, 2007.

[6] U.S. Government Accountability Office, "Critical Infrastructure Protection: DHS List of Priority Assets Needs to be Validated and Reported to Congress," Government Accountability Office, Washington, DC, 2013.

[7] U.S. Department of Homeland Security, "Infrastructure Protection Gateway," [Online]. Available: http://www.dhs.gov/ipgateway. [Accessed 11 October 2015].

[8] U.S. Department of Homeland Security, "Protective Security Advisors," [Online]. Available: http://www.dhs.gov/protective-security-advisors. [Accessed 11 October 2015].

[9] U.S. Government Accountability Office, "Critical Infrastructure Protection: DHS Could Better Manage Security Surveys and Vulnerability Assessments," Washington, DC, 2012.

[10] U.S. Department of Homeland Security, "Water Sector-Specific Plan," US Department of Homeland Security, Washington, DC, 2010.

[11] U.S. Department of Homeland Security, "Transportation Systems Sector-Specific Plan," US Department of Homeland Security, Washington, DC, 2010.

[12] U.S. Department of Homeland Security, "Energy Sector-Specific Plan," US Department of Homeland Security, Washington, DC, 2010.

[13] U.S. Department of Homeland Security, "National Infrastructure Protection Plan," Department of Homeland Security, Washington, DC, 2006.

[14] American Water Works Association, "RAMCAP Standard for Risk and Resilience Management of Water and Wastewater Systems," American Water Works Association, Denver, CO, 2010.

[15] U.S. Department of Homeland Security, "The National CI/KR Protection Annual Report," Department of Homeland Security, Washington, DC, 2006.

[16] United States Congress, "Government Performance and Results Act of 1993," Washington, DC, 1993.

Chapter 15: Counter WMD Strategy

[1] Wikipedia Contributors, "Geneva Conventions," Wikipedia, The Free Encyclopedia, 14 October 2015. [Online]. Available: https://en.wikipedia.org/w/index.php?title=Geneva_Conventions&oldid=685737583. [Accessed 15 October 2015].

[2] Wikipedia Contributors, "Hague Conventions of 1899 and 1907," Wikipedia, The Free Encyclopedia, 18 September 2015. [Online]. Available: https://en.wikipedia.org/w/index.php?title=Hague_Conventions_of_1899_and_1907&oldid=681668727. [Accessed 13 October 2015].

[3] Wikipedia Contributors, "Chemical Weapons in World War I," Wikipedia, The Free Encyclopedia, 8 October 2015. [Online]. Available: https://en.wikipedia.org/w/index.php?title=Chemical_weapons_in_World_War_I&oldid=684798762. [Accessed 13 October 2015].

[4] Wikipedia Contributors, "Chemical Weapons Convention," Wikipedia, The Free Encyclopedia, 14 October 2015. [Online]. Available: https://en.wikipedia.org/w/index.php?title=Chemical_Weapons_Convention&oldid=685635433. [Accessed 15 October 2015].

[5] Wikipedia Contributors, "Biological Weapons Convention," Wikipedia, The Free Encyclopedia, 18 August 2015. [Online]. Available: https://en.wikipedia.org/w/index.php?title=Biological_Weapons_Convention&oldid=676666937. [Accessed 15 October 2015].

[6] Wikipedia Contributors, "Treaty on the Nonproliferation of Nuclear Weapons," Wikipedia, The Free Encyclopedia, 8 October 2015. [Online]. Available: https://en.wikipedia.org/w/index.php?title=Treaty_on_the_Non-Proliferation_of_Nuclear_Weapons&oldid=684687461. [Accessed 15 October 2015].

[7] Counterproliferation Program Review Committee, "Report on Activities and Programs for Countering Proliferation and NBC Terrorism, Vol 1, Executive Summary," Department of Defense, Washington, DC, 2011.

[8] The White House, "National Strategy to Combat Weapons of Mass Destruction," Washington, DC, 2002.

[9] Counterproliferation Program Review Committee, "Report on Activities and Programs for Countering Proliferation of NBC Terrorism," Department of Defense, Washington, DC, 2013.

[10] U.S. Department of Defense, "DoDD 2060.02, DoD Combating WMD Policy," Department of Defense, Washington, DC, 2007.

[11] U.S. Department of Defense, "DoD Strategy for Countering Weapons of Mass Destruction," Department of Defense, Washington, DC, 2014.

[12] U.S. Department of Defense, "Unified Command Plan," [Online]. Available: http://www.defense.gov/Sites/Unified-Combatant-Commands. [Accessed 14 October 2015].

[13] National Guard Bureau, "Homeland Response Force," National Guard Bureau, Washington, DC, 2014.

[14] Chairman of the Joint Chiefs of Staff, "Joint Publication 3-40: Countering Weapons of Mass Destruction," Washington, DC, 2014.

[15] National Nuclear Security Administration, "Emergency Response," [Online]. Available: http://nnsa.energy.gov/aboutus/ourprograms/emergencyoperationscounterterrorism. [Accessed 14 October 2015].

[16] U.S. Customs and Border Protection, "Radiation Portal Monitors Safeguard America from Nuclear Devices and Radiological Materials," [Online]. Available: http://www.cbp.gov/border-security/port-entry/cargo-security/cargo-exam/rad-portal1. [Accessed 15 October 2015].

[17] Business Insider, "The Staggering Cost of the Last Decade's US War in Iraq - In Numbers," [Online]. Available: http://www.businessinsider.com/the-iraq-war-by-numbers-2014-6. [Accessed 15 October 2015].

Chapter 16: Cybersecurity

[1] Wikipedia Contributors, "List of Disasters in the United States by Death Toll," Wikipedia, The Free Encyclopedia, 8 October 2015. [Online]. Available: https://en.wikipedia.org/w/index.php?title=List_of_disasters_in_the_United_States_by_death_toll&oldid=684817383. [Accessed 15 October 2015].

[2] US-Canada Power System Outage Task Force, "Final Report on the Implementation of Task Force Recommendations," 2006.

[3] G. B. Anderson and M. L. Bell, "Lights Out: Impact of the August 2003 Power Outage on Mortality in New York, NY," Epidemiology, vol. 23, no. 2, pp. 189-193, 2012.

[4] Center for the Study of the Presidency and Congress, "Securing the US Electrical Grid," Center for the Study of the Presidency & Congress, Washington, DC, 2014.

[5] North American Electric Reliability Corporation, "High-Impact, Low-Frequency Risk to the North American Bulk Power System," 2010.

[6] Wikipedia Contributors, "Three Mile Island Accident," Wikipedia, The Free Encyclopedia, 5 October 2015. [Online]. Available: https://en.wikipedia.org/w/index.php?title=Three_Mile_Island_accident&oldid=684282213. [Accessed 15 October 2015].

[7] Wikipedia Contributors, "Chernobyl Disaster," Wikipedia, The Free Encyclopedia, 9 October 2015. [Online]. Available: https://en.wikipedia.org/w/index.php?title=Chernobyl_disaster&oldid=684924238. [Accessed 15 October 2015].

[8] Wikipedia Contributors, "Stuxnet," Wikipedia, The Free Encyclopedia, 11 October 2015. [Online]. Available: https://en.wikipedia.org/w/index.php?title=Stuxnet&oldid=685198804. [Accessed 15 October 2015].

[9] Wikipedia Contributors, "Federal Reserve System," Wikipedia, The Free Encyclopedia, 15 October 2015. [Online]. Available: https://en.wikipedia.org/w/index.php?title=Federal_Reserve_System&oldid=685935407. [Accessed 16 October 2015].

[10] U.S. Department of Homeland Security, "Explore Terms: A Glossary of Common Cybersecurity Terminology," National Initiative for Cybersecurity Careers and Studies, [Online]. Available: https://niccs.us-cert.gov/glossary#letter_d. [Accessed 16 October 2015].

[11] Rutgers University, "Internet Technology: Understanding Autonomous Systems," [Online]. Available: https://www.cs.rutgers.edu/~pxk/352/notes/autonomous_systems.html. [Accessed 14 December 2014].

[12] Akamai, "The Internet from 100,000 feet," [Online]. Available: https://developer.akamai.com/stuff/Content_Delivery/Object_Delivery.html. [Accessed 14 December 2014].

[13] DrPeering International, "Who are the Tier 1 ISPs?," [Online]. Available: http://drpeering.net/FAQ/Who-are-the-Tier-1-ISPs.php. [Accessed 14 December 2014].

[14] Wikipedia Contributors, "Tier 1 Network," 11 August 2015. [Online]. Available: https://en.wikipedia.org/w/index.php?title=Tier_1_network&oldid=675610498. [Accessed 16 October 2015].

[15] Middle East Network Operations Group, "Promoting the Use of Internet Exchange Points," 2012.

[16] Kalliola, Aapo, "Network Security: Routing Security," Aalto University, 2012.

[17] Internet Society, "Internet Ecosystem: Naming and addressing, shared global services and operations, and open standards development," 2014.

[18] Wikipedia Contributors, "Computer Fraud and Abuse Act," Wikipedia, The Free Encyclopedia, 13 October 2015. [Online]. Available: https://en.wikipedia.org/w/index.php?title=Computer_Fraud_and_Abuse_Act&oldid=685479743. [Accessed 18 October 2015].

[19] O. A. Hathaway, R. Crootof, P. Levitz, H. Nix, A. Nowlan, W. Perdue and J. Spiegel, "The Law of Cyber-Attack," California Law Review, 2012.

[20] Center for Strategic and International Studies, "Net Losses: Estimating the Global Cost of Cybercrime," McAffee, Santa Clara, CA, 2014.

[21] J. R. McCumber, "Information Systems Security: A Comprehensive Model," in Proceedings of the 14th National Computer Security Conference, 1991.

[22] R. N. Charette, "Why Software Fails," IEEE Spectrum, [Online]. Available: http://www.spectrum.ieee.or/pring/1685. [Accessed 14 January 2009].

[23] C. Simmons, C. Ellis, S. Shiva, D. Dasgupta and Q. Wu, "AVOIDIT: A Cyber Attack Taxonomy," 2009.

[24] P. L. 107-296, "Homeland Security Act of 2002," Washington, DC, 2002.

[25] The White House, "The National Strategy to Secure Cyberspace," The White House, Washington, DC, 2003.

[26] Wikipedia Contributors, "Distributed Denial-of-Service Attacks on Root Nameservers," Wikipedia, The Free Encyclopedia, 27 July 2015. [Online]. Available: https://en.wikipedia.org/w/index.php?title=Distributed_denial-of-service_attacks_on_root_nameservers&oldid=673326697. [Accessed 18 October 2015].

[27] US Department of Homeland Security, "Information Technology Sector Specific Plan," Department of Homeland Security, Washington, DC, 2010.

[28] US Department of Homeland Security, "Securing Voice and Data Systems in the Emergency Services Sector," Department of Homeland Security, Washington, DC, 2012.

[29] Transportation Sector Working Group, "Roadmap to Secure Control Systems in the Transportation Sector," Department of Homeland Security, Washington, DC, 2012.

[30] U.S. Department of Homeland Security, "Interim National Cyber Incident Response Plan," Department of Homeland Security, Washington, DC, 2010.

[31] U.S. Department of Defense, "The Department of Defense Cyber Strategy," [Online]. Available: http://www.defense.gov/News/Special-Reports/0415_Cyber-Strategy. [Accessed 19 October 2015].

[32] U.S. Department of Defense, "Mission Analysis for Cyber Operations of Department of Defense," Department of Defense, Washington, DC, 2014.

[33] J. D. Moteff, "Critical Infrastructures: Background, Policy, and Implementation," Congressional Research Service, Washington, DC, 2014.

[34] U.S. Department of Homeland Security, "White Paper: DHS Response to the NIST Cybersecurity Framework Request for Information," US Department of Homeland Security, Washington, DC, 2013.

[35] National Institute of Standards and Technology, "Framework for Improving Critical Infrastructure Cybersecurity," 2014.

Chapter 17: Counterterrorism

[1] Anti-Defamation League, "Extremism in America: The Militia Movement," [Online]. Available: http://archive.adl.org/learn/ext_us/militia_m.html. [Accessed 15 January 2016].

[2] Wikipedia Contributors, "Al-Qaeda," Wikipedia, The Free Encyclopedia, 9 January 2016. [Online]. Available: https://en.wikipedia.org/w/index.php?title=Al-Qaeda&oldid=698974736. [Accessed 15 January 2016].

[3] Wikipedia Contributors, "Islamic State of Iraq and the Levant," Wikipedia, The Free Encyclopedia, 15 January 2016. [Online]. Available: https://en.wikipedia.org/w/index.php?title=Islamic_State_of_Iraq_and_the_Levant&oldid=699999884. [Accessed 15 January 2016].

[4] The White House, "PDD-39, U.S. Policy on Counterterrorism," The White House, Washington, DC, 1995.

[5] Chairman of the Joint Chiefs of Staff, "Joint Publication 3-26: Counterterrorism," Department of Defense, Washington, DC, 2014.

[6] The White House, "National Strategy for Counterterrorism," White House, Washington, DC, 2011.

[7] The White House, "HSPD-5, Management of Domestic Incidents," The White House, Washington, DC, 2003.

[8] Bjelopera, Jerome P., "The Federal Bureau of Investigation and Terrorism Investigations," Congressional Research Service, Washington, DC, 2013.

[9] P. L. 107-296, "Homeland Security Act of 2002," Washington, DC, 2002.

[10] Randol, Mark A., "The Department of Homeland Security Intelligence Enterprise: Operational Overview and Oversight Challenges for Congress," Congressional Research Service, Washington, DC, 2010.

[11] M. J. Garcia, "Renditions: Constraints Imposed by Laws on Torture," Congressional Research Service, Washington, DC, 2009.

[12] Wikipedia Contributors, "Extraordinary Rendition," Wikipedia, The Free Encyclopedia, 12 October 2015. [Online]. Available: https://en.wikipedia.org/w/index.php?title=Extraordinary_rendition&oldid=685396385. [Accessed 3 November 2015].

[13] American Civil Liberties Union, "Fact Sheet: Extraordinary Rendition," [Online]. Available: https://www.aclu.org/fact-sheet-extraordinary-rendition. [Accessed 3 November 2015].

[14] Wikipedia Contributors, "Qaed Salim Sinan al-Harethi," Wikipedia, The Free Encyclopedia, 23 February 2015. [Online]. Available: https://en.wikipedia.org/w/index.php?title=Qaed_Salim_Sinan_al-Harethi&oldid=648479246. [Accessed 3 November 2015].

[15] R. A. Best Jr. and A. Feickert, "Special Operations Forces (SOF) and CIA Paramilitary Operations: Issues for Congress," Congressional Research Service, Washington, DC, 2009.

[16] Wikipedia Contributors, "Taliban," Wikipedia, The Free Encyclopedia, 1 November 2015. [Online]. Available: https://en.wikipedia.org/w/index.php?title=Taliban&oldid=688546297. [Accessed 4 November 2015].

[17] Wikipedia Contributors, "General Atomics MQ-1 Predator," Wikipedia, The Free Encyclopedia, 3 October 2015. [Online]. Available: https://en.wikipedia.org/w/index.php?title=General_Atomics_MQ-1_Predator&oldid=683971612. [Accessed 4 November 2015].

[18] Air Force Historical Support Division, "Operation Enduring Freedom," [Online]. Available: http://www.afhso.af.mil/topics/factsheets/factsheet.asp?id=18634. [Accessed 4 November 2015].

[19] Wikipedia Contributors, "Osama bin Laden," Wikipedia, The Free Encyclopedia, 2 November 2015. [Online]. Available: https://en.wikipedia.org/w/index.php?title=Osama_bin_Laden&oldid=688606671. [Accessed 4 November 2015].

[20] . A. Best Jr., "The National Counterterrorism Center (NCTC) - Responsibilities and Potential Congressional Concerns," Congressional Research Service, Washington, DC, 2011.

[21] The White House, "National Security Strategy," The White House, Washington, DC, 2015.

Chapter 18: Emergency Preparedness & Response

[1] Office of Homeland Security, "National Strategy for Homeland Security," The White House, Washington, DC, 2002.

[2] P. L. 107-296, "Homeland Security Act of 2002," Washington, DC, 2002.

[3] U.S. Department of Homeland Security, "History: Who Became Part of the Department?," [Online]. Available: http:// www.dhs.gov/dhspublic/display? theme=59&ontent=4081&print=true. [Accessed 7 April 2005].

[4] The White House, "HSPD-5, Management of Domestic Incidents," The White House, Washington, DC, 2003.

[5] U.S. Department of Homeland Security, "National Response Framework," Washington, DC, 2008.

[6] U.S. Department of Homeland Security, "National Response Plan," Department of Homeland Security, Washington, DC, 2004.

[7] B. R. Lindsay, "The National Response Framework: Overview and Possible Issues for Congress," 2008, Washington, DC, November.

[8] F. X. McCarthy and J. T. Brown, "Congressional Primer on Responding to Major Disasters and Emergencies," Congressional Research Service, Washington, DC, 2015.

[9] S. Maguire and S. Reese, "Department of Homeland Security Grants to State and Local Governments: FY2003 to FY2006," Congressional Research Service, Washington, DC, 2006.

[10] K. Bea, "The National Preparedness System: Issues in the 109th Congress," Congressional Research Service, Washington, DC, 2005.

[11] The White House, "PPD-8, National Preparedness," The White House, Washington, DC, 2011.

[12] U.S. Department of Homeland Security, "National Preparedness Goal," Department of Homeland Security, Washington, DC, 2011.

[13] U.S. Department of Homeland Security, "National Preparedness System," Department of Homeland Security, Washington, DC, 2011.

[14] U.S. Department of Homeland Security, "Overview of the National Planning Frameworks," Department of Homeland Security, Washington, DC, 2014.

[15] Federal Emergency Management Agency, "Information Sheet: National Preparedness Goal, Second Edition - What's New," Washington, DC, 2015.

[16] U.S. Department of Homeland Security, "Homeland Security Exercise and Evaluation Program," Department of Homeland Security, Washington, DC, 2007.

[17] U.S. Department of Homeland Security, "Homeland Security Exercise and Evaluation Program (HSEEP)," Department of Homeland Security, Washington, DC, 2013.

[18] The White House, "HSPD-8, National Preparedness," The White House, Washington, DC, 2003.

[19] E. R. Petersen, B. R. Lindsay, L. Kapp, E. C. Liu and D. R. Peterman, "Homeland Emergency Preparedness and the National Exercise Program: Background, Policy Implications, and Issues for Congress," Congressional Research Service, Washington, DC, 2008.

[20] Federal Emergency Management Agency, "National Exercise Program," Washington, DC, 2011.

[21] CNN, "National Exercise Program Fast Facts," CNN, [Online]. Available: http://www.cnn.com/2013/10/30/us/operation-topoff-national-level-exercise-fast-facts/. [Accessed 11 November 2015].

Chapter 19: Aviation Security

[1] U.S. Department of Homeland Security, "Transportation Systems Sector-Specific Plan," US Department of Homeland Security, Washington, DC, 2010.

[2] B. Elias, D. R. Peterman and J. Frittelli, "Transportation Security: Issues for the 114th Congress," Congressional Research Service, Washington, DC, 2015.

[3] Transportation Sector Working Group on Secure Control Systems, "Roadmap to Secure Control Systems in the Transportation Sector," US Department of Transportation, Washington, DC, 2012.

[4] K. Zetter, "Is It Possible for Passengers to Hack Commercial Aircraft?," 26 May 2015. [Online]. Available: http:// www.wired.com/2015/05/possible-passengers-hack-commercial-aircraft/. [Accessed 14 November 2015].

[5] D. D. P. Johnson, "Civil Aviation and Cybersecurity," Honeywell, 2013.

[6] DrPeering International, "Who are the Tier 1 ISPs?," [Online]. Available: http://drpeering.net/FAQ/Who-are-the-Tier-1-ISPs.php . [Accessed 14 December 2014].

Chapter 20: Maritime Security

[1] U.S. Department of Homeland Security, "Transportation Systems Sector-Specific Plan," US Department of Homeland Security, Washington, DC, 2010.

[2] United States Coast Guard, "CGP-3.0 Operations," United States Coast Guard, Washington, DC, 2012.

[3] United States Coast Guard, "CGP 1.0 Doctrine for the U.S. Coast Guard," United States Coast Guard, Washington, DC, 2014.

[4] B. Elias, D. R. Peterman and J. Frittelli, "Transportation Security: Issues for the 114th Congress," Congressional Research Service, Washington, DC, 2015.

Chapter 21: Surface Transportation Security

[1] U.S. Department of Homeland Security, "Transportation Systems Sector-Specific Plan," US Department of Homeland Security, Washington, DC, 2010.

[2] U.S. Department of Transportation, "Federal Transit Administration," [Online]. Available: http://www.fta.dot.gov/about/14103.html. [Accessed 19 November 2015].

[3] B. Elias, D. R. Peterman and J. Frittelli, "Transportation Security: Issues for the 114th Congress," Congressional Research Service, Washington, DC, 2015.

Chapter 22: Border Security

[1] M. R. Rosenblum, J. P. Bjelopera and K. M. Finklea, "Border Security: Understanding Threats at U.S. Borders," Congressional Research Service, Washington, DC, 2013.

[2] C. C. Haddal, "Border Security: Key Agencies and Their Missions," Congressional Research Service, Washington, DC, 2010.

[3] L. Seghetti, "Border Security: Immigration Inspections at Ports of Entry," Congressional Research Service, Washington, DC, 2015.

[4] U.S. Customs and Border Protection, "SBInet Program," Washington, DC, 2009.

[5] L. Seghetti, "Border Security: Immigration Enforcement Between Ports of Entry," Congressional Research Service, Washington, DC, 2014.

[6] A. Lipowicz, "Boeing's SBInet Contract Gets The Axe," Washington Technology, 14 January 2011. [Online]. Available: https://washingtontechnology.com/articles/2011/01/14/dhs-cancels-rest-of-sbinet-and-plans-mix-of-new-technologies-at-border.aspx. [Accessed 22 November 2015].

[7] U.S. Government Accountability Office, "Arizona Border Surveillance Technology Plan," Washington, DC, 2014.

[8] C. C. Haddal, "Border Security: The Role of the U.S. Border Patrol," Congressional Research Service, Washington, DC, 2010.

Chapter 23: Immigration Enforcement

[1] W. A. Kandel, "U.S. Immigration Policy: Chart Book of Key Trends," Congressional Research Service, Washington, DC, 2014.

Part IV: Mission Components

Chapter 24: National Protection & Programs Directorate

[1] The White House, "Reorganization Plan for the Department of Homeland Security," Government Printing Office, Washington, DC, 2002.

[2] J. D. Moteff, "Critical Infrastructures: Background, Policy, and Implementation," Congressional Research Service, Washington, DC, 2015.

[3] U.S. Department of Homeland Security, "Budget-in0-Brief; Fiscal Year 2016," Department of Homeland Security, Washington, DC, 2015.

[4] U.S. Department of Homeland Security, "NPPD Organization Chart," 12 December 2014. [Online]. Available: http://www.dhs.gov/sites/default/files/publication/nppd-or-chart-12122014.pdf. [Accessed 8 December 2015].

[5] U.S. Department of Homeland Security, "National Protection and Programs Directorate: Office of Infrastructure Protection," [Online]. Available: http://www.dhs.gov/office-infrastructure-protection. [Accessed 8 December 2015].

[6] U.S. Department of Homeland Security, "National Infrastructure Protection Plan: Partnering for Critical Infrastructure Security and Resilience," US Department of Homeland Security, Washington, DC, 2013.

[7] U.S. Department of Homeland Security, "Supplemental Tool: Connecting to the NIC and NCCIC," Washington, DC, 2015.

[8] U.S. Department of Homeland Security, "National Protection and Programs Directorate: Infrastructure Information Collection Division," [Online]. Available: http://www.dhs.gov/about-infrastructure-information-collection-division. [Accessed 8 December 2015].

[9] U.S. Department of Homeland Security, "National Protection and Programs Directorate: Office of Cybersecurity and Communications," [Online]. Available: http://www.dhs.gov/office-cybersecurity-and-communications. [Accessed 8 December 2015].

[10] W. L. Painter, J. D. Moteff, S. A. Lister, B. R. Lindsay, F. X. McCarthy and L. G. Kruger, "DHS Appropriations FY2016: Protection, Preparedness, Response, and Recovery," Congressional Research Service, Washington, DC, 2015.

[11] U.S. Department of Homeland Security, "National Protection and Programs Directorate," [Online]. Available: http://www.dhs.gov/national-protection-and-programs-directorate. [Accessed 8 December 2015].

[12] U.S. Department of Homeland Security, "National Protection and Programs Directorate: Office of Biometric Identity Management Identification Services," [Online]. Available: http://www.dhs.gov/obim-biometric-identification-services. [Accessed 8 December 2015].

[13] U.S. Department of Homeland Security, "National Protection and Programs Directorate: The Federal Protective Service," [Online]. Available: http://www.dhs.gov/topic/federal-protective-service. [Accessed 8 December 2015].

[14] U.S. Department of Homeland Security, "National Protection and Programs Directorate: Office for Bombing Prevention," [Online]. Available: http://www.dhs.gov/obp. [Accessed 8 December 2015].

Chapter 25: Science & Technology Directorate

[1] D. A. Shea, "The DHS S&T Directorate: Selected Issues for Congress," Congressional Research Service, Washington, DC, 2014.

[2] U.S. Department of Homeland Security, "About Capability Development Support," [Online]. Available: http://www.dhs.gov/science-and-technology/about-cds. [Accessed 21 January 2016].

[3] U.S. Department of Homeland Security, "S&T Organizational Chart," 22 November 2015. [Online]. Available: http://www.dhs.gov/publication/st-organizational-chart. [Accessed 21 January 2016].

[4] U.S. Department of Homeland Security, "About the First Responders Group," [Online]. Available: http://www.dhs.gov/science-and-technology/about-first-responders. [Accessed 21 January 2016].

[5] U.S. Department of Homeland Security, "About Research and Development Partnerships," [Online]. Available: http://www.dhs.gov/science-and-technology/about-research-and-development-partnerships. [Accessed 21 January 2016].

[6] U.S. Department of Homeland Security, "Homeland Security Science and Technology Advisory Committee," [Online]. Available: The Homeland Security Science and Technology Advisory Committee (HSSTAC) serves as a source of. [Accessed 21 January 2016].

[7] U.S. Department of Homeland Security, "Homeland Security Science and Technology Advisory Committee Charter," [Online]. Available: http://www.dhs.gov/science-and-technology/homeland-security-science-and-technology-advisory-committee-charter. [Accessed 21 January 2016].

[8] U.S. Department of Homeland Security, "International Cooperative Programs Office," [Online]. Available: http://www.dhs.gov/science-and-technology/st-icpo. [Accessed 21 January 2016].

[9] U.S. Department of Homeland Security, "About the Office of National Laboratories," [Online]. Available: http://www.dhs.gov/science-and-technology/office-national-laboratories. [Accessed 21 January 2016].

[10] Energy.Gov, "Department of Energy National Laboratories," [Online]. Available: http://energy.gov/maps/doe-national-laboratories. [Accessed 22 January 2016].

[11] U.S. Department of Homeland Security, "DHS InnoPrize Program - Prize Competitions," [Online]. Available: http://www.dhs.gov/science-and-technology/prize-competitions. [Accessed 21 January 2016].

[12] U.S. Department of Homeland Security, "Small Business Innovation Research Program," [Online]. Available: http://www.dhs.gov/science-and-technology/sbir. [Accessed 21 January 2016].

[13] U.S. Department of Homeland Security, "The Office of SAFETY Act Implementation," [Online]. Available: http://www.dhs.gov/science-and-technology/safety-act. [Accessed 21 January 2016].

[14] U.S. Department of Homeland Security, "Technology Transfer Program," [Online]. Available: http://www.dhs.gov/science-and-technology/technology-transfer-program. [Accessed 21 January 2016].

[15] U.S. Department of Homeland Security, "Long-Range Broad Agency Announcement," [Online]. Available: http://www.dhs.gov/science-and-technology/st-lrbaa. [Accessed 21 January 2016].

[16] U.S. Department of Homeland Security, "Welcome to the Centers of Excellence," [Online]. Available: http://www.dhs.gov/science-and-technology/centers-excellence. [Accessed 21 January 2016].

[17] U.S. Department of Homeland Security, "Office of University Programs," [Online]. Available: http://www.dhs.gov/science-and-technology/office-university-programs. [Accessed 21 January 2016].

[18] U.S. Department of Homeland Security, "Science and Technology Directorate Review 2014," Washington, DC, 2014.

Chapter 26: Domestic Nuclear Detection Office

[1] D. A. Shea, "The Global Nuclear Detection Architecture: Issues for Congress," Congressional Research Service, Washington, DC, 2009.

[2] U.S. Department of Homeland Security, "Domestic Nuclear Detection Office," [Online]. Available: http://www.dhs.gov/domestic-nuclear-detection-office. [Accessed 23 January 2016].

[3] U.S. Department of Homeland Security, "Domestic Nuclear Detection Office Organizational Chart," 8 August 2015. [Online]. Available: http://www.dhs.gov/publication/dndo-organizational-chart. [Accessed 23 January 2016].

[4] J. Medalia, "Detection of Nuclear Weapons and Materials: Science, Technologies, Observations," Congressional Research Service, Washington, DC, 2010.

Chapter 27: Intelligence & Analysis

[1] M. A. Randol, "The Department of Homeland Security Intelligence Enterprise: Operational Overview and Oversight Challenges for Congress," Congressional Research Service, Washington, DC, 2010.

[2] M. A. Randol, "The Department of Homeland Security Intelligence Enterprise: Operational Overview and Oversight Challenges for Congress," Congressional Research Service, Washington, DC, 2009.

[3] "Office of Intelligence and Analysis," [Online]. Available: http://www.dhs.gov/office-intelligence-and-analysis. [Accessed 23 January 2016].

[4] U.S. Department of Homeland Security, "Department of Homeland Security Interaction with State and Local Fusion Centers; Concept of Operations," Washington, DC, 2008.

[5] U.S. Department of Homeland Security, "Office of Intelligence and Analysis Organizational Chart," 7 June 2011. [Online]. Available: http://www.dhs.gov/publication/office-intelligence-and-analysis-organizational-chart. [Accessed 23 January 2016].

[6] M. A. Randol, "Homeland Security Intelligence: Perceptions, Statutory Definitions, and Approaches," Congressional Research Service, Washington, DC, 2009.

[7] U.S. Department of Homeland Security, "Office of Intelligence and Analysis Mission," [Online]. Available: http://www.dhs.gov/office-intelligence-and-analysis-mission. [Accessed 25 January 2016].

[8] U.S. Department of Homeland Security, "Office of Cyber & Infrastructure Analysis (OCIA)," [Online]. Available: http://www.dhs.gov/office-cyber-infrastructure-analysis. [Accessed 25 January 2016].

[9] U.S. Department of Homeland Security, "Office of Operations Coordination," [Online]. Available: http://www.dhs.gov/office-operations-coordination. [Accessed 26 January 2016].

[10] U.S. Department of Homeland Security, "National Network of Fusion Centers Fact Sheet," [Online]. Available: http://www.dhs.gov/national-network-fusion-centers-fact-sheet. [Accessed 26 January 2016].

[11] U.S. Department of Homeland Security, "National Terrorism Advisory System," [Online]. Available: http://www.dhs.gov/national-terrorism-advisory-system. [Accessed 26 January 2016].

[12] U.S. Department of Homeland Security, "Fact Sheet: Update to the National Terrorism Advisory System," [Online]. Available: http://www.dhs.gov/news/2015/12/16/update-national-terrorism-advisory-system. [Accessed 26 January 2016].

[13] U.S. Government Accountability Office, "DHS Intelligence Analysis: Additional Actions Needed to Address Analytic Priorities and Workforce Challenges," Washington, DC, 2014.

Chapter 28: FEMA

[1] Federal Emergency Management Agency, "About the Agency," [Online]. Available: https://www.fema.gov/about-agency. [Accessed 22 December 2015].

[2] E. S. Blake, T. B. Kimberlain, R. J. Berg, J. P. Gangialosi and J. L. Beven II, "Tropical Cyclone Report: Hurricane Sandy," National Hurricane Center, 2013.

[3] J. T. Brown, F. X. McCarthy and E. C. Liu, "Analysis of the Sandy Recovery Improvement Act of 2013," Congressional Research Service, Washington, DC, 2013.

[4] Federal Emergency Management Act, "Sandy Recovery Act of 2013," 2015. [Online]. Available: http://www.fema.gov/sand-recovery-improvement-act-2013. [Accessed 22 December 2015].

[5] Federal Emergency Management Agency, "FEMA: Prepared. Responsive. Committed.," 2008. [Online]. Available: http://www.fema.gov/pdf/about/brochuer.pdf. [Accessed 22 December 2015].

[6] Federal Emergency Management Agency, "FEMA Leadership Organizational Structure," [Online]. Available: https://www.fema.gov/media-library/assets/documents/28183. [Accessed 27 February 2016].

[7] Federal Emergency Management Agency, "Regional Contact Information," [Online]. Available: https://www.fema.gov/regional-contact-information. [Accessed 22 December 2015].

[8] Federal Emergency Management Agency, "National Preparedness," [Online]. Available: http://www.fema.gov/media-library-data/1443799615171-2aae90be55041740f97e8532fc680d40/National_Preparedness_Goal_2nd_Edition.pdf. [Accessed 22 December 2015].

[9] U.S. Department of Homeland Security, "National Preparedness Goal: Second Edition," Department of Homeland Security, Washington, DC, 2015.

[10] Federal Emergency Management Agency, "Whole Community," [Online]. Available: http://www.fema.gov/whole-community#. [Accessed 22 December 2015].

[11] Federal Emergency Management Agency, "Reservist Program," [Online]. Available: http://www.fema.gov/reservist-program. [Accessed 22 December 2015].

[12] Federal emergency Management Agency, "Community Emergency Response Teams," [Online]. Available: http://www.fema.gov/community-emergency-response-teams. [Accessed 22 December 2015].

[13] Federal Emergency Management Agency, "Urban Search and Rescue," [Online]. Available: http://www.fema.gov/urban-search-rescue. [Accessed 22 December 2015].

[14] Federal Emergency Management Agency, "Voluntary, Faith Based, & Community-Based Organizations," [Online]. Available: http://www.fema.gov/voluntary-faith-based-community-based-organizations . [Accessed 22 December 2015].

[15] Federal Emergency Management Agency, "Disaster Recovery Centers," [Online]. Available: http://www.fema.gov/disaster-recovery-centers. [Accessed 22 December 2015].

[16] Federal Emergency Management Agency, "About the Ready Campaign," [Online]. Available: http://www.ready.gov/about-us. [Accessed 22 December 2015].

[17] Federal Emergency Management Agency, "Climate Change," [Online]. Available: http://www.fema.gov/climate-change. [Accessed 22 December 2015].

[18] The White House, "Executive Order 13653: Recommendations to the President," [Online]. Available: https://www.whitehouse.gov/sites/default/files/docs/task_force_report_0.pdf. [Accessed 22 December 2015].

Chapter 29: U.S. Coast Guard

[1] R. I. Johnson, "Guardians of the Sea, History of the United States Coast Guard," Naval Institute Press, Annapolis, MD, 1988.

[2] United States Coast Guard, "U.S. Coast Guard History," [Online]. Available: http://www.Coast Guard.mil/history/articles/h_COAST GUARDhistory.asp. [Accessed 3 October 2015].

[3] United States Coast Guard, "Timeline of the Coast Guard History," [Online]. Available: http://www.Coast_Guard.mil/history/faqs/when.asp. [Accessed 3 October 2015].

[4] United States Coast Guard, "Historic Missions," [Online]. Available: http://www.Coast_Guard.mil/history/Missionindex.asp. [Accessed 3 October 2015].

[5] United States Coast Guard, "Coast Guard Publication 1: Doctrine for the U.S. Coast Guard," 2014.

[6] United States Coast Guard, "Organization," [Online]. Available: http://www.uscg.mil/top/about/organization.asp. [Accessed 3 October 2015].

[7] United States Coast Guard, "Units," [Online]. Available: http://www.uscg.mil/top/units/. [Accessed 3 October 2015].

[8] T. Coburn, "A Review of the Department of Homeland Security's Missions and Performance," 2015.

Chapter 30: Transportation Security Administration

[1] Transportation Security Administration, "Transportation Security Overview," [Online]. Available: http://www.dhs.gov/transportation-security-overview. [Accessed 22 December 2015].

[2] Transportation Security Administration, "Transportation Security Results," [Online]. Available: http://www.dhs.gov/transportation-security-results. [Accessed 22 December 2015].

[3] "Public Law 107-71: Aviation and Transportation Security Act," Washington, DC, 2001.

[4] Transportation Security Administration, "Mission," [Online]. Available: https://www.tsa.gov/about/tsa-mission. [Accessed 22 December 2015].

[5] U.S. Government Accountability Office, "Transportation Security Administration has strengthened planning to guide investments in key aviation security programs, but more work remains," Government Accountability Office, Washington, DC, 2008.

[6] M. Grabell, "Federal Air Marshal Service," Pro Publica, 2008.

[7] Office of Inspector General, "Effectiveness of TSA's Surface Transportation Security Inspectors," Transportation Security Administration, Washington, DC, 2009.

[8] U.S. Government Accountability Office, "TSA's explosives detection canine program: Status of increasing the number of canine teams," Government Accountability Office, Washington, DC, 2008.

[9] All America Auto Transport, "What is TSA?," [Online]. Available: https://www.aaat.com/transport-security-administration.cfm. [Accessed 27 February 2016].

[10] U.S. Department of Homeland Security, "Budget in Brief FY2016," Department of Homeland Security, Washington, DC, 2015.

[11] Transportation Security Administration, "Aviation Security," [Online]. Available: http://www.dhs.gov/aviation-security . [Accessed 22 December 2015].

[12] Transportation Security Administration, "Security Screening," [Online]. Available: http://www.tsa.gov/travel/security-screening . [Accessed 22 December 2015].

[13] Department of Homeland Security, "DHS Traveler Redress Inquiry Program (TRIP)," [Online]. Available: http://www.dhs.gov/dhs-trip . [Accessed 22 December 2015].

[14] Transportation Security Administration, "Training," [Online]. Available: https://www.tsa.gov/for-industry/training . [Accessed 22 December 2015].

[15] U.S. Department of Homeland Security, "Privacy Impact Assessment for the Alien Flight Student Program," Department of Homeland Security, Washington, DC, 2014.

[16] U.S. Department of Homeland Security, "Cargo Screening," [Online]. Available: http://www.dhs.gov/cargo-screening . [Accessed 22 December 2015].

[17] Office of the Inspector General, "TSA's preparedness for mass transit and passenger rail emergencies," Transportation Security Administration, Washington, DC, 2010.

Chapter 31: U.S. Customs & Border Protection

[1] H. C. Relyea and H. B. Hogue, "Department of Homeland Security Reorganization: The 2SR Initiative," Congressional Research Service, Washington, DC, 2005.

[2] V. C. Jones and L. Seghetti, "U.S. Customs and Border Protection: Trade Facilitation, Enforcement, and Security," Congressional Research Service, Washington, DC, 2015.

[3] L. Seghetti, "Border Security: Immigration Enforcement Between Ports of Entry," Congressional Research Service, Washington, DC, 2014.

[4] U.S. Department of Homeland Security, "U.S. Customs and Border Protection: Leadership/Organization," [Online]. Available: http://www.cbp.gov/about/leadership-organization. [Accessed 27 January 2016].

[5] U.S. Department of Homeland Security, "U.S. Customs and Border Protection: Assistant Commissioners' Office," [Online]. Available: http://www.cbp.gov/about/leadership/assistant-commissioners-offices. [Accessed 27 January 2016].

[6] U.S. Department of Homeland Security, "CBP Organization Chart," 9 April 2015. [Online]. Available: http://www.cbp.gov/document/publications/cbp-organization-chart. [Accessed 27 January 2016].

[7] U.S. Department of Homeland Security, "U.S. Customs and Border Protection," [Online]. Available: http://www.cbp.gov/about/leadership/commissioners-staff-offices. [Accessed 27 January 2016].

[8] C. C. Haddal, "Border Security: The Role of the U.S. Border Patrol," Congressional Research Service, Washington, DC, 2010.

Chapter 31: U.S. Secret Service

[1] S. Reese, "The U.S. Secret Service: History and Missions," Congressional Research Service, Washington, DC, 2014.

[2] White House Press Office, "President to Propose Department of Homeland Security," The White House, Washington, DC, 2002.

[3] M. A. Randol, "The Department of Homeland Security Intelligence Enterprise: Operational Overview and Oversight Challenges for Congress," Congressional Research Service, Washington, DC, 2010.

[4] U.S. Department of Homeland Security, "U.S. Secret Service Organization Chart," 7 June 2011. [Online]. Available: https://www.dhs.gov/xlibrary/assets/org-chart-usss.pdf. [Accessed 29 January 2016].

[5] GOP.gov, "House Republicans: Legislative Digests," [Online]. Available: http://www.gop.gov/bill/h-r-1656-secret-service-improvements-act-of-2015-as-amended/. [Accessed 29 January 2016].

[6] CONGRESS.GOV, "H.R. 1656 - Secret Service Improvements Act of 2015," [Online]. Available: https://www.congress.gov/bill/114th-congress/house-bill/1656. [Accessed 29 January 2016].

Chapter 33: U.S. Immigration & Customs Enforcement

[1] U.S. Immigration and Customs Enforcement, "Who We Are," [Online]. Available: https://www.ice.gov/about. [Accessed 28 February 2016].

[2] U.S. Immigration and Customs Enforcement, "History," [Online]. Available: https://www.ice.gov/history. [Accessed 29 February 2016].

[3] U.S. Immigration and Customs Enforcement, "What We Do," [Online]. Available: https://www.ice.gov/overview#wcm-survey-target-id. [Accessed 28 February 2016].

[4] U.S. Department of Homeland Security, "U.S. Immigration & Customs Enforcement," [Online]. Available: https://www.dhs.gov/xlibrary/assets/org-chart-ice.pdf. [Accessed 28 February 2016].

[5] U.S. Immigration and Customs Enforcement, "Human Trafficking," [Online]. Available: https://www.ice.gov/human-trafficking. [Accessed 28 February 2016].

[6] U.S. Immigration and Customs Enforcement, "Human Smuggling," [Online]. Available: https://www.ice.gov/human-smuggling. [Accessed 28 February 2016].

[7] U.S. Immigration and Customs Enforcement, "Money Laundering," [Online]. Available: https://www.ice.gov/money-laundering. [Accessed 28 February 2016].

[8] U.S. Immigration and Customs Enforcement, "Bulk Cash Smuggling Center," [Online]. Available: https://www.ice.gov/bulk-cash-smuggling-center. [Accessed 28 February 2016].

[9] U.S. Immigration and Customs Enforcement, "Firearms, Ammunition, and Explosives Smuggling Investigations," [Online]. Available: https://www.ice.gov/firearms-explosives-smuggling. [Accessed 28 February 2016].

[10] U.S. Immigration and Customs Enforcement, "Border Enforcement Security Task Force (BEST)," [Online]. Available: https://www.ice.gov/best. [Accessed 28 February 2016].

[11] U.S. Immigration and Customs Enforcement, "Cultural Property, Art and Antiquities Investigations," [Online]. Available: https://www.ice.gov/cultural-art-investigations. [Accessed 28 February 2016].

[12] U.S. Immigration and Customs Enforcement, "HSI Forensic Laboratory," [Online]. Available: https://www.ice.gov/hsi-fl. [Accessed 28 February 2016].

[13] U.S. Immigration and Customs Enforcement, "Cyber Crimes Center," [Online]. Available: https://www.ice.gov/cyber-crimes. [Accessed 28 February 2016].

[14] U.S. Immigration and Customs Enforcement, "Child Exploitation Investigations Unit," [Online]. Available: https://www.ice.gov/predator. [Accessed 28 February 2016].

[15] U.S. Immigration and Customs Enforcement, "National Security Unit," [Online]. Available: https://www.ice.gov/national-security-unit. [Accessed 28 February 2016].

[16] U.S. Immigration and Customs Enforcement, "Counterterrorism and Criminal Exploitation Unit," [Online]. Available: https://www.ice.gov/counterterrorism-and-criminal-exploitation-unit. [Accessed 28 February 2016].

[17] U.S. Immigration and Customs Enforcement, "Student and Exchange Visitor Program," [Online]. Available: https://www.ice.gov/sevis. [Accessed 28 February 2016].

[18] U.S. Immigration and Customs Enforcement, "Counter-Proliferation Investigations Program," [Online]. Available: https://www.ice.gov/cpi. [Accessed 28 February 2016].

[19] U.S. Immigration and Customs Enforcement, "Export Enforcement Coordination Center," [Online]. Available: https://www.ice.gov/eecc. [Accessed 28 February 2016].

[20] U.S. Immigration and Customs Enforcement, "Project Shield America," [Online]. Available: https://www.ice.gov/project-shield-america. [Accessed 28 February 2016].

[21] U.S. Immigration and Customs Enforcement, "Visa Security Program," [Online]. Available: https://www.ice.gov/visa-security-program. [Accessed 28 February 2016].

[22] U.S. Immigration and Customs Enforcement, "Illicit Pathways Attack Strategy," [Online]. Available: https://www.ice.gov/ipas. [Accessed 28 February 2016].

[23] U.S. Immigration and Customs Enforcement, "Enforcement and Removal Operations," [Online]. Available: https://www.ice.gov/ero. [Accessed 28 February 2016].

[24] U.S. Immigration and Customs Enforcement, "IMAGE," [Online]. Available: https://www.ice.gov/image. [Accessed 28 February 2016].

[25] U.S. Immigration and Customs Enforcement, "Worksite Enforcement," [Online]. Available: https://www.ice.gov/worksite. [Accessed 28 February 2016].

[26] U.S. Immigration and Customs Enforcement, "Detention Management," [Online]. Available: https://www.ice.gov/detention-management. [Accessed 28 February 2016].

[27] U.S. Immigration and Customs Enforcement, "Fugitive Operations," [Online]. Available: https://www.ice.gov/fugitive-operations. [Accessed 28 February 2016].

[28] U.S. Immigration and Customs Enforcement, "Criminal Alien Program," [Online]. Available: https://www.ice.gov/criminal-alien-program. [Accessed 28 February 2016].

[29] U.S. Immigration and Customs Enforcement, "Identity and Benefit Fraud," [Online]. Available: https://www.ice.gov/identity-benefit-fraud. [Accessed 28 February 2016].

[30] U.S. Immigration and Customs Enforcement, "ICE Enforcement and Removal Operations Report," Department of Homeland Security, Washington, DC, 2015.

[31] M. R. Rosenblum and W. A. Kandel, "Interior Immigration Enforcement: Programs Targeting Criminal Aliens," Congressional Research Service, Washington, DC, 2013.

[32] A. Bruno, "Immigration-Related Worksite Enforcement: Performance Measures," Congressional Research Service, Washington, DC, 2015.

[33] U.S. Department of Homeland Security, "Written testimony of CBP Deputy Commissioner Keven McAleenan and ICE Deputy Director Daniel Ragsdale," [Online]. Available: https://www.dhs.gov/news/2014/04/08/written-testimony-cbp-and-ice-house-homeland-security-subcommittee-border-and. [Accessed 29 February 2016].

[34] U.S. Immigration and Customs Enforcement, "Joint Terrorism Task Force," [Online]. Available: https://www.ice.gov/jttf. [Accessed 28 February 2016].

Chapter 34: U.S. Citizenship & Immigration Services

[1] W. A. Kandel, "U.S. Citizenship and Immigration Services (USCIS) Functions and Funding," Congressional Research Service, Washington, DC, 2015.

[2] U.S. Citizenship and Immigration Services, "Our History," [Online]. Available: https://www.uscis.gov/about-us/our-history. [Accessed 3 March 2016].

[3] U.S. Citizenship and Immigration Services, "What We Do," [Online]. Available: https://www.uscis.gov/about-us/what-we-do. [Accessed 3 March 2016].

[4] U.S. Citizenship and Immigration Services, "USCIS Organizational Chart," [Online]. Available: https://www.uscis.gov/about-us/uscis-organizational-chart. [Accessed 2 March 2016].

[5] U.S. Citizenship and Immigration Services, "Office of Public Engagement to Customer Service and Public engagement Directorate," [Online]. Available: https://www.uscis.gov/about-us/directorates-and-program-offices/customer-service-and-public-engagement-directorate/office-public-engagement-customer-service-and-public-engagement-directorate. [Accessed 3 March 2016].

[6] U.S. Citizenship and Immigration Services, "Field Operations Directorate," [Online]. Available: https://www.uscis.gov/about-us/directorates-and-program-offices/field-operations-directorate. [Accessed 3 March 2016].

[7] U.S. Citizenship and immigration Services, "Fraud Detection and National Security Directorate," [Online]. Available: https://www.uscis.gov/about-us/directorates-and-program-offices/fraud-detection-and-national-security/fraud-detection-and-national-security-directorate. [Accessed 3 March 2016].

[8] U.S. Citizenship and Immigration Services, "Refugee, Asylum, and International Operations Directorate," [Online]. Available: https://www.uscis.gov/about-us/directorates-and-program-offices/refugee-asylum-and-international-operations-directorate. [Accessed 3 March 2016].

[9] U.S. Citizenship and Immigration Services, "Service Center Operations Directorate," [Online]. Available: https://www.uscis.gov/about-us/directorates-and-program-offices/service-center-operations-directorate/service-center-operations-directorate. [Accessed 3 March 2016].

[10] U.S. Citizenship and Immigration Services, "The Administrative Appeals Office (AAO)," [Online]. Available: https://www.uscis.gov/about-us/directorates-and-program-offices/administrative-appeals-office-aao/administrative-appeals-office-aao. [Accessed 3 March 2016].

[11] U.S. Citizenship and Immigration Services, "Office of Intake and Document Production," [Online]. Available: https://www.uscis.gov/about-us/directorates-and-program-offices/lockbox-intake/office-intake-and-document-production. [Accessed 3 March 2016].

[12] U.S. Citizenship and Immigration Services, "Office of Citizenship," [Online]. Available: https://www.uscis.gov/about-us/directorates-and-program-offices/office-citizenship. [Accessed 3 March 2016].

[13] U.S. Citizenship and Immigration Services, "Office of Communications," [Online]. Available: https://www.uscis.gov/about-us/directorates-and-program-offices/office-communications. [Accessed 3 March 2016].

[14] U.S. Citizenship and Immigration Services, "Office of Legislative Affairs," [Online]. Available: https://www.uscis.gov/about-us/directorates-and-program-offices/office-legislative-affairs. [Accessed 3 March 2016].

[15] U.S. Citizenship and Immigration Services, "Office of Privacy," [Online]. Available: https://www.uscis.gov/about-us/directorates-and-program-offices/office-privacy-0. [Accessed 3 March 2016].

[16] U.S. Citizenship and Immigration Services, "Office of Transformation Coordination," [Online]. Available: https://www.uscis.gov/about-us/directorates-and-program-offices/office-transformation-coordination. [Accessed 3 March 2016].

[17] M. R. Rosenblum and R. E. Wasem, "Comprehensive Immigration Reform in the 113th Congress: Major Provisions in Senate-Passed S. 744," Congressional Research Service, Washington, DC, 2013.

Part V: Mission Partners

Chapter 35: Congress

[1] F. M. Kaiser, "American National Government: An Overview," Congressional Research Service, Washington, DC, 2004.

[2] W. J. Oleszek, "Congressional Oversight: An Overview," Congressional Research Service, Washington, DC, 2010.

[3] National Commission on Terrorist Attacks Upon the United States, "The 9/11 Commission Report," Government Printing Office, Washington, DC, 2004.

[4] The Annenberg Public Policy Center of the University of Pennsylvania, "Reflections on the Tenth Anniversary of the 9/11 Commission Report," Annenberg Public Policy Center, Philadelphia, PA, 2014.

[5] J. Zuckerman, "Politics Over Security: Homeland Security Congressional Oversight in Dire Need of Reform," Heritage Foundation, September 2012. [Online]. Available: http://www.heritage.org/research/reports/2012/09/homeland-security-congressional-oversight-in-dire-need-of-reform/. [Accessed 12 January 2016].J. Markon, "Department of Homeland Security has 120 Reasons to Want Streamlined Oversight," The Washington Post, 25 September 2014. [Online]. Available: https://www.washingtonpost.com/news/federal-eye/2014/09/25/outsized-congressional-oversight-wighting-down-department-of-homeland-security/. [Accessed 12 January 2016].

[6] H. H. Willis, "Streamlining Congressional Oversight of DHS," The Rand Corporation, July 2014. [Online]. Available: HTTP://WWW.RAND.ORG/BLOG/2014/07/STREAMLINING-CONGRESSIONAL-OVERSIGHT-OF-DHS.HTML. [Accessed 12 January 2016].

Chapter 36: National Security Council

[1] J. R. A. Best, "The National Security Council: An Organizational Assessment," Congressional Research Service, Washington, DC, 2011.

[2] A. G. Whittaker, S. A. Brown, F. C. Smith and E. McKune, "The National Security Process: The Security Council and Interagency System," Industrial College of the Armed Forces, National Defense University, Washington, DC, 2011.

[3] H. C. Relyea, "The Executive Office of the President: An Historical Overview," Congressional Research Service, Washington, DC, 2008.

Chapter 37: Intelligence Community

[1] Office of the Director of National Intelligence, "Intelligence Community," [Online]. Available: http://www.dni.gov/index.php. [Accessed 20 March 2016].

[2] M. Warner, "Wanted: A Definition of "Intelligence"," Central Intelligence Agency, 2007. [Online]. Available: https://www.cia.gov/library/center-for-the-study-of-intelligence/csi-publications/csi-studies/studies/vol46no3/article02.html. [Accessed 20 March 2016].

[3] U.S. Central Intelligence Agency, "History of the CIA," 10 April 2007. [Online]. Available: https://www.cia.gov/about-cia/history-of-the-cia. [Accessed 20 March 2016].

[4] Federation of American Scientists, "The Evolution of the U.S. Intelligence Community - An Historical Overview," 23 February 1996. [Online]. Available: http://fas.org/irp/offdocs/int022.html. [Accessed 20 March 2016].

[5] 50 U.S.C 401, "National Security Act of 1947," Washington, DC, 1947.

[6] Foreign Policy, "The Ten Biggest American Intelligence Failures," 3 January 2012. [Online]. Available: http://foreignpolicy.com/2012/01/03/the-ten-biggest-american-intelligence-failures/. [Accessed 20 March 2016].

[7] R. A. Best Jr., "Director of National Intelligence Statutory Authorities: Status and Proposals," Congressional Research Service, Washington, DC, 2011.

[8] M. C. Erwin, "Intelligence Issues for Congress," Congressional Research Service, Washington, DC, 2013.

[9] Office of the Director of National Intelligence, "U.S. National Intelligence," Washington, DC, 2011.

[10] Office of the Director of National Intelligence, "ODNI FAQ," [Online]. Available: http://www.dni.gov/index.php/about/faq?start=2. [Accessed 21 March 2016].

[11] U.S. Department of Justice, Bureau of Justice Assistance, "The Foreign Intelligence Surveillance Act of 1978," [Online]. Available: https://it.ojp.gov/PrivacyLiberty/authorities/statutes/1286. [Accessed 21 March 2016].

[12] J. K. Elsea, "Criminal Prohibitions on the Publication of Classified Defense Information," Congressional Research Service, Washington, DC, 2013.

[13] J. W. Rollins and E. C. Liu, "NSA Surveillance Leaks: Background and Issues for Congress," Congressional Research Service, Washington, DC, 2013.

[14] Congressional Research Service, "Legal Sidebar: USA FREEDOM Act Reinstates Expired USA PATRIOT Act Provisions but Limits bulk Collection," Congressional Research Service, Washington, DC, 2015.

[15] Randol, Mark A., "Homeland Security Intelligence: Perceptions, Statutory Definitions, and Approaches," Congressional Research Service, Washington, DC, 2009.

Chapter 38: Department of Defense

[1] Chairman of the Joint Chiefs of Staff, "JP-1, Doctrine for the Armed Forces of the United States," Washington, DC, 2013.

[2] U.S. Department of Defense, "JP 3-27, Homeland Defense," Chairman of the Joint Chiefs of Staff, Washington, DC, 2013.

[3] U.S. Department of Defense, "Strategy for Homeland Defense and Defense Support of Civil Authorities," Washington, DC, 2013.

[4] M. J. Reents, "Operation Noble Eagle and The Use of Combat Air Patrols for Homeland Defense," Naval Postgraduate School, Monterey, CA, 2008.

[5] B. Wilson, "Interagency Collaboration on the High Seas," InterAgency Journal, vol. 2, no. 1, Winter 2011, pp. 58-65, 2011.

[6] Chairman of the Joint Chiefs of Staff, "JP 3-28: Defense Support of Civil Authorities," Washington, DC, 2013.

[7] U.S. Department of Homeland Security, "National Response Framework," Department of Homeland Security, Washington, DC, 2013.

[8] U.S. Department of Homeland Security, "Emergency Support Function Annexes: Introduction," Department of Homeland Security, Washington, DC, 2008.

[9] W. Knight, "Homeland Security: Roles and Mission for United States Northern Command," Congressional Research Service, Washington, DC, 2008.

Chapter 39: National Guard

[1] National Governors' Association, "NGA Policy Statement HHS-03, Army and Air National Guard," National Governors Association, 2010.

[2] S. Bowman, L. Kapp and A. Belasco, "Hurricane Katrina: DOD Disaster Response," Congressional Research Service, Washington, DC, 2005.

[3] U.S. Government Accountability Office, "Defense Management: Actions Needed to Ensure National Guard and Reserve Headquarters Are Sized to be Efficient," GAO, Washington, DC, 2013.

[4] A. Feickert and L. Kapp, "Army Active Component (AC) / Reserve Component (RC) Force Mix: Considerations and Options for Congress," Congressional Research Service, Washington, DC, 2014.

[5] U.S. Government Accountability Office, "Reserve Forces: Army National Guard and Army Reserve Readiness for 21st Century Challenges," GAO, Washington, DC, 2006.

[6] Commission on the National Guard and Reserves, "Second Report to Congress," 2007.

[7] Chairman of the Joint Chiefs of Staff, "JP 3-28: Defense Support of Civil Authorities," Washington, DC, 2013.

[8] Wikipedia, The Free Encyclopedia, "State Adjutant General," Wikipedia Contributors, 8 March 2016. [Online]. Available: https://en.wikipedia.org/w/index.php?title=State_adjutant_general&oldid=708869138. [Accessed 25 March 2016].

[9] The White House, "The Federal Response to Hurricane Katrina: Lessons Learned," Washington, DC, 2006.

[10] Emergency Management Assistance Compact, "What is EMAC?," [Online]. Available: http://www.emacweb.org/index.php/learnaboutemac/what-is-emac. [Accessed 25 March 2016].

[11] Wikipedia, The Free Encyclopedia, "Hurricane Katrina," Wikipedia Contributors, 15 March 2016. [Online]. Available: https://en.wikipedia.org/w/index.php?title=Hurricane_Katrina&oldid=710204583. [Accessed 25 March 2016].

[12] R. Burke and S. McNeil, "Toward a Unified Military Response: Hurricane Sandy and the Dual Status Commander," United States Army War College Press, Carlisle, PA, 2015.

[13] Commission on the National Guard and Reserves, "Final Report to Congress and the Secretary of Defense," Washington, DC, 2008.

[14] W. Knight, "Homeland Security: Roles and Mission for United States Northern Command," Congressional Research Service, Washington, DC, 2008.

[15] R. C. Mason, "Securing America's Borders: The Role of the Military," Congressional Research Service, Washington, DC, 2013.

[16] U.S. Government Accountability Office, "Homeland Defense: National Guard Bureau Needs to Clarify Civil Support Teams' Mission and address Management Challenges," GAO, Washington, DC, 2006.

[17] Wikipedia Contributors, "Civil Support Team," Wikipedia, The Free Encyclopedia, 29 September 2015. [Online]. Available: https://en.wikipedia.org/w/index.php?title=Civil_Support_Team&oldid=683234224. [Accessed 26 March 2016].

[18] National Guard Bureau, "Homeland Response Force Fact Sheet," NGB, Washington, DC, 2014.

[19] L. Kapp and N. Serafino, "The National Guard State Partnership Program: Background, Issues, and Options for Congress," Congressional Research Service, Washington, DC, 2011.

Chapter 40: Federal Bureau of Investigation

[1] J. P. Bjelopera, "The Federal Bureau of Investigation and Terrorism Investigations," Congressional Research Service, Washington, DC, 2013.

Chapter 41: State & Local Law Enforcement

[1] U.S. Department of Homeland Security, "DHS' Role in State and Local Fusion Centers is Evolving," DHS Office of Inspector General, Washington, DC, 2008.

[2] U.S. Senate Permanent Subcommittee on Investigation, "Federal Support For and Involvement in State and Local Fusion Centers," Washington, DC, 2012.

[3] U.S. Department of Homeland Security, "State and Major Urban Area Fusion Centers," [Online]. Available: https://www.dhs.gov/state-and-major-urban-area-fusion-centers. [Accessed 26 March 2016].

[4] J. Rollins, "Fusion Centers: Issues and Options for Congress," Congressional Research Service, Washington, DC, 2008.

[5] U.S. Department of Homeland Security, "Fusion Center Locations and Contact Information," [Online]. Available: https://www.dhs.gov/fusion-center-locations-and-contact-information. [Accessed 26 March 2016].

[6] U.S. Department of Justice, "Fusion Center Guidelines," Washington, DC, 2008.

[7] U.S. Department of Homeland Security, "Department of Homeland Security Interaction with State and Local Fusion Centers Concept of Operations," Washington, DC, 2008.

Chapter 42: First Responders

[1] Office of Homeland Security, "National Strategy for Homeland Security," The White House, Washington, DC, 2002.

[2] National Commission on Terrorist Attacks Upon the United States, "The 9/11 Commission Report: Executive Summary," Government Printing Office, Washington, DC, 2004.

[3] K. Bea, W. Krouse, D. Morgan, W. Morrissey and C. S. Redhead, "Emergency Preparedness and Response Directorate of the Department of Homeland Security," Congressional Research Service, Washington, DC, 2003.

[4] K. Bea, "The National Preparedness System: Issues in the 109th Congress," Congressional Research Service, Washington, DC, 2005.

[5] U.S. Department of Homeland Security, "National Preparedness Goal," Washington, DC, 2005.

[6] Federal Emergency Management Agency, "CPG-101: Developing and Maintaining Emergency Operations Plans," Washington, DC, 2010.

[7] U.S. Department of Homeland Security, "National Preparedness Guidelines," Washington, DC, 2007.

[8] Homeland Security Council, "National Strategy for Homeland Security," Washington, DC, 2007.

[9] K. Bea, "Federal Emergency Management Policy Changes After Hurricane Katrina: A Summary of Statutory Provisions," Congressional Research Service, Washington, DC, 2007.

[10] U.S. Department of Homeland Security, "National Preparedness Goal," Washington, DC, 2011.

[11] J. T. Brown, "Presidential Policy Directive 8 and the National Preparedness System: Background and Issues for Congress," Congressional Research Service, Washington, DC, 2011.

[12] U.S. Department of Homeland Security, "National Preparedness System," Washington, DC, 2011.